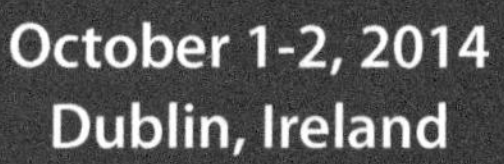

October 1-2, 2014
Dublin, Ireland

Association for
Computing Machinery

Advancing Computing as a Science & Profession

COSN'14

Proceedings of the 2014 ACM

Conference on Online Social Networks

Sponsored by:

ACM

Supported by:

NSF, Microsoft Research, Prof. Ram Kumar Memorial Foundation, Bell Labs Acatel-Lucent, and Akamai

Advancing Computing as a Science & Profession

The Association for Computing Machinery
2 Penn Plaza, Suite 701
New York, New York 10121-0701

Notice to Past Authors of ACM-Published Articles
ACM intends to create a complete electronic archive of all articles and/or other material previously published by ACM. If you have written a work that has been previously published by ACM in any journal or conference proceedings prior to 1978, or any SIG Newsletter at any time, and you do NOT want this work to appear in the ACM Digital Library, please inform permissions@acm.org, stating the title of the work, the author(s), and where and when published.

ISBN: 978-1-4503-3198-2 (Digital)

ISBN: 978-1-4503-3369-6 (Print)

Additional copies may be ordered prepaid from:

ACM Order Department
PO Box 30777
New York, NY 10087-0777, USA

Phone: 1-800-342-6626 (USA and Canada)
+1-212-626-0500 (Global)
Fax: +1-212-944-1318
E-mail: acmhelp@acm.org
Hours of Operation: 8:30 am – 4:30 pm ET

Printed in the USA

Welcome from the Program Co-Chairs

Welcome to the second edition of ACM Conference on Online Social Networks (COSN) in Dublin, Ireland. The second conference builds upon the success of the first COSN last year in providing a premier publication venue that features high quality research across multiple disciplines focused around the study of OSNs. The 25 papers that will be presented over the next two days represent some of the best research covering a wide variety of topics related to OSNs ranging from privacy and anonymity to social advertising and commerce, from detecting social communities to understanding diffusion of information and influence within them, and from proposing efficient and scalable network algorithms to large-scale empirical studies of user opinions in social networks.

We solicited full papers (up to 12 pages) describing original research in detail and short papers (6 pages) conveying promising work and high-level vision. We received 87 submissions from over 20 countries, of which 65 were full papers and 22 were short papers. The final program includes 20 full papers and 5 short papers.

The PC consisted of 24 members (including the two of us). In addition, we sought and received additional reviews for some papers from over 20 external reviewers. On average, every PC member reviewed around 12 papers and read a few more. Every submission received at least 3 reviews. Reviewing was single blind. The reviewers knew who the authors were, but the authors will not know who the reviewers are. We were careful to ensure that reviewers did not review papers with which they were conflicted. The reviewing process included extensive on-line discussions followed by a day long face-to-face PC meeting. The PC met in Stanford University on July 25th. The face-to-face PC meeting was beneficial as it brought various representatives of the OSN community together, some of whom were meeting others for the first time.

As Program Co-Chairs our job was largely that of orchestrating the hard work of others. Our greatest thanks are due to the members of the Program Committee. We would also like to thank the Steering Committee, particularly Balachander Krishnamurthy and Ben Zhao, for always being available with valuable advice when we needed it. We would also like to thank Alessandra Sala, our general chair, Öznur Özkasap, our proceedings chair, Christo Wilson, our posters chair, Ponnurangam Kumaraguru, the COSN'14 website manager and publicity chair, and Mainack Mondal, the COSN'14 submission site manager for helping with logistics. Finally, we wish to thank all our sponsors and supporters for making COSN'14 possible.

Ashish Goel
COSN'14 TPC Co-Chair
Stanford / Twitter

Krishna P. Gummadi
COSN'14 TPC Co-Chair
MPI for Software Systems

Table of Contents

Session 5: Social Advertising and Commerce

Session 6: Social Communities

Session 7: Network Identity

Session 8: Security in Social Networks

COSN 2014 ACM Conference on Online Social Networks Organization

General Chair: Alessandra Sala *(Bell Laboratories, Ireland)*

Program Chairs: Ashish Goel *(Stanford / Twitter, USA)*
Krishna Gummadi *(MPI-SWS, Germany)*

Local Arrangements Chair: Neil Hurley *(University College, Dublin, Ireland)*

Registration Chair: Simon Wilson *(Trinity College, Dublin, Ireland)*

Publicity Chair: Ponnurangam Kumaraguru *(IIIT Delhi, India)*

Budget Chair: Christo Wilson *(Northeastern University, USA)*

Publications Chair: Oznur Ozkasap *(Koc University, Turkey)*

Travel Grant Chairs: Gonca Gursun *(Ozyegin University, Turkey)*
Augustin Chaintreau *(Columbia University, USA)*

Steering Committee Chair: Balachander Krishnamurthy *(AT&T Labs-Research, USA)*

Steering Committee: Virgilio Almeida *(Federal Univ of Minais Gerais, Brazil)*
Jon Crowcroft *(Univ of Cambridge, United Kingdom)*
Ben Zhao *(Univ of California Santa Barbara, USA)*

Technical Advisory Committee: Rakesh Agrawal *(Microsoft Search Labs)*
Meeyoung Cha *(KAIST, Korea)*
Krishna Gummadi *(MPI-SWS, Germany)*
Anne-Marie Kermarrec *(INRIA, France)*
Jon Kleinberg *(Cornell University, USA)*
Ponnurangam Kumaraguru *(IIIT Delhi, India)*

Program Committee: Alessandro Acquisti *(CMU, USA)*
Fabricio Benevenuto *(UFMG, Brazil)*
Jim Blomo *(UC Berkeley / Yelp, USA)*
Paolo Boldi *(University of Milano, Italy)*
Francesco Bonchi *(Yahoo Labs Barcelona, Spain)*
Ceren Budak *(Microsoft Research NYC, USA)*
Carlos Castillo *(QCRI, Qatar)*
Meeyoung Cha *(KAIST, Korea)*
Anirban Dasgupta *(IIT Gandhinagar, India)*
Xiaoming Fu *(University of Goettingen, Germany)*
Ashish Goel *(Stanford / Twitter, USA)*
Krishna Gummadi *(MPI-SWS, Germany)*
Nick Koudas *(University of Toronto, Canada)*
Ponnurangam Kumaraguru *(IIIT Delhi, India)*
Cecilia Mascolo *(Cambridge University, UK)*
Winter Mason *(Facebook, USA)*
Alan Mislove *(Northeastern University, USA)*
Mirco Musolesi *(University of Birmingham, UK)*
Prateek Mittal *(Princeton University, USA)*
Sue Moon *(KAIST, Korea)*
Alessandro Panconesi *(Sapienza, University of Rome, Italy)*
Manuel Gomez Rodriguez *(MPI for Intelligent Systems, Germany)*
Aneesh Sharma *(Twitter, USA)*
Ben Zhao *(UC Santa Barbara, USA)*

Additional reviewers: Cigdem Aslay
Xu Chen
Yang Chen
Alain Forget
Jim Graves
Ralph Gross
Sara Hajian
Hong Huang
Lei Jiao
David Koll
Nicolas Kourtellis
Jun Li
Wenzhong Li
Andrea Marino
Veronica Marotta
Yasir Mehmood
Sonam Samat
Florian Schaub
Giovanni Stilo
Carmen Vaca
Konglin Zhu

COSN 2014 Sponsor & Supporters

Sponsor:

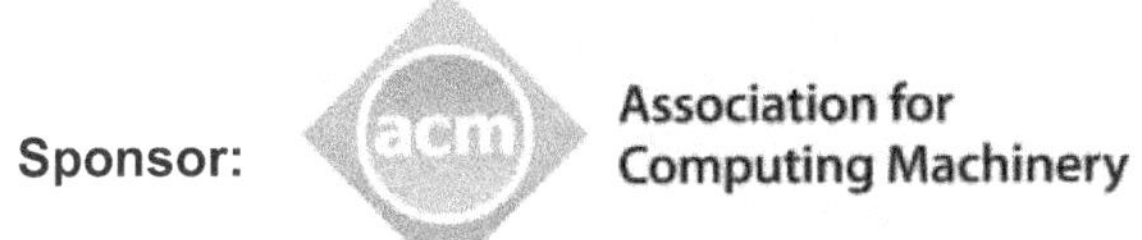

Platinum Supporter:

Gold Supporter:

Silver Supporter:

Conference Reception supported by:

Mining Democracy

Vincent Etter* Julien Herzen* Matthias Grossglauser Patrick Thiran
School of Computer and Communication Sciences
École Polytechnique Fédérale de Lausanne (EPFL), Lausanne, Switzerland
firstname.lastname@epfl.ch

ABSTRACT

Switzerland has a long tradition of direct democracy, which makes it an ideal laboratory for research on real-world politics. Similar to recent *open government* initiatives launched worldwide, the Swiss government regularly releases datasets related to state affairs and politics. In this paper, we propose an exploratory, data-driven study of the political landscape of Switzerland, in which we use opinions expressed by candidates and citizens on a web platform during the recent Swiss parliamentary elections, together with fine-grained vote results and parliament votes.

Following this purely data-driven approach, we show that it is possible to uncover interesting patterns that would otherwise require both tedious manual analysis and domain knowledge. In particular, we show that traditional cultural and/or ideological idiosyncrasies can be highlighted and quantified by looking at vote results and pre-election opinions. We propose a technique for comparing the candidates' opinions expressed before the elections with their actual votes cast in the parliament after the elections. This technique spots politicians that do not vote consistently with the opinions that they expressed during the campaign. We also observe that it is possible to predict surprisingly precisely the outcome of nationwide votes, by looking at the outcome in a single, carefully selected municipality. Our work applies to any country where similar data is available; it points to some of the avenues created by user-generated data emerging from open government initiatives, which enable new data-mining approaches to political and social sciences.

Categories and Subject Descriptors

H.2.8 [**Database Applications**]: Data Mining

General Terms

Algorithms; Experimentation

*These authors contributed equally to this work.

COSN'14, October 1–2, 2014, Dublin, Ireland.

ACM ACM 978-1-4503-3198-2/14/10$15.00.
http://dx.doi.org/10.1145/2660460.2660476.

Keywords

Political data; voting advice application; dimensionality reduction; vote results prediction

1. INTRODUCTION

In order to promote transparency and accountability, as well as to stimulate citizen awareness, an increasing number of governments across the world are adopting *open government* directives [20]. As of 2014, the website Datacatalogs [1] references more than 350 such local, regional and national datasets. These initiatives result in the release of massive amounts of structured data about multiple aspects of state affairs, politics, and governmental agencies in various countries.

In parallel to these efforts, several governments, organizations and academic groups set up *voting advice applications* (VAA's) in the form of websites that allow politicians and interested citizens to express their preferences on political issues, by answering a series of pre-determined questions spanning a variety of topics. The candidates have public profiles containing their responses (as well as various other information, such as their birthdate, interests, or Facebook profile), and the voters are matched with candidates based on their own responses. Examples of such VAA's include *Vote Compass* [6] in Canada, the USA and Australia, *Stemwijzer* [5] in the Netherlands, *Wahl-O-Mat* [7] in Germany, *Stemtest* [4] in Belgium and *smartvote* [3] in Switzerland.

In this paper, we propose an exploratory, data-mining approach that uses some of the data released by governments, together with data obtained from VAA's, to analyze a country's democracy and political trends. We consider the case of Switzerland: This country has a diversified party landscape, with frequent votes on a wide variety of topics, both at parliamentary and citizen levels. We use three different datasets:

1. The set of all vote results in each municipality, for each national vote between 1981 and 2011.
2. The set of all votes in the parliament, by all parliament members, during the current legislature (which started in 2011).
3. The set of opinions given on the smartvote VAA [3] by hundreds of thousands of citizens, as well as more than 82% of candidates for parliamentary elections.

We give more details on our datasets in Section 2.2. The initial reason for the existence of these datasets was to increase government accountability and citizen participation.

abbreviation	full name	ideology	obtained votes
SVP	Swiss People's Party	National conservatism	26.6%
SP	Social Democratic Party	Social democracy	18.7%
FDP	Free Democratic Party	Classical liberalism	15.1%
CVP	Christian Democratic People's Party	Christian democracy	12.3%
Greens	Green Party	Green politics	8.4%
BDP	Conservative Democratic Party	Conservatism, economic liberalism	5.4%
GL	Green Liberal Party	Green liberalism	5.4%

Table 1: The seven major parties after the Swiss National Council elections of 2011. The last column lists the percentage of votes each party obtained during these elections.

Yet, as a byproduct, they also provide researchers with new ways of mining and (re-)discovering patterns that are peculiar to political life, but that usually require tedious manual analysis and domain knowledge. Although the nature of this data (e.g., the individual opinions of politicians or votes in municipalities) is not new, its scale is unprecedented. It enables us to address interesting questions such as

- What are the similarities between the ideological trends of parliament candidates (the representatives) and voters?
- Considering *all* votes at the municipality level over a period of 30 years, are there some clear patterns linking geography and voting behaviors?
- Is it possible to predict nationwide vote outcomes by looking only at the outcome in a single municipality?
- How "redundant" are political parties, given the opinions expressed by their candidates in smartvote surveys?
- How should a candidate fill a VAA survey during the campaign, in order to maximize her likelihood to appear at the top of the voting recommendations?
- In order to hold a candidate accountable for her public statements, can we use the survey she filled out during the election campaign, once she has been elected at the parliament?

Our intent is to exploit the scale of the data to tackle these questions from a statistical perspective. Of course, our results are not universal, and they are valid only in the contexts for which our datasets are representative. Yet, our various procedures apply to any context where similar data is available, and our main intent in this paper is to show how systematic data mining can shed new light on questions related to political and social sciences.

The remainder of the paper is organized as follows. In Section 2, we give some background information on Swiss politics and the datasets we use. In Section 3, we study the ideological landscape and the differences between parliament candidates and voters. In Section 4, we study trends at a geographical level and observe to what extent vote results of individual municipalities can be used to predict national vote outcomes. In Section 5, we show that voting advice applications can be abused by candidates to obtain better ranks in voting recommendations. We also propose a technique to use these same VAA surveys in order to check on the consistency of the votes at the parliament. Finally, we discuss some related work in Section 6, and we give some concluding remarks in Section 7.

2. BACKGROUND

In this section, we briefly describe the Swiss political system, and its various components. We list the main political parties on which we focus, and then describe the three datasets we use in this paper. The first dataset contains vote outcomes at the municipality level, the second consists of votes of the members of the parliament, and the last dataset contains political opinions of candidates and voters, gathered on an online voting advice application.

2.1 Politics of Switzerland

The political system of Switzerland consists of a *Federal Council* (7 seats) and a bicameral parliament, which is composed of the *Council of States* (46 seats) and the *National Council* (200 seats). The Federal Council serves as head of state and executive power, and the parliament possesses the legislative power (together with citizens, as per the constitutional right for citizens to launch initiatives[1]). The Council of States represents the *cantons* (which are the states of the federal state), and each canton is attributed two seats (except six "half" cantons that have only one seat). The National Council represents the people, and each canton is attributed a number of seats proportional to its population.

The National Council and the Council of States are elected at the same time every four years, most recently in 2011. Several political parties are represented in the parliament. In this paper, we focus on the seven largest parties (in terms of votes obtained during the National Council elections in 2011) shown on Table 1.

2.2 Description of the Datasets

In this section, we describe the three datasets that we use for our analysis. We provide a summary in Table 2.

2.2.1 Municipality Votes

Our first dataset consists of the outcomes of the federal (i.e., nationwide) votes for each municipality between January 1981 and December 2011. There were 245 such votes on various topics, including military, finances, transportation, culture, integration of foreigners, public health, education, equality of rights, working conditions, energy policies, abortion, etc. The results (i.e., the proportions of "yes") are publicly available for each Swiss municipality[2]. In December 2011, there were 2,515 municipalities in Switzerland. We discard the results

[1]Initiatives, similar to propositions in California, allow any citizen or organization to gather a predetermined number of signatures to propose a new piece of legislation [36].

[2]`http://www.bfs.admin.ch/bfs/portal/de/index/themen/17/03/blank/data/01.html`

dataset	content
Municipality votes	Outcomes (percentage of "yes") for 245 nationwide votes in 2,389 municipalities between 1981 and 2011. This amounts to 585,305 outcomes.
Votes in the parliament	2,494 votes (yes/no/abstention) by 181 of the 200 national councilors, since the beginning of the current legislature in 2011. This amounts to 451,414 votes.
Smartvote pre-electoral opinions	Responses given by 2,985 candidates (82.4% of all candidates) and 229,133 citizens (~9% of total turnout) on the smartvote VAA [3] during the campaign of the 2011 parliamentary elections.

Table 2: Specifications of our three datasets.

smartvote 2011 statistics	
Number of questions in the short survey	32
Number of questions in the long survey	75
Number of candidates who took the long survey	2985
Approximate number of unique voters that requested recommendations	436,726
Number of voters who completed all questions of the short survey	229,133
Number of voters who completed all questions of the long survey	80,067

Table 3: Statistics about the political opinions dataset, that contains the responses given on the smartvote VAA by the citizens and candidates during the Swiss parliamentary elections of 2011.

for all the municipalities that have merged during the period 1981-2011, and our final dataset contains the vote results for 2,389 municipalities.

2.2.2 *Votes in the Parliament*

Our second dataset consists of all the votes of the members of the National Council since the beginning of the current legislature, between December 2011 and December 2013. There were 2,494 votes by the 200 national councilors during this period[3]. In order to compare the opinions given on smartvote with the votes in the National Council, we discard the votes of the councilors that did not reply to the smartvote survey, hence our final dataset contains the votes (or abstentions) of 181 national councilors.

2.2.3 *Opinions Expressed on Smartvote*

Our third dataset consists of the responses given on the smartvote VAA [3] by the citizens and candidates during the Swiss parliamentary elections of 2011[4]. Smartvote proposes a long and a short survey. The short survey is composed of 32 questions and the long survey is composed of 75 questions, that include the 32 questions from the short survey. The *voters* (i.e., the visitors of the website) had the freedom to choose which survey to answer, but the candidates had to answer all the questions of the long survey. The questions address various topics ranging from society to economy and finance, and they were carefully selected to cover topics as representative as possible of current political issues. An answer consists in selecting one of the following options: *strongly agree - agree - disagree - strongly disagree.* An additional set of "budget questions" require selecting one of the options: *less - no change - more.* Finally, the voters can also select "no answer" (an option not available to the candidates). Each possible answer is mapped internally by smartvote to a number in the set $\{0, 0.25, 0.75, 1\}$ for regular questions, and in the set $\{0, 0.5, 1\}$ for budget questions. The final recommendation given to each voter is a list of candidates, in decreasing order of distance (using the l_2-norm) to this voter [32].

2,985 candidates filled out the survey, which represents about 82.4% of all the candidates. Unless otherwise specified, we consider the responses given by voters who participated in the short survey (which was the most popular survey). This amounts to about 229,000 voters[5], which corresponds to 9.3% of the total voter turnout of 2011. Detailed statistics about this dataset are summarized in Table 3.

3. IDEOLOGICAL SPACE

In this section, we provide a first analysis of the political landscape of Switzerland. We observe that simple dimensionality-reduction techniques can produce useful visual representations of political positions. We then analyze the difference of distribution and polarization between voters and candidates (before and after the elections), in such political spaces. Finally, we compute pairwise similarities between political parties, as measured by the opinions expressed by their members.

3.1 Dimensionality Reduction

In this section, we consider the dataset of opinions expressed on smartvote. Each candidate who took the short survey can be represented as a point in a space of 32 dimensions. Because it is likely that some politicians tend to think similarly on several questions, we can expect that some of these dimensions are strongly correlated. For instance, it could be the case that two persons who answer similarly to the question "Should access to naturalization be made more difficult?" also answer similarly to the question "Are you in favor of legalizing the status of illegal immigrants?". Therefore, one of the first questions that we could ask concerns the intrinsic dimensionality of this dataset. In the following, we use principal component analysis (PCA) [28, 30] in order to compute the sets of questions that best capture these correlations.

Denote by $\mathcal{A}$ the set of possible responses to any question on smartvote[6]. Let n be the number of questions and C the number of candidates. Using this notation, we define $\mathbf{C}$ as the $C \times n$ matrix of candidates' responses, whose $(i, j)^{\text{th}}$ entry $\mathbf{C}_{i,j} \in \mathcal{A}$ is the response of the i-th candidate to the

[3]The data is publicly available via a dedicated web-service: `http://ws.parlament.ch/votes`.

[4]The smartvote dataset can be obtained on demand for research purposes, by sending a request to `contact@smartvote.ch`.

[5]Note that obtaining a precise figure for the number of unique voters is difficult, as one voter can ask several recommendations on the website. This number is an estimate, obtained after filtering out identical web sessions.

[6]We merge budget and regular questions, and take $\mathcal{A} = \{0, 0.25, 0.5, 0.75, 1\}$ for all questions.

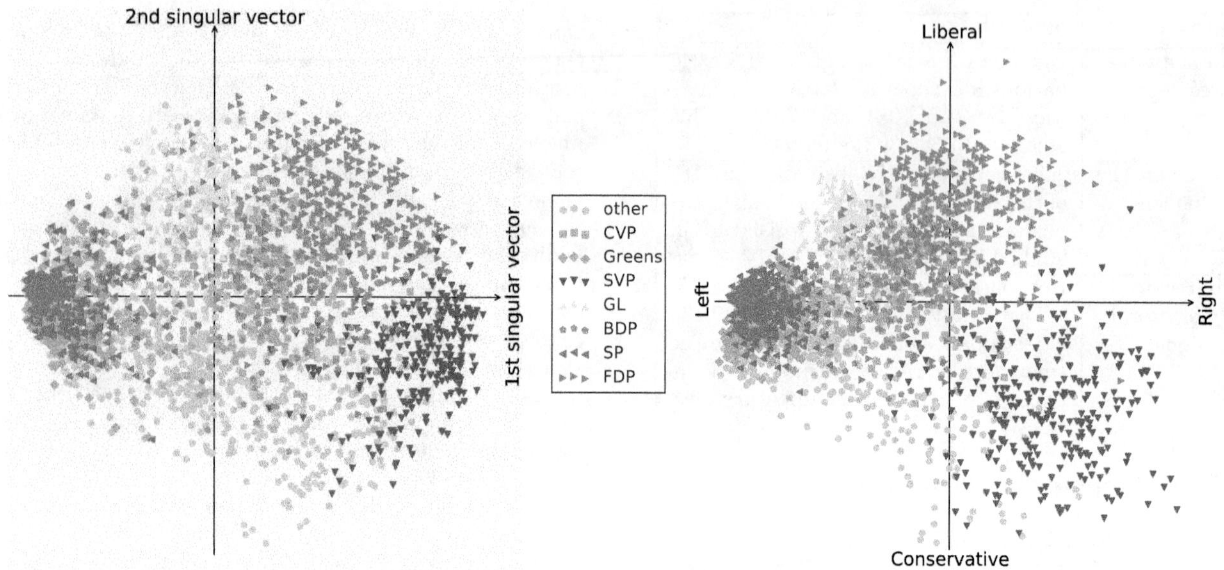

Figure 1: Left: 2-D projection of candidates onto the first two singular vectors of the matrix of their smartvote responses. Right: projection obtained by the smartvote *Smartmap*, with qualitative axes referring to traditional ideological separations.

j-th question. We start by centering $\mathbf{C}$ so that it has zero mean. We then compute the SVD factorization of $\mathbf{C}$ as

$$\mathbf{C} = \mathbf{U}\mathbf{\Sigma}\mathbf{W}^T,$$

where $\mathbf{U}$ is the $C \times C$ matrix whose columns are the left-singular vectors of $\mathbf{C}$, $\mathbf{\Sigma}$ is a $C \times n$ diagonal matrix, whose n non-zero entries are given by the singular values of $\mathbf{C}$, and $\mathbf{W}$ is the $n \times n$ matrix whose columns are the right-singular vectors of $\mathbf{C}$. We adopt the usual convention, according to which the columns of $\mathbf{U}$ and $\mathbf{W}$, and the diagonal elements of $\mathbf{\Sigma}$ are ordered by decreasing amplitude of the corresponding singular values. The projection of $\mathbf{C}$ onto the basis constituted by its singular vectors is given by $\mathbf{C}' := \mathbf{CW}$. The matrix $\mathbf{C}'$ has a diagonal covariance matrix, i.e., all its dimensions are uncorrelated. Furthermore, if we denote s_i the singular value associated with the i-th singular vector, the variance of the data along the i-th dimension of $\mathbf{C}'$ is proportional to s_i^2. It follows that, for any $k \leq n$, the first k dimensions of $\mathbf{C}'$ are the k dimensions that capture most of the variance of the data.

We use this property in Figure 1 (left) to obtain a graphical representation of the candidates on the plane, by showing the first two columns of $\mathbf{C}'$, i.e., the projection of $\mathbf{C}$ onto its first two singular vectors. In Figure 1 (right), we also show the representation of the same candidates using the *Smartmap* provided by smartvote [3]. The Smartmap employs a similar dimensionality-reduction technique based on correspondence analysis, and it has been manually validated in order to obtain the correspondence with traditional left/right and liberal/conservative directions.

The relative positions of candidates and political parties are qualitatively similar in both cases, which confirms that our dimensionality-reduction approach is consistent with traditional ideological representations.

Interestingly, PCA easily recovers the usual left/right and liberal/conservative divisions, by looking *only* at the responses (and not at the questions themselves). In Table 4,

Singular vector	First two questions
1st	1. Would you support foreigners who have lived for at least ten years in Switzerland being given voting and electoral rights at municipal level? 2. Are you in favour of legalizing the status of illegal immigrants?
2nd	1. Are you in favour of the complete liberalization of shop opening times? 2. Should Switzerland conclude an agricultural free trade agreement with the EU?
3rd	1. Should Switzerland legalize the consumption of hard and soft drugs? 2. Should same-sex couples who have registered their partnership be able to adopt children?

Table 4: Two most important questions of the first three singular vectors, for the dataset of candidates' responses to the smartvote survey. These questions are those that contribute the most, in absolute value, to each of the singular vectors. They can be used to interpret the different themes on which the candidates tend to disagree the most.

we show the two most important questions corresponding to the first three singular vectors (i.e., the two questions with the largest absolute weights for each axis). It very clearly appears that the first two axes refer, broadly speaking, to openness and integration of foreigners, and to economic liberalism. Interestingly, the third axis (not used for the 2-D representation in Figure 1) seems dominated by "ethical" issues, such as drug consumption and adoption by same-sex couples.

Candidate density

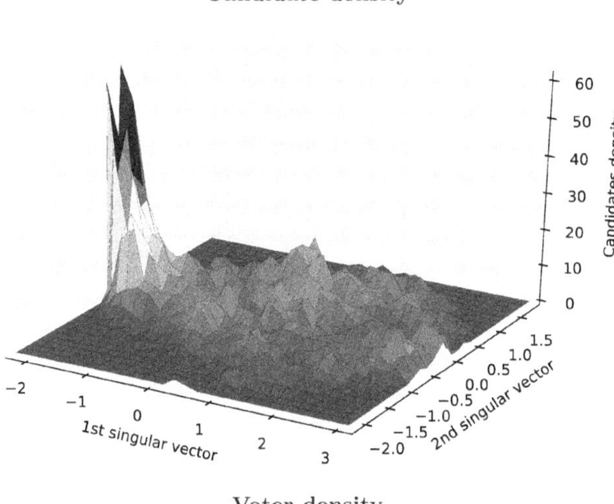

Voter density

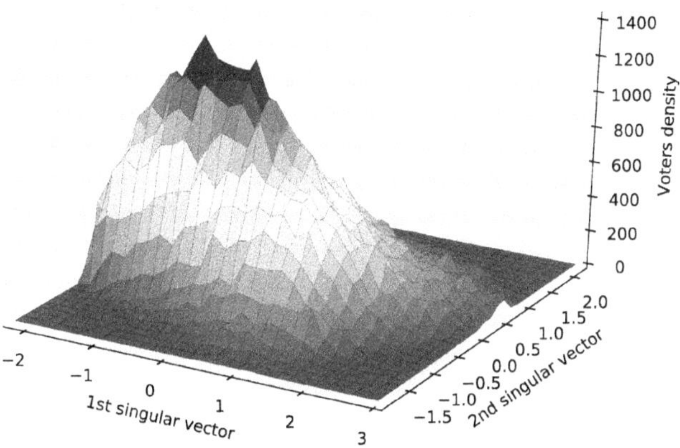

Figure 2: Density of candidates and voters in the ideological space, computed from their smartvote responses. The distributions are very different, and the candidates at the "left" of the space exhibit especially low variance.

3.2 Candidates, Voters, and Polarization

Using the dimensionality-reduction approach presented in the previous section, we can compare the distribution of candidates with that of voters in the ideological space. To this end, we divide the 2-D region of Figure 1 in a 30×30 grid and compute the candidate density as the number of candidates falling into each cell. We follow the same procedure for voters and show both densities in Figure 2. Perhaps the most striking feature of this figure is the comparatively large density of candidates residing on the "left" of the political space. As has already been observed [13], left-wing candidates appear to be very consistent in their responses and exhibit little variance. It seems to be that these candidates, more than the others, tend to strongly agree on the issues raised in the first two singular vectors. It is also possible that this is partly an artifact due to the (publicly admitted [17]) existence of "guidelines" provided by some parties and used by their candidates to answer smartvote questions.

The difference between the two densities of Figure 2 also suggests that politicians are somewhat more polarized than citizens. This fact has often been observed by political scientists, in particular in Switzerland [21]. It is confirmed by the first two plots in Figure 4 that show the proportion of total variance that is captured by each of the first three singular vectors (as well as the remaining variance, captured by the remaining singular vectors). We see that the first three singular vectors capture about a third of the variance in the voters responses, while candidates have 58% of their variance captured in these first three dimensions.

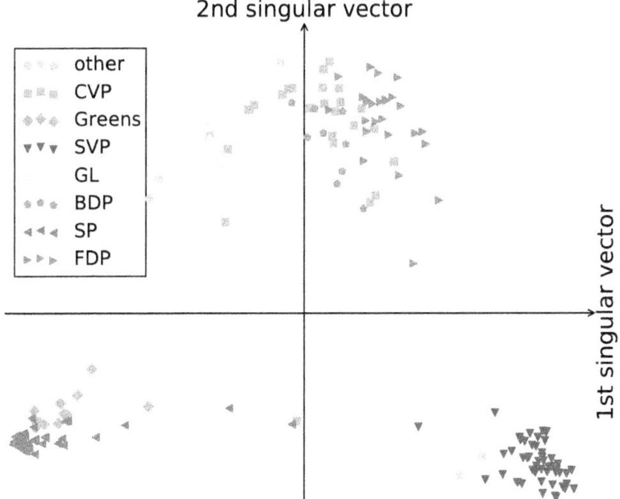

Figure 3: 2-D representation of parliament members, obtained from the dataset of votes in the parliament. The votes in the parliament are more clustered and polarized than the pre-electoral opinions given by candidates and represented in Figure 1.

To further investigate the polarization of politicians, we apply the same dimensionality-reduction approach to the dataset of parliament votes. The resulting 2-D representation of the members of the parliament is shown in Figure 3. Once elected, politicians are much more clustered (which is essentially explained by the existence of coalitions in the parliament). We also show in the last plot of Figure 4 the variance captured by the singular vectors of the dataset of the parliament votes. It confirms that votes in the parliament are strongly polarized, with 66% of the total variance explained by only the first three axes. The candidates, in contrast, are somewhat less polarized during the pre-electoral campaign, but still significantly more than the voters.

3.2.1 Party Overlaps

Figure 1 shows that some subsets of the political parties significantly overlap with each other. In order to check whether such overlaps still exist in the original 32-dimensional space, we compute, for each party, the proportion of candidates of this party who are closer to the median answer of the candidates of *at least* one other party, than to the median of their own party. These proportions are shown in Figure 5. It appears that several of the main parties have a large proportion of their candidates who are closer to at least one other party. This concerns more than 20% of the candidates of four of the seven parties. The FDP, CVP and BDP show exceptionally large figures; more than 35% of FDP, 45% of CVP and 50% of BDP candidates are closer to the median

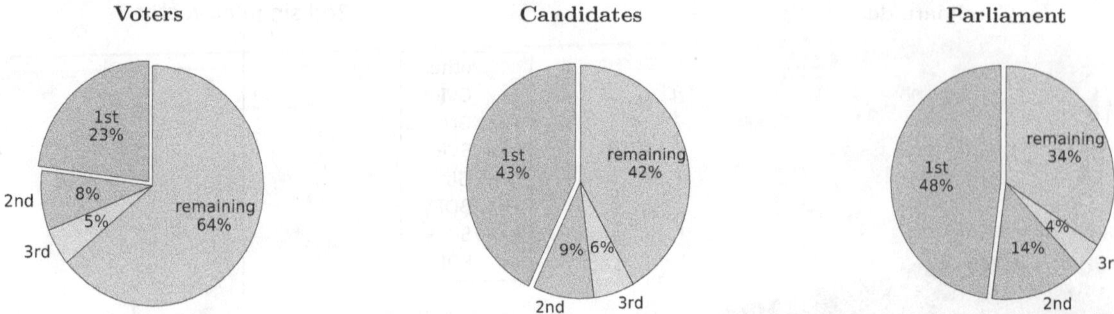

Figure 4: Proportion of the variance captured by the first three singular vectors of candidates, voters, and parliament members. Votes at the parliament are more polarized than the opinions given on smartvote. In turn, the opinions given by the candidates are more polarized than the opinions given by the voters.

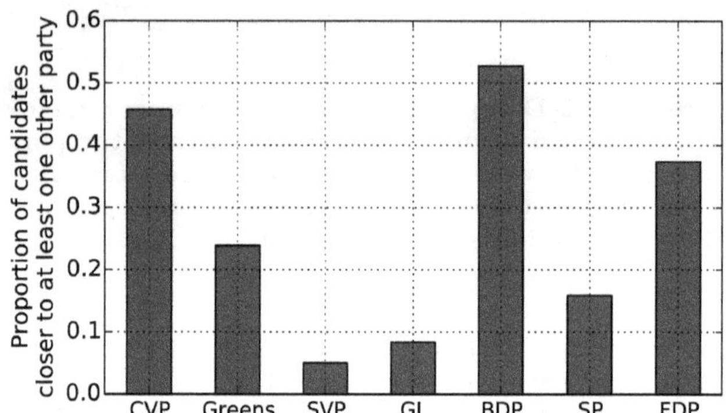

Figure 5: Proportions of candidates of each party that are closer to the median of *at least* one other party than to the median of their own party.

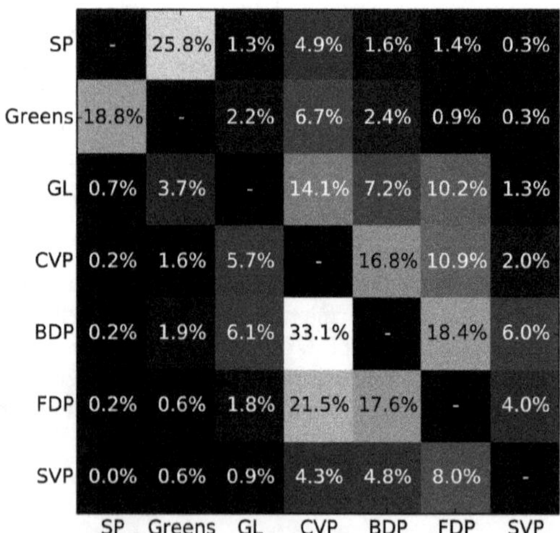

Figure 6: Inter-party overlaps. The number in row i and column j indicates the percentage of candidates of party i that are closer to the median position of party j.

answer of at least one other party. These parties do not belong to political extremities, but rather share a region near the center of the political space, which partly explains why they largely overlap. In practice, this means that using smartvote questions, it is hard to determine which party suits best a person with centrist opinions.

In order to gain more insights into which parties are actually closer, we look at detailed pairwise overlaps. Specifically, for each pair of parties (i, j), we show in Figure 6 the proportion of candidates of party i who are closer to the median of party j than to the median of their own party i. Note that here too, these proportions are computed in the original space, and are thus not subject to distortion due to dimensionality reduction. It is surprising that even opposite parties (such as SVP and SP, or SVP and Greens) have a few overlapping candidates.

4. MUNICIPALITIES

In this section, we take a closer look at the voting patterns of municipalities, with respect to both their main language and their geographical location. Then, we compare the outcome of votes in municipalities with the outcome at the federal (national) level, and show that it is possible to identify unique municipalities that have a great predictive power.

Throughout this section, we use the dataset of votes at the municipality level, described in Section 2.2. It contains the results of federal votes in Swiss municipalities, as well as the result at the federal level (whether the object was accepted or not). We denote by $\mathbf{M}$ the $M \times V$ matrix containing, for each municipality $m \in \{1, \dots, M\}$ and federal vote $v \in \{1, \dots, V\}$, the proportion $\mathbf{M}_{mv}$ of *yes* obtained in the municipality for this vote. Finally, we write $\mathbf{o} = \{o_v, v = 1, \dots, V\}$ for the outcome of these votes at the federal level. We have $M = 2,389$ municipalities and $V = 245$ votes.

4.1 The Infamous "Röstigraben"

Following the dimensionality reduction procedure described in Section 3.1, we project each line of $\mathbf{M}$, corresponding to the results of all votes in each municipality, onto the first two singular vectors of $\mathbf{M}$, and show the result in Figure 8. In this figure, each municipality is represented by a point whose shape indicates the language spoken by the majority.

The figure shows two clear clusters, corresponding to the French-speaking municipalities on one side, and the remaining municipalities on the other, separated by what Swiss people humorously call the *Röstigraben*[7] (literally *hashbrown curtain*). The gap between the two clusters reflects the difference in votes that often arise during federal elections in

[7]This term describes the cultural difference between the German-speaking Switzerland, on one side, and the French-speaking part (sometimes together with the Italian-speaking part) on the other.

Switzerland, where the results from French-speaking cantons are different from those of German-speaking cantons. It is interesting to note that while the Italian-speaking municipalities are culturally closer to the French-speaking ones (and are usually placed on the same side of the Röstigraben), their voting patterns seem to be closer to those of German-speaking municipalities in this projection.

To investigate the relationship between the geographical location of a municipality and its voting pattern, we map each point of the two-dimensional space represented in Figure 8 to a color, illustrated by the gradient in the upper-right corner of Figure 9. We then draw the map of Switzerland in Figure 9, where each municipality is shown with the color corresponding to its location in Figure 8. Thus, two municipalities having similar voting patterns have a similar color on the map. Lakes and municipalities for which some vote results are missing (e.g., due to a merging of municipalities) are shown in white[8].

Again, the separation between the French and German-speaking parts is clearly visible. Moreover, it is possible to identify different types of municipalities: urban centers, such as the greater areas of Geneva, Lausanne, Bern and the Zürich area have relatively similar tints of green, indicating that they share similar voting patterns, whereas rural areas in the German-speaking part share a deep purple color. It is interesting that the French-speaking part of the mountainous canton of *Valais*, located in the southwestern part of Switzerland, has its own unique voting pattern, shown in light blue.

4.2 Vote Outcome Prediction

We have seen in Section 4.1 that municipalities vary substantially in their voting patterns. One question that arises from this observation is whether it is possible to find one municipality whose voting behavior is representative of the global national outcomes. To answer this question, we study in this subsection the predictability of the outcome of votes at the federal level, using the outcome in a single municipality as unique feature.

We therefore define the following learning problem: Given the outcome $\mathbf{M}_{mv} \in [0, 1]$ of vote v in a municipality m, can we predict its outcome $o_v \in \{\text{yes}, \text{no}\}$ at the federal level? We split our dataset of 245 votes by taking the first 80% (196 votes) as a training set, and the remaining 20% (49 votes) as a test set. We train one binary classifier[9] for each municipality $m \in \{1, \ldots, M\}$. The parameters of the classifiers are selected using a 10-fold cross-validation on the training set. Figure 7 shows the cumulative distribution function of the accuracy of these M classifiers, averaged over the 10 validation sets (i.e., over the 10 cross-validation folds).

The results are quite surprising: about 10% of municipalities correspond to an accuracy higher than 90%, which means that knowing their results allows us to predict the outcome at the federal level with less than 10% of mistakes. Moreover, some municipalities reach accuracies of more than 96% on the validation set. The municipality reaching the highest average prediction accuracy on the validation sets is *Ebikon*, a town of 12,000 inhabitants in the canton of Lucerne. We evaluated the accuracy of the predictor which uses the vote outcome of Ebikon as feature, and we found that it obtains

[8]A more detailed map can be found online [2].

[9]We use a Gradient Boosted Decision Tree, implemented in Python with `scikit-learn` [23].

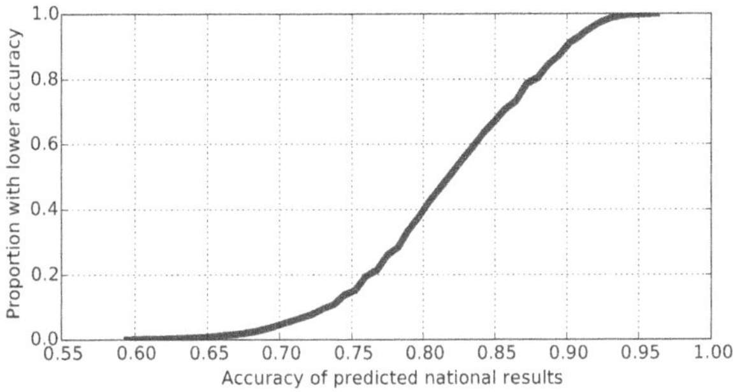

Figure 7: Cumulative distribution function of the accuracy of the prediction of the outcome of votes at the federal level, given the outcome of a single municipality. The accuracies are averaged over 10 cross-validation folds. 10% of municipalities allow to predict vote results at the national level with an accuracy higher than 90%.

a prediction accuracy of 95.9% on the test set. This means that out of the 49 votes of our test set, only 2 are incorrectly predicted by the classifier of Ebikon.

Although surprising[10], these results can be partly explained by the characteristics of Ebikon: located in the heart of Switzerland, it is quite representative of the overall diversity of the country. During the 2007 National Council elections, it had overall demographic features similar to that of Switzerland, and the proportion of votes for the different parties related relatively closely to the proportion of seats obtained. Moreover, as pointed in Figure 8, its voting pattern falls in the bulk of the German-speaking cluster.

Having such a representative sample would be extremely useful to many: Polling institutes, political parties and even news agencies would be able to target this municipality instead of sampling the population at random, thus maximizing the utility of their opinion surveys.

5. OTHER USES OF VAA'S

We showed in Section 3 that the data obtained from VAA's can be used to dress a fairly interesting portrait of the political landscape of the country. In this section, we show that an unscrupulous candidate could turn the public opinions of her adversaries to her advantage, by crafting a specific profile that would gather more voting recommendation than any other candidate. Moreover, we also show how a concerned citizen could turn these public profiles against potential cheaters, by comparing their votes after their election with their advertised opinion in order to spot changes of opinion.

5.1 Crafting the Ideal Opinion

As explained in Section 2.2, the smartvote VAA emits voting recommendations to each visitor by first computing the l_2-distance between her responses and those of each candidate, and then recommending the candidates who are the closest. This means that the responses a candidate gives to each question in the smartvote survey influences directly the number of voting recommendations she gets. Hence, it

[10]A similar effect was observed in the USA for the presidential elections, with the state of Ohio.

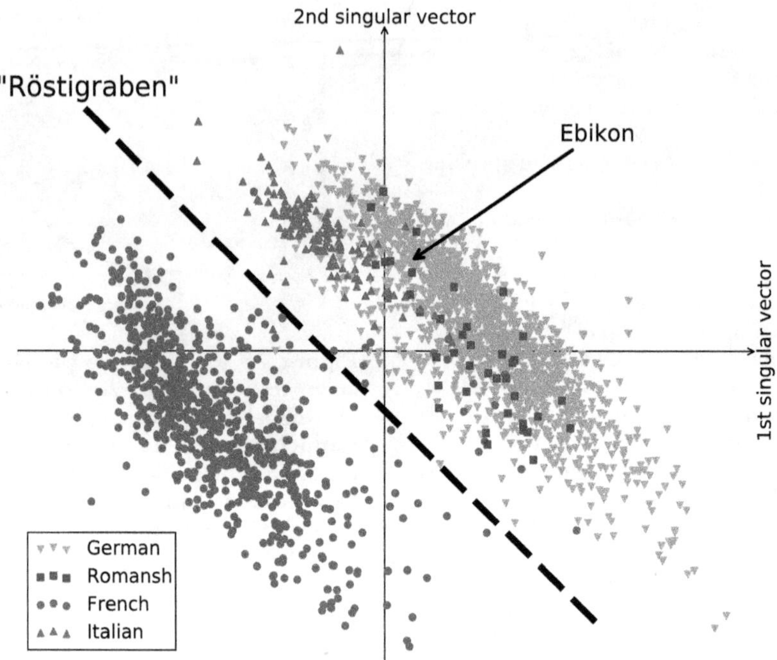

Figure 8: Projection of the vote results in each municipality onto the first two singular vectors of the municipality votes matrix M. The shape of each point indicates the language spoken by the majority in the municipality. A clear separation is visible between the French-speaking municipalities and the remaining municipalities.

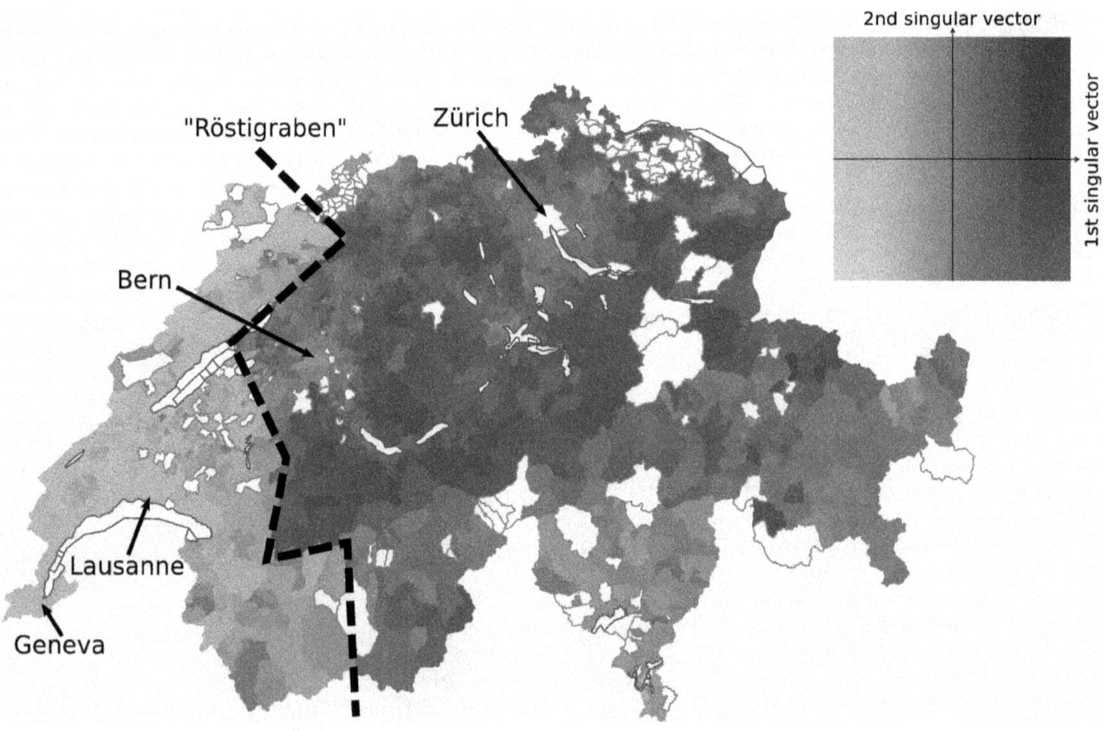

Figure 9: Voting patterns of Swiss municipalities. The color of a municipality is assigned using its location in Figure 8 and the color gradient shown in the upper right corner. Two municipalities with similar colors have similar voting patterns. The *Röstigraben*, corresponding to the cultural difference between French-speaking municipalities and German-speaking ones, is clearly visible from the difference in voting patterns. Regions shown in white are lakes or municipalities for which some vote results are missing (due to a merging of municipalities, for example). A more detailed map can be found online [2].

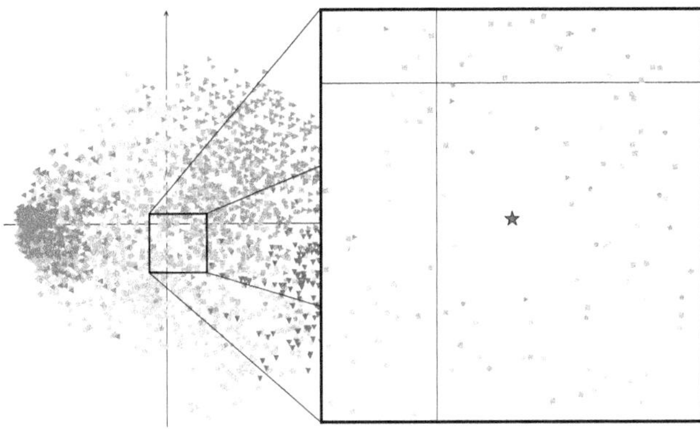

Figure 10: Zoom in the 2-D representation of candidates shown in Figure 1. We clearly see an area with no candidates, which we choose for the location of our crafted opinion, represented as a star.

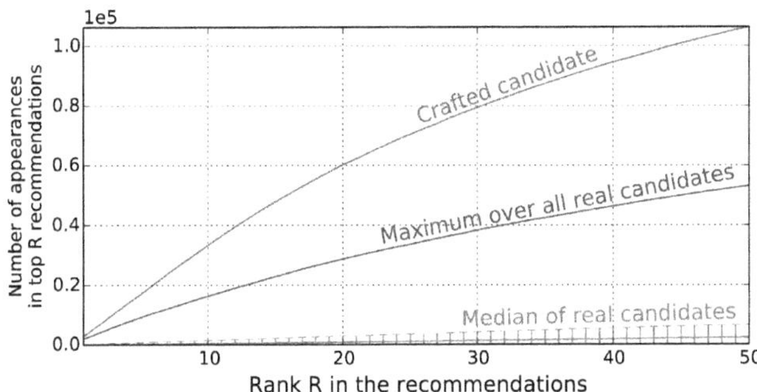

Figure 11: Number of appearances of candidates in the top recommendations. The curves show how many times the median, best, and crafted candidates appear in the top R recommendations for voters. The crafted candidate uses responses corresponding to the star shown in Figure 10. It gets more recommendations than any other candidates, appearing in the top 50 recommendations for close to half of the 230,000 voters.

is interesting to see if it is possible to create an "optimized" profile, in order to get as many recommendations as possible.

Computing the optimal set of answers that maximize the likelihood of a candidate to appear on top of recommendations would require to know both the answers of candidates and voters. However, at the time of completing the survey, a candidate can only access the answers given by her fellow candidates (which are publicly listed on the website). Furthermore, even if the set of answers given by voters were known in advance, the computation of an optimal profile is of combinatorial complexity; if there are n questions with k possible choices, an exhaustive search requires $O(k^n)$ computations. More efficient techniques (e.g., based on geometric approximation [16]) could be used to solve this problem. We leave a more formal study of this optimization problem for future work.

Instead, we propose a simple but efficient heuristic to craft a new candidate profile, by looking only at the answers of the other candidates. Our method consists in inspecting the distribution of candidates in the two-dimensional ideological space depicted in Figure 1. We see that there are several spots where the density of candidates is quite low. However, from Figure 2, we know that voters tend to have a more uniform distribution, thus suggesting that these spots might correspond to "unrepresented" citizens. Thus, we choose to place our crafted candidate in one of those spots, filling a gap in the ideological space but staying far from the extremes.

Such an "optimal" positioning problem has been studied from a game-theoretical point of view in simpler settings [10, 22], and it has been shown that choosing the median position leads to the best results. However, selecting the median answer to each question as our crafted profile did not give satisfactory results in this setting.

To compute the actual responses this crafted candidate should give to the smartvote survey, we proceed as follows: First, we get the coordinates of an empty spot in the ideological space, represented in Figure 1, that is still close to the center of the space. The intuition behind this choice is that we want to be as far as possible from any other candidate, and still be close to the majority of voters. Such a location is illustrated in Figure 10. Then, we perform the inverse operation of the projection explained in Section 3.1, to project a 2-dimensional point back onto the 32-dimensional space of smartvote responses. Because the responses can only take values in $\mathcal{A}$, we round each component of the resulting projected answer to the closest value.

Finally, we add this crafted set of responses (obtained from the point shown in Figure 10) to the list of candidates and compute recommendations for each voter. We count, for each candidate, the number of times she appears in the top R recommendations of a voter, for $R \in \{1, \ldots, 50\}$ and show the results in Figure 11. The lower curve shows how many times the median candidate appears in the top R recommendations, and the error bars indicate the standard deviation. The middle curve shows the maximum number of times a real candidate appears in the top R recommendations. The upper curve shows how many times our crafted profile appears in the top R recommendations.

We see that our crafted profile appears significantly more often in the top recommendations than any other candidate. For example, it appears more than 100,000 times in the top 50 recommendations, about twice as much as the best real candidate. As our dataset consists of around 230,000 voters, this means that our crafted profile is recommended to almost half of the voters. Although the effect of these recommendations on direct votes has not been clearly determined [34], Ladner et al. indicate that 67% of smartvote users state that smartvote had an influence on their choice of party [18]. This influence is even more significant for swing voters [19]. Thus, both parties and individual candidates would benefit from an increased number of recommendations.

5.2 Detecting Opinion Shifts

We showed above how an unscrupulous candidate could craft a profile that would gather more recommendations than any other. This could result in the election of this candidate, who would then have to vote daily in the parliament. However, in this case, the votes she would cast in the parliament may not be in accordance with the opinion expressed by her crafted smartvote responses. As all votes of the members of the parliament are publicly disclosed, a concerned citizen could monitor legislators in order to detect *flip-floppers*, i.e., candidates changing their opinion after they are elected. We

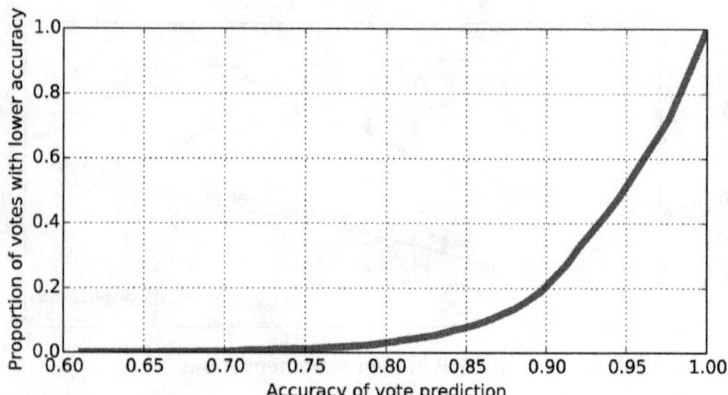

Figure 12: Cumulative distribution function of the predictability of parliament votes from smartvote responses. For each issue in the parliament dataset, we use the smartvote profile of candidates to predict their votes, and report the average accuracy over 10 folds, where 90% of the candidates are used for training and 10% for evaluation. We see that close to 50% of votes can be predicted with an accuracy of 95% or more, using only the smartvote profiles of legislators.

propose here a method to measure the shift in opinion of candidates, between the profile they advertised on smartvote (or any other VAA) during an electoral campaign, and their voting patterns in the parliament once they are elected. Note that our method aims only at quantifying opinion shifts. Of course, there are many contexts where politicians can be reasonably expected to change opinions with time, and moderate opinions shifts need not always be interpreted as bad signals.

5.2.1 *Predicting Parliament Votes*

The first step towards detecting changes of opinion is to map a set of smartvote responses to votes in the parliament. To do so, we identify parliament votes that can be predicted by smartvote responses. Indeed, the intuition is that, as smartvote responses are a good indicator of a candidate's political opinion, some votes can be accurately predicted from a set of smartvote responses. Therefore, we define the following learning problem: Given the smartvote profile of all candidates $\mathbf{C}$ and their votes $\mathbf{v}$ at the parliament on a given issue, learn a model that predicts the vote $\mathbf{v}_c \in \{\text{yes}, \text{no}\}$ of a candidate $c \in \{1, \ldots, C\}$ on this issue, from her smartvote opinion $\mathbf{C}_{c \cdot}$.

We train a linear classifier[11] for each of the 2,494 votes in the parliament dataset. For each vote, we filter candidates to keep those that actually voted (some are sometimes absent, or abstain) as learning samples. We evaluate the predictability of each vote by computing the prediction accuracy of our linear classifier using on 10 folds, where, for each fold, the classifier is trained on 90% of the candidates and evaluated on the remaining 10%. We then compute the average accuracy on these 10 folds, and report the results in Figure 12.

Figure 12 shows the cumulative distribution function of the prediction accuracy for each vote. We observe that the vast majority of votes at the parliament can be predicted with a high accuracy from smartvote profiles; more than 90% of votes can be predicted with an accuracy higher than 85%, and close to 50% of the votes can be predicted with an accuracy higher than 95%.

[11]We use Logistic Regression, implemented in Python with `scikit-learn` [23].

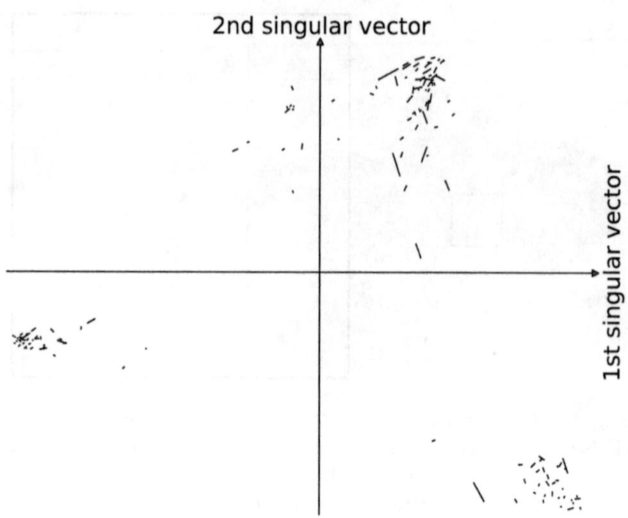

Figure 13: Opinion shifts of parliament members. Each segment represents a legislator, and goes from her expected votes (according to her smartvote profile) to her actual votes. The median legislator has only 0.3% of votes that are different than what is expected from her advertised opinion. The largest difference is 3.75%. Interestingly, the magnitudes of the shifts seem to be different for the three coalitions.

5.2.2 *Computing Opinion Shifts*

Now that we have a way to map smartvote opinions to parliament votes, we can compute the expected votes of legislators, based on their smartvote profile, and compare them with their actual votes. To do so, we first choose the 1,000 most predictable votes, in order to maximize the confidence in our predicted votes. This corresponds to the top 40% of votes, meaning that each of them can be predicted with an accuracy higher than about 96% (see Figure 12).

We then use the predictors trained in Section 5.2.1 to predict the expected votes of each candidate on these 1,000 issues. This means that, for each candidate, we use her smartvote profile to compute her expected votes on these issues, and we compare them with her actual votes. We compute the proportion of actual votes that differ from the expected votes. This proportion corresponds to the shift in opinion of the candidate, between her smartvote profile and her actual voting behavior in the parliament.

The 181 legislators voted on a median number of 906 issues. The median discrepancy between the votes predicted from smartvote profiles and the actual votes is only 0.3%. This means that the median candidate votes coherently with her advertised smartvote opinion 99.7% of the time. The candidate with the largest discrepancy has 3.75% of her votes in opposition to her advertised opinion. While this distance is an order of magnitude larger than the median distance, it still means that 96 votes out of 100 are coherent with what she advertised, which is a somewhat reassuring observation. A larger distance could mean that she falsely advertised her opinion on smartvote, or that she "flip-flopped", i.e., she changed her opinion significantly after being elected. However, it can also be expected that legislators sometimes divert from their advertised positions, for example to follow their party on a specific issue. Thus, one should be careful when interpreting such differences between expected and actual votes.

To visualize these opinion shifts, we show in Figure 13 the 2-D representation[12] of the expected and actual votes of each councilor, computed as explained in Section 3.1. Each candidate is represented as a segment, with one end corresponding to her expected votes, and the other to her actual votes. The longer a segment, the more significant the shift in opinion between her smartvote profile and her votes in the parliament. Interestingly, the magnitudes of the shifts seem to be different for the three coalitions.

6. RELATED WORK

Spatial approaches are often used to represent politicians or parties, most often using one or two dimensions. Some papers use dimensionality reduction techniques similar to ours [13, 31, 35]. However, to the best of our knowledge, we are the first to apply it on datasets of this scale. Furthermore, we show how it can be used to craft ideal VAA profiles, and put it in contrast with parliamentary and municipal votes.

Some researchers studied roll calls at the U.S. Congress [26, 25, 9]. For instance, Poole et al. study voting patterns at the Congress [26], and find that legislators can be described in a space of low dimensionality. Based on spatial voting theory [11], Enelow et al. propose a method to predict congressional votes. Their method relies only on past congressional votes to make predictions. While we study the predictability of votes, we do not use our predictors to predict future votes. Instead, we propose a method that permits to map one space (the opinions expressed on a VAA) onto another (the votes in the parliament), in order quantify opinion shifts.

Hansen et al. [15] explore the cohesiveness of political parties using VAA data, by measuring the agreement among party members. We propose a different approach, which allows us to measure the overlap between each pair of parties.

While we focus on predicting the results of national *issue voting* in Section 4.2, there is a large body of work that focuses on predicting the results of *elections*. For instance, Armstrong et al. [8] use biographical information about candidates to predict U.S. election results. In addition, several studies focus on Twitter data to predict the outcome of elections, from Germany [33] to the Netherlands [27] and Singapore [29]. However, some researchers (see e.g., Gayo [12]) have warned against relying only on tweets to predict election results, arguing that the data is inherently biased and that missing signals could be more important than observed ones.

Related to the votes prediction and the opinion shifts measurement that we propose in Section 5, Gerrish et al. [14] study the prediction of lawmakers' position on a bill, using the text of the bill. The authors use the resulting model to explore how lawmakers deviate from their expected voting patterns. Finally, Poole studies members of the U.S. Congress [24], and finds that they "adopt a consistent ideological position and maintain it over time".

[12]We restrict the parliament dataset to the 1,000 most predictable votes, instead of all 2,494 votes, resulting in a projection slightly different than that shown in Figure 3.

7. CONCLUSION

We proposed a data-mining approach towards using massive open government and VAA datasets to study different aspects of a country's politics. We considered the case of Switzerland, as this country has a strong democratic culture with a diversified political landscape. We observed that the scale of the data enables statistical approaches to uncover patterns that usually require manual investigations by domain experts.

We compared the polarization of voters with that of politicians, before and after the elections. We found out that some parties have more than 40% of their candidates that are closer to at least one other party. We showed that it is possible to learn models that predict vote outcomes at the national level with an accuracy higher than 95%, by looking at the outcome in a single municipality.

We described how an unscrupulous candidate could craft a synthetic VAA profile, in order to gather a very large number of voting recommendations. However, we also proposed a technique to hold a legislator accountable for her opinions expressed on a VAA, by mapping VAA responses to votes in the parliament and comparing her expected vote with her actual votes. Our technique can be used to spot legislators that vote in contradiction to the opinions that they expressed on a VAA.

Overall, our work applies to any country where similar data is available, and it points to some avenues created by open government initiatives that enable new data-mining approaches to political and social sciences.

8. ACKNOWLEDGMENTS

We would like to thank Jan Fivaz, Julien Fiechter and the rest of the smartvote team for providing us with their dataset, and answering the many questions we had about its format and use. We would also like to thank Olivier Dousse for the several insightful initial discussions on this topic.

9. REFERENCES

[1] Datacatalogs.org. `http://datacatalogs.org/`.

[2] Predikon eigenmap. `http://www.predikon.ch/eigenmap`.

[3] Smartvote. `http://www.smartvote.ch`.

[4] Stemtest. `http://www.stemtest2014.be/`.

[5] Stemwijzer. `http://www.stemwijzer.nl/`.

[6] Vote compass. `http://votecompass.com/`.

[7] Wahl-o-mat. `http://www.bpb.de/politik/wahlen/wahl-o-mat/`.

[8] J Scott Armstrong and Andreas Graefe. Predicting elections from biographical information about candidates: A test of the index method. *Journal of Business Research*, 64(7):699–706, 2011.

[9] Joshua Clinton, Simon Jackman, and Douglas Rivers. The statistical analysis of roll call data. *American Political Science Review*, 98(02):355–370, 2004.

[10] Anthony Downs. An economic theory of political action in a democracy. *The Journal of Political Economy*, pages 135–150, 1957.

[11] James M Enelow and Melvin J Hinich. *The spatial theory of voting: An introduction*. CUP Archive, 1984.

[12] Daniel Gayo-Avello. Don't turn social media into another 'literary digest' poll. *Communications of the ACM*, 54(10):121–128, 2011.

[13] Micha Germann, Fernando Mendez, Uwe Serdult, and Jonathan Wheatley. Exploiting smartvote data for the ideological mapping of swiss political parties. In *XXVI Congress of the Italian Political Science Association*, pages 13–15, 2012.

[14] Sean Gerrish and David M. Blei. How they vote: Issue-adjusted models of legislative behavior. In *NIPS*, pages 2762–2770, 2012.

[15] Martin Ejnar Hansen and Niels Erik Kaaber Rasmussen. Does running for the same party imply similar policy preferences? evidence from voting advice applications. *Representation*, 49(2):189–205, 2013.

[16] Sariel Har-Peled. *Geometric approximation algorithms*. Number 173. American Mathematical Soc., 2011.

[17] 24 heures. Sur smartvote, certains partis aident les candidats à répondre, August 2011. `http://goo.gl/Uru3Gt`.

[18] Andreas Ladner, Gabriela Felder, and Jan Fivaz. More than toys? a first assessment of voting advice applications in switzerland. *Voting Advice Applications in Europe. The State of the Art*, pages 91–123, 2010.

[19] Andreas Ladner, Jan Fivaz, and Joëlle Pianzola. Voting advice applications and party choice: evidence from smartvote users in switzerland. *International Journal of Electronic Governance*, 5(3):367–387, 2012.

[20] Daniel Lathrop and Laurel Ruma. *Open government: Collaboration, transparency, and participation in practice.* O'Reilly Media, Inc., 2010.

[21] Philipp Leimgruber, Dominik Hangartner, and Lucas Leemann. Comparing candidates and citizens in the ideological space. *Swiss Political Science Review*, 2010.

[22] Roger B Myerson and Robert J Weber. A theory of voting equilibria. *American Political Science Review*, 87(01):102–114, 1993.

[23] F. Pedregosa, G. Varoquaux, A. Gramfort, V. Michel, B. Thirion, O. Grisel, M. Blondel, P. Prettenhofer, R. Weiss, V. Dubourg, J. Vanderplas, A. Passos, D. Cournapeau, M. Brucher, M. Perrot, and E. Duchesnay. Scikit-learn: Machine learning in Python. *Journal of Machine Learning Research*, 12:2825–2830, 2011.

[24] Keith T Poole. Changing minds? not in congress! *Public Choice*, 131(3-4):435–451, 2007.

[25] Keith T Poole and Howard Rosenthal. A spatial model for legislative roll call analysis. *American Journal of Political Science*, pages 357–384, 1985.

[26] Keith T Poole and Howard Rosenthal. Patterns of congressional voting. *American Journal of Political Science*, pages 228–278, 1991.

[27] Erik Tjong Kim Sang and Johan Bos. Predicting the 2011 dutch senate election results with twitter. In *Proceedings of SASN 2012*, pages 53–60. EACL, 2012.

[28] Jonathon Shlens. A tutorial on principal component analysis. *Systems Neurobiology Laboratory, University of California at San Diego*, 2005.

[29] Marko Skoric, Nathaniel Poor, Palakorn Achananuparp, Ee-Peng Lim, and Jing Jiang. Tweets and votes: A study of the 2011 singapore general election. In *HICSS 2012*, pages 2583–2591. IEEE, 2012.

[30] Lindsay I Smith. A tutorial on principal components analysis. *Cornell University, USA*, 51:52, 2002.

[31] Jaakko Talonen and Mika Sulkava. Analyzing parliamentary elections based on voting advice application data. In *IDA X*, pages 340–351. Springer, 2011.

[32] Luis Terán, Jan Fivaz, and Stefani Gerber. Using a fuzzy-based cluster algorithm for recommending candidates in e-elections. *Fuzzy Methods for Customer Relationship Management and Marketing*, page 115, 2012.

[33] Andranik Tumasjan, Timm Sprenger, Philipp Sandner, and Isabell Welpe. Predicting elections with twitter: What 140 characters reveal about political sentiment. In *ICWSM*, 2010.

[34] Kristjan Vassil. *Voting Smarter? The Impact of Voting Advice Applications on Political Behavior.* PhD thesis, European University Institute, 2011.

[35] Jonathan Wheatley, Christopher Carman, Fernando Mendez, and James Mitchell. The dimensionality of the scottish political space: Results from an experiment on the 2011 holyrood elections. *Party Politics*, 2012.

[36] Wikipedia. Ballot measure, 2013. `https://en.wikipedia.org/wiki/Ballot_measure`.

Partisan Sharing: Facebook Evidence and Societal Consequences

Jisun An
Qatar Computing Research Institute, Qatar
jan@qf.org.qa

Daniele Quercia
Yahoo Labs Barcelona, Spain
dquercia@acm.org

Jon Crowcroft
University of Cambridge, UK
Jon.Crowcroft@cl.cam.ac.uk

ABSTRACT

The hypothesis of selective exposure assumes that people seek out information that supports their views and eschew information that conflicts with their beliefs, and that has negative consequences on our society. Few researchers have recently found counter evidence of selective exposure in social media: users are exposed to politically diverse articles. No work has looked at what happens after exposure, particularly how individuals react to such exposure, though. Users might well be exposed to diverse articles but share only the partisan ones. To test this, we study *partisan sharing* on Facebook: the tendency for users to predominantly share like-minded news articles and avoid conflicting ones. We verified four main hypotheses. That is, whether partisan sharing: 1) exists at all; 2) changes across individuals (e.g., depending on their interest in politics); 3) changes over time (e.g., around elections); and 4) changes depending on perceived importance of topics. We indeed find strong evidence for partisan sharing. To test whether it has any consequence in the real world, we built a web application for BBC viewers of a popular political program, resulting in a controlled experiment involving more than 70 individuals. Based on what they share and on survey data, we find that partisan sharing has negative consequences: distorted perception of reality. However, we do also find positive aspects of partisan sharing: it is associated with people who are more knowledgeable about politics and engage more with it as they are more likely to vote in the general elections.

Categories and Subject Descriptors

J.4 [**Computer Applications**]: Social and behavioral sciences

General Terms

Experimentation, Measurement

Keywords

Facebook; Twitter; Social media; Online social network; Politics; Selective exposure; Partisan sharing; News aggregators

COSN'14, October 1 – 2, 2014, Dublin, Ireland.

http://dx.doi.org/10.1145/2660460.2660469.

1. INTRODUCTION

The media landscape affords people the opportunity to control which political messages they consume. With freedom of choice comes responsibility, especially that of having a balanced news diet. Unfortunately, the opposite of a balanced diet – selective exposure – is likely to happen when consuming news. The theory of selective exposure holds that people tend to seek out political information confirming their beliefs and avoid challenging information. With a mix of experiments, surveys, and content analysis, decades of research have proved its existence across a variety of media – in newspapers, magazines, (cable) TV, radio, and online news sites [16,17,21,36].

Selective exposure is thought to be highly problematic for democracy – for example, it is often associated with "echo chambers" [37], whereby citizens befriend only like-minded others and do not talk to anyone else, resulting in segregated and polarized communities. Computer scientists have proposed different news aggregators that encourage politically diverse news consumption and try to mitigate the effect of selective exposure [11,18,24,28,29].

The problem is that, based on previous work, we do not know what happens after exposure – how individuals react to it. People might be exposed to diverse articles but share only the partisan ones. Social media offers us a unique opportunity to study how people react upon exposure. We thus go beyond selective exposure and study *partisan sharing* in an unobtrusive way and in large-scale: the tendency for users to predominantly *share* (not only be exposed to) like-minded news articles and avoid conflicting ones.

Political scientists have been focusing on building a "theory" of news consumption and they have done so upon either *self-reported* data of media *consumption* (and self-reporting can be inaccurate and error-laden [32, 41]), media *selection* data (often generated from small-scale experiments) or *actual* data of media *exposure*, which does not necessarily translate into consumption – one might well be exposed to a TV show without paying too much attention.

Computer scientists, on the other hand, have been studying online news consumption for a while now [23,25,29]. Individuals are increasingly turning to social networking sites to read and share political news, especially on Twitter and Facebook [2, 31]. Researchers have been able to get hold of data on those sites and unobtrusively analyze sharing patterns of a large number of users during long periods of time. They have produced reliable data-driven analyses of sharing behavior without, however, focusing on the theoretical side. That is why hypothesis driven analyses, so common in political science, represent the next natural step for social media research.

To this end, we formulate a set of hypotheses from the political science literature (Figure 1), analyze data from Facebook (44,999 news articles from 37 popular US news sites and 12,495 Facebook user profiles) and gather evidence for or against partisan sharing. In so doing, we make the following main contributions:

- We derive a set of well-grounded and coherent hypotheses related to partisan sharing in social media from the literature in political science (Section 3). These hypotheses are about whether or not partisan sharing exists in social media; changes across individuals; changes over time; and impacts on society by being associated with specific people's political attitudes.
- We gather a representative US sample of Facebook users (Section 4) and test some of those hypotheses with that data (Section 5). We investigate the news media sources individuals share and we find that partisan sharing exists. Based on a measure of partisanship we will define, only 33% of US Facebook news readers in our test sample can be considered moderate. Contrary to what the literature has posited, especially among conservatives, partisan sharing applies only to political news and disappears for non-political news (e.g., entertainment). We find that those who are partisan tend to be interested in politics. We have also been able to study how partisanship changes over time: we found that partisanship among Facebook users within a US state tends to be stable, and changes only during primary elections to then go back to the original value.
- Since Facebook data allows us to test most of the hypotheses but not all, we build a political site that recruits UK BBC viewers on Twitter and allows them to express their opinions about a weekly BBC political debate called Question Time (Section 6). Since Twitter differs from Facebook, we consider the hypotheses we have already tested on Facebook and find that they equally hold on the Twitter data. After this validity check, we test three new hypotheses regarding societal aspects of partisan sharing. We firstly find that people perceive a news outlet to be politically biased depending on their own political leanings (regardless of the objective bias) – the farther their leaning from the outlet's, the more biased they perceive the outlet to be. This results in partisan individuals having a distorted perception of how biased news outlets are. However, partisanship has a positive aspect too. We indeed find that the more partisan individuals, the more politically knowledgeable they are (second hypothesis), and the more likely to participate to political life (e.g., to vote).

We brought data to bear on the phenomenon of partisan sharing. Contrary to popular belief, social media have done little to broaden political discourse. Despite the political diversity social media have brought into one's news diet [2], individual news sharing has not been changed much contrary to traditional media. On one hand, social media users share news that matches their political beliefs and, as a result, may become increasingly divided; on the other hand, partisan sharing may encourage participation and news posting on social media sites. To mitigate the effect of partisan sharing, one might think of new ways of making sharing a bit less partisan and a bit more serendipitous, and this work offers an experimental basis for such future work.

2. RELATED WORK

Selective exposure. By analyzing news consumption on a variety of media (which included TV, radio, magazines, newspapers, online), Stroud [36] concluded that people tend to preferentially choose, read, and enjoy partisan news. A large body of literature shows supportive evidence for her findings [9,16,17,21,27]. More recently, some researchers have reported situations in which selective exposure is lower than expected or totally missing. LaCour did not find any evidence for it in the TV and radio consumption of 920 individuals in Chicago and New York [19]; Shapiro found an extremely low level of it online [13]; and An et al. even found that Twitter friends expand one's diversity of political news [2].

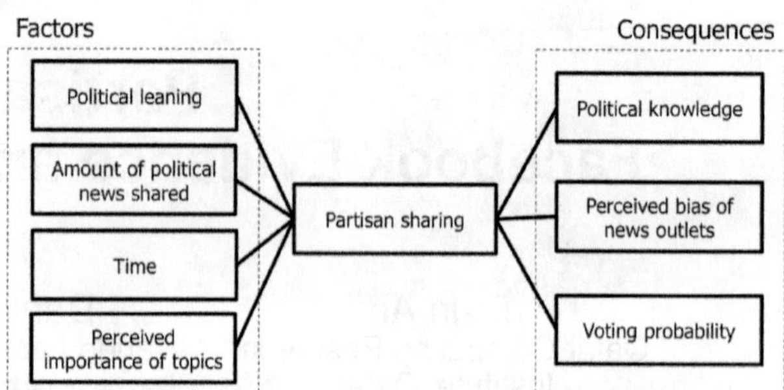

Figure 1: Factors and Consequences of Partisan Sharing.

However, despite its breadth, such a work and, for that matter, similar others suffer from the data under study: self-reported (and, as such, error-prone) data of news consumption. Starting from this criticism, LaCour directly measured how 920 individuals from New York and Chicago have been exposed to news for 85 days [19]. These measurements were taken by cell phones that recorded participants' audio. He showed that self-reported data grossly overestimates exposure. It turns out that most people do not care much about politics and are thus on a meager news diet – consequently, it does not really matter whether that diet is balanced or not. The problem is that audio-recording cell phones report what people are exposed to but not necessarily what they are paying attention to. A similar problem applies to An et al.'s work [2]. The authors analyzed Twitter streams and found that Twitter friends greatly expand one's diversity of political news. However, it is not possible to quantify the extent to which a Twitter user is actually paying attention to his/her own stream.

Why it matters. Selective exposure is often considered a threat to political and societal life. That is because it might influence people's beliefs in whom they should vote for [26,42]. It also encourages intolerance of dissent and results into ideological segregation [3,14]. Adamic et al. [1] showed that the political discourse on the blogsphere is not only partisan but also highly-polarized. The same pattern (i.e., polarized communities) has been observed in social media when looking at: usage of political hashtag [7] and a distribution of tweets different stories receive [39]. Political selective exposure also influences opinion formation on matters that have little to do with politics [36]. However, selective exposure is not always bad. It is also associated with political participation and political knowledge (i.e., factual information about politics) [36]: the more one is exposed, the more one is interested in politics and is knowledgeable about it.

What to do. Computer scientists have proposed different news aggregating systems that encourage politically diverse news consumption. For example, BLEWS [11] and NewsCube [29] gather and visualize news articles on the same subject matter but with different political leanings, making people aware of the existence of media bias. Munson and Resnick have studied how different presentation techniques make politically diverse news articles more

Hypothesis	Facebook	Twitter
Dynamics		
[H1] Existence	✓	✓
[H2.1] Political leaning	✓	✓
[H2.2] Amount of news shared	✓	✓
[H3] Changes over time	✓	
[H4] Perceived importance	✓	
Societal consequences		
[H5.1] Perceived bias		✓
[H5.2] Political knowledge		✓
[H5.3] Voting probability		✓

Table 1: List of Hypotheses. ✓indicates the hypothesis tested with Facebook/Twitter data.

appealing than others. It turns out that making hostile news more appealing is quite challenging [24].

Considering the literature, we conclude that no work has studied one of the results of (selective) exposure: what people do after being exposed. Unlike traditional experiments, social media sites offers us a unique opportunity to observe sharing for a long period of time in unobtrusive ways. We set out to explore partisan sharing in the context of Facebook and Twitter, and we firstly do so by connecting sharing behavior to factors of selective exposure.

3. PARTISAN SHARING

To begin with, we define partisan sharing as the tendency for users to predominantly share like-minded news articles and avoid conflicting ones.[1] Then, we derive five main hypotheses which were related to selective exposure in the literature and we now related to partisan sharing. That is, whether partisan sharing: 1) exists at all; 2) changes across individuals (i.e., depending on their interest in politics); 3) changes over time (i.e., around elections); 4) depends on perceived importance of topic; and 5) has any consequence in the real world (i.e., whether people vote or not).

Existence of partisan sharing. Its existence has been hitherto debated, as discussed in the previous section. Given that we will study news sharing in the context of Facebook and Twitter, our first hypothesis is: *[H1] Individual's news sharing in social media is not balanced but suffers from partisan sharing.*

Partisan sharing changes across individuals. It has been found that those who have a settled tendency of reading about politics tend to seek out news confirming their political proclivities, mainly because they do not like to pay attention to information challenging their views [36]. It is thus the case that ideological selectivity is predominant among partisan people and news junkies [4, 36]. Thus, our next hypothesis is: *[H2] An individual's level of partisan sharing depends on*: *[H2.1] political leaning*; and *[H2.2] amount of political news shared.* Those three factors are listed, for convenience, in the block on the left in Figure 1. That block collates factors associated with partisan sharing, which also include time, discussed next.

Partisan sharing changes over time. People tend to pay more attention to politics during specific periods of time, for example, during elections when the attention to the political agenda is high. More generally we might hypothesize that *[H3] Partisan sharing is highly prevalent in politically salient periods.*

Partisan sharing changes depending on the perceived importance of certain topic. People have their own preferences of which issues are important and ought to be in the political agenda. These preferences are often formed based on consumption of information from politically-biased outlets. Different outlets are associated with different topical priorities [22, 38]. Consequently, we hypothesize that *[H4]. Partisan sharing is associated with one's perceived importance of certain topic.*

Consequence of partisan sharing. After having formulated hypotheses regarding the dynamics associated with partisan sharing, we now formulate three hypotheses regarding its societal consequences. Recent research has found that selective exposure results into polarization and societal fragmentation [36, 37]. Our next hypothesis is then *[H5]. Partisan sharing is related to polarized political attitudes and, as such, affects one's:*

> *[H5.1] Perceived political bias of news outlets.* Partisanship often influences perceptions, including perception of how biased a news outlet is. It has been shown that the same outlet is considered very differently by people depending on their political leanings [36]. A left-leaning outlet is perceived moderately (if not at all) biased by left-leaning people, while it is perceived highly biased by right-leaning people.
>
> *[H5.2] Political knowledge.* Partisanship is associated with political knowledge: the more partisan, the more knowledgeable about politics [36].
>
> *[H5.3] Voting probability.* When people decide for whom to vote, they again rely on partisan media, which exert considerable influence [26, 42].

Having a list of factors and of consequences associated with partisan sharing, we are now ready to test their importance and we do so by using two datasets: Facebook and Twitter datasets. Table 1 summarizes the hypotheses and report which dataset is used to test which hypothesis. We mainly use Facebook data for the analysis, and we validate and complement results with Twitter data (Section 6).

4. METHODOLOGY

To begin with, we perform the following steps: gather a Facebook dataset of news sharing, consider only articles about politics, determine the media slant of the corresponding outlets, and compute each user's partisan skew. The higher an individual's partisan skew score, the higher his/her partisan sharing.

Facebook news sharing. More than five million Facebook users have been able to take a variety of genuine personality and ability tests by installing an application called myPersonality.[2] Users can also opt in and give their consent to share their personality scores and profile information, and 40% have chosen to do so. We gather news sharing information from a random subset of those users: 228,064 Facebook users who shared (i.e., posted) 4.9M links.

To avoid temporal biases generated by the adoption of the Facebook application, we focus on a specific period of time that is stable enough: from April to September 2010. During that period, we gathered 44,999 articles posted by 12,495 users: 37% of links are successfully classified as political news articles through Alchemy

[1] In this work, we only consider what people initially post (referred as 'share') on social media.

[2] http://www.mypersonality.org/wiki

Facebook			
Liberal		Conservative	
huffingtonpost	11,236 (45.2%)	foxnews	3,774 (51.5%)
nytimes	10,083 (41.3%)	online.wsj	2,767 (54.1%)
msnbc.msn	4,892 (30.7%)	nydailynews	1,433 (26.8%)
abcnews.go	2,752 (23.2%)	nypost	695 (31.9%)
washingtonpost	2,468 (58.3%)	politico	670 (87.3%)
time	2,104 (34.9%)	forbes	565 (20.7%)
cbsnews	1,868 (22.8%)	washingtontimes	432 (73.4%)
bostonglobe	1,260 (29.3%)	townhall	426 (91.3%)
latimes	1,239 (37.3%)	nationalreview	288 (65.9%)
salon	967 (64.8%)	chicagotribune	239 (36.4%)
slate	923 (44.9%)	bostonherald	118 (50.1%)
sfgate	779 (34.1%)	usnews	130 (36.2%)
wnd	441 (72.1%)	newsmax	93 (76.6%)
newyorker	368 (33.9%)	weeklystandard	60 (79.5%)

Table 2: List of the News Sites Shared by Facebook Users. We remove ".com" from domain name of news sites. Each outlet comes with its total number and proportion of political news articles.

API (discussed shortly). The articles they post come from 37 news sites (a few representative news sites are displayed in Table 2.[3]). The demographic of these users reflects the general Facebook population in USA [4]: their number of social contacts is between 30 and 1000 and whose age is comprised between 18 and 54. This group is composed of 7,372 women (59%) and 5,037 men (41%) with a median age of 23. Table 3 reports the demographic details of Facebook users in our dataset.

Each user has posted 2.85 articles on average; while 66.5% of users have posted only one article. Based on their activity level (i.e., number of news shared), we find 4,710 users who posted more than two news articles, 2,113 users who posted more than four news articles, and 950 users who posted more than eight news articles on Facebook. We confirm that demographic information of those groups are consistent with that of general Facebook population.

Only news articles about politics. To select only the articles about politics, we need to be able to classify articles into categories, and select those that fall into politics. To that end, we use Alchemy text classification API.[5] We use this API because it has been shown that it entails superior classification performance compared to other popular classifiers [33]. Alchemy API is a suite of natural language processing tools. It is capable of assigning a plain English category to any given string of text (a tweet, for instance), along with a certainty score from 0.0 to 1.0, which represents the API's degree of belief that the text pertains to that category. It can also take a URL as an argument – it then classifies the textual content of the document it finds there. Alchemy can choose from the following 12 topics: Arts Entertainment, Business, Computer Internet, Culture Politics, Gaming, Health, Law Crime, Recreation, Religion, Science Technology, Sports, and Weather. Hence we are using Alchemy topics as a gold standard in our work. We excluded 5,705 URLs

[3]6 news outlets are considered to be at the center of the political spectrum: CNN (13,753 (39.7%)), NewsWeek (1,101 (45.8%)), Arizona Central (363 (37.2%)), The Atlantic (384 (44.2%)), PBS (808 (51.2%)), and Christian Science Monitor (603 (31.2%))

[4]Ugander et al. have reported that the age of 140M USA Facebook users ranges from 13 to 60+ where 20s and 30s are the dominant. Also the median number of social contacts is 100, yet, the distribution is highly skewed (there are few people having more than 1000 social contacts), resulting in 190 as an average value [40].

[5]http://www.alchemyapi.com

	Facebook
Age	<20(25%), <30(31%), <40(18%), ≥40(16%)
Gender	Male (41%), Female (59%)
Partisanship	Partisan (59.6% (Lib (69.9%),Con (30.1%))), Non-partisan (40.4%)

Table 3: Details for our 12,855 Facebook Users.

that are categorized as "None" (e.g., broken link) and URLs that have low confidence values (< 0.5 on Alchemy's scale of $[0, 1]$). Then we take the remaining ones that are classified under "Culture/Politics" for our analysis (16,729 news articles).

Determining media slant. We need to classify news outlets into liberal, conservative, or center. Since the outlets in the Facebook dataset are mainly in US (Table 2), we consider four classification schemes previously used in the literature of political science: 1) *Left-Right*, which classifies a large number of news outlets, including those with online presence only[6]; 2) *MondoTimes*, which classifies news outlets based on user votes on a crowdsourcing platform[7] (this has been used in Gentzkow and Shapiro's work [12]); 3) *Gentzkow and Shapiro*'s novel classification, which relies on term similarity between political speeches and news articles [12]; and 4) *Larcinese* et al.'s classification, which relies on the amount of coverage media outlets give to U.S. political scandals [20]. The results reported later on do not change depending on which of the four classification we use. That is largely because the four schemes show high agreement, as we shall discuss in Section 8. Thus we report the results only for the first classification.

Measuring partisanship: Net partisan skew. To measure partisan sharing, in line with previous work [19], we focus on news posting from partisan sources (i.e., those that are classified as either conservative or liberal) and compute the *net partisan skew* as the number of conservative news postings minus that of liberal news (news counts, being skewed, undergo a logarithm transformation):

$$leaningScore_{conservative} - leaningScore_{liberal} \quad (1)$$

$$leaningScore_p = ln(\#\text{news articles of } p) \quad (2)$$

$leaningScore_p$ is 0 when the news count of p is 0. The partisan skew is our main measure of partisan sharing and reflects how balanced a user's news sharing is – for example, it is zero if the user posts an equal amount of conservative and liberal news; it is $\pm$ 1 if, for every 2.7 ($\approx e^1$) conservative (liberal) articles, the user posts 1 liberal (conservative) article; and it is $\pm$ 2 if, for every 7.4 ($\approx e^2$) conservative (liberal) articles, the user posts 1 liberal (conservative) article. We use this metric to be able to compare our result to that of previous work [19], which has incidentally shown limited evidence of selective exposure.

5. PARTISAN SHARING IN FACEBOOK

We will test to which extent partisan sharing exists (Section 5.1) and how it changes across individuals (Section 5.2) and over time (Section 5.3), we will then study its association with perceived importance of topics (Section 5.4). Table 1 reports which hypotheses has been tested upon Facebook dataset.

[6]http://left-right.us

[7]http://mondotimes.com

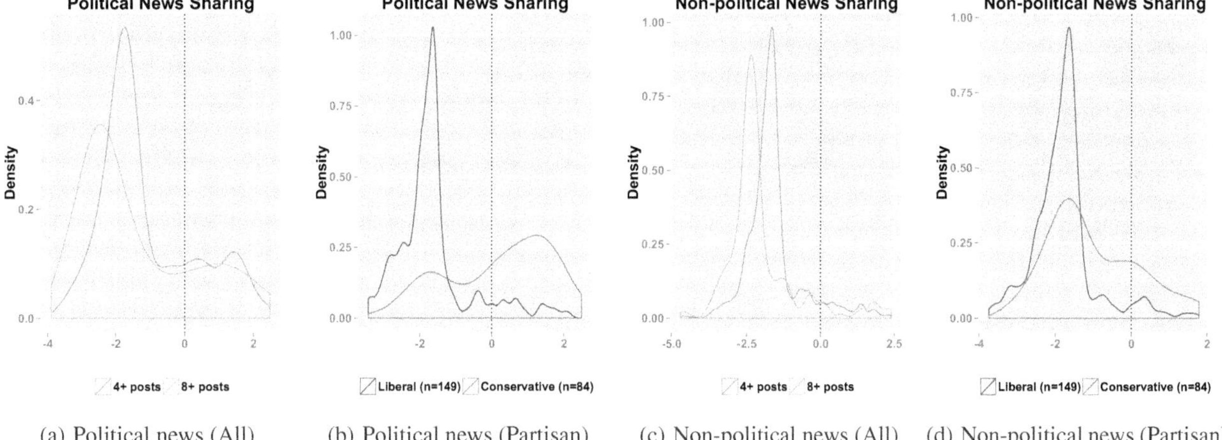

(a) Political news (All) (b) Political news (Partisan) (c) Non-political news (All) (d) Non-political news (Partisan)

Figure 2: Net Partisan Skew of political news by *(a) Activity Level*. For any of the two activity levels (4+ articles and 8+ articles posted), there are two peaks reflecting liberal views (left peak) and conservative views (smaller right peak), respectively. The majority of our Facebook users are liberal. *(b) Party*. We consider users who share 4+ political articles. Liberal users share more liberal news outlets and are centered around a net partisan skew of -1.8, while conservative users share more conservative news and are centered around 1.4. Net Partisan Skew of soft news (e.g., Arts Entertainment) by *(c) Activity Level*. For any of the two activity levels (4+ articles and 8+ articles posted), the distribution is unimodal and centered around -1.7 and -2.43, respectively. Both Liberal and Conservative are sharing soft news coming from liberal outlets. *(d) Party*. We consider users who share 4+ political articles. Liberal users post more liberal news outlets and are thus centered around a net partisan skew of -1.8.

5.1 Existence

[H1] Individuals' news sharing in social media is not balanced but suffers from partisan sharing.

To measure the extent to which partisan sharing exists, we analyze news sharing for articles coming from partisan news outlets – that is, from outlets that can be labeled as either conservative or liberal. We compute net partisan skew using expression (1) (how balanced one's news sharing is): a positive score represents users sharing news from conservative outlets, while a negative one indicates sharing from liberal outlets. The theory of partisan sharing suggests that we should find a binomial distribution, with conservative users sharing predominantly conservative news articles, and liberal users sharing predominantly liberal ones. Figure 2(a) displays the distribution of net partisan skew in the form of kernel density estimates for two sets of users – low-activity users who posted at least 4 articles and high-activity ones who posted more than 8 articles. Each curve shows two peaks, reflecting two user segments – one sharing exclusively liberal news, and the other sharing exclusively conservative news. This is true for both curves, suggesting that partisan sharing holds not only for high-activity users but also for low-activity ones. Based on self-reported political affiliations, clearly denoted as either "liberal" or "conservative", on Facebook, we separate liberal users ($N = 149$) from conservative ones (N=84) and compute their partisan skew (Figure 2(b)). We find that all of them share a considerable number of like-minded news and systematically avoid counter-attitudinal news. The majority of liberals (conservatives) read one counter-attitudinal article every 6 (4) like-minded articles.

Finally, since it has been shown that selective exposure to political news ends up influencing news sharing on matters that are not strictly related to politics [36], we analyze sharing of not only political news but of any type of news. We find that, when sharing news about, say, Arts Entertainment, people do not constraint their general (non-political) news sharing to outlets matching their political beliefs, resulting in a unimodal (skewed to the left) distribution (Figure 2(c)). Surprisingly, conservatives tend to share non-political news from liberal outlets (Figure 2(d)).

5.2 Changes across individuals

Despite the evidence that partisan sharing occurs, it is clear that not everyone shares like-minded news to the same extent – after all, 32.8% of users have a net partisan skew in the range as low as [-1,1]. Does partisan sharing change depending on users' characteristics? Previous studies in political science have posited that *an individual's level of partisan sharing depends on: **[H2.1]** political leaning*; and ***[H2.2]** amount of news sharing*.

We test whether partisan sharing changes depending on one's political leaning (*H2.1*). For a fair comparison, we first check whether the activity level of liberals and conservative are comparable. We find that they are similar – on average liberals share 9 news articles, while it is 8.2 news articles shared for conservative. Also unpaired t-test confirms that there is no difference on their activity level (the hypotheses was rejected). Then, we plot the (absolute value) of partisan skew for conservative and liberals (Figure 3(a)). By running unpaired t-test on these values, we find that liberals tend to be more partisan (with net skew of 1.82) than conservative (with net skew of 1.26) ($t(166.535) = 5.805$, $p < 0.0005$). For every counter-attitudinal news article shared, liberals will also share 6.2 like-minded articles, while conservative will only share 3.5 like-minded articles. This means that conservative users are less polarized than liberal ones, sharing 43% less like-minded articles. This is in line with work by LaCour who found that "Democrats, as a group, watch slightly more like-minded news, while on average Republicans have a more balanced media diet" [19].

Next, to test *H2.2*, we plot the net partisan skew (absolute value) against news sharing (i.e., the logarithm of number of shared news articles) in Figure 3(b). The higher the news sharing, the higher the partisan skew. For example, users who shared 4 articles ($\approx$ 1.2 on the x-axis) have an average partisan skew of 1.2: for every 3.3 ($\approx e^{1.2}$) conservative (liberal) articles, those users share 1 liberal (conservative) article. Higher-level activity users, say,

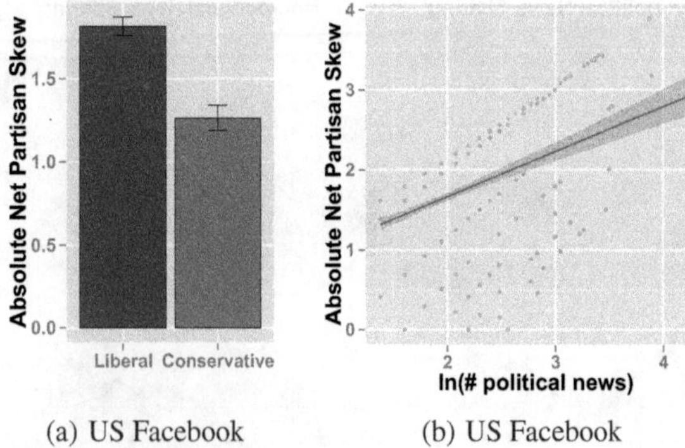

(a) US Facebook (b) US Facebook

Figure 3: Net Partisan Skew by *(a)* Party and *(b)* Activity. The absolute value of partisan skew is for US Facebook users who have shared 4+ articles.

those who shared 20 articles ($\approx$ 3 on the x-axis) have partisan skew of 2: for every 7.4 ($\approx e^2$) like-minded articles, those users share only 1 counter-attitudinal article. As users share more news, they also share more partisan news. For statistical test, we run two popular correlation with a Pearson's correlation coefficients of $r = .41$ ($p < 0.0005$) and with a Spearman's correlation coefficients of $r = .46$ ($p < 0.0005$). This finding runs contrary to what recent work has found [19] and confirms the partisan sharing hypothesis: as news sharing increases, readers tune out the other side.

5.3 Changes over time

From February to September 2010, primary elections were held in the USA (elections in which each political party nominates candidates for an upcoming general election), and different States held them in different months (e.g., Indiana in May, California in June).[8] We consider the time window in which our Facebook data overlaps with the election period and obtain news sharing data for two sets – States that voted in May (10 states out of 10 that held elections) and those that voted in June (12 out of 13). We then test the following hypothesis:

***[H3]** Partisan sharing is prevalent in politically salient periods (e.g., during elections).*

Figure 4 shows the average partisan skew (absolute value) for the two sets – for both of them, partisanship is minimum in the election month and tends to *increase* to a stable point outside that period. For the States voting in May, the absolute average partisan skew is 1.4 in the election month and is around 1.6 outside it. This means that, during elections, for every 4 ($\approx e^{1.4}$) conservative (liberal) articles, users post 1 liberal (conservative) article. Outside elections, partisan skew increases: users need to post 5 ($\approx e^{1.6}$) conservative (liberal) articles to then post 1 liberal (conservative) article. The same pattern holds for the States voting in June, where the ratios are 3.3-to-1 during elections and 4-to-1 outside them. Contrary to our expectation, this result (i.e., minimum partisanship during elections) seems to suggest that Facebook users tend to make their news diets both richer and more balanced during elections. Or it might well be that partisans share news articles from hostile outlets, just to make fun of them. If we were to have comments associated with the act of sharing, we would have studied their sentiment. Unfortunately, we do not have such data. However, we should stress that temporal evolution of partisanship has never been studied before, and this result, albeit preliminary, suggests that it is a research direction that ought to be in the agenda.

[8] http://www.bbc.co.uk/news/world-us+canada-10634453

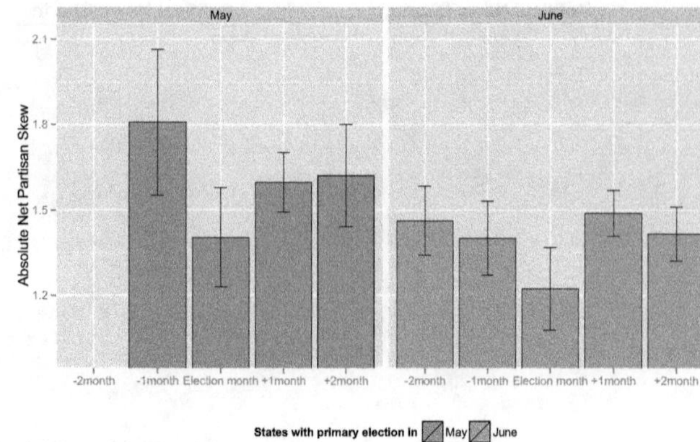

Figure 4: Absolute Net Partisan Skew by voting US states. That had primary elections in May (first barplot), and those in June (second barplot).

5.4 Changes depending on perceived importance

[H4] Partisan sharing is associated with one's perceived importance of certain topic.

To test *H4*, i.e., whether media news supply is tailored to partisan consumption (e.g., whether Fox News tailors its offering to its partisan readers as opposed to moderate ones), we identify two different classes of users – those who are partisan (high net skew) and those who are moderate (low net skew) – and see whether they consume different topics to a different extent. To do so, we match (moderate and partisan) conservative users with conservative outlets, and (moderate and partisan) liberal ones with liberal outlets. We then compute the total supply-demand divergence for four subgroups of the form user&outlet: partisan&conservatives, moderate& conservatives, partisan&liberals, and moderate&liberals. The divergence for any of the four sets is then:

$$\text{divergence} = \sum_{\text{topic}} |\text{demand}_{\text{topic}} - \text{supply}_{\text{topic}}| \quad (3)$$

computed over all topics covered by Alchemy API (Section 4), $\text{demand}_{\text{topic}}$ is the proportion of news articles a certain type of users (e.g., moderate) have consumed in that topic, and $\text{supply}_{\text{topic}}$ is the proportion of news articles the partisan media have supplied for that topic. If an outlet supplies articles consumed by a certain class of users (e.g., partisan vs. moderate), then the divergence is zero for that class. By contrast, it is highest when the supplied articles do not meet the demand of that class of users at all. We expect that supply matches the partisans' news demand (lower divergence) rather than the moderates' (higher divergence). News outlets tend to meet the demand of partisan users twice as much as (1.7 x) the demand of moderate ones.

5.5 Summary

We have found that partisan sharing: 1) exists, but contrary to the literature, such selectivity is limited to political news; 2) changes across individuals – people who are interested in politics tend to have stronger partisanship; 3) changes over time, in particular, their political diversity increases during the election period; and 4) is associated with perceived importance of topic – news outlets match the information needs of partisan rather than moderate online readers.

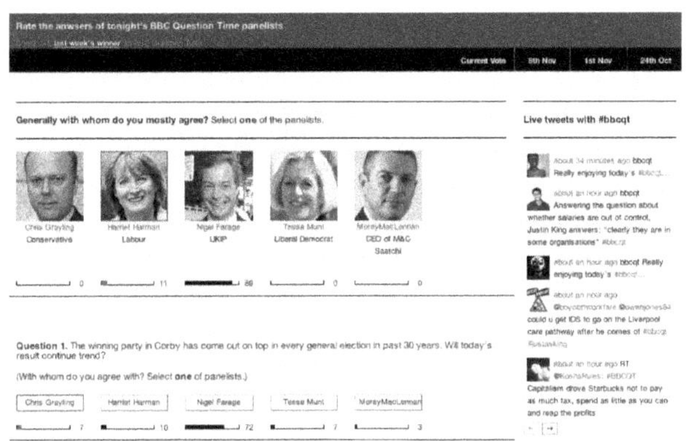

Figure 5: Screenshot of our application.

6. PARTISAN SHARING IN TWITTER

We first analyzed a Facebook dataset of shared news articles. Since we can test only part of the hypotheses on Facebook data, we also build a political engagement site connected to Twitter to perform the remaining hypotheses. As shown in Table 1, we validate the first three hypotheses and we newly investigate the last three hypotheses with a Twitter dataset.

6.1 Methodology

To conduct the study, we follow steps similar to those described in Section 4: gather a Twitter dataset, extract political news articles, determine media slant, and measure net partisan skew of each user.

Twitter news sharing of BBC audience. Question Time is a topical debate television program in UK. The show typically features five panelists – three UK politicians from the major parties plus two public figures – who answer pre-selected questions. On 24 September 2009, the show launched its Twitter presence and, by June 2011, it became one of the most-tweeted shows in the UK, with more than 5K tweets using the #bbcqt hashtag during each week. We have implemented a web application[9] with which BBC viewers could select the panelist they found more convincing (see Figure 5). These viewers were recruited by posting messages on the Twitter stream of #bbcqt hashtag. We made the application available during three weekly programs in 2012 (Oct 24, Nov 1, and Nov 7). During this period, we had 102 users who voted, among whom 71 reported their Twitter usernames and 35 answered survey questions (e.g., *which party is closest to your political preference?, how politically biased are the following news outlets? did you vote in the last general election?*). Table 4 reports details of those user who responded. For the 71 users who reported their valid usernames, we crawled their tweets. We gathered 1,008 political news articles posted by the 71 users for the last 5 months of data collection, which happened to come from 10 different UK news sites reported in Table 2.[10] The average number of articles per individual is 14 and the median is 10.

Determining media slant. In the Twitter dataset, we have mainly UK outlets, for which the literature does not offer any classification. We thus contacted three UK political journalists and ask them to classify the outlets into liberal, conservative, or neutral for us (Table 5). We measure the inter-rater agreement using Cohen's kappa coefficient [5], which results in 1 if two raters are in complete agreement. The overall kappa score among them on the 10 UK news sites was as high as 0.918. Under majority rule, we take a political leaning for a media source that is preferred by a majority of journalists.

[9] http://www.votingtime.org.uk

[10] BBC News (375 (48%)) was one of the popular news sources among our users, and it is known to be neutral.

	Twitter
Age	<20 (8%), <30 (7%), <40 (33%), <50 (22%), $\geq$ 50 (30%)
Gender	Male (65%), Female (35%)
Partisanship	Partisan (81.2% (Labour (40%), Lib(17%), Ind (31%), Con (12%))), Non-partisan (18.8%)

Table 4: Details for our 35 Twitter Users interviewed.

Twitter			
Liberal		Conservative	
guardian	482 (40.6%)	telegraph	350 (45.7%)
independent	141 (37.4%)	dailymail	149 (31.9%)
mirror	67 (34.1%)	thesun	64(36.4%)

Table 5: List of the News Sites Shared by Twitter Users. We remove ".co.uk" from domain name of news sites.

6.2 Validation

The goal of building this platform and integrating it with Twitter is to test whether partisan sharing has any read-world impact. Before meeting this goal, we need to verify whether the hypotheses that hold on Facebook also hold on Twitter. From the Twitter data, we are able to verify the first two sets of hypotheses (i.e., *H1* and *H2*).

Existence.
[H1] Individuals' news sharing in social media is not balanced but suffers from partisan sharing.

To test *[H1]*, we plot the distribution of net partisan skew of Twitter users. There is no bimodal distribution as in the case of Facebook (Figure 6(a)). There are two possible explanations: 1) Twitter itself is known to predominantly liberal [30]; or 2) conservative users in Twitter share also liberal articles. However, if we consider only partisan users, the bimodal distribution (reflecting the existence of partisan sharing) is back in the picture (Figure 6(b)).

Changes across individuals.
An individual's level of partisan sharing depends on: [H2.1] political leaning *and* [H2.2] amount of news shared.

First, to test *[H2.1]*, we compare absolute net partisan skew of liberal users to that of conservative users (Figure 7(a)). The result confirms our previous observation: liberals tend to be more partisan (with net skew of 1.5). When we examine how absolute net partisan skew varies by amount of political news shared (*[H2.2]*), we find a positive correlation between these two variables (Figure 7(b)) with a Pearson's correlation coefficients of $r = .31$ ($p < 0.005$) and with a Spearman's correlation coefficients of of $r = .30$ ($p < 0.01$), indicating that those who share more are the ones with stronger partisanship.

6.3 Additional hypotheses

Having ascertained the existence of partisan sharing also on Twitter, we now determine whether it is associated with one's polarized political attitude by administering a survey to the participants of our TV experiment.
[H5] Partisan sharing will relate to polarized political attitudes and, as such, affects one's:

[H5.1] perceived political bias of news outlets;
[H5.2] political knowledge;
[H5.3] voting probability.

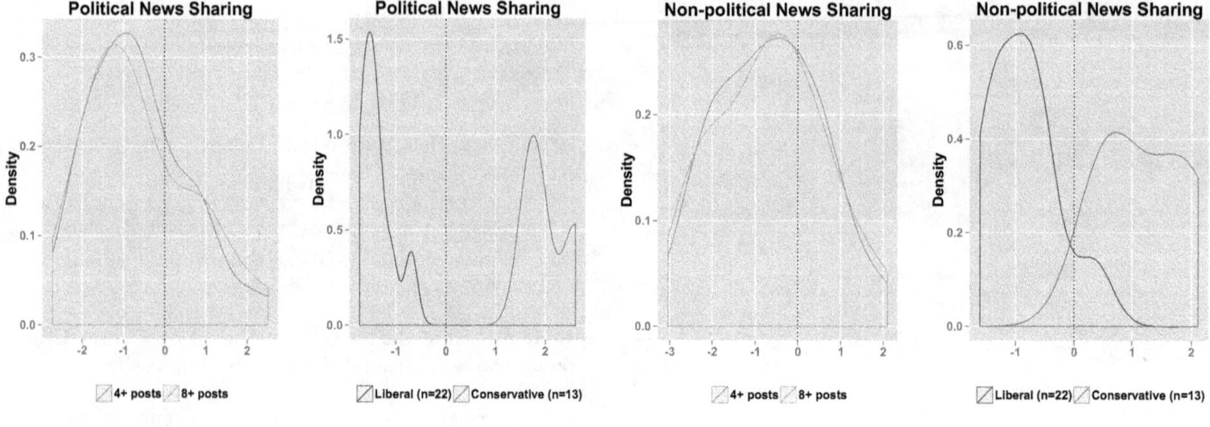

(a) Political news (All) (b) Political news (Partisan) (c) Non-political news (All) (d) Non-political news (Partisan)

Figure 6: Net Partisan Skew of political news in Twitter: *(a)* The majority of our Twitter users are liberal; *(b)* Liberals and conservatives share like-minded news; *(c)* Both share soft news from outlets of no particular leaning (peak is centered around -0.5); *(d)* Partisanship for soft news.

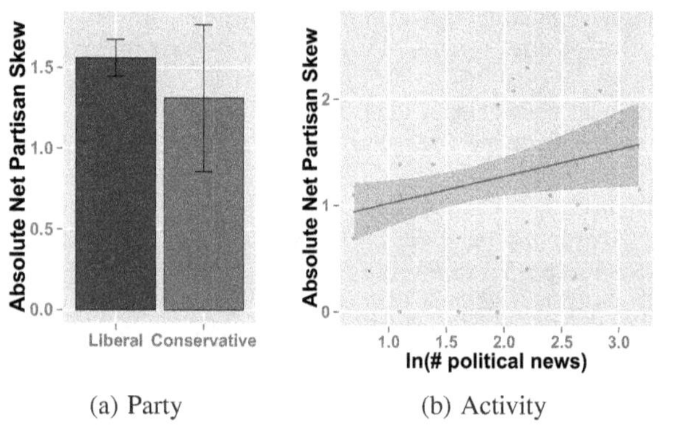

(a) Party (b) Activity

Figure 7: Net Partisan Skew by *(a)* Party and *(b)* Activity. The absolute value of partisan skew is for UK Twitter users who have shared 4+ articles.

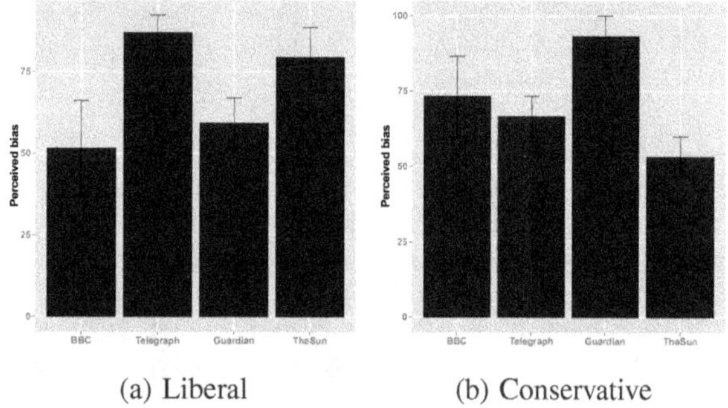

(a) Liberal (b) Conservative

Figure 8: Perceived Bias of News Outlets by Party.

To test the relationship between perceived bias and partisanship (*H5.1*), we ask our application survey's respondents to which extent they thought four news outlets – BBC, Telegraph, Guardian, and The Sun – were politically biased (the score ranges from 0 to 100, where 0 means 'neutral' and 100 means 'strongly biased'). We then compare perceived bias by users with different political leanings. We find that liberal and conservative users significantly differ in their perceptions of the media's leanings (Figure 8). For example, liberals perceive the Guardian to be far less biased (56 on a [0,100] scale) than conservatives do (93). People need to objectively recognize biased reporting to discount it. The problem is that they are not able to do so: they scrutinize hostile news outlets (those holding views different to their own), while they turn a blind (cognitive) eye to "friendly" news outlets. The ominous consequence of all this is that like-minded information is often perceived to be unbiased and is thus accepted with little scrutiny.

To test the relationship between political knowledge and partisan sharing (*H5.2*), we need to test one's knowledge. The users of our application administer to a survey. The survey contains 11 questions, 4 of which form together a small political knowledge quiz about general UK political facts: *Which position is now held by George Osborne? Is the Queen above the law? When does the House of Commons scrutinise the government? Which party has the most members in the House of Commons?* 35 Twitter users answered the survey and the quiz. Given the low number of people, the results need to be taken with caution, but we will see that they confirm previous evidence about news consumption offline, and that deviations from average (error bars) are limited.

We anticipate that political knowledge (number of correct answers) would be related to partisan sharing. That is because Stroud anticipated that "partisan selective exposure enhances political knowledge" [36]. The results of net partisan skew against number of correct answers in the quiz are shown in Figure 9(a). As expected, the politically knowledgeable tended to be more partisan than those less knowledgeable.

Finally, to test the relationship between voting probability and partisan sharing (*H5.3*), we contrast two types of Twitter users – those who have declared to have reached a decision about whether they will vote at the next UK general election in our survey, and those who remain undecided. In line with previous findings in USA [36], UK people who have decided whether to vote are also more partisan than those who remain undecided ($t(4.558) = 4.566$, $p < 0.01$). Despite the small Twitter sample size, the difference is enough not to leave any room for alternative interpretations.

Having their decisions about whether they will vote at the next UK general election, we run a linear regression that predicts one's partisanship based on voting probability:

$$|netpartisanskew| = \alpha + \beta_1 \text{voting}_{\text{GeneralElection}}$$

The regression has an adjusted R^2 of 0.49 and the beta coefficient of $\text{voting}_{\text{GeneralElection}}$ is 0.98 ($p < 0.005$). This result indicates that

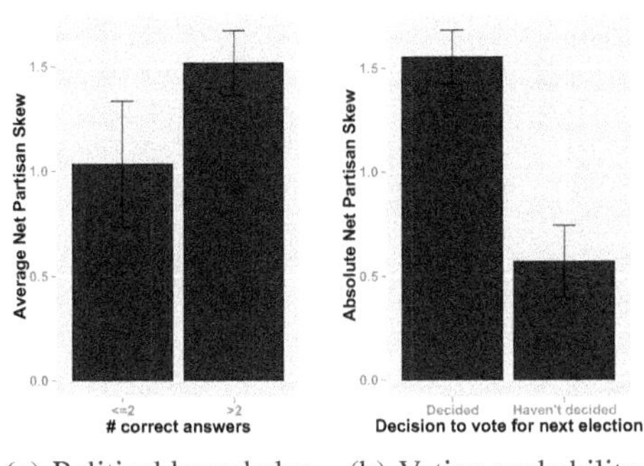

(a) Political knowledge (b) Voting probability

Figure 9: Net Partisan Skew by *(a)* Political Knowledge and *(b)* Probability of Voting. The absolute value of partisan skew is for UK Twitter users who have shared 4+ articles.

individual's partisanship could be predicted only by whether they have decided to vote or not.

6.4 Summary

After having ascertained the existence of partisan sharing, we studied the real-world impact of it. As one expects, it is negative as it is strongly related to distorted perceptions of which news outlets are politically biased and which not. However, it is also positive: it is associated with people who are knowledgeable about politics and are actively engaged in political life.

7. PREDICTING PARTISANSHIP

Not everyone values diversity [24]. Thus, to build tools that counter partisan sharing, one would need to identify partisan users first, so that they can adopt a personalized strategy. Several studies have attempted to predict the political leanings of users in SNSs, particularly by their social networks [35] and by the usage of political hashtag in Twitter [6]. Unlike previous work, we attempt to predict a level of partisanship with our Facebook and Twitter datasets.

7.1 A case study of Facebook

Since we have rich demographic data for our Facebook users, we will try to predict their levels of partisanship. More specifically, we consider. The following predictors:

- Three Facebook variables: number of Facebook friends, number of postings, and number of likes received from their social contacts.
- Three personal attributes: sex, age, and size of the city s(he) lives in.
- Five personality traits: for our users, we have data from the five-factor model of personality, or the big five, which is the most comprehensive, reliable and useful set of personality concepts [8, 15]. An individual is associated with five scores that correspond to the five main personality traits and that form the acronym of OCEAN. Imaginative, spontaneous, and adventurous individuals are high in $Openness$. Individuals who are ambitious, resourceful and persistent individuals are high in $Conscientiousness$. Individuals who are sociable and tend to seek excitement are high in $Extraversion$. Those high in $Agreeableness$ are trusting, altruistic, tender-minded, and are motivated to maintain positive relationships with others. Finally, emotionally liable and impulsive individuals are high in $Neuroticism$.

All predictors undergo a logarithmic transformation, when necessary (e.g., when they are skewed) and are then correlate with net partisan skew. We find that conservatives (high in net partisan skew) tend to be older ($r = 0.24$), have less likes from friends ($r = -0.13$), live in smaller town than liberals ($r = -0.15$), are more emotionally stable and less spontaneous than liberals ($r_{Openness} = -0.20$, $r_{Conscientiousness} = -0.15$, and $r_{Neuroticism} = -0.21$) All coefficients are statistically significant at level $p < 0.005$. Next, we study how these predictors are correlated with partisanship. To this end, we correlate them with the absolute value of net partisan skew - the higher his/her absolute value, the more partisan a user. Out of the eleven predictors, none of them was correlated for conservatives, while only sex was correlated for liberals ($r = 0.30$), suggesting that liberal men tend to be more partisan than liberal women. To sum up, it turns out that predicting political leaning (the area which most existing research in computer science has gone into) is far easier than predicting partisanship, which appears to be quite challenging. As a result, it might be very difficult to create tools that effectively counter partisan sharing without being able to identify partisan users.

7.2 A case study of Twitter

The relationship between partisanship and perceived bias also suggests an interesting practical application: knowing how an individual perceives four news outlets to be biased, one could potentially predict the individual's political leaning. To test this, we ask our application survey's respondents to report their partisanship on a scale [0,100], where 0 is Labour, 25 is Liberal, 75 is conservative, and 100 is British National Party (BNP) or UK Independence Party (UKIP).[11]

Having their views on how they perceived the four outlets to be biased, we run a linear regression that predicts one's partisanship based on perceived biases[12]:

$$partisanship = \alpha + \beta_1 bias_{BBC} + \beta_2 bias_{Telegraph} + \beta_3 bias_{Guardian} + \beta_4 bias_{TheSun}$$

The regression has an adjusted R^2 of 0.44, which means that as much as 44% of the variability of an individual's partisanship is explained only by how the individual perceives four news outlets to be biased. The strongest beta coefficients are registered for the left-leaning The Guardian ($bias_{Guardian}$ = 0.62) and right-leaning The Sun ($bias_{TheSun}$=-0.61). The different signs suggest that what differentiates conservatives from liberals is how they perceive The Guardian and The Sun: the two groups will perceive biased (reliable) a different news outlet. The best way to quickly assess whether one is conservative or not would be to ask him/her how biased The Guardian is and how reliable The Sun is. Indeed, knowing the perceived biases for these two outlets, one could predict partisanship with an adjusted R^2 of 0.41. The remaining coefficients are of less importance: $bias_{Telegraph}$=-0.17 (right-leaning newspaper considered biased by left-leaning people); and $bias_{BBC}$= 0.11 (neutral news media corporation considered biased by right-leaning people). All coefficients are statistically significant at level $p < 0.01$.

[11] BNP is far-right political party and UKIP is known to right-wing populist political party in UK.

[12] Given that Twitter users were recruited through web application, connectivity among them was very low (a probability a user is following another was 4%), allowing us to apply a linear regression model.

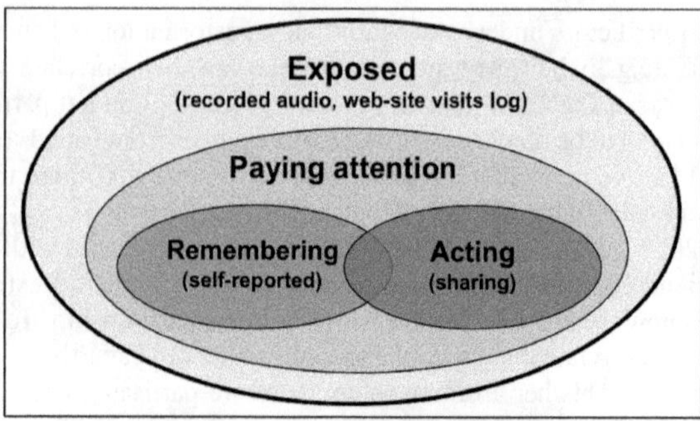

Figure 10: Attention Dynamics.

8. DISCUSSION

Validating media slant. To categorize news outlets, we have used four measures of media slant. Had only one been used, we might have been unsure whether our results hold true in general, or whether they are the product of classification artifacts. The four measures are: *scheme1:* `http://left-right.org` ; *scheme2:* crowdsourcing platform `http://mondotime.com`; *scheme3:* classification based on scandals [20] ; and *scheme4:* classification based on congressmen's speeches [12]. All the results we have presented hold for all the four scheme. That is largely because, for any pair of schemes, the two tend to be in agreement. To show this, we consider all possible unordered scheme pairs, and compute their agreement. By agreement, we mean the number of concordant classifications of the two schemes divided by the total number of classifications. Table 6 shows that agreement scores are above 80%, suggesting that the four schemes are all likely to return very similar classification of media slant.

Agreement	*scheme1*	*scheme2*	*scheme3*	*scheme1*
scheme1	100	93.67	81.48	100
scheme2	93.67	100	81.48	95.83
scheme3	81.48	81.48	100	100
scheme4	100	95.83	100	100

Table 6: Pairwise-Agreement of Media Slant Measures.

Being exposed does not necessarily translate into actions. Previous work that supports selective exposure has mostly measured news consumption from self-reported survey data. The little work that has gone into the direct and unobtrusive measurement of news consumption has conflated active with passive exposure. By active exposure, we refer to a situation in which one is either paying attention to news to which (s)he is exposed and, eventually, is translating that attention into action (e.g., calling a friend to chat about the latest political scandal) or is able to recall (e.g., telling an interviewer about the latest political scandal one has read). Instead, by passive exposure, we refer to a situation in which one is exposed to news (s)he is not paying attention to (because, e.g., (s)he is multitasking). In this work, we have measured how people act upon a piece of news by analyzing what Facebook users actually *share* with their social contacts. Our results are in line with those produced upon self-reported data [36] and are in contrast with studies of direct measurements [13, 19]. One possible explanation is that direct measurements capture exposure to news but not necessarily attention (Figure 10) – one might be exposed to a piece of news without paying attention to it. By contrast, telling to have read a piece of news or posting it on Facebook can only happen if one has paid attention to the piece of news in the first place. By studying news sharing, we have moved the literature forward by measuring active (as opposed to passive) exposure and found evidence for partisan sharing.

Limitations. This work has some main limitations. First, our Twitter and Facebook users represent a specific subgroup. Our Twitter users are individuals who are definitely interested in politics as they watch Question Time and tweet about it. Since cultural guidelines clearly exist about political behavior and attitude, one should best consider that our results are likely to hold for that specific group of Twitter users. Similarly, we do not attempt to generalize our Facebook results – they apply to Facebook users who live in the United States. Secondly, the sample size of Twitter users is limited. As such, the results should only be considered to be preliminary. Yet, they seem to be reasonable for two main reasons: 1) error bars allow us to distinguish which results are more definite than others; 2) results on Twitter and Facebook are consistent, and that speaks to their *external validity*: it is no coincidence that two different platforms in two different countries show similar results. The third limitation of our work is that we do not have any data on why a user shares an article. If a user share a news article of an hostile media outlet, it does not necessarily mean that (s)he is vouching for it – (s)he might simply make fun of it. However, given the large sample size on Facebook, such an effect would be likely randomized. The fourth limitation of our work is that the assumption that articles published by a news outlet matches the outlet's political slant. This is reasonable based on the literature of political science, which suggests that even a factual article, as opposed to an op-ed (opinion-editorial) article, often follows a political slant of its source. The last limitation is that we could not test causality for our hypotheses as we do not hold enough data.

Engaging undecided voters through social media. Social media have been used by US political campaigners to engage the public. Since past elections have been determined by independent and undecided voters, "especially those women voters who decide late" [10], it might be beneficial to identify the undecided, indifferent, procrastinating, and nonparticipating voters. To do so, this work has suggested that one could search for social media users who have shared only a limited number of political news articles before the election. That strategy would directly target undecided voters. More sophisticated targeting strategies could tap into social influence [34]. One could, for example, identify users who are both partisan (with a simple computation of their net partisan skew) and have a considerable number of social contacts who are undecided: they are in the best (social networking) position to influence a large fraction of undecided voters.

9. CONCLUSION

In large part, political views in the United States are formed nowadays by either television or the Internet. In the past, the structure of television news was built around a broader electorate, and that has changed with the introduction of cable TV: people crave like-minded news channels and avoid politically hostile ones. Do online habits keep up with television ones? This question is too important to be left to the unknown, not least because of the recent decline of national networks and newspapers and the rise of ever more online social media in news industry. This is the first study to unobtrusively measure partisan sharing in the context of online news consumption. We have shown that partisan sharing still exists and does depend on a variety of factors. Consequently, in the near future, as the current structure of online media consolidates, we might be left with a political discourse driven by echo chambers. It is important, then, to create alternative media that brings together left, right, and center.

Acknowledgment Jisun An was supported in part by the Google European Doctoral Fellowship in Social Computing.

10. REFERENCES

[1] L. A. Adamic and N. Glance. The political blogosphere and the 2004 U.S. election: Divided they blog. In *SIGKDD*, 2005.

[2] J. An, M. Cha, K. Gummadi, and J. Crowcroft. Media landscape in twitter: A world of new conventions and political diversity. In *ICWSM*, 2011.

[3] B. Bishop. *The Big Sort: why the clustering of likeminded America is tearing us apart*. New York, New York: Houghton Mifflin Company, 2008.

[4] S. H. Chaffee, M. N. Saphir, J. Graf, C. Sandvig, and K. S. Hahn. Attention to counter-attitudinal messages in a state election campaign. *Political Communication*, 18(3):247–272, 2001.

[5] J. Cohen. A coefficient of agreement for nominal scales. *Educational and Psychological Measurement*, 20(1):7–46, 1960.

[6] M. D. Conover, B. Gonçalves, A. F. Jacob Ratkiewicz, and F. Menczer. Predicting the political alignment of twitter users. In *SocialCom*, 2011.

[7] M. D. Conover, J. Ratkiewicz, M. Francisco, B. Goncalves, F. Menczer, and A. Flammini. Political polarization on Twitter. In *ICWSM*, 2011.

[8] P. Costa and R. Mccrae. The revised neo personality inventory (neopi-r). *SAGE Publications*, 2005.

[9] S. Dilliplane. All the news you want to hear: The impact of partisan news exposure on political participation. *Public Opinion Quarterly*, 75(2):287, 2011.

[10] Economist. An aggressive rematch. 2012.

[11] M. Gamon, S. Basu, D. Belenko, D. Fisher, M. Hurst, and A. C. Konig. Blews: Using blogs to provide context for news articles. In *ICWSM*, 2008.

[12] M. Gentzkow and J. M. Shapiro. What drives media slant? evidence from u.s. daily newspapers. *Econometrica Econometric Society*, 78(1):35–71, 2010.

[13] M. Gentzkow and J. M. Shapiro. Ideological segregation online and offline. *Quarterly Journal of Economics*, 2011.

[14] C. J. Glynn, S. Herbs, G. J. OKeefe, and R. Y. Shapiro. *Public Opinion*. Boulder CO: Westview Press, 1999.

[15] L. Goldberg, J. Johnson, H. Eber, R. Hogan, M. Ashton, R. Cloninger, and H. Gough. The international personality item pool and the future of public-domain personality measures. *Journal of Research in Personality*, 40, 2006.

[16] S. K. Goldman and D. C. Mutz. The friendly media phenomenon: A cross-national analysis of cross-cutting exposure. *Political Communication*, 28(1):42–66, 2011.

[17] S. Iyengar and K. S. Hahn. Red media, blue media: Evidence of ideological selectivity in media use. *Journal of Communication*, 59(1):19–39, 2009.

[18] M. Jiang and S. Argamon. Exploiting Subjectivity Analysis in Blogs to Improve Political Leaning Categorization. In *SIGIR*, 2008.

[19] M. LaCour. A balanced news diet, not selective exposure: Evidence from a direct measure of media exposure. *APSA 2012 Annual Meeting Paper*, 15(5):795–825, 2012.

[20] V. Larcinese, R. Puglisi, and J. M. S. Jr. Partisan bias in economic news: Evidence on the agenda-setting behavior of u.s. newspapers. *Journal of Public Economics*, 95(9-10):1178–1189, 2011.

[21] E. Lawrence, J. Sides, and H. Farrell. Self-segregation or deliberation? blog readership, participation, and polarization in american politics. *Perspectives on Politics*, 8(01):141–157, 2010.

[22] M. E. McCombs and D. L. Shaw. The agenda-setting function of mass media. *Public Opinion Quarterly*, 36(2):176–187, 1972.

[23] S. Munson and P. Resnick. Sidelines: An Algorithm for Increasing Diversity in News and Opinion Aggregators. In *ICWSM*, 2009.

[24] S. Munson and P. Resnick. Presenting diverse political opinions: How and how much,. In *ACM CHI*, 2010.

[25] S. Munson and P. Resnick. The Prevalence of Political Discourse in Non-Political Blogs. In *ICWSM*, 2011.

[26] D. C. Mutz. *Political persuasion and attitude change*. University of Michigan Press, 1996.

[27] H. N. Nie, D. W. I. Miller, S. Golde, D. M. Butler, and K. Winneg. The world wide web and the u.s. political news market. *American Journal of Political Science*, 54(2):428–439, 2010.

[28] A. Oh, H. Lee, and Y. Kim. User Evaluation of a System for Classifying and Displaying Political Viewpoints of Weblogs. In *ICWSM*, 2009.

[29] S. Park, S. Kang, S. Chung, and J. Song. Newscube: Delivering multiple aspects of news to mitigate media bias. In *CHI*, 2009.

[30] PewResearch. Digital politics. *PewResearch center, Infographic*, 2012.

[31] PewResearch. In changing news landscape, even television is vulnerable. trends in news consumption: 1991-2012. *PewResearch Technical Report*, 2012.

[32] M. Prior. The immensely inflated news audience: Assessing bias in self-reported news exposure. *Public Opinion Quarterly*, 73(1):130, 2009.

[33] D. Quercia, H. Askham, , and J. Crowcroft. Tweetlda: Supervised topic classification and link prediction in twitter. *Web Science Conference*, 2012.

[34] L. Rainie, A. Smith, K. L. Schlozman, H. Brady, and S. Verba. Social media and political engagement. *PewResearch Technical Report*, 2012.

[35] D. Sparks, A. King, and F. Orlando. Ideological extremity in social networks. 2011. http://dsparks.wordpress.com/2011/03/22/ideological-extremity-in-social-networks.

[36] N. Stroud. *Niche News*. Boulder CO: Westview Press, 2011.

[37] C. Sunstein. *Republic.com*. Princeton University Press, 2001.

[38] P. C. Survey. Where do you fit? the political party quiz. *PewResearch Center*, 2012.

[39] D. SÃąez-Trumper, C. Castillo, and M. Lalmas. Social Media News Communities: Gatekeeping, Coverage, and Statement Bias. In *CIKM*, 2013.

[40] J. Ugander, B. Karrer, L. Backstrom, and C. Marlow. The anatomy of the facebook social graph. *CoRR*, abs/1111.4503, 2011.

[41] L. Vavreck. The exaggerated effects of advertising on turnout: The dangers of self-reports. *Quarterly Journal of Political Science*, 2(4):325–342, 2007.

[42] S. D. Vigna and E. Kaplan. The Fox News effect: Media bias and voting. *Quarterly Journal of Economics*, 2007.

Role of Conformity in Opinion Dynamics in Social Networks

Abhimanyu Das
Microsoft Research
Mountain View, CA
abhidas@microsoft.com

Sreenivas Gollapudi
Microsoft Research
Mountain View, CA
sreenig@microsoft.com

Arindam Khan*
School of Computer Science
Georgia Tech, Atlanta, GA
akhan67@gatech.edu

Renato Paes Leme*
Google Research
New York, NY
renatoppl@google.com

ABSTRACT

Social networks serve as important platforms for users to express, exchange and form opinions on various topics. Several opinion dynamics models have been proposed to characterize how a user iteratively updates her expressed opinion based on her innate opinion and the opinion of her neighbors. The extent to how much a user is influenced by her neighboring opinions, as opposed to her own innate opinion, is governed by a measure of her "conformity' parameter. Characterizing this degree of conformity for users of a social network is critical for several applications such as debiasing online surveys and finding social influencers. In this paper, we address the problem of estimating these conformity values for users, using only the expressed opinions and the social graph. We pose this problem in a constrained optimization framework and design efficient algorithms, which we validate on both synthetic and real-world Twitter data. Using these estimated conformity values, we then address the problem of identifying the smallest subset of users in a social graph that, when seeded initially with some non-neutral opinions, can accurately explain the current opinion values of users in the entire social graph. We call this problem seed recovery. Using ideas from compressed sensing, we analyze and design algorithms for both conformity estimation and seed recovery, and validate them on real and synthetic data.

1. INTRODUCTION

The widespread use of online social networks has a very direct bearing on how users form and express opinions on various issues such as politics, technology, consumer products, healthcare etc. Though users are increasingly spending more time on these networks, not all of them adopt and propagate ideas and opinions in a homogeneous way. Understanding how users in an online social network shape and influence each other's opinions is important in the context of viral marketing, behavioral targeting and information dissemination of users in the network.

There has been a plethora of work on modeling opinion dynamics in social networks [8, 11, 33, 22] in the sociology and economics literature. Specifically, these works model how an individual user updates her opinion in the context of information learned from her neighbors in her social network, and then use the model to characterize the evolution of opinions in the network in terms of equilibria, convergence time, and the emergence of a consensus or polarization.

More recent models [12, 2, 21] explicitly incorporate the notion of an *innate opinion* – i.e., an endogenous opinion of each user about a certain topic – as opposed to her *expressed opinion*, which is a result of a social process. These models describe how the opinion of each user in a social network evolves (i.e. how she changes her opinion over time) based on the following: (i) her innate opinion, which is an immutable property of the user, (ii) the expressed opinion of users in her social circle and (iii) internal parameters of the model. In the case of the Friedkin and Johnsen [12] model, the model parameters correspond to a real quantity for each user which measures her *conformity*, i.e., the likelihood of this user adopting the opinions of her neighbors in the network.

While the expressed opinion of users are readily observable in the social network (e.g. from a user's tweets or Facebook posts), both the innate opinion and conformity parameter of users are hidden and can only be inferred by reverse engineering the opinion dynamics process. In particular, identifying these endogenous conformity values of users are a critical component toward enabling several interesting applications that leverage opinion dynamics processes. Salient examples include efficient sampling of innate user opinions [5], seeding opinions to maximize opinion adoption [13], and identifying candidates for viral marketing or targeting.

Inferring the conformity parameter for each user by simply analyzing the history of opinions emitted by the user is not practical largely due to lack of availability of a reasonable amount of historical opinion formation data for each user. Therefore, we ask the following question, that we call ConformityExtraction : *Can we reliably estimate con-*

*Work done at Microsoft Research

COSN'14, October 1–2, 2014, Dublin, Ireland.
Copyright 2014 ACM 978-1-4503-3198-2/14/10 ...$15.00.
http://dx.doi.org/10.1145/2660460.2660479.

formity parameters of users in a social network from a single snapshot of the stationary state of the opinion dynamic?

Mathematically this is an under-determined problem since it involves n constraints (the fact that the dynamic is in a stationary state for each user) and $2n$ variables (the innate opinion and conformity parameter for each user). We overcome this problem by relying on two natural assumptions, *viz.*,

- *homophily*: we assume that if two users are close in the social network, then their innate opinions are likely to be also close.
- *access to a coarse conformity distribution*: we assume that we have access to a coarse-grained estimate of the distribution of conformity parameters in the entire network.

We next define a novel problem, which we call SEEDRECOVERY , that is fundamentally different from the well-studied problem of influence maximization [24, 32]. While the motivating application for both the problems is finding influencers, the influencers from SEEDRECOVERY are a small set of users whose early adoption (in the past) of an opinion has been critical in shaping the current snapshot of opinions in the network. On the other hand, the users computed via influence maximization are individual who, when currently seeded with the opinion, will be critical in shaping (or maximizing) the future spread of the opinion in the network, agnostic to any historical opinion dynamics.

We note that the study of SEEDRECOVERY is enabled by our estimates of the conformity parameters. More formally, we are given the current state of expressed opinions in the social network and we want to identify if there is a sparse set of innate opinions in the network that can explain the current expressed opinions. This enables us to distinguish opinions that might have been seeded, i.e., are the result of a small number of planted opinions (say by means of a viral market campaign) from opinions that arise naturally. It also helps capture a measure of the "heterogeneity" or "richness" of the opinion dynamics process in a social network. In fact, we identify this problem as a special case of the sparse recovery problem that is commonly studied in the compressed sensing and signal processing literature [3, 9, 37] and for which greedy strategies are known to work well[1]. We apply a similar GREEDY algorithm for the SEEDRECOVERY problem, and validate it for a special case analytically and more general, using experimental analysis on synthetic and Twitter data.

Contributions of this study

Our contributions in the study are three-fold:

- We address the CONFORMITYEXTRACTION problem of recovering the conformity values of users in a social network, using only the stationary snapshot of the opinion dynamics, along with assumptions on homophily and a coarse-grained empirical distribution of user conformity.
- We formulate the problem of SEEDRECOVERY in a social network, show that it is related to the well-studied sparse recovery problem, and propose a GREEDY algorithm for recovering the seed set of users for the opinion dynamics.
- We perform extensive experiments on both synthetic graphs and a large set of real-world Twitter data to validate the performance of our algorithms for both CONFORMITYEXTRACTION and SEEDRECOVERY .

[1]We note here that unlike the influence maximization problem, the sparse recovery objective is not submodular

2. RELATED WORK

The broad research area of opinion formation is quite classical, and we refer the interested reader to [22] for a survey. The earliest work in this domain comes from the sociology and statistics literature [33, 8, 11].

Several models for opinion formation and consensus have been studied in the sociology community. One notable example is the work by DeGroot [8] which studies how consensus is formed and reached when individual opinions are updated using the average of the neighborhood opinions in a network. The work of Friedkin and Johnsen (FJ) [12], is perhaps the first study to extend the DeGroot model to include both disagreement and consensus, by associating with each node an innate opinion in addition to her expressed opinion. In their model, a user adheres to her initial opinion with a certain weight α_i, while she is socially influenced by others in her network with a weight $1 - \alpha_i$.

On the subject of conformity, recent work [35] focused on computing conformity parameters under three different notions of *individual*, *peer*, and *group* conformities. We differ from this line of work in that our focus is on leveraging the underlying opinion dynamics in a social network to estimate user specific conformity parameters. Further, estimating conformity values in the context of opinion dynamics also allows us to identify sparse seeded opinions (SEEDRECOVERY).

There has been a large body of work on modeling the adoption or spread of ideas, rumors or content among online users. Well known models in this domain include Threshold [19], Cascade models [15], and conformity-aware cascade models [27] that specify how a node adopts a particular idea or product based on the adoption pattern prevalent in its neighborhood. Subsequently, several papers studied, both theoretically [24] and empirically [14, 17, 31], the phenomenon of diffusion of ideas or content in a social network and the related problem of identifying influential nodes to seed, in order to maximize adoption rates. Several of these papers are mainly concerned with binary-valued propagation of an idea or products where a user decides to either adopt or not adopt the idea, instead of a more continuous opinion dynamics model where a user opinion is influenced by her neighboring opinions to varying degrees. However a recent paper by Terzi et al. [13] considers influence maximization in the context of opinion adoption based on the Friedkin-Johnsen model. They pose the problem of selecting a small set of nodes and seeding them with a single positive opinion to maximize the adoption of the overall positive opinion in the network. They show that the resulting problem is submodular and can hence be maximized efficiently. However, they assume knowledge of the user conformity values in the opinion dynamics model and do not address the problem of how to estimate these parameters.

As mentioned previously, the SEEDRECOVERY problem that we introduce is fundamentally different from the above influence maximization problems, since the goal is not to seed users with products or opinions to maximize adoption, but rather to understand if the current state of expressed opinions in the social network can be explained (from the opinion dynamics process) using the opinions of a small set of seed nodes, and if so, to recover these seed nodes. Several results in the sparse recovery literature have shown [3, 9, 37, 6] that greedy and L_1-relaxation techniques can recover the linear combination efficiently as long as the matrix formed by taking the vectors x_i as columns is well-conditioned and k is sufficiently small. However, we are not aware of any prior application of sparse recovery techniques for opinion formation problems.

In other related work, Das et al [5] addresses the problem of sampling users in a social graph to estimate the average innate opinion of users, using only the expressed opinion of the sampled nodes. However, they too require knowledge of the per-user conformity values for their sampling algorithms.

For the cascade-based models for diffusion of an idea or product-adoption, the problem of estimating the adoption probabilities of a user has been studied in [18], [10] and [34]. Most of these papers use a probabilistic model, along with historical data of user adoption activity, to estimate adoption probabilities for each edge in the social graph. However, for the case of social opinion dynamics, to the best of our knowledge, we are not aware of any related work for estimating the user conformity parameters for applications that use opinion dynamics models.

3. OPINION MODEL

We consider a (possibly directed) social network graph $G = (V, E)$ with nodes $V = \{1, 2, \dots, n\}$, corresponding to individuals and edges E corresponding to social interactions. We will say that $(i, j) \in E$ if i *is influenced by* j. We will denote by $N_i = \{j; (i, j) \in E\}$, the set of neighbors of node i and $d_i = |N_i|$, the out-degree of node i.

It will be convenient to express the graph in terms of its adjacency matrix $\mathbf{A}$, which corresponds to an $n \times n$ matrix such that $\mathbf{A}_{ij} = 1$ if $(i, j) \in E$ and $\mathbf{A}_{ij} = 0$ otherwise. We will also use $\mathbf{I}$ to represent the $n \times n$ identity matrix, $\mathbf{1}$ to represent the vector in $\mathbb{R}^n$ with all components 1 and given a vector $v \in \mathbb{R}^n$, we will represent by $\mathtt{dg}(v)$ the matrix with the components of v in the diagonal and zero elsewhere.

We are interested in studying opinion formation processes in social networks. We will distinguish between an agent's *innate opinion*, which reflects the agent's interval belief, and the agent's *expressed opinion*, which is the opinion an agent chooses to express in the network as a result of a social influence process. Here we encode the opinions as a single real quantity. Let $y_i^t \in \mathbb{R}$ be the opinion *expressed* by node i on time t. We express by z_i the innate opinion of agent i.

The classic model due to Friedkin and Johnsen [12] proposes a dynamic governing the opinion formation process. In their model, each agent is associated with conformity parameter α_i in the $[0, 1]$ range, which measures how strong her innate opinions are, and how likely will she be influenced by her neighborhood opinions. An α_i value close to 1 implies that the individual is highly opinionated, and her expressed opinion is similar to her innate opinion. While a value close to 0 implies that the individual has a very weak innate opinion and consequently her expressed opinion is largely governed by the opinions of neighbors around her. According to their model, in every timestep, each agent updates her expressed opinion to a convex combination between her innate opinion and the average of expressed opinions of her neighbors in the previous timestep. The weight of each term in the

$$y_i^{t+1} = \alpha_i \cdot z_i + (1 - \alpha_i) \cdot \frac{1}{d_i} \sum_{j \in N_i} y_j^t \tag{1}$$

In matrix form, we can re-write it as:

$$y^{t+1} = \mathtt{dg}(\alpha) \cdot z + (\mathbf{I} - \mathtt{dg}(\alpha)) \cdot \mathtt{dg}(d)^{-1} \mathbf{A} y^t \tag{2}$$

It has been shown in [5] that the above opinion formation dynamics converge to an equilibrium that depends only on the innate opinions and the structure of the network and not on the original opinions, as long as $\alpha_i > 0$ for all $i \in V$, i.e., each individual holds an innate opinion that has some impact on what they express.

The equilibrium can be obtained as the unique fixed point of equation (2), i.e.:

$$y = (\mathbf{I} - (\mathbf{I} - \mathtt{dg}(\alpha)) \cdot \mathtt{dg}(d)^{-1} \mathbf{A})^{-1} \mathtt{dg}(\alpha) \cdot z \tag{3}$$

We will denote by $\mathbf{F}$ the matrix governing the Friedkin-Johnsen dynamic, i.e., $\mathbf{F} = (\mathbf{I} - (\mathbf{I} - \mathtt{dg}(\alpha)) \cdot \mathtt{dg}(d)^{-1} \mathbf{A})^{-1} \mathtt{dg}(\alpha)$. Also, given any matrix $\mathbf{M}$ of size $m \times n$ and a subset $S \subseteq [n]$, we denote by $\mathbf{M}_S$ the matrix of size $m \times |S|$ corresponding to the columns of $\mathbf{M}$ with indices in S. Similarly, given a vector $x \in \mathbb{R}^n$, we will denote by x_S the vector in $\mathbb{R}^S$ corresponding to the components of x with indices on S.

4. CONFORMITY EXTRACTION

Based on the Friedkin-Johnsen opinion dynamics model described in the previous section, we now address the problem of estimating the conformity parameter α_i of a user in a social network. Since we expect that these per-user conformity parameters depend on the topic that is being opined, in the remainder of this section we formulate the conformity extraction problem in the context of a particular topic. We then present a Linear Programming based approach for this problem.

We only assume knowledge of the current steady state expressed opinions of users in the social network. In practice, these opinions can be obtained from opinion mining [28] of recent content posted by the user on the social network, for example, her recent tweets on Twitter or posts on Facebook. We are also given the directed social graph among these users, which could correspond to, say, the Twitter follow graph or Facebook friend graph.

Using these two pieces of information, we would like to estimate each user's α_i value. Clearly, as seen from Equation 1, if we knew the user's innate opinion z_i, we could directly calculate her α_i based on how far is her expressed opinion compared to her innate opinion and the mean of her neighboring expressed opinions. However, in practice, it is very hard to glean information about an individual user's innate opinions. Hence, the main technical challenge is that we have an under-determined system of equations where we have two unknowns per user: α_i and z_i while the opinion dynamics model only gives us one equation per user.

To overcome the underdeterminacy of this system, we devise two score functions and pick the candidate (α, z) pair that optimizes a combination of such scores:

Homophily score: We first assume that users in the graph exhibit some degree of homophily in their innate opinions. That is, if two users are "close" to each other in the social network, then their innate opinions are likely to be close to each other. Homophily property in social networks is well-studied [25, 30, 29, 36, 1]. However, instead of treating the homophily property as a hard constraint, we will define a score or measure of the amount of homophily in the graph, and try to favor solutions that have a large homophily score over other solutions. In particular, we define the following homophily score function:

$$H(z) = \sum_{i,j \in V} |z_i - z_j| \cdot (1 - D_{ij}/n)$$

where D_{ij} is the distance from node i to node j in the social graph.

Conformity distribution score: We bucket the range of α_i into three categories: low $B_1 = [0, 1/3]$, medium $B_2 = (1/3, 2/3]$ and high $B_3 = (2/3, 1]$ and assume that we have a coarse-grained estimate of the empirical distribution of the conformity values across buckets: let λ_j be the estimate of what fraction of the α_i values fall in bucket j. Then, given a vector α of conformity parameters, the *log-likelihood* that this vector was generated by a distribution with bucket estimates $(\lambda_1, \lambda_2, \lambda_3)$ is given by:

$$L(\alpha) = \beta_1(\alpha) \cdot \log \lambda_1 + \beta_2(\alpha) \cdot \log \lambda_2 + \beta_3(\alpha) \cdot \log \lambda_3$$

where $\beta_i(\alpha) = \sum_{j=1}^{n} \beta_{ij}$ and $\beta_{ij} = 1$ if $\alpha_i \in B_j$ and zero otherwise.

Note that the assumption about knowledge of the coarse-grained conformity distribution across the three buckets is much weaker than an assumption about the exact distribution of the α_i values. Furthermore, in practice this is not an unrealistic assumption, since one can manually go through a small set of users who have tweeted or created a post about the topic, peruse their past postings and use human judgment to infer what fraction of them are likely to be highly conforming, moderately conforming, or stubborn.

4.1 Mathematical Program for Identifying Conformity

Based on the score functions identified, we propose identifying conformity via the following Mathematical Program:

$$\begin{aligned}
&\textsc{Minimize}_{\alpha,z} \quad H(z) - c \cdot L(\alpha) \\
&\text{s.t} \\
&\quad y = \mathtt{dg}(\alpha) \cdot z + (\mathbf{I} - \mathtt{dg}(\alpha))\mathtt{dg}(d)^{-1}\mathbf{A}y \\
&\quad \alpha_i \in (0,1), \qquad \forall i \in V
\end{aligned}$$

where $\mathtt{dg}$ is the diagonal matrix and c is a regularization constant that adjust the trade-off between the score functions, and that is set in our experiments using cross validation. By rearranging the update rule of the Friedkin-Johnsen model and denoting the average opinion of neighbors of node i by $m_i = \frac{1}{d_i} \sum_{j \in N_i} y_i$, we can write:

$$\begin{aligned}
&\textsc{Minimize}_{\alpha,z} \quad H(z) - c \cdot L(\alpha) \\
&\text{s.t} \\
&\quad \alpha_i(z_i - m_i) = y_i - m_i, \quad \forall i \in V \\
&\quad \alpha_i \in (0,1), \qquad \forall i \in V
\end{aligned}$$

Observe that this is not a Linear Program since both terms α_i and z_i are variables and the product $\alpha_i \cdot z_i$ appears in the constraints. Now we describe how to change the program to get rid of the product. We note that the objective function doesn't depend on α_i directly, but rather on β_{ij} which are indicators of the event $\alpha_i \in B_j$. Therefore, we propose to substitute the constraint $\alpha_i(z_i - m_i) = y_i - m_i$ by

$$\beta_{ij} = 1 \Rightarrow \frac{y_i - m_i}{z_i - m_i} \in B_j$$

and enforce integrality constraints on β_{ij} as well as $\sum_{j=1}^{3} \beta_{ij} = 1$. We note that this doesn't affect the value of the mathematical program, since for any solution of the program on (z, β), it is possible to recover a solution (z, α) with the same objective simply by taking $\alpha_i = (y_i - m_i)/(z_i - m_i)$.

Now, we re-write the newly introduced constraints in a more amenable form. First, we enforce the constraint that the ratio $(y_i - m_i)/(z_i - m_i)$ is non-negative. Given this constraint, we can rephrase $\beta_{ij} = 1 \Rightarrow \underline{b}_j \leq \frac{y_i - m_i}{z_i - m_i} \leq \bar{b}_j$ where $B_j = [\underline{b}_j, \bar{b}_j]$ as follows:

$$\bar{b}_j \cdot \mathtt{sgn}(y_i - m_i) \cdot (z_i - m_i) \geq \beta_{ij} |y_i - m_i|$$

$$\underline{b}_j \cdot \mathtt{sgn}(y_i - m_i) \cdot (z_i - m_i) \leq \beta_{ij} |y_i - m_i| + K \cdot (1 - \beta_{ij})$$

where $\mathtt{sgn}(x) = 1$ if $x \geq 0$ and $\mathtt{sgn}(x) = -1$ otherwise and $K = c_1(\mathtt{sgn}(y_i - m_i) \cdot (z_i - m_i))$ where c_1 is a constant $\geq 2/3$. To see that those are equivalent, notice that if $\beta_{ij} = 1$, this gives exactly $\underline{b}_j \leq \frac{y_i - m_i}{z_i - m_i} \leq \bar{b}_j$. If $\beta_{ij} = 0$, then both constraints are trivially satisfied for $c_1 \geq 2/3$.

This leads to the following Integer Program:

$$\begin{aligned}
&\textsc{Minimize} \quad H(z) - c \cdot \textstyle\sum_{j=1}^{3} (\sum_i \beta_{ij}) \log \lambda_i \\
&\text{s.t} \\
&(y_i - m_i)(z_i - y_i) \geq 0, \forall i \\
&\bar{b}_j \cdot \mathtt{sgn}(y_i - m_i) \cdot (z_i - m_i) \geq \beta_{ij} |y_i - m_i|, \forall i, j \\
&\underline{b}_j \cdot \mathtt{sgn}(y_i - m_i) \cdot (z_i - m_i) \leq \beta_{ij} |y_i - m_i| + K \cdot (1 - \beta_{ij}), \forall i, j \\
&\textstyle\sum_{j=1}^{k} \beta_{ij} = 1, \forall i \in V \\
&\beta_{ij} \in \{0, 1\}, \forall i, j
\end{aligned}$$

Relaxation and rounding. We refer to the solution of this integer program as the IPRECOVERY . However, since integer program is **NP**-hard and thus solving an integer program is not practically feasible for large instances, we begin with an LP relaxation, LPRECOVERY , and offer a simple rounding technique for the solution of LPRECOVERY to obtain the final solution. Our approach consists of relaxing the integrality constraints to $\beta_{ij} \in [0, 1]$, solving the resulting Linear Program, obtaining z and β_{ij} and then recovering the values of α_i by setting:

$$\alpha_i = \frac{y_i - m_i}{z_i - m_i}$$

Note that in the LP objective, there are no α_i's. We assign node i to bucket B_j based on its α_i value. This in a way, is a rounding of β_{ij} based on only α_i values. In the analysis, we show that original β_{ij} values from the LP and the rounded β_{ij}'s from α_i's are quite close. Therefore, the objective value resulting from the rounding is also close to the objective value of IPRECOVERY since the solution to LPRECOVERY is a lower bound to the objective function. Further, we also show empirically (see Section 6) our approach performs comparably to IPRECOVERY .

Analysis. In the above linear program, we show that the parameters β_{ij} and the α_i derived using the equation $\alpha_i = (y_i - m_i)/(z_i - m_i)$, are closely related.

LEMMA 1. $\alpha_i \in [0, 1]$.

PROOF. From the constraint $(y_i - m_i)(z_i - y_i) \geq 0$, $\mathtt{sgn}(y_i - m_i) = \mathtt{sgn}(z_i - y_i) = \mathtt{sgn}(z_i - m_i)$.
Thus y_i lies between z_i and m_i. Hence, $|y_i - m_i| \leq |z_i - m_i|$. Thus $\alpha_i = (y_i - m_i)/(z_i - m_i) \leq 1$.
On the other hand, from the same constraint we get,

$$\begin{aligned}
\frac{(y_i - m_i)(z_i - y_i)}{(z_i - m_i)^2} &\geq 0 \\
\Rightarrow (y_i - m_i)/(z_i - m_i) &\geq 0 \\
\Rightarrow |y_i - m_i|/|z_i - m_i| &\geq 0 \\
\Rightarrow \alpha_i &\geq 0
\end{aligned}$$

□

LEMMA 2. *If* $\beta_{i1} > c_2$ *then* $\alpha_i < \frac{1}{3c_2}$.

PROOF. From $\overline{b}_j \cdot \mathtt{sgn}(y_i - m_i) \cdot (z_i - m_i) \geq \beta_{ij}|y_i - m_i|$,
$\frac{1}{3}|z_i - m_i| \geq \beta_{i1}|y_i - m_i| > c_2|y_i - m_i|$
$\Rightarrow \frac{1}{3c_2} > \frac{|y_i - m_i|}{|z_i - m_i|} = \alpha_i$. □

COROLLARY 1. *If* $\beta_{i1} > 1/2$ *then* $\alpha_i < \frac{2}{3}$.

LEMMA 3. *If* $\beta_{i3} > c_3$ *then* $\alpha_i > c_1 - \frac{3c_1 - 2}{3c_3}$.

PROOF. From $\underline{b}_j \cdot \mathtt{sgn}(y_i - m_i) \cdot (z_i - m_i) \leq \beta_{ij}|y_i - m_i| + K \cdot (1 - \beta_{ij})$,
$\Rightarrow \frac{2}{3} \leq \beta_{i3} \cdot \alpha_i + c_1(1 - \beta_{i3})$.
$\Rightarrow (c_1 - \frac{2}{3}) \geq \beta_{i3}(c_1 - \alpha_i) > c_3(c_1 - \alpha_i)$
$\Rightarrow \alpha_i > c_1 - \frac{3c_1 - 2}{3c_3}$. □

COROLLARY 2. *If* $\beta_{i3} > 1/2$ *and* $c_1 = 1$ *then* $\alpha_i > \frac{1}{3}$.

THEOREM 1. *If* $\beta_{ij} > 1/2$ *for some* $j \in \{1, 2, 3\}$ *and derived* $\alpha \in B_k$, *then* $|j - k| \leq 1$.

PROOF. For $j = 2$, the theorem is trivially true. For $j = 1, 3$ the proof follows from Corollary 1 and Corollary 2. □

In words, Theorem 1 says that if β has reasonable weight ($> 1/2$) on some bucket B_j, then the derived bucket B_k from α is very close to B_j.

5. SEED RECOVERY

In the previous section, we discussed how to infer the conformity parameters α_i for users in a social network. The knowledge of those parameters enables various interesting applications. In this section, we discuss one such application called the SEEDRECOVERY problem.

Consider the scenario where y_i represents the opinion about a certain product. By means of a marketing campaign, a company might try to influence the general opinions on this product by planting few nodes with very high innate opinions about such products. This could be done, for example, by paying celebrities to tweet about certain products or events. The problem of how to choose a few nodes to seed an opinion on a network has been extensively studied [24, 13]. In the context of SEEDRECOVERY , we ask the following question: given the expressed opinions in a network, how likely it is that those were seeded by a small number of nodes ?

We assume that opinions are normalized in such a way that $z_i = 0$ represents a default neutral opinion, i.e., the node hasn't heard about that particular product or has neither positive nor negative innate opinions about it. Now, given a certain observed expressed opinions y, is there a vector z with a small number of innate non-neutral opinions that could have produced y as an outcome of the Friedkin-Johnsen dynamic ? In other words, for a given k, can we estimate:

$$\mathtt{error}_k = \min_z \|y - \mathbf{F}z\|_2^2 \text{ s.t. } \|z\|_0 = k$$

This can be cast as an instance of the *sparse recovery problem* from compressed sensing. The two main approaches to solve this problem are convex relaxation [3, 9] and greedy algorithms [37, 6]. We take the latter route and apply the well-known *Forward Regression algorithm* that was analyzed in [6]. Davis et al. [7] showed that the problem of minimizing $\mathtt{error}_k$ admits no multiplicative approximation, by showing that it is NP-hard to check for a given instance if $\mathtt{error}_k = 0$. As a result, approximation guarantees for this problem are usually given in terms of the squared multiple correlation or R^2 objective ($\mathrm{R}^2 = 1 - \mathtt{error}_k/\|y\|_2^2$), which is a well known measure of goodness-of-fit in statistics [23].

We note that since $0 \leq \mathtt{error}_k \leq \|y\|_2^2$, the R^2-objective is in the $[0, 1]$ range, where $\mathrm{R}^2 = 1$ corresponds to a solution of $\mathtt{error}_k = 0$. We will say that a solution z is an α-approximation if $\mathrm{R}^2(z) \geq \alpha \cdot \mathrm{R}^2(z')$ for any $z' \in \mathbb{R}^n$ with $\|z'\|_0 = k$.

Now we describe the Forward Regression algorithm and derive its approximation guarantees for the SEEDRECOVERY problem. First, we note that the problem can be re-written as:

$$\mathtt{error}_k = \min_{S:|S|=k} \left[\min_{z_S} \|y - \mathbf{F}_S z_S\|_2^2 \right]$$

For a fixed $S \subseteq [n]$, it is a classic result in Linear Algebra (see [16] for example) that $\|y - \mathbf{F}_S z_S\|_2^2$ is minimized by the vector $z_S = (\mathbf{F}_S^T \mathbf{F}_S)^{-1} \mathbf{F}_S^T y$, therefore the error can be written as:

$$\begin{aligned}
\mathtt{error}_k &= \min_{S:|S|=k} \|y - \mathbf{F}_S(\mathbf{F}_S^T \mathbf{F}_S)^{-1}\mathbf{F}_S^T y\|_2^2 \\
&= \min_{S:|S|=k} \|y\|_2^2 - y^T \mathbf{F}_S(\mathbf{F}_S^T \mathbf{F}_S)^{-1}\mathbf{F}_S^T y
\end{aligned}$$

since $\mathbf{F}_S(\mathbf{F}_S^T \mathbf{F}_S)^{-1}\mathbf{F}_S^T y$ and $y - \mathbf{F}_S(\mathbf{F}_S^T \mathbf{F}_S)^{-1}\mathbf{F}_S^T y$ are perpendicular vectors. This transformation allows us to write the problem in terms of the R^2 objective as:

$$\mathrm{R}^2 = \max_{S:|S|=k} f(S) \text{ where } f(S) = \hat{y}^T \mathbf{F}_S(\mathbf{F}_S^T \mathbf{F}_S)^{-1}\mathbf{F}_S^T \hat{y}$$

and $\hat{y} = y/\|y\|_2$. The Forward Regression algorithm builds a family of sets incrementally by adding the element that provides the maximum increase in value for f. The algorithm is initialized with $S_0 = \emptyset$ and for each $k = 1\ldots,n$, we define $S_{k+1} = S_k \cup \{i\}$ for some $i \in \text{argmax}_{j\notin S_k} f(S_k \cup \{j\})$.

We will provide a two-fold validation for the Forward Regression algorithm for the Seed Recovery problem: the first is theoretical. We will use a result due to Das and Kempe [6] to give a theoretical approximation guarantee for this problem for a special case. The Forward Regression algorithm notoriously performs much better in practice than its theoretical bounds [6], however the theoretical guarantee is useful to highlight the dependency of the algorithm on parameters of the instance. In particular, we will show that the approximation guarantee improves for higher values of α_i. In Section 7, we also perform experimental validation of this algorithm: we construct synthetic instances of the problem for which the innate opinions form a sparse vector and evaluate the outcome of the Forward Regression algorithm against the ground truth.

The theoretical guarantee on the approximation of the Forward Regression algorithm can be obtained from spectral properties of the matrix $\mathbf{F}$:

THEOREM 2 (DAS AND KEMPE [6]). *For each $k = 1, 2, \ldots, n$,*

$$f(S_k) \geq \left[1 - \exp\left(\frac{-\lambda^k_{\min}(\mathbf{F}^T\mathbf{F})}{\max_i \|\mathbf{F}^i\|_2^2}\right)\right] \cdot \max_{S:|S|=k} f(S)$$

where F^i is the i-th column of matrix $\mathbf{F}$ and $\lambda^k_{\min}(\mathbf{F}^T\mathbf{F})$ is the smallest k-sparse eigenvalue of the matrix $\mathbf{F}^T\mathbf{F}$, i.e., $\lambda_{k,\min}(\mathbf{F}^T\mathbf{F}) = \min_{x\in\mathbb{R}^n\backslash 0, \|x\|_0=k} \|\mathbf{F}x\|_2^2/\|x\|_2^2$

Since $\lambda^k_{\min}(\mathbf{F}^T\mathbf{F})$ is non-increasing in k, the approximation guarantee is better for smaller values of k, which are the ones we are specially interested, since our objective is to verify if the expressed opinion can be explained by an initial sparse seed. In what follows, we provide a lower bound on the exponent $\lambda^k_{\min}(\mathbf{F}^T\mathbf{F})/\max_i \|\mathbf{F}^i\|_2^2$ for the special case of regular undirected graphs and uniform α_i values, i.e., we will assume that α_i is the same for all i and that the graph is undirected and all nodes have the same degree. Since α_i is the same and d_i is the same for all nodes, we drop the subscript i for the rest of the section. The Friedkin-Johnsen matrix $\mathbf{F}$ in this case is symmetric and can be written as:

$$\mathbf{F} = \alpha \cdot \left(\mathbf{I} - \frac{1-\alpha}{d} \cdot \mathbf{A}\right)^{-1} = \alpha \sum_{k=0}^{\infty} (1-\alpha)^k \left(\frac{1}{d}\mathbf{A}\right)^k$$

using the matrix identity $(\mathbf{I}-\mathbf{M})^{-1} = \sum_{k=0}^{\infty} \mathbf{M}^k$. From this we can observe that the entries of $\mathbf{F}$ are non-negative. We use this fact to show the following result:

LEMMA 4. *If $\mathbf{F}$ is the Friedkin-Johnsen matrix associated with an undirected regular graph with degree d and uniform values $\alpha_i = \alpha(> 0)$, then all columns of the matrix $\mathbf{F}$ have their norm bounded by 1.*

PROOF. Let $\mathbf{1}$ be the vector with all components equal to 1. Then if $\mathbf{A}$ is the matrix associated with the regular graph, then clearly $\frac{1}{d}\mathbf{A}\mathbf{1} = \mathbf{1}$. Therefore $\mathbf{F}\mathbf{1} = \alpha \sum_{k=0}^{\infty} (1-\alpha)^k (\frac{1}{d}\mathbf{A})^k \mathbf{1} = \mathbf{1}\alpha \sum_{k=0}^{\infty} (1-\alpha)^k = \mathbf{1}$. Therefore, for all rows i, $\sum_j \mathbf{F}_{ij} = 1$. Since the entries are non-negative, it means that all entries are in the $[0, 1]$ range. Finally, we use the symmetry of $\mathbf{F}$ to see that:

$$\|\mathbf{F}^i\|_2^2 = \sum_j \mathbf{F}_{ij}^2 \leq \sum_j \mathbf{F}_{ij} = 1$$

□

The remaining term in Theorem 2 is $\lambda^k_{\min}(\mathbf{F}^T\mathbf{F})$, which we bound by the smallest eigenvalue of $\mathbf{F}^T\mathbf{F}$:

$$\lambda^k_{\min}(\mathbf{F}^T\mathbf{F}) \geq \lambda_{\min}(\mathbf{F}^T\mathbf{F}) = \min_{x\neq 0} \frac{\|\mathbf{F}x\|_2^2}{\|x\|_2^2}$$

In the subsequent proof, we use the concept of the operator norm of a matrix. Given a square matrix $\mathbf{M}$, we define its operator norm $\|\mathbf{M}\|_2 = \max_{x\in\mathbb{R}^n\backslash\{0\}} \|\mathbf{M}x\|_2/\|x\|_2$ and use the following matrix inequalities:

$$\|\mathbf{M}_1 + \mathbf{M}_2\|_2 \leq \|\mathbf{M}_1\|_2 + \|\mathbf{M}_2\|_2 \tag{4}$$

$$\|\mathbf{M}_1 \cdot \mathbf{M}_2\|_2 \leq \|\mathbf{M}_1\|_2 \cdot \|\mathbf{M}_2\|_2 \tag{5}$$

We refer to [16] for an extensive exposition on matrix norms and spectral properties of matrices.

Also, given the adjacency matrix $\mathbf{A}$ of a regular graph of degree d. We will use the fact [4] that the operator norm of the adjacency matrix is at most the maximum degree of its vertices, hence,

$$\|\frac{1}{d}\mathbf{A}\|_2 \leq 1. \tag{6}$$

LEMMA 5. *If $\mathbf{F}$ is the Friedkin-Johnsen matrix associated with an undirected regular graph d and uniform values $\alpha_i = \alpha(> 0)$, then*

$$\lambda_{\min}(\mathbf{F}^T\mathbf{F}) \geq \frac{\alpha^2}{4}$$

PROOF. Since $\alpha > 0$ then $\mathbf{F}$ is invertible, therefore:

$$\lambda_{\min}(\mathbf{F}^T\mathbf{F}) = \min_{x\neq 0} \frac{\|\mathbf{F}x\|_2^2}{\|x\|_2^2} = \min_{y\neq 0} \frac{\|y\|_2^2}{\|\mathbf{F}^{-1}y\|_2^2}$$
$$= \left[\max_{y\neq 0} \frac{\|\mathbf{F}^{-1}y\|_2}{\|y\|_2}\right]^{-2} = \|\mathbf{F}^{-1}\|_2^{-2}$$

By the definition of $\mathbf{F}$ we have that:

$$\mathbf{F}^{-1} = \alpha^{-1} \cdot (\mathbf{I} - (1-\alpha) \cdot \frac{1}{d}\mathbf{A})$$

Therefore:

$$\|\mathbf{F}^{-1}\|_2 \leq \alpha^{-1}(\|\mathbf{I}\|_2 + (1-\alpha)\|\tfrac{1}{d}\mathbf{A}\|_2) \leq \alpha^{-1}(1 + 1 - \alpha) \leq 2\alpha^{-1}$$

Here the first inequality follows from the matrix inequalities 4 and 5 and the second inequality follows from inequality 6. Thus, $\lambda_{\min}(\mathbf{F}^T\mathbf{F}) \geq \frac{\alpha^2}{4}$ □

Thus from Theorem 2, Lemma 4 and 5, we get the following theorem:

THEOREM 3. *For each $k = 1, 2, \ldots, n$,*

$$f(S_k) \geq \left[1 - \exp\left(-\alpha^2/4\right)\right] \cdot \max_{S:|S|=k} f(S).$$

6. CONFORMITY EXTRACTION EXPERIMENTS

In this section, we present the results for our experiments for the CONFORMITYEXTRACTION problem on both real world Twitter data and synthetic data.

6.1 Conformity in Synthetic Data

We first conduct synthetic experiments (where we have complete access to ground truth and can therefore obtain fine-grained validation) to show that our algorithms described in Section 4 can extract conformity values with high accuracy. Toward this end, we generated graphs having regular, random and power law degree distributions. The number of nodes in the graph was varied from 100 to 1000. The degree in the regular graph case was set to 20 while the maximum degree in the power-law and random graph was set to 100.

Every node was assigned one of 10 innate opinions in $\{0, 1, 2, \ldots, 9\}$. To capture a homophily effect on the innate opinions, we imposed a Lipschitz constraint on the assignment of innate opinions to nodes, such that for 85% of the graph edges, the difference in opinions between the nodes forming the edge is at most 1.

For assigning α values to nodes, we used three different distributions: α values distributed uniformly in $[0, 1]$, α values taken from a power-law distribution with most of the values close to 0, and a bimodal Gaussian distribution with peaks close to 0 and 0.5. Finally, we note that all results are averaged over 10 runs.

Using the α distribution and innate opinions of nodes in the graph, we ran 5000 rounds of the Friedkin-Johnsen opinion dynamics, and considered the final opinions of the nodes as their expressed opinions.

Based on these expressed opinions and the graph structure, we then estimated the α values of all nodes in the graph, using our LPRecovery and IPRecovery algorithms for ConformityExtraction described in Section 4. For all our experiments, we used a commercial optimization solver [20] to run LPRecovery and IPRecovery . To measure the effectiveness of our algorithms, we compared the estimated α values with the ground-truth α parameters. We first categorized the nodes into three buckets based on their ground truth α values: low, medium, and high corresponding to the ranges $[0, 1/3]$, $(1/3, 2/3]$, and $(2/3, 1]$ respectively. Then, we plotted the performance of our algorithms (separately for each bucket and also for for the overall set of nodes) using two metrics: 1) a fine-grained measure corresponding to the absolute error between the ground truth α and the estimated α; 2) a coarse-grained measure corresponding to the accuracy or percentage of nodes for which we estimated their buckets correctly.

Figure 1 illustrates the results for random graphs using the LPRecovery algorithm. We varied the number of nodes in $\{100, 250, 500, 750, 1000\}$ and ran the experiments with the three different types of α distributions. In almost all the cases, the absolute error in estimating the conformity parameters was less then 0.12. In general, we observe that the accuracy of our algorithm is slightly better for the sparse α distribution where most of the nodes have low α values, than with other distributions. This is because the LPRecovery algorithm has a slight bias towards assigning low α values, since this allows for a greater degree of freedom in minimizing the objective function of the linear program (Section 4). We also note that the estimation error for the α values is lower for large graphs than for small graphs. This is likely due to the fact that as we increase the number of nodes in the random graph, the expected degree of a node increases, which then strengthens the homophily assumptions used by the linear program to prune its feasible solution space.

The results for the accuracy measure are qualitatively similar. As seen from the figure, we recover at least 80% of the values in each bucket. Again, in the natural case of sparse α distribution, this number increases to 90%.

We observe that we obtained qualitatively similar results for the case of regular and power-law graphs and for the case where we used the IPRecovery algorithm instead of LPRecovery . The results are omitted due to lack of space.

6.2 Conformity in Twitter Data

Next, we ran our algorithms for ConformityExtraction on real world social network data from Twitter. Our data set comprised of user opinions extracted from a large set of tweets corresponding to one of three topics, namely: *organic food*, *weight loss* and *electric cars*. We considered all tweets related to these topics (using simple keyword-based classifiers) within a 6-month timeline from 12/1/2012 to 5/31/2013. The total number of tweets in each topic varied between 100000 and 2000000. We then ran each tweet through a commercial sentiment analyzer [26] to obtain sentiment values ranging from -1 (corresponding to negative sentiment) to 1 (corresponding to positive sentiment), which was then smoothed into one of 10 opinion buckets. We treated the median of a user's last three opinion values as her expressed opinion. Using the Twitter follow graph, we obtained the induced subgraph over the nodes (across all topics) with around 1 million nodes and 100 million edges. As before, our goal is to extract α values of the users using the expressed opinions and graph structure.

One significant difference in this experiment is that, unlike the synthetic experiments, there is no explicit ground truth α values available for the users. To overcome this problem, we identified, using tweet histories, a small set of ground truth consisting of users with high α and low α. To obtain this ground truth for each topic, we first extract users with at least 5 tweets on the topic, and have at least 5 neighbors in the Twitter graph who have also tweeted about the topic. We categorize a user's tweet into a positive, negative or neutral opinion based on the sentiment value. We then define a stubborn user (high α bucket) as one whose opinions differs from her majority neighboring opinion for ϵ fraction of her tweets. Similarly a user is conforming (low α bucket) if her final opinion is different from her initial opinion and whose set of opinions is the same as the final majority opinion in her neighborhood for γ fraction of her tweets. We ignored the nodes that do not satisfy these conditions in our analysis. For our experiments we set ϵ to be 0.7 and γ to be 0.3.

Note that the above method to compute the ground truth cannot be used as a general algorithm to extract conformity values for *all* users since only a small set of users satisfy the aforementioned criteria to reliably measure their conformity. This necessitates the design of algorithms such as the ones proposed in this paper.

For each of the topics, we ran our IPRecovery and LPRecovery algorithms using the expressed opinions and the induced graph structure on all Twitter users who have tweeted about the topic at least 5 times and have at least 5 neighbors, and estimated their conformity parameter α. This yielded around 2000 to 15000 users for each topic. From among these users, we then extracted a smaller ground truth set of stubborn users and conforming users. We considered the estimated α value for each user in the ground truth set, and

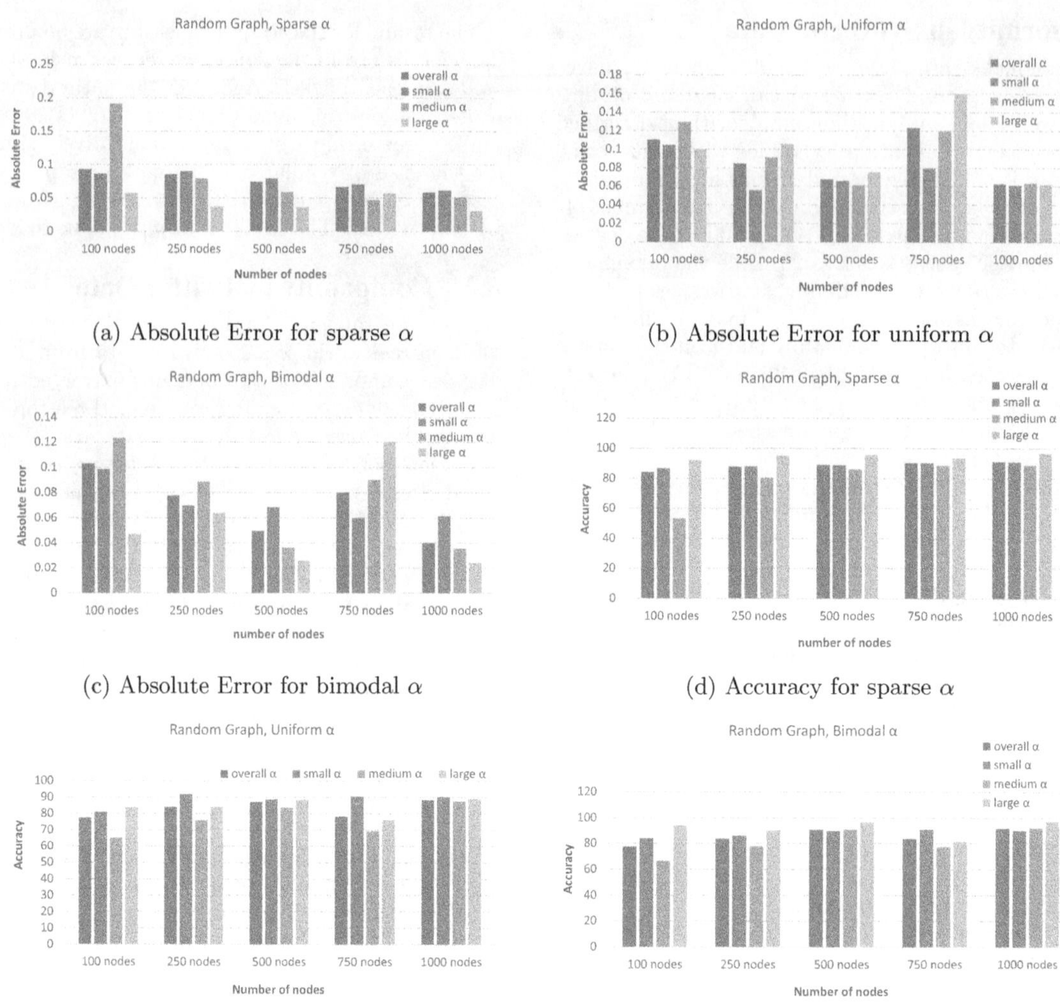

(a) Absolute Error for sparse α

(b) Absolute Error for uniform α

(c) Absolute Error for bimodal α

(d) Accuracy for sparse α

(e) Accuracy for uniform α

(f) Accuracy for bimodal α

Figure 1: Effectiveness of LPRecovery on random graphs

Topic	Algorithm	Percentage of stubborn nodes recovered	Percentage of conforming nodes recovered
Electric Car	LPRecovery	75	65
Electric Car	IPRecovery	77	82.5
Organic Food	LPRecovery	87.5	66.7
Organic Food	IPRecovery	89	59
Weight Loss	LPRecovery	55	65
Weight Loss	IPRecovery	55	61

Table 1: Conformity Extraction on Twitter

used a threshold of 0.66 and 0.33 on their estimated α to predict whether these users are stubborn, conforming, or neither. We observe that since the associated α values are either large or small, respectively, they can be more readily extracted from the data. We then measure the recall with respect to the stubborn user set (i.e., what fraction of ground truth stubborn users were correctly recovered by our algorithm) and similarly with respect to the conforming user set. Table 1 summarizes the results.

As the table shows, our algorithms perform well in recovering the stubborn users from the ground truth set for many instances. In particular, for the topic of organic food, our algorithms recover almost 90% of the stubborn users, but recover a lesser (60%) fraction of the conforming user. On the other hand, for weight loss, the performance of the algorithms in recovering the conforming users (65%) is better than that for the stubborn users (55%). This correlated with the observed skew toward stubborn users for *organic food* and conforming users for *weight loss* (see Figure 3).

The table above also validates empirically that the LPRecovery algorithm is a good approximation to the (much slower) IPRecovery algorithm, since the gap in performance between the two algorithms for most cases is less than 10%.

6.3 Validation of homophily in Twitter

The assumption of homophily in the innate opinions of users in a social networks is crucial in our LPRecovery and IPRecovery algorithms, since it helps us solve an underdetermined system of equations. To validate this assumption, we set out to observe the difference between the innate

Topics	Avg gap in neighboring opinions	Fraction of edges with gap < 1
Electric Car	0.75	64%
Weight Loss	0.79	69%
Organic Food	0.60	83%

Table 2: Homophily in Twitter data

values of neighbors in the Twitter follow graph for the three topics. For the homophily experiments, we define a user's innate opinion on a particular topic to be the average of the sentiment values associated with the first three tweets posted by the user in the 6 month time period. Recall that the user's opinion values as extracted from our sentiment analyser are bucketed into $\{0, 1, 2, \ldots, 9\}$. Table 2 reports the average difference in opinions between every pair of users connected by an edge in the Twitter graph, as well as the total fraction of edges in the graph for which this difference in opinions is less than 1. As seen in the table for our topics of interest, we observe that for more than 64% of the users, the difference in opinions across an edge is less than 1. Furthermore the average difference between a pair of neighboring users is less than 1 for all the topics.

7. SEED RECOVERY EXPERIMENTS

In the next set of experiments, we used the α values from our previous ConformityExtraction experiments to address the SeedRecovery problem for both synthetic as well as Twitter graphs. Thus, we would like to compute a small set of nodes with a given innate opinion (and assuming neutral innate opinion on all other nodes) that can best explain the current expressed opinions in the network resulting from Friedkin-Johnsen dynamics. As described in Section 5, we measure the discrepancy in the predicted expressed opinions using this seed set versus the ground truth expressed opinion across all the nodes in the graph. As mentioned earlier, for measuring this discrepancy, we use the squared multiple correlation (R^2) metric, which lies in $[0, 1]$ and is essentially equal to $1 - L2Error$, where $L2Error$ is the normalized L_2 norm error between the predicted expressed opinion vector and the ground truth expressed opinion vector. Our goal is to recover a seed set of k nodes in the graph that can maximize the R^2 measure.

We use the Greedy algorithm (defined in Section 5) to recover the best seed sets of size k (we vary k from 1 to 20) for both synthetic and Twitter data. We also report the characteristics of the computed seed set as we vary its size k. We compare the performance of the Greedy algorithm against two natural baselines that have been used in similar problems ([24]): selecting nodes with the highest α-values and selecting nodes with the highest degrees in the graph.

7.1 Synthetic Data

Similar to Section 6, we generated synthetic graphs of 1000 nodes with regular, random and power law degree distributions, and assigned innate opinions in a similar manner as earlier. We also used the same three distributions of α values as earlier: uniform, bimodal and sparse. We only report the result of random graphs (the regular and power-law graphs had qualitatively similar results). In Figure 2(a), we plot the R^2 metric as a function of k for the various α distributions for the Greedy algorithm.

First, as expected, the R^2 increases as the size of the seed set increases. More interestingly, even for as low as 6 seed nodes, we get an R^2 value of close to 0.92 indicating a very good agreement between the original and predicted expressed opinions. For comparison, we also plot the corresponding R^2 values using the two baseline algorithms (selecting nodes according to the α values and degrees respectively) for each of the α distributions. Clearly, our Greedy algorithm performs significantly better than both the baselines. Secondly, in terms of the characteristics of the seed set selected by Greedy , we observe that the algorithm starts off by initially selecting high-degree, stubborn nodes, and then moves to nodes with lower α and degree values (Figures 2(b) and 2(d)) as the size of the seed set increases. We also measured the difference in the α values between a node in the seed set and its average neighboring α. Figure 2(c) indicates that our algorithm favors selecting seed nodes that have high α but whose neighbors have low α values. These observations agree with our intuitive expectation that the most likely seed nodes are ones that are stubborn and have a large number of conforming neighbors. Interestingly, similar behaviour has also been observed previously in [5] in the context of selecting nodes to best estimate the average innate opinion in the network.

In a more direct experiment (Figures 2(e) and 2(f)), we "planted" 10 seed nodes in a 1000 node random graph with $\alpha = 0.95$ for all the 10 nodes. Further, these 10 nodes were initialized with non-neutral innate opinions while those of the remaining nodes had neutral opinions. As before, the α values of the remaining nodes were drawn from three different distributions – sparse, bimodal, and uniform. The goal of this experiment was to validate if our algorithm can indeed "recover" the planted seed nodes, purely based on the expressed opinions and alpha values of all the nodes. Note that the graph also contained several (based on the specific α distribution) stubborn nodes that were not seeds, and hence it is not sufficient to simply pick nodes with large α values as the seeds. This is corroborated by Figure 2(e) which shows that the R^2 value of the seed set obtained by the Greedy algorithm outperforms the α-based algorithm. The α-based algorithm in turn outperforms the degree-based algorithm, due to the fact that the seed nodes in this case have high *alpha* values.

In particular, Figure 2(e) shows that the Greedy algorithm finds exactly the right set of 10 seed nodes. This is because for any size ≥ 10, the R^2 value is 1.0, implying that the selected seed set actually contains all the 10 seed nodes! This observation is further corroborated by Figure 2(f) where we see that the average value of α for the seed set of size 10 is precisely 0.95 which is indeed the α value for each of the planted stubborn node.

7.2 Twitter Data

Next, we repeated the SeedRecovery experiments using Twitter data for various topics. The dataset and resulting social graph are exactly the same as in Section 6.2. As earlier, we used the α values generated from the conformity extraction experiments described in Section 6.2. Figure 3 shows the distribution of these α values for different topics. The α distributions for all the topics resemble either sparse

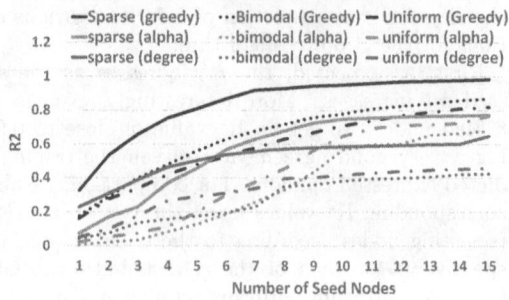

(a) Squared multiple correlation R^2

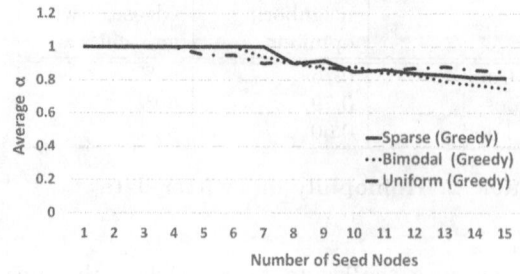

(b) Average α of the seed set

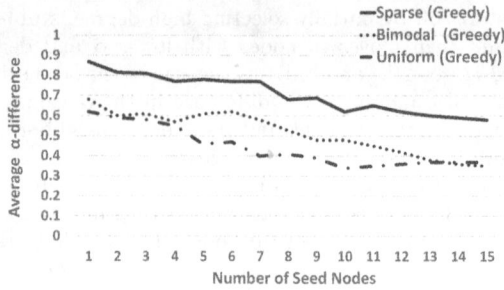

(c) Avg difference in α values of the seed set node and its neighborhood

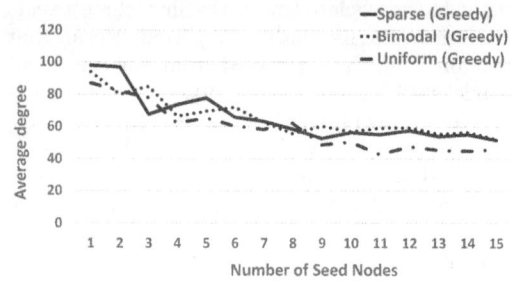

(d) Average degree of seed set for a power-law graph

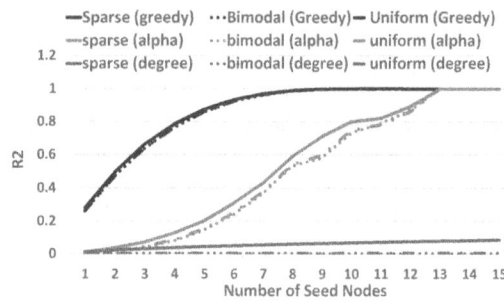

(e) Squared multiple correlation R^2 of the recovered seed set

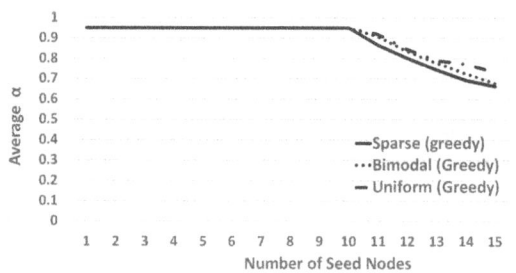

(f) Average α of the recovered seed set

Figure 2: Characteristics of the seed set for synthetic random graphs, with uniform, bimodal, and power-law α-distributions. Figures 2(e) and 2(f) show results for the "planted" seed set experiment.

or bimodal distributions, and we remind the reader that we covered both of them in our simulations.

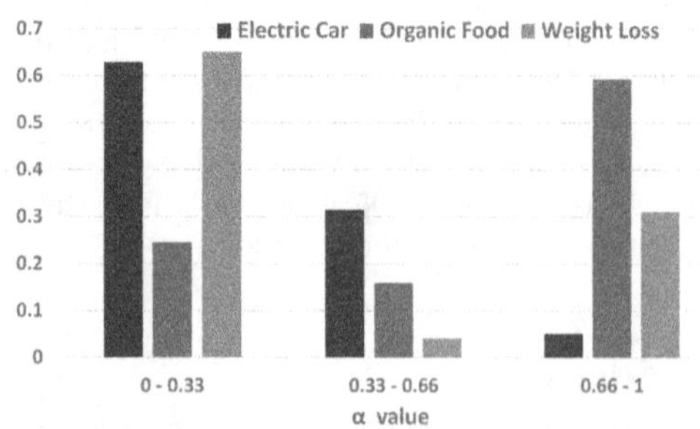

Figure 3: Distribution of α across the three buckets

The results are summarized in Figure 4. Qualitatively, even for this data, we observe similar results to the simulations. The R^2 of the selected seed set is much larger than the α-based and degree-based baseline algorithms, for all the topics. Similarly, based on the plots showing the average α value, average degree, and average neighborhood difference in α values for the seed set, the GREEDY algorithm shows a clear preference for selecting seed nodes that are moderately stubborn and have a large number of conforming neighbors. (Note that just selecting seed nodes based on high alpha values alone does not suffice, as shown by the corresponding baseline performance in 4(a)).

However, we do see interesting differences in the R^2 plots between various topics. For example, while the squared multiple correlation for *Electric cars* is around 0.6 for $k = 20$, it is only around 0.2 for the case of *Organic food* or *Weight loss*. This suggests that for the Twitter data, the equilibrium opinions for Electric cars is much more likely to have been generated by a small number of seed nodes, as compared to those for organic food or weight loss. We therefore surmise that the R^2 measure of the seed set for a topic might provide

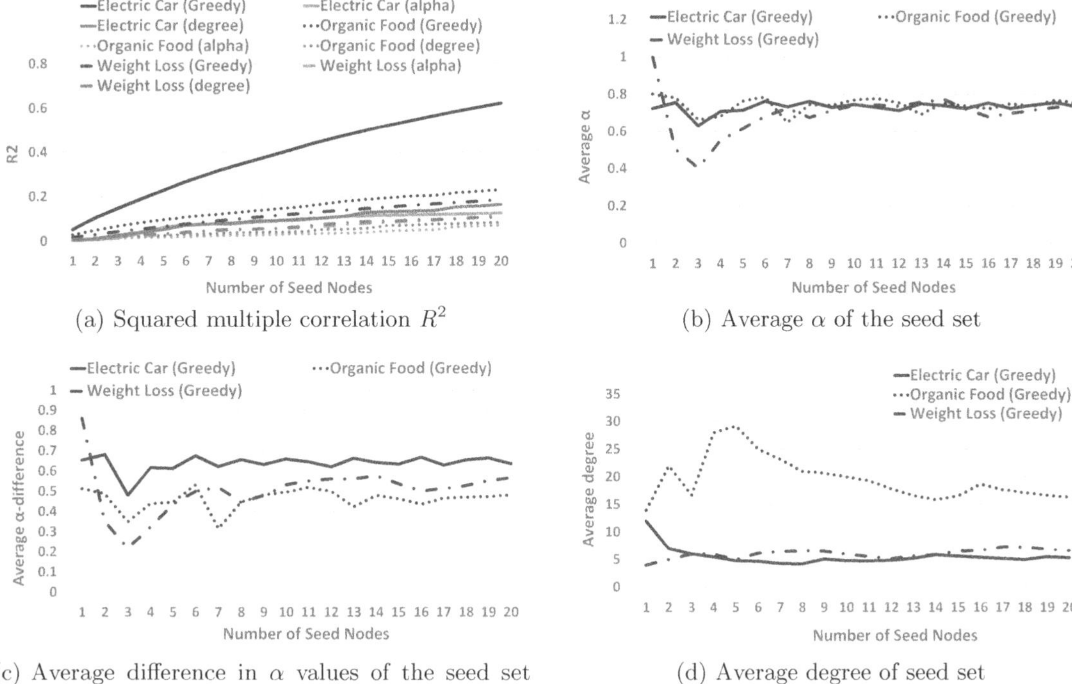

(a) Squared multiple correlation R^2

(b) Average α of the seed set

(c) Average difference in α values of the seed set node and its neighborhood

(d) Average degree of seed set

Figure 4: Characteristics of seed set for the three different topics on Twitter

insights into a notion of how "heterogenous" or "diverse" is the opinion dynamics for that topic in a social network.

8. CONCLUSIONS

The notion of conformity plays a central role in shaping of users opinions in online social networks. In this study, we proposed algorithms for estimating conformity of users using only the expressed opinions of users resulting from the underlying opinion dynamics and the social graph. Under some natural conditions, we show using both simulations and Twitter data that our algorithms perform well on extracting the conformity values of the users.

Further, we propose efficient algorithms to recover the smallest set of source nodes in the graph that best explain the current distribution of opinions in the entire graph. We refer to this problem as *seed recovery* and we believe this and similar problems have many applications in running effective marketing campaigns, understanding information flow in social networks etc. As before, we validate our algorithms for this problem using both simulations and Twitter data. An interesting open question is to generalize the conformity extraction problem to other well-studied opinion dynamics models.

9. REFERENCES

[1] A. Anagnostopoulos, R. Kumar, and M. Mahdian. Influence and correlation in social networks. In *Proceedings of the 14th ACM SIGKDD international conference on Knowledge discovery and data mining*, pages 7–15. ACM, 2008.

[2] D. Bindel, J. M. Kleinberg, and S. Oren. How bad is forming your own opinion? In *FOCS*, pages 57–66, 2011.

[3] E. J. Candès, J. Romberg, and T. Tao. Stable signal recovery from incomplete and inaccurate measurements. *Communications on Pure and Applied Mathematics*, 59:1207–1223, 2005.

[4] F. Chung. *Spectral Graph Theory*. Number no. 92 in CBMS Regional Conference Series. American Mathematical Society, 1997.

[5] A. Das, S. Gollapudi, R. Panigrahy, and M. Salek. Debiasing social wisdom. In *Proceedings of the 19th ACM SIGKDD*, pages 500–508. ACM, 2013.

[6] A. Das and D. Kempe. Submodular meets spectral: Greedy algorithms for subset selection, sparse approximation and dictionary selection. In *ICML*, pages 1057–1064, 2011.

[7] G. Davis, S. Mallat, and M. Avellaneda. Adaptive greedy approximations. *Constructive Approximation*, 13(1):57–98, Mar. 1997.

[8] M. H. DeGroot. Reaching a consensus. *Journal of the American Statistical Association*, 69(345):118–121, 1974.

[9] D. Donoho. For most large underdetermined systems of linear equations, the minimal 11-norm near-solution approximates the sparsest near-solution. *Communications on Pure and Applied Mathematics*, 59:1207–1223, 2005.

[10] X. Fang, P. J.-H. Hu, Z. L. Li, and W. Tsai. Predicting adoption probabilities in social networks. *Information Systems Research*, 24(1):128–145, 2013.

[11] J. Fowler and N. Christakis. Cooperative behavior cascades in human social networks. *Proc. Nat. Acad. Sci.*, 107(12):5334–8, 2010.

[12] N. E. Friedkin and E. C. Johnsen. Social influence and opinions. *Journal of Mathematical Sociology*, 15(3-4):193–206, 1990.

[13] A. Gionis, E. Terzi, and P. Tsaparas. Opinion maximization in social networks. *arXiv preprint arXiv:1301.7455*, 2013.

[14] S. Goel, D. J. Watts, and D. G. Goldstein. The structure of online diffusion networks. In *Proc. of the 13th ACM EC*, pages 623–638. ACM, 2012.

[15] J. Goldenberg, B. Libai, and E. Muller. Talk of the network: A complex systems look at the underlying process of word-of-mouth. *Marketing letters*, 12(3):211–223, 2001.

[16] G. H. Golub and C. F. Van Loan. *Matrix computations (3rd ed.)*. Johns Hopkins University Press, Baltimore, MD, USA, 1996.

[17] M. Gomez Rodriguez, J. Leskovec, and A. Krause. Inferring networks of diffusion and influence. In *Proc. of the 16th ACM SIGKDD*, pages 1019–1028. ACM, 2010.

[18] A. Goyal, F. Bonchi, and L. V. Lakshmanan. Learning influence probabilities in social networks. In *Proceedings of the third ACM international conference on Web search and data mining*, pages 241–250. ACM, 2010.

[19] M. Granovetter. Threshold models of collective behavior. *American journal of sociology*, pages 1420–1443, 1978.

[20] Gurobi. Optimizer - http://www.gurobi.com/products/gurobi-optimizer/gurobi-overview.

[21] R. Hegselmann and U. Krause. Opinion dynamics and bounded confidence models, analysis, and simulation. *Journal of Artificial Societies and Social Simulation*, 5(3), 2002.

[22] M. O. Jackson. *Social and Economic Networks*. Princeton University Press, Princeton, NJ, USA, 2008.

[23] R. A. Johnson and D. W. Wichern. *Applied multivariate statistical analysis*, volume 5. Prentice hall Upper Saddle River, NJ, 2002.

[24] D. Kempe, J. Kleinberg, and É. Tardos. Maximizing the spread of influence through a social network. In *Proc. of the ninth ACM SIGKDD*, pages 137–146. ACM, 2003.

[25] C. R. Langford, M. L. Lengnick-Hall, and M. Kulkarni. How do social networks influence the employment prospects of people with disabilities? *Employee Responsibilities and Rights Journal*, 25(4):295–310, 2013.

[26] Lexalytics. Salience engine - http://www.lexalytics.com/technical-info/salience-engine-for-text-analysis.

[27] H. Li, S. S. Bhowmick, and A. Sun. Cinema: conformity-aware greedy algorithm for influence maximization in online social networks. In *Proceedings of the 16th International Conference on Extending Database Technology*, pages 323–334. ACM, 2013.

[28] B. Liu. Sentiment analysis and opinion mining. *Synthesis Lectures on Human Language Technologies*, 5(1), 2012.

[29] P. V. Marsden. Homogeneity in confiding relations. *Social networks*, 10(1):57–76, 1988.

[30] M. McPherson, L. Smith-Lovin, and J. M. Cook. Birds of a feather: Homophily in social networks. *Annual review of sociology*, pages 415–444, 2001.

[31] S. A. Myers, C. Zhu, and J. Leskovec. Information diffusion and external influence in networks. In *Proc. of the 18th ACM SIGKDD*, pages 33–41. ACM, 2012.

[32] M. Richardson and P. Domingos. Mining knowledge-sharing sites for viral marketing. In *Proceedings of the eighth ACM SIGKDD*, pages 61–70. ACM, 2002.

[33] T. C. Schelling. Models of segregation. *American Economic Review*, 59(2):488–493, 1969.

[34] J. Tang, J. Sun, C. Wang, and Z. Yang. Social influence analysis in large-scale networks. In *Proceedings of the 15th ACM SIGKDD*, pages 807–816. ACM, 2009.

[35] J. Tang, S. Wu, and J. Sun. Confluence: Conformity influence in large social networks. In *Proceedings of the 19th ACM SIGKDD international conference on Knowledge discovery and data mining*, pages 347–355. ACM, 2013.

[36] D. J. Watts, P. S. Dodds, and M. E. Newman. Identity and search in social networks. *science*, 296(5571):1302–1305, 2002.

[37] T. Zhang. On the consistency of feature selection using greedy least squares regression. *Journal of Machine Learning Research*, 10:555–568, 2009.

Computing Classic Closeness Centrality, at Scale

Edith Cohen
Microsoft Research
editco@microsoft.com

Daniel Delling
Microsoft Research
dadellin@microsoft.com

Thomas Pajor
Microsoft Research
tpajor@microsoft.com

Renato F. Werneck
Microsoft Research
renatow@microsoft.com

ABSTRACT

Closeness centrality, first considered by Bavelas (1948), is an importance measure of a node in a network which is based on the distances from the node to all other nodes. The classic definition, proposed by Bavelas (1950), Beauchamp (1965), and Sabidussi (1966), is (the inverse of) the average distance to all other nodes.

We propose the first highly scalable (near linear-time processing and linear space overhead) algorithm for estimating, within a small relative error, the classic closeness centralities of all nodes in the graph. Our algorithm applies to undirected graphs, as well as for centrality computed with respect to round-trip distances in directed graphs.

For directed graphs, we also propose an efficient algorithm that approximates generalizations of classic closeness centrality to outbound and inbound centralities. Although it does not provide worst-case theoretical approximation guarantees, it is designed to perform well on real networks.

We perform extensive experiments on large networks, demonstrating high scalability and accuracy.

1. INTRODUCTION

Closeness centrality is a structural measure of the importance of a node in a network, which is based on the ensemble of its distances to all other nodes. It captures the basic intuition that the closer a node is to all other nodes, the more important it is. Structural centrality in the context of social graphs was first considered in 1948 by Bavelas [4].

The classic definition measures the closeness centrality of a node as the inverse of the average distance from it and was proposed by Bavelas [5], Beauchamp [6], and Sabidussi [44]. On a graph $G = (V, E)$ with $|V| = n$ nodes, the centrality of v is formally defined by

$$B^{-1}(v) = (n-1)/\sum_{u \in V} d_{vu}, \quad (1)$$

COSN'14, October 1–2, 2014, Dublin, Ireland.

ACM 978-1-4503-3198-2/14/10 ...$15.00.
http://dx.doi.org/10.1145/2660460.2660465.

where d_{vu} is the shortest-path distance between v and u in G. This textbook definition is also referred to as *Bavelas closeness centrality* or as the *Sabidussi Index* [26, 27, 50].

The classic closeness centrality of a node v can be computed exactly using a single-source shortest paths computation (such as Dijkstra's algorithm). In general, however, we are interested not only in the centrality of a particular node, but rather in the set of all centrality values. This is the case when centrality values are used to obtain a relative ranking of the nodes. Beyond that, the distribution of centralities captures important characteristics of a social network, such as its *centralization* [27, 50].

When we would like to perform many centrality queries (in particular when we are interested in centrality values for all nodes) on graphs with billions of edges, such as large social networks and Web crawl graphs, the exact algorithms do not scale. Instead, we are looking for scalable computation of approximate values, with small relative error.

The node with maximum classic closeness centrality is known as the 1-median of the network. A near-linear-time algorithm for finding an approximate 1-median was proposed by Indyk and Thorup [29, 47]. Their algorithm samples k nodes at random and performs Dijkstra's algorithm from each sampled node. They show that the node with minimum sum of distances to sampled nodes is with high probability an approximate 1-median of the network. The same sampling approach was also used to estimate the centrality values of all nodes [25] and to identify the top k centralities [40]. When the distance distribution is heavy-tailed, however, the sample average is a very poor estimator of the average distance: The few very distant nodes that dominate the average distance are likely to be all excluded from the sample C, resulting in a large expected error for almost all nodes.

Contributions

We present the first near-linear-time algorithm for estimating, with a small relative error, the classic closeness centralities of all nodes. Our algorithm provides probabilistic guarantees that hold for all instances and for all nodes.

Computationally, our algorithm selects a small uniform sample C of k nodes and performs single-source shortest paths computation from each sampled node. We provide a high-level description, illustrated in Figure 1, of how we use this information to estimate centralities of all nodes.

From the single-source computations, we know the distances from nodes in C to all other nodes and therefore the exact value of $B(u)$ for each $u \in C$, but we need to estimate

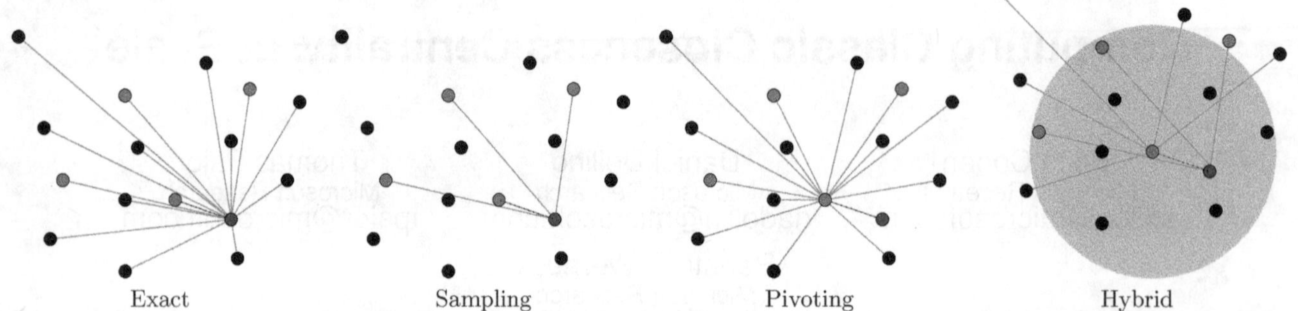

Figure 1: Exact: Average distance from blue node to all other nodes. Sampling: Average distance to sampled (red) nodes. Pivoting: Average distance from pivot (closest sampled node). Hybrid: Distances outside the threshold radius from pivot are estimated through the pivot (but distances to sampled nodes outside the threshold are exact). Shorter distances, within the threshold radius, are estimated through sampled nodes.

the centrality of other nodes. As we mentioned, a natural way to use this information is *sampling* [25, 29, 40, 47]: Estimate the centrality of a node v using the sample average $\hat{B}(v) = \sum_{u \in C} d_{vu}/k$. As we argued, however, the expected relative error can be very large when the distribution of distances from the node v to all other nodes is skewed.

A second basic approach, which we propose here, is *pivoting*, which builds on techniques from approximate shortest-paths algorithms [15, 48]. We define the *pivot* $c(v) \in C$ of a node v as the node in the sample which is closest to v. We can then estimate the centrality of v by that of its pivot, $B(c(v))$, which we computed exactly. By the triangle inequality, the value of $B(v)$ is within $\pm\, d_{vc(v)}$ of $B(c(v))$.

A large error, however, can be realized even on natural instances: The centrality of the center node in a star graph would be estimated with an error of almost 100%, using average distance of approximately 2 instead of 1. If we use the *pivoting upper bound*

$$\hat{B}(v) = B(c(v)) + d_{vc(v)}$$

as our estimator, we obtain an estimate that is about three times the value of the true average. We can show, however, that this is just about the worst case: On all instances and nodes v, the pivoting upper bound estimate is, with high probability, not much less than $B(v)$ or much more than three times the value, that is, the estimate is within a factor of 3 of the actual value. Since the argument is both simple and illuminating, we sketch it here. When the sample has size k, it is likely that the distance between v and its pivot $c(v)$ is one of the $1/k$ closest distances from v. Actually, with very high probability, $d_{vc(v)}$ is one of the $(\log n)/k$ closest distances to v. Since $B(v)$ is the average value of a set of values such that $(1 - (\log n)/k)$ of them are at least as large as $d_{vc(v)}$, we obtain that

$$B(v) \geq (1 - (\log n)/k) d_{vc(v)}. \tag{2}$$

We next apply the triangle inequality to obtain

$$B(c(v)) \leq B(v) + d_{vc(v)}. \tag{3}$$

Finally, we combine (2) and (3) to obtain that our estimate $\hat{B}(v) \equiv B(c(v)) + d_{vc(v)} \leq B(v) + 2d_{vc(v)}$ is not likely to be much larger than $3B(v)$.

Therefore, the pivoting estimator has a bounded error with high probability, regardless of the distribution of distances, a property we could not get with the sampling estimator. Neither method, sampling or pivoting, however, is satisfactory to us, since we are interested in a *small relative* error, for *all* nodes, on all instances, and with (probabilistic) guarantees.

Our key algorithmic insight is to carefully combine the sampling and pivoting approaches. When estimating centrality for a node v, we apply the pivoting estimate only to nodes u that are "far" from v, that is, nodes that have distance d_{vu} much larger than the distance to the pivot $c(v)$. The sampling approach is applied to the remaining "closer" nodes. By doing so, our hybrid approach obtains an estimate with a small relative error with high confidence, something that was not possible when using only one of the methods in isolation. Moreover, the computation needed by our hybrid algorithm is essentially the same as with the basic approaches: k single-source shortest paths computation for a small value of k. Our hybrid estimator is presented and analyzed in Section 2. The estimator is applicable to points in a general metric space and is therefore presented in this context. An efficient algorithm which computes the hybrid centrality estimate for all nodes in an undirected graphs is presented in Section 3.

The effectiveness of our hybrid estimate in practice depends on setting a threshold correctly between pivoting and sampling. Our analysis sets a threshold with which we obtain guarantees with respect to worst-case instances, i.e., for any network structure and distances distribution of a node. In our implementation, we experiment with different settings. We also propose a novel *adaptive* approach, which estimates the error for several (or effectively all relevant) choices of threshold values, on a node per node basis. The sweet spot estimate which has the smallest estimated error is then used. Our error estimator for each threshold setting and our adaptive approach are detailed in Section 4.

In applications, we are often interested in measuring centrality with respect to a particular topic or property which has a different presence at each node. Nodes can also intrinsically be heterogeneous, with different activity or importance levels. These situations are modeled by an assignment of weights $\beta(i) \geq 0$ to nodes. Accordingly, one can naturally define *weighted* classic closeness centrality of a node i as

$$B_\beta^{-1}(i) = \frac{\sum_{j \neq i} \beta(i)}{\sum_{j \neq i} \beta(i) d_{ij}}. \tag{4}$$

In Section 5, we present and analyze an extension of our algorithm designed for approximating weighted centralities. The approach is based on weighted sampling of nodes, which, for any weighting β, ensures a good approximations (small relative error) of Equation (4). The handling of weighted nodes is supported with almost no cost to scalability or accuracy when compared to unweighted instances.

In Section 6 we consider directed networks. When the graph is strongly connected, meaning that all nodes can reach all other nodes, it is often natural to consider closeness centrality with respect to *round-trip* distances. The round-trip distance between two nodes is defined as the sum $d_{uv} + d_{vu}$ of the shortest-paths distances. We show that a small modification of our hybrid algorithm, which requires both forward and reverse single-source shortest-paths computations from each sampled node, approximates round-trip centralities for all nodes with a small relative error. This follows because our hybrid estimator and its analysis apply in any metric space, and round-trip distances are a metric.

When the graph is not strongly connected, however, classic closeness centrality is not well defined: All nodes that have one or more unreachable nodes have centrality value of 0. We may also want to separately consider inbound or outbound centralities, based on outbound distances from a node or inbound distances to a node, since these can be very different on directed graphs. Proposed modification of classic centrality to directed graphs are based on a combination of the average distance within the outbound or inbound reachability sets of a node, as well as on the cardinalities of these sets [12, 35]. We therefore consider scalable estimation of these quantities, proposing a sampling-based solution which provides good estimates when the distance distribution is not too skewed.

Section 7 briefly describes other relevant related work, including other important centrality measures. The results of our experimental evaluation are provided in Section 8, demonstrating the scalability and accuracy of our algorithms on benchmark networks with up to tens of millions of nodes.

2. THE HYBRID ESTIMATOR

We present our hybrid centrality estimator, which applies for a set V of $n = |V|$ points in a metric space.

We use parameters k and ϵ, whose setting determines a tradeoff between computation and approximation quality. We sample k points uniformly at random from V to obtain a set C. We then obtain the distances d_{ij} from each point $i \in C$ to all points $j \in V$. The estimators we consider are applied to this set of nk computed distances.

Specifically, we consider estimators $\hat{S}[j]$ for $j \in V$ of the sum $S(j) = \sum_{i \in V} d_{ij}$. We then estimate the centrality of j as (the inverse of) $\hat{B}[j] \leftarrow \hat{S}[j]/(n-1)$.

For points $j \in C$, we can compute the exact value of $S(j)$, since the exact distances d_{ji} are available to all i. For $j \notin C$ we are interested in estimating $S(j)$. We define the *pivot* of j (closest node in the sample):

$$c(j) = \arg\min_{i \in C} d_{ij}$$

and the distance $\Delta(j) = d_{jc(j)}$ to the pivot.

In the introduction we discussed three basic estimators: The *sample average*

$$\hat{B}(j) = \frac{1}{k} \sum_{i \in C} d_{ij} , \qquad (5)$$

the *pivot* estimator, $\hat{B}(j) \equiv B(c(j))$, and the *pivoting upper bound*

$$\hat{B}(j) \equiv B(c(j)) + \Delta(j) .$$

We argued that neither one can provide a small relative error with high probability.

The hybrid estimate $\hat{S}[j]$ for a point $j \in V \setminus C$ is obtained as follows (efficient computation is discussed in the next section). We first compute the pivot $c(j)$ and its distance $\Delta(j)$. We then partition the points $V \setminus \{j\}$ to three parts $L(j)$, $HC(j)$, and $H(j)$, where the placement of a node i is determined according to its distance $d_{ic(j)}$ from the pivot $c(j)$.

- The points $L(j)$ (L stands for "low") have distance at most $\Delta(j)/\epsilon$ from $c(j)$. The sum of distances to these points is estimated using the sum of distances to the sampled points which are in $L(j)$. Since these points are a uniform sample from $L(j)$, we compute the *effective* sampling probability $p(j) \equiv |L(j) \cap C|/|L(j)|$, and divide the sum by $p(j)$ to obtain an unbiased estimate.
- The set $HC(j)$ ("high in C") includes sampled points $i \in C$ that have distance greater than $\Delta(j)/\epsilon$ from the pivot $c(j)$. The distances from v to these points are accounted for exactly.
- The set $H(j) \subset V \setminus C$ ("high") are the points that are not sampled whose distance to the pivot $c(j)$ is greater than $\Delta(j)/\epsilon$. The sum of distances to these points is estimated by the exact sum of their distances to $c(j)$.

The estimate $\hat{S}[j]$ for $S(j)$ is thus

$$\hat{S}[j] = \sum_{i \in H(j)} d_{c(j)i} + \sum_{i \in HC(j)} d_{ji} + \frac{|L(j)|}{|L(j) \cap C|} \sum_{i \in L(j) \cap C} d_{ji}. \qquad (6)$$

Since $c(j) \in L(j) \cap C$, the denominator satisfies $|L(j) \cap C| \geq 1$ and thus the estimator is well defined. It is easy to verify that the estimate $\hat{S}[j]$ for all points j can be computed from the nk distances we collected.

2.1 Quality Guarantees

We now analyse the quality of the hybrid estimator and show that the estimate $\hat{S}[j]$ has a small relative error for any point j:

THEOREM 2.1. *Using $k = 1/\epsilon^3$, the hybrid estimator (6) has a normalized root mean square error (NRMSE) of $O(\epsilon)$. Using $k = \frac{\log n}{\epsilon^3}$, when applying the estimator to all points in V, we get a maximum relative error of $O(\epsilon)$ with high probability.*

PROOF. We consider the error we obtain by using $\hat{S}[j]$ instead of $S[j]$ for a point $j \in V \setminus C$. Error can be accumulated on accounting for distances to $H(j)$ or to $L(j)$.

The first set, $H(j)$, includes all non-sample points that have distance greater than $\Delta(j)/\epsilon$ from $c(j)$. The accumulated error on the sum is bounded by $\pm\Delta(j)$ for each point in $H(j)$. Since the distance from j to a point in $i \in H(j)$ is at least

$$d_{c(j)i} - \Delta(j) = \Delta(j)(1/\epsilon - 1),$$

the relative error on all of $H(j)$ is at most $\Delta(j)/[\Delta(j)(1/\epsilon - 1)] = 1/(1/\epsilon - 1) = \epsilon/(1-\epsilon)$.

We now turn to $L(j)$, where we use a sampling estimator: We estimate the sum of distances to points in $L(j)$ using the sum of distances to sample points that are in $L(j)$. The sample points constitute a random sample of $L(j)$, which includes each point in $L(j)$ with probability $p = k/n$.

We compute the variance of estimating $\sum_{i \in L(j)} d_{ji}$ using the estimate $\frac{1}{p}\sum_{i \in L(j) \cap C} d_{ji}$. Consider the ratio of the variance to the square of the sum. The ratio is maximized when the set $L(j)$ includes all points (otherwise the contribution of $H(j)$ increases the denominator but not the numerator). Therefore, since we are upper bounding the error, we can assume that the set $L(j)$ contains all points.

The points in $L(j)$ are of distance at most $\Delta(j)(1/\epsilon + 1)$ from j.

We first consider the total contribution to the centrality of the set of points A that are of distance smaller than $\Delta(j)$ from j. Since $\Delta(j)$ is the distance to the pivot, the expected number of such points is not more than n/k. Their expected total relative contribution to $B(j)$ is at most their relative fraction, which in expectation is $1/k \ll \epsilon$. Moreover, for an integer $a > 1$, the probability of there being more than an/k such points is the probability that all k sampled points selected among the $n(1-a/k)$ farthest points from j, which is at most $(1-a/k)^k \approx e^{-a}$. So the contribution of points A to centrality (and to the variance) is also well concentrated.

We now consider the contribution to variance of points that have distance between $\Delta(j)$ and $(1/\epsilon + 1)\Delta(j)$. For convenience we use $s \equiv 1/\epsilon + 1$ and $\Delta \equiv \Delta(j)$. Repeating the same argument as before, since we are computing an upper bound we can assume that this set contains all points. Given the sum of distances of these points, the "worst case" for variance is when all distances are at one of the extremes; we thus further assume that the distance of each point is either Δ or $s\Delta$. The variance contribution of a point is $(1/p - 1)$ times its distance squared. We now define $x \in [0,1]$ to be the fraction of points are of distance Δ; the remaining have distance $s\Delta$. The sum of distances is

$$n(x\Delta + (1-x)s\Delta) = n\Delta(x + (1-x)s)$$

and the variance is

$$\begin{aligned}
&((1/p) - 1)n(x\Delta^2 + (1-x)s^2\Delta^2) \\
&= ((1/p) - 1)n\Delta^2(x + (1-x)s^2) \\
&\le \frac{n^2\Delta^2}{k}(x + (1-x)s^2).
\end{aligned}$$

We now consider the maximum over choices of n and x of the ratio of the variance to the square of the mean, which is

$$\max_{x \in [0,1]} \frac{1}{k}\frac{x + (1-x)s^2}{(x + (1-x)s)^2}.$$

This is maximized at $x = s/(s+1) = (1+\epsilon)/(1+2\epsilon)$. The maximum is $\frac{1}{k}\frac{(s+1)^2}{4s} = \frac{(1+2\epsilon)^2}{4k\epsilon(1+\epsilon)} \approx \frac{1}{4k\epsilon}$. This means that the Coefficient of Variation (CV) is about $\frac{1}{2\sqrt{k\epsilon}}$.

Balancing the sampling CV with the pivoting relative error of ϵ we obtain $k \approx \frac{1}{2\epsilon^3}$. □

In our implementation, we worked with parameter settings of $\epsilon = \sqrt{k}$. This setting means that the relative error on the pivoting component is at most $\epsilon/(1-\epsilon)$. We can typically expect it to be much smaller, however. First, because distances in $H(j)$ can be much larger than $\Delta(j)/\epsilon$. Second, the estimates of different points are typically not "one sided" (the estimate is one sided when the pivot happens to be on or close to the shortest path from j to most other points), so errors can cancel out. For the sampling component, the analysis was with respect to a worst-case distance distribution, where all values lie at the extremes of the range, but in practice we can expect an error of $\approx 1/\sqrt{k} \approx \epsilon$. Moreover, when the population variance of $L(j)$ is small, we can expect a smaller relative error.

In Section 4 we propose adaptive error estimation, which for each point j, uses the sampled distances d_{ij} to obtain a tighter estimate on the actual error.

3. COMPUTING ESTIMATES

We now consider closeness centrality on undirected graphs, with a focus on efficient computation, both in terms of running time and the (run-time) storage we use, Specifically, we would like to compute estimates $\hat{S}[v]$ of $S(v) = \sum_j d_{vj}$ for all nodes $v \in V$.

All the estimators we consider, the basic sampling (5) and pivoting estimates and the hybrid estimate (6) are applied to a set of (at most) kn sampled distances. To compute these distances, we can first sample a set C of k nodes uniformly at random and then run Dijkstra's single-source shortest path algorithm from each node $u \in C$ to compute the distances d_{uv} from u to all other nodes. The computation of the estimates $\hat{S}[v]$ given these distances is linear. The issue with this approach is a run-time storage of $O(nk)$.

We first observe that both the basic sampling and the basic pivoting estimates can be computed using only $O(1)$ run-time storage per node. With sampling, we accumulate, for each node v, the sum of distances from the nodes in C. We initialize the sum to 0 for all v and then when running Dijkstra from $u \in C$, we add d_{uv} to each scanned node v. The additional run-time storage used here is the state of Dijkstra and $O(1)$ additional storage per node. With pivoting, we initialize $\Delta(v) \leftarrow \infty$ for all nodes. When running Dijkstra from u, we accumulate the sum of distances as $S(v)$. We also update $\Delta(v) \leftarrow \min\{d_{uv}, \Delta(v)\}$ when a node v is scanned. When $\Delta(v)$ is updated, we also update the pivot $c(v) \leftarrow u$. Finally, for each node v, we estimate $S(v)$ by the precomputed $S(c(v))$.

The pseudocode provided as Algorithm 1 computes the hybrid estimates (6) for all nodes using $O(1)$ additional storage per node. To do so with only $O(1)$ storage, we use an additional run of Dijkstra: For each node $v \in V$, we first compute its pivot $c(v)$ and the distance $\Delta(v) = d_{vc(v)}$. This can be done with a single run of Dijkstra's algorithm having all sampled nodes as sources.

We then run Dijkstra's algorithm from each sampled node $u \in C$. For the sampled nodes $u \in C$, the sum $S(u)$ is computed exactly; for such cases, we have $\hat{S}[u] = S(u)$. For the nodes $v \notin C$ we compute an estimate $\hat{S}[v]$.

The computation of the estimate is based on identifying the three components of the partition of $V \setminus \{v\}$ into $L(v) \cup HC(v) \cup H(v)$, which is determined according to distances from the pivot $c(v)$. The pivot mapping computed in the additional run is used to determine this classification.

The contributions to the sum estimates $\hat{S}[v]$ are computed during the single-source shortest paths computations from C. In particular, the contribution to $\hat{S}[v]$ of sampled nodes $u \in L(v) \cup HC(v)$ are computed when we run Dijkstra from u. The contribution of $H(v)$ is computed when we run Dijkstra from the pivot $c(v)$ of v.

When running Dijkstra from a sampled node $u \in C$ and visiting v, we need to determine whether u is in $L(v)$ or $HC(v)$ in order to compute its contribution. If $u \in HC(v)$, we increase $\hat{S}[v]$ by d_{uv}. If $u \in L(v)$, we would like to increase $\hat{S}[v]$ by $d_{uv}/p[v]$. At that point, however, $p[v]$, which depends on $|L(v)|$ and $|C \cap L(v)|$, may not be available. We therefore add d_{uv} to LCSUM$[v]$, which tracks the sum of distances to nodes in $C \cap L(v)$. We also increment LCNUM$[v]$, which tracks the cardinality $|C \cap L(v)|$. When the k Dijkstra runs terminate, we can compute $p[v]$ and increase $\hat{S}[v]$ by LCSUM$[v]/p[v]$.

Deciding whether u is in $L(v)$ or $HC(v)$ can sometimes be done only after the pivot $c(v)$ was visited by the Dijkstra run from u. If $d_{uv} > \Delta(v)(1/\epsilon + 1)$ then from the triangle inequality $d_{uc(v)} > \Delta(v)/\epsilon$ and we can determine that $u \in HC(v)$. Similarly, if $d_{uv} \le \Delta(v)(1/\epsilon - 1)$ we can determine that $u \in L(v)$. Otherwise, we can classify u only after we visit $c(v)$ and know the distance $d_{c(v)u}$. In this case, the accounting of u to $\hat{S}[v]$ is postponed: We place the pair (v, d_{uv}) in LIST$[c(v)]$. Each time a sampled node $z \in C$ is visited by u, we process the list LIST$[z]$ and for each entry (v, d_{vu}) we use $d_{uz} \equiv d_{uc(v)}$ to classify v and accordingly increase $\hat{S}[v]$ or LCSUM$[v]$. LIST$[z]$ is then deleted.

The accounting for $H(v)$ is done when running Dijkstra from the pivot $c(v)$. During Dijkstra from u, we record information on each node v for which $c(v) \equiv u$. The threshold values $\Delta(v)/\epsilon$ are recorded in increasing order in the THRESH array, as nodes are visited. The set of nodes with pivot u and a threshold value is recorded in the entry of NODES which corresponds to the threshold value. The sum of distances from u to all nodes in $V \setminus C$ with distances that are between entries in the THRESH array is computed in the corresponding entries of the BIN array. After Dijkstra's algorithm from u is completed, we process these arrays in reverse, computing for each node v such that $c(v) \equiv u$ the contribution of $H(v)$ to the estimate $\hat{S}[v]$.

This algorithm performs $k+1$ runs of Dijkstra's algorithm and uses running storage that is linear in the number of nodes (does not depend on k). This means the algorithm has very little computation overhead over the basic estimators.

4. ADAPTIVE ERROR ESTIMATION

Algorithm 1 also computes, for each node v, an estimate on the error of our estimate $\hat{S}[v]$. This estimate is *adaptive*, that is, it depends on the input. This is in contrast to the error bounds in Theorem 2.1, which are with respect to *worst-case* instances and, if used, will typically grossly overestimate the actual error and provide weak and pessimistic confidence bounds. We explain how these adaptive estimates are computed.

We also propose *adaptive error minimization* as Algorithm 2: Instead of working with a fixed value of ϵ, as in Algorithm 1, the new algorithm chooses the estimate that has the smallest estimated error.

4.1 Error Estimation

In Algorithm 1, error estimates are computed separately for each of the two components: one from the pivoting on the "distant" nodes $H(v)$, and one from the sampling, on the "closer" nodes $L(v)$.

The pivoting error is estimated by considering distant sampled nodes, that is, nodes in $HC(v)$. These nodes are treated as a representative sample of $H(v)$. For these nodes, we take the average of the squared difference between the distance of the node from v and its distance from the pivot $c(v)$:

$$\widehat{SQ}(H(v)) = \frac{1}{|HC(v)|} \sum_{u \in HC(v)} \left(d_{uv} - d_{c(v)u}\right)^2. \qquad (7)$$

Note that for nodes in $HC(v)$, both these distances are available from the single-source shortest-paths computations we performed. Finally, to obtain an estimate on the contribution of the pivoting component to the squared error of $\hat{S}[v]$, we multiply by the magnitude $|H(v)|$ of the set $H(v)$, which we know exactly. In cases when there are not enough or no samples (when $HC(v)$ is empty), we instead compute the average squared difference over a "suffix" of the farthest nodes in C.

The sampling error applies to the remaining "closer" nodes $L(v)$ and depends on the distribution of distances in $L(v)$, that is, on the population variance of $L(v)$, and on the sample size from this group, which is $L(v) \cap C$. We first estimate the population variance of the set of distances from v to the set of nodes $L(v)$. This is estimated using the sample variance of the uniform sample $L(v) \cap C$, as

$$\begin{aligned} \hat{\sigma^2}(L(v)) &= \frac{1}{|C \cap L(v)|} \sum_{u \in C \cap L(v)} \left(d_{uv} - \frac{\sum_{u \in C \cap L(v)} d_{uv}}{|C \cap L(v)|} \right)^2 \\ &= \frac{\sum_{u \in C \cap L(v)} d_{uv}^2}{|C \cap L(v)|} - \left(\frac{\sum_{u \in C \cap L(v)} d_{uv}}{|C \cap L(v)|} \right)^2. \qquad (8) \end{aligned}$$

We then divide the estimated population variance by the number of samples $|L(v) \cap C|$ (variable LCNUM in the pseudocode) to estimate the variance of the average of $|L(v) \cap C|$ samples from the population. To estimate the variance contribution of the sampling component to the sum estimate $\hat{S}[v]$, we multiply by $|L(v)|$ (variable LNUM in the pseudocode). The combined square error of $\hat{S}[v]$ is estimated by summing these two components:

$$|H(v)| \widehat{SQ}(H(v)) + \frac{|L(v)|}{|L(v) \cap C|} \hat{\sigma^2}(L(v)).$$

4.2 Adaptive Error Minimization

In order to get the most mileage from the k single source shortest paths computations we performed, we would like to adaptively select the best "threshold" between pivoting and sampling, rather than work with a fixed value.

For a node $v \in V$ and a threshold value T let

$$\begin{aligned} H(v,T) &= \{u \in V \setminus C \mid d_{c(v)u} > T\} \\ HC(v,T) &= \{u \in C \mid d_{c(v)u} > T\} \\ L(v,T) &= \{u \in V \mid d_{c(v)u} \le T\}. \end{aligned}$$

The set $H(v,T)$ contains all non-sampled nodes with distance from $c(v)$ greater than T, the set $HC(v,T)$ contains all sampled nodes with distance from $c(v)$ greater than T,

Algorithm 1 Centrality estimation for all nodes: undirected

Input: Network G, integer $k > 0$, $\epsilon > 0$

select uniformly at random k nodes $C = \{c_1, \ldots, c_k\} \subset V$

for $v \in V$ **do** ▷ Computation equivalent to a single Dijkstra

$c[v] \leftarrow \arg\min_{i=1,\ldots,k} d_{c_i v}$ ▷ Pivot of v

$\Delta[v] \leftarrow d_{v, c_{c[v]}}$ ▷ distance of v to its pivot

$\hat{S}[v] \leftarrow 0$; LCsum$[v] \leftarrow 0$; LCnum$[v] \leftarrow 0$; LCsumSq$[u] \leftarrow 0$; HCsum$[u] \leftarrow 0$; HCsumSqErr$[u] \leftarrow 0$;

for $i = 1, \ldots, k$ **do**

$t \leftarrow 0$; $curt \leftarrow 0$; Thresh$[0] \leftarrow 0$ ▷ Initialize thresholds array and counters

Run Dijkstra from the sampled node c_i

for each new node u visited by Dijkstra **do**

$d \leftarrow d_{c_i u}$ ▷ distance from c_i to u

$\hat{S}[c_i] \leftarrow \hat{S}[c_i] + d$

if $u \in C$ **then** ▷ equivalently, $c_{c[u]} = u$

$j \leftarrow c[u]$ ▷ a sampled node is its own pivot, we get its index

last$[j] \leftarrow i$; dist$[j] \leftarrow d$ ▷ c_j was visited from c_i and has distance dist$[j]$

for $z \in$ List$[j]$ **do**

if $d > \Delta[z.node]/\epsilon$ **then** HCsum$[z.node] \overset{+}{\leftarrow} z.d$ ▷ $c_i \in HC(z.node)$

HCsumSqErr$[z.node] \overset{+}{\leftarrow} (z.d - d)^2$

else LCsum$[z.node] \overset{+}{\leftarrow} z.d$; LCnum$[z.node] \overset{+}{\leftarrow} 1$; LCsumSq$[z.node] \overset{+}{\leftarrow} z.d^2$ ▷ $c_i \in L(z.node)$

Delete List$[j]$

else ▷ $u \notin C$

if $(d \le \Delta[u](1/\epsilon - 1))$ **or** (last$[c[u]] = i$) **and** (dist$[c[u]] \le \Delta[u]/\epsilon$) **then** ▷ $c_i \in L(u)$

LCsum$[u] \overset{+}{\leftarrow} d$; LCnum$[u] \overset{+}{\leftarrow} 1$

LCsumSq$[u] \overset{+}{\leftarrow} d^2$

else ▷ We can not determine if $c_i \in L(u)$ or we know $c_i \in HC(u)$ but $c[u]$ was not yet visited

$z.node \leftarrow u$; $z.d \leftarrow d$

List$[c[u]] \leftarrow$ List$[c[u]] \cup \{z\}$

if $c[u] = i$ **then** ▷ c_i is the pivot of u

if Thresh$[t] = d/\epsilon$ **then** ▷ same threshold as previous

nodes$[t] \leftarrow$ nodes$[t] \cup \{u\}$

else $t \leftarrow t + 1$; Thresh$[t] \leftarrow d/\epsilon$; nodes$[t] \leftarrow \{u\}$; bin$[t] \leftarrow 0$; count$[t] \leftarrow 0$

while $curt < t$ **and** $d >$ Thresh$[curt + 1]$ **do** $curt \overset{+}{\leftarrow} 1$

if $d >$ Thresh$[curt]$ **then** bin$[curt] \overset{+}{\leftarrow} d$; count$[curt] \overset{+}{\leftarrow} 1$

▷ Compute tail sums for nodes for which c_i is pivot

tailsum $\leftarrow 0$; tailnum $\leftarrow 0$

while $t > 0$ **do**

tailsum $\overset{+}{\leftarrow}$ bin$[t]$

tailnum $\overset{+}{\leftarrow}$ count$[t]$

for $u \in$ nodes$[t]$ **do**

Hsum$[u] \leftarrow$ tailsum

Hnum$[u] \leftarrow$ tailnum ▷ Hnum$[u] = |H(u)|$; Hsum$[u] = \sum_{v \in H(u)} d_{c(u)v}$

$t \leftarrow t - 1$

for $u \in V \setminus C$ **do**

Lnum $\leftarrow n - 1 -$ Hnum$[u] - k +$ LCnum$[u]$; HCnum $\leftarrow k -$ LCnum

$p \leftarrow \frac{\text{LCnum}[u]}{\text{Lnum}}$ ▷ Fraction of sampled nodes that are in $L(u)$

$\hat{S}[u] \leftarrow$ Hsum$[u] +$ HCsum$[u] +$ LCsum$[u]/p$

SqErrEst$[u] \leftarrow \frac{1}{\text{LCnum}[u]}\left(\frac{\text{LCsumSq}[u]}{\text{LCnum}[u]} - \left(\frac{\text{LCsum}[u]}{\text{LCnum}[u]}\right)^2\right)\text{Lnum}[u] + \frac{\text{HCsumSqErr}[u]}{\text{HCnum}}\text{Hnum}[u]$

return For all u: $(u, \hat{S}[u], \text{SqErrEst}[u])$

and the set $L(v,T)$ contains all nodes with distance from $c(v)$ at most T.

We can then define an estimator with respect to a threshold T, as in Equation (6):

$$\hat{S}(v,T) = \sum_{u \in H(v,T)} d_{c(v)u} + \sum_{u \in HC(v,T)} d_{vu} + \frac{|L(v,T)|}{|L(v,T) \cap C|} \sum_{u \in L(v,T) \cap C} d_{vu}. \tag{9}$$

In Algorithm 1 we used the threshold value $T_v = \Delta(v)/\epsilon$ for a node v. Here we choose T_v adaptively so as to balance the estimated error of the first and third summands.

One way to achieve this is to apply Algorithm 1 simultaneously with several choices of ϵ. Then, for each node, we take the value with the smallest estimated error. We propose here Algorithm 2, which maintains $O(k)$ state per node but looks for the threshold sweet spot while covering the full range between pure pivoting and pure sampling.

Algorithm 2 computes estimates and corresponding error estimates as in Algorithm 1. The estimates, however, are computed for k values of the threshold T_v which correspond to the distances from $c(v)$ to each of the other sampled nodes. From these k estimates, the algorithm selects the one which minimizes the estimated error.

The reason for considering only these k threshold values (for each pivot) is that they represent all the possible assignments of sampled nodes to $L(v)$ or $HC(v)$.

Finally, we note that the run-time storage we use depends linearly in the sets of threshold values and therefore it can be advantageous, when run-time storage is constrained, to reduce the size further. One way to do this is, for example, to only use values of T_v which correspond to discretized distances.

5. WEIGHTED CENTRALITY

We now consider weighted classic closeness centrality with respect to node weights $\beta : V \geq 0$, as defined in Equation (4). We limit our attention to estimating the denominator

$$S_\beta(i) = \sum_{j \neq i} \beta(i) d_{ij},$$

since the numerator $\sum_{j \neq i} \beta(i)$ can be efficiently computed exactly for all nodes by computing the sum $\sum_i \beta(i)$ once and, for each node j, subtracting the weight of the node j itself from the total. We show how to modify Algorithm 1 to compute estimates for $S_\beta(i)$ for all nodes. We will also argue that the proof of Theorem 2.1 goes through with minor modifications, that is, we obtain a small relative error with high probability.

If the node weights are in $\{0,1\}$, the modification is straightforward. We obtain our sample C only from nodes i with weight $\beta(i) = 1$ and account only for these nodes in our estimate of S.

We now provide details on the modification needed to handle general weights β. The first component is the node sampling. We apply a weighted sampling algorithm; in particular, we use VarOpt stream sampling [13, 17], which is a weighted version of reservoir sampling [30, 49]. We obtain a sample of exactly k nodes so that the inclusion probability of each node is proportional to its weight. More precisely, VarOpt computes a threshold value τ (which depends on k and on the distribution of β values). A node v is sampled with probability $\min\{1, \beta(v)/\tau\}$. These sampling probabilities are PPS (Probability Proportional to Size), but with VarOpt we obtain a sample of size exactly k (whereas independent PPS only guarantees an expected size of k). For each sampled node we define its *adjusted weight* $\hat{\beta}(v) = \max\{\tau, \beta(v)\}$, where τ is the VarOpt threshold.

The weighted algorithm is very similar to Algorithm 1, but requires the modification stated as Algorithm 3. The contributions to $\hat{S}[u]$ of nodes v that are in $H[u]$ (accounted for in the tail sums computed in the BIN array) or in $HC[u]$ are multiplied by $\beta(v)$. For nodes in $L(v)$, we compute the inverse probability estimate with respect to the inclusion probability $\min\{1, \beta(v)/\tau\}$. We divide the contribution, which is $\beta(v)d_{uv}$, by the inclusion probability, obtaining $\hat{\beta}(v)d_{uv}$.

Our error estimates can also be easily modified to work with weighted centralities. Instead of the cardinality of each set, we use the total β weight of the set; instead of a sum of distances, we use the β-weighted sum.

Algorithm 3 Modifications of Alg. 1 for weighted centrality

$\hat{S}[c_i] \overset{+}{\leftarrow} \beta(u)d_{c_i u}$ ▷ when computing $\hat{S}$ for $c_i \in C$
$\hat{S}[u] \overset{+}{\leftarrow} \beta(c_i)d_{c_i u}$ ▷ when $c_i \in HC(u)$
$\hat{S}[u] \overset{+}{\leftarrow} \hat{\beta}(c_i)d_{c_i u}$ ▷ when $c_i \in L(u)$
if $\beta(c_i) < \tau$ **then** VAREST$[u] \overset{+}{\leftarrow} d^2_{c_i u}(\tau - \beta(c_i))\tau$ ▷ when $c_i \in L(u)$; when $\beta(c_i) > \tau$ then c_i is included with probability 1 and its contribution to variance is 0.
BIN$[curt] \overset{+}{\leftarrow} \beta(u)d_{c_i u}$; COUNT$[curt] \overset{+}{\leftarrow} \beta(u)$ ▷ when computing tail sums/counts for c_i

The analysis of the approximation quality of $\hat{S}$ in Algorithm 3 carries over to the weighted algorithm. In fact, the skewness of β can only improve estimation quality: intuitively, the sample would contain in expectation more than k/n fraction of the total β weight, since heavier items are more likely to be sampled.

6. DIRECTED GRAPHS

6.1 Round-trip Centralities

For a strongly connected directed graph, it is natural to consider the round-trip distances $\overleftrightarrow{d}_{ij} \equiv d_{ij} + d_{ji}$, and *round-trip centrality* values computed with respect to these round-trip distances.

Since round-trip distances are a metric, the hybrid estimator (6) applies, as does Theorem 2.1, which provides the strong guarantees on approximation quality. Moreover, a simple modification of the algorithms we presented for undirected graphs applies to estimation of round-trip centralities in strongly connected directed graphs. We choose a uniform random sample of k nodes, as we did in the undirected case. Then, for each sampled node $u \in C$, we perform two single-source shortest paths computations, to compute the forward and a backward distances to all other nodes. Then for each node $v \in V \setminus C$, we compute the sum $\overleftrightarrow{d}_{uv} = d_{uv} + d_{vu}$ of these distances. We sort the nodes v by increasing $\overleftrightarrow{d}_{uv}$. We then use the sorted order and round-trip distances the same way we used the Dijkstra order in the undirected version of the algorithm.

Algorithm 2 Classic closeness centralities with adaptive error minimization

```
select a set C = {c_1, ..., c_k} ⊂ V of sampled nodes, uniformly at random; for j = 1, ..., k, use c[c_j] ← j.
for v ∈ V do Δ[v] ← ∞
for i = 1, ..., k do
    Δ[c_i] ← 0                                   ▷ pivot of c_i is itself, distance to pivot is 0
    cvisited ← 1; vvisited ← 0                   ▷ number of nodes in C and V \ C, respectively, visited so far
    distsumvisited ← 0                           ▷ sum of distances to nodes in V \ C visited so far
    δ[i, i] ← 0                                  ▷ δ[i, j] is the distance between sampled nodes c_i and c_j
    π[i, 1] ← i                                  ▷ π[i, *] is the permutation of sampled nodes by increasing distance from c_i
    Run Dijkstra's algorithm from c_i
    for v ∈ V in order of first visit by Dijkstra do
        d ← d_{c_i v}
        if v ∈ C then
            j ← c[v]                             ▷ index of sampled node v
            cvisited ← cvisited + 1; π[i, cvisited] ← j; δ[i, j] ← d
            TAILNUM[i, cvisited] ← vvisited
            TAILSUM[i, cvisited] ← distsumvisited
        else                                     ▷ v ∉ C
            if d < Δ[v] then
                Δ[v] ← d, c[v] ← i
            D[v, i] ← d                          ▷ (n − k) × k matrix of distances of v ∈ V \ C to sampled nodes 1, ..., k
            vvisited +← 1; distsumvisited +← d
    After Dijkstra ends:
    for j = 1, ..., k do
        TAILNUM[j, cvisited] ← vvisited − TAILNUM[j, cvisited]
        TAILSUM[j, cvisited] ← distsumvisited − TAILSUM[j, cvisited]
    Ŝ[c_i] ← distsumvisited + Σ_{j=1}^{k} δ[i, j]          ▷ Exact S[c_i] of sampled node c_i
    ESTERR[c_i] ← 0;                             ▷ estimated errors (no errors) for Ŝ[c_i].
for v ∈ V \ C do                                 ▷ Compute Ŝ, ESTERR for all remaining nodes
    LCSUM ← 0; HCSUM ← Σ_{i=1}^{k} D[v, i]; HCSUMSQERR ← Σ_{i=1}^{k} (D[v, i] − δ[c(v), i])^2
    Ŝ[v] ← Ŝ[c[v]]; ESTERR[v] ← HCSUMSQERR · (n − 1 − k)/k
    MinErr ← ESTERR[v]
    for i = 1, ..., k do                         ▷ scan sampled nodes π[c(v), i] by increasing distances from c(v)
        LCSUMSQ +← D[v, π[c(v), i]]^2
        HNUM ← TAILNUM[c(v), π[c(v), i]]
        LNUM ← n − 1 − HNUM − k + i              ▷ |L(v)| for current threshold
        LCNUM ← i; p ← LCNUM/LNUM
        LCSUM +← D[v, π[c(v), i]]                ▷ sum of distances to sampled nodes within threshold
        HCSUM −← D[v, π[c(v), i]]                ▷ sum of distances to sampled nodes outside threshold
        HSUM ← TAILSUM[c(v), π[c(v), i]]
        HCSUMSQERR −← (D[v, π[c(v), i]] − δ[c(v), π[c(v), i]])^2
        EST ← LCSUM/p + HSUM + HCSUM             ▷ estimated S[v]
        ESTERR ← (1/LCNUM)(LCSUMSQ/LCNUM − (LCSUM/LCNUM)^2) LNUM + (HCSUMSQERR/HCNUM) HNUM
                                                 ▷ est. error for threshold δ[c(v), π[c(v), i]]
        if ESTERR < MinErr then
            MinErr ← ESTERR                      ▷ Look for the estimation sweet spot
            Ŝ[v] ← EST; SQERREST[v] ← ESTERR
return Ŝ, SQERREST
```

6.2 Inbound and Outbound Centralities

As mentioned in the introduction, for general (not necessarily strongly connected) directed graphs, we may also be interested in separating *outbound* or *inbound centralities*. In particular, we are interested in the average distance from a particular node v to all nodes it can reach (outbound centrality) or from nodes that can reach v (inbound centrality), as well as in the cardinalities of these sets.

The size of the outbound reachability set of v is

$$\overrightarrow{R}[v] = |\{u \in V \setminus \{v\} \mid v \leadsto u\}| ,$$

where $v \leadsto u$ indicates that u is reachable from v. Similarly, the size of the inbound reachability set of v is

$$\overleftarrow{R}[v] = |\{u \in V \setminus \{v\} \mid u \leadsto v\}| .$$

Accordingly, we define the total distance to the outbound reachability set of v as

$$\overrightarrow{S}[v] = \sum_{u|v \leadsto u} d_{vu},$$

and the total distance to the inbound reachability set of v as

$$\overleftarrow{S}[v] = \sum_{u|u \leadsto v} d_{uv}.$$

The outbound and inbound centralities are accordingly defined as the (inverse of the) ratios $\overrightarrow{S}[v]/\overrightarrow{R}[v]$ and $\overleftarrow{S}[v]/\overleftarrow{R}[v]$.

Unfortunately, the hybrid estimator, and even the special case of the pivoting estimator, do not work well with direction. This is because directed distances are not a metric (they are not symmetric). Intuitively, distances from the pivot (closest sampled node) can be much larger than distances from the node for which we estimate centrality.

Sampling can be used with direction, but, when naively applied, will not provide relative error guarantees even when the distance distribution is not skewed. The reason is that it is not enough to use all distances from a small sample of nodes. For sampling to work, we need to obtain a sample of a certain size from the reachability set of each node. Some nodes, however, may reach few or no nodes from this sample. Therefore the sample provides very little information (or none at all) for estimating the centrality of these nodes.

We extend the basic sampling approach to directed graphs using an algorithm of Cohen [14] that efficiently computes for each node a uniform sample of size k from its reachability set (for outbound centrality) or from nodes that can reach it (for inbound centrality). We modify the algorithm so that respective distances are computed as well. (We apply Dijkstra's algorithm instead of generic graph searches.) This algorithm also computes nk distinct distances, but does so adaptively, so that they are not all from the same set of sources.

The same algorithm also provides approximate cardinalities of these sets [14]. This means that, when the distance distribution is not too skewed, we can obtain good estimates of the average distance to reachable nodes (or from nodes our node is reachable from).

Algorithm 4 contains pseudocode for estimating outbound average distance ($\overrightarrow{B} = \overrightarrow{S}/\overrightarrow{R}$) and reachability ($\overrightarrow{R}$) for all nodes. By applying the same algorithm on G instead of the reverse graph G^T, we can obtain estimates for the inbound quantities.

Algorithm 4 Estimate for all $v \in V$ average distance to reachable nodes $\hat{B}$ and cardinality $\hat{R}$: directed graphs

```
t ← 0,
for v ∈ V do MARK[v] ← False; COUNT[v] ← 0; T[V] ←
0; DISTSUM[v] ← 0
for nodes u ∈ V in random order do
    t ← t + 1; MARK[u] ← True
    Perform pruned Dijkstra from u on G^T
    for each scanned node v of distance d_vu do
        if COUNT[v] = k then Prune Dijkstra at v
        else
            if u ≠ v then
                DISTSUM[v] +← d_vu
                COUNT[v] +← 1
                if COUNT[v] = k then
                    T[v] ← t
                    if MARK[v] then T[v] ← t − 1
for v ∈ V do
    if COUNT[v] = 0 then B̂[v] ← 0
    else B̂[v] ← DISTSUM[v]/COUNT[v]
    if COUNT[v] < k then R̂[v] ← COUNT[v]
    else R̂[v] ← 1 + (k−1)(n−2)/(T[v]−1)
```

The algorithm computes for each node a uniform random sample of size k from its reachability set. It does so by running Dijkstra's algorithm from each node u in random order, adding u to the sample of all nodes it reaches. Since these searches are pruned at nodes whose samples already have k nodes, no node is scanned more than k times during the entire computation. The total cost is thus comparable to k full (unpruned) Dijkstra computations. This algorithm does not offer worst-case guarantees. However, on realistic instances, where centrality is in the order of the median distance, it performs well.

The algorithm applies a bottom-k variant [19] of the reachability estimation algorithm of Cohen [14] and also computes distances. The cardinality estimator is unbiased with coefficient of variation (CV) at most $1/\sqrt{k-2}$ [14]. The quality of the average distance estimates depends on the distribution of distances and we evaluate it experimentally.

We also consider non-uniform node weights and the respective weighted definitions, $\overrightarrow{S}_\beta[v] = \sum_{u|v \leadsto u} \beta(u) d_{vu}$ and $\overrightarrow{R}_\beta[v] = \sum_{u|v \leadsto u} \beta(u)$. A pseudocode for a weighted version is provided as Algorithm 5. The algorithm assigns nodes with ranks that depend on their weight, effectively having each node count for a bottom-k sample of its reachability set, as proposed by Cohen and Kaplan [14, 19]. The pseudocode uses priority sampling [24, 39]. The algorithm then processes nodes according to increasing rank order. The weighted reachability estimate is applied to the rank of the kth sample (this is a bottom-k estimator).

7. RELATED WORK

Closeness centrality is only one of several common definitions of importance rankings. These include degree centrality, intended to capture activity level, betweenness centrality, which captures power, and eigenvalue centralities, which capture reputation [27, 50].

Table 1: **Evaluating algorithms on *undirected* instances. For each instance, we report its number of nodes and edges, and for several algorithms the running time and average relative error.**

				Exact	Sampling		Pivoting		Hyb.-0.1		Hyb.-ad	
type	instance	$\lvert V\rvert$ $[\cdot 10^3]$	$\lvert E\rvert$ $[\cdot 10^3]$	time $\approx$ [h:m]	err. [%]	time [sec]	err. [%]	time [sec]	err. [%]	time [sec]	err. [%]	time [sec]
road	fla-t	1 070	1 344	59:30	5.4	24.4	3.2	21.6	2.5	28.3	2.8	73.2
	usa-t	23 947	28 854	44 222:06	2.9	849.4	3.7	736.4	2.0	2 344.3	2.6	9 937.9
grid	grid20	1 049	2 095	70:34	4.3	26.5	3.5	26.8	2.9	29.2	3.3	69.7
triang	buddha	544	1 631	19:07	3.6	14.5	3.3	13.6	2.4	15.9	3.2	30.7
	buddha-w	544	1 631	21:25	3.5	16.4	2.6	15.5	2.2	18.5	2.9	38.1
	del20-w	1 049	3 146	72:06	2.7	27.4	3.6	26.7	2.6	32.6	2.7	71.0
	del20	1 049	3 146	67:54	4.1	25.6	5.3	25.2	3.7	27.0	3.6	54.7
game	FrozenSea	753	2 882	38:25	3.0	22.1	4.1	20.2	2.1	24.0	3.4	49.3
sensor	rgg20	1 049	6 894	137:36	1.6	54.2	3.8	49.3	2.1	63.7	2.2	123.3
	rgg20-w	1 049	6 894	160:29	1.6	61.2	3.8	57.1	2.1	73.3	2.3	142.3
comp	Skitter	1 695	11 094	248:27	0.7	59.7	14.3	55.2	0.7	61.6	3.6	109.5
	MetroSec	2 250	21 643	269:51	0.6	52.1	2.3	47.5	0.6	53.2	0.3	93.2
social	rws20	1 049	3 146	113:40	0.9	45.6	3.0	41.3	0.9	49.4	0.9	98.6
	rba20	1 049	6 291	132:35	0.8	56.8	9.7	48.4	0.8	60.2	1.0	117.4
	Hollywood	1 069	56 307	226:42	1.0	86.5	14.6	81.8	1.0	85.7	1.9	117.6
	Orkut	3 072	117 185	2 973:09	1.7	377.4	7.2	367.6	1.7	376.4	2.1	553.0

Algorithm 5 Estimate for all $v \in V$ weighted sum of distances to reachable nodes $\hat{S}$ and weighted sum of reachable nodes $\hat{R}$: directed graphs

for $v \in V$ **do** COUNT$[v] \leftarrow 0$; BCOUNT$[v] \leftarrow 0$; DISTSUM$[v] \leftarrow 0$
$V_+ \leftarrow \{v \in V \mid \beta[v] > 0\}$
for $u \in V_+$ **do** $r[v] \leftarrow$ RAND$()/\beta[v]$ $\triangleright$ RAND$() \sim U[0,1]$ is uniform at random from $[0,1]$
for $u \in V_+$ in increasing r order **do**
  Perform pruned Dijkstra from u on G^T
  for each scanned node v of distance d_{vu} **do**
    if COUNT$[v] = k$ **then** Prune Dijkstra at v
    else
      if $u \neq v$ **then**
        COUNT$[v] \stackrel{+}{\leftarrow} 1$
        if COUNT$[v] < k$ **then**
          DISTSUM$[v] \stackrel{+}{\leftarrow} \beta[u]d_{vu}$
          BCOUNT$[v] \stackrel{+}{\leftarrow} \beta[u]$
        if COUNT$[v] = k$ **then**
          T$[v] = r[u]$
for $v \in V$ **do**
  if COUNT$[v] = 0$ **then** $\hat{R}[v] \leftarrow 0$; $\hat{S}[v] \leftarrow 0$
  else if COUNT$[v] < k$ **then** $\hat{R}[v] \leftarrow$ BCOUNT$[v]$; $\hat{S}[v] \leftarrow$ DISTSUM$[v]$
  else $\hat{S}[v] \leftarrow \frac{\text{DISTSUM}}{T[v]}$; $\hat{R}[v] \leftarrow \frac{k-1}{T[v]}$

We only consider the classic definition of closeness centrality. A well-studied alternative is *distance-decay* closeness centrality, where the contribution of each node to the centrality of another is discounted (is non-increasing) with distance [11,12,16,18,21,41]. The subtle difference between distance-decay and classic closeness centrality is that the latter emphasizes the penalties for far nodes, whereas the distance-decay measures instead emphasize the reward from closer nodes. Distance-decay centrality is well defined on disconnected or directed graphs. In terms of scalable computation, efficient algorithms with a small relative error guarantee were known for two decades and engineered to handle graphs with billions of edges [2,8,9,14,16,18,20,42]. These algorithms, however, provide no guarantees for estimating classic closeness centrality. The intuitive reason is that they are based on sampling that is biased towards closer nodes, whereas correctly estimating classic closeness centrality requires accounting for distant nodes, which can be missed by such a sample.

8. EXPERIMENTS

We implemented our algorithms in C++ using Visual Studio 2013 with full optimization. We conducted all tests on a machine with two Intel Xeon E5-2690 CPUs and 384 GiB of DDR3-1066 RAM, running Windows 2008R2 Server. Each CPU has 8 cores (2.90 GHz, 8×64 kiB L1, 8×256 kiB, and 20 MiB L3 cache), but all runs are sequential. We use 32-bit integers to represent arc lengths.

We test a variety of instances, including *social networks* (Epinions [43], WikiTalk [31,32], Flickr [38], Hollywood [7, 10], Twitter [22], LiveJournal [34], and Orkut [52]), *computer networks* (Gnutella [37], Skitter [33], Slashdot [34], MetroSec [36]), and *web graphs* (NotreDame [1], Indo [7,10], Indochina [7,10]). All these instances are unweighted, and some are directed. We consider two additional synthetic instances: rws20 is generated according to a preferential attachment model [51] and rba20 is a small-world graph [3].

We also test *road networks* [23]. Instances fla-t (Florida) and usa-t (USA) are undirected and use TIGER data; eur-t and eur-d are directed and represent Western Europe. For these instances, the suffix indicates whether edge costs represent travel times (-t) or distances (-d). Instance grid20 is a 1024×1024 unweighted grid.

The buddha instance is a computer graphics mesh representing a three-dimensional object [45]. Instance del20 is a Delaunay triangulation of 2^{20} random points on the unit square [28]. Nodes also represent random points in the unit square for rgg20, but now two nodes are connected by an edge if the corresponding Euclidean distance is below a given threshold (chosen to ensure the graphs are almost connected [28]). Such *random geometric graphs* often model

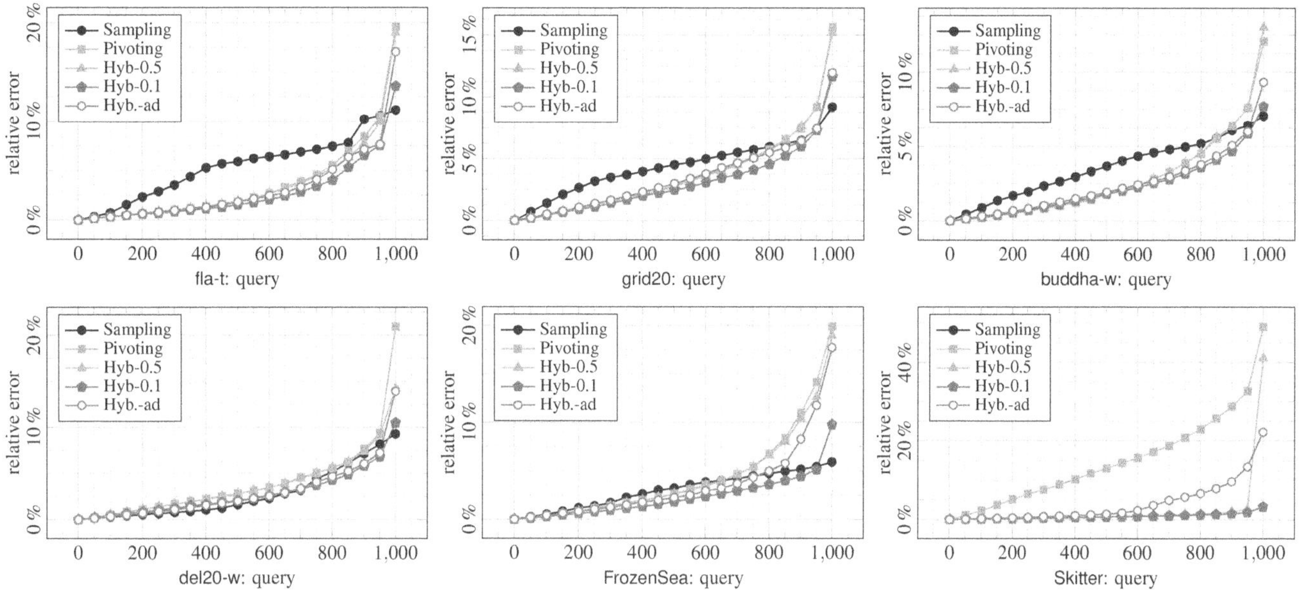

Figure 2: Cumulative quality distribution (over 1000 queries) for varying ϵ.

sensor networks. These three instances are unweighted; their counterparts with a -w suffix have edge lengths corresponding to Euclidean distances. Instance FrozenSea is a grid with obstacles from Starcraft (a computer game) available from `movingai.com` [46]. Edge lengths are set to 408 for axis-aligned moves and 577 for diagonal moves ($577/408 \approx \sqrt{2}$).

8.1 Undirected Closeness Centrality

Table 1 summarizes the main results for undirected instances. We set $k = 100$ for this experiment. We evaluate sampling, pivoting, and our novel hybrid algorithm with respect to running time and solution quality. We consider two versions of our algorithm, both based on Algorithm 1: the first uses $\epsilon = \sqrt{1/k} = 0.1$; the *adaptive* version picks, for each node, the ϵ value from {0.001, 0.025, 0.05, 0.1, 0.2, 0.5, 0.99} that minimizes the estimated error.

For each instance, Table 1 shows the number of nodes and edges it contains (in thousands), followed by the estimated time needed to compute exact centralities for all nodes. Then, for each approximate algorithm, we show its average relative error (over 1000 random nodes queried) and the total time for computing centrality estimates for all nodes (including preprocessing).

We observe that the exact algorithm is prohibitively time-consuming for large graphs, justifying our settling for approximations. Among those, all methods do reasonably well, with average relative error always below 15%. The sampling algorithm is in general more robust than pivoting, with average relative error below 6%. For some high-diameter graphs (such as road networks and meshes), however, pivoting finds better results. Our hybrid algorithm successfully achieves a good tradeoff between these two approaches. Its quality usually matches the best among pivoting and sampling, and often outperforms them.

The adaptive version of our algorithm goes one step further and actually uses different values of ϵ to obtain even finer tradeoffs. This can occasionally be helpful (as in MetroSec), but in general using fixed ϵ is better in terms of running time and quality. Although Algorithm 2 uses additional space to make even finer choices, it leads to very similar results (not shown in the table). We conclude that fixing $\epsilon = \sqrt{1/k}$ is a good strategy: It is more robust than either sampling or pivoting, with very little overhead. On the biggest graph we tested (Orkut), with 117 million edges, we obtained centrality estimates with approximation guarantees for all nodes in about six minutes.

Figure 2 examines the quality of the algorithms in Table 1 in more detail. For comparison, we also show results for the hybrid algorithm with $\epsilon = 0.5$. Once again, we compute the relative error for 1000 queries, plotted in order of increasing error. In other words, for each value $1 \leq i \leq 1000$, we report the i-th smallest relative error observed for each algorithm. We consider six representative instances. For fla-t, grid20, and buddha-w, sampling yields better results than pivoting; for del20-w, FrozenSea, and Skitter, sampling behaves better. On all cases, our default hybrid algorithm (with $\epsilon = 0.1$) is generally better than either method. We note that, unsurprisingly, pivoting tends to have more outliers than pure sampling (i.e., the worst queries for pivoting are worse than the worst for sampling). Although some of this effect is transferred to the hybrid algorithm, it is much less pronounced. This is not true with higher ϵ, which causes the hybrid algorithm to rely more heavily on pivoting.

8.2 Directed Centrality

We now consider centrality on arbitrary directed graphs. Table 2 gives the results obtained by Algorithm 4. Once again, we use $k = 100$ and evaluate the algorithm with 1000 random queries. The "Exact" column shows the estimated time for computing all n outbound centralities using Dijkstra computations. We then show the average relative error (over the 1000 random queries) and the total running time to compute all n centralities using Algorithm 4. Although this algorithm has no theoretical guarantees, its average relative error is consistently below 6% in practice. Moreover,

Table 2: Evaluating algorithms on *directed* instances. As in Table 1, we report the number of nodes and directed edges and for several algorithms the running time and average relative error.

type	instance	$\|V\|$ [$\cdot 10^3$]	$\|E\|$ [$\cdot 10^3$]	Exact time $\approx$[h:m]	Sampling err. [%]	Sampling time [sec]
road	eur-t	18 010	42 189	28 399:47	3.2	655.9
	eur-d	18 010	42 189	22 306:20	3.2	517.0
web	NotreDame	326	1 470	0:54	2.4	1.5
	Indo	1 383	16 540	58:46	4.1	21.1
	Indochina	7 415	191 607	2 884:19	4.7	174.7
comp	Gnutella	63	148	0:02	2.8	0.6
social	Epinions	76	509	0:07	5.4	1.1
	Slashdot	82	870	0:18	2.2	2.2
	Flickr	1 861	22 614	227:01	4.3	65.1
	WikiTalk	2 394	5 021	22:01	0.5	5.4
	Twitter	457	14 856	28:16	1.2	26.1
	LiveJournal	4 848	68 475	2 757:01	1.9	276.8

it is quite practical, taking less than three minutes even on a graph with almost 200 million edges.

9. CONCLUSION

We presented a comprehensive solution to the problem of approximating, within a small relative error, the classic closeness centrality of all nodes in a network. We proposed the first near-linear-time algorithm with theoretical guarantees and provide a scalable implementation. Our experimental analysis demonstrates the effectiveness of our solution.

Our basic design and analysis apply in any metric space: Given the set of distances from a small random sample of the nodes to all other nodes, we can estimate, for each node, its average distance to all other nodes, with a small relative error. We therefore expect our estimators to have further applications.

10. REFERENCES

[1] R. Albert, H. Jeong, and A.-L. Barabási. Internet: Diameter of the World-Wide Web. *Nature*, 401:130–131, September 1999.

[2] L. Backstrom, P. Boldi, M. Rosa, J. Ugander, and S. Vigna. Four degrees of separation. In *WebSci*, pp. 33–42, 2012.

[3] A.-L. Barabási and R. Albert. Emergence of scaling in random networks. *Science*, 286(5439):509–512, 1999.

[4] A. Bavelas. A mathematical model for small group structures. *Human Organization*, 7:16–30, 1948.

[5] A. Bavelas. Communication patterns in task oriented groups. *Journal of the Acoustical Society of America*, 22:271–282, 1950.

[6] M. A. Beauchamp. An improved index of centrality. *Behavioral Science*, 10:161–163, 1965.

[7] P. Boldi, M. Rosa, M. Santini, and S. Vigna. Layered label propagation: A multiresolution coordinate-free ordering for compressing social networks. In *Proceedings of the 20th international conference on World Wide Web*, pp. 587–596. 2011.

[8] P. Boldi, M. Rosa, and S. Vigna. HyperANF: Approximating the neighbourhood function of very large graphs on a budget. In *WWW*, 2011.

[9] P. Boldi, M. Rosa, and S. Vigna. Robustness of social networks: Comparative results based on distance distributions. In *SocInfo*, pp. 8–21, 2011.

[10] P. Boldi and S. Vigna. The WebGraph framework I: Compression techniques. In *Proceedings of the 13th international conference on World Wide Web*, pp. 595–602. 2004.

[11] P. Boldi and S. Vigna. In-core computation of geometric centralities with hyperball: A hundred billion nodes and beyond. In *ICDM workshops*, 2013. `http://arxiv.org/abs/1308.2144`.

[12] P. Boldi and S. Vigna. Axioms for centrality. *Internet Mathematics*, 2014.

[13] M. T. Chao. A general purpose unequal probability sampling plan. *Biometrika*, 69(3):653–656, 1982.

[14] E. Cohen. Size-estimation framework with applications to transitive closure and reachability. *J. Comput. System Sci.*, 55:441–453, 1997.

[15] E. Cohen. Undirected shortest-paths in polylog time and near-linear work. *J. Assoc. Comput. Mach.*, 47:132–166, 2000. Extended version of a STOC 1994 paper.

[16] E. Cohen. All-distances sketches, revisited: HIP estimators for massive graphs analysis. In *PODS*. ACM, 2014.

[17] E. Cohen, N. Duffield, C. Lund, M. Thorup, and H. Kaplan. Efficient stream sampling for variance-optimal estimation of subset sums. *SIAM J. Comput.*, 40(5), 2011.

[18] E. Cohen and H. Kaplan. Spatially-decaying aggregation over a network: Model and algorithms. *J. Comput. System Sci.*, 73:265–288, 2007. Full version of a SIGMOD 2004 paper.

[19] E. Cohen and H. Kaplan. Summarizing data using bottom-k sketches. In *ACM PODC*, 2007.

[20] P. Crescenzi, R. Grossi, L. Lanzi, and A. Marino. A comparison of three algorithms for approximating the distance distribution in real-world graphs. In *TAPAS*, 2011.

[21] C. Dangalchev. Residual closeness in networks. *Phisica A*, 365, 2006.

[22] M. De Domenico, A. Lima, P. Mougel, and M. Musolesi. The anatomy of a scientific rumor. *Scientific Reports*, 3:2980, 2013.

[23] C. Demetrescu, A. V. Goldberg, and D. S. Johnson, editors. *The Shortest Path Problem: Ninth DIMACS Implementation Challenge*, DIMACS Book 74. American Mathematical Society, 2009.

[24] N. Duffield, M. Thorup, and C. Lund. Priority sampling for estimating arbitrary subset sums. *J. Assoc. Comput. Mach.*, 54(6), 2007.

[25] D. Eppstein and J. Wang. Fast approximation of centrality. In *SODA*, pp. 228–229, 2001.

[26] L. C. Freeman. A set of measures of centrality based on betweeness. *Sociometry*, 40:35–41, 1977.

[27] L. C. Freeman. Centrality in social networks: Conceptual clarification. *Social Networks*, 1, 1979.

[28] M. Holtgrewe, P. Sanders, and C. Schulz. Engineering a scalable high quality graph partitioner. In *24th International Parallel and Distributed Processing*

Symposium (IPDPS'10), pp. 1–12. IEEE Computer Society, 2010.

[29] P. Indyk. Sublinear time algorithms for metric space problems. In *STOC*. ACM, 1999.

[30] D. E. Knuth. *The Art of Computer Programming, Vol 2, Seminumerical Algorithms*. Addison-Wesley, 1st edition, 1968.

[31] J. Leskovec, D. Huttenlocher, and J. Kleinberg. Predicting positive and negative links in online social networks. In *Proceedings of the 19th international conference on World wide web*, pp. 641–650. ACM, 2010.

[32] J. Leskovec, D. Huttenlocher, and J. Kleinberg. Signed networks in social media. In *Proceedings of the SIGCHI Conference on Human Factors in Computing Systems*, pp. 1361–1370. ACM, 2010.

[33] J. Leskovec, J. Kleinberg, and C. Faloutsos. Graphs over time: Densification laws, shrinking diameters and possible explanations. In *Proceedings of the eleventh ACM SIGKDD international conference on Knowledge discovery in data mining*, pp. 177–187. ACM, 2005.

[34] J. Leskovec, K. J. Lang, A. Dasgupta, and M. W. Mahoney. Community structure in large networks: Natural cluster sizes and the absence of large well-defined clusters. *Internet Mathematics*, 6(1):29–123, 2009.

[35] N. Lin. *Foundations of Social Search*. McGraw-Hill Book Co., New York, 1976.

[36] C. Magnien, M. Latapy, and M. Habib. Fast computation of empirically tight bounds for the diameter of massive graphs. *Journal of Experimental Algorithmics (JEA)*, 13:10:1–10:9, 2009.

[37] R. Matei, A. Iamnitchi, and I. Foster. Mapping the Gnutella network: Properties of large-scale peer-to-peer systems and implications for system design. *IEEE Internet Computing Journal*, 2002.

[38] A. Mislove, M. Marcon, K. P. Gummadi, P. Druschel, and B. Bhattacharjee. Measurement and analysis of online social networks. In *Proceedings of the 7th ACM SIGCOMM conference on Internet measurement*, pp. 29–42. 2007.

[39] E. Ohlsson. Sequential poisson sampling. *J. Official Statistics*, 14(2):149–162, 1998.

[40] K. Okamoto, W. Chen, and X. Li. Ranking of closeness centrality for large-scale social networks. In *Proc. 2nd Annual International Workshop on Frontiers in Algorithmics*, FAW. Springer-Verlag, 2008.

[41] T. Opsahl, F. Agneessens, and J. Skvoretz. Node centrality in weighted networks: Generalizing degree and shortest paths. *Social Networks*, 32, 2010. `http://toreopsahl.com/2010/03/20/`.

[42] C. R. Palmer, P. B. Gibbons, and C. Faloutsos. ANF: A fast and scalable tool for data mining in massive graphs. In *KDD*, 2002.

[43] M. Richardson, R. Agrawal, and P. Domingos. Trust management for the semantic web. In *The Semantic Web - ISWC 2003*, pp. 351–368. Springer, 2003.

[44] G. Sabidussi. The centrality index of a graph. *Psychometrika*, 31(4):581–603, 1966.

[45] P. V. Sander, D. Nehab, E. Chlamtac, and H. Hoppe. Efficient traversal of mesh edges using adjacency primitives. *ACM Transactions on Graphics (TOG)*, 27(5):144, 2008.

[46] N. R. Sturtevant. Benchmarks for grid-based pathfinding. *IEEE Transactions on Computational Intelligence and AI in Games*, 4(2):144–148, 2012.

[47] M. Thorup. Quick k-median, k-center, and facility location for sparse graphs. In *ICALP*. Springer-Verlag, 2001.

[48] J. D. Ullman and M. Yannakakis. High-probability parallel transitive closure algorithms. *SIAM J. Comput.*, 20:100–125, 1991.

[49] J. Vitter. Random sampling with a reservoir. *ACM Trans. Math. Softw.*, 11(1):37–57, 1985.

[50] S. Wasserman and K. Faust, editors. *Social Network Analysis: Methods and Applications*. Cambridge University Press, 1994.

[51] D. J. Watts and S. H. Strogatz. Collective dynamics of 'small-world' networks. *Nature*, 393(6684):440–442, 1998.

[52] J. Yang and J. Leskovec. Defining and evaluating network communities based on ground-truth. In *Proceedings of the ACM SIGKDD Workshop on Mining Data Semantics*, MDS '12, pp. 3:1–3:8, New York, NY, USA, 2012. ACM.

Analysis of the Semi-synchronous Approach to Large-scale Parallel Community Finding

Erika Duriakova, Neil Hurley
Insight Centre for Data Analytics
School of Computer Science and Informatics
University College Dublin
Dublin, Ireland
first.last@insight-centre.org

Deepak Ajwani, Alessandra Sala
Bell Laboratories, Dublin
Dublin, Ireland
first.last@alcatel-lucent.com

ABSTRACT

Community-finding in graphs is the process of identifying highly cohesive vertex subsets. Recently the vertex-centric approach has been found effective for scalable graph processing and is implemented in systems such as GraphLab and Pregel. In the vertex-centric approach, the analysis is decomposed into a set of local computations at each vertex of the graph, with results propagated to neighbours along the vertex's edges. Many community finding algorithms are amenable to this approach as they are based on the optimisation of an objective through a process of *iterative local update* (ILU), in which vertices are successively moved to the community of one of their neighbours in order to achieve the highest local gain in the quality of the objective. The sequential processing of such iterative algorithms generally benefits from an asynchronous approach, where a vertex update uses the most recent state as generated by the previous update of vertices in its neighbourhood. When vertices are distributed over a parallel machine, the asynchronous approach can encounter race conditions that impact on its performance and destroy the consistency of the results. Alternatively, a semi-synchronous approach ensures that only non-conflicting vertices are updated simultaneously. In this paper we study the semi-synchronous approach to ILU algorithms for community finding on social networks. Because of the heavy-tailed vertex distribution, the order in which vertex updates are applied in asynchronous ILU can greatly impact both convergence time and quality of the found communities. We study the impact of ordering on the distributed label propagation and modularity maximisation algorithms implemented on a shared-memory multicore architecture. We demonstrate that the semi-synchronous ILU approach is competitive in time and quality with the asynchronous approach, while allowing the analyst to maintain consistent control over update ordering. Thus, our implementation results in a more robust and predictable performance and provides control over the order in which the node labels are updated, which is crucial to obtaining the correct trade-off between running time and quality of communities on many graph classes.

COSN'14, October 1–2, 2014, Dublin, Ireland.

http://dx.doi.org/10.1145/2660460.2660474.

Categories and Subject Descriptors

G.2.2 [**DISCRETE MATHEMATICS**]: Graph Theory — Graph algorithms;
G.1.0 [**NUMERICAL ANALYSIS**]: General — Parallel algorithms

Keywords

Parallel Graph Algorithms; Community Detection Algorithms; Iterative Local Update; Semi-synchronous Graph Algorithms

1. INTRODUCTION

The problem of identifying communities in large and complex networks has received ample attention in recent years, owing to its application in the analysis of social networks, citation networks, the world-wide web, biological networks and so on. Many different definitions of community structure have been proposed and various algorithms have been developed to extract such structure from the complex networks that arise in real-world applications. Common to all definitions is the notion that a community is a cohesive subset of the nodes or vertices of the network graph. Such cohesive subsets often correspond to meaningful structure in the underlying real-world problem. When the network is a social network, they can be interpreted as social communities, but may be understood, in the case of biological networks for instance, as important functional units. Metrics such as modularity and conductance have been proposed to quantify the cohesiveness of communities. Other metrics, such as normalised mutual information, allow a community assignment to be compared against a set of ground-truth communities. (See [4] for a comprehensive overview.)

In the last decade, one of the most studied metrics for community detection is *modularity* [13] of a partition of the graph vertices into a set of non-overlapping communities. Modularity measures the cohesiveness of the given partition on the given graph against the cohesiveness of the same partition on a "null model" consisting of a random graph with the same degree distribution. An alternative approach [16] models community finding as an information theoretic problem of finding a set of modules or communities that minimise the number of bits required in a particular encoding of a random walk over the graph, resulting in an objective they call the *map equation.* While in many ways very different models of community, both of these approaches propose an objective function over the set of possible partitions, whose optimum corresponds to the 'best' community structure under the model. A number of other methods also seek a community assignment to optimise a functional objective over the set of possible assignments, including methods for overlapping community detection, such as MOSES [12]. Given any such model, we face the computational task of proposing an algorithm to optimise its associated objective.

It transpires that among the best strategies for optimising any of these objectives, an algorithm based on *iterative local update* (ILU) has proven particularly effective, both in run-time performance and quality of the resulting communities. In this approach, the community assignment is initialised by assigning a unique community label to each vertex. Each vertex is visited in some order; the communities of its neighbours are considered and the vertex is moved to the neighbouring community that results in the largest improvement in the objective, if it exists. Several passes through the vertices are made, until no further moves generate an improvement in the objective, or more generally until a threshold α of vertex updates fails to be reached. This algorithm constitutes a single phase of the algorithm. In [1, 16], further phases are applied in which the network is rebuilt by merging connected nodes that share a community and the algorithm is re-applied on the community graph thus formed. The phases are repeated until no further improvement in the objective is obtained.

The most basic community-finding algorithm based on the ILU method described above is the *label propagation* (LP) algorithm [15]. LP does not depend on any explicit objective function, but rather, in each iteration, a vertex is assigned the most frequent label (or the heaviest label in case of weighted graph) among its neighbours and itself. Ties can be broken arbitrarily, randomly, or in favour of the maximum label. As above, this iterative process terminates at an iteration in which no more than a threshold α of vertices has moved. LP has emerged as a particularly effective technique, that has been shown to result in good quality community structure and has since been also used as a fundamental block in many other complex community detection ensemble schemes (e.g., [14]).

In many of the current *parallel* label-propagation implementations (e.g., [17]), the labels of the vertices are asynchronously updated. In the shared-memory context, this implies that whether an old or new label value of neighbours is read at the update stage depends on the architecture and systems-level details, such as when the cores flush their private caches to memory and how is the memory hierarchy shared between the different cores. This makes it impossible to control the sequential order in which the vertices are updated in the ILU algorithm for community detection and precludes any analysis of the outcome of the algorithm in terms of this update ordering.

In this paper, we demonstrate that, for social network graphs with highly non-uniform degree distributions, the vertex update ordering has a large impact on the run-time of the analysis and the quality of the resulting communities. It is thus a key parameter of the computation. This suggests that analysts wishing to explore the structural properties of the network, should be able to control this update order, independently of the details of the machine on which the algorithm is run. Even if the analyst prefers a certain amount of randomisation for the ensemble approaches to work better with the ILU based approaches as basic building blocks, she would prefer to control this randomisation and not leave such a crucial aspect to the architecture and systems-layer details. Thus we explore semi-synchronous parallel ILU algorithms that use an input graph colouring to *impose* a vertex update order. While the set of possible input orderings is restricted by the requirement that it be efficiently computable on the parallel machine, we address the question of how to choose a colouring given a particular desired update order and explore the convergence and run-time characteristics of different colouring strategies.

Our Contribution Differently from previous work on this topic, we explore the use of *independent sets* to compromise between processor data independence and good mixing of community labels during the course of the algorithm. This so-called *semi-synchronous* approach was previously proposed in [9] but not fully implemented and evaluated on a parallel architecture. Specifically,

- We extend the semi-synchronous approach to a general framework for community-finding using the ILU method that includes objectives such as modularity and the map equation.
- We perform a detailed empirical evaluation of various design parameters on the performance of ILU method and the quality of the resultant communities. We show that the vertex update ordering and the colouring technique has a significant effect on the outcome of the ILU algorithms.
- The empirical evaluation of design parameters enables us to carefully engineer the semi-synchronous ILU that is comparable in running time to the state-of-the-art asynchronous implementations and yet provides the consistent control of node update ordering to the developer. Our approach uses many optimisation tricks such as keeping track of active nodes and a blocked colouring strategy.

Outline Section 2 describes the iterative local update methodology and the synchronous, asynchronous and semi-synchronous techniques to parallelize it. Section 3 generalizes the semi-synchronous approach to parallelize iterative local update algorithms for optimising modularity and the map equation as well. After outlining the datasets and machine architectures on which we carry out our study, in Section 4, we examine the effect of different vertex visit orderings on the performance of an ILU algorithm in Section 5. Section 6 discusses vertex ordering based on graph colouring. Finally, Section 7 presents the results of our empirical analysis.

1.1 Related Work

While we focus in this paper on implementation on shared memory multicores, the ILU framework has formed the basis of so-called *vertex-centric* scalable graph processing systems such as Pregel [11], GraphLab [10] and GraphChi [8]. These systems solve graph-based data analytics problems by iterating the computation of a vertex kernel function over all vertices in the graph. Pregel and GraphLab can be distinguished by the type of synchronisation they support. Pregel supports synchronous algorithms in which computations proceed in a set of *super-steps* followed by a synchronisation. Each vertex kernel running independently in parallel in a super-step cannot access any state changes made by other vertices until the end of the super-step. GraphLab supports asynchronous computations, where vertex kernels can modify state shared with neighbouring vertices, during an update sweep. Recognising the need for analysts to maintain consistency in their results, GraphLab enables *serialisable* asynchronous computations, ensuring that the parallel asynchronous computation is equivalent to some sequential update order.

The original GraphLab system supports a *Chromatic Engine*, analogous to the semi-synchronous approach we explore in this paper. This work was further extended in [7] using colouring techniques to acquire independent sets while also supporting dynamic data-graph computations. However, the recent PowerGraph [5] enhanced system relies instead on a dynamic locking mechanism to ensure that conflicting assesses to shared data are resolved. While this guarantees that the computation is serialisable, the equivalent sequential computation is difficult for the analyst to discern as it is dependent on the parallel architecture.

Another distributed implementation of a constrained variant of the LP algorithm has been used in the graph partitioning system for Facebook's "People You May Know" (PMYK) service [18]. None of these works has considered the semi-synchronous approach to parallelisation.

In other relevant state-of-the-art, different approaches to the parallelisation of LP and greedy modularity maximisation have been evaluated in [17]. In fact, some of the engineering tricks in our work (e.g., the use of *active/inactive* flag described in section 3.1) are similar to those considered in [17]. However the fundamental difference between the two works is that while the implementations in [17] are based on an asynchronous approach, our implementation is based on semi-synchronous ILU algorithms (algorithm framework 2). The engineering of the semi-synchronous algorithm necessitates the study of the impact of graph colouring techniques to identify independent sets and different node orderings, which was not considered in [17].

1.2 Notation

In the rest of the text, we use the following notations. A graph $G(V, E)$ consists of a set of vertices V of size n and a set of edges $E \subseteq V \times V$ of size m. In this paper we consider undirected graphs, such that $(v, w) \in E \Leftrightarrow (w, v) \in E$ with, optionally, an associated edge *weight* $w : E \rightarrow \mathbb{R}^+$, with $w(e) = 1 \forall e \in E$ in the *unweighted* case. Moreover, we write $\forall v \in V, N_v = \{w \in V | \exists e = (v, w)\}$ for the *neighbourhood* of v; $d_v = |N(v)|$ for the *degree* of v; and $k_v = \sum_{w \in N_v} w(e)$ for the *weighted degree* of v. With a node numbering $l : V \rightarrow \{1, \ldots, n\}$ giving a unique integer identifier $i = l(v)$ for each v, we can use i to represent v and interchangeably write k_i for k_v etc. The *adjacency matrix* of the graph is the $n \times n$ matrix, $A = \{a_{ij}\}$, such that $a_{ij} = w(e)$ whenever $(i, j) \in E$ and $a_{ij} = 0$ otherwise. The output of a community finding algorithm may be represented as the assignment of a community label to each node in the graph, which we write as $\zeta : V \rightarrow \mathbb{N}$, where $\zeta(v)$ is the community label of node v. It will be convenient to write $\zeta(A)$ for the set of all labels on a subset of vertices A.

2. PARALLEL ILU

The algorithmic framework of the ILU method is shown in Algorithm 1. Due to its local update of the node labels, the ILU approach is considered to be well suited for a fast and scalable implementation. In the ILU method, the work carried out per vertex is a function of the vertex's neighbourhood size. A natural approach to parallelisation is to partition the vertices among the available processors, updating vertex labels in parallel. Provided the sum of the neighbourhood sizes in each partition is balanced, then the total work should be evenly balanced across the machine, with little interprocessor communication required in the label update. However, this analysis neglects the fact that in the serial algorithm, labels are updated in sequential order. As shown in Algorithm 1, the label applied to vertex v at iteration i, depends on the most recent labels obtained for those neighbours, $N^p(v)$, visited previously to v on the current iteration, and on the old labels for those neighbours, $N^s(v)$, visited later in the loop. In fact, the use of the most recent label values during update is critical to allow fast mixing of the labels, reducing the total number of required iterations for the algorithm to converge to a stable set of communities.

Algorithm 1 Iterative Local Update (ILU)

Input: $G(V, E)$, $\alpha \geq 0$.
1: Initialize labels: $\forall (v \in V), \zeta_0(v) \leftarrow l(v)$ ($l : V \rightarrow \{1, \ldots, n\}$ gives a unique integer identifier)
2: $i \leftarrow 0$, updated $\leftarrow n$
3: **while** updated $> \alpha$ **do**
4: $\quad i \leftarrow i + 1$, updated $\leftarrow 0$
5: $\quad$ **for** $\forall (v \in V)$ **do**
6: $\quad\quad \zeta_i(v) = f(\zeta_i(N^p(v)), \zeta_{i-1}(N^s(v))$ ($f(.)$ is the local update function)
7: $\quad\quad$ **if** $\zeta_i(v) \neq \zeta_{i-1}(v)$ **then**
8: $\quad\quad\quad$ updated $\leftarrow$ updated $+ 1$
9: $\quad\quad$ **end if**
10: $\quad$ **end for**
11: **end while**
Output: $\forall \zeta_i(v), v \in V$

2.1 Levels of Synchronisation

We summarise the different strategies for parallelisation of an ILU algorithm for community-finding on a shared-memory multicore as follows:

Synchronous Parallelisation In this approach the labels $\zeta_i(v)$ are updated based on the label values from the previous iteration only i.e. line 7 of Algorithm 1 becomes $\zeta_i(v) = f(\zeta_{i-1}(N(v)))$ and parallelisation is achieved by replacing line 5 of Algorithm 1 with a `parallel for` to distribute the vertices among the shared threads for processing. This approach is preferable from the perspective of minimising shared memory access and avoiding race-conditions. However, it comes at the penalty of poorer mixing of labels.

Asynchronous Parallelisation This strategy is simply to ignore the race conditions incurred by a direct parallelisation of the serial algorithm, by using a single shared data structure from which to read label values and write label updates. In this case, when updating $\zeta_i(v)$, the label value read for a neighbour w may correspond to $\zeta_i(w)$ or $\zeta_{i-1}(w)$, depending on whether the thread processing w has written

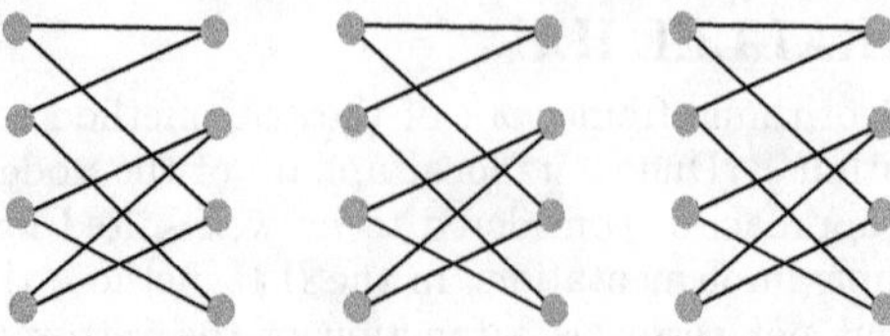

Figure 1: Illustration of label oscillation problem on a bipartite graph, showing the node labels (represented by colours) in iteration i, $i+1$ and $i+2$

its label before that processing v reads it. The update ordering of vertices becomes dependent on the architecture of the machine and moreover, may not correspond to *any* sequential ordering of vertex updates, since race conditions can lead to a situation where two neighbouring vertices *both* use their old values in their update step.

Semi-synchronous Parallelisation The key to this strategy [9] is the use of a *proper graph colouring* i.e. a partitioning of the vertex set V into a set of independent subsets $\{C_1, \dots C_k\}$ such that $C_i \subset V$, $C_i \cap C_j = \emptyset$, $1 \leq i < j \leq k$ and $\bigcup_i C_i = V$; where, $\forall i$, no two vertices in C_i share an edge. Vertex updates occur in order of colour, i.e. the vertices in C_1 are updated before those in C_2 and so on, leading to a parallel algorithm which we call PSILU, of the form shown in Algorithm 2.

Algorithm 2 Parallel Semi-synchronous Iterative Local Update (PSILU)

Input: $G(V, E)$, $\alpha \geq 0$, $\{C_1, \dots, C_k\}$
Initialize labels: $\forall (v \in V), \zeta_0(v) \leftarrow l(v)$
$i \leftarrow 0$, updated $\leftarrow n$
while updated $> \alpha$ **do**
  $i \leftarrow i + 1$, updated $\leftarrow 0$
  Initialize shared quantities
  for $\forall C_j$, $j = 1, \dots, k$ **do**
    ParallelFor $\forall (v \in C_j)$
      $\zeta_i(v) = f\left(\zeta_i(N^p(v)), \zeta_{i-1}(N^s(v)\right)$ ($f(.)$ is the local update function)
      if $\zeta_i(v) \neq \zeta_{i-1}(v)$ **then**
        updated $\leftarrow$ updated $+ 1$
      end if
    EndParallelFor
    Parallel Reduce *shared quantities*
  end for
end while
Output: $\forall \zeta_i(v), v \in V$

2.2 Limitations of Synchronisation Levels

Synchronous Parallelisation The main problem of synchronous parallelisation is the poor mixing of labels. An extreme, but common, consequence of this poor mixing is that there may be a cyclic oscillation of the labels of some vertices (already observed in [15]). For instance, Figure 1 shows a bi-partite graph and the node labels represented by colours. In this scenario, the labels of the vertices in the two parts of the graph oscillate from one iteration to another. This problem prevents the convergence to a stable community structure. Current parallel implementations side-step this issue either by terminating when the number of nodes to be updated is below a certain arbitrary threshold or by doing a certain degree of asynchronous updating or both (e.g., [17]).

Asynchronous Parallelisation While updating vertices in a particular serial order is beneficial for mixing of the labels, race conditions in the asynchronous approach make it impossible to control update ordering and thus preclude an analysis of the performance in terms of this ordering. The performance of the algorithm is highly dependent on the low-level details of the architecture. In the shared-memory context, whether an old or new label value is read at the update stage depends on the timing of when the new label value is flushed to memory. If many such updates occur before the neighbourhood values have flushed, it can effectively lead to a synchronous update. Such a behaviour can push the number of iterations required to converge higher than would be expected. Moreover, when new label values do flush to memory, the writing of such shared label values that must subsequently be read by another thread, destroys cache coherency, requiring reads from memory rather than cache.

Semi-synchronous Parallelisation Liu and Murata [9] show that in the semi-synchronous variation of LP, the label oscillation problem disappears in a range of bipartite graphs. This is later extended by Cordasco and Gargano [3] to general graphs. The latter result formally proves that this variant is guaranteed to converge. It also shows that the communities identified by this variant have roughly the same modularity score as the asynchronous approach on a range of graphs. Furthermore, the results of the semi-synchronous variant were shown to be more stable than the asynchronous variant – the standard deviation of the modularity obtained for different test settings was smaller.

Due to the independence property of each colour set, the order in which the vertices are processed within a colour does not affect the outcome of the algorithm. Moreover, as only the vertices within a single colour set are processed in parallel, label values of neighbours are never updated during the parallel loop, removing race conditions from the outcome of the algorithm and avoiding the cache coherency issues of the fully asynchronous approach. Finally, the algorithm still allows for significant label mixing during a single pass of the algorithm through the vertex set, thus reducing the number of iterations required by a synchronous algorithm, while avoiding its convergence issues.

The considerable gains of the semi-synchronous parallelisation in terms of convergence and consistency of results are attained at the cost of additional synchronisation barriers. For this reason, it was assumed to be too slow to be of much practical merit and therefore, was not considered in earlier parallel implementations of ILU in general and label-propagation in particular. We analyse the effects of colouring algorithms and vertex updated orderings on the performance of the semi-synchronous approach and use it to engineer an implementation based on a careful design choices. In Section 7, we show the experimental results analysing the performance of our engineered semi-synchronous implementation.

3. SEMI-SYNCHRONOUS ILU FOR MODULARITY MAXIMISATION AND MAP EQUATION

In this section, we present our extension of the semi-synchronous ILU for modularity maximisation (MM). The key issue in this extension is that MM requires more states to be maintained in order to compute the change in modularity that drives the vertex update function. In particular, while modularity depends on the adjacency matrix of the given graph, it also depends on the *volume* of each community, where $\text{Vol}_c = \sum_{i \in c} k_i$. The change in modularity when moving a node v from its current community c to the community of a neighbouring node, d is:

$$\Delta m_{vcd} = \frac{2}{M}(k_{v,d} - k_{v,c}) - \frac{2}{M^2} k_v(\text{Vol}_d - \text{Vol}_c + k_v)$$

where $k_{v,d}$ is the sum of the edge weights from v to d and $M = \sum_i k_i$. The second component of this expression is non-local. Its existence implies that the order of vertex updates even over independent vertex sets impacts on the outcome of the algorithm and moving two vertices simultaneously on different threads may not be equivalent to any sequential ordering. In fact, when vertices are moved simultaneously by different threads, the overall change in modularity can be expressed as $\Delta m = \sum_{t=1}^{T} \Delta m_t - I$, where T is the number of threads, Δm_t is the change in modularity due to moving vertices assigned to thread t and I is a term that expresses the interaction between vertices moved by different threads, which is unknown until threads synchronise after a set of local updates.

The semi-synchronous strategy of restricting parallel updates to independent sets restricts I to

$$I = \frac{1}{M^2} \sum_c \left(\Delta \text{Vol}_c^2 - \sum_{t=1}^{T} (\Delta \text{Vol}_c^t)^2 \right) \quad (1)$$

where ΔVol_c^t is the overall change in the volume of community c due to the movement of vertices by thread t and ΔVol_c is the overall change in the volume of c. The interaction term is small in comparison to that which would apply if non-independent sets of vertices were moved and, if desired, can be easily corrected at each synchronisation point. Vol_c (and I) may be updated by reduction after a set of local updates (line 13 of Algorithm 2). Since in the ILU approach we initialise with a community per node, rather than reduce over such a large number of local values, it is better to recompute the volume using the new community labels.

Similarly, the objective function for the map equation [16] depends on two sets of quantities, namely p_c, the probability that a random walk visits community c and q_c, the exit probability from community c, where these probabilities are based on a random walk over the graph. When an independent set of vertices is updated in parallel, the use of independent sets reduces the error in state during parallel update and the overall change to these shared quantities after the update is simply the sum of the change as calculated independently on each thread.

3.1 Algorithm Optimisations

As the LP and MM algorithm approach convergence, the last number of sweeps through the vertices result in just a few vertices changing their label values. This phase of the algorithm can be needlessly expensive. A key optimisation used in [17], which we adopt in both our LP and MM algorithms, is the maintenance of an `active` flag for each vertex. Only active vertices are considered for update. Whenever a vertex leaves its label unchanged, its active flag is set to `false`; whenever a vertex changes its label, it sets the active flags of its neighbours to `true`, so that they are considered for update in the next pass. Even so, when the stopping criterion is based on the fraction of vertices that move in each sweep, the MM algorithm can perform a large number of update steps as it approaches convergence, resulting in only a very small change in the overall modularity. Hence, we stop the algorithm when the perceived change in modularity (i.e. the estimated Δm, excluding the interaction term I) after an update sweep is less than a given threshold ($= 10^{-4}$ in our experiments).

4. DATASETS AND ARCHITECTURES

Graphs considered Table 1 shows the graphs that we consider in our experimental evaluation. Pokec, Orkut and Livejournal [1] are online social networks and exhibit the complex structure of such networks, such as high clustering and heavy-tailed degree distribution. UK 2002[2] is obtained from a crawl of the `.uk` domain. We choose this network to contrast with the social networks.

Architectures considered To evaluate the performance of the shared memory implementation, we use the following architecture:

- (Config A) A system with 2 x 10-core Intel Xeon E5-2470 v2 2.4GHz processors, each with a shared 25MB L3 cache and 256KB L2 cache per core and a total of 128GB RAM.
- (Config B) A system with 2 x 16-core 2.6 GHz AMD Opteron 6282 SE processors and a total of 96GB RAM. Each core has its private 2MB L2 cache while the 16 MB L3 cache is shared between 16 cores.
- (Config C) A system with 4-core (× 2 with hyper-threading) 3.6GHz Intel(R) Core i7-3820 processor with a shared 10MB L3 cache and 64GB RAM.
- (Config D) A system with 6-cores (× 4) 2.4GHz Intel(R) Xeon E7450 processor with a shared 12 MB L3 cache and 128GB RAM.

For the sake of brevity, we only highlight the key findings on Config A and note that the results on Config B, C and D are along similar lines.

Software designed We implemented our ILU LP and MM code, using C++ and OpenMP. The OS has a Linux Ubuntu (12.04 release) installation. We used the option -O3 with the gnu C++ compiler version 4.6.

5. EFFECT OF VERTEX VISIT ORDER ON ASYNCHRONOUS ILU

The performance of the LP and MM ILU algorithms depends intimately on how fast the labels mix, which in turn is dependent on the order in which vertices are updated. Social network graphs generally consist of a core of inter-connected high degree nodes, along with low-degree 'whiskers' outside the core. The node degrees are highly non-uniform, following a heavy-tailed scale-free distribution. For such graphs, in particular, we can expect highly different behaviour of the LP algorithm depending on the ordering in which nodes are traversed. Intuitively, ordering the nodes in decreasing degree so that high-degree nodes are processed first should

[1] downloaded from `http://snap.stanford.edu`
[2] downloaded from `http://law.di.unimi.it`

Table 1: Networks used

Network	# nodes	# edges	Avg. clustering coefficient	Diameter	Effective Diameter
UK 2002	18,520,486	298,113,762	-	218	19.8
Orkut	3,072,441	117,185,083	0.16	9	4.8
Live Journal	4,847,571	42,851,237	0.2742	16	6.5
Pokec	1,632,803	22,301,964	0.1094	11	5.2

allow the labels to mix quickly from the core to the periphery of the network. Alternatively, choosing a breadth-first search (BFS) ordering from a chosen starting node allows the labelling to mix outward from that node. Such orderings can lead to fast convergence of the LP algorithm. We use the Pokec social network to study this mixing issue.

5.1 LP on Pokec

We introduce a work-load measure, W, to quantify the work carried out during the full execution of the algorithm. We define,

$$W = \sum_{i=1}^{\#\text{sweeps}} \sum_{v \in V^i_{\text{active}}} k_v;$$

the sum over all sweeps through the vertices of the degrees of the vertices, V^i_{active}, that are active during sweep i. This is a reasonable approximation of the computation that is carried out in these ILU algorithms. For each active vertex v, the labels of its k_v neighbours are considered for a potential move to the corresponding community, an $O(k_v)$ operation, considering that selecting the best move involves a maximisation of k_v terms. We ignore the constant overhead of processing inactive vertices and the fact that active vertices that change their label must carry out a further $O(k_v)$ operation to set the active flag of their neighbours. In practise, with all other conditions fixed, we find empirically that runtime and W follow an approximately linear relationship and W gives a measure of how much useful computation is carried out, excluding the overhead.

In Figures 2 and 3 we show the modularities and workload that result from running the LP algorithm on the Pokec graph, under a number of different node traversal orderings, as box-plots based on 100 trial runs. Six orderings are chosen,

1. Random ordering;
2. Increasing degree ordering;
3. Decreasing degree ordering;
4. BFS starting from the node of maximum degree and ordering the nodes in each level set in order of decreasing degree;
5. BFS starting from the node of minimum degree and ordering the nodes in each level set in order of increasing degree;
6. BFS starting with a random node and ordering the nodes in each level set randomly.

The wide variation in results is striking. Choosing the nodes from high to low degree results in fast mixing and

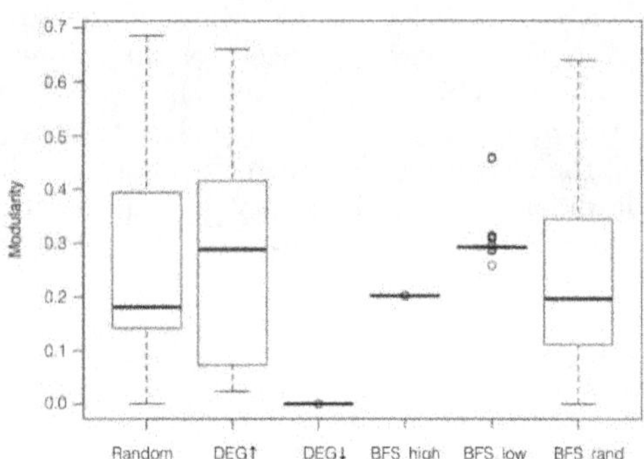

Figure 2: Modularity of LP communities for different traversal Orderings on the Pokec network.

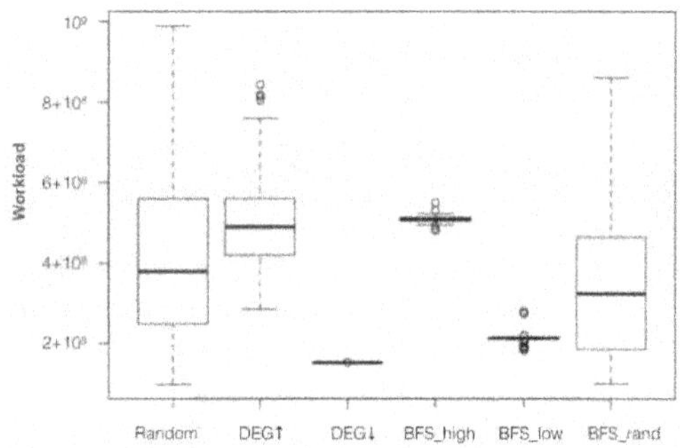

Figure 3: Workload of LP algorithm for different traversal Orderings on the Pokec network.

hence low workload, but also results in low modularity, because the labels mix into a giant community. A random ordering gives a wide variation of workloads and modularities.

BFS starting from a random node results in lower workload on average than a fully random ordering and a similar range of modularities. On the other hand BFS starting from low degree node results in low workload and high modularity with practically no variance. It would appear to be the best compromise in terms of workload and quality.

5.2 MM on Pokec

The MM algorithm is less prone to getting trapped in undesirable local maxima than LP. We find that, running on the above orderings, the algorithm converges to solutions that vary in modularity in a range between 0.658 and 0.676. Nevertheless, the work required to reach this solution varies according to update order. The decreasing degree order requires $W = 2.058 \times 10^8$, while the increasing degree order requires more than twice as much work ($W = 5.369 \times 10^8$). Random ordering requires $W = 3.784 \times 10^8$ on average while a BFS from a random node requires slightly less work on average ($W = 3.682 \times 10^8$) and from the highest degree node, less again ($W = 3.481 \times 10^8$)

Similar behaviour is seen in other social network graphs of highly non-uniform degree distribution such as the Orkut social network graph. It follows that an analyst may prefer the decreasing degree order to speed convergence.

5.3 Asynchronous Ordered Computations

On a shared-memory multicore, a simple approach to approximating a desired update order is to apply an asynchronous update by parallelising the sequential loop that iterates through the vertices in the desired order using a `parallel for` operation, on the assumption that race conditions will have only a minor impact on the outcome. However, the impact is quite dramatic. On the Orkut network, the workload experienced by the asynchronous version of the decreasing degree ordering on 4 threads is on average 3.7 times greater than on a single thread and this grows to 4.6 times when 16 threads are used. Moreover, it is clear that a static scheduling of the loop would assign all the high-degree (and therefore work-intensive) vertices to the same thread, leading to high load imbalance. Our empirical evaluation shows that even an adaptive dynamic schedule (using the OpenMP `guided` scheduler) still leads to high load imbalance. The result is that a speed-up of only 1.17 is achieved on eight threads.

It transpires that much better control of the work-load can be achieved by adopting the semi-synchronous approach. Nevertheless, this also introduces extra overhead, through the synchronisation steps – this trade-off will be explored later in the paper.

6. COLOURING ALGORITHMS

The performance of the semi-synchronous algorithm is highly dependent on the choice of colouring algorithm. A commonly used heuristic is the *greedy* heuristic [2] summarised in Algorithm 3, which depends, firstly, on the ordering in which the vertices are visited and, secondly, on how a colour is chosen from amongst those not forbidden. Hasenplaugh et. al. provide a comprehensive overview of sequential an parallel graph colouring algorithms using a number of different node ordering heuristics [6]. In many applications, an optimal colouring is considered to be one in which the total number of colours is minimised. In this case, a good choice for the choose(.) function is min(.) and vertices may be traversed in order of degree. Using the minimum function can lead to a highly unbalanced colouring, in which a few colour sets contain many more vertices than the others. For the PSILU algorithms considered here, each colour set is separately parallelised by distributing its vertices among the available threads. Thus, a highly unbalanced colouring does not necessarily mean an unbalanced workload, as the work carried out by each thread is proportional to the sum of the degrees of the vertices allocated to the thread in a complete pass through the vertex set. In fact, if `static` scheduling is used to distribute the vertices within each colour, then the ordering of the vertices *within* each colour has a larger impact on the load balance. In particular, if vertices were ordered by degree within each colour set, then some threads would get a disproportional amount of work. A `guided` schedule over a randomly ordered colour set is found to be the most effective in ensuring small load imbalance.

A further consideration is the total number of iterations required for the algorithm to converge and the total workload, W. Iterating over an independent set slows mixing as, by construction, no vertex in the colour set shares a neighbour with any vertex. In particular, if the first colour set traversed is very large (as may be typical of an algorithm that seeks to minimise the total number of colours), then all the vertices within this set are effectively updating in synchronous mode, as their updates all depend on the labels of neighbours from the previous pass. This suggests that to speed mixing, the colour sets should not be too large, while if they are too small, the speed of a single pass through the algorithm will be affected by a large number of synchronisations after each colour is processed. Thus, an effective heuristic for colouring for ILU community-finding algorithms is

1. To minimise the number of iterations, choose a *balanced* colouring algorithm, in which the work per colour is as balanced as possible across all colours;

2. To minimise the load imbalance per iteration, choose an vertex ordering within each colour set, so that the work per thread is as balanced as possible and use a dynamic scheduling of work.

Given a particular vertex visit preference order, we can also ask if a colouring strategy can be found that adheres to that preference as closely as possible. For instance, if decreasing degree update order is preferred in the ILU algorithm, then colouring the vertices in order of decreasing degree, ensures that high-degree vertices in general get low colour values and hence are processed early in the ILU update sweep. Thus a simple strategy is to colour the vertices in the order in which we would like them to be processed by the ILU algorithm.

As for choosing the non-forbidden colour, we distinguish between three variants:

- **Random Greedy Heuristic** (RG): choose(.) = a randomly chosen non-forbidden colour.

- **First Greedy Heuristic** (FG): choose(.) = min(.) – This variant aims at minimising the total number of colours. However, this can lead to a highly unbalanced colouring.

- **Smallest Greedy Heuristic** (SG): choose(.) = the non-forbidden colour, such that the number of nodes associated with the colour is minimised. This leads to highly balanced colours, though the number of colours can be larger than First greedy approach.

6.1 Analysis of Coloured Orderings on Pokec

For each of the RG, FG and SG colouring strategies, we form the colour sets using three different node traversal orderings – namely a BFS ordering starting from a random node and decreasing and increasing degree ordering. We examine the modularity and workloads that are obtained using the LP algorithm and the different resulting vertex orderings in Figures 4 and 5. For SG, the BFS traversal ordering leads to a similar set of modularity values and workloads as using

Algorithm 3 Sequential Greedy Colouring

Input: $G(V, E)$

$\forall v \in V,\ c(v) \leftarrow 0,\ i \leftarrow 1$
$\pi \leftarrow$ ordering of the vertices
while $i \neq n$ **do**
  $v \leftarrow \pi(i),\ i \leftarrow i+1,\ F \leftarrow \emptyset$ (F holds the forbidden colours for v)
  for each $n \in N(v)$ **do**
    $F \leftarrow F \cup c(n)$
  end for
  $c_m = \text{choose}\{j > 0 : j \notin F\},\ c(v) = c_m,$
end while

Output: $\forall v \in V\ c(v)$

the asynchronous LP with BFS ordering starting from random source (as presented in figures 2 and 3), though with greater variance. The decreasing degree visit ordering leads to small workload, but also low modularities. These low modularity values are avoided while low work-load is maintained when MM is used. It would appear that FG with decreasing degree node ordering would be the best choice as it results in the highest modularity value on average. However this approach also results in the highest workload. On the other hand RG with increasing degree node ordering seems to be the best compromise between high average modularity and low average workload.

It is important to note that the workload is independent of the number of threads and hence the coloured orderings have the potential to achieve greater speed-up in semi-synchronous mode, than that achieved by the asynchronous method.

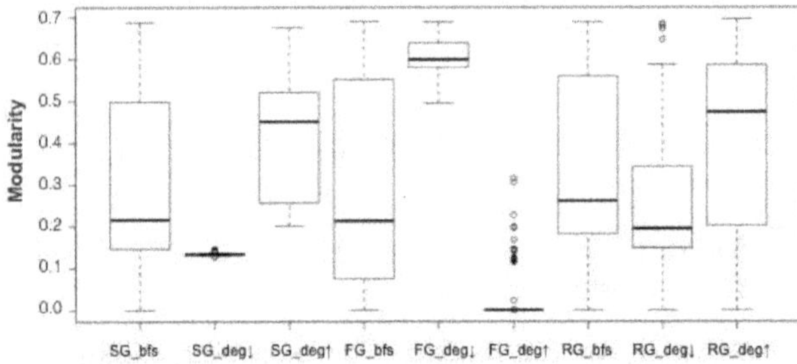

Figure 4: Modularity and workload for different colour orderings on the Pokec network.

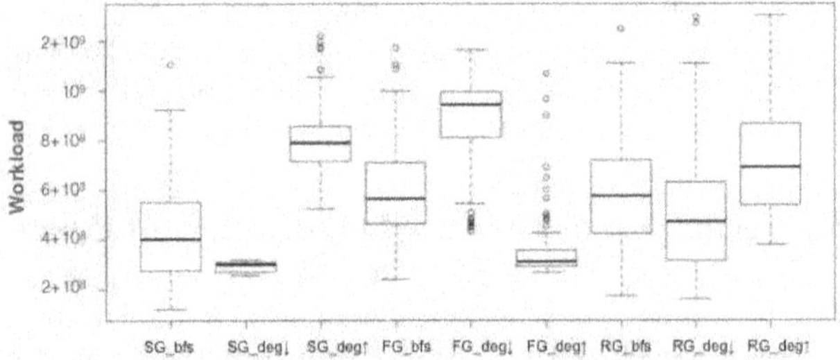

Figure 5: Modularity and workload for different colour orderings on the Pokec network.

6.2 Blocked Colouring Strategy

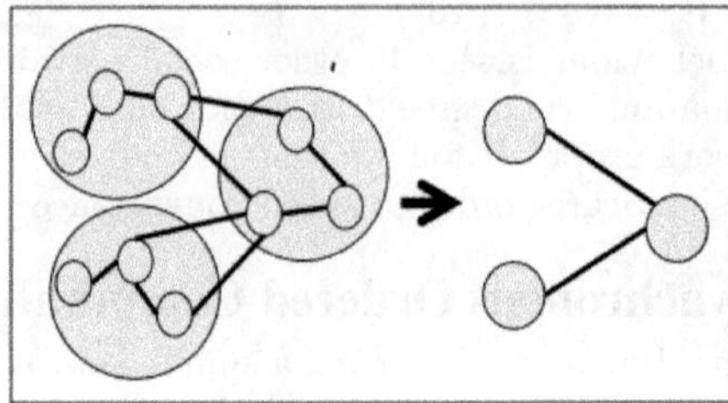

Figure 6: Merging vertices into larger units of work

Another strategy to mitigate against slow mixing when updating on independent sets of vertices is to carry out a blocked colouring strategy. In the standard ILU, the tasks that are allocated to each thread consist of a single vertex update. A generalisation is to combine multiple vertices into a single task. See Figure 6 in which a block graph is formed by merging groups of three vertices. A colouring of the block graph allows non-conflicting tasks to be updated in parallel. As each block of vertices is updated on a single thread, vertex updates within a block are immediately available to their neighbours in the same block – thus, label mixing can begin even in the first colour update. One drawback of this approach is that task unbalance can be exacerbated when a number of high degree vertices are allocated to the same block. Also, depending on the network, the block graph may be significantly more dense than the original graph, hence requiring more colours. On the other hand, when the network exhibits hierarchical structure, blocking can be an effective way to ensure fast mixing in the lower levels of the hierarchy. In our implementation, given a block size, we visit vertices in a given order and form blocks by merging them with neighbouring vertices in a breadth-first manner.

7. EVALUATION

In this section, we report our analysis on the performance of our semi-synchronous implementation and the design choices involved in its engineering. In the LP algorithm, we use random tie breaking and whenever there is a random element to the algorithm, e.g. when random colouring is applied, we report average run-times, speed-up over multiple runs. Note that we have carefully benchmarked our code with that presented in [17] and have confirmed that our asynchronous implementation on a single thread produces identical output with that code.

Our evaluation attempts to answer the following questions:

- How is the work-load W affected by different vertex traversal orderings?
- How does the overhead of synchronisation affect the performance of semi-synchronous algorithms?
- To what extent does load imbalance affect the speed-up of the algorithms?

While the total work-load W provides a measure of the total amount of computation that is carried out by the algorithms, run-time is also affected by overhead. In the asynchronous method, threads synchronise after each pass

Table 2: LP on 1 and 8 Processors : RG and Asynchronous with Decreasing Degree Ordering.

Network	Method	# Cols	# Sweeps	$W_{\times 10^9}$	t_{col}	t_1	t_8	S	m_1	m_8
Orkut	Async Deg ↓	1	4.4/28.6	0.46/1.37	$0s$	$24.4s$	$37.2s$	0.65	~ 0	0.07
Orkut	RG Deg ↓	40.6	25.8	1.00	$8.65s$	$174.4s$	$35.5s$	4.90	0.53	0.55
Pokec	Async Deg ↓	1	15.4/16.3	0.15/0.13	$0s$	$7.87s$	$3.48s$	2.25	0.0003	0.01
Pokec	RG Deg ↓	39	52.25	0.45	$1.33s$	$33.8s$	$7.55s$	4.47	0.17	0.30
UK 2002	Async Deg ↓	1	30.2/30.2	1.15/1.41	$0s$	$51.4s$	$41.5s$	1.23	0.97	0.95
UK 2002	RG Deg ↓	944	30	1.23	$4.5s$	$120.7s$	$29.7s$	4.06	0.96	0.96

through the vertices; the semi-synchronous methods have more synchronisation points by a factor of the number of colours. Hence the number of colours and the number of sweeps through the vertices give an indication of the amount of overhead. Semi-synchronous methods also have the overhead of computing the colouring.

7.1 LP Algorithm

We summarise results obtained for 1 and 8 threads on the two social network graphs and on the UK 2002 network in Tables 2 and 3, contrasting the decreasing degree ordering with increasing degree ordering. In the case of the asynchronous method, the two values given for # sweeps and W correspond to the averages obtained on 1 and 8 threads; t_1, t_8 are the total run-times; t_{col} is the time taken to colour the graph; S is the speedup on 8 threads with respect to the same algorithm run on a single thread; m_1, m_8 are the modularity values obtained on the corresponding number of threads.

Note the larger speed-up obtained for the semi-synchronous algorithms, compared with the asynchronous approach. Except for the Pokec network, the run-time obtained on 8 processors is smaller with semi-synchronous method, despite the greater number of synchronisation points and colouring overhead. Moreover, the RG coloured ordering avoids the giant community local minimum that LP falls into when run in a strictly decreasing degree ordering on the social network graphs. As pointed out in Section 5.1, the results on the social network graphs are highly volatile. On the other hand, the UK 2002 graph shows much more stability, with modularity values generally robust to the ordering of the algorithm. When increasing degree order is used, generally there is significantly more work done in order for LP to converge, which leads to large run-times. Colouring in increasing degree order tends to result in more colours and hence more synchronisation points for the semi- synchronous algorithm. Furthermore, the work is much more balanced by the dynamic scheduler in the asynchronous method, resulting in an increase in speed-up. The overhead of the semi-synchronous method now means that it lags behind the asynchronous method in run-time.

7.2 MM Algorithm

In terms of work-load and scalability, we can reach many of the same conclusions with the MM algorithm as are reached with the LP algorithm. The convergence criterion is important in this case. Generally, if the MM algorithm was allowed to complete to full convergence (i.e. until no more vertex updates occur in a sweep of the algorithm), then all orderings would reach similar modularity scores, but the decreasing degree ordering does so much more quickly. For instance, on the Orkut network, decreasing degree ordering reaches a modularity score of 0.66 with a work-load of 2.11×10^9 ($160s$ on a single thread) while increasing degree ordering reaches a slightly smaller modularity of 0.63, but with a work-load of 3.37×10^9 ($282s$). On the other hand, if we apply a stopping condition based on Δm, then decreasing degree ordering still succeeds in reaching the high modularity score, while the other orderings exit with comparably lower modularity scores (see Figure 8). If synchronisation is applied after each colour update to keep Δm exact, then semi-synchronous cannot compete with asynchronous in terms of run-time. However, with synchronisation applied only at the end of a full vertex sweep, we can see the advantage of a coloured ordered ordering. The run-time of the asynchronous and RG decreasing degree strategies is shown in Figure 7. Again, asynchronous decreasing degree ordering fails to achieve speed-up on multiple threads due to the load imbalance and varying work-loads that it incurs when running on multiple threads. The peak at 8 threads, is due to the fact that, on our architecture, race conditions lead to the method requiring more than twice as much work as on a single thread. In contrast, the semi-synchronous strategy maintains a relatively consistent work-load, which is larger than that of pure decreasing degree ordering on a single thread, but yields better performance after 4 threads.

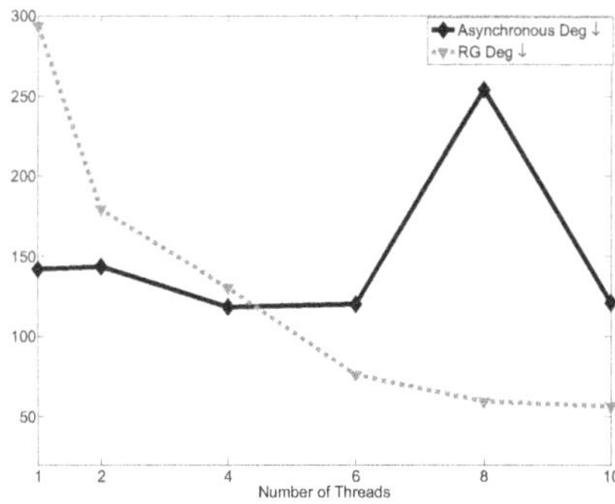

Figure 7: Asynchronous Runtime v RG Runtime on the Orkut Network

7.3 Blocked Colouring

We explore the effect of blocking with two of the networks, Orkut and UK 2002. Following a decreasing degree order, we merge neighbouring vertices in a breadth-first manner to form blocks. Using the RG colouring strategy in decreasing degree order, we run a single thread LP algorithm on the Orkut and UK 2002 graphs for block sizes in the range 1 to 128. The results are shown in Figure 9. Grouping just two vertices together results in more thaw a halving of the run-time after which further increases in block-size give just

Table 3: LP on 1 and 8 Processors : RG and Asynchronous with Increasing Degree Ordering.

Network	Method	# Cols	# Sweeps	$W_{\times 10^9}$	t_{col}	t_1	t_8	S	m_1	m_8
Orkut	Async Deg ↑	1	32.4/57.6	1.60/1.76	$0s$	$88.4s$	$23.1s$	3.81	0.51	0.54
Orkut	RG Deg ↑	304.6	56	2.8	$7.4s$	$195.0s$	$41.0s$	4.75	0.52	0.52
Pokec	Async Deg ↑	1	76/80	0.5/0.58	$0s$	$33.18s$	$5.94s$	5.58	0.24	0.39
Pokec	RG Deg ↑	90.75	86	0.57	$1.14s$	$48.5s$	$8.5s$	5.71	0.48	0.55
UK 2002	Async Deg ↑	1	40/38	1.54/1.551	$0s$	$70.8s$	$20.0s$	3.54	0.92	0.95
UK 2002	RG Deg ↑	944	44.4	1.57	$6.1s$	$145.5s$	$40.89s$	4.19	0.92	0.92

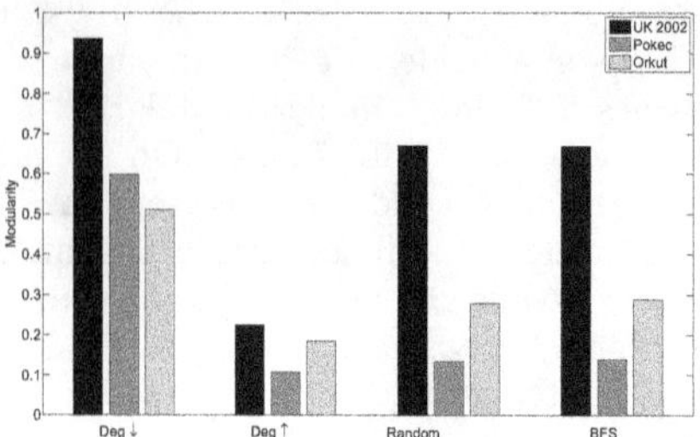

Figure 8: Modularities Achieved with RG colouring and different orderings.

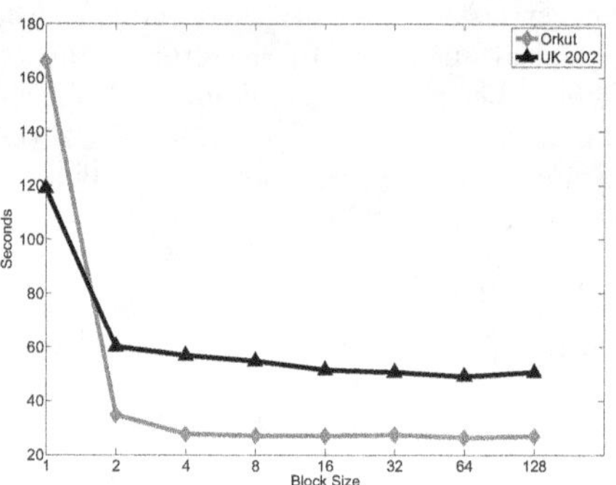

Figure 9: Comparison of Runtime of LP against Block Size, Single Thread, RG with Deg ↓ ordering

small gains in run-time. Based on these results, we choose a block size of 4 for the Orkut network and 16 for the UK 2002 network and run the algorithm on multiple threads, in Figure 10. The strong interconnectedness of vertices at the core of social networks, means that blocking tends to group high-degree nodes together which are very highly connected within the rest of the core. This results in a blocked graph that is more dense than the original graph. As a result, more colours are required to colour the graph. On Orkut, while on average 117 colours are required for the original graph, 545 are required when vertices are merged into blocks of size 4. On the other hand, UK 2002 web graph has a more hierarchical structure which blocking helps to reveal, resulting in a blocked graph which can be coloured with 92 colours on average with blocks of size 16, compared with the 944 required on the original graph. The resulting fewer synchronisation points, along with the fact that labels can immediately mix between connected vertices within blocks gives the blocked strategy an advantage over the non-blocked method. On the other hand, scalability is hampered by the larger work units, which can lead to more imbalance. While both networks maintain their performance improvement over a block size of 1, the UK 2002 network maintains a better speed-up (3.05 on 8 processors) compared with Orkut (only 1.71 on 8 processors).

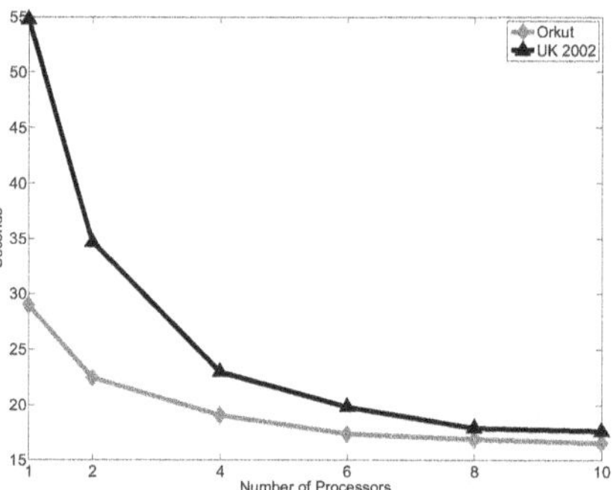

Figure 10: Comparison of Runtime of LP against # Threads, RG with Deg ↓ ordering, Block Size=4 (Orkut), =16(UK 2002)

8. CONCLUSION

In the past, the parallel and distributed ILU implementations did not consider using a semi-synchronous approach, as it was considered to be too slow to be practically viable. In this paper, we have shown that on shared-memory platforms, this algorithm can be engineered to be as fast (and sometimes even faster than) the asynchronous approach, without the race conditions and the related cache-coherency issues associated with the latter. A major advantage of our engineered approach is that it gives the control of node update ordering back to the algorithm developer. The number of iterations and the quality of the resulting clusters produced by our approach is invariant to architecture and systems layer issues.

We find that node ordering and graph colouring techniques have a significant impact on the running time of the semi-synchronous approach and the quality of the resulting communities. Thus, to achieve good performance, a user needs to carefully select the node ordering and graph colouring technique based on the structure of the graph being considered (if known in advance) and the overall application objective.

For the node ordering, our results show that decreasing node ordering results in fast label mixing but it often results in one giant community yielding low modularity values. On the other hand, increasing degree node ordering produces a large variation in results, requiring multiple runs of the algorithm in order to maximise the modularity value. For social network graphs, the BFS with increasing degree node ordering seems to be the best choice, as it reduces the variation both in modularity and workload.

The modularity of the communities identified by the MM algorithm is more robust to node ordering than the LP algorithm. However, similar to LP, the workload for MM algorithm varies a lot with the node update ordering. Thus, a decreasing degree ordering is preferable for the MM algorithm, to speed the convergence.

Using the right colouring strategy one can preserve the preferred node ordering while the LP algorithm is run in parallel on a number of threads. That is the semi-synchronous LP is completely deterministic and therefore it returns the control over the node ordering back to the developer. Our findings suggest that even simple and highly parallelisable colouring strategies can achieve the desired node ordering. For instance the SG colouring with BFS node ordering strategy results in similar modularity and workload values as pure BFS node ordering.

Our blocked colouring strategy can speed the asynchronous LP considerably if used on networks with hierarchical structure.

Our engineering of the semi-synchronous approach is based on a careful selection of node ordering and graph colouring strategy in order to maximise the run time performance and the quality of the resulting communities.

Most scalable graph processing systems proposed in recent years (e.g., Pregel [11], GraphLab [10], GraphChi [8]), are based on a vertex-centric model of computation. In this model, each node and edge is associated with some labels and the computation consists of iteratively updating these labels. ILU is a natural framework for community detection in this computation model. The insights learnt from our work can be particularly useful in engineering ILU for these systems. In fact, our results can be more generally useful for designing and engineering many other algorithms in the vertex-centric computation model, where the mixing rate of labels is an important concern.

Acknowledgements

The Insight Centre for Data Analytics is supported by Science Foundation Ireland under Grant Number SFI/12/RC/2289.

9. REFERENCES

[1] Blondel, V.D., Guillaume, J.L., Lambiotte, R., Lefebvre, E.: Fast unfolding of communities in large networks. Journal of Statistical Mechanics: Theory and Experiment 2008(10), P10008 (2008), `http://stacks.iop.org/1742-5468/2008/i=10/a=P10008`

[2] Çatalyürek, Ü.V., Feo, J., Gebremedhin, A.H., Halappanavar, M., Pothen, A.: Graph coloring algorithms for multi-core and massively multithreaded architectures. Parallel Computing (2012)

[3] Cordasco, G., Gargano, L.: Label propagation algorithm: a semi-synchronous approach. International Journal of Social Network Mining (IJSNM) 1(1), 3–26 (2012)

[4] Fortunato, S.: Community detection in graphs. CoRR abs/0906.0612 (2009)

[5] Gonzalez, J.E., Low, Y., Gu, H., Bickson, D., Guestrin, C.: Powergraph: Distributed graph-parallel computation on natural graphs. In: Proceedings of the 10th USENIX Symposium on Operating Systems Design and Implementation (OSDI) (2012)

[6] Hasenplaugh, W., Kaler, T., Schardl, T.B., Leiserson, C.E.: Ordering heuristics for parallel graph coloring. In: Proceedings of the 26th ACM symposium on Parallelism in algorithms and architectures. pp. 166–177. ACM (2014)

[7] Kaler, T., Hasenplaugh, W., Schardl, T.B., Leiserson, C.E.: Executing dynamic data-graph computations deterministically using chromatic scheduling. In: Proceedings of the 26th ACM symposium on Parallelism in algorithms and architectures. pp. 154–165. ACM (2014)

[8] Kyrola, A., Blelloch, G., Guestrin, C.: Graphchi: Large-scale graph computation on just a pc. In: Proceedings of the 10th USENIX Conference on Operating Systems Design and Implementation (OSDI'12). pp. 31–46. USENIX Association (2012)

[9] Liu, X., Murata, T.: How does label propagation algorithm work in bipartite networks? In: Proceedings of the 2009 IEEE/WIC/ACM International Joint Conference on Web Intelligence and Intelligent Agent Technology. pp. 5 – 8. IEEE (2009)

[10] Low, Y., Gonzalez, J., Kyrola, A., Bickson, D., Guestrin, C., Hellerstein, J.M.: Graphlab: A new framework for parallel machine learning. In: Proceedings of the Twenty-Sixth Conference on Uncertainty in Artificial Intelligence (UAI). pp. 340–349 (2010)

[11] Malewicz, G., Austern, M.H., Bik, A.J., Dehnert, J.C., Horn, I., Leiser, N., Czajkowski, G.: Pregel: A system for large-scale graph processing. In: Proceedings of the 2010 ACM SIGMOD International Conference on Management of Data (SIGMOD'10). pp. 135–146. ACM (2010)

[12] McDaid, A., Hurley, N.: Detecting highly overlapping communities with model-based overlapping seed expansion. In: Advances in Social Networks Analysis and Mining (ASONAM), 2010 International Conference on. pp. 112–119. IEEE (2010)

[13] Newman, M.E.: Modularity and community structure in networks. Proc Natl Acad Sci U S A 103(23), 8577–8582 (2006)

[14] Ovelgönne, M., Geyer-Schulz, A.: An ensemble learning strategy for graph clustering. In: Graph Partitioning and Graph Clustering. Contemporary Mathematics, vol. 588, pp. 187–206. American Mathematical Society (2012)

[15] Raghavan, U.N., Albert, R., Kumara, S.: Near linear time algorithm to detect community structures in large-scale networks. Physical Review E 76(036106), 1 – 12 (2007)

[16] Rosvall, M., Bergstrom, C.T.: Maps of random walks on complex networks reveal community structure. Proceedings of the National Academy of Sciences 105(4), 1118–1123 (2008)

[17] Staudt, C., Meyerhenke, H.: Engineering high-performance community detection heuristics for massive graphs. In: Proceedings of the 42nd International Conference on Parallel Processing (ICPP). pp. 180–189. IEEE (2013)

[18] Ugander, J., Backstrom, L.: Balanced label propagation for partitioning massive graphs. In: Proceedings of the Sixth ACM International Conference on Web Search and Data Mining (WSDM). pp. 507–516. ACM (2013)

WTF, GPU! Computing Twitter's Who-To-Follow on the GPU

Afton Geil, Yangzihao Wang, and John D. Owens
University of California, Davis

ABSTRACT

In this paper, we investigate the potential of GPUs for performing link structure analysis of social graphs. Specifically, we implement Twitter's WTF ("Who to Follow") recommendation system on a single GPU. Our implementation shows promising results on moderate-sized social graphs. It can return the top-K relevant users for a single user in 172 ms when running on a subset of the 2009 Twitter follow graph with 16 million users and 85 million social relations. For our largest dataset, which contains 75% of the users (30 million) and 50% of the social relations (680 million) of the complete follow graph, this calculation takes 1.0 s. We also propose possible solutions to apply our system to follow graphs of larger sizes that do not fit into the on-board memory of a single GPU.

Categories and Subject Descriptors

H.4 [**Information Systems**]: World Wide Web—*social networks*; E.1 [**Data**]: Data Structures—*graphs and networks*; D.1.3 [**Software**]: Programming Techniques: Concurrent Programming—*parallel programming*.

Keywords

Online Social Networks; GPU Computing; Recommendation Systems; Graph Processing; Twitter

1. INTRODUCTION

Many web service providers use recommendation systems to sell products or to increase the value of their service. Shopping services like Amazon suggest products users may be interested in buying, news sites recommend articles based on a user's reading history, and streaming services like Netflix recommend movies and television shows to watch. Social networking services recommend people that the current user may want to connect with. In a social network, where the content is entirely user-generated, a good recommendation system is key in retaining and engaging users.

COSN'14, October 1–2, 2014, Dublin, Ireland.

ACM 978-1-4503-3198-2/14/10 ...$15.00.
http://dx.doi.org/10.1145/2660460.2660481.

Twitter is a social media service that allows users to broadcast short, 140-character *tweets* to all users who choose to *follow* them. Twitter's success depends on acquiring and maintaining an active user base. A user's satisfaction with the service depends almost entirely on the content generated by the other users in their social network. They need to subscribe to the tweets of users they are interested in reading updates from. Finding users to follow can be difficult, especially for new users, so Twitter provides them with recommendations of accounts they may be interested in subscribing to. This service is called "Who to Follow", or WTF. Twitter calculates these recommendations by analyzing the link structure of the follow graph [4]. Recommendations should be provided and updated in real time to keep up with changes in the follower graph. For a graph with hundreds of millions of nodes and billions of edges, this is no small problem. Graphics processing units (GPUs) have a highly parallel architecture that is potentially well-suited for this kind of large-scale graph analysis.

GPUs are throughput-oriented, highly parallel architectures that have proven to be very efficient for solving many large-scale problems with plenty of available parallelism. The modern GPU has become the most cost-effective way to perform massive amounts of computation. A single GPU can often outperform a cluster of CPUs; however, they have not yet been able to gain a foothold in data centers. This is due to various issues, such as programmability, limited memory size, and communication costs. GPUs have a very different architecture from CPUs. This makes GPUs efficient at solving large problems, but also creates unique programming challenges.

Solving graph problems on a GPU is particularly difficult because although these problems usually have a large amount of parallelism, that parallelism is irregular: in social graphs, nodes typically have widely varying connectivity and thus wildly varying work per node. As well, graph algorithms usually involve traversing the graph, including paths that split and join along the way; this complicates the control flow, because paths could intersect at any time. Nonetheless, some work has been done on implementing PageRank, a popular graph analysis algorithm, on GPUs [12, 14]; however, this work does not confront the irregular challenges of graph traversal because they use the linear algebra formulation of the PageRank algorithm. GPUs can work well on native graph representations: Merrill et al. used GPUs to achieve $4x$ speedups over multicore CPUs with breadth-first search [9]. Our work leverages some of Merrill et al.'s traversal strategies, but maps a more complex graph algorithm to GPUs. Very

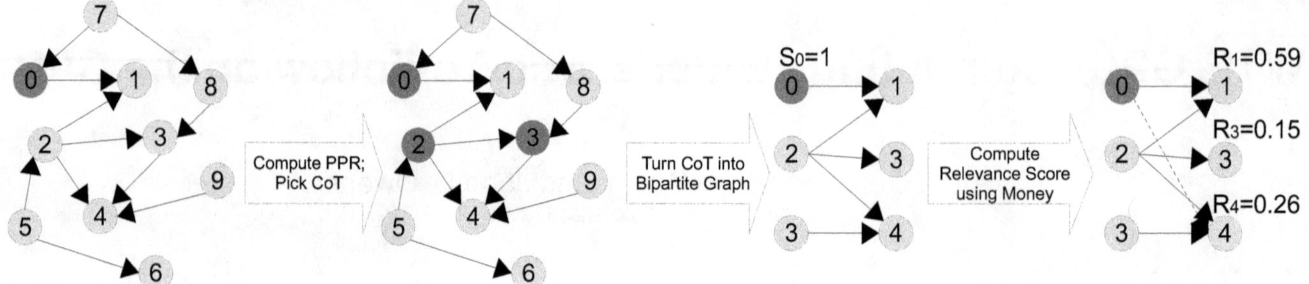

Figure 1: Overview of Twitter's WTF algorithm. ***Frame 1:*** **The initial graph (red [dark] node is the user for whom recommendations are being computed).** ***Frame 2:*** **The Circle of Trust (nodes in pink [dark]) is found using Personalized PageRank.** ***Frame 3:*** **The graph is pruned to include only the CoT and the users they follow.** ***Frame 4:*** **The relevance scores of all users on the right side are computed with Twitter's Money algorithm. Node 4 will be suggested for Node 0 to follow because it has the highest value of all nodes the user is not already following.**

little work has been done using GPUs for recommendation systems. Srinivasa et al. implemented the friends-of-friends algorithm on a GPU [13]. Friends-of-friends is a basic recommendation algorithm that takes a user and nodes adjacent to the user and returns the set of second level nodes that are adjacent to these nodes. Srinivasa et al. only tested their algorithm on small graphs (fewer than 40,000 nodes), but they did achieve a speedup of about $2x$ over a basic CPU implementation.

2. TWITTER'S WTF ALGORITHM

Two main stages comprise the WTF recommender. In the first stage, Twitter calculates a Personalized PageRank (PPR) for the user. PPR assigns a ranking to all nodes in the network based on how closely connected they are to the main node (the user interested in recommendations). This ranking is used to find the top 1000 ranking nodes. These nodes form the user's "Circle of Trust" (CoT), which consists of the 1000 nodes closest to the user. Pruning the graph in this way increases the personalization of the recommendation and reduces spam. Next, they create a bipartite graph with the CoT on one side, and the users followed by the CoT on the other. All other nodes are pruned from the graph. The final step is Twitter's "Money" algorithm, a graph analysis algorithm that determines which accounts the user is most likely to be interested in following. Figure 1 shows a schematic of the entire WTF algorithm.

2.1 Personalized PageRank

PageRank is an algorithm for ranking nodes in a graph based on the structure of the graph [11]. It was originally used on the web graph to rank webpages for search engines. The PageRank of a node can be thought of as the probability that a random walker traversing the graph along the edges will land on that node. It is a measure of how well-connected the node is, and therefore, how important it is to the graph. A Personalized PageRank (PPR) calculation relative to node A is identical to the normal PageRank calculation, except all random walks begin at node A, rather than a random node. Overall, a Personalized PageRank calculation for A shows which nodes are most closely related to A.

PageRank can be calculated using Monte Carlo methods or power iteration. A Monte Carlo method for Personalized PageRank would be to actually perform many random walks on the graph and maintain a count of the number of times each node is visited, then use these counts to estimate the stationary distribution. Power iteration methods formulate the problem as a system of linear equations and use linear algebra techniques to solve for the ranking values. Twitter chose a Monte Carlo method for their PPR, while we chose a power iteration method for our implementation. We discuss the reasoning for this decision in Section 6.

2.2 Money

Twitter's Money algorithm [3] is similar to a combination of Kleinberg's HITS algorithm [5] and Lempel and Moran's SALSA [7]. First, the graph is transformed into a bipartite graph, with the CoT on the left side, and the users the CoT follows on the right side, as shown in the second and third stages of Figure 1. If a user is both in the CoT and followed by someone in the CoT, this node will appear on both sides of the bipartite graph. The CoT nodes are assigned a *similarity* value, and the users they follow are assigned a *relevance* value. Initially, the user we are trying to get recommendations for, C, has their similarity score set to 1, and all others have their similarity or relevance scores set to 0. The Money algorithm distributes each CoT member's similarity score to the relevance scores of all the users they follow. The followers then distribute their relevance scores back across the graph to all of their followers. As in PPR, the Money algorithm can also be written as a system of linear equations. From the solution of this system of equations, Twitter finds the nodes with the highest relevance scores. These are the accounts they recommend to the user in the Who to Follow feature. The similarity scores are used for other features, such as the "similar to you" feature and targeted advertising.

3. PARALLELIZING GRAPH ALGORITHMS ON THE GPU

Both PPR and Money are link prediction algorithms that traverse the graph and assign rank values for a subset of nodes. Like many other graph algorithms, they can be viewed as iterative convergent processes. There is a data dependency between iterative steps, but within each step, a large number of independent edge-centric or vertex-centric operations can be parallelized. However, to fully exploit the compute capabilities of GPUs, we need special strategies to handle irregular memory access and work distribution.

For compact and efficient memory access, we use the compressed sparse row (CSR) format to represent the follow graph on the GPU. It uses a column-indices array, C, to store a list of neighbor vertices and a row-offsets array, R, to store the offset of the neighbor list for each vertex. This representation enables us to use parallel primitives such as prefix sum to reorganize sparse and uneven workloads into dense and uniform ones in all phases of graph processing.

3.1 Graph Primitives

To solve the issue of irregular work distribution, we design two graph primitives: *graph traversal* and *filtering*. Graph traversal starts with a queue of vertices we call the *frontier*. Traversal then takes several iterations to advance toward other vertices by visiting the neighbor list of all vertices in the current frontier in parallel and adding the neighbor vertices to the new frontier. Filtering starts with a frontier that contains either edges or vertices, does a user-defined validation test for every item in the frontier in parallel, then generates a new frontier containing only the items that have passed the validation test.

In PPR, graph traversal and filtering alternate until all the rank values converge and there are no vertices in the frontier for the graph traversal primitive. In Money, we use the graph traversal primitive to bounce back and forth between two disjoint sets in a bipartite graph: the CoT and the union of all CoT vertices' neighbor lists. Since in graph traversal primitives, the neighbor lists can vary greatly in size, traversing these neighbor lists in parallel efficiently and in a load-balanced way is critical for the performance of our system. Merrill et al. [9] uses specialized strategies according to neighbor list size in the context of a parallel breadth-first search (BFS) algorithm. The algorithm efficiently reduces the amount of overhead within each kernel and better utilizes the GPU. Our implementation extends this strategy with two important improvements. First, we add inline device functions to perform user-specific computations and to reuse graph traversal primitives for both PPR and Money by just replacing the function we load when visiting edges and vertices. Second, BFS's operations on vertices are idempotent, but ours are not, so we guarantee the correctness of both algorithms by adding atomics to resolve race conditions between edges converging on a vertex.

3.2 Application to Other Graph Algorithms

The graph traversal primitive distributes the parallel workload per edge or per node in a graph to tens of thousands of threads on the GPU to process in parallel, and the filtering primitive reorganizes the elements we want to process in parallel for the next iteration. By reusing these two primitives, we have implemented several graph-traversal-based ranking algorithms such as PageRank, PPR, Money, HITS, and SALSA with minimal programming cost. Several of these algorithms run on bipartite graphs, which are key abstractions in several ranking and link prediction algorithms. As far as we know, we are the first to target bipartite graph algorithms on the GPU.

We implement bipartite graphs in the following way. A directed bipartite graph is similar to a normal undirected graph, except in a directed bipartite graph, we need to consider the outgoing edges and the incoming edges of a vertex separately. We achieve this by reversing the source and destination vertex ID for each edge while constructing the CSR data structure to record the incoming edges and using an additional prefix sum pass to compute the incoming degree for each vertex. In our graph primitives, we also added a feature to switch between visiting the outgoing edges of a vertex and visiting the incoming edges of a vertex. We use this method in our SALSA implementations. In our Money and HITS implementation, we do not need to calculate the in-degree of every node in the graph, but just the ones connected to the CoT. We take advantage of this by finding the incoming degree values for neighbors of the CoT on the fly with an additional pass of the graph traversal primitive. Because of the small size of the CoT, this extra pass takes negligible time but saves us gigabytes of memory for large datasets.

4. WTF IMPLEMENTATION

In our implementation, we start by putting all the graph topology information on the GPU. First, we compute the PPR value for each vertex in the follow graph with a user-defined seed vertex. Then we radix-sort the PPR values and take the vertices with the top k PPR values (in our implementation, $k = 1000$) as the CoT and put them in a frontier. We then run the Money algorithm, sort the vertices that the CoT follows, and finally extract the vertices with the top relevance scores to use for our recommendation.

4.1 Personalized PageRank

Algorithm 1 shows our implementation of PPR using the graph primitives and functors we design. We update PPR using the following equation:

$$PPR(v_i) = \begin{cases} (1-\delta) + \delta \cdot \sum\limits_{v_j \in pred(v_i)} \frac{PPR(v_j)}{d_{\mathrm{OUT}}(v_j)} & v_i \text{ is seed} \\ \delta \cdot \sum\limits_{v_j \in pred(v_i)} \frac{PPR(v_j)}{d_{\mathrm{OUT}}(v_j)} & \text{otherwise} \end{cases}$$

where δ is a constant damping factor (typically set to 0.85), $d_{\mathrm{OUT}}(v_j)$ is the number of outbound edges on vertex v_j, and N is the total number of vertices in the graph.

The PPR algorithm starts by initializing problem data (line 1). It assigns the initial rank value for each vertex as $\frac{1}{N}$, and puts all vertices in the initial frontier. The main loop of the algorithm contains two steps. For each iteration, we first use GraphTraversal to visit all the edges for each vertex in the frontier and distribute each vertex's PPR value to its neighbors (line 7). Then we use Filtering to update the PPR value for the vertices that still have unconverged PPR values. We give the seed vertex an extra value (line 10) as in the equation. Then we remove the vertices whose PPR values have converged from the frontier (line 12). The algorithm ends when all the PPR values converge and the frontier is empty.

4.2 Twitter's Money Algorithm

Algorithm 2 shows our implementation of Twitter's Money algorithm. We treat people in the CoT and people they follow as two disjoint sets X and Y in the bipartite graph $G = (X \cup Y, E)$ they form. For each node in X (the CoT), the Money algorithm computes its similarity score; for each node in Y, the Money algorithm computes its relevance score.

Algorithm 1 Personalized PageRank

```
procedure SET_PROBLEM_DATA(G, P, seed, delta)
    P.ranks_curr[1..G.verts] ← 1/N
    P.src ← seed, P.delta ← delta
    P.frontier.Insert(G.nodes)
end procedure
procedure DISTRIBUTEPPRVALUE(s_id, d_id, P)
    atomicAdd(P.rank_next[d_id], P.rank_curr[s_id] / P.out_degree[s_id])
end procedure
procedure UPDATEPPRVALUE(node_id, P)
    P.rank_next[node_id] ← (P.delta · P.rank_next[node_id]) + (P.src == node_id)?(1.0 − P.delta) : 0
    diff ← fabs(P.rank_next[node_id] − P.rank_curr[node_id])
    return diff > P.threshold
end procedure
procedure COMPUTE_PPR(G, P, seed, delta, max_iter)
    SET_PROBLEM_DATA(G, P, seed, delta)
    while P.frontier.Size() > 0 do
        GRAPHTRAVERSAL(G, P, DistributePPRValue)
        FILTERING(G, P, UpdatePPRValue)
        swap(P.rank_next, P.rank_curr)
    end while
end procedure
```

Algorithm 2 Twitter's Money Algorithm

```
1: procedure SET_PROBLEM_DATA(G, P, seed, alpha)
2:     P.relevance_curr[1..G.verts] ← 0
3:     P.sim_curr[1..G.verts] ← 0
4:     P.src ← seed, P.alpha ← alpha
5:     P.sim_curr[seed] ← 1
6:     P.frontier.Insert(G.cot_queue)
7: end procedure
8: procedure DISTRIBUTERELEVANCE(s_id, d_id, P)
9:     atomicAdd(P.relevance_next[d_id], P.sim_curr[s_id] / P.out_degree[s_id])
10: end procedure
11: procedure DISTRIBUTESIM(s_id, d_id, P)
12:     val ← (1 − P.alpha) · P.relevance_curr[d_id] / P.in_degree[d_id] + (P.src == s_id)?(P.alpha / P.out_degree[s_id]) : 0
13:     atomicAdd(P.sim_next[d_id], val)
14: end procedure
15: procedure COMPUTE_MONEY(G, P, seed, alpha)
16:     SET_PROBLEM_DATA(G, P, seed, alpha)
17:     for iter++ < 1/alpha do
18:         GRAPHTRAVERSAL(G, P, DistributeRelevance)
19:         swap(P.relevance_next, P.relevance_curr)
20:         GRAPHTRAVERSAL(G, P, DistributeSim)
21:         swap(P.sim_next, P.sim_curr)
22:     end for
23: end procedure
```

We use the following equations in our implementation:

$$sim(x) = \begin{cases} \alpha + (1-\alpha) \cdot \sum_{(x,y) \in E} \frac{relevance(y)}{d_{\mathrm{IN}}(y)} & x \text{ is seed} \\ (1-\alpha) \cdot \sum_{(x,y) \in E} \frac{relevance(y)}{d_{\mathrm{IN}}(y)} & \text{otherwise} \end{cases}$$

$$relevance(y) = \sum_{(x,y) \in E} \frac{sim(x)}{d_{\mathrm{OUT}}(x)}$$

In the Money algorithm, we also initialize problem data first (line 1). We set the similarity score for the seed vertex to 1, and set the similarity and relevance scores for all other vertices to 0. We then put all vertices in the CoT in the initial frontier. The main loop of the algorithm contains two steps of GraphTraversal, for each iteration we use the first GraphTraversal to visit all the edges for each vertex in the CoT and distribute each vertex's similarity score to its neighbors' relevance scores (line 9). After this step, we update the relevance scores so that they may be used in the computation of similarity scores (line 19). The second GraphTraversal will visit all the edges for each vertex in the CoT again, but this time it will distribute the neighbors' relevance scores back to each CoT vertex's similarity score (line 12). Again, we treat the seed vertex differently so that it can get more similarity score during each iteration, which in turn will affect its neighbors' relevance scores and other CoT vertices' similarity scores. After the second GraphTraversal step, we update the similarity scores (line 21). As Twitter does in their Money algorithm [3], we end our main loop after $1/\alpha$ iterations.

5. EXPERIMENT

We ran all experiments in this paper on a Linux workstation with 2 × 2.53 GHz Intel 4-core E5630 Xeon CPUs, 12 GB of main memory, and an NVIDIA K40c GPU with 12 GB on-board memory. The parallel programs were compiled with NVIDIA's nvcc compiler (version 6.0.1) with the -O3 flag. The sequential programs were compiled using gcc 4.6.3 with the -O3 flag. The datasets used in our experiments are shown in Table 1, and Table 2 shows the runtimes of our GPU recommendation system on these datasets. Runtimes are for GPU computation only and do not include CPU-GPU transfer time; we discuss why in Section 6. The wiki-Vote dataset is a real social graph dataset that contains voting data for Wikipedia administrators; all other datasets are follow graphs from Twitter and Google Plus [6,8]. Twitter09 contains the complete Twitter follow graph as of 2009; we extract 75% of its user size and 50% of its social relation edge size to form a partial graph that can fit into the GPU's memory.

Table 1: Experimental Datasets

Dataset	Vertices	Edges
wiki-Vote	7.1k	103.7k
twitter-SNAP	81.3k	2.4M
gplus-SNAP	107.6k	30.5M
twitter09	30.7M	680M

Table 2: Runtimes for Different Graph Sizes

Time (ms)	wiki-Vote	twitter	gplus	twitter09
PPR	0.45	0.84	4.74	832.69
CoT	0.54	1.28	2.11	51.61
Money	2.70	5.16	18.56	158.37
Total	4.37	8.36	26.57	1044.99

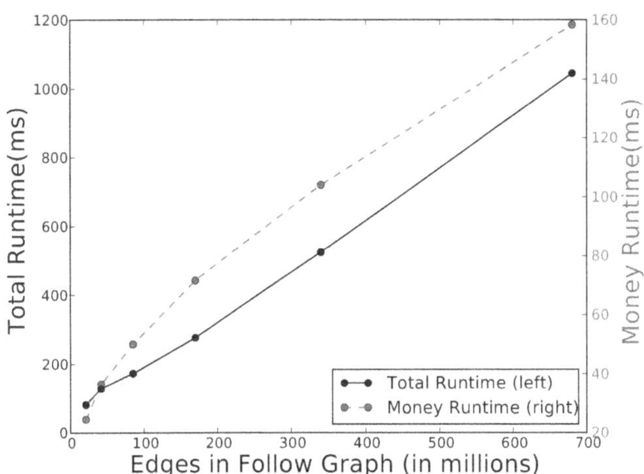

Figure 2: Scalability of runtime versus edge count for our GPU recommendation system.

In order to test the scalability of our WTF-on-GPU recommendation system, we ran WTF on six differently-sized subsets of the twitter09 dataset. The results are shown in Figure 2. We see that the implementation scales sublinearly with increasing graph size. As we double the graph size, the total runtime increases by an average of $1.684x$, and the runtime for Money increases by an average of $1.454x$. The reason lies in our work-efficient parallel implementation. By doing per-vertex computation exactly once and visiting each edge exactly once, our parallel algorithm performs linear $O(m+n)$ work. The reason that we have better scalability for the Money algorithm is that although we are doubling the graph size each time, the CoT size is fixed at 1000. We address scalability beyond a single GPU in Section 6.

6. DISCUSSION

On a graph with more than 175 million nodes and 20 billion edges, the WTF algorithm currently takes around 500 ms in Twitter's data center [10]. In contrast, our implementation can process a graph with 25 million nodes and 340 million edges in a similar amount of time (524 ms), and it takes 1 second to process our largest dataset, which is still significantly smaller than the complete Twitter graph.

The Personalized PageRank calculation takes up the vast majority of the runtime for larger graphs (Table 2). This is because PPR runs on the entire graph, but Money only runs on the pruned CoT graph, which does not grow as quickly. One possible way to reduce the runtime would be to precompute the CoT, and only run Money to update WTF. In this scheme, PPR would only be run periodically, and it could be an offline process. Alternatively, an incremental PPR calculation, as in Bahmani et al. [2], could provide an estimate of the new CoT without needing to iterate through the entire graph. With the precomputed CoT, we would only need to run Twitter's Money algorithm to get the result. According to our sublinear scalability model of Twitter's Money algorithm runtime, we could compute the result in 300 ms on Twitter's circa-2009 follow graph.

We also note that our PPR calculation uses a power iteration method, while Twitter's is a Monte Carlo method. Both methods are quite accurate, but there are a few trade-offs [1]. The power iteration method is deterministic. Every time the algorithm runs on the same set of data, we will get the same results. Monte Carlo methods involve actually performing random walks to compute the probability distribution, so the outcome will not be exactly the same every time. In terms of performance, Monte Carlo methods give a reasonable approximation after only the first iteration, but the error decreases very slowly with more iterations. Power iteration, on the other hand, starts with a much more inaccurate estimation, but the error decreases and converges quicker than for Monte Carlo. We chose power iteration because it is both efficient and easy to implement on a GPU; however, it is possible that a Monte Carlo method would perform better on a GPU. Because Monte Carlo methods involve many independent walks, they are potentially well-suited to the GPU's massively parallel architecture.

One major limitation of our current implementation is the size of GPU memory. Today's GPUs have at most 12 GB of memory, whereas a CPU system can easily have ten times as much memory. This means that the entire current Twitter follow graph cannot fit in GPU memory. The twitter09 dataset is close to the maximum size that can fit on a single GPU. To compute WTF on the full graph, we would need to partition the graph and/or distribute it across multiple nodes. Scaling any large-scale parallel data analysis system, especially online social network system, beyond a single GPU remains a major challenge today. The unstructured and highly irregular connectivity of power-law graphs like social graphs makes it difficult to design partitioning and synchronization strategies for such graphs.

Another limitation is the bandwidth of the connection between main memory and GPU memory. Results in Section 5 do not include the data transfer time from CPU memory to the GPU. For our largest graph, the transfer time is 852.24 ms—about 85% of the compute time. In our experiments, we assume that graph data will be resident on the GPU, because it will be used to run a variety of algorithms on the follow graph, so transfer time will not be significant overall; however, for a different use case or very frequent updates to the graph, data transfer time could seriously limit performance.

Fortunately, future GPU systems have potential solutions for the modest size of today's GPU memories. The next node on NVIDIA's GPU roadmap is "Pascal" (2016), which can be connected to the CPU via a high-speed "NVLink" connection that allows access to the CPU's main memory at CPU-main-memory speeds (as well as supporting unified virtual memory across CPU and GPU). While such systems will still require careful memory management, they eliminate the current performance disadvantage in the case data fits in CPU memory but not GPU memory.

7. CONCLUSIONS AND FUTURE WORK

In this work, we have shown that it is possible to use a GPU for recommendation algorithms on social graphs, but there are still many ways in which the performance could be improved. Software platforms for large-scale online social network analysis on hybrid CPU-GPU architectures could potentially offer better throughput and performance on systems that are more cost-effective than today's CPU-based cluster architectures. However, moving workloads to GPUs is challenging for the following reasons:

- Designing parallel algorithms for such systems is both difficult and time consuming.
- Today, limited PCIe bandwidth is a constraint for using discrete GPUs for communication-bounded tasks.
- The limited memory size on current GPUs makes it difficult to run algorithms on datasets that cannot fit in the GPU memory.

With the appearance of more graph processing libraries on the GPU, the design and implementation of online social network analysis software on the GPU is becoming easier and more efficient. Today, most online social network analysis algorithms are still compute-bound when running on large datasets. This makes a multi-CPU/multi-GPU architecture running across multiple nodes a promising solution.

We propose a two-layer framework running on a three-layer memory hierarchy where GPU memory serves as the fast cache, and CPU main memory serves as the second level cache, sitting atop data stored on hard disks/SSDs. In our case of building a recommendation system, the entire follow graph will be stored in CPU memory with disk as backing store. Multiple nodes, each containing one or more GPUs, will store the CoT for each user in the graph. Currently Twitter has 250 million users. If we keep the size of CoT at 1000 and use unsigned integers for vertex IDs, then we will need 2 TB to store CoTs for all users. That can be easily partitioned by user ID to fit on 4 or more machines with 512 GB or less of main memory. In this case, we can run PPR as an offline algorithm that runs only once per day or after a certain number of graph updates. The recommendation system can then work in real time with around 100 ms running time. Because the number of vertices in CoT is a constant 1000, the pruned graph that contains only vertices in CoT and vertices they connect to will be much smaller than the original follow graph. This set-up would reduce both the computational workload and GPU memory requirements.

Acknowledgments

Thanks to Brian Larson and Pankaj Gupta (Twitter) for helpful comments and guidance on this work. We appreciate the financial support of UC Lab Fees Research Program Award 12-LR-238449, the DARPA XDATA program under AFRL Contract FA8750-13-C-0002, by NSF awards CCF-1017399 and OCI-1032859, and by the National Science Foundation Graduate Research Fellowship Program.

8. REFERENCES

[1] K. Avrachenkov, N. Litvak, D. Nemirovsky, and N. Osipova. Monte Carlo methods in PageRank computation: When one iteration is sufficient. *SIAM Journal of Numerical Analysis*, 45(2):890–904, Feb. 2007.

[2] B. Bahmani, A. Chowdhury, and A. Goel. Fast incremental and personalized PageRank. *Proceedings of the VLDB Endowment*, 4(3):173–184, Dec. 2010.

[3] A. Goel. The "who-to-follow" system at Twitter: Algorithms, impact, and further research. WWW 2014 industry track, 2014.

[4] P. Gupta, A. Goel, J. Lin, A. Sharma, D. Wang, and R. Zadeh. WTF: The who to follow service at Twitter. In *Proceedings of the International Conference on the World Wide Web*, pages 505–514, May 2013.

[5] J. M. Kleinberg. Authoritative sources in a hyperlinked environment. *Journal of the ACM*, 46(5):604–632, Sept. 1999.

[6] H. Kwak, C. Lee, H. Park, and S. Moon. What is Twitter, a social network or a news media? In *Proceedings of the International Conference on the World Wide Web*, pages 591–600, Apr. 2010.

[7] R. Lempel and S. Moran. SALSA: The stochastic approach for link-structure analysis. *ACM Transactions on Information Systems*, 19(2):131–160, Apr. 2001.

[8] J. Leskovec. SNAP: Stanford large network dataset collection. `http://snap.stanford.edu/data/`. Accessed: 2014-05-18.

[9] D. Merrill, M. Garland, and A. Grimshaw. Scalable GPU graph traversal. In *Proceedings of the 17th ACM SIGPLAN Symposium on Principles and Practice of Parallel Programming*, PPoPP '12, pages 117–128, Feb. 2012.

[10] S. A. Myers, A. Sharma, P. Gupta, and J. Lin. Information network or social network?: The structure of the Twitter follow graph. In *Proceedings of the Companion Publication of the International Conference on the World Wide Web*, WWW Companion '14, pages 493–498, Apr. 2014.

[11] L. Page, S. Brin, R. Motwani, and T. Winograd. The PageRank citation ranking: Bringing order to the web. Technical Report 1999-66, Stanford InfoLab, Nov. 1999.

[12] A. Rungsawang and B. Manaskasemsak. Fast PageRank computation on a GPU cluster. In *Proceedings of the 2012 20th Euromicro International Conference on Parallel, Distributed and Network-Based Processing (PDP)*, pages 450–456, Feb. 2012.

[13] K. G. Srinivasa, K. Mishra, C. S. Prajeeth, and A. M. Talha. GPU implementation of friend recommendation system using CUDA for social networking services. In *Proceedings of the International Conference on Emerging Research in Computing, Information, Communication, and Applications*, pages 890–895, Aug. 2013.

[14] T. Wu, B. Wang, Y. Shan, F. Yan, Y.Wang, and N. Xu. Efficient PageRank and SpMV computation on AMD GPUs. In *Proceedings of the 39th International Conference on Parallel Processing*, pages 81–89, Sept. 2010.

Fighting Authorship Linkability with Crowdsourcing

Mishari Almishari
College of Computer and Information Sciences
King Saud University
mialmishari@ksu.edu.sa

Ekin Oguz
Computer Science Department
University of California, Irvine
eoguz@uci.edu

Gene Tsudik
Computer Science Department
University of California, Irvine
gts@ics.uci.edu

ABSTRACT

Massive amounts of contributed content – including traditional literature, blogs, music, videos, reviews and tweets – are available on the Internet today, with authors numbering in many millions. Textual information, such as product or service reviews, is an important and increasingly popular type of content that is being used as a foundation of many trendy community-based reviewing sites, such as TripAdvisor and Yelp. Some recent results have shown that, due partly to their specialized/topical nature, sets of reviews authored by the same person are readily linkable based on simple stylometric features. In practice, this means that individuals who author more than a few reviews under different accounts (whether within one site or across multiple sites) can be linked, which represents a significant loss of privacy.

In this paper, we start by showing that the problem is actually worse than previously believed. We then explore ways to mitigate authorship linkability in community-based reviewing. We first attempt to harness the global power of crowdsourcing by engaging random strangers into the process of re-writing reviews. As our empirical results (obtained from Amazon Mechanical Turk) clearly demonstrate, crowdsourcing yields impressively sensible reviews that reflect sufficiently different stylometric characteristics such that prior stylometric linkability techniques become largely ineffective. We also consider using machine translation to automatically re-write reviews. Contrary to what was previously believed, our results show that translation decreases authorship linkability as the number of intermediate languages grows. Finally, we explore the combination of crowdsourcing and machine translation and report on results.

Categories and Subject Descriptors

K.4.1 [**Computers and Society**]: Public Policy Issues—*Privacy*

COSN'14, October 1–2, 2014, Dublin, Ireland.

ACM 978-1-4503-3198-2/14/10 ...$15.00.
http://dx.doi.org/10.1145/2660460.2660486.

Keywords

authorship attribution; author linkability; author identification; author anonymization; crowdsourcing; stylometry

1. INTRODUCTION

The Internet has become a tremendous world-wide bazaar where massive amounts of information (much of it of dubious quality and value) are being disseminated and consumed on a constant basis. Sharing of multimedia content is one of the major contributors to Internet's growth and popularity. Another prominent source of shared information is textual, e.g., blogs, tweets and various discussion fora. Among those, community reviewing has carved out an important niche. This category includes well-known sites, such as: Yelp, CitySearch, UrbanSpoon, Google Places and TripAdvisor. There are also many others that include customer-based reviewing as a side-bar, e.g., Amazon or Ebay.

Regardless of their primary mission and subject coverage, community reviewing sites are popular, since many are free and contain lots of useful content voluntarily contributed by multitudes of regular people who document their experience with products, services, destinations, and attractions. Larger sites, e.g., TripAdvisor and Yelp, have tens of millions of users (readers) and millions of contributors [9].

Certain features distinguish community reviewing sites from other contributory Internet services:

- Discussion Fora: these vary from product or topic discussions to comment sections in on-line news media. They are often short and not very informative (even hostile).
- Body of Knowledge: the best-known and most popular example is Wikipedia – a huge amalgamation of communal knowledge on a very wide range of subjects. However, unlike reviewing sites where each review is atomic and discernable, related contributions to body-of-knowledge sites are usually mashed together, thus (by design) obscuring individual prose.
- Online Social Networks (OSNs): such sites are essentially free-for-all as far as the type and the amount of contributed information. Since most OSNs restrict access to content provided by a user to "friends" (or "colleagues") of that user, opinions and reviews do not propagate to the rest of Internet users.

Some recent work [20] has shown that many contributors to community reviewing sites accumulate a body of authored content that is sufficient for creating their stylometric profiles, based on rather simple features (e.g., digram frequency). A stylometric profile allows probabilistic linkage among reviews generated by the same person. This could be used to link reviews from different accounts (within a site or across sites) operated by the same user. On one hand, tracking authors of spam reviews can be viewed as a useful service. On the other hand, the ease of highly accurate linkage between different accounts is disconcerting and ultimately detrimental to privacy. Consider, for example, a vindictive merchant who, offended by reviews emanating from one account, attempts to link it to other accounts held by the same person, e.g., for the purpose of harrassment. We consider both sides of this debate to be equally valid and do not choose sides. However, we believe that the privacy argument deserves to be considered, which triggers the motivation for this paper:

> *What can be done to mitigate linkability of reviews authored by the same contributor?*

Roadmap:.
Our goal is to develop techniques that mitigate review account linkability. To assess efficacy of proposed techniques, we need accurate review linkage models. To this end, we first improve state-of-art author review linkage methods. We construct a specific technique, that offers 90% accuracy, even for a small number of identified reviews (e.g., 95) and a smaller set (e.g., 5) of anonymous reviews.

Our second direction is the exploration of techniques that decrease authorship linkability. We start by considering crowdsourcing, which entails engaging random strangers in rewriting reviews. As it turns out, our experiments using Amazon MTurk [1] clearly demonstrate that authorship linkability can be significantly inhibited by crowdsourced rewriting. Meanwhile, somewhat surprisingly, crowd-rewritten reviews remain meaningful and generally faithful to the originals. We then focus on machine translation tools and show that, by randomly selecting languages to (and from) which to translate, we can substantially decrease linkability.

Organization:.
The next section summarizes related work. Then, Section 3 overviews some preliminaries, followed by Section 4 which describes the experimental dataset and review selection process for subsequent experiments. Next, Section 5 discusses our linkability study and its outcomes. The centerpiece of the paper is Section 6, which presents crowdsourcing and translation experiments. It is followed by Section 7 where we discuss possible questions associated with the use of crowdsourcing. Finally, summary and future work appear in Section 8.

2. RELATED WORK

Related work generally falls into two categories: Authorship Attribution/Identification and Author Anonymization.

Authorship Attribution:.
There are many studies in the literature. For example, [20] shows that many Yelp's reviewers are linkable using only very simple feature set. While the setting is similar to ours, there are some notable differences. First, we obtain high linkability using very few reviews per author. Second, we only rely on features extracted from review text. A study of blog posts achieves 80% linkability accuracy [22]. Author identification is also studied in the context of academic paper reviews achieving accuracy of 90% [21]. One major difference between these studies and our work is that we use reviews, which are shorter, less formal and less restrictive in choice of words than blogs and academic papers. Abbasi and Chen propose a well-known author attribution technique based on Karhunen-Loeve transforms to extract a large list of Writeprint features (assessed in Section 5) [10]. Lastly, Stamatatos provides a comprehensive overview of authorship attribution studies [26].

Author Anonymization:.
There are several well-known studies in author anonymization [24, 17, 19]. Rao and Rohatgi are among the first to address authorship anonymity by proposing using round-trip machine translation, e.g., English → Spanish → English, to obfuscate authors [24]. Other researchers apply round-trip translation, with a maximum of two intermediate languages and show that it does not provide noticeable anonymizing effect [15, 13]. In contrast, we explore effects (on privacy) of increasing and/or randomizing the number of intermediate languages.

Kacmarcik and Gamon show how to anonymize documents via obfuscating writing style, by proposing adjustment to document features to reduce the effectiveness of authorship attribution tools [17]. The main limitation of this technique is that it is only applicable to authors with a fairly large text corpus, whereas, our approach is applicable to authors with limited number of reviews.

Other practical-counter-measures for authorship recognition techniques such as obfuscation and imitation attacks are explored [14]. However, it is shown that such stylistic deception can be detected with 96.6% accuracy [11].

The most recent relevant work is Anonymouth [19] – a framework that captures the most effective features of documents for linkability and identifies how these feature values should be changed to achieve anonymization. Our main advantage over Anonymouth is usability. Anonymouth requires the author to have two additional sets of documents, on top of the original document to be anonymized: 1) sample documents written by the same author and 2) a corpus of sample documents written by other authors. Whereas, our approach does not require any such sets.

3. BACKGROUND

This section overviews stylometry, stylometric characteristics and statistical techniques used in our study.

Merriam-Webster dictionary defines `Stylometry` as: *the study of the chronology and development of an author's work based especially on the recurrence of particular turns of expression or trends of thought* [7]. We use stylometry in conjunction with the following two tools:

Writeprints feature set: well-known stylometric features used to analyze author's writing style.

Chi-Squared test: a technique that computes the distance between each author's review in order to assess linkability.

3.1 Writeprints

Writeprints is essentially a combination of static and dynamic stylometric features that capture lexical, syntactic, structural, content and idiosyncratic properties of a given body of text [10]. Some features include:

- Average Character Per Word: Total number of characters divided by total number of words.
- Top Letter Trigrams: Frequency of contiguous sequence of 3 characters, e.g. $aaa, aab, aac, ..., zzy, zzz$. There are 17576 ($26^3$) possible permutation of letter trigrams in English.
- Part of Speech (POS) Tag Bigrams: POS tags are the mapping of words to their syntactic behaviour within sentence, e.g. noun or verb. POS tag bigrams denotes 2 consecutive parts of speech tags. We used Stanford POS Maxent Tagger [27] to label each word with one of 45 possible POS tags.
- Function Words: Set of 512 common words, e.g. *again*, *could*, *himself* and etc, used by Koppel et al. in Koppel, 2005.

Writeprints has been used in several stylometric studies [10, 22, 21]. It has been shown to be an effective means for identifying authors because of its capability to capture even smallest nuances in writing.

We use Writeprints implementation from JStylo – a Java library that includes 22 stylometric features [19].

3.2 Chi-Squared Test

Chi-Squared (CS) test is used to measure the distance between two distributions [25]. For any two distributions P and Q, it is defined as:

$$CS_d(P, Q) = \sum_i \frac{(P(i) - Q(i))^2}{P(i) + Q(i)}$$

CS_d is a symmetric measure, i.e., $CS_d(P, Q) = CS_d(Q, P)$. Also, it is always non-negative; a value of zero denotes that P and Q are identical distributions. We employ Chi-Squared test to compute the distance between contributor's anonymous and identified reviews.

4. LINKABILITY STUDY PARAMETERS

This section describes the dataset and the problem setting for subsequent linkability analysis.

4.1 Dataset

We use a large dataset of reviews from Yelp[1] that contains 1,076,850 reviews authored by 1,997 distinct contributors. We selected this particular dataset for two reasons:

1. Large number of authors with widely varying numbers of reviews: average number of reviews per author is 539, with a standard deviation of 354.
2. Relatively small average review size – 149 words – which should make linkability analysis more challenging.

4.2 Problem Setting

Informally, our main goal is to link a given set of anonymous set reviews R to a set of identified reviews, perhaps with a known author.[2] The problem is more challenging when the sets of anonymous and identified reviews are relatively small. The exact problem setting is as follows:

We first select 40 authors at random. Although this is a relatively small number, we pick it in order to make subsequent crowdsourcing experiments feasible, as described in Section 6. Then, we randomly shuffle each author's reviews and select the first N. Next, we split selected reviews into two sets:

- First X reviews form the **Anonymous Record** (AR) set. We experiment with AR sets of varying sizes.
- Subsequent $(N-X)$ reviews form the **Identified Record** (IR) set.

Our problem is then reduced to linking ARs to their corresponding IRs. We set N=100 and vary X from 1 to 5. This makes IRs and ARs quite small compared to an average of 539 reviews per author in the original dataset. As a result, the linking problem becomes very challenging.

Next, we attempt to link ARs to their corresponding IRs. Specifically, for each AR, we rank – in descending order of likelihood – all possible authors, i.e., IRs. Then, the top-ranked IR (author) is the one most similar to the given AR. If the correct author is among top-ranked T IRs, we say that the linking model has a hit; otherwise, it is a miss. For a given value of T, the fraction of hits of all ARs (over the total of 40) is referred as Top-T linkability ratio (LR). The linkability analysis boils down to finding a model that maximizes LR for different T and AR sizes. We consider two integer values of T: 1 denotes a perfect-hit and 4 stands for an almost-hit.

LR	Linkability Ratio
AR	Anonymous Records
IR	Identified Records
CS	Chi-Squared Distance Model
F	A feature
F_T	The set of tokens in feature F
S_F	Set of selected features
WP_i	Writeprint feature i
WP_{all}	Combination of all Writeprints
$CS_d(IR, AR)$	CS distance between IR and AR

Table 1: Notation and abbreviations

5. LINKABILITY ANALYSIS

We first apply a subset of the popular Writeprints feature set[3] to convert each AR and IR into a token set. We then use Chi-Square[4] to compute distances between these token sets.

We now describe experimental methodology in more detail. Notation and abbreviations are reflected in Table 1.

[1]See: www.yelp.com.

[2]Identification of the author might not be the only goal. It might suffice to simply link two disparate bodies of reviews, thus establishing that they were authored by the same person.

[3]We initially experimented with the Basic-9 feature set, which is known to provide useful information for author identification for less than 10 potential authors [13]. However, its performance was really poor, since we have 40 authors in the smallest set.

[4]We tried others tests including: Cosine, Euclidean, Manhattan, and Kullback-Leibler Divergence. However, Chi-Squared Test outperformed them all.

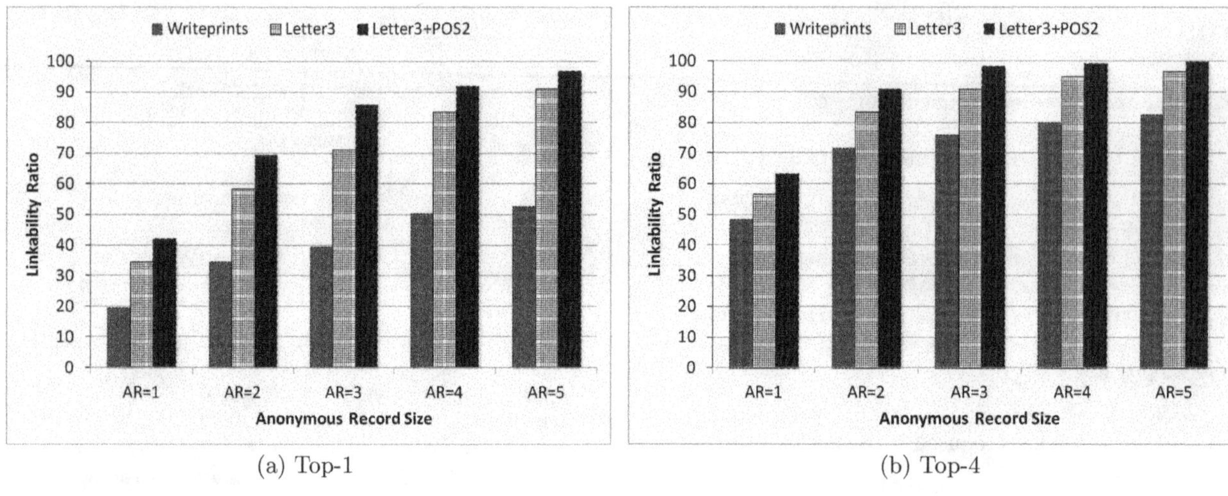

(a) Top-1

(b) Top-4

Figure 1: LRs of Writeprints, Letter3 and Letter3+POS2

5.1 Methodology

First, we tokenize each AR and IR sets using every feature – F – in our set of selected features – S_F – to obtain a set of tokens $F_T = \{F_{T_1}, F_{T_2}, ..., F_{T_n}\}$, where F_{T_i} denotes the i-th token in F_T. Then, we compute distributions for all tokens. Next, we use CS model to compute the distance between AR and IR using respective token distributions. Specifically, to link AR with respect to some feature F, we compute CS_d between the distribution of tokens in F_T for AR and the distribution of tokens in F_T for each IR. Next, we sort the distances in ascending order of $CS_d(IR, AR)$ and return the resulting list. First entry corresponds to the IR with the closest distance to AR, i.e., the most likely match. For the sake of generality, we repeat this experiment 3 times, randomly picking different AR and IR sets each time. Then, we average the results. Note that S_F is initially empty and features are gradually added to it, as described next.

5.2 Feature Selection

We use a general heuristics – a version of greedy hill-climbing algorithm – for feature selection [23]. The main idea is to identify most influential features and gradually combine them in S_F, until encountering a high LR.

5.2.1 WP_{all}

As a benchmark, we start with setting S_F to WP_{all}, which combines all 22 Writeprint features. We compute LR using WP_{all} in CS model with $|AR| = 5$. Unfortunately, WP_{all} results in low LRs – only 52.5% in Top-1 and 82.5% in Top-4. We believe that, because of the small AR set, the combination of many features increases noise, which, in turn, lowers linkability.

5.2.2 Improving WP_{all}

Next, we use each feature from WP_{all} individually, i.e., we try each WP_i with $|AR| = 5$. Table 2 shows the best five features together with WP_{all} after ranking LRs in Top-1 and Top-4. First five features perform significantly better than all others, especially, better than WP_{all} which landed in 9-th place. Interestingly, LR increases drastically – from 52.5% to 91% in Top-1 – with the best feature. Since Top Letter Trigrams performs best individually, we add it to S_F. Then we proceed to considering the combination of other four features with Top Letter Trigrams.

		Linkability Ratio	
Ranking	Feature	Top-1(%)	Top-4(%)
1	Top Letter Trigrams	91	96
2	POS Bigrams	89	96
3	Top Letter Bigrams	86	94
4	Words	79	94
5	POS Tags	78	90
9	WP_{all}	52.5	82.5

Table 2: LRs of best five Writeprint features individually and WP_{all}, with $|AR| = 5$

5.2.3 Improving Top Letter Trigrams

Next, we combine each feature from the set {POS Bigrams, Top Letter Bigrams, Words, POS Tags} with S_F to see whether it yields a higher LR. It turns out that combining POS Bigrams yields the best LR gain: from 91% to 96% in Top-1, and 96% to 100% in Top-4. Since we achieve 100% LR in Top-4, we set S_F as {Top Letter Trigrams, POS Bigrams}.

Figures 1(a) and 1(b). show LR comparisons of experimented features with varying AR sizes. For all AR sizes, there is a significant improvement with Top Letter Trigrams over Writeprints. A similar trend occurs with {Top Letter Trigrams, POS Bigrams} over only Top Letter Trigrams in both Top-1 and Top-4.

5.3 Scalability of the Linkability Technique

So far, our small-scale study assessed linkability of 40 authors within a set of 40 possible authors. This is partly because computation of WP_{all} in bigger author sets is very expensive. However, 40 is a very small number in a real-world scenario. Therefore, we need to verify that high LRs identified with S_F still hold for larger number of possible authors. To this end, we vary author set size between 40 and 1000. In particular, we consider set sizes of $[40, 100, 250, 500, 750, 1000]$ authors. In each experiment, we assess linkability of 40 authors when mixing them with others.

Figure 2 shows Top-1 and Top-4 LR of S_F with $|AR| = 5$. Our preferred selection of features – Top Letter Trigram and

POS Bigrams – achieves high LR, 77.5% in Top-1 and 90% in Top-4, even in a set of 1000 possible authors.

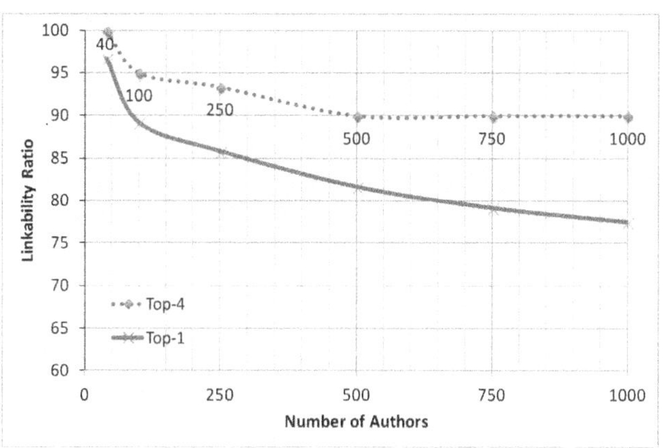

Figure 2: LRs of Letter3+POS2 in varying size of author sets

5.4 Summary

To summarize, key results are:

1. Starting with a well-known Writeprints feature set we achieved modest LRs of up to 52.5% in Top-1 and 82.5% in Top-4 using the CS model. (See Section 5.2.1)

2. Then, we tried each Writeprint feature individually with the intuition that the combination of multiple features would have more noise, thus decreasing linkability. Surprisingly, using only Top Letter Trigrams or POS Bigrams, we achieved significantly better LR than all Writeprints features. (See Section 5.2.2)

3. Next, we selected Top Letter Trigrams, which yields 91% and 96% LR in Top-1 and Top-4, as our rising main. Then, we increased linkability to 96% in Top-1, and 100% in Top-4 by adding POS Bigrams. (See Section 5.2.3)

4. Even when assessing linkability within a large number of possible authors sets, the preferred combination of features maintains high LR, e.g. 77.5% in Top-1 and 90% in Top-4 among 1000 possible authors (See Section 5.3). Thus, we end up setting S_F as {Top Letter Trigrams, POS Bigrams}, which will be used for evaluation of anonymization techniques.

6. FIGHTING AUTHORSHIP LINKABILITY

We now move on to the main topic of this paper: techniques that could mitigate authorship linkability. We consider two general approaches:

1. Crowdsourcing: described in Section 6.1.

2. Machine Translation: described in Section 6.2.

6.1 Crowdsourcing to the Rescue

We begin by considering what it might take, in principle, to anonymize reviews. Ideally, an anonymized review would exhibit stylometric features that are not linkable, with high accuracy, to any other review or a set thereof. At the same time, an anonymized review must be as meaningful as the original review and must remain faithful or "congruent" to it. (We will come back to this issue later in the paper). We believe that such perfect anonymization is probably impossible. This is because stylometry is not the only means of linking reviews. For example, if a TripAdvisor contributor travels exclusively to Antarctica and her reviews cover only specialized cruise-ship lines and related products (e.g., arctic-quality clothes), then no anonymization technique can prevent linkability by topic without grossly distorting the original review. Similarly, temporal aspects of reviews might aid linkability[5]. Therefore, we do not strive for perfect anonymization and instead confine the problem to the more manageable scope of reducing stylometric linkability. We believe that this degree of anonymization can be achieved by rewriting.

6.1.1 How to Rewrite Reviews?

There are many ways of rewriting reviews in order to reduce or obfuscate stylometric linkability. One intuitive approach is to construct a piece of software, e.g., a browser plug-in, that alerts the author about highly linkable features in the prospective review. This could be done in real time, as the review is being written, similarly to a spell-checker running in the background. Alternatively, the same check can be done once the review is fully written. The software might even proactively recommend some changes, e.g., suggest synonyms, and partition long, or join short, sentences. In general, this might be a viable and effective approach. However, we do not pursue it in this paper, partly because of software complexity and partly due to the difficulty of conducting sufficient experiments needed to evaluate it.

Our approach is based on a hypothesis that the enormous power of global crowd-sourcing can be leveraged to efficiently rewrite large numbers of reviews, such that:

(1) Stylometric authorship linkability is appreciably reduced, and

(2) Resulting reviews remain sensible and faithful to the originals.

The rest of this section overviews crowdsourcing, describes our experimental setup and reports on the results.

6.1.2 Crowdsourcing

Definition: according to the Merriam-Webster dictionary, `Crowdsourcing` is defined as: *the practice of obtaining needed services, ideas, or content by soliciting contributions from a large group of people, and especially from an online community, rather than from traditional employees or suppliers* [7].

There are numerous crowdsourcing services ranging in size, scope and popularity. Some are very topical, such as `kickstarter` (creative idea/project funding) or `microworkers` (web site promotion), while others are fairly general, e.g., `taskrabbit` (off-line jobs) or `clickworker` (on-line tasks). We selected the most popular and the largest general crowdsourcing service – Amazon's Mechanical Turk (MTurk) [1]. This choice was made for several reasons:

- We checked the types of on-going tasks in various general crowdsourcing services and MTurk was the only one where we encountered numerous on-going text rewriting tasks.

[5]Here we mean time expressed (or referred to) within a review, not only time of posting of a review.

Rewrite the following review

* You have to keep meaning similar to original review.
* You have to use your own sentences.
* Your submission must be at least 92 words long but no more than 132 words.
* Duplicate submissions will not be accepted.
* Your writing must be original and can not simply be a copy of part of a website.
* Please do not change proper names

Thanks for your time

**********************Original Review Starts Below***********************

The line was all the way down the block. We were willing to sit with other people. That wasn't the problem. It was that we were seated at a table WAY IN THE BACK of beyond. So if the cart pushers even bothered to get back to us, they had run of out food (Oddly, they still had chicken feet). When we finally flagged down some food, a half hour had gone by. The food was good. Nothing whets the appetite like hunger. The stuffed eggplant is better at China Garden. And yes, the pretty Sino-American gals with their moms come here. Plus the cart pusher lady NEVER smiles. Authentic. Super.

**********************Original Review Finishes Here**********************

Figure 3: Sample rewriting task in MTurk

- We need solid API support in order to publish numerous rewriting tasks. We also need a stable and intuitive web interface, so that the crowdsourcing service can be easily used. Fortunately, MTurk offers a user-friendly web interface for isolated users and API support to automate a large number of tasks.
- Some recent research efforts have used MTurk in similar studies [28, 16, 18].

In general, we need crowdsourcing for two phases: (1) rewriting original reviews, and (2) conducting a readability and faithfulness evaluation between original and rewritten reviews. More than 400 random MTurkers participated in both phases.

6.1.3 Rewriting Phase

Out of three randomly created AR and IR review sets we used in Section 5, we randomly selected one as the target for anonymization experiments. We then uploaded all reviews in this AR set to the crowdsourcing service and asked MTurkers to rewrite them using their own words. We asked 5 MTurkers to rewrite each review, in order to obtain more comprehensive and randomized data for the subsequent linkability study. While rewriting, we explicitly instructed participants to keep the meaning similar and not to change proper names from the original review. Moreover, we checked whether the number of words in each new review is close to that of the original before accepting a rewritten submission; divergent rewrites were rejected. A sample rewriting task and its submission are shown in Figure 3.

We published reviews on a weekly basis in order to vary the speed of gathering rewrites. Interestingly, most tasks were completed during the first 3 days of week, and the remaining 4 days were spent reviewing submissions. We finished the rewriting phase in 4 months. Given 40 authors and AR size of 5 (200 total original reviews), each review was rewritten by 5 MTurkers, resulting in 1,000 total submissions. Of these, we accepted 882. The rest were too short or too long, not meaningful, not faithful enough, or too similar, to the original. Moreover, out of 200 originals, 139 were rewritten 5 times. All original and rewritten reviews can be found at our publicly shared folder [6].

We paid US$0.12, on average, for each rewriting task. Ideally, a crowdsourcing-based review rewriting system would be free, with peer reviewers writing their own reviews and helping to re-writing others. However, since there was no such luxury at our disposal, we decided to settle on a low-cost approach[6]. Initially, we offered to pay US$0.10 per rewritten review. However, because review size ranges between 2 and 892 words, we came up with a sliding-price formula: $0.10 for every 250 words or a fraction thereof, e.g., a 490-word review pays $0.20 while a 180-word one pays $0.10. In addition, Amazon MTurk charges a 10% fee for each task.

One of our secondary goals was assessment of efficacy and usability of the crowdsourcing service itself. We published one set of 40 reviews via the user interface on the MTurk website, and the second set of 160 reviews – using MTurk API. We found both means to be practical, error-free and easy to use. Overall, anyone capable of using a web browser can easily publish their reviews on MTurk for rewriting.

After completing the rewriting phase, we continued with a readability study to assess sensibility of rewritten reviews and their correspondence to the originals.

6.1.4 Readability Study

Readability study proceeded as follows: First, we pick, at random, 100 reviews from 200 reviews in the AR set. Then,

[6]We consider the average of US$0.12 to be very low per review cost.

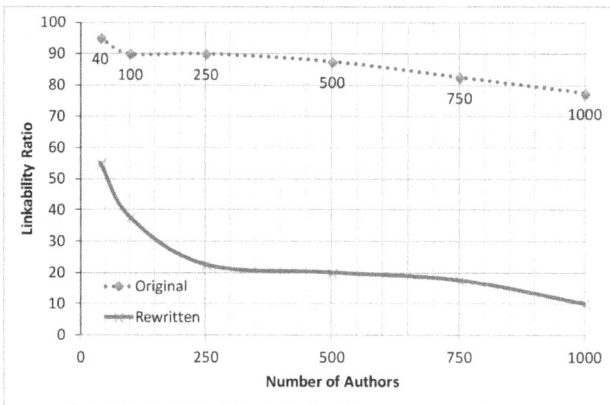

(a) Top-1 while varying the size of author set

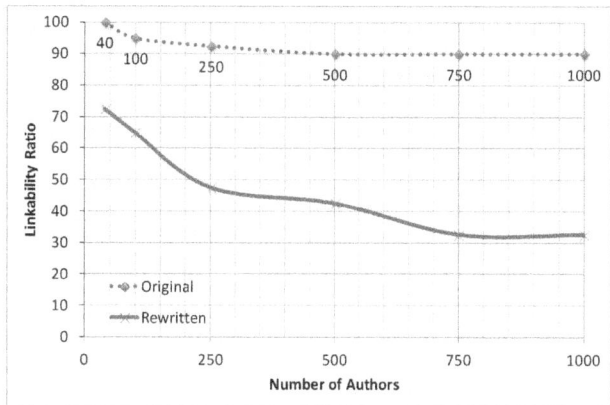

(b) Top-4 while varying the size of author set

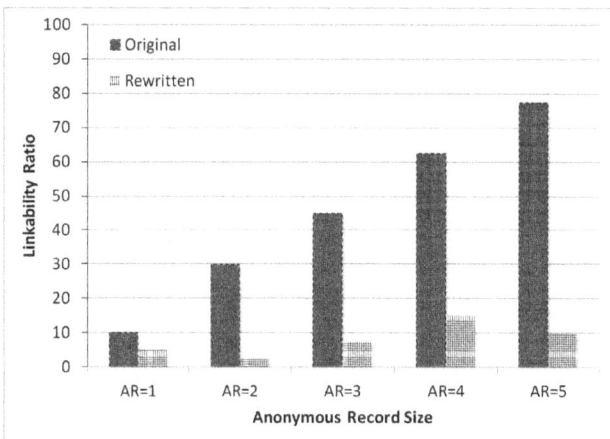

(c) Top-1 in a set of 1000 authors

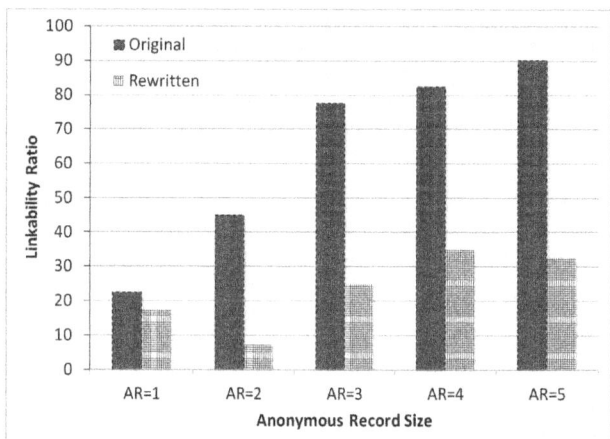

(d) Top-4 in a set of 1000 authors

Figure 4: LRs of Original and Rewritten Reviews

for each review, we randomly select one rewritten version. Next, for every [*original*, *rewritten*] review-pair, we publish a readability task on MTurk. In those tasks, we ask two distinct MTurkers to score rewritten reviews by comparing its similarity and sensibility to the original one. We define the scores as Poor(1), Fair(2), Average(3), Good(4), Excellent(5), where Poor means that the two reviews are completely different, and Excellent means they are essentially the same meaning-wise. We also ask MTurkers to write a comprehensive result which explains the differences (if any) between original and rewritten counterparts. A sample readability study task and its submission are given in Figure 5.

This study took one week and yielded 142 valid submissions. Results are reflected in Figure 6. The average readability score turns out to be 4.29/5, while 87% of reviews are given scores of Good or Excellent. This shows that rewritten reviews generally retain the meaning of the originals. Next, we proceed to re-assess stylometric linkability of rewritten reviews.

6.1.5 *Linkability of Rewritten Reviews*

Recall that the study in Section 5 involved 3 review sets each with 100 reviews per author. For the present study, we only consider the first set since we published anonymous reviews from first set to MTurk. In this first set, we replace AR with the corresponding set of MTurk-rewritten reviews where we pick a random rewritten version of each review, while each author's IR remains the same.

Figures 4(a) and 4(b) compare LRs between original - rewritten reviews with varying number of authors. Interestingly, we notice a substantial decrease in LRs for all author sizes. For $|AR| = 5$ in a set of 1000 authors, Top-1 and Top-4 LR drop from 77.5% to 10% and from 90% to 32.5% respectively. Even only in 40 authors set, Top-1 LR decreases to 55%, which is significantly lower than 95% achieved with original reviews.

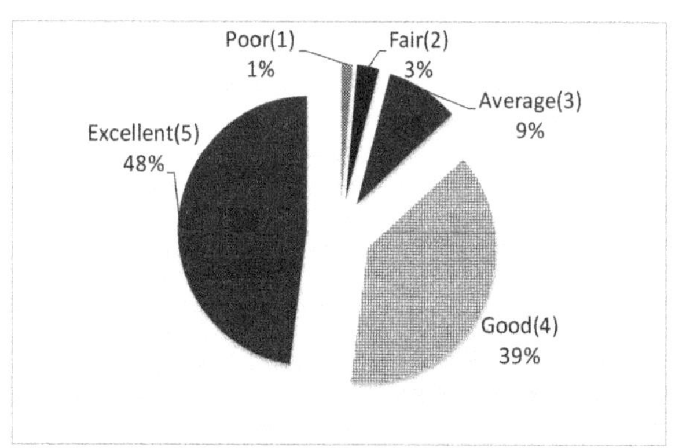

Figure 6: Readability Results of Rewritten Reviews

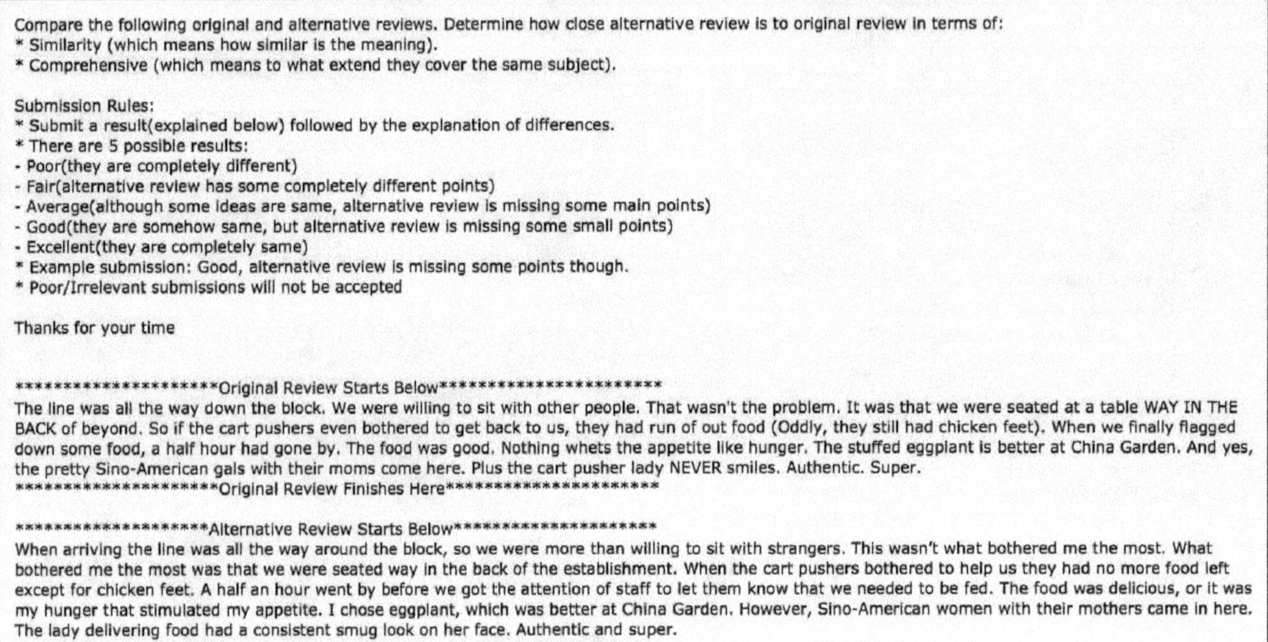
Compare the following original and alternative reviews. Determine how close alternative review is to original review in terms of:
* Similarity (which means how similar is the meaning).
* Comprehensive (which means to what extend they cover the same subject).

Submission Rules:
* Submit a result(explained below) followed by the explanation of differences.
* There are 5 possible results:
- Poor(they are completely different)
- Fair(alternative review has some completely different points)
- Average(although some ideas are same, alternative review is missing some main points)
- Good(they are somehow same, but alternative review is missing some small points)
- Excellent(they are completely same)
* Example submission: Good, alternative review is missing some points though.
* Poor/Irrelevant submissions will not be accepted

Thanks for your time

********************Original Review Starts Below***********************
The line was all the way down the block. We were willing to sit with other people. That wasn't the problem. It was that we were seated at a table WAY IN THE BACK of beyond. So if the cart pushers even bothered to get back to us, they had run of out food (Oddly, they still had chicken feet). When we finally flagged down some food, a half hour had gone by. The food was good. Nothing whets the appetite like hunger. The stuffed eggplant is better at China Garden. And yes, the pretty Sino-American gals with their moms come here. Plus the cart pusher lady NEVER smiles. Authentic. Super.
*********************Original Review Finishes Here**********************

*******************Alternative Review Starts Below*********************
When arriving the line was all the way around the block, so we were more than willing to sit with strangers. This wasn't what bothered me the most. What bothered me the most was that we were seated way in the back of the establishment. When the cart pushers bothered to help us they had no more food left except for chicken feet. A half an hour went by before we got the attention of staff to let them know that we needed to be fed. The food was delicious, or it was my hunger that stimulated my appetite. I chose eggplant, which was better at China Garden. However, Sino-American women with their mothers came in here. The lady delivering food had a consistent smug look on her face. Authentic and super.
********************Alternative Review Finishes Here*******************

Figure 5: Sample readability task in MTurk

We also present a detailed comparison of original and rewritten reviews' LRs with different AR sizes in Figures 4(c) and 4(d). Notably, both Top-1 and Top-4 LR decrease dramatically for all AR sizes. 35% is the highest LR obtained with rewritten reviews, which is substantially less than those achieved with original counterparts.

After experiencing this significant decrease in linkability, we analyze rewritten reviews to see what might have helped increase anonymity. We notice that most MTurkers do not change the skeleton of original review. Instead, they change the structure of individual sentences by modifying the order of subject, noun and verb, converting an active sentence into a passive one, or vice versa. We also observe that MTurkers swap words with synonyms. We believe that these findings can be combined into an automated tool, which can help authors rewrite their own reviews. This is one of the items for future work, discussed in more detail in Section 7.

6.1.6 Crowdsourcing Summary

We now summarize key findings from the crowdsourcing experiment.

1. MTurk based crowdsourcing yielded rewritten reviews that were:

   Low-cost – we paid only \$0.12 including 10% service fee for rewriting each 250-word review.

   Fast – we received submissions within 3-4 days, on average.

   Easy-to-use – based on experiences with both user-interface and API of MTurk, an average person who is comfortable using a browser, Facebook or Yelp can easily publish reviews to MTurk.

2. As the readability study shows, crowdsourcing produces meaningful results: rewrites remain faithful to originals. (See Section 6.1.4).

3. Most importantly, rewrites substantially reduce linkability. For an $|AR| = 5$ where we previously witnessed the highest LR, Top-1 LR shrunk from 95% to 55% in a set of 40 authors and from 77.5% to 10% in a set of 1000 authors. (See Section 6.1.5).

6.2 Translation Experiments

We now consider an alternative approach that uses on-line translation to mitigate linkability discussed in Section 5. The goal is to assess the efficacy of translation for stylometric obfuscation and check whether translation and crowdsourcing can be blended into a single socio-technological linkability mitigation technique.

It is both natural and intuitive to consider machine (automated, on-line) translation for obfuscating stylometric features of reviews. One well-known technique is to incrementally translate the text into a sequence of languages and then translate back to the original language. For example, translating a review from (and to) English using three levels of translation (two intermediate languages) could be done as follows: English → German → Japanese → English. The main intuition is to use the on-line translator as an external re-writer, so that stylometric characteristics would change as the translator introduces its own characteristics.

Using a translator to anonymize writing style has been attempted in prior work [13, 15]. However, prior studies did not go beyond three levels of translation and did not show significant decreases in linkability. Also, it was shown that that translation often yields non-sensical results, quite divergent from the original text [13]. Due to recent advances in this area, we revisit and reexamine the use of translation. Specifically, we explore effects of the number of intermediate languages on linkability and assess readability of translated outputs. In the process, we discover that translators are actually effective in mitigating linkability, while readability

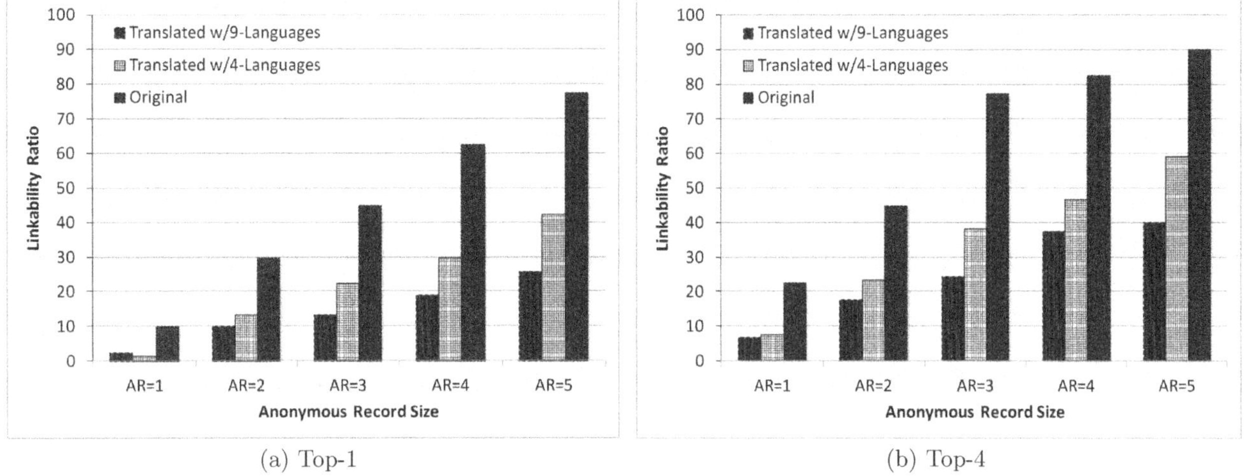

(a) Top-1

(b) Top-4

Figure 7: Comparison of Original-Translated Reviews LRs in a set of 1000 authors

is (though not great) is reasonable and can be easily fixed by crowdsourcing.

6.2.1 *Translation Framework*

We begin by building a translation framework to perform a large number of translations using any number of languages. Currently, Google [4] and Bing [2] offer the most popular machine translation services. Both use statistical machine translation techniques to dynamically translate text between thousands of language pairs. Therefore, given the same text, they usually return a different translated version. Even though there are no significant differences between them, we decided to use Google Translator. It supports more languages: 64 at the time of this writing [5], while Bing supports 41 [3]).

Google provides a translation API as a free service to researchers with a daily character quota, which can be increased upon request. The API provides the following two functions:

- $translate(text, sourceLanguage, targetLanguage)$: Translates given text from source language to target language.
- $languages()$: Returns the set of source and target languages supported in the *translate* function.

Using these functions, we implement the algorithm, shown in Algorithm 1. We first select N languages at random. Then, we consecutively translate text into each of the languages, one after the other. At the end, we translate the result to its original language, English, in our case. We consider the final translated review as the anonymized version of the original.

We also could have used a fixed list of destination languages. However, it is easy to see that translated reviews might then retain some stylometric features of the original (This is somewhat analogous to deterministic encryption.). Thus, we randomize the list of languages hoping that it would make it improbable to retain stylometric patterns. For example, since Google translator supports 64 languages, we have more than $\prod_{n=0}^{N-1}(64-n) \approx 2^{53}$ distinct lists of languages for $N = 9$.

After implementing the translation framework, we proceed to assessing linkability of the results.

Algorithm 1 Round-Translation of *Review* with N random languages

```
Obtain all supported languages via languages()
RandomLanguages ← select N languages randomly
Source ← "English"
for Language language in RandomLanguages do
    Review ← translate(Review, Source, language)
    Source ← language
end for
Translated ← translate(Review, Source, "English")
return Translated
```

6.2.2 *Linkability of Translated Reviews*

Using Algorithm 1, we anonymized the AR review set[7]. We varied N from 1 to 9 and re-ran linkability analysis with translated reviews as the AR. In doing so, we used S_F identified in Section 5. To assert generality of linkability of translated texts, we performed the above procedure 3 times, each time with a different list of random languages and then ran linkability analysis 3 times as well. Average linkability results of all 3 runs are plotted in Figures 8, 7(a) and 7(b).

For the number of intermediate languages, our intuition is that increasing the number of levels of translation (i.e., intermediate languages) causes greater changes in stylometric characteristics of original text. Interestingly, Figure 8 supports this intuition: larger N values yield larger decreases of linkability. While the decrease is not significant in Top-4 for N: $[1, 2]$, it becomes more noticeable after 3 languages. For $|AR| = 5$, we have Top-1 & Top-4 linkabilities of 42.5% & 59% with 4 languages, 31% & 47% with 7 languages and 25% & 40% with 9 languages, respectively. These are considerably lower than 77.5% & 90% achieved with original ARs. Because Top-1 linkability decreases to 25% after 9 languages, we stop increasing N and settle on 9.

[7]Translated example reviews are shown in Appendix B.

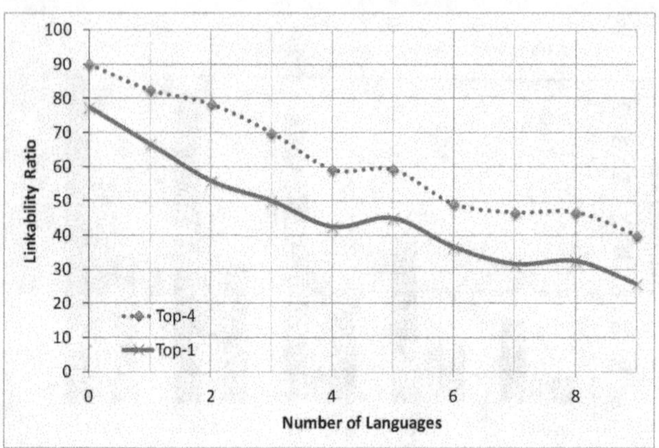

Figure 8: LRs with $|AR| = 5$ while varying number of languages in a set of 1000 authors

Figures 7(a) and 7(b) show reduction in Top-1 and Top-4 linkability for varying AR sizes. In all of them, original reviews have higher LRs than ones translated with 4 languages; which in turn have higher LRs than those translated with 9 languages. This clearly demonstrates that when more translations are done, the more translator manipulates the stylometric characteristics of a review.

6.2.3 *Readability of Translated Reviews*

So far, we analyzed the impact of using on-line translation on decreasing stylometric linkability. However, we need to make sure that the final result is readable. To this end, we conducted a readability study. We randomly selected a sample of translated reviews for $N = 9$. We have 3 sets of translated reviews, each corresponding to a random selection of 9 languages. From each set, we randomly selected 20 translated reviews, which totals up to 60 translated reviews. Then, for each [*original*, *translated*] review-pair, we published readability tasks on MTurk (as in Section 6.1.4) and had it assessed by 2 distinct MTurkers, resulting in 120 total submissions.

Results are shown in Figure 9. As expected, results are not as good as those in Section 6.1.4. However, a number of reviews preserve the original meaning to some extent. The average score is 2.85 out of 5 and most scores were at least "Fair".

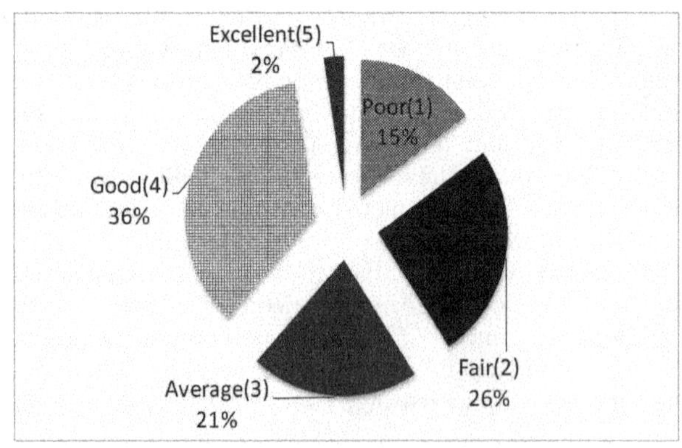

Figure 9: Readability Results of Translated Reviews

6.2.4 *Fixing the Translated Reviews*

Even though machine translation is continuously getting better at producing readable output, the state-of-the-art is far from ideal. After manually reviewing some [*original*, *translated*] pairs, we realized that most translated reviews retained the main idea of the original. However, because of: (1) frequently weird translation of proper nouns, (2) mis-organization of sentences, and (3) failure of translating terms not in the dictionary, translated review are not easy to read. We decided to provide translated reviews along with their original versions to MTurkers and asked them to fix unreadable parts[8]. As a task, this is easier and less time-consuming than rewriting the entire review.

Out of 3 translated review sets, we selected one at random and published all 200 ($|AR| = 5$ for 40 authors) translated reviews from our AR set to MTurk. We received 189 submissions; only 31 authors had their full AR's translated reviews completely fixed. We then performed the same linkability assessment with these 31 authors while we update their AR's by translated-fixed reviews.

Comparison of linkability ratios between original, translated, and fixed version of the same translated reviews is plotted in Figure 10(a). It demonstrates that, fixing translations does not significantly influence linkability. In AR-5, Top-1 linkability of fixed translation is 19% while non-fixed translations 25%. Meanwhile, both are significantly lower than 74% LR of original counterparts.

Finally, we perform a readability study on fixed translations. Out of 189 submissions, we select 20 randomly and publish to MTurk as a readability task. Average readability score increased from 2.85 to 4.12 after fixing the machine translation. Detailed comparison of readability studies between translated and translated-fixed reviews is given in Figure 11. We notice high percentage of translated reviews has Average score, while fixed counterparts mostly score as Good or Excellent. Results are really promising since they show that the meaning of a machine translated review can be fixed while keeping it unlinkable.

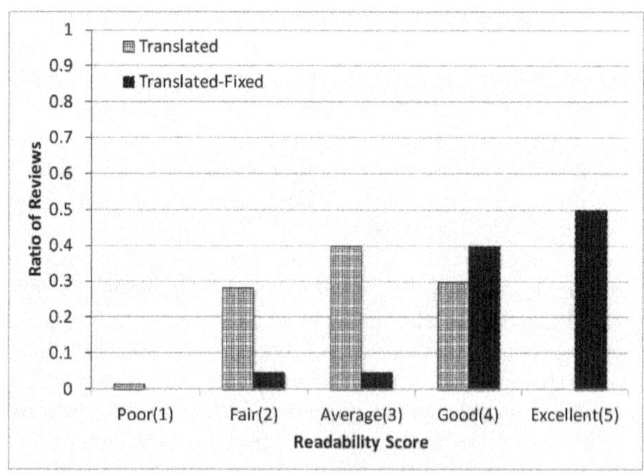

Figure 11: Readability study comparison between Translated and Translated-Fixed Reviews

[8]Sample submission to a translation-fix task is presented in Appendix B.

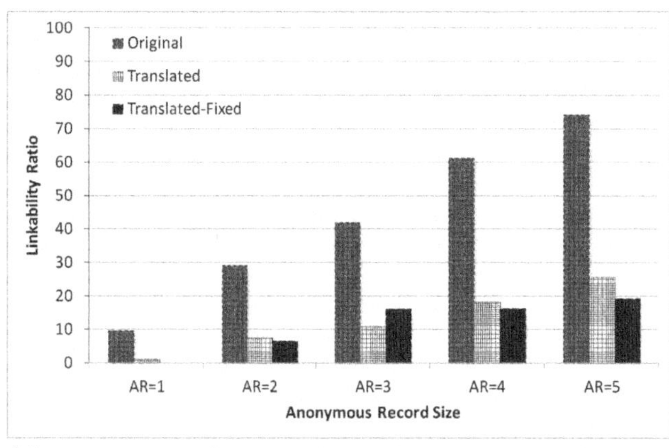

(a) LRs in a set of 1000 authors while varying the AR size

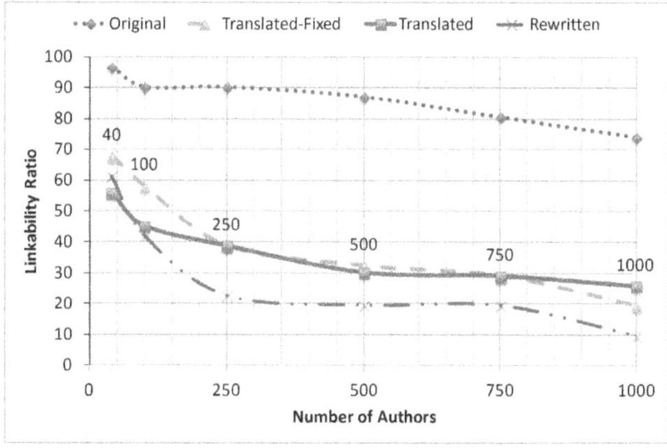

(b) LRs with $|AR| = 5$ while varying the number of authors

Figure 10: Top-1 LRs for Original, Translated, Translated-Fixed and Rewritten Reviews

6.2.5 *Comparison of Anonymization Techniques*

We present the comparison of linkability results achieved using crowdsourcing, machine translation and combination of both [9]. in Figure 10(b). Regardless of the size of author set, we achieve substantial decrease in linkability. Our techniques show that people are good at rewriting and correcting reviews while introducing their own style, keeping the meaning similar, and, most importantly, reducing linkability. While purely rewritten reviews have the lowest linkability, both translated and translated-fixed reviews perform comparable to each other. As far as readability, crowdsourcing (mean score of 4.29/5) performed much better than translation (mean score of 2.85/5). However, results show that low readability scores can be fixed (resulting in a mean score of 4.12/5) using crowdsourcing while keeping linkability low. We summarize results as follows:

- Crowdsourcing: Achieves better anonymity and readability. However, it takes longer than translation since it is not an automated solution. Moreover, though not expensive, it is clearly not free.
- Machine Translation: Completely automated and cost-free approach which takes less time than crowdsourcing. However, poor readability is the main disadvantage.

7. DISCUSSION

In spite of its usefulness in decreasing linkability and enhancing readability, there are some open questions associated with the use of crowdsourcing.

1. **How applicable is crowdsourcing to other OSNs?** In some other OSNs penalties for deanonymization would be higher than Yelp. However we chose Yelp dataset for the reasons given in Section 4.1. The same technique can be presumably applied to other settings, e.g., anonymous activist blogs, tweets in Twitter and TripAdvisor reviews.

2. **How might authors get their reviews rewritten?** This could be addressed by integrating a plug-in into a browser. When an author visits an OSN and writes a review, this plug-in can ease posting of a task to a crowdsourcing platform and return the result back to the author via one-time or temporary email address. On the system side, plug-in would create a rewriting task and relay it to the crowdsourcing system. A possible building block can be the recent work in [12] that proposes a crowdsourcing task automation system. It automates task scheduling, pricing and quality control, and allows tasks to be incorporated into the system as a function call.

3. **How feasible is crowdsourcing in terms of latency and cost?** We believe that a delay of couple of days would not pose an inconvenience since review posting does not need to occur in real time. Many popular OSNs does not publish reviews instantly, e.g., TripAdvisor screens each review to make sure it meets certain guidelines. This moderation can take as long as several weeks [8].

   As far as costs, we paid US$0.12, on average for each rewriting task. We consider this amount is extremely low which can be easily subsidized by the advertizing revenue, with ads in the plug-in.

4. **Is there a privacy risk in posting reviews to strangers?** It is difficult to assess whether there is a privacy risk since an adversary does not learn both posted and rewritten reviews, unless she is registered as a worker, completes the task, and her submission gets published. However, this clearly does not scale for the adversary when the number of posted reviews is large and requires manual follow-up with the posts. Also, MTurk Participation Agreement[10] involves conditions that protect privacy of both worker and requester.

5. **Is there a chance of having a rewriter's writing style recognized?** We believe that this is not the case. First, there are many workers to choose from and we can force the system not to select the same worker more than a specific number of times. Second, we expect that a worker would rewrite many reviews

[9]See: https://github.com/ekinoguz/JGAAP-Sprout and https://github.com/ekinoguz/hiding for the source code of our experiments and anonymization techniques.

[10]See: https://www.mturk.com/mturk/conditionsofuse

from different sources. This will widen the range of topics that rewritten reviews would cover and would make rewritten reviews more difficult to recognize. Finally, the identities of workers are expected to remain private since the only party who can see worker details for a given task is the person who posted it.

6. **Is there a chance of using crowdsourcing to generate fake content?** If our work is adopted, it might actually help spammers to make fake content easier to generate and avoid detection. However, the real effect is yet to be tested. Although real and fake reviews are generated by the same means, they are generated for different purposes with different content. Real reviews are generated to preserve anonymity and they hold on the meaning of the original review, whereas fake ones are generated to give fake assessments. Despite stylometric similarities, fake reviews could possibly hold many features that would distinguish them from real ones; such as multiple copies, similarities in ratings with other fake reviews, exaggerations in assessments, etc. But the real effect is yet to be assessed.

8. CONCLUSIONS AND FUTURE WORK

This paper investigated authorship linkability in community reviewing and explored some means of mitigating it. First, we showed, via a linkability study using a proper subset of the Writeprints feature set, that authorship linkability is higher than previously reported. Then, using the power of global crowdsourcing on the Amazon MTurk platform, we published reviews and asked random strangers to rewrite them for a nominal fee. After that, we conducted a readability study showing that rewritten reviews are meaningful and remain similar to the originals. Then, we re-assessed linkability of rewritten reviews and discovered that it decreases substantially. Next, we considered using translation to rewrite reviews and showed that linkability decreases while number of intermediary languages increases. After that, we evaluated readability of translated reviews, and realized that on-line translation does not yield results as readable as those from rewritings. Next, we take advantage of crowdsourcing to fix poorly readable translations and still achieve low linkability.

This line of work is far from being complete and many issues remain for future consideration:

- We need to explore detailed and sophisticated evaluation techniques in order to understand stylometric differences between original, rewritten and translated reviews. If this succeeds, more practical recommendations can be given to review authors.
- As discussed in Section 7, we want to parlay the results of our study into a piece of software or a plug-in intended for authors.
- We need to conduct the same kind of study in the context of review sites other than Yelp, e.g., Amazon, TripAdvisor or Ebay. Also, cross-site studies should be undertaken, e.g., using a combination of Amazon and Yelp reviews.

Acknowledgments

This research was conducted as part of NSF CSR Award 1213140: "Collaborative Research: Enabling Privacy-Utility Trade-offs in Pervasive Computing Systems".

9. REFERENCES

[1] Amazon Mechanical Turk. `https://www.mturk.com/mturk/`.

[2] Bing Translator. `http://www.bing.com/translator`.

[3] Bing Translator Language Codes. `http://msdn.microsoft.com/en-us/library/hh456380.aspx`.

[4] Google Translate. `http://translate.google.com/`.

[5] Google Translator API. `https://developers.google.com/translate/`.

[6] Original, Rewritten, Translated and Translated-Fixed Reviews. `http://sprout.ics.uci.edu/projects/aaa/dataset_userhiding.tar.gz`.

[7] Reference book and online dictionaries. `http://www.merriam-webster.com/`.

[8] TripAdvisor Review Moderation. `http://www.tripadvisor.com/vpages/review_mod_fraud_detect.html`.

[9] Yelp By The Numbers. `http://officialblog.yelp.com/2010/12/2010-yelp-by-the-numbers.html`.

[10] A. Abbasi and H. Chen. Writeprints: A Stylometric Approach to Identity-Level Identification and Similarity Detection in Cyberspace. In *ACM Transactions on Information Systems*, 2008.

[11] S. Afroz, M. Brennan, and R. Greenstadt. Detecting hoaxes, frauds, and deception in writing style online. In *IEEE Symposium on Security and Privacy*, 2012.

[12] D. W. Barowy, C. Curtsinger, E. D. Berger, and A. McGregor. Automan: A platform for integrating human-based and digital computation. In *OOPSLA*, 2012.

[13] M. Brennan, S. Afroz, and R. Greenstadt. Adversarial stylometry: Circumventing authorship recognition to preserve privacy and anonymity. *ACM Transactions on Information and System Security (TISSEC)*, 2012.

[14] M. R. Brennan and R. Greenstadt. Practical attacks against authorship recognition techniques. In *IAAI*, 2009.

[15] A. Caliskan and R. Greenstadt. Translate once, translate twice, translate thrice and attribute: Identifying authors and machine translation tools in translated text. In *ICSC*, 2012.

[16] E. Hayashi, J. Hong, and N. Christin. Security through a different kind of obscurity: evaluating distortion in graphical authentication schemes. In *Proceedings of the SIGCHI Conference on Human Factors in Computing Systems*, CHI, 2011.

[17] G. Kacmarcik and M. Gamon. Obfuscating document stylometry to preserve author anonymity. In *ACL*, 2006.

[18] P. G. Kelley. Conducting usable privacy & security studies with amazon's mechanical turk. In *Symposium on Usable Privacy and Security (SOUPS)(Redmond, WA*, 2010.

[19] A. W. E. McDonald, S. Afroz, A. Caliskan, A. Stolerman, and R. Greenstadt. Use fewer instances of the letter "i": Toward writing style anonymization. In *Privacy Enhancing Technologies*, 2012.

[20] M. A. Mishari and G. Tsudik. Exploring linkability of user reviews. In *ESORICS*, 2012.

[21] M. Nanavati, N. Taylor, W. Aiello, and A. Warfield. Herbert West – Deanonymizer. In *6th USENIX Workshop on Hot Topics in Security*, 2011.

[22] A. Narayanan, H. Paskov, N. Z. Gong, J. Bethencourt, E. Stefanov, E. C. R. Shin, and D. Song. On the Feasibility of Internet-Scale Author Identification. In *IEEE Symposium on Security and Privacy*, 2012.

[23] P. Pudil, J. Novovičová, and J. Kittler. Floating search methods in feature selection. *Pattern recognition letters*, 15(11):1119–1125, 1994.

[24] J. R. Rao and P. Rohatgi. Can pseudonymity really guarantee privacy. In *Proceedings of the Ninth USENIX Security Symposium*, 2000.

[25] R. Schumacker and S. Tomek. Chi-square test. In *Understanding Statistics Using R*, pages 169–175. Springer, 2013.

[26] E. Stamatatos. A Survey of Modern Authorship Attribution Methods. In *Journal of the American Society for Information Science and Technology*, 2009.

[27] K. Toutanova, D. Klein, C. D. Manning, and Y. Singer. Feature-rich part-of-speech tagging with a cyclic dependency network. In *Proceedings of the 2003 Conference of the North American Chapter of the Association for Computational Linguistics on Human Language Technology-Volume 1*, pages 173–180. Association for Computational Linguistics, 2003.

[28] B. Ur, P. G. Kelley, S. Komanduri, J. Lee, M. Maass, M. L. Mazurek, T. Passaro, R. Shay, T. Vidas, L. Bauer, N. Christin, L. F. Cranor, S. Egelman, and J. López. Helping users create better passwords. *USENIX*, 2012.

APPENDIX

A. CROWDSOURCING EXAMPLES

We present two example submissions from our rewriting and readability tasks in MTurk. Note that the full collection of original and rewritten reviews can be accessed in [6].

A.1: Rewriting Example

Sample rewritten review for the task given in Figure 3: *"When arriving the line was all the way around the block, so we were more than willing to sit with strangers. This wasn't what bothered me the most. What bothered me the most was that we were seated way in the back of the establishment. When the cart pushers bothered to help us they had no more food left except for chicken feet. A half an hour went by before we got the attention of staff to let them know that we needed to be fed. The food was delicious, or it was my hunger that stimulated my appetite. I chose eggplant, which was better at China Garden. However, Sino-American women with their mothers came in here. The lady delivering food had a consistent smug look on her face. Authentic and super."*

A.2 Readability Example

Sample readability study submission for a task given in Figure 5:
"Good, they are similar on the main points. When discussing the Sino-American women and their mothers, the alternative left out 'pretty' which seemed like a point that appealed to original reviewer. Also, by using the word 'smug' to describe the lady delivering food, the alternative review depicts her more negatively than the original."

B. TRANSLATION EXAMPLES

We present the round-trip machine translation of original review in Figure 3 with three, six and nine random selection of intermediate languages, and also translated-fixed version by MTurk below:

Random round-trip machine translation with three languages *English → Welsh → Irish → Ukrainian → English*: *"The line was all the way down the block. We are ready to sit with other people. This was not a problem. It was that we were sitting at the table, and the way in the back longer. So if the cart pushers even bother to get back to us, they run out of food (surprisingly, still chicken feet). When we finally gave up a little food half an hour passed. Food was good. Nothing stimulates the appetite like hunger. Best stuffed eggplants in the garden China. And many Chinese-American girls and their mothers to come here. Plus a woman pushing a cart ever smiles. Authentic. Super."*

Random round-trip machine translation with six languages *English → Welsh → Irish → Ukrainian → Yiddish → French → Korean → English*: *"The line at the bottom of the box is We sit down with other people who are prepared. It was not a problem. Pusherz basket even if you do not bother coming back to us, we have it sitting on the table, and how I was back in May, they (surprisingly, many chicken feet) to food shortages. Some food when we passed an hour and a half. The food was good. Nothing like hunger and appetite stimulation. China stuffed in the garden of the. Many Chinese-American women and their mothers come here. The woman pushing a cart does not smile. True. More."*

Random round-trip machine translation with nine languages *English → Welsh → Irish → Ukrainian → Yiddish → French → Korean → Esperanto → Norwegian → Malay → English*: *"Line at the bottom of the box, we sit down with other people who are willing. It's not a problem. Pusherz cart even if you do not bother to come back to us, we have it sitting on the table, and as I was back in May, (surprisingly, a lot of chicken feet) to food shortages. Some foods when they pass an hour and a half. Food is good. Nothing like hunger and appetite stimulation. China filling the park. Many Chinese-American women and their mothers come here. Woman pushing a trolley is not smiling. Sant. More."*

Fixed version of previous machine translated review with nine languages: *"The problem wasn't that we weren't willing to sit with other people but the line was still all the way down the block. The problem was that we were seated a table as far away as could be. Even if the servers made it to our table, their trays were empty (except for the chicken feet). It was a half an hour before we were able to get any of the food but it tasted good because we were so hungry; although, the China Garden has better stuffed eggplant. The pretty Sino-American girls come here with their mothers and the woman server never smiles. Traditional. Awesome."*

Note that the full collection of translated reviews can be found in [6].

"On the Internet, Nobody Knows You're a Dog": A Twitter Case Study of Anonymity in Social Networks

Sai Teja Peddinti*
psaiteja@nyu.edu

Keith W. Ross*†
keithwross@nyu.edu

Justin Cappos*
jcappos@nyu.edu

*Dept. of Computer Science and Engineering, NYU
Brooklyn, New York, USA

†NYU Shanghai
Shanghai, China

ABSTRACT

Twitter does not impose a Real-Name policy for usernames, giving users the freedom to choose how they want to be identified. This results in some users being *Identifiable* (disclosing their full name) and some being *Anonymous* (disclosing neither their first nor last name).

In this work we perform a large-scale analysis of Twitter to study the prevalence and behavior of Anonymous and Identifiable users. We employ Amazon Mechanical Turk (AMT) to classify Twitter users as Highly Identifiable, Identifiable, Partially Anonymous, and Anonymous. We find that a significant fraction of accounts are Anonymous or Partially Anonymous, demonstrating the importance of Anonymity in Twitter. We then select several broad topic categories that are widely considered sensitive–including pornography, escort services, sexual orientation, religious and racial hatred, online drugs, and guns–and find that there is a correlation between content sensitivity and a user's choice to be anonymous. Finally, we find that Anonymous users are generally less inhibited to be active participants, as they tweet more, lurk less, follow more accounts, and are more willing to expose their activity to the general public. To our knowledge, this is the first paper to conduct a large-scale data-driven analysis of user anonymity in online social networks.

Categories and Subject Descriptors

J.4 [**Social And Behavioral Sciences**]: Sociology; K.4.1 [**Public Policy Issues**]: Privacy; H.4 [**Information Systems Applications**]: Miscellaneous

General Terms

Measurement, Human Factors

Keywords

Online Social Networks; Twitter; Anonymity; Quantify; Behavioral Analysis

COSN'14, October 1–2, 2014, Dublin, Ireland.

http://dx.doi.org/10.1145/2660460.2660467.

1. INTRODUCTION

Many online social networks, including Facebook and Google+, enforce a Real-Name policy, requiring users to use their real names when creating accounts [3, 2]. The cited reasons for the Real-Name policy include that it improves the quality of the content and the service (helping decrease spam, bullying, and hacking), increases accountability, and helps people to find each other. The Real-Name policy, however, also enables the social networks to tie user interests–as reflected from their use of the online services–with their true names, generating a treasure trove of consumer data. This has resulted in many debates [13] and petitions [6], with privacy advocates claiming that Real-Name policy erodes online freedom [31]. Privacy-conscious users have started finding ways to bypass the policy, hiding their real identity while continuing to use these social networks [22].

Twitter, on the other hand, does not impose strict rules for users to provide their real names, although it does require them to register with and employ unique pseudonyms. Taking advantage of this lack of Real-Name policy, many Twitter users choose to employ pseudonyms that have no relation to their real names. Some users choose such a pseudonym only because they enjoy being associated with a particular fun or interesting pseudonym. But many users likely choose pseudonyms with no relation to their real names because they want to be anonymous on Twitter. For example some users may desire the ability to tweet messages without revealing their actual identities. Other users may desire to follow sensitive and controversial accounts without exposing their real identities. The lack of Real-Name policy enforcement has turned Twitter into a popular information exchange portal where users share and access information without being identifiable–as is evident by Twitter's role in Egyptian revolution [25] and for reporting news in Mexico [34]. However, there is a meaningful debate about the pros and cons of online anonymity, as it allows people to more easily spread false rumours [14], defame individuals [12], attack organizations [33], and even spread spam [41, 17].

In this work we use Twitter to study the *prevalence* and *behavior* of Identifiable users (those disclosing their full name) and Anonymous users (those disclosing neither their first nor last name). Although both on-line and off-line anonymity has been considered by researchers in psychology and sociology, as discussed in Section 7, these studies have generally been carried out with small data sets and surveys. There have also been a few data-driven studies of anonymity in blogs and postings to Web sites [16, 5, 36]. To our knowledge, this paper is the first to conduct a large-scale data-driven analysis of user anonymity in online social networks. The potential benefits of such a study include: (i) a deeper understanding of the importance and role of anonymity in our society; (ii) guidance for the incorporation of privacy and anonymity features in existing and future online social networks; (iii) and as we shall discuss in the body of the paper, the discovery of illegal (such as child-porn and terrorism) or controversial (such as ethnic or religious hate) activities.

Contributions

- We first analyze a large random sample of 100,000 Twitter users. After removing ephemeral users (active on Twitter for less than six months) and spam users, we employ Amazon Mechanical Turk (AMT) to classify Twitter users as Highly Identifiable, Identifiable, Partially Anonymous, and Anonymous based on whether their first and last names are given in their profiles and whether they link to other social networks with a Real-Name policy. We find that 5.9% of the accounts are Anonymous and 20% of the accounts are Partially Anonymous, demonstrating the importance of Anonymity for a large fraction of Twitter Users. Leveraging this same data set, we find Identifiable and Anonymous users exhibit distinctly different behavior in choosing which accounts to follow.

- We evaluate whether content sensitivity has any correlation with users choosing to be anonymous. For this analysis we select several broad topic categories that are widely considered sensitive and/or controversial–pornography, escort services, sexual orientation, religious and racial hatred, online drugs, and guns. We also consider several generic non-sensitive categories. For each of these broad categories we identify Twitter accounts that tweet about these categories. We observe that the different categories contain greatly different percentages of Anonymous and Identifiable followers. Strikingly, all but one of the sensitive aggregate categories have the largest percentage of Anonymous users. We also examine each of the non-sensitive and sensitive accounts individually and observe that there is a general pattern of having larger percentages of Anonymous followers for the sensitive accounts and larger percentages of Identifiable followers for the non-sensitive accounts. As we discuss in the body of the paper, this observation can potentially lead to a new mechanism for identifying sensitive and controversial accounts, as well as helping to determine what types of categories people consider to be sensitive.

- We combine the two datasets and analyze some of the behavioral issues associated with Anonymous and Identifiable users. We find that Anonymous users are generally less inhibited to be active participants, as they tweet more, lurk less, follow more accounts, and are more willing to expose their activity to the general public. However, the Highly Identifiable users, who publicly link to OSNs with a Real-Name policy, typically have many more friends and followers than Identifiable users, demonstrating a high degree of online social activity and visibility.

The following sections of the paper are organized as follows. Section 2 provides a brief background on Twitter and its terminology. Section 3 gives details about the user categories we are interested in and the classification procedure. We describe our collected dataset statistics in Section 4. Our findings on the use of non-identifying pseudonyms, correlation with following sensitive accounts, and group behavioral differences are reported in Section 5. Section 6 discusses future work. Section 7 describes the related work and Section 8 concludes the paper.

2. BACKGROUND

Every Twitter account is comprised of four main pieces of information.

- First is the account *Profile* which includes the details provided by the user about him/her. These include the *screen name*, which is a user-chosen unique alphanumeric ID (also referred to as the username); the *name*, which may be the user's actual first and last name; and (optionally) a small textual description, a profile picture, the user's city/location and a URL (either linking to another social network profile or to something the user supports). It is to be noted that the details provided in the profile need not always be true (e.g., the name field can contain a fake first and/or last name).

- Second is the list of *Tweets* (i.e., messages) posted by the user. A tweet is a message restricted to 140 characters and can contain text, URLs (URL shortening is generally applied to limit the URL size to 20 characters) and *HashTags* (which is a metadata tag used to group messages).

- Third is the *Friends* list of the user. When a Twitter user follows another user (a "friend"), he/she receives the tweets from that friend. This relationship is unidirectional, so if A is a friend of B, B need not be a friend of A.

- Fourth is the *Followers* list of the user. All the users who follow a particular Twitter user are termed his/her followers. They receive all the tweet updates posted by the particular user.

By default, all of this information is publicly available from the Twitter web site. Twitter provides a *protected* privacy feature, to enable users to hide their tweets, friend lists, and follower lists.

Twitter provides a free API to obtain nearly unrestricted access to the social network data, which is only limited by the number of requests that can be sent during a time interval. In this work, we limit our analysis to the profile information, friends and followers listing and do not analyze the tweets posted by the user.

Ephemeral and Spam Accounts

In order to not bias the results, we remove from our data sets all user accounts that show signs of being ephemeral or spam. We say an account is *non-ephemeral* if the sum of friends and followers is at least five *and* it has had some activity–either (i) posting a tweet or (ii) adding a friend–at least six months after its creation. As the API doesn't give the dates that friends are added, we take a conservative approach for meeting condition (ii). For a given account Bob, we examine the account creation dates of all the friends of Bob. If Bob has at least one friend with an account creation date that is six months after Bob's account creation date, then Bob clearly added a friend at least six months after creating his account.

Various entities frequently attempt to create spam accounts in Twitter for spreading spam or malware [17, 41]. Twitter puts significant effort into identifying and blocking these spam accounts. Indeed, a recent study of suspended accounts on Twitter shows that Twitter is fairly successful in blocking almost 92% of the spam accounts within 3 days of the first tweet and all of the spam accounts (including those belonging to big spam campaigns) within 6 months [41]. However, to be on the safe side, we do eliminate accounts that have some resemblance to spam account behavior, as reported in [41] (such as followers-to-friends ratio being less than 0.1).

3. CLASSIFYING USERS

In this study, we rely on human knowledge to classify user accounts as Anonymous and Identifiable. In particular, we leverage Amazon Mechanical Turk (AMT). For each Twitter account, we present the account *name* and *screen name* to Mechanical Turk workers and ask them to determine whether these two fields collectively contain (a) just a first name, (b) just a last name, (c) both a first name and a last name, or (d) neither a first nor a last name. The worker can also indicate (e) not sure. We instructed the Mechanical Turk workers to choose 'neither a first nor a last name' and 'both a first name and a last name' options only when they are completely confident, to avoid mis-labelling in situations when there is a lack of clarity (for example due to unusual international names). This enables us to have high confidence in the accounts labelled as not containing names and those containing complete (both first and last) names. To account for human error, we have each account labelled by two Mechanical Turk master workers (those with high ratings). When there is a disagreement, we ask a third master worker to assign the label and use the majority. If there is still a tie among the labels, we (the authors) manually look into the disagreements and finalize the label for the account.

Using these AMT labelings, we define each user account in our data sets as follows:

- **Anonymous** – A Twitter account containing neither the first nor last name (as labelled by AMT) and not containing a URL in the profile (which may point to a web page that identifies or partially identifies the user).
- **Identifiable** – A Twitter account containing both a first name and a last name (as labelled by AMT).
- **Highly Identifiable** – A Twitter account that is Identifiable *and* contains a URL reference to another social network account employing a Real-Name policy (such as Facebook or Google+). It is a subset of the Identifiable group.
- **Partially Anonymous** – A Twitter account having a first name or last name but not both (as labelled by AMT).
- **Unclassifiable** – A Twitter account that is neither Anonymous, Identifiable nor Partially Anonymous. Accounts which have neither a first nor last name but have a URL fall under this category. Also, Twitter accounts that belong to an organization or a company belong here.

We recognize that pseudonymity is different from anonymity, and that Twitter does not support complete anonymity (where the messages are not associated with any pseudonym). However, we prefer to use the more commonly employed term *Anonymous* rather than the more obscure term *Pseudonymous*.

Drawbacks

We mention here that a small fraction of the accounts labelled Anonymous may not be fully anonymous, in that they may provide an identifiable profile photo. However, it has been shown that Twitter profile pictures are often misleading, making it hard to even deduce ethnicity or gender, and are often virtual characters (such as cartoons) or belong to celebrities [37]. Also, a small fraction of the Anonymous users may provide their real identities in their tweets. Furthermore, some users may use fake first and last names, so that a fraction of Identifiable users are effectively Anonymous users. Thus there is some noise in the user classification, noise which is difficult to completely remove. Our results will show, however, that even in the presence of this noise, the Anonymous and Identifiable groups have distinctly different behaviors.

We also point out that employing Amazon Mechanical Turk for user classification is costly in both money and time. (Even if we charge as low as one cent for each account classification, getting multiple workers to label every account adds up for a large-scale study). This limits the number of accounts we can classify, forcing us to optimize our efforts. We are currently exploring techniques for automatic account classification.

4. DATASET COLLECTION AND CHARACTERISTICS

We make use of two distinct data sets in our study.

4.1 Random Accounts

For measuring the prevalence of anonymity in Twitter, we make use of a recent public Twitter dataset released in 2010 containing 41.7 million Twitter accounts [28]. Of the 41.7 million accounts we randomly pick 100,000 accounts and use them as the dataset for this study. It is to be noted that the 2010 public dataset is only used for picking a random subset of Twitter usernames; we use the Twitter API to gather the latest profile information and the friends and follower lists for each of these 100,000 accounts.

We preprocess our initial list of 100,000 users by eliminating all the deactivated accounts, non-English accounts (which do not report English as the language of preference), spam accounts, and ephemeral accounts. The statistics are shown in Table 1. The remaining 50,173 Twitter accounts are passed on to Mechanical Turk for labelling.

4.2 Followers of Sensitive and Non-Sensitive Accounts

We evaluate whether content sensitivity has any correlation with users choosing to be anonymous, by classifying the followers of sensitive and non-sensitive Twitter accounts as

Table 1: Dataset for Measuring Anonymity

Category	# of Twitter Accounts
Deactivated	864
Non-English	5,113
Ephemeral	42,515
Spam	1,335
Remaining	50,173
Total	100,000

Anonymous and Identifiable. As pointed out in [36], there is no universal definition of what constitutes sensitive content. For this analysis, we create a second dataset by selecting several broad topic categories that are widely considered sensitive and/or controversial by many–pornography, escort services, sexual orientation, religious and racial hatred, online drugs, and guns. We also consider several generic non-sensitive broad categories–news sites, family recreation, movies/theater, kids/babies, and companies/organizations producing household items. For each of these broad categories we identify a few distinctive search terms, and manually pick Twitter accounts that show up when we search for the chosen terms on the Twitter page. When selecting specific accounts in the sensitive categories, we manually look into the account activity to ensure they have high levels of sensitive or controversial tweets.

Most of our short-listed highly-sensitive accounts turned out to have relatively few followers. Among these short-listed accounts, we selected accounts that had at least 200 followers. In total, we picked 50 Twitter accounts related to the different sensitive categories, and 20 accounts related to non-sensitive categories. (Fewer accounts related to nonsensitive categories were needed since those accounts typically have many more followers.) The entire list of chosen Twitter *screen names* in each category and their follower counts are provided in Table 2. Similar to the earlier data collection, to reduce noise we eliminate all non-English, spam and ephemeral followers of these accounts. Because most of the non-sensitive accounts had millions of followers, we conducted our analysis on 1,000 randomly-chosen followers for each Twitter account in the non-sensitive category (to reduce Mechanical Turk costs). All the non-ephemeral followers are again categorized as Identifiable, Partially Anonymous, Anonymous and Unclassifiable using AMT. When comparing different categories, we focus on percentages to ensure that the different numbers of followers do not skew the results.

5. EXPERIMENTAL RESULTS

In this section we report and interpret the results of our experiments.

5.1 Quantifying Anonymity

From our first data set, all the 50,173 accounts (remaining after pre-processing the randomly selected 100,000 Twitter accounts) were labelled using AMT and then categorized as described in Section 3. The distribution of Twitter users across each category is shown in Table 3.

Among the total 50,173 active accounts, we find 5.9% of the accounts are Anonymous. It is to be noted that some of the Identifiable users may contain fake user names and hence actually be anonymous. *Thus, we conclude that anonymity is an important feature for many Twitter users, with at least 5.9% of Twitter users using non-identifiable pseudonyms.* Furthermore, over 25% of the users are semi-anonymous in that they do not provide both their first and last names. *This signifies that online anonymity is important in Twitter, and not having a Real-Name policy could be a strong selling point for a social network.*

Table 3: Labelled Data for Quantifying Anonymity

Label	# of Twitter Accounts
Highly Identifiable	906 (1.8%)
Identifiable	34,085 (67.9%)
Partially Anonymous	10,019 (20%)
Anonymous	2,934 (5.9%)
Unclassifiable	3,135 (6.2%)
Total	50,173

The Identifiable user group has 67.9% of the accounts, although as just mentioned, an unknown fraction of these users may actually be anonymous. The Highly Identifiable users, who provide first and last names and link to other social networks with Real-Name policy, constitute 1.8% of the accounts. Although the Highly Identifiable users make up only a small percentage of the Twitter users, we will see they exhibit interesting behavior.

5.1.1 Interests Overlap Between Labelled Groups

To measure whether accounts exhibit similar interests compared to other accounts within the same group, we analyzed the popular friends in the Anonymous and Identifiable categories. We split the Identifiable group into two subsets and compare the friends overlap between the two Identifiable groups, and between the Identifiable and Anonymous groups. Since the Identifiable group is larger, in order to not skew the results, we randomly pick two Identifiable group subsets containing the same number of accounts as the Anonymous group.

Let A denote the set of friends for the accounts in the Anonymous group, and I_1 and I_2 denote the set of friends for the accounts in the two Identifiable groups. For each of the sets of friends, we rank order the friends by popularity. In particular, for each friend $f \in A$, we determine the number of accounts that have f as a friend, and then rank these friends from highest value to lowest value. In an analogous manner, we rank the friends in I_1 and I_2. Then for every top-ranked N friends in each of the three sets, where N varies between 20 and 1000, we determine the overlap. The results are shown in Table 4, where we report the fraction of overlap between the different lists.

Table 4 shows that although there is significant overlap among the popular friends in the Anonymous and the Identifiable groups, for all values of N, the overlap between the Identifiable subsets is always greater. This clearly shows that Anonymous users' interests often deviate from those of Identifiable users. We explore this issue in greater depth in the next subsection.

5.2 Anonymity in Sensitive Accounts

As described in Section 4.2, our second data set consists of 70 accounts (20 non-sensitive and 50 sensitive) along with

Table 2: Sensitive and Non-sensitive Twitter Accounts

Label	Category	Total Followers	Active Followers	Twitter Accounts
Sensitive	Gay/Lesbian	27,315	17,022	GayFollowBack_, blahblah1113, GayDatingFree, GayFlirt, GDates, LorenzoDavids2, GayJock-Studs, LoveNudeSelfies, Monstrous10, FreshSX
	Escort Services	11,977	7,113	Escort_Dubai, bocaratonescort, newarkescorts, 001Escort, NYEscorts_Posh, sexinleeds, SapphireEscort, theEscortWeb, glamourescortz, TheEroticGroup
	Pornography	40,261	18,722	bustybethx, MyGayXXXPorn, _youwanna-fuck, gal_nawty, essexbukkakepar, tattianax, NaughtyTerror, Eritoporn, PeekShowsModels, mysexywifeXXX
	Antisemitism	828	597	againstzionism, We_Hate_Israel
	White Supremacy	3,903	2,218	NiggerHanger, kkkofficial, KKKlan
	Islamophobia	13,834	12,081	banquran2, MuhammadThePig, barenakedislam, KafirCrusaders, IslamExposer
	Marijuana	14,195	11,786	buy_marijuana, BhangChocolate, growweedeasy
	Online Drugs	1,383	1,103	BuyGenericDrugs, buyviagranow, securerxpills
	Guns	8,602	6,835	MyGunsForSale, GunBroker, FirearmsforSale
	Antichristian	1,921	1,292	PriestsRapeBoys
Non-Sensitive	Movies/ Theater	4,000	2,656	aladdin, TheLionKing, DespicableMe, StarTrek-Movie
	Family Recreation	4,000	2,933	FamilyFun, FamilyDotCom, NatlParkService, SixFlags
	Companies/ Organizations	4,000	2,242	World_Wildlife, Nestle, LAYS, AOL
	News	4,000	2,634	ReutersLive, abcnews, HuffPostTech, intlCES
	Kids/Babies	4,000	2,929	BabyZone, BabiesRUs, Creativity4Kids, PB-SKIDS

Table 4: Popular Friends Overlap Between Anonymous and Identifiable Groups

# of Top Popular Friends (N)	Fraction of Overlap		
	$\frac{I_1 \cap I_2}{N}$	$\frac{A \cap I_1}{N}$	$\frac{A \cap I_2}{N}$
20	0.9	0.55	0.55
30	0.93	0.57	0.57
50	0.88	0.62	0.64
70	0.87	0.66	0.66
100	0.84	0.65	0.64
200	0.87	0.68	0.71
500	0.87	0.69	0.71
1000	0.84	0.66	0.69

all the followers of these accounts, as summarized in Table 2. Leveraging AMT, each follower is categorized as Anonymous, Partially Anonymous, Identifiable, or Unclassifiable. Figure 1 shows the average percentage of followers who are Anonymous, Identifiable and Highly Identifiable (subset of Identifiable) for each category of sensitive and non-sensitive accounts. The categories are arranged in order from the highest percentage to the lowest percentage of Anonymous followers.

We first observe that the different categories contain greatly different percentages of Anonymous and Identifiable followers. The percentage of Anonymous users varies from 6.6% to 37.3%; the percentage of Identifiable users varies from 26.9% to 59.6%. Strikingly, the sensitive categories have the largest percentage of Anonymous users. Except for Online Drugs, all of the sensitive categories have more than 10.3% of Anonymous followers and all the non-sensitive categories have at most 8.9% of Anonymous followers. Pornography, Marijuana, Islamophobia and Gay/Lesbian all have more than 21.6% of Anonymous followers, with pornography far exceeding the rest with 37.3% of Anonymous followers.

For the percentages of Identifiable followers, there are also patterns, although not as clearly demarcated as for the Anonymous percentages. The categories with fewer than 40% of Identifiable followers (Pornography, Marijuana, Gay/ Lesbian, Escort Groups) are all sensitive; and most of the categories with more than 50% of Identifiable followers are non-sensitive categories. But some of the sensitive categories have a surprisingly large percentage of Identifiable followers (e.g. White Supremacy and Guns). We believe one reason the patterns may be less strong for Identifiable users is because the Identifiable category may be noisier than the Anonymous category, as a significant fraction of the Identifiable users may be using fake names and are in actuality Anonymous. It is also possible that many followers in the White Supremacy and Guns categories take "pride" in being

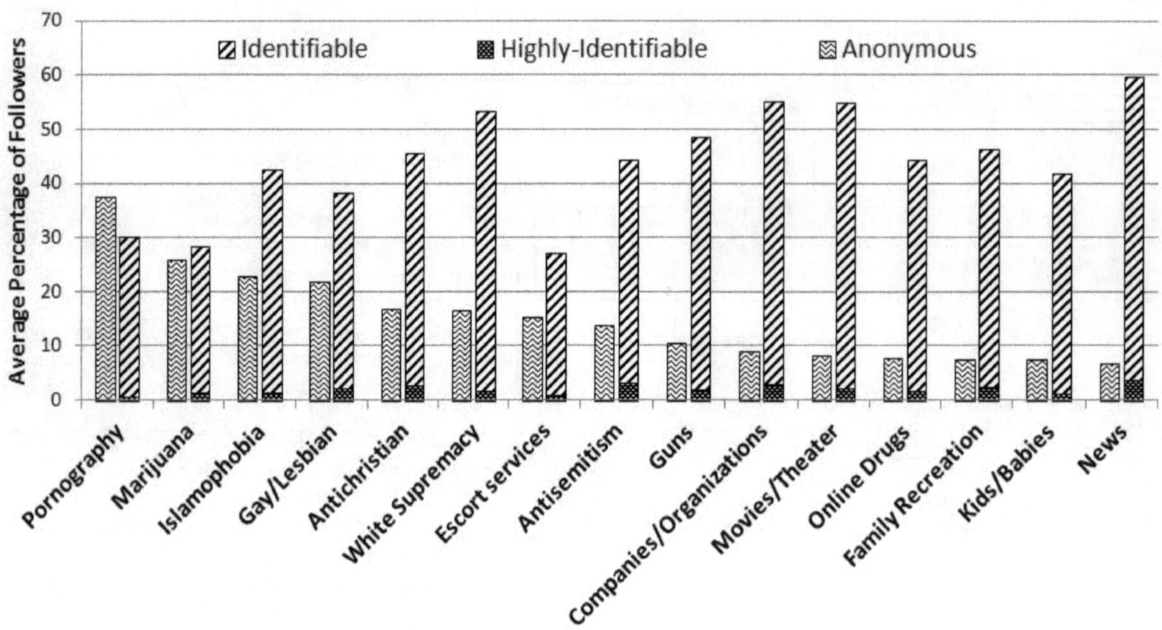

Figure 1: Sensitive and Non-Sensitive Twitter Account Categories: Follower Distribution

members of these groups and do not feel the need to hide their identities. This shows that there are different types of sensitive content–while some generate secrecy, others may influence people to be open (resulting in having many Identifiable followers rather than Anonymous). This establishes that content sensitivity is quite nuanced and complex. For the Highly Identifiable users, there is less of a pattern, although Pornography and Escort Services have the lowest percentages.

Based on these patterns, we can define a simple sensitive *topic* classifier that relies on the percentage of Anonymous and Identifiable followers (for example, (i) a topic with more than 10% of Anonymous followers is potentially sensitive or controversial, and (ii) a topic with more than 40% of Identifiable followers and fewer than 10% of Anonymous followers is likely non-sensitive). In future work, we expect to build an automated mechanism to determine whether an account is Anonymous, Identifiable, or Unclassifiable, which can then be used for topic sensitivity classification.

Even non-sensitive categories have 6.6% – 8.9% of Anonymous followers. This is an important observation that validates that users do not create anonymous profiles for the *sole* purpose of following sensitive accounts. To avoid maintaining multiple profiles, an Anonymous user might follow both sensitive and non-sensitive Twitter accounts using the same profile, leaking out his interests on Twitter. For example, by following the *Star Wars Movie* Twitter account, a user indicates that he is interested in the *Star Wars* franchise. These non-sensitive interest disclosures can potentially be used to deanonymize the Anonymous users using techniques similar to [45] (which shows that a user's group membership sets in a social network are generally unique and can be used to identify the user).

Figure 1 presents results for the accounts aggregated over each category. To gain further insight, we now consider the *individual* accounts instead of the account categories. We consider all of the non-sensitive accounts and all of the highly-sensitive accounts, except those belonging to the online drugs category (which appears from the data to not actually be a highly-sensitive category). Figure 2 shows a scatterplot with one point for each of these accounts. The x-axis of the plot indicates the fraction of Identifiable followers, the y-axis indicates the fraction of Anonymous followers. From the figure we can see that there is a general trend to have more Anonymous followers for the sensitive accounts and more Identifiable followers for the non-sensitive accounts. In fact, we see that the line $y = 0.905 \times x - 0.305$ (obtained using linear regression) separates the points belonging to the two classes–all but three of the sensitive accounts are above the line, and all but one of the non-sensitive accounts are below this line. In future work, we expect to build an automated mechanism to determine whether an account is Anonymous, Identifiable, or Unclassifiable. Figure 2 provides hope that we may be able to develop a sensitive account detector based on the percentages of detected Anonymous and Identifiable followers.

Twitter's popularity has resulted in an increase in its misuse. With the help of legal authorities, Twitter management is actively fighting spam [17, 41], spread of pirated media content [26], child porn [1], and terrorism [44]. As most of the miscreants already employ evasion techniques against current detection mechanisms–such as keyword based detection or URL spam/phishing detection–it becomes important to identify new signals that can be leveraged. Figures 1 and 2 show there is indeed a strong correlation between follower anonymity and the account sensitivity. This validates that analyzing Anonymous followers can help us detect these sensitive accounts–helping narrow down the illegal and controversial account search space. This approach does not replace existing detection techniques, but is complementary and helps raise the bar for miscreants.

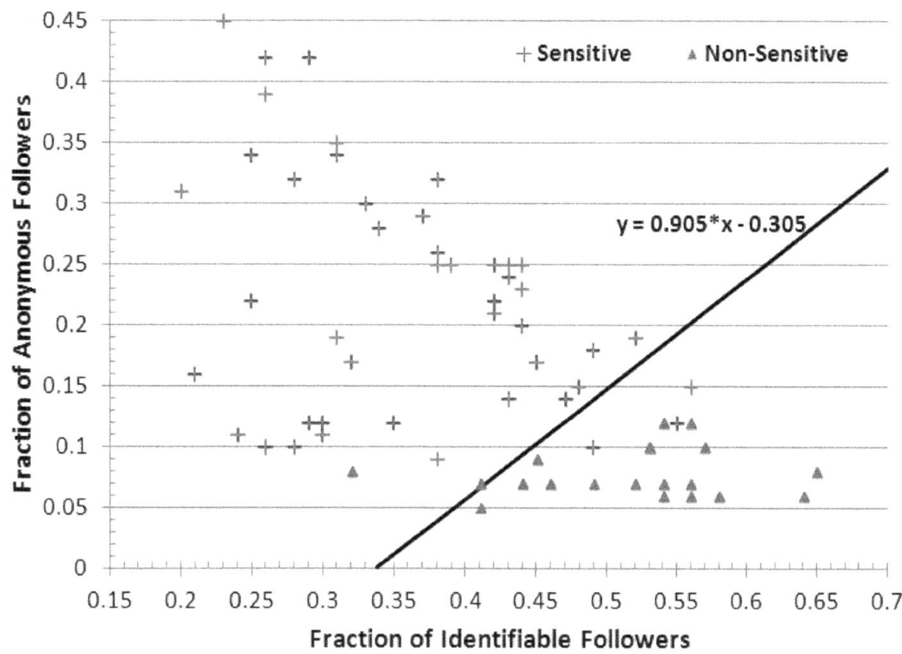

Figure 2: Sensitive and Non-Sensitive Twitter Accounts: Scatter Plot

Table 3 indicates that the percentage of Anonymous users is 5.9%, whereas Figure 1 shows that even non-sensitive accounts have Anonymous users going up to 8.9%. Similarly, the percentage of Identifiable users in Table 3 is 68%, where as in the second dataset they do not go beyond 60%. One reason for these small differences could be the difference in the age of the accounts in the two datasets. The second dataset has many recently created accounts (median account creation date is *Jan 09, 2011*) compared to the first dataset (median is *Apr 22, 2009*).

5.3 Behavioral Analysis

For the behavioral analysis of Twitter accounts we combine the datasets from the earlier two studies. After eliminating all the non-English, spam and ephemeral accounts, the distribution of labelled accounts across each category is shown in Table 5.

5.3.1 Lurker and Protected Accounts

Many OSNs have silent participants. We categorize a Twitter user as *Lurker* if the user does not post any tweets. Since ephemeral users have been removed in this study, a Lurker therefore is a user who has been active for at least six months (as evidenced by adding a friend at least six months after account creation) but yet has never posted a tweet.

As stated in Section 2, Twitter supports a *protected* privacy feature that enables users to protect their activity from being publicly visible. We investigate whether Anonymous users make use of this *protected* feature. Table 5 shows the distribution of Protected and Lurker accounts across the different labelled groups (Unclassifiable and Partially Anonymous are not shown).

We see from Table 5 that Identifiable users have a greater tendency to be private as compared to Anonymous users. A reasonable explanation for this is that, because an Identifiable user makes his identity known through his profile, he may be more reluctant to publicly share his tweets and friend list with the public at large. We also see that Identifiable users have a greater tendency to lurk as compared to Anonymous users. An Anonymous user may be less inhibited about tweeting, and hence is more willing to tweet than an Identifiable user.

Table 5: Protected and Lurker Twitter Account Statistics

Label	# of Twitter Accounts	Protected Accounts	Lurker Accounts
Highly Identifiable	2,082	301 (14.5%)	7 (0.3%)
Identifiable	65,293	8,547 (13.1%)	2,895 (4.4%)
Anonymous	19,942	2,035 (10.2%)	592 (3%)

Combining the datasets in Section 5.1 and Section 5.2 (containing many sensitive accounts), the Anonymous users increase from 5.9% to 15.3%. The Identifiable users decrease from 67.9% to 50%. This re-emphasizes that content sensitivity has a strong correlation with user anonymity. However, currently we do not know which is the cause and which is the effect, i.e., do users create Anonymous accounts because they want to follow sensitive topics (we identified that it is not the *sole* reason earlier in Section 5.2), or is it because they have an Anonymous account they do not shy away and are more open in expressing sensitive interests. This causality issue remains an open question.

5.3.2 Friends, Followers, and Tweets

To measure how different labelled groups use Twitter product features, we look at the friend, follower and tweet statistics, shown in Figure 3.

From the graphs, we can see that Highly Identifiable users have more friends, more followers and even post more tweets –implying that they are very socially active. The Identifiable users are at the other extreme–they have fewer friends, followers, and tweets. The Anonymous users have some similarities with the Highly Identifiable users, but are distinct compared to the Identifiable users.

From Figure 3a, we can see that Anonymous users tend to have many more friends (i.e., follow many more people) than Identifiable users. Being unidentifiable allows them to follow many accounts, including sensitive accounts, without worrying about the repercussions. The Identifiable users are perhaps more conservative in choosing who to follow, as it is possible to trace back their online actions to their real world identities. The kink in the CDFs at 2000 is due to Twitter's famous *follow limit*[1]–preventing people from following more than 2000 accounts, only exceedable by having many followers.

Figure 3b also shows that being Anonymous does not negatively impact the online user experience, as users are still able to obtain many followers. As Anonymous users do not hold back when sharing information or expressing opinions online, they seem to be much better at building an "online brand" for themselves, thereby attracting more users to follow them. Figure 3c indicates that Anonymous users post more tweets than Identifiable users, but they are not as socially active as Highly Identifiable users.

The median number of friends for Highly Identifiable and Anonymous groups are at 432 and 456.6, whereas the Identifiable group is far behind at 151. Similarly, the median number of followers of Highly Identifiable and Anonymous groups are very close–184.5 and 184. The median number of followers for Identifiable group is just 59. In the number of tweets, we see some distinction between Anonymous and Highly Identifiable groups–the medians of Identifiable, Anonymous and Highly Identifiable are at 145, 423 and 790 respectively.

Table 6 shows the friends and followers statistics for the Lurkers belonging to different labelled categories. Anonymous Lurkers are very active compared to Lurkers in Identifiable group–on average, they have nearly double the number of friends and followers. The strange behavior of many people following an Anonymous account, which does not post any tweets, is likely due to the attractiveness of the profile information and the expectation that something interesting (or sensitive) might be posted by that account. The same excitement does not hold for an Identifiable account.

The main takeaway message in this subsection is that Anonymous users are generally more active participants than Identifiable users, as they tweet more, lurk less, follow more accounts, and are more willing to expose their activity to the general public. These findings indicate that Anonymous and Identifiable users exhibit different online behaviors, and shows the feasibility of using these behaviors in developing an automatic Anonymous and Identifiable account classifier.

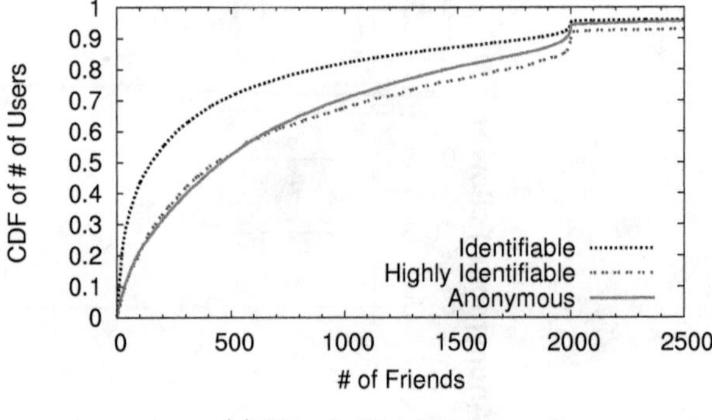

(a) Friends Distribution

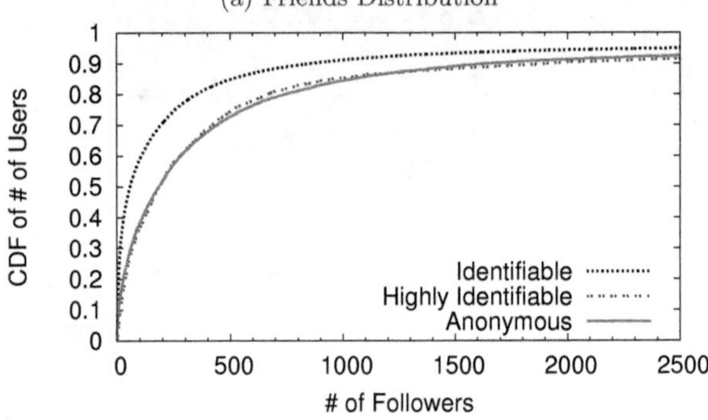

(b) Followers Distribution

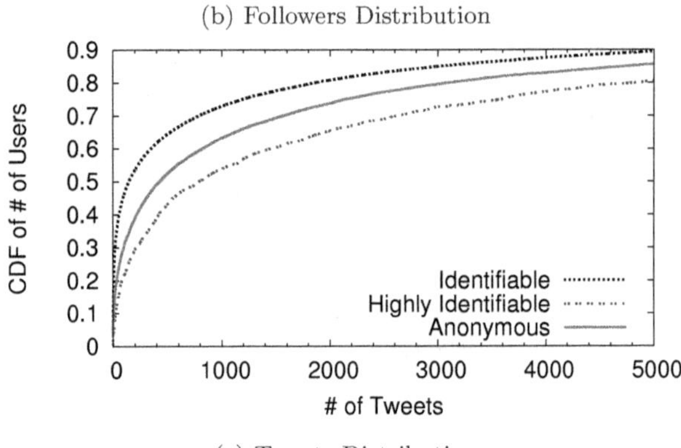

(c) Tweets Distribution

Figure 3: Friends, Followers and Tweets Statistics

6. FUTURE DIRECTIONS

As mentioned in Section 3, relying on AMT significantly limits the number of accounts we can analyze. Having a larger sample of labelled accounts can help us (i) automatically detect sensitive accounts (such as those spreading child porn–as outlined in Section 5.2), (ii) better understand the nuances of content sensitivity and its influence on online user behavior, (iii) better understand the reasons for choosing anonymous pseudonyms or evaluate the after effects of the choice, or (iv) identify behavioral traits that can be used to deanonymize the Anonymous Twitter users. Automatic user classification–possible through building large first and last name lists (e.g., crawling Facebook/Google+ user directories), or building efficient machine learning classifiers after studying a small ground truth labelled set–can help us overcome the limitations. We expect to pursue this direction in the future.

Tweets are a very important source of information that we did not exploit in this work. A user may reveal many of the user's private attributes–such as name, gender, age, sexual preference, etc.–in the tweets. Incorporating tweets into our anonymity study can help reduce the noise in the dataset. Furthermore, studying tweets can help evaluate whether anonymity has any correlation with making controversial posts on Twitter.

[1] `https://support.twitter.com/articles/66885-why-can-t-i-follow-people`

Table 6: Friends and Followers Statistics for Different Lurker Categories

	# of Friends			# of Followers		
Label	**Mean**	**Median**	**Standard Deviation**	**Mean**	**Median**	**Standard Deviation**
Identifiable Lurkers	64.8	20	217.2	15.9	5	76.8
Anonymous Lurkers	182.6	39	437.8	57.4	5	361.9

7. RELATED WORK

7.1 Surveys and Interviews

Employing surveys and interviews, many social scientists, economists, psychologists have taken interest in online anonymity [29, 42, 11, 23, 39, 10]. Our study differs from these approaches in that we employ a large-scale data-driven approach, rather than rely on surveys and interviews. The large-scale approach not only allows us to quantify issues in anonymity and reduce statistical errors, but also permits us to explore new issues, such as the importance of following sensitive topics as a motivation for anonymity. Moreover, as argued in the paper, the data-driven approach may allow us to automatically identify sensitive topics and controversial accounts (and perhaps illegal activity).

In particular, a recent survey-based study points out that people are actively seeking anonymity on the web, and that it increases online engagement [24]. This result mirrors our data driven results in Section 5.2, where we show that Anonymous users are generally less inhibited to be active participants, as they tweet more, lurk less, follow more accounts, and are more willing to expose their activity to the general public. Acquisti et al. employ an analytical framework to investigate the economics of anonymity, so it can be introduced as a feature in many online applications [4].

7.2 Data Driven Studies

There are several recent data-driven studies of anonymity using blogs and web sites. Gomez et al. studied anonymous user comments on the technology news website, Slashdot, and found that fully anonymous comments made up 18.6% of the total, and that pseudonymity is the norm when reputation mechanisms are enforced [16]. A study about 4chan, an image board website, showed that online communities can succeed despite being fully anonymous and extremely ephemeral [5]. By analyzing a question-and-answer website–Quora, Peddinti et al. show that it is possible to gain a novel understanding of users' perspectives on content sensitivity via a data-driven analysis of their usage of anonymity features of the website [36].

In our work, we focus on anonymity in online social networks. We measure the extent to which people exercise anonymity when provided with a choice of being identifiable or anonymous, as well as evaluate the behavior of anonymous and identifiable users. To our knowledge, we are the first to perform a data-driven analysis of user anonymity in online social networks.

7.3 Anonymization and Deanonymization

While some researchers have been trying to improve the anonymity guarantees in a social network [40, 7], there is a large body of research work on deanonymizing users and linking users across different social networks. Some deanonymization techniques link different social network accounts using usernames [38, 46], whereas others rely on social connection graphs [35].

Techniques such as [19] and [43], compare profile information across multiple websites to identify and link accounts belonging to the same user, thereby generating a richer user profile than is possible to infer from a single website. [15] and [20] make use of the user posted content on the website to link different social network profiles. Solutions involving machine learning techniques have also been proposed to disambiguate profiles belonging to the same user across different social networks [32, 30, 27].

Some of these techniques can potentially be used to deanonymize anonymous users on Twitter. However, the focus of our work has not been on deanonymizing users, but rather on quantifying people's desire to be anonymous and to study the behavior of anonymous users.

7.4 Studies on Twitter

Due to the availability of an API, many have extensively studied different aspects of Twitter–Java et al. focus on how Twitter users choose others to follow [21], Kwak et al. study information dissemination [28], Cha et al. measure user influence [9], and Castillo et al. study information credibility [8]. Studies have also been undertaken to improve usability of Twitter, such as developing a user recommendation service [18]. We study how Twitter users utilize the in-built privacy features.

8. CONCLUSION

We performed a large-scale analysis of Twitter to study the prevalence and behavior of Anonymous and Identifiable users. We employed Amazon Mechanical Turk (AMT) to classify Twitter users as Highly Identifiable, Identifiable, Partially Anonymous, and Anonymous. We quantified the importance of Anonymity for a large fraction of online users. We then selected several broad topic categories that are widely considered sensitive and found that there is a correlation between content sensitivity and a user's choice to be anonymous. Finally, we found that Anonymous users are generally less inhibited to be active participants, as they tweet more, lurk less, follow more accounts, and are more willing to expose their activity to the general public.

9. ACKNOWLEDGEMENTS

We thank Aleksandra Korolova for valuable feedback on the paper draft.

This work was supported in part by the NSF (under grant CNS-1318659). The views and conclusions contained in this document are those of the authors and should not be interpreted as necessarily representing the official policies, either expressed or implied, of any of the sponsors.

10. REFERENCES

[1] Child pornography via Tweet: pedophiles abuse Twitter as a distribution channel. http://www.naiin.org/en/news/Child-pornography-via-Tweet-pedophiles-abuse-Twitter-as-a-distribution-channel-75.html.

[2] Create your Google+ profile name. https://support.google.com/plus/answer/1228271?hl=en. Accessed: Feb 8th, 2014.

[3] Facebook's Name Policy. https://www.facebook.com/help/292517374180078. Accessed: Feb 8th, 2014.

[4] A. Acquisti, R. Dingledine, and P. Syverson. On the economics of anonymity. In *Financial Cryptography*, Lecture Notes in Computer Science, 2003.

[5] M. S. Bernstein, A. Monroy-Hernández, D. Harry, P. André, K. Panovich, and G. G. Vargas. 4chan and/b: An analysis of anonymity and ephemerality in a large online community. In *Proceedings of the 5th International AAAI Conference on Weblogs and Social Media (ICWSM)*, 2011.

[6] V. Blue. Forced Google Plus integration on YouTube backfires, petition hits 112,000. http://www.zdnet.com/forced-google-plus-integration-on-youtube-backfires-petition-hits-112000-7000023196/.

[7] A. Campan and T. Truta. Data and structural k-anonymity in social networks. In *Proceedings of Privacy, Security, and Trust in KDD*, 2009.

[8] C. Castillo, M. Mendoza, and B. Poblete. Information credibility on twitter. In *Proceedings of the 20th International Conference on World Wide Web (WWW)*, 2011.

[9] M. Cha, H. Haddadi, F. Benevenuto, and K. Gummadi. Measuring user influence in twitter: The million follower fallacy. In *Proceedings of 4th International AAAI Conference on Weblogs and Social Media (ICWSM)*, 2010.

[10] T. Chesney and D. K. Su. The impact of anonymity on weblog credibility. *International Journal of Human-Computer Studies*, 68(10), 2010.

[11] T. Connolly, L. M. Jessup, and J. S. Valacich. Effects of anonymity and evaluative tone on idea generation in computer-mediated groups. *Management Science*, 36(6), 1990.

[12] B. Dowell. Rise in defamation cases involving blogs and Twitter. http://www.theguardian.com/media/2011/aug/26/defamation-cases-twitter-blogs.

[13] C. GAYLORD. Facebook's Forgotten Rule: No Fake Names Allowed. http://abcnews.go.com/Technology/facebooks-forgotten-rule-fake-names-allowed/story?id=15509496.

[14] D. GEERE. Twitter spread misinformation faster than truth in UK riots. http://www.wired.co.uk/news/archive/2011-08/09/twitter-misinformation-riots.

[15] O. Goga, H. Lei, S. H. K. Parthasarathi, G. Friedland, R. Sommer, and R. Teixeira. Exploiting innocuous activity for correlating users across sites. In *Proceedings of the 22nd International Conference on World Wide Web (WWW)*, 2013.

[16] V. Gómez, A. Kaltenbrunner, and V. López. Statistical analysis of the social network and discussion threads in slashdot. In *Proceedings of the 17th International Conference on World Wide Web (WWW)*, 2008.

[17] C. Grier, K. Thomas, V. Paxson, and M. Zhang. @spam: The underground on 140 characters or less. In *Proceedings of the 17th ACM Conference on Computer and Communications Security (CCS)*, 2010.

[18] P. Gupta, A. Goel, J. Lin, A. Sharma, D. Wang, and R. Zadeh. Wtf: The who to follow service at twitter. In *Proceedings of the 22nd International Conference on World Wide Web (WWW)*, 2013.

[19] D. Irani, S. Webb, K. Li, and C. Pu. Large online social footprints–an emerging threat. In *Proceedings of International Conference on Computational Science and Engineering (CSE)*, 2009.

[20] P. Jain, P. Kumaraguru, and A. Joshi. @I Seek 'Fb.Me': Identifying Users Across Multiple Online Social Networks. In *Proceedings of the 22nd International Conference on World Wide Web Companion (WWW Companion)*, 2013.

[21] A. Java, X. Song, T. Finin, and B. Tseng. Why we twitter: Understanding microblogging usage and communities. In *Proceedings of the 9th WebKDD and 1st SNA-KDD Workshop on Web Mining and Social Network Analysis*, 2007.

[22] A. Jeffries. Facebook's fake-name fight grows as users skirt the rules. http://www.theverge.com/2012/9/17/3322436/facebook-fake-name-pseudonym-middle-name.

[23] L. M. Jessup, T. Connolly, and J. Galegher. The effects of anonymity on gdss group process with an idea-generating task. *MIS Q.*, 14(3), 1990.

[24] R. Kang, S. Brown, and S. Kiesler. Why do people seek anonymity on the internet?: informing policy and design. In *Proceedings of the SIGCHI Conference on Human Factors in Computing Systems (CHI)*, 2013.

[25] A. Kavanaugh, S. Yang, S. Sheetz, L. T. Li, and E. Fox. Microblogging in crisis situations: Mass protests in Iran, Tunisia, Egypt. In *Workshop on Transnational Human-Computer Interaction, CHI*, 2011.

[26] S. Knafo and J. Bialer. How Twitter Handles Piracy – An Inside Look. http://www.huffingtonpost.com/2012/02/02/how-twitter-handles-piracy_n_1251167.html.

[27] M. Korayem and D. J. Crandall. De-anonymizing users across heterogeneous social computing platforms. In *Proceedings of 7th International AAAI Conference on Weblogs and Social Media (ICWSM)*, 2013.

[28] H. Kwak, C. Lee, H. Park, and S. Moon. What is twitter, a social network or a news media? In *Proceedings of the 19th International Conference on World Wide Web (WWW)*, 2010.

[29] Y. Lelkes, J. A. Krosnick, D. M. Marx, C. M. Judd, and B. Park. Complete anonymity compromises the accuracy of self-reports. *Journal of Experimental Social Psychology*, 48(6), 2012.

[30] J. Liu, F. Zhang, X. Song, Y.-I. Song, C.-Y. Lin, and H.-W. Hon. What's in a name?: an unsupervised approach to link users across communities. In

Proceedings of the 6th ACM International Conference on Web Search and Data Mining (WSDM), 2013.

[31] N. Lomas. Facebook Users Must Be Allowed To Use Pseudonyms, Says German Privacy Regulator; Real-Name Policy 'Erodes Online Freedoms'. `http://techcrunch.com/2012/12/18/facebook-users-must-be-allowed-to-use-pseudonyms-says-german-privacy-regulator-real-name-policy-erodes-online-freedoms/`.

[32] A. Malhotra, L. C. Totti, W. M. Jr., P. Kumaraguru, and V. Almeida. Studying user footprints in different online social networks. *CoRR*, abs/1301.6870, 2013.

[33] E. Munoz. NYPD Twitter campaign implodes, flooded with photos of police abuse. `http://rt.com/usa/154120-nypd-hashtag-twitter-police/`.

[34] E. Mustafaraj, P. T. Metaxas, S. Finn, and A. Monroy-HernÃąndez. Hiding in plain sight: A tale of trust and mistrust inside a community of citizen reporters. In *Proceedings of 6th International AAAI Conference on Weblogs and Social Media (ICWSM)*, 2012.

[35] A. Narayanan and V. Shmatikov. De-anonymizing social networks. In *Proceedings of 30th IEEE Symposium on Security & Privacy*, 2009.

[36] S. T. Peddinti, A. Korolova, E. Bursztein, and G. Sampemane. Cloak and swagger: Understanding data sensitivity through the lens of user anonymity. In *Proceedings of the 35th IEEE Symposium on Security & Privacy*, 2014.

[37] M. Pennacchiotti and A.-M. Popescu. A machine learning approach to twitter user classification. In *Proceedings of 5th International AAAI Conference on Weblogs and Social Media (ICWSM)*, 2011.

[38] D. Perito, C. Castelluccia, M. Kaafar, and P. Manils. How unique and traceable are usernames? In *Proceedings of the 11th International Conference on Privacy Enhancing Technologies (PETS)*. 2011.

[39] T. Postmes, R. Spears, K. Sakhel, and D. de Groot. Social influence in computer-mediated communication: The effects of anonymity on group behavior. *Personality and Social Psychology Bulletin*, 27(10), 2001.

[40] K. P. Puttaswamy, A. Sala, and B. Y. Zhao. Starclique: Guaranteeing user privacy in social networks against intersection attacks. In *Proceedings of the 5th International Conference on Emerging Networking Experiments and Technologies (CoNEXT)*, 2009.

[41] K. Thomas, C. Grier, D. Song, and V. Paxson. Suspended accounts in retrospect: An analysis of twitter spam. In *Proceedings of the 2011 ACM SIGCOMM Conference on Internet Measurement Conference (IMC)*, 2011.

[42] P. A. Thompsen and D.-K. Ahn. To be or not to be: An exploration of e-prime, copula deletion and flaming in electronic mail. In *ETC: A Review of General Semantics;Summer92, Vol. 49 Issue 2, p146*, 1992.

[43] J. Vosecky, D. Hong, and V. Shen. User identification across multiple social networks. In *Proceedings of First International Conference on Networked Digital Technologies (NDT)*, 2009.

[44] D. Wiener-Bronner. Twitter Is the Preferred Social Media Platform Among Terrorists. `http://www.businessinsider.com/terror-groups-twitter-2014-5`.

[45] G. Wondracek, T. Holz, E. Kirda, and C. Kruegel. A practical attack to de-anonymize social network users. In *Proceedings of 31st IEEE Symposium on Security & Privacy*, 2010.

[46] R. Zafarani and H. Liu. Connecting corresponding identities across communities. In *Proceedings of 3rd International AAAI Conference on Weblogs and Social Media (ICWSM)*, 2009.

Online Privacy as a Collective Phenomenon

Emre Sarigol
ETH Zurich
Weinbergstrasse 56/58
Zurich, Switzerland
semre@ethz.ch

David Garcia
ETH Zurich
Weinbergstrasse 56/58
Zurich, Switzerland
dgarcia@ethz.ch

Frank Schweitzer
ETH Zurich
Weinbergstrasse 56/58
Zurich, Switzerland
fschweitzer@ethz.ch

ABSTRACT

The problem of online privacy is often reduced to individual decisions to hide or reveal personal information in online social networks (OSNs). However, with the increasing use of OSNs, it becomes more important to understand the role of the social network in disclosing personal information that a user has not revealed voluntarily: How much of our private information do our friends disclose about us, and how much of our privacy is lost simply because of online social interaction? Without strong technical effort, an OSN may be able to exploit the assortativity of human private features, this way constructing shadow profiles with information that users chose not to share. Furthermore, because many users share their phone and email contact lists, this allows an OSN to create full shadow profiles for people who do not even have an account for this OSN.

We empirically test the feasibility of constructing shadow profiles of sexual orientation for users and non-users, using data from more than 3 Million accounts of a single OSN. We quantify a lower bound for the predictive power derived from the social network of a user, to demonstrate how the predictability of sexual orientation increases with the size of this network and the tendency to share personal information. This allows us to define a *privacy leak factor* that links individual privacy loss with the decision of other individuals to disclose information. Our statistical analysis reveals that some individuals are at a higher risk of privacy loss, as prediction accuracy increases for users with a larger and more homogeneous first- and second-order neighborhood of their social network. While we do not provide evidence that shadow profiles exist at all, our results show that disclosing of private information is not restricted to an individual choice, but becomes a collective decision that has implications for policy and privacy regulation.

COSN'14, October 1–2, 2014, Dublin, Ireland.

http://dx.doi.org/10.1145/2660460.2660470

Categories and Subject Descriptors

H.1.2 [**Information Systems**]: Models and principles—*User/machine Systems*

General Terms

Data mining, Privacy, Social Systems

Keywords

Privacy; Shadow Profiles; Prediction

1. INTRODUCTION

Our society is increasingly grounded on information and communication technologies, in which protecting one's privacy might not be an individual choice [12]. In online social networks (OSNs), the characteristics of each user is determined primarily by its connections, rather than by its intrinsic properties. Hence, from an individual's perspective, isolation is often not a desirable option [42]. To that end, the issue of protecting one's privacy within the OSN relates largely to the community the individual is embedded in, and how it is handled, if at all, by the community at large.

Although the existence of mass surveillance and the imminent threats it poses are known by many, studies in a number of fields show that people do little to protect their privacy against surveillance [42]. In an OSN, users are often incentivised to share personal data, e.g. by offering some sort of benefit or personalization as a service (e.g. recommender systems). But incentives also arise from social influences, e.g. from social surveillance of peers to receive attention and to reinforce existing relationships [33]. When an OSN provider has access to the contacts of users, it gains stronger predictive power. Together with the content willingly produced by users, there are ways to extract probabilistic profiles of other users, even about persons who did not have an account in the given OSN [9].

On the aggregated level, this leads to an imbalance between the knowledge that a single user has about the OSN provider and the knowledge that the provider has, or is able to deduce, about individual users and even about persons that are not users. There is no way of knowing how the information provided by an everyday user to the OSN can be utilized, and there are no clear policies about this either. The usage often stretches from personalization to social discrimination, without the user's knowledge [31]. A `Facebook` bug revealed in 2013 is an appropriate example for one of the many ways the information provided by users may be utilized. According to the reported bug, `Facebook` attempted to obtain users' off-site email addresses and phone numbers, gathered from the contact lists shared by other users. It appeared that the covertly collected information was then being stored in each Facebook user's invisible *Shadow Profile* that is somehow attached to accounts [1]. Digital trends [3] defines a Facebook Shadow Profile as *"a file that Facebook keeps on you containing data it pulls up from looking at the information that a user's friends voluntarily provide. You're not supposed to see it, or even know it exists."* Facebook reacted to the incident to fix the leak as soon as possible. However, what has remained not fixed until now is their policy. In a set of interviews, Facebook officials claimed that obtaining third party user data on individuals in this manner was not a privacy breach since the data has been submitted voluntarily by members of Facebook, which make the data a property of Facebook [2]. This argument is backed up by the following statement in Facebook Terms of Service:

We receive information about you from your friends and others, such as when they upload your contact information, post a photo of you, tag you in a photo or status update, or at a location, or add you to a group. When people use Facebook, they may store and share information about you and others that they have, such as when they upload and manage their invites and contacts [4].

Facebook for Mobile alone has over one billion users that agreed to their terms of service, which allows the application to *"read data about your contacts stored on your phone, including the frequency with which you've called, emailed, or communicated in other ways with specific individuals"*. It is not difficult to imagine the massive amount of ongoing data acquisition based on such intact privacy policies. Therefore, it becomes an imminent question to what extent can an OSN be turned into a tool that acquires data to profile the whole society, just because some individuals have become members of that OSN. Our main contribution to this discussion is to demonstrate to what extent the information of an OSN provider about its users can be used to quantify knowledge about the individuals of our society, at large. We use an empirical dataset from Friendster, a large online social networking site that preceded Facebook. This dataset, which is publicly accessible in the Internet Archive[1], allowed us to evaluate the power that Friendster had to create shadow profiles.

Our aim is not to provide new tools or algorithms to improve the accuracy of the knowledge that an OSN provider can possess. Instead, we aim to apply state of the art statistical analyses and machine learning techniques to quantify the extent to which individual privacy is leaked by the activity of others in an OSN, and to empirically test how the individual decision to reveal information turns into a collective phenomenon to disclose privacy. In our analysis, we study two interrelated problems. First we explore the *Partial Shadow Profile* problem, in which an OSN infers private information that its users chose not to share. Second, we address the *Full Shadow Profile* problem, in which an OSN provider discovers private information about individuals who do not even have an account there, solely based on personal information and contact lists shared by its actual users.

[1] https://archive.org/details/archive-team-friendster

In this work, we focus on sexual orientation as a relevant and sensitive private information the disclosure of which should be in control of the users. The combination of gender and sexual orientation creates a set of classes that appear with inhomogeneous frequencies, which is often the case in real-life prediction problems of different domains (e.g. political affiliation). For each user, we construct a simple social context based on frequency measures on the neighborhood at increasing distances. We quantify privacy leak factors for different sexual orientation groups and analyze how they are affected by two main factors, the network size and the disclosure parameter, i.e. the ratio of users sharing their contact lists and/or private information with the OSN. We further analyze how the coefficients of larger (i.e. majority) and smaller (i.e. minority) sexual orientation groups compare with respect to these two factors.

2. RELATED WORK

Understanding privacy in OSNs starts with the individual motivation to share personal information and its associated risk of sharing this information with undesired contacts [6, 24]. Most OSNs include highly customizable modules to control privacy settings, which can lead to higher efforts and uncertainty how to use the site [29], or to distancing from those users that have a lower awareness of possible data leakage [32, 26, 10]. Recent technologies promise to alleviate user privacy concerns. For example, distributed recommender systems can put a limit to privacy disclosure [21], deployment of OSNs in the cloud can avoid the centralization of user data [44, 46], techniques for picture encryption [43] and content anonymization [38] can prevent undesired access to private content.

Private information about users can be a source of wealth, e.g. by significantly increasing the revenue of personalized advertisement [19]. This creates incentives for OSNs to share private user information with third parties, from which the user does not necessarily benefit. A possible solution for this dilemma is to create monetization schemes that allow users to set up the price they request for companies to access their private information [41], effectively creating *privacy butlers* that automatically control privacy [45, 27]. This approach can be criticized for its ethics about the value of privacy, asking if market dynamics would push less wealthy individuals to have no privacy [36]. Additionally, the monetization of privacy relies on systems that would allow an individual to have full access control of its privacy, which is hardly realistic.

Even with full individual control, the possibility of third-parties to infer private attributes still exists [35]. The discovery of unknown/hidden parts of a network based on its visible properties is a well studied problem, in particular with respect to *link prediction* [15, 5, 28]. Such hidden links have been shown to be predictable by geographic coincidences [14], using geotagged photo data from Flickr. The method introduced in [14] utilizes the number and proximity in time and space of co-occurences among pairs of individuals to infer the likelihood of a social tie between them. The link prediction problem has also been applied to predict links between non-users of Facebook [20], given only the link information towards non-members from the known network. Additionally, the *network completion* problem aims to infer both missing links and nodes, where it has been shown that the missing part of the network can be inferred based only on the connectivity patterns of the observed part [5].

Previous studies of user privacy have focused on *sensitive attribute inference* problems, where user private attributes are detected based on a mix of public profiles in the network, friendship links and group membership information of private users [47]. Specifically, within the *friendship identification and inference* attack [23], a user might aim to infer private attributes of another user. Given that the attacker and the target are direct or 2-distant neighbors, the success of such attacks depends on network topological properties, such as the position of the attacker in the network. Furthermore, iterative algorithms can effectively label nodes by propagating information to their neighborhoods [18]. A wide variety of models have aimed at predicting different private features, such as gender, age, political orientation [39], home location [37], and academic profiles [34]. In the context of sexual and romantic relationships, two previous works are especially relevant. First, the *"gaydar"* experiment [22] showed that homosexual male users can be detected based on the amount of friends of the same type they had on `Facebook`. Second, a recent article [7] proposes a new measure of *dispersion* and applies it to a large `Facebook` dataset in order to predict which of a user's friends is their romantic partner.

In this article, we evaluate the accuracy of partial and full shadow profiles for the sexual orientation of users and non-users of the `Friendster` social network. Our analysis builds on the sequence of users joining `Friendster` to evaluate predictions over individuals without a user account in a similar manner as done in [20] where the links between non-users are inferred. Knowing in which sequence the users joined `Friendster` has freed us from having to utilize a network growth model in our analysis. Furthermore, we pay special attention to the ratios of friends belonging to each orientation in the neighborhood of users at a given time in the growth of the network. Our results should be compared with previous work on sexual orientation of users in smaller datasets [22]. To our knowledge, our work is the first to address the possibility of creating full shadow profiles for the sexual orientation of non-users from a large scale OSN.

3. DATA DESCRIPTION

Before its social networking functionalities were discontinued, `Friendster` was crawled by the `Internet Archive`, leaving a snapshot of all the publicly available information at that moment. Our previous analysis of the connectivity patterns of the network [16] reveals that the first 20 Million users of `Friendster` were largely located in the US, before the OSN spread to other countries. The growth of `Friendster` in the US stopped because of the competition with `MySpace` and `Facebook` [40]. This allows us to analyze these initial 20 Million users as a subset of US users of the OSN.

The amount of information about each user available in the `Friendster` dataset depends on the privacy settings of the user. Most of them allowed their friendship lists to be publicly available, and some of them also let other users to see private features explicitly given by the user, such as age and gender. Within the subset we considered, 3,431,335 users had public profiles which were captured by the crawl, including the personal information explained in Table 1. This subset contains a total of 11,074,009 undirected friendship links among these public profiles only, resulting in an average degree of 3.23.

Feature	Description
User ID	integer
Name	string
Birth date	date
Gender	*Male*, *Female*, or *Unspecified*
Interests*	*Friends*, *Activity Partners*, *Just looking around*, *Fans*, *Dating Women*, *Relationship with Women*, *Dating Men*, *Relationship with Men*, *Dating Men and Women*, *Relationship with Men and Women*
Relationship status	*Single*, *Married*, *In a Relationship*, *Domestic Partners*, *It's Complicated*

Table 1: `Friendster` public profile features. The interests feature contains one or more of its possible values.

In addition, each user has an id number that indicates the order in which the user joined the social network, allowing us to construct time-dependent vectors of feature distributions in user neighborhoods, as described in the following section.

The network in Figure 1 displays the `Friendster` network among a randomly selected 10% of the users with public profiles, where node colors represent the sexual orientation class, and the colored edges represent assortativity where two endpoints share the same sexual orientation class. About 30% of all the edges are assortative in this representative network, which suggests that it is common to form links based on sexual orientation.

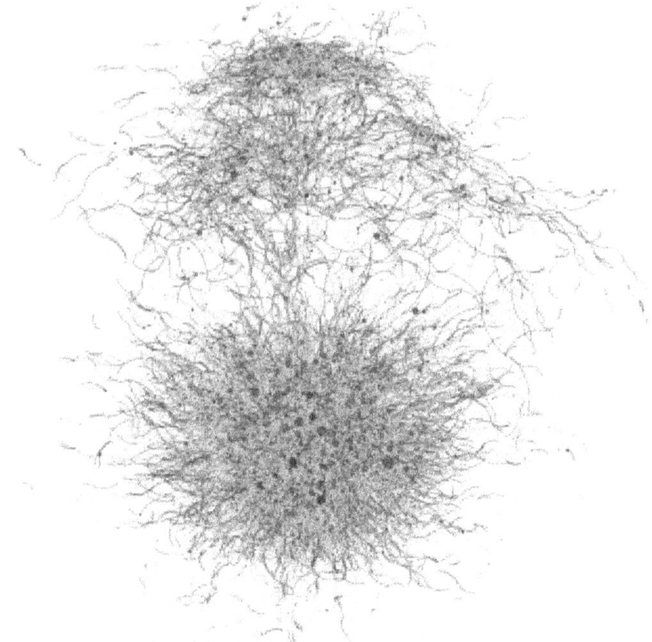

Figure 1: The network for a subset of Friendster users. The red edges represent assortativity, where the endpoint nodes are in the same sexual orientation class. The node colors correspond to the sexual orientation class.

Gender	M	F	Class	Label	% users
Female	No	No	Female without interest	**FF**	28.2
Male	No	No	Male without interest	**FM**	26.4
Female	Yes	No	Heterosexual female	**HeF**	9.3
Male	Yes	No	Homosexual male	**HoM**	1.9
Female	No	Yes	Homosexual female	**HoF**	1.0
Male	No	Yes	Heterosexual male	**HeM**	19.9
Female	Yes	Yes	Bisexual female	**BiF**	6.8
Male	Yes	Yes	Bisexual male	**BiM**	6.5

Table 2: User orientation classification. An "interested in" relationship may stand for interested in dating or having a relationship.

4. METHODS

Being aware that sexual orientation and gender can be defined in a variety of ways [8], we use the simplest classification available in our data: gender as birth sex (male or female) and sexual orientation simplified to the set of possible combinations of interest towards the two genders. This way, we combine gender with the explicit romantic interest in other genders, as specified by *Dating* and *Relationship* interests towards different genders introduced in Table 1. Each user can be assigned to one of the eight classes with respect to their sexual orientations, which are described in Table 2. Additional features of sexual orientation can capture other activities, group identities, or political standpoints, and other features that cannot be empirical measured in our dataset.

Features	Description
Profile	Age, gender, relationship status, Sexual orientation
n_k	Number of users at distance k
a_k	Average age of friends at distance k
g_k	Gender counts at distance k
r_k	Relationship counts at distance k
i_k	Romantic interest counts at distance k
x_k	Sexual orientation counts at distance k
x_w	Weighted frequency of friends of each sexual orientation

Table 3: Features of the user vector. Neighborhood frequencies are computed for distances 1, 2, and 3, for each possible value of the profile features.

For each user in the dataset, we built a feature vector including their profile information, and different metrics of the distribution of features in their neighborhood at distances up to 3. For each distance k, we calculated the amount of users at that exact distance (n_k), and within those users, we counted the amounts of users with each possible value of gender, relationship status, romantic interest, and sexual orientation. To measure age in the neighborhood, we computed the average age of the users at distance k (a_k). Since previous research suggests that the most indicative factor is the sexual orientation of the first neighbors of the user [22], we computed an additional weighted count of friends of each sexual orientation, weighting each link by the amount of common friends that the two users have. The features of this vector are summarized in Table 3.

5. PARTIAL SHADOW PROFILES

Our first step was to explore the *partial shadow profiles* problem. We define partial shadow profiles as enhanced data of an OSN provider about its users, covering personal information these users did not initially agree to share. We test the OSN provider's ability to construct partial shadow profiles over the set of users that have initially disclosed their romantic interest towards at least one gender, leaving out users of the classes FF and FM. This leaves us with 1,027,400 users and six classes, with feature vectors built over the network including all 3.3 Million users to reach neighborhoods at larger distances.

We arrange the data of these users as follows: We choose a *partial disclosure parameter* $R \in \{x/10 : x \in \mathbb{N}, x < 10\}$, defined as the probability that a user has shared sexual interest information with the social network. For a given R, we include users in the *training* set with probability R, and leave them for the *test* set with probability $1 - R$. The training set contains those users whose sexual orientation class are known, and the test set contains those users whose class or other user features (e.g. gender and age) are hidden. This reproduces the problem setup that the OSN provider faces when constructing partial profiles: a set of its users have disclosed their orientation, but others chose not to. We preserve the friendship links of all users, including those in the *test* set and build the user vector for the *training* set of users, using all the links and only the user features within the *training* set, since the user features of the *test* set of users are hidden. We use this vector to train a Random Forest Classifier, and use the resulting classifier to predict the sexual orientation of users in the *test* set. Since both the training and the test cases are randomly chosen, we repeat this 10 times for each R.

Through these 10 repetitions, we aim at understanding the dependence between the tendency to share personal information of the users of an OSN, and the predictability of the sexual orientation of those users who chose not to share that information. In particular we want to understand under which conditions this prediction would outperform a random estimator and by what factor.

5.1 Prediction Results

For each value of R and random samplings of training and test users, we computed the *Precision* and *Recall* values for each of the six sexual orientation classes. Figure 2 shows the mean values over the 10 runs of each value of R.

We observe that for all classes, *Recall* can reach values much higher than the base rate, which is equivalent to the percentage of users that belong to each class. This holds for low values of R for all classes but homosexual females and bisexual males, which require $R > 0.3$ to have a precision above the base rate. For the case of homosexual females, which constitutes 2% of all users, the *Precision* increases up to 60% but the *Recall* values increase marginally between 2% and 4%, showing that some homosexual females can be detected with high *Precision*, but the vast majority of them cannot be predicted by the Random Forest Classifier. The most striking results are for homosexual males, where both *Precision* and *Recall* are several times above the base rate, and for the majority classes of heterosexual males and females, which also show large values of *Precision* and *Recall.*

Precision values alone indicate that the accuracy of predictions increases significantly with higher values of R. To

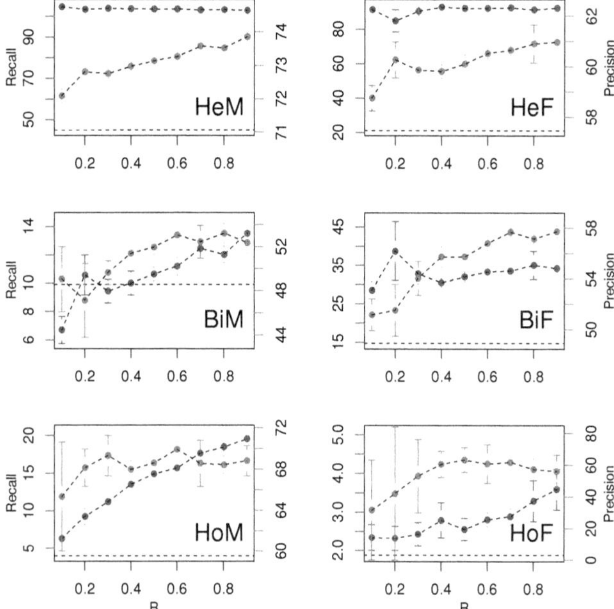

Figure 2: Recall and Precision (%) for each class versus R for the partial shadow profile problem. The blue lines and the left y-axis show the recall values, whereas the red lines and the right y-axis show the precision values as R, the partial disclosure parameter, grows. The dashed black line shows the base rate, the percentage of users for each class within the whole data set.

empirically test the relationship between prediction results and the partial disclosure parameter, we computed Cohen's Kappa Coefficient [13] for each class and classification run:

$$\kappa = \frac{Pr(a) - Pr(e)}{1 - Pr(e)} \quad (1)$$

where $Pr(a)$ is the relative observed agreement between classification and test data, and $Pr(e)$ is the hypothetical probability of chance agreement, using the observed data to calculate the probabilities of each observer randomly saying each category.

If the raters are in complete agreement then $\kappa = 1$. If there is no agreement among the raters other than what would be expected by chance (as defined by $Pr(e)$), $\kappa = 0$. Cohen's Kappa κ captures a combination of *Precision* and *Recall* similar to the F_1 value, but includes the comparison to the baseline of a random classifier in its calculation. Thus, the performance of a random classifier would tend towards $\kappa = 0$, while the value of F_1 would depend on the distribution of classes in the dataset.

Since Kappa's coefficient is independent of class size and thus is resilient to biases introduced by differing class sizes, we aggregate the performance of the classifier for individual classes into a single average κ. Figure 3 displays the average Cohen's Kappa coefficient over all classes.

We observe that as the partial disclosure parameter R grows, an OSN provider would be able to predict, with higher accuracy, the sexual orientation of those users that did not share it. We statistically test this observation through

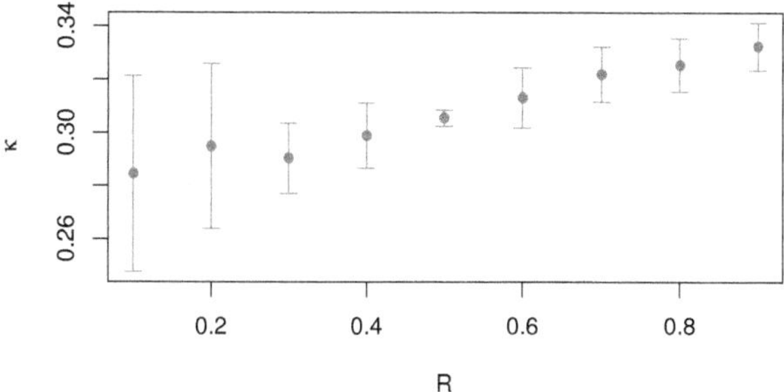

Figure 3: Cohen's Kappa coefficient versus R for the partial shadow profile problem.

a *privacy leak factor* for each user class, computed as the weight of R in a linear regressor with an intercept and κ as dependent variable. Table 4 shows the statistical results for each of the six fits, as well as the fit for the privacy leak factor computed for all classes on the average κ.

Class	Class %	priv. leak. factor	p-value
HeM	47	0.02	2.9×10^{-7}
HeF	23	0.04	2.1×10^{-3}
BiM	9	0.09	4.9×10^{-4}
BiF	16	0.06	5.2×10^{-2}
HoM	4	**0.24**	7.1×10^{-6}
HoF	2	0.02	8.6×10^{-3}
$\overline{\kappa}$	-	0.12	1.1×10^{-3}

Table 4: privacy leak factors for each class and average κ in the partial shadow profiles problem. All estimates are below the 0.01 significance level, with the exception of BiF.

This statistical analysis demonstrates that all classes have a significant and positive privacy leak factors, with the exception of bisexual females, for which the p-value was above 0.01. The size estimates of the privacy leak factor differ across classes, having relatively low values for heterosexual male and female, and for the homosexual female class. The largest values are present for the homosexual and bisexual male classes. Homosexual males have low predictability under $R = 0.1$, since they constitute about 4% of all users, but the privacy leak factor is much higher than for other classes, being estimated as 0.24, 12 times larger than for the largest class of heterosexual males. This suggests that homosexual male users that do not disclose their sexual orientation are at a larger risk of privacy leakage if the tendency of other users to share their sexual orientation becomes stronger.

Finally, the standard errors for the average κ, and the *Precision* and *Recall* of individual classes reveal that, across the 10 runs for each R, the prediction accuracy does not vary much for a given R, especially for higher values of R. This suggests that the prediction accuracy does not rely on which users of the OSN have revealed their sexual orientation, given that large enough ($R \simeq 0.3$) percentage of the population share personal information.

6. FULL SHADOW PROFILES

Full shadow profiles are the profiles that an OSN provider can generate about individuals that do not have an account for this OSN. The idea is, when a user shares its contact list with the OSN, the provider can find out which email addresses do not have an associated account and can generate a full shadow profile for these non-users. If those non-users appear in many contact lists of OSN users, data mining techniques can be used to infer the home location, age, gender, etc, of the non-users.

For the Full Shadow Profiles problem, we arrange our data as follows: We select a parameter $a \in \{x/10 : x \in \mathbb{N}, x < 10\}$, where each a divides the whole user data of N users into two sets:

- *Inside* user set, which is of size $a \times N$ users
- *Outside* user set, which is of size $(1 - a) \times N$ users

In Figure 4, the *Inside* user set is represented by the combination of the black and gray nodes, and is the set of members of the OSN at time t. The *Outside* user set is represented by the combination of red and white nodes, which are the set of users that are not part of the network at time t, hereafter denoted as *non-users*.

Furthermore, we introduce a *disclosure parameter* $\rho \in \{0.5, 0.7, 0.9\}$ which is the fraction of users in the *Inside* user set that shared all of their contacts with `Friendster`. For `Facebook`, given the fact that every user of the `Facebook for Mobile` initially has to agree that `Facebook` can access their contact list, ρ would be closer to 1.0.

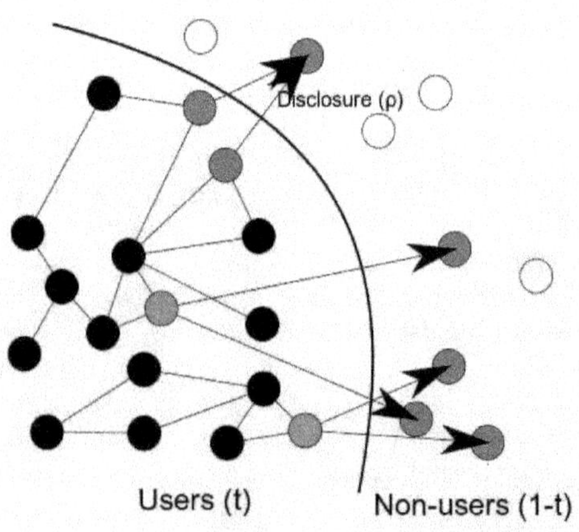

Figure 4: Schema of the full shadow profile construction problem.

Given a combination of a and ρ, we measure: a) To what degree is the OSN provider able to find out about the sexual orientation of the *non-users*; b) How much is the social network confident about its findings about the *non-users*, by measuring how much it can predict about its actual user base, i.e. *Inside*. To that end, we pursue the following method in three steps:

1. We build a user vector for each user in the *Inside* user set as described in Section 3 [2], discarding all their links to the non-users. We then use this user vector to build a Random Forest classifier [11] over the user class of sexual orientation (hereby referred to as RF_a).
2. For each user in the *Inside* user set, we flip a biased coin where the outcome is heads with probability ρ and for those users that got tails, we discard all their links to the non-users. Using the remaining links, we build the user vector of the non-users who have at least one link to *Inside*. This user vector represents the vector that the social network can construct for the non-users, using only the contacts of its users that shared their contact lists.
3. We use RF_a to predict the sexual orientation of the non-users.

While building the feature vectors for non-users in step 2, we discard all user attributes (relationship status, age and gender) from the feature vector, and keep only neighborhood information for each user. The reason we discard user attributes is to represent the real life situation where the social network knows nothing at all about the non-users at t. Since RF_a will be used to classfy the resulting vector, RF_a must also be built using the same features available in for the non-users. Therefore, we discard all user attributes also from the user feature vector in step 1.

Step 1 is run once for each a where we acquire a corresponding RF_a Step 2 and 3 are repeated 10 times for each (a, ρ) pair, such that for each run, a different ρ fraction of users share their contact lists, and hence a different set of links are preserved to the non-users.

6.1 Prediction Results

In the full shadow profiles problem, non-users are subject of losing privacy as other individuals join the OSN, potentially revealing their contacts. We evaluate the performance of the RF_a classifier over the set of non-users, for increasing values of a, to test if prediction accuracy correlates with the size of the OSN. Since these results are subject to increase with the disclosure parameter ρ, we repeat the analysis for three different values of ρ. We measured precision and recall over the complete set of non-users, and report their mean values over 10 resamples in Figure 5.

For all classes, there is an increasing trend in recall values with a, as well as with ρ. ρ plays a more significant role for recall than for precision. This is because as ρ grows, feature vectors for more non-users can be constructed, leaving out less and less non-users from the predictions, which impacts recall over all non-users. Larger values of a also contribute to precision in most of the cases, but this increase seems negligible compared to the distance between precision and base rate of each class. To further understand these trends, we computed Cohen's Kappa for all classes over each evaluation. The average values of κ versus a are shown in Figure 6, showing that the predictive power of the classifier increases with a and slightly increases with ρ.

To statistically test for the presence of an increase of prediction quality with a, we calculated privacy leak factors for

[2]For the full shadow profile analysis, we did not use 3-order neighborhood information due to the large number of simulations needed and computational limitations that were introduced

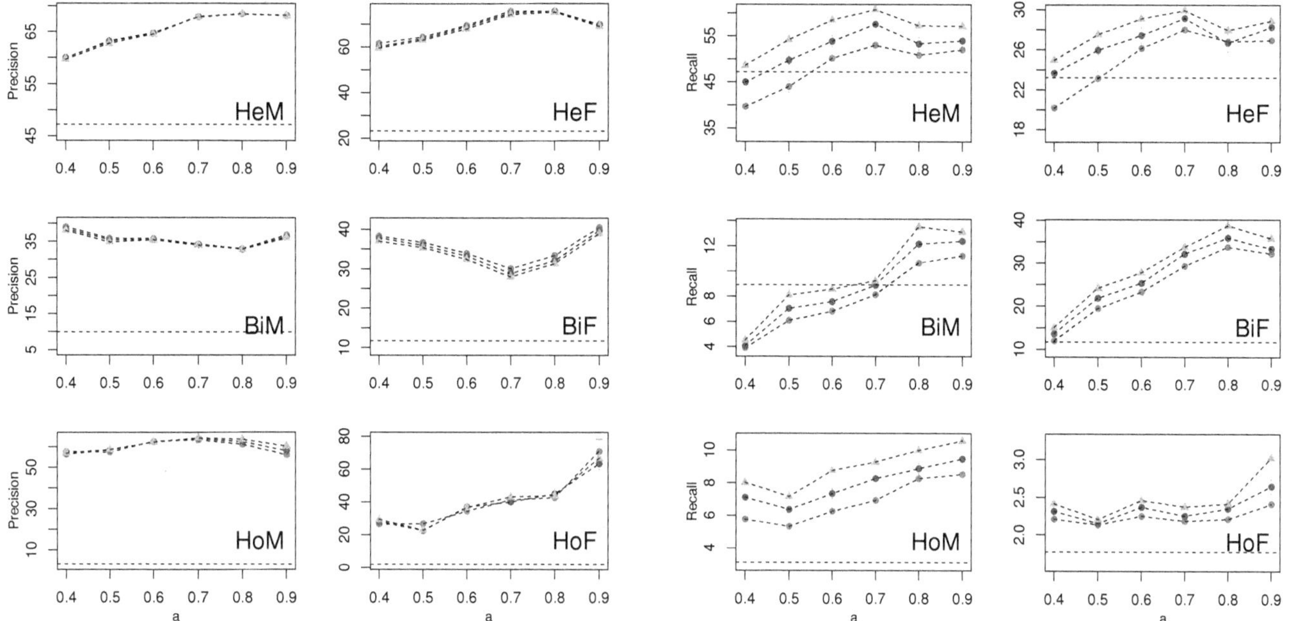

Figure 5: Precision and recall for each class in the full shadow profiles problem, for $\rho = 0.5$ (red), $\rho = 0.7$ (blue), and $\rho = 0.9$ (green). The base rate of each class is given by the dashed black line.

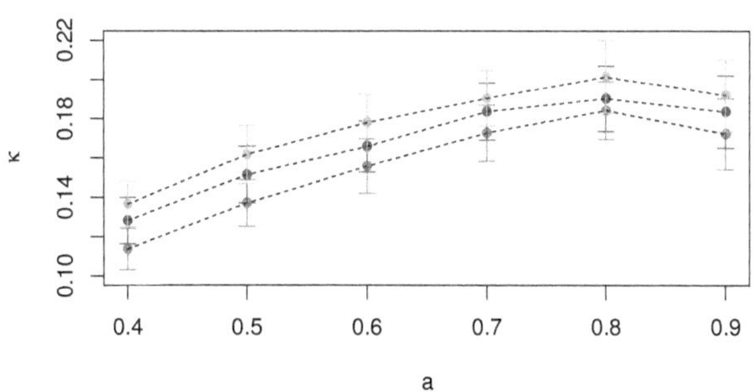

Figure 6: Cohen's Kappa in full shadow profiles for all classes versus a, for $\rho = 0.5$ (red), $\rho = 0.7$ (blue), and $\rho = 0.9$ (green).

ρ	privacy leak factor (all classes)	p-value
0.5	0.12	0.007
0.7	0.13	0.002
0.9	0.16	0.002

Table 5: Privacy leak factor in full shadow profiles, calculated over κ for all classes.

the full shadow profiles problem. In contrast with the partial shadow profiles problem, where we linked the decision of users to disclose their personal information, in the full shadow profiles problem we are interested in knowing how the decision of some users to join the OSN can influence the privacy of non-users. Thus, we compute privacy leak factor as the regression weight of a in the κ of the classifier for different values of ρ. As shown in Table 5, the privacy leak factor is positive and significant for the three values of ρ, suggesting that an overall privacy loss for non-users as the OSN grows.

The privacy leak factor for full shadow profiles is not homogeneous for all sexual orientations. Table 6 shows the privacy leak factors, which are positive and significant for all classes but homosexual female. The values of the privacy leak factor do not greatly differ for the three values of ρ, suggesting that the main driving factor of privacy loss of non-users is network growth. Comparing across classes, the sexual orientation with the strongest privacy leak factor is bisexual females, which had the least significant counterpart for partial shadow profiles, as shown in Table 4. This suggests that bisexual females can be detected with higher accuracy when other users join the OSN, rather than by disclosure of private attributes within the OSN.

ρ	Class	priv.leak f.	p-value	Class	priv.leak f.	p-value
0.5		0.21	0.015		0.23	0.021
0.7	**HeM**	0.18	0.035	**HeF**	0.15	0.059
0.9		0.21	0.030		0.15	0.051
0.5		0.17	0.00021		0.35	0.0012
0.7	**BiM**	0.19	0.0011	**BiF**	0.32	0.0024
0.9		0.21	0.0037		0.30	0.0055
0.5		0.11	0.029		0.0012	0.71
0.7	**HoM**	0.087	0.048	**HoF**	0.0036	0.57
0.9		0.097	0.046		0.0037	0.61

Table 6: Privacy leak factor in full shadow profiles for each class.

6.2 Analyzing Prediction Results

We analyzed the properties that correctly predicted non-users have in common, in order to shed light to other factors that may have played a role in predictions. Figure 7 shows the distribution of the first order neighborhood size in the *Inside* for all non-users at $a = 0.6$ and $\rho = 0.9$, and the

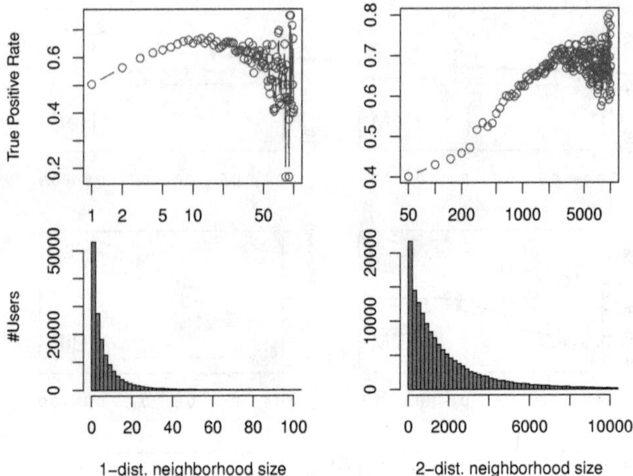

Figure 7: Bottom left: First order neighborhood size distribution where the sizes are the number of friends in the known part of the network who shared their contact lists. Top left: True Positive rate (TPR) for different first order neighborhood sizes where TPR is given by the ratio of number of correctly predicted users to the number of users that fall into each neighborhood size range. Bottom right: Second order neighborhood size distribution. Top right: TPR for different second order neighborhood sizes. All figures are derived from 10 simulations where $a = 0.6$ and $\rho = 0.9$.

corresponding *true positive rate* (TPR) for each neighborhood size range, calculated as the ratio of correctly classified users over all classified users. Non-users with at least one friend in the *Inside* are more likely to be predicted correctly (TPR = 0.52). In addition, the TPR increases with neighborhood size. At first sight, this would mean that one friend in the *Inside* set gives the OSN provider enough power to accurately profile a non-user. But looking at Figure 7 (right column), which shows the TPR distribution for different second order neighborhood sizes of non-users, we observe a new dependence: Although the second order neighborhood size is more heterogeneous, the TPR increases significantly for larger sizes. Therefore, from a non-user's perspective, not only the amount of friends in the OSN is a critical factor, but how well connected those friends are.

We explored the assortativity of sexual orientation between users and non-users, and how this can increase prediction accuracy. As an example, we look at homosexual male users, which is one of the smallest classes. Figure 8 displays the distribution of homosexual male user ratios in the first order neighborhood of non-users of the same orientation, and the corresponding TPR for each ratio of assortative links. It is more likely that homosexual male non-users will be classified correctly as the ratio of links of the same kind increases in their first order neighborhood, suggesting that assortativity plays a significant role in privacy leakage. An ratio of homosexual male friends of 0.1 is quite common, and displays no significant affect on TPR (TPR = 0.09), although it is still larger than the base rate. For a ratio of homosexual male friends between 0.2 and 0.5, there is a clear increase in the TPR.

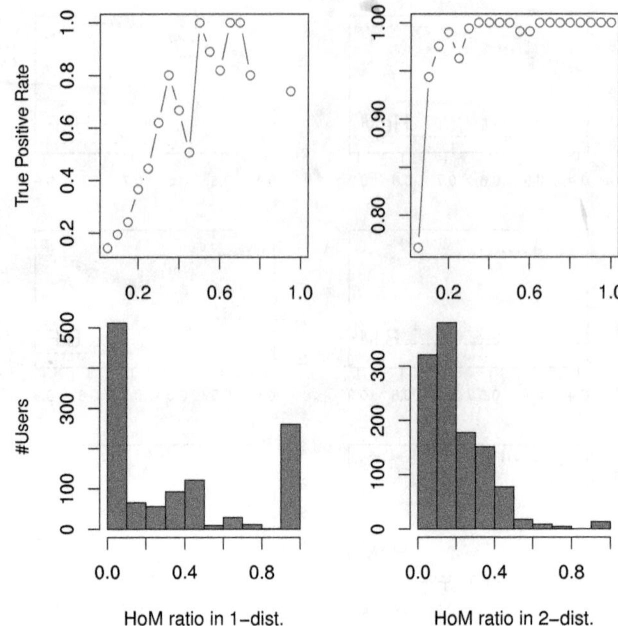

Figure 8: (bottom left) Distribution of HoM user ratios in the first order neighborhood of HoM non-users. (top left) TPR for HoM non-users in each HoM ratio range, where TPR is given by the ratio of number of correctly predicted HoM non-users to all HoM non-users. (bottom right) Distribution of HoM user ratios in the second order neighborhood of HoM non-users. (top right) TPR for HoM non-users in each second order HoM ratio range. All figures are derived from 10 simulations where $a = 0.6$ and $\rho = 0.9$.

Noise is present between 0.5 and 0.6, due to the fact that there are only very few non-users that fall in these categories. Figure 8 suggests that the ratios of homosexual male friends in the second order neighborhoods of non-users also correlate with the respective TPR values, suggesting that higher order assortative ties also influence privacy leakage.

These figures help us understand further what kind of dynamics contribute to privacy leakage in an OSN. The privacy leakage seems to be influenced by the size of the first order neighborhood, how many highly connected users exist within the first order neighborhood, and the assortativity across the first and second order neighborhoods with respect to the user's sexual orientation. The cross-dependence among these three factors seem to result in a large amount of privacy leakage. In this section we have looked at only a few of the possible factors and analyzed assortative relationships of only one sexual orientation class. The analysis can certainly be extended by looking into network features of known and unknown users and into different different classes.

7. DISCUSSION

The privacy leak factor is not homogeneous for all sexual orientations. We showed that the privacy leak factors for large and small groups respond differently to changing network size and disclosure behavior. For example, the amount by which precision and recall digress away from their respective base rates for HoM individuals is much larger than and HeM individuals. Often, it is more risky for smaller groups to be compromised within the society, whereas larger groups are often not concerned by this risk. This is mostly due to peer pressure or to the fact that minority rights are legally not represented.

There are multiple factors that put individuals under privacy risk. We have shown that network size and disclosure parameter influence privacy risk for non-users. We have also suggested that this risk varies depending on how connected a non-user is to the network, and the nature of their connection (i.e. the homophilic nature of connections).

The simulations are representative of a realistic network growth scenario and disclosure behavior. Our simulations are representative of a realistic network growth since we used `Friendster` user IDs, which are sequential with respect to the member's joining time, thus freeing our analysis to consult different growth models. Furthermore, the choice for the range of disclosure parameter, $\rho \in [0.5, 0.7, 0.9]$, corresponds to a realistic scenario for the fraction of members sharing their contact lists. $\rho = 0.9$ is closer to reality as most people share their contact lists (either voluntarily or due to the accepted terms of use) when they subscribe to an online social network, as reports about `Facebook` reveal. Finally, since we have made 10 runs for each a and ρ pair, and since standard errors are quite marginal, we can conclude that the findings are rather representative of the conditions a and ρ.

Since the data of the first 20 Million `Friendster` users have been downloaded from the `Internet Archive`, the completeness of the dataset can only be guaranteed based on what the `Internet Archive` offers. Furthermore, we are bounded by about 3.3 Million of these users that disclosed any sort of sexual orientation, which results in a sparser network than that of all 20 Million users. Although the resulting network and user data is much bigger than the datasets that have been used in other works, a more comprehensive study can take into account all 20 Million profiles and study the 3.3Mil using all their links in the 20 Million. This would mean analyzing some 70 Million edges. However, given the number of user vectors computed for full shadow profiles alone where a user vector for the non-users is computed 10 times for each (a, ρ) pair, resulting in 180 user vectors; and given the number of links that had to be traversed for computing each vector and the computational limitations introduced thereof, we believe that our results do provide a comprehensive analysis of privacy leakage. We have also not provided further analysis of factors that may play a role in prediction accuracy other than the ones discussed in Section 6.2. A more comprehensive analysis at this stage can answer the question which neighborhoods in larger distances still play a significant role in putting users under privacy leakage risk.

8. CONCLUSIONS

We presented an analysis of the social component of privacy, and how the decisions of some users to disclose private information impacts the chances of other users to maintain their privacy. This provides an indirect coupling between seemingly unrelated user decisions, as it was also observed in other online communities where the decision of some users to become incative influences other the activity of other users [16]. Users in isolation face lower risks of losing privacy than when they interact with each other. The same way as social interaction leads to the emergence of conventions [25], it can also undermine the quality of collective decisions [30], posing the question of how much private information a user loses just for interacting with others. Our work focused on sexual orientation, resonating within works on gender-aligned interaction in online communities [17]. But it keeps open to study privacy leakage in other kinds of private information, such as age or marital status.

We showed that the privacy leak factors for large and small groups respond differently to changing network size and disclosure behavior. For example, privacy leak factors are higher for homosexual males than for heterosexual males in the partial shadow profiles problem, showing that the former group loses more privacy as other users share their sexual orientation with the OSN provider. We have shown that network size and disclosure parameter influence privacy risk for non-users in the full shadow profiles problem, and that this risk varies depending on how connected a non-user is to the network, and the assortative nature of their connections. This poses a simple conclusion: not having an account in an OSN does not guarantee a higher level of privacy, as long as one has enough friends who already are in the OSN.

In an interlinked community, an individual's privacy is a complex property, where it is in constant mutual relationship with the systemic properties and behavioral patterns of the community at large. We provided quantitative insights into the dependence of an individual's privacy to their respective community, and how far an OSN provider can utilize this dependency to create shadow profiles. Our work does not improve the methods to create shadow profiles; we limited ourselves to the application of existing methods to underline an already existing risk. We showed that, as the network grows and its members share their contact lists with the provider, the risk of privacy leakage increases. Given the fact that this dependency is present under generalized social interaction, we should consider privacy as a collective concept, where individual privacy policies are not sufficient to control private information.

9. REFERENCES

[1] Anger mounts after facebook's 'shadow profiles' leak in bug. `http://zd.net/1vuzDly`, June 2013.

[2] Facebook: Where your friends are your worst enemies. `http://bit.ly/1jiMQJ7`, June 2013.

[3] What's a facebook shadow profile and why should you care? `http://bit.ly/1p7e5ag`, July 2013.

[4] Facebook data use policy. `http://www.facebook.com/about/privacy/your-info`, May 2014.

[5] M. K. 0002 and J. Leskovec. The network completion problem: Inferring missing nodes and edges in networks. In *SDM*, pages 47–58. SIAM / Omnipress, 2011.

[6] A. Acquisti and J. Grossklags. Privacy and rationality in individual decision making. *IEEE Security & Privacy*, 2:24–30, 2005.

[7] L. Backstrom and J. M. Kleinberg. Romantic partnerships and the dispersion of social ties: a network analysis of relationship status on facebook. In *CSCW*, pages 831–841, 2014.

[8] D. Boyd. Sexing the internet: Reflections on the role of identification in online communities. In *Sexualities, Medias, Technologies*, 2001.

[9] D. Boyd. Networked privacy. *Surveillance & Society*, 10:348–350, 2012.

[10] L. Brandimarte, A. Acquisti, and G. Loewenstein. Misplaced confidences privacy and the control paradox. *Social Psychological and Personality Science*, 4(3):340–347, 2013.

[11] L. Breiman. Random forests. *Machine Learning*, 45(1):5–32, 2001.

[12] M. Castells. *The Rise of the Network Society.* Blackwell Publishers, January 2000.

[13] J. Cohen. Weighted kappa: Nominal scale agreement provision for scaled disagreement or partial credit. *Psychological bulletin*, 70(4):213–220, 1968.

[14] D. J. Crandall, L. Backstrom, D. Cosley, S. Suri, D. Huttenlocher, and J. Kleinberg. Inferring social ties from geographic coincidences. *Proceedings of the National Academy of Sciences*, 2010.

[15] D. Erdós, R. Gemulla, and E. Terzi. Reconstructing graphs from neighborhood data. In M. J. Zaki, A. Siebes, J. X. Yu, B. Goethals, G. I. Webb, and X. Wu, editors, *ICDM*, pages 231–240. IEEE Computer Society, 2012.

[16] D. Garcia, P. Mavrodiev, and F. Schweitzer. Social resilience in online communities: The autopsy of friendster. In *Proceedings of the First ACM Conference on Online Social Networks*, COSN '13, pages 39–50, New York, NY, USA, 2013. ACM.

[17] D. Garcia, I. Weber, and R. V. K. Garimella. Gender asymmetries in reality and fiction: The bechdel test of social media. In *International AAAI Conference on Weblogs and Social Media*, 2014.

[18] D. Gayo Avello. All liaisons are dangerous when all your friends are known to us. In *Proceedings of the 22Nd ACM Conference on Hypertext and Hypermedia*, HT '11, pages 171–180, New York, NY, USA, 2011. ACM.

[19] P. Gill, V. Erramilli, A. Chaintreau, B. Krishnamurthy, K. Papagiannaki, and P. Rodriguez. Best paper – follow the money: Understanding economics of online aggregation and advertising. In *Proceedings of the 2013 Conference on Internet Measurement Conference*, IMC '13, pages 141–148, New York, NY, USA, 2013. ACM.

[20] E. Á. Horvát, M. Hanselmann, F. A. Hamprecht, and K. A. Zweig. One Plus One Makes Three (for Social Networks). *PLoS One*, 7(4), 2012.

[21] S. Isaacman, S. Ioannidis, A. Chaintreau, and M. Martonosi. Distributed rating prediction in user generated content streams. In *Proceedings of the ACM RecSys*, Oct. 2011.

[22] C. Jernigan and B. F. T. Mistree. Gaydar: Facebook friendships expose sexual orientation. *First Monday*, 14(10), 2009.

[23] L. Jin, X. Long, and J. Joshi. A friendship privacy attack on friends and 2-distant neighbors in social networks. *CoRR*, abs/1309.6204, 2013.

[24] M. Johnson, S. Egelman, and S. M. Bellovin. Facebook and Privacy : It's Complicated. In *Symposium on Usable Privace and Security*, 2012.

[25] F. Kooti, W. A. Mason, K. P. Gummadi, and M. Cha. Predicting emerging social conventions in online social networks. In *Proceedings of the 21st ACM International Conference on Information and Knowledge Management*, CIKM '12, pages 445–454, New York, NY, USA, 2012. ACM.

[26] B. Krishnamurthy and C. E. Wills. Privacy leakage in mobile online social networks. In *Proceedings of the 3rd Conference on Online Social Networks*, WOSN'10, pages 4–4, Berkeley, CA, USA, 2010. USENIX Association.

[27] J. Lanier. *Who owns the future?* Simon and Schuster, 2013.

[28] D. Liben-Nowell and J. Kleinberg. The link prediction problem for social networks. In *Proceedings of the Twelfth International Conference on Information and Knowledge Management*, CIKM '03, pages 556–559, New York, NY, USA, 2003. ACM.

[29] Y. Liu, K. P. Gummadi, B. Krishnamurthy, and A. Mislove. Analyzing facebook privacy settings. In *IMC '11*, 2011.

[30] J. Lorenz, H. Rauhut, F. Schweitzer, and D. Helbing. How social influence can undermine the wisdom of crowd effect. *Proceedings of the National Academy of Sciences (PNAS)*, 108(22):9020– 9025, 2011.

[31] D. Lyon. *Surveillance as Social Sorting: Privacy, Risk and Automated Discrimination.* Routledge, Dec. 2002.

[32] D. Malandrino, A. Petta, V. Scarano, L. Serra, R. Spinelli, and B. Krishnamurthy. Privacy awareness about information leakage: Who knows what about me? In *Proceedings of the 12th ACM Workshop on Workshop on Privacy in the Electronic Society*, WPES '13, pages 279–284, New York, NY, USA, 2013. ACM.

[33] A. Marwick. The public domain: Surveillance in everyday life. *Surveillance & Society*, 9:378–393, 2012.

[34] A. Mislove, B. Viswanath, K. P. Gummadi, and P. Druschel. You are who you know: Inferring user profiles in online social networks. In *Proceedings of the Third ACM International Conference on Web Search and Data Mining*, WSDM '10, pages 251–260, New York, NY, USA, 2010. ACM.

[35] M. Mondal, P. Druschel, K. P. Gummadi, and A. Mislove. Beyond access control: Managing online privacy via exposure. In *Proceedings of the Workshop on Usable Security*, USEC ' 14, 2014.

[36] E. Morozov. The real privacy problem. *TECHNOLOGY REVIEW*, 116(6):32–43, 2013.

[37] T. Pontes, G. Magno, M. Vasconcelos, A. Gupta, J. Almeida, P. Kumaraguru, and V. Almeida. Beware of What You Share: Inferring Home Location in Social Networks. *ICDM '12*, pages 571–578, 2012.

[38] K. P. Puttaswamy, A. Sala, and B. Y. Zhao. Starclique: Guaranteeing user privacy in social networks against intersection attacks. In *Proceedings of the 5th International Conference on Emerging Networking Experiments and Technologies*, CoNEXT '09, pages 157–168, New York, NY, USA, 2009. ACM.

[39] D. Rao, D. Yarowsky, A. Shreevats, and M. Gupta. Classifying latent user attributes in twitter. In

Proceedings of the 2Nd International Workshop on Search and Mining User-generated Contents, SMUC '10, pages 37–44, New York, NY, USA, 2010. ACM.

[40] B. Ribeiro and C. Faloutsos. Modeling website popularity competition in the attention-activity marketplace. *arXiv preprint arXiv:1403.0600*, 2014.

[41] C. Riederer, V. Erramilli, A. Chaintreau, B. Krishnamurty, and P. Rodriguez. For sale : Your Data, By : You. *Proceedings of ACM SIGCOMM HotNets*, pages 1–6, July 2011.

[42] F. Stalder. The Failure of Privacy Enhancing Technologies (PETs) and the Voiding of Privacy. *Sociological Research Online*, 7(2), 2002.

[43] M. Tierney, I. Spiro, C. Bregler, and L. Subramanian. Cryptagram: Photo privacy for online social media. In *Proceedings of the First ACM Conference on Online Social Networks*, COSN '13, pages 75–88, New York, NY, USA, 2013. ACM.

[44] C. Wilson, T. Steinbauer, G. Wang, A. Sala, H. Zheng, and B. Y. Zhao. Privacy, availability and economics in the polaris mobile social network. In *Proceedings of the 12th Workshop on Mobile Computing Systems and Applications*, pages 42–47. ACM, 2011.

[45] R. Wishart, D. Corapi, A. Madhavapeddy, and M. Sloman. Privacy butler: A personal privacy rights manager for online presence. In *Pervasive Computing and Communications Workshops (PERCOM Workshops), 2010 8th IEEE International Conference on*, pages 672–677, March 2010.

[46] L. Zhang and A. Mislove. Building confederated web-based services with priv.io. In *Proceedings of the First ACM Conference on Online Social Networks*, COSN '13, pages 189–200, New York, NY, USA, 2013. ACM.

[47] E. Zheleva and L. Getoor. To join or not to join: The illusion of privacy in social networks with mixed public and private user profiles. In *Proceedings of the 18th International Conference on World Wide Web*, WWW '09, pages 531–540, New York, NY, USA, 2009. ACM.

Spreading Rumours without the Network

Paweł Brach*
University of Warsaw
pawel.brach@mimuw.edu.pl

Alessandro Epasto†
Sapienza University of Rome
epasto@di.uniroma1.it

Alessandro Panconesi‡
Sapienza University of Rome
ale@di.uniroma1.it

Piotr Sankowski§
University of Warsaw
sank@mimuw.edu.pl

ABSTRACT

In this paper we tackle the following question: is it possible to predict the characteristics of the evolution of an epidemic process in a social network on the basis of the degree distribution alone? We answer this question affirmatively for several diffusion processes– Push-Pull, Broadcast and SIR– by showing that it is possible to predict with good accuracy their average evolution. We do this by developing a space efficient predictor that makes it possible to handle very large networks with very limited computational resources. Our experiments show that the prediction is surprisingly good for many instances of real-world networks. The class of real-world networks for which this happens can be characterized in terms of their neighbourhood function, which turns out to be similar to that of random networks. Finally, we analyse real instances of rumour spreading in Twitter and observe that our model describes qualitatively well their evolution.

Categories and Subject Descriptors

H.2.8 [**Database Management**]: Database Applications—*Data mining*; G.3 [**Probability and Statistics**]: Stochastic processes

General Terms

Algorithms

*Partly supported by ERC StG project PAAl 259515, FET IP project MULTIPEX 317532 and NCN grant N N206 567940.

†Partially supported by a Google Europe PhD Fellowship in Algorithms and by the EU FET project MULTIPLEX 317532.

‡Partially supported by a Google Faculty Research Award, the CASPUR HPC Std Grant 2012 and by the EU FET project MULTIPLEX 317532.

§Partly supported by ERC StG project PAAl 259515, FET IP project MULTIPEX 317532 and NCN grant N N206 567940.

COSN'14, October 1–2, 2014, Dublin, Ireland.

ACM 978-1-4503-3198-2/14/10 ...$15.00.
http://dx.doi.org/10.1145/2660460.2660472.

Keywords

rumour spreading; degree distribution; configuration model; social networks; push-pull; sir; neighbourhood function.

1. INTRODUCTION

In recent years, we have witnessed the emergence of many sophisticated web services that allow people to interact on an unprecedented scale. The wealth of data produced by these new ways of communication holds the promise to increase our understanding of human social behaviour, but a fundamental hurdle is posed by the sensitivity of these data. It could be available in principle, but its access must be severely constrained to protect the privacy of users and the confidentiality of data. In some contexts, e.g. sociological and epidemiological studies, the network topology for which the diffusion processes are to be evaluated might simply be unknown, or impossible to be determined with any accuracy. It is often possible, however, to gain relatively unconstrained access to some crude statistical information about the data. For instance, while the exact network topology of a social graph could be unavailable, some aggregate information such as its degree distribution can be disclosed and made public. A broad question arises naturally: can non-trivial conclusions about various social processes be inferred based only on such limited access to the data?

We tackle this question in the case of diffusion processes. We study some classical models of information diffusion (which we henceforth refer collectively as rumour spreading[1]) – gossiping in its PUSH and PULL variants, broadcast and SIR– and ask the following question: is it possible to predict the average evolution of the epidemic as it spreads in a given real-world network on the basis of its degree distribution alone? Furthermore, given the size of current data sets, we want to perform such a prediction in a space efficient manner, to make the prediction for very large graphs possible with limited computational resources. Note that on the basis of the degree information alone, we can only hope to predict how the process will evolve on average, for there can be graphs with the same degree distribution for which the epidemic will evolve at very different speeds.

Surprisingly, we show that our goal is achievable for a large class of real-world networks. This is the class of real networks whose neighbourhood function [6] closely resembles that of a random graph with the same degree distribution.

[1]We stress that, contrary to the common meaning of the word "rumour", in the context of the literature on information diffusion processes rumour simply means a generic information.

The above discussion gives the gist of our results. Before describing them in detail, let us review the diffusion models we will be considering.

Push, Pull and SIR.

Gossip (a.k.a. random-call model) is a fundamental communication primitive inspired by the dynamics of viral diffusion and word-of-mouth. It comes in three guises known as PUSH, PULL and PUSH-PULL. In each, the process starts at time $t = 0$ with one source node with a message. The process evolves in a sequence of discrete, synchronous rounds. In the PUSH variant, in round $t \geq 0$, every informed node selects a neighbour uniformly at random to which the message is forwarded. The PULL variant is symmetric, i.e., in round $t \geq 0$, every node that does not yet know the message selects a neighbour uniformly at random and asks for the information to be transferred, provided that the queried neighbour has it. The PUSH-PULL variant is a combination of both, in each round informed nodes execute a PUSH and uniformed ones a PULL.

From a computer science perspective these models provide simple-to-implement tools for the dissemination of information across a network [12] and for this reason they have been studied extensively in practice and theory. More generally, they provide a very simple model for the dynamics of viral diffusion that, in spite of their simplicity, can offer some insight into more realistic processes in sociology [26], economics [21], and epidemiology [20]. There is a rich theoretical literature the studies the speed of these protocols. To draw a few paradigmatic examples from a rich body of literature, Feige *et al.* [13] showed that, in any connected network, PUSH delivers the message to every node within $O(n \log n)$ many rounds, where n denotes the number of nodes. These results have been extended to PUSH-PULL over random graphs with power law degree distribution with exponent α in [14]. It has been shown that when $2 < \alpha < 3$ the rumour spreads to almost all nodes in $O(\log \log n)$ time, whereas when $\alpha > 3$ one needs $\Omega(\log n)$ rounds. In a series of relatively recent papers [11, 10, 15] a tight relationship was established between the speed of diffusion of PUSH-PULL and the conductance of the network, denoted as φ, culminating with the optimal $O(\log n/\varphi)$ bound [15]. Notice that all these results are asymptotic while our focus here is different. We want to predict the expected number of informed nodes at time t, on the basis of the degree distribution of the network.

In this paper we also evaluate a classical diffusion model inspired by mathematical epidemiology studies [20, 16], the SIR process. In this process, a node in the network can be either *susceptible*, *infected* or *removed*. At time $t = 0$ a single node is infected and all the others are susceptible. At time $t \geq 0$, infected nodes transmit at each step the rumour to each susceptible neighbour, independently with probability p. After one step, nodes that were infected in the previous step are removed and stop the transmission. Notice that SIR generalizes broadcast, to which it is equivalent when $p = 1$. For consistency with the PUSH-PULL model we will define informed nodes in SIR as the ones either in infected or removed state (i.e. the ones that already received the rumour). One of the most striking results concerning SIR is that the diffusion is governed by reproduction number $R_0 = p\bar{d}$, where $\bar{d}$ is the average degree of the nodes. In random networks with degree distribution of finite variance, $R_0 = 1$ is a critical threshold below which the process extinguishes before infecting a negligible fraction of the nodes. For $R_0 > 1$, instead, the process grows exponentially fast. Such threshold effect is absent in certain random graphs with scale-free (for instance power law) degree distribution [8].

These rumour spreading processes can be regarded as the simplest models for information (or epidemic) diffusion. We can now describe our results and methods more precisely.

Problem definition, methodology and results.

The goal of the paper is to develop a space-efficient predictor that is capable of estimating as precisely as possible the expected number of infected nodes at time t when an epidemic spreads across a real-world social network, where the expectation is taken over all possible runs of the diffusion process under consideration. The input to the predictor is not the network itself but its degree distribution only.

A recent paper by Goel *et al.* [16] shows that the well-known random configuration model can be surprisingly good at predicting qualitatively the shape and evolution of viral processes in Twitter. We explore this insight further by adopting the configuration model as the basis for our predictor. In a nutshell, our approach is, first, to develop a provably exact and space-efficient estimator for the configuration model and, second apply it to real-world networks.

Let us recall the definition of the *configuration model* [37, 16]. We are given m *stubs*, m an even number, partitioned into n *buckets* according to a given *degree sequence* $D := (d_1, d_2, \ldots, d_n)$, where d_i is the number of stubs in bucket i, i.e., the degree of node i in the graph. An undirected (multi)graph is generated by the following random process: a pair of stubs is chosen uniformly at random; let i and j be the buckets these stubs belong to; an edge connecting nodes i and j is inserted in the (multi)graph. The procedure is repeated until there are no more free stubs. Observe that m is even so this procedure ends. The model can be easily generalized to the case of directed (multi)graphs.

In contrast to real social networks, random graphs generated by the configuration model have very few triangles. And yet, as the results in [16] and in this paper show, it can be the basis for accurate predictions of diffusion processes in real-world networks. A very positive feature of the model is its simplicity, which opens the way to a rigorous mathematical analysis. We will make use of this feature by proving that our space-efficient estimator is exact for the configuration model.

By using a random graph model our problem becomes mathematically well-defined: given a degree distribution D, we want to estimate, for each time t, the expected number of nodes that are informed by rumour spreading in a random graph drawn from the configuration model with degree distribution D, starting from a random source.

Notice now that this problem admits a trivial solution via sampling: it is enough to generate "many" random graphs with the given degree distribution and, for each one of them, to simulate rumour spreading (itself a random process) "many" times. If we accumulate the results by computing averages for each value of $t = 0, 1, \ldots,$ by the law of large numbers the averages will converge to the expected values. We shall refer to this procedure as the *naive estimator*.

The naive estimator can be easily parallelized, as each sample is independent, but has one clear bottleneck: space. The scale of current social networks would force the use external memory – namely disk storage – unless special hardware is available, resulting in prohibitive running times. Moreover, the naive predictor cannot scale efficiently in distributed computation paradigms like MapReduce, due to the network communication bottleneck, as such paradigms are not suited to run jobs that requires a large shared memory (i.e. the graph).

In this paper, we develop a predictor along the same lines of the naive estimator, but such that, by generating each graph locally "on the fly", it can keep everything in main memory even for very large graphs. In terms of space, our predictor needs only $O(n)$ instead of $O(n+m)$ space which for real-world social graphs is a very significant improvement (m denotes number of edges in the graph). For undirected graphs, further optimization is possible which allows spectacular savings in memory usage. To give a rough idea, storing the entire Facebook network would require 480GB of memory[2], whereas our estimator can be run on less than a gigabyte of memory.

The design of such space efficient algorithms poses interesting algorithmic challenges. In particular the algorithms need to be able to sample a constantly changing distribution in an efficient way. To this end we develop a simple variation of the well-known Walker's method [35] (see Appendix A) which proves to be practically very efficient.

More specifically, our results are as follows. We develop a predictor such that, given as input a degree distribution:

- It gives the correct prediction for our diffusion processes in the configuration model, i.e., given a degree distribution D, for each time t, it correctly computes the average number of nodes that are informed at time t when the rumour starts from a random source of a random graph with degree distribution D;

- It gives good predictions for real-life social networks, provided that the neighbourhood function of the network is not "too far" from that of random networks with the same degree distribution. We also show the converse: when the neighbourhood functions differ the predictor performs poorly.

- It is efficient in terms of space and, in the case of undirected networks, exceptionally efficient.

In their study of the neighbourhood function, Boldi *et al.* show that the neighbourhood function of real networks is an informative statistics able to distinguish social graphs from the web graph [6]. More generally, as we do in this paper, it can be used to tell apart social from non-social graphs. Seen in this light our result is especially intriguing, as it shows that, in the case of gossiping and SIR, social networks behave like an average instance of a random graph.

The rest of the paper is organized as follows. In Section 2 we develop the estimator for the configuration model, and show that it is provably exact. Next section discusses how the estimator can be improved in the undirected case. In Section 4 we describe its performance, which is very good for real-life directed and undirected social networks. In Section 5 we recap and hint at possible interesting research directions stemming from our work. Finally, in Appendix A we describe the technical details of our sampling procedure.

[2]Estimated as $\log(n)$ bits per edge for this snapshot [3].

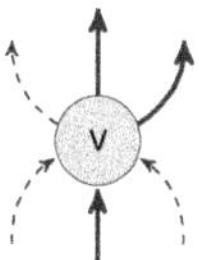

Figure 1: A privy node v during the execution of the algorithm. Solid stubs connect v to (resp. from) other privy nodes. Dashed stubs are free, i.e., represent edges that have not yet been drawn. Node v has $\text{rank}_{\text{in}} = 1$, $\text{rank}_{\text{out}} = 2$, $\text{free}_{\text{in}} = 2$ and $\text{free}_{\text{out}} = 1$.

2. MODEL FOR DIRECTED GRAPHS

In this section we develop a space efficient estimator for the configuration model [37]. In the introduction we have already defined the model for undirected graphs. The directed model that we consider here is essentially identical except that, for each vertex v, we need to specify two quantities, the in and out degree, i.e., the pair $(\text{deg}_{\text{in}}(v), \text{deg}_{\text{out}}(v))$. These pairs must satisfy the obvious requirement that the sum of the in-degrees must be equal to the sum of the out-degrees. If this requirement is satisfied the sequence is called *graphical.*

It is useful to think of each vertex as having $\text{deg}_{\text{in}}(v)$ in-stubs and $\text{deg}_{\text{out}}(v)$ out-stubs. Edges are generated by selecting without replacement a random in-stub and a random out-stub. Doing this can create parallel edges and self-loops but they make for a negligible fraction of the total number of edges when $n \to \infty$ (by a balls-and-bins argument). Hence, the error introduced this way is negligible. Note that the efficient and unbiased generation of simple (as opposed to multi) graphs is an open problem [4].

Let us now switch to the estimator, which will be described for the PUSH process only for lack of space. The discussion for PULL, SIR and broadcast (which is essentially a special case of SIR) is similar, and omitted from this extended abstract.

In what follows by *sample* we mean a run of rumour spreading for a randomly generated graph and a random source. Our goal is to execute each sample efficiently in terms of space. This is achieved by simulating rumour spreading without storing the edges of the graph. The rough idea is to generate edges in a piecemeal fashion when needed, i.e., when an edge is actually used to send the rumour across. We observe that once the edge is used for the transmission of the rumour it can be immediately forgotten, because both endpoints will know the rumour afterwards. Hence, we do not need to store it, but only the fact that its two endpoints now have, respectively, one more out-edge and one more in-edge. The resulting saving, as we shall see, is significant. This approach is similar to the ones used for the analysis of random graph processes [37].

Let us now describe the algorithm that executes samples in a space efficient way. For every vertex u, we shall keep track of whether it is *privy* (it knows the rumour) or *out-of-the-loop* (it does not know the rumour) and the following quantities:

1. $\text{rank}_{\text{in}}(t, v)$, the number of in-neighbours at time t that are privy;

2. $\text{rank}_{\text{out}}(t, v)$, the number of out-neighbours at time t that are privy.

As discussed, the algorithm does not keep track of the edges that are generated – they are effectively forgotten. Instead, for each vertex v, we will remember just how many in and out edges respectively have been generated so far, without knowing which edges exactly they represent. We can think of stubs as being *used* or *free*, and keep track of the following quantities:

1. $\text{free}_{\text{in}}(t, v)$, the number of in-edges that are still undetermined at time t;

2. $\text{free}_{\text{out}}(t, v)$, the number of out-edges that are still undetermined at time t.

In the sequel, we will drop the dependency on time, when it is clear from the context. Clearly, these quantities are somewhat redundant since $\text{deg}_{\text{in}} = \text{rank}_{\text{in}} + \text{free}_{\text{in}}$ and $\text{deg}_{\text{out}} = \text{rank}_{\text{out}} + \text{free}_{\text{out}}$. The algorithm for PUSH actually stores, for each node, only the values deg_{out}, rank_{out}, and free_{in}. The values deg_{in} are only used to initialize the values $\text{free}_{\text{in}} := \text{deg}_{\text{in}}$, the value rank_{in} is not actually used. The other quantities can be simply computed from these, but it is useful to write them explicitly for clarity of the exposition (see Figure 1). Likewise, it is useful for explanatory purposes to think of vertices as having in and out stubs attached to them. They are not actually stored, but they help explaining the algorithm, which we do next.

Its input consists of a graphical sequence D and an integer parameter τ. Its goal is to simulate one run of rumour spreading for τ rounds for a random graph taken from the configuration model given by degree sequence D. It proceeds in a sequence of synchronous rounds $t = 0, 1, 2, \ldots, \tau$ (in practice, as soon as all nodes become privy we can stop the simulation). Initially one node s, the source, is made privy uniformly at random.

For $[0 \leq t \leq \tau]$: (Refer to Figure 2). All nodes that are privy in the current round are processed in an arbitrary order. Let u be the current privy node to be processed. One of its out-stubs is selected uniformly at random. If the stub is used nothing happens (this corresponds to the fact that the rumour will be sent to another privy node). Otherwise, the selected out-stub of u is free and becomes used. Then, a free in-stub is selected uniformly at random. Let v be the node to which this free in-stub belongs. Next, we increment $\text{rank}_{\text{out}}(u)$, decrement $\text{free}_{\text{in}}(v)$ and mark one of the free in-stubs of v as used. If v is out-of-the-loop, it becomes privy at round $t+1$ (notice that v remains out-of-the-loop during this round and may be selected several times).

We remark once again that the graphical operations concerning stubs are not necessary for the algorithm but we describe them for clarity of exposition. In particular, we *do not* store the stubs explicitly, but only the quantities deg_{out}, rank_{out} and free_{in}. Note that the probability that a used out-stub is selected in round t for a given vertex u is $p = \frac{\text{rank}_{\text{out}}(u)}{\text{deg}_{\text{out}}(u)}$.

Time complexity.

We start by analysing the time needed to simulate a single round of the algorithm. We make the standard assumptions [27] that we can sample in constant time for a uniform distribution over $[0, 1]$ and that basic arithmetic operations require $O(1)$ time.

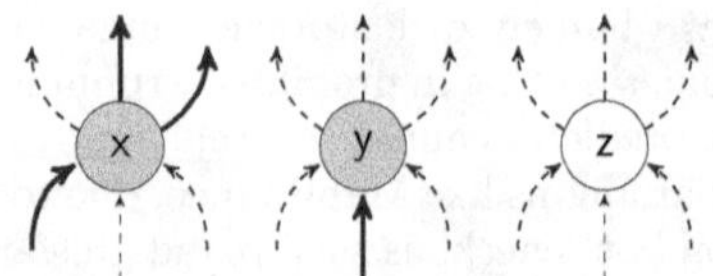

Figure 2: The situation at time t. Privy nodes are dark. Notice that stubs of out-of-the-loop nodes are all free.

The main difficulty in implementing a round is the selection of free in-stubs uniformly at random. This would be easy if we stored the free in-stubs explicitly, which we do not. But since we know, for each vertex, their number, we can equivalently pick a vertex with a probability proportional to the number of its free in-stubs. Performing such random selection efficiently is a non trivial task as the probability distribution of all nodes changes at each edge drawing. This problem is known in literature as dynamic variate sampling [36, 27] and several solutions provides different space-time trade-off. As we provide more details about this operation in Appendix A, here we only summarize the most important results.

The asymptotically optimal Mathias et al. [27] algorithm implements such operations using $O(n)$ space and in $O(1)$ time for each in-stub selection. Wong et al. [36] presented an easy to implement $O(n)$ size data structure that requires $O(\log(n))$ time per sampling. In our experiments we actually use [36] or simple variant of the Walker [35] method that we have developed and which provides almost constant time for $O(n)$ space (more details in Appendix A).

All the remaining updates and random choices (e.g., selection of out-stubs for a given node uniformly at random) can be implemented in $O(1)$ time per node processed. The total number of nodes processed in one step is given by the number of informed nodes. Hence this cost is equal to the number of PUSH messages exchanged. Let $\mu(\tau)$ be the number of messages exchanged by the rumour spreading process in the first τ steps of the process (or up to when all nodes are informed). The complexity of the algorithm is simply $O(\mu(\tau))$. Note that the exact estimation of the message complexity of PUSH and PULL is a challenging problem, for which only partial answers are known [10]. Clearly we have the trivial upper bound of $\mu(\tau) = O(\tau \cdot n)$. On the other hand, note that the simulation of PUSH on a given graph clearly cannot take less than $\mu(\tau)$ time, thus proving the algorithm has the same complexity as simulating the rumour spreading process in a graph. For the PULL and SIR algorithms, not presented in this paper, similar argument shows that our algorithm needs $O(\mu(\tau) + m)$ time to simulate the rumour spreading process for given graph. Nevertheless, the most important advantage of our simulation is the small space requirement, which makes it possible to run each sample in main memory. Simulating samples with external memory would make the task computationally demanding.

Space complexity.

The PUSH algorithm requires for each node in the graph $O(1)$ space to store the necessary information: in and out degrees, in and out ranks and the number of in and out free stubs. This gives $O(n)$ space in total. To select in-stubs uniformly at random, the algorithm employs an additional data structure. As already mentioned with both Mathias et al. [27] and Wong et al. [36] algorithms such data structure requires $O(1)$ space per element of the sampling set, thus the total cost is again $O(n)$. We can conclude that the algorithm requires for directed graphs $O(n)$ space. The same conclusion holds for the PULL and SIR algorithms.

This asymptotic analysis shows the reason why in practice the savings are quite substantial compared to representing the entire graph. We will see later that undirected graphs allow for further optimizations with very interesting results.

Correctness of the algorithm.

In the introduction we discussed pros and cons of the configuration model. One of the crucial properties that we pointed out is its simplicity, which opens the way to rigorous mathematical reasoning. In this section, we take full advantage of this feature by proving the correctness of the algorithm. To proceed formally with the proof we need to introduce the following definitions.

Let D be a fixed graphical sequence. Consider the naive estimator, defined in the introduction: pick a random graph from the configuration model according to D, pick a random source inside this graph, and run rumour spreading for τ rounds. This generates a sequence of privy sets A_i, $i = 0, 1, \ldots, \tau$, where A_i is the set of vertices that are privy at round i. And, let B_i, $i = 0, 1, \ldots, \tau$, the analogous sequence of privy sets generated by the algorithm for the same D.

Theorem 1. For every $i = 0, 1, \ldots, \tau$, the sets A_i and B_i have the same probability distribution.

For lack of space we can only sketch the proof. The details will appear in the full version of the paper. The claim of the theorem holds at the start for the sets A_0 and B_0. They contain only the source, which is selected uniformly at random in both cases.

Effectively the algorithm determines an underlying graph with degree sequence D by drawing its edges when needed by the PUSH process. As the algorithm keeps track, of the number of nodes currently informed in the neighbourhood of each node, we observe that the rumour spreading process is correctly simulated on the underlying graph produced. However, what needs to be proved is that the underlying graph is actually drawn with a probability given by the configuration model. It is actually possible to prove this for a wider class of algorithms. Consider an algorithm where the order of nodes that perform PUSH is arbitrary, i.e., we select an arbitrary privy node with free out-stub and then we choose the destination node by taking u.a.r. a free in-stub. By applying the deferred decision principle on the choices of the in-stubs it is possible to prove that graphs obtained in this way are sampled from the configuration model distribution, which concludes the proof of Theorem 1.

3. MODEL FOR UNDIRECTED GRAPHS

The algorithm described in the previous section can be simplified for the case of undirected graphs. In this section we briefly sketch the main differences between the two algorithms, deferring the complete discussion to the full paper, while pointing out a remarkable feature of the undirected case namely, its economy in terms of space.

In the undirected case, each vertex only has stubs, as opposed to in- and out-stubs. Consequently we only need to keep track of the rank of a node and the number of free edges incident to it. The main difference between the directed and the undirected case is that it is convenient to use the following matrix representation to store the current state of the algorithm. We can encode the current state of all nodes in a matrix of size $O(\Delta^2)$, where cell (i, j) stores the number of nodes with degree i and rank j. Note that only the $i \geq j$ cells are necessary. Because we still need to remember whether the node is privy or out-of-the-loop, we use two such matrices. In other words, we group nodes by degree and rank. To perform the simulation we only need the cardinality of these groups. This is also possible in the directed case, but only if the network is undirected we can achieve significant space optimization.

In particular, this is the case for graphs whose degree distribution follows a power law or heavy tail distribution, as it is typical of real social graphs [30]. In order to give an idea of the kinds of savings involved, let us assume that the degree distribution follows a power law with $\alpha > 1$ (i.e. the fraction $f(k)$ of nodes with degree k is $f(k) = k^{-\alpha} Z(\alpha)^{-1}$, where $Z(\alpha)$ is a normalization constant). Information for nodes of degree $\deg(v) < \gamma$, for a carefully chose threshold γ, is stored in two $\gamma \times \gamma$ matrices. Higher degree nodes are treated individually in a linear array (as in the previous algorithm). Let us now analyse the cost of this representation.

Definition 1. Let $E(\gamma)$ be the cost of the rank data structure with parameter γ. $E(\gamma) = M(\gamma) + H(\gamma)$ where $M(\gamma)$ is the cost of representing the matrices and $H(\gamma)$ is the cost for the information of the high degree nodes.

We have $M(\gamma) = \frac{1}{2}(\gamma)(\gamma + 1) = O(\gamma^2)$, while

$$H(\gamma) = n \sum_{k=\gamma+1}^{\infty} f(k) = O\left(n \int_{k=\gamma+1}^{\infty} x^{-\alpha} dx\right) = O(n\gamma^{1-\alpha}).$$

We can see that the minimum of $E(\gamma)$ is reached for $M(\gamma^*) = H(\gamma^*)$, which gives $\gamma^* = n^{\frac{1}{1+\alpha}}$ and optimal cost $O(n^{\frac{2}{1+\alpha}})$. Since $\alpha > 1$ the cost is always $o(n)$. Moreover, for real networks α is typically in the $(2, 4)$ range (see for instance Table II in [30]). Hence, we can achieve a significant space improvement with respect to storing the entire graph that requires $O(n + m)$ space.

To provide an understanding on the orders of magnitude of the saving, we report in Table 1, a back-of-the-envelope calculation of the number of memory cells needed by the data structure for the best gammas. We need three cells for each entry of the $\gamma^* \times \gamma^*$ matrix and three cells for each high degree node (details are omitted from this paper). The space requirements of each graph are estimated with their number of edges. It is apparent that the space savings with this optimization are very significant.

The data for Facebook (world) is referred to a snapshot of Facebook with 7.2×10^8 active users and 1.4×10^{11} edges, analysed by Backstrom et al. [3]. While we do not have access to the graph, for obvious reasons, the degree distribution was made available by Ugander et al. [33]. Perhaps, this is another confirmation that the access to such statistical information for the research community is easier than the access to the graph.

Note that with [36] algorithm, the additional data structure required to sample edges in such huge graph easily fits in less than 300 MB of memory. This justifies our claim in the introduction that less than 1 GB of memory is sufficient to run our algorithms on such huge graph.

Graph	$\gamma*$	#Cells used	#Edges
AstroPh	54	10,080	393,944
Dblp	91	24,111	6,418,218
Enron	44	7,581	361,622
Facebook (dataset)	84	22,266	1,456,818
Facebook (world)	2,183	1.4×10^7	1.4×10^{11}
Renren	85	27,726	1,410,496

Table 1: Optimal γ values and cost of the compressed representation for real undirected networks (in terms of memory cells used).

The matrix representation can also be used for the directed case, but in this case, as we need $O(\gamma^3)$ space, the savings appear to be modest.

4. EVALUATION

In this section we evaluate the predictive power of our model in real social networks. We have executed the following experiments whose goal is to compare the actual process with the prediction of our estimator. Given a specific real network G we use it to compute the ground truth by means of the naive estimator described in the introduction: for $0 \leq t \leq \tau$, we compute the expected number of privy nodes at time t by simulating the rumour spreading process on the graph r times. The same approach is used to determine the output of the predictor.

The number r of samples necessary for a certain precision can be determined by standard statistics techniques. Roughly, the variance of the process can be determined empirically through sampling. Knowing the variance, a standard application of the central limit theorem, provides an estimation of the number of samples necessary. Concretely, in the PULL process for instance, a confidence interval of $\pm 0.5\%$ of the nodes in the graph, with probability 0.95, requires for the ground truth approximately between 300 and 5,000 samples depending on the network. On the other hand between 1,000 and 5,000 samples are needed for the predictor. However, to show the most accurate results possible, we have used a number of samples that greatly exceed these numbers, as in most graphs we employed 10,000 samples.

All the diffusion processes analysed can spread the information only to nodes connected to the starting node. For this reason, to be able to measure the accuracy of the estimator in a reliable way, we restrict the analysis to the largest strongly connected component in each graph. Otherwise, depending on the starting node, the number of informed nodes at the end of the process would vary greatly in a way that is not related to the actual rumour spreading process.

Accuracy measures.

The literature on prediction accuracy is vast and several different measures have been defined (see [17] for instance). In this paper, we report results for two well-known measures: the L_2 distance and the Mean Absolute Percentage Error, or MAPE [17].

To introduce formally the accuracy measures employed let us begin with the following definition.

Definition 2. For $t = 0, \ldots, \tau$, let $s_t \in R$ be the average number of nodes informed time step t in the rumour spreading process (i.e., the ground truth). Similarly, at the same time let $p_t \in R$ be the average number of nodes informed as predicted by the algorithm.

Note that for consistency of notation, for SIR, we define s_t and p_t as the number of nodes currently in state infected or removed at time t – i.e. the nodes that have received the rumour – in the ground-truth and in the prediction, respectively.

Given these definitions, the well-known L_2 distance of the two series is defined as

$$L_2(S, P) = \sqrt{\sum_{t=1}^{T} |s_t - p_t|^2}.$$

The L_2 distance intuitively measures how far the two curves are from each other in the plane. An L_2 value of 0 shows a perfectly correct prediction (i.e., $s_t = p_t$ for all t) while the maximum error is unbounded. As the two curves s_t and p_t range in $[0, n]$, the L_2 distance clearly depends on the size of the graph and is not well suited to compare directly the prediction error across different graphs (we can expect larger errors on larger graphs). If we consider, however, the two curves scaled down by n, i.e., the fraction of nodes informed in each time step, both $\frac{p_t}{n}$ and $\frac{s_t}{n}$ will range in $[0, 1]$ and the L_2 distance applied to the two scaled vectors will be not dependent on the size of the graph any more. Notice that this measure is exactly equivalent to dividing the L_2 distance of the two (unscaled) curves by n. For this reason, in this section we report the L_2 distance value normalized by the number of nodes.

To complement our analysis we assess the prediction error with another widely-used measure, the Mean Absolute Percentage Error, or MAPE [17], which is defined as follows

$$\text{MAPE}(S, P) = \frac{1}{T} \sum_{t=1}^{T} \left| \frac{s_t - p_t}{s_t} \right|.$$

The measure intuitively assesses the average percentage of the prediction error with respect to the ground truth and contrary to the L_2 distance it does not require normalization.

While easy to interpret, the use of MAPE (or any other measure based on averages such as RMSPE, GMRAE to name a few [17]) requires a certain care in our context.

Observe that in PUSH and PULL s_t converges to n for $t \to \infty$, but it never reaches this value because the probability that there is an uninformed (out-of-the-loop) node is always non-zero. To see why this is problem, consider the trivial prediction: $p_t = n$ uniformly for all t. For large enough t, s_t is arbitrary close to n (in connected graphs) and thus the MAPE of the trivial prediction converges to 0 as T tends to infinity. Similar considerations apply to SIR where s_t.

In order to overcome this problem we need to compute MAPE for a fixed, and finite, interval $[0, T]$. Intuitively, we want to measure the MAPE only for the part of the curve that is informative – i.e. when the process is still evolving. For this reason we report MAPE for the range $[1, T(\epsilon)]$ where $T(\epsilon)$, in the PUSH and PULL case, is defined as the largest time for which the ground truth has at most $(1-\epsilon)n$ informed nodes. Similarly for SIR, where the ground-truth curve s_t converges for $t \to \infty$ to certain value δ in $[0, n]$ we define $T(\epsilon)$ as the largest time in which at most $(1-\epsilon)\delta$ nodes informed. We estimate δ by executing the process for a large τ number of steps after which a negligible fraction of nodes are still actively infected in expectation. By choosing ϵ, for instance in the interval $[1\%, 5\%]$, we can evaluate the

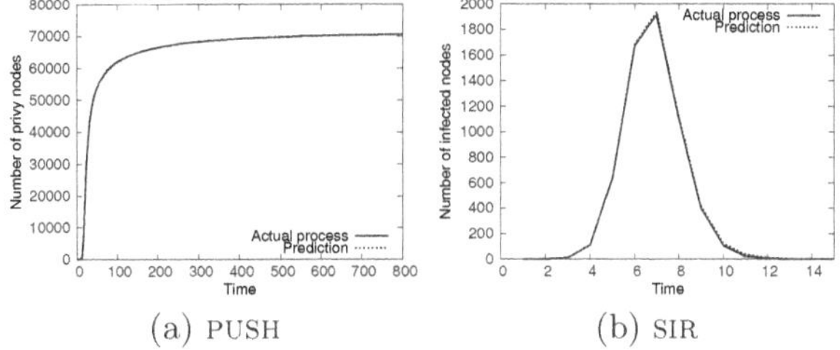

(a) PUSH (b) SIR

Figure 3: Prediction on directed random graph. Results for PULL are very similar to PUSH

prediction for the interesting part of the trajectory of the process. In Table 3 we report values for MAPE using $\epsilon = 2\%$.

Random graphs.

In this section we report the performance of our predictor for the configuration model. Figure 3 exemplifies the results obtained for directed graphs: confirming Theorem 1 the prediction is essentially perfect (the results in the undirected case are similar). The plots show the outcome of a simulation for which the degree sequence was extracted from a Slashdot snapshot [24]. In both this picture and the following the time represents the number of steps in the process. Both prediction and the actual process have been averaged over 100 random graphs for which we run 100 times the rumour spreading process. We obtained the following L_2/n values for the three processes: 0.0014 for PUSH, 0.0345 for PULL and 0.0095 for SIR. Note that we observed that the PULL and SIR process exhibits an higher variance than PUSH and this is reflected by the higher L_2 norm. Intuitively, this is determined by the large dependence on the degree of the source node in the first steps of the process with respect to the PUSH process. Finally, we need to state that in a series of experiments we have observed that the evolution of the process depends strongly on the degree distribution when n and m are fixed – the results will be included in the full version of the paper.

Real networks.

Let us now discuss the predictions of the model for real networks. We consider both graphs whose nodes and edges represent people and human relationships (henceforth social graphs) and graphs whose nodes do not represent human beings (non-social). Our social graphs can be roughly divided into several groups by their origin:

- *Friendship and trust networks*: to this group belong snapshots of the undirected trust network of Epinions [31]; the undirected friendship networks of Facebook [34] (New Orleans community) and Renren [18]; and the directed friendship networks of Pokec [32], LiveJournal [9] and Slashdot [24];
- *Collaboration networks*: here belong the undirected co-authorship networks in astrophysics (AstroPh [23]) and computer science (DBLP [7]); and the directed communication network of Wikipedia's users (Wiki-Talk [22]);

Graph	$\|V\|$	$\|E\|$	d_{eff}	cc	ϕ
AstroPh	17903	393944	5.05	0.63	1.01×10^{-2}
DBLP	805021	6418218	7.35	0.65	4.41×10^{-3}
Epinions	32223	443506	5.34	0.24	4.00×10^{-2}
Enron	33696	361622	4.82	0.51	4.52×10^{-3}
EuAll	34203	151132	4.35	0.26	9.38×10^{-2}
Facebook	59691	1456818	5.14	0.24	2.13×10^{-2}
LiveJournal	3828682	65349587	6.70	0.31	2.40×10^{-4}
Pokec	1304537	29183655	5.85	0.12	3.45×10^{-2}
Renren	33294	1410496	4.26	0.20	3.22×10^{-2}
Slashdot	71307	841201	4.77	0.07	2.33×10^{-2}
Wiki-Talk	111881	1477893	3.97	0.18	1.60×10^{-1}
Amazon	241761	1131217	25.5	0.40	4.27×10^{-3}
BerkStan	334857	4523232	16.21	0.64	1.55×10^{-4}
Google	434818	3419124	13.99	0.64	4.56×10^{-4}
NotreDame	53968	296228	14.27	0.55	1.29×10^{-4}
Stanford	150532	1576314	16.31	0.64	1.47×10^{-4}
RoadNet	1957027	5520776	503.44	0.05	2.04×10^{-3}

Table 2: Properties of the graphs analysed. For all graphs we consider only the biggest (strongly) connected component. Light and dark grey cells represents, respectively, social and non-social networks.

- *Email networks*: undirected mail exchange networks of Enron [24] and of a research institution (EuAll [23]);

For what concerns the non-social graphs we evaluated:

- *Web networks*: here we have directed snapshots of the Notre Dame university (NotreDame [1]), Stanford university (Stanford [24]) and Google [24] websites and a crawl of the pages of Stanford and Berkley university (BerkStan [24]).
- *Product networks*: here belong a directed product co-purchasing network form Amazon websites (Amazon [21]).
- *Road networks*: here we consider a directed graph representing the connections of the roads of California (RoadNet [24]).

All graphs analysed are available online or on request. For each graph, we considered only the largest (strongly) connected component. Table 2 reports some statistics for these graphs: d_{eff}, cc and ϕ indicate, respectively, an estimation of the 90-th percentile effective diameter [23], the clustering coefficient and conductance [24], obtained with the SNAP graph library.[3] The conductance was estimated with the method of Andersen et al. [2], removing orientations in the case of directed networks.

In what follows, for lack of space, we report results that exemplify our main conclusions. The full data sets are available on request and will be publicly distributed with our code and appear in the full paper.

The main qualitative conclusion that our experiments warrant is that the accuracy of the prediction of the estimator follows a very different trend in the two main categories of network analysed. For all instances of what we dubbed social graphs the prediction matches qualitatively well the evolution of the process in the actual graphs. Remarkably, the prediction is especially accurate for friendship and trust networks (Epinions, Facebook, LiveJournal, Renren, Slashdot) – i.e., ones that could be considered to be more "genuine" social networks (See Figure 6 for some examples). For

[3] Available at `snap.stanford.edu/snap`, the same website provided many of the graphs used.

Graph	PUSH L_2/n	PUSH MAPE	SIR L_2/n	SIR MAPE	Neighbourhood F. L_2/n	Neighbourhood F. MAPE
AstroPh	0.549	0.208	0.647	0.470	0.508	0.222
DBLP	1.32	0.614	0.698	0.521	0.564	0.263
Epinions	0.536	0.032	0.256	0.286	0.314	0.100
Enron	2.74	0.062	0.327	0.316	0.212	0.056
EuAll	2.05	0.093	0.576	0.368	0.342	0.069
Facebook	0.476	0.105	0.448	0.316	0.428	0.182
LiveJournal	0.688	0.216	0.467	0.423	0.632	0.455
Pokec	0.356	0.005	0.631	0.137	0.359	0.188
Renren	0.490	0.042	0.235	0.147	0.249	0.099
Slashdot	0.378	0.019	0.048	0.044	0.118	0.035
WikiTalk	1.17	0.029	0.061	0.070	0.094	0.024
Amazon	5.24	15.9	0.023	67.3	2.87	4.70
BerkStan	3.61	0.187	0.755	51.3	1.89	0.104
Google	4.05	0.648	2.15	225.4	1.78	2.67
NotreDame	4.79	0.267	2.03	19.3	1.41	0.338
Stanford	4.07	0.162	0.401	11.3	1.70	0.200
RoadNet	23.9	67.9	2.623	24412.2	14.8	48.9

Table 3: Accuracy of the algorithms presented (MAPE is calculated for $\epsilon = \%2$). We report the results of undirected algorithm for undirected graph and directed algorithm for directed graphs. Light and dark grey cells represents, respectively, social and non-social networks. Notice the much higher prediction errors for non-social graphs. Results for PULL are very similar to PUSH and omitted for lack of space.

other social graph classes, the prediction error is comparably larger, but still is qualitatively close to the ground-truth. In particular for some instances of collaboration networks such as DBLP and the mail networks (EuAll, Enron) it works rather well.

In sharp contrast, the prediction in non-social graphs (web graphs, product networks and road networks) is very inaccurate. Figure 6 exemplifies these findings in the case of PUSH. Similar results are obtained for PULL and SIR (omitted from this extended abstract). In all the reported experiments involving SIR we report the experiments where the parameter p was set such that the reproduction number $R_0 = p\bar{d}$ is 1. Similar results are obtained for other parameter settings. Table 3 reports the MAPE and L_2 errors for all our networks.

For each network we have averaged over 10,000 samples, except for LiveJournal for which 1,000 samples were used due to running time constraints. The number of steps simulated was $\tau = 3{,}000$, after which the all processes simulated change by only a negligible fraction in expectation.

Discussion.

The sharp distinction in the prediction accuracy between social and non-social graphs is intriguing as it suggests that the two classes of graphs behave differently with respect to the rumour spreading process. The former shows a close similarity to the evolution of the rumour spreading processes in the configuration model graphs while the latter does not. Is there some specific property of these type of networks that makes our prediction accurate?

Several properties are known to distinguish friendship graphs from non-social networks: diameter (look at Table 2), assortativity [28][4], and compressibility [7], some of which has been already reported to influence epidemic processes [5].

But the key to interpret the results is the neighbourhood function [6]. The neighbourhood function $f_G(t)$ of a graph $G = (V, E)$, for $t \in 1, \ldots n$, is a defined as the number of ordered node pairs (u, v) such that v can be reached from u by a directed path of length at most t. This function, and in particular its so-called index of dispersion [6], has been shown to be able to tell apart social graphs from the web graph. Hence it is a good candidate to explain the different behaviour observed in our experiments.

Moreover, consider the SIR process with probability of transmission 1 (i.e., the broadcast). It is possible to prove that the expected number s_t of nodes informed at time t, for a u.a.r. chosen source node, is linearly related to the neighbourhood function $f_G(t)$ of the graph, more precisely $s_t = \frac{f_G(t)}{n}$.

Hence, if we observe that a real network G has a neighbourhood function that closely resemble that of an average instance of configuration model graphs with the same degree distribution, this would imply that our prediction for the broadcast process in such network is accurate. The opposite is also true, the broadcast process in a graph with a neighbourhood function very different (in a way that has to be formally specified) with respect to the configuration model graphs will be predicted inaccurately by our model. Notice that this mathematical implication holds only for the broadcast model. However, in any of the process evaluated (PUSH, PULL and SIR with arbitrary probability) it is still possible to notice that the expected number of nodes informed s_t, starting from a random source, is upper-bounded by the neighbourhood function, more precisely $s_t \leq \frac{f_G(t)}{n}$.

It is hence possible to expect a close relationship between the similarity of the neighbourhood function of a graph with that of configuration model graphs and the precision of our prediction method in such graph. We tested this hypothesis with the following experiment. For each real graph G, we computed the neighbourhood function $f_G(t)$ of the graph and the average neighbourhood function over random configuration model graphs with the same degree distribution as G. Then we measured the distance between the two functions (for instance with the L_2 norm) and compared this distance with our prediction error.

The main message is exemplified by Figure 7. On the left hand side we see what happens for the Slashdot network: its neighbourhood function is very close to that of a random network and the prediction of the average number of infected nodes (in this case by SIR) is very accurate. In contrast, on the right, we see that when the neighbourhood functions are far apart the prediction is off. Notice that for the random networks we use the average of the neighbourhood function over 10 instances of the configuration model. In both real and random graphs we compute the neighbourhood function using the method of Boldi et al. [6].

Table 3 reports the full data of our experiments. The results show a clear and strong correlation between the distance of the two functions and the approximation error. The last two columns in the table report the distance of the two neighbourhood functions for our real networks. Notice that the distance is much higher in non-social graph than in social graph (for instance L_2/n is at most ~ 0.6 in the former and at least ~ 1.4 in the latter).

To further validate the hypothesis, for the 17 real graphs in our dataset, we tested the Pearson correlation coefficient between the L_2/n distance of $f_G(t)$ and $c_G(t)$ in a graph G and the MAPE error of the prediction. This coefficient is 0.98, 0.98, 0.97 for PUSH, PULL and SIR, respectively. We

[4]For an illuminating discussion on the correct way to define and use this concept see [25].

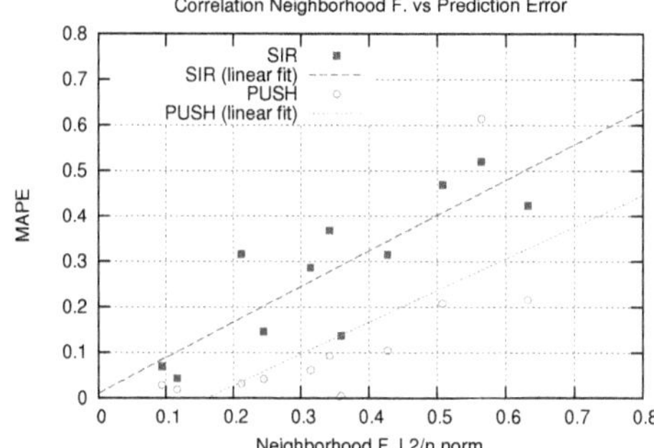

Figure 4: Correlation between prediction error and L_2/n distance between the graph and the average configuration model neighbourhood function. Results for PULL are very similar to PUSH.

Graph	Ground-Truth	Estimated	Error
AstroPh	4.45	5.53	0.24
DBLP	5.74	6.90	0.20
Enron	2.53	2.64	0.04
Epinions	3.18	3.38	0.06
EuAll	2.61	2.06	0.21
Facebook	5.13	5.60	0.09
LiveJournal	6.17	6.11	0.01
Pokec	10.03	13.57	0.35
Renren	5.12	5.55	0.08
Slashdot	2.83	2.69	0.05
WikiTalk	1.79	1.69	0.06

Table 4: Accuracy of the prediction of the average structural virality of SIR in our social graphs. Notice the small relative with the ground-truth.

checked that the correlation remains strong even considering only graph in the single category (social or non-social). For instance in the case of SIR, the coefficient is 0.84 and 0.99 in social and non-social graphs, respectively. Figure 4 shows the correlation for social graphs only. Notice that all these Pearson coefficients are significant with p-value lower than 0.5%.

Finally, we also checked that these observations are not explained by simpler graph statistics such the clustering coefficient or the diameter. We did not found any statistically significant correlation between MAPE error and conductance or clustering coefficient. On the other hand, the effective diameter has a strong positive correlation with the MAPE over the entire dataset but this correlation becomes non-significant (p-value $>$ 0.5% in SIR) when looking at single network classes (i.e., only for social or non-social networks).

This result can suggest that, despite its simplicity, the configuration model qualitatively matches real social graphs in terms of their neighbourhood function and hence it justifies the good prediction of our model in such networks and conversely the poor results for non-social graphs.

Structural virality.

We run an additional experiment to verify the predictive power of our model in real networks. In their study Goel *et al.* [16] introduce a scalar quantity called structural virality and argue that to some extent it captures the shape of a diffusion process. Consider a *diffusion tree* T where an edge (u, v) is present if u informed v. The virality of the tree T is defined as

$$v(T) = \frac{1}{n(n-1)} \sum_{i,j} d_{ij},$$

where d_{ij} is the distance in the tree of the nodes i and j. They find this measure to be close in the case of real twitter propagations and SIR in the configuration model.

This measure can be computed efficiently on-the-fly in our framework without affecting the computational complexity of our algorithms. In particular we run the following experiment for the SIR model on our social networks. The results show that the average virality predicted by our model is close to the one observed in the ground-truth process. In our social graphs (see Table 4) the relative error with the ground-truth in the estimation of the virality is between $\sim 1\%$ in Livejournal to $\sim 35\%$ in Pokec. This shows that the model is able to predict qualitatively well not only the average number of informed nodes at each time step but also the viral structure of the diffusion.

Real rumours.

Finally, we have also analysed some real instances of rumour spreading in Twitter. We have collected the tweets for selected hashtags that are related to instances of viral information diffusions.[5] For each of the rumours we tried to fit the prediction of the SIR model on a configuration model graph with power law distribution to the real data with a linear transformation. Figure 5 shows the fraction of nodes informed in the actual twitter process (with respect to the peak value) and in the fitted SIR one. Similar to the experiments in [16] we run SIR on a configuration model graph with power law distribution (we used the Snapshot degree distribution as a reference). In all instances we used the same SIR estimation obtained with parameter $R_0 = 1$ and optimized the linear transformation for the lowest L_2 error.

Notice that the parameters of the linear transformation that best fit the process varies from rumour to rumour (as the number of informed nodes and the speed of the diffusion can be vastly different) so this result is clearly not to be intended that a single instance of SIR can predict *all* instances of rumour diffusions in Twitter. The takeaway observation however is that the SIR model on configuration model graph qualitatively matches the evolution of some viral rumours in real networks, as previously observed by S. Goel et al. [16], thus further validating our approach.

5. CONCLUSIONS

In this paper we have developed a space efficient estimator that is able to predict with good accuracy the average growth of rumour spreading in a given social network. The results are especially accurate for friendship and trust networks. Remarkably, in our opinion, the only information that the predictor needs is the degree distribution of the network. The estimator is based on the configuration model, for which it was formally proven to be correct. We would like to remark that we will make the code and our results available online when the paper is published. This could facilitate to explore the following further avenues of research that our work points to.

[5]For instance tweets related to important world-wide events, e.g., tweets containing hashtag *#conclave* in the latest Pope election.

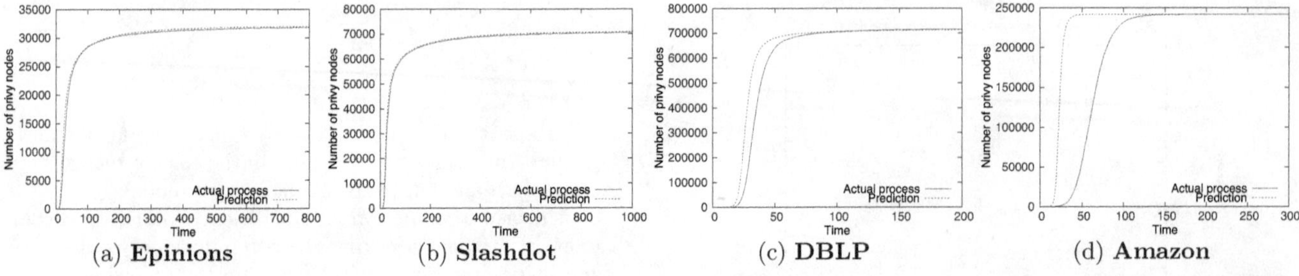

(a) **Epinions** (b) **Slashdot** (c) **DBLP** (d) **Amazon**

Figure 6: Prediction for the PUSH model. Epinions and Slashdot exemplify the very good prediction obtained for friendship and trust networks; the performance for DBLP is typical of email networks and the worst instances of collaboration networks; finally, Amazon shows the typical result for non social networks.

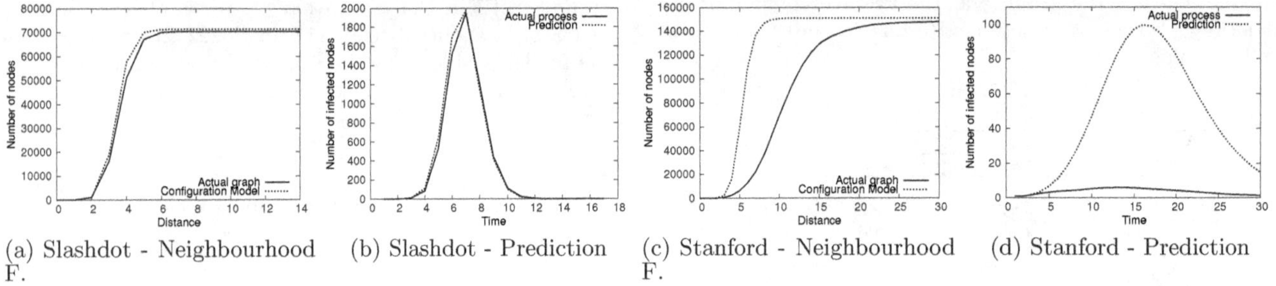

(a) Slashdot - Neighbourhood F. (b) Slashdot - Prediction (c) Stanford - Neighbourhood F. (d) Stanford - Prediction

Figure 7: Neighbourhood function and prediction for SIR in social and non-social graphs. Notice how the social graph Slashdot shows both a Neighbourhood function close to the average one in configuration model graphs and good prediction. The web graph Stanford shows a substantially different neighbourhood function with respect to configuration model and a poor prediction.

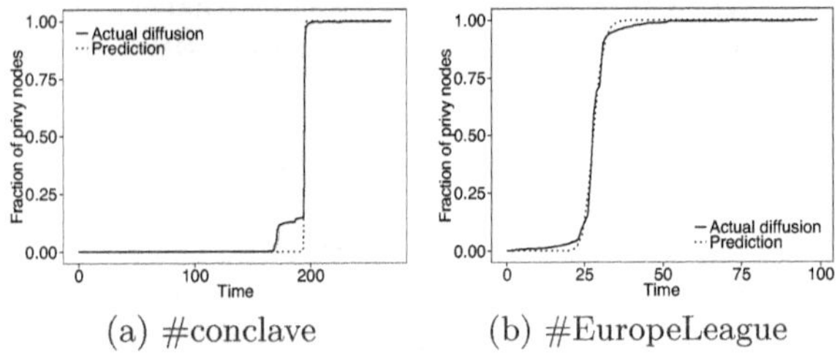

(a) #conclave (b) #EuropeLeague

Figure 5: Fitting of SIR model prediction with selected hashtags diffusion from Twitter in March 2013. The data contains tweets with keywords "#conclave *signaling*" (2108 tweets) and "#EuropeLeague *Steaua*" (2351 tweets).

The first question is whether it is possible to come up with much more compact predictors, for instance based on systems of differential equations [29]. Another interesting direction is to consider a similar approach but for other diffusive processes. For which processes can we predict their growth based only on limited information? In addition, it would be interesting to apply similar techniques to the influence maximization [19] in networks for which the topology is unavailable. Finally, it could be worthwhile trying to develop similar predictors based on more nuanced graph models, that would allow for more accurate predictions and to extend successfully the approach to larger classes of real networks.

Acknowledgements

We thank Flavio Chierichetti and Silvio Lattanzi for many insightful comments, and Nelly Litvak for some useful pointers to the literature.

APPENDIX

A. SAMPLING

The most crucial and time consuming operation in our algorithms is drawing an element form a set with a probability proportional to some dynamic integer value. This problem is known in literature as dynamic variate sampling and several solutions are known [36, 27]. More precisely, we are interested in a data structure that, for a sequence of N non-negative weights summing up to M, provides two operations: *get* (that retrieves an element) and *update* (that modifies its associated weight)[6]. Ideally, we would like to have a data structures that require $O(N)$ space while providing $O(1)$ amortized time for *get* and *update*.

A well-known data structure based on binary trees [36] provides $O(N)$ space and $O(\log(N))$ time for both *get* and *update*. While slower than optimal, this data structure, has the clear advantage of having very low hidden multiplicative constants, making possible to retain almost all the memory saving described in the previous sections. Nevertheless, there are solutions that use slightly more space but support both operations in $o(\log N)$ time.

[6]In our context, $M = m$ is the number of edges m and N is the number of equivalences classes of nodes ($N = n$ for directed graphs, $N = o(n)$ for undirected ones).

Dynamic sampling.

For the case in which weights are fixed, the well known Walker's alias method [35] provides an elegant and optimal solution. The algorithm requires an $O(N)$-time preprocessing step that has to repeated for each update operation. However, for the case of monotone decreasing weights, which applies to directed graph algorithms, we can define a simple and efficient variants of the algorithm based on rejection sampling. Each element is associated with an additional *reject* probability, given by the amount weight reduced by the previous extractions. Every time an element i is drawn, we reject it with $reject_i$ probability and repeat the sampling.

It is easy to show that this reproduces the right distribution, and that the extraction per *get* operation can be constrained to $O(1)$ in expectation. Suppose, in fact, that overall the *reject* probability is less than $\frac{1}{2}$, then each *get* operation would require less than 2 samples in expectation. We can then repeat the $O(N)$ time preprocessing every time the total weight has been decreased by half. The total cost for $O(M)$ *get* and *updates* is then $O(M)$ plus $N \log(M)$ for the initializations. In our algorithms this gives $O(1 + \frac{\log(m)}{d})$ amortized cost per *get*, where d is the average degree. This is practically $O(1)$ because d is in general larger or comparable to $\log(m)$.

This algorithm while easy to implement and very efficient, cannot be applied to the case where the matrix data structure is used. In such case, weights can increase as well – nodes can be moved to a new class. However, for this case, Matias et. al [27] algorithm provide a constant time solution which uses space $O(N)$. This general purpose data structure can be applied to all our algorithms proving that $O(1)$ time and $O(N)$ is achievable as stated in the previous sections. Although optimal in the asymptotic sense, this data structure is rather complex to implement. While we have not conducted a thorough experimental evaluation, we found that the simpler data structures discussed previously behave quite well in practice, and are easy to implement.

B. REFERENCES

[1] R. Albert, H. Jeong, and A. L. Barabasi. The diameter of the world wide web. Nature, 1999.

[2] R. Andersen, F. Chung, and K. Lang. Local graph partitioning using pagerank vectors. In FOCS, 2006.

[3] L. Backstrom, P. Boldi, M. Rosa, J. Ugander, and S. Vigna. Four degrees of separation. In WebSci, 2012.

[4] M. Bayati, J. Kim, and A. Saberi. A sequential algorithm for generating random graphs. Algorithmica, 2010.

[5] M. Boguá, R. Pastor-Satorras, and A. Vespignani. Epidemic spreading in complex networks with degree correlations. Statistical mechanics of complex networks, 2003.

[6] P. Boldi, M. Rosa, and S. Vigna. HyperANF: Approximating the neighbourhood function of very large graphs on a budget. In WWW, 2011.

[7] P. Boldi and S. Vigna. The WebGraph framework I: Compression techniques. In WWW, 2004.

[8] S. Chatterjee, R. Durrett, et al. Contact processes on random graphs with power law degree distributions have critical value 0. The Annals of Probability, 2009.

[9] F. Chierichetti, R. Kumar, S. Lattanzi, M. Mitzenmacher, A. Panconesi, and P. Raghavan. On compressing social networks. In KDD, 2009.

[10] F. Chierichetti, S. Lattanzi, and A. Panconesi. Almost tight bounds for rumour spreading with conductance. In Proc. 42nd STOC, 2010.

[11] F. Chierichetti, S. Lattanzi, and A. Panconesi. Rumour spreading and graph conductance. In SODA, 2010.

[12] A. Demers, D. Greene, C. Hauser, W. Irish, J. Larson, S. Shenker, H. Sturgis, D. Swinehart, and D. Terry. Epidemic algorithms for replicated database maintenance. In PODC, 1987.

[13] U. Feige, D. Peleg, P. Raghavan, and E. Upfal. Randomized broadcast in networks. In Algorithms. Springer, 1990.

[14] N. Fountoulakis, K. Panagiotou, and T. Sauerwald. Ultra-fast rumor spreading in social networks. In SODA, 2012.

[15] G. Giakkoupis. Tight bounds for rumor spreading in graphs of a given conductance. In T. Schwentick and C. Dürr, editors, STACS, 2011.

[16] S. Goel, A. Anderson, J. Hofman, and D. Watts. The structural virality of online diffusion. Under review 5harad.com/papers/twiral.pdf, 2014.

[17] R. J. Hyndman and A. B. Koehler. Another look at measures of forecast accuracy. Int. J. Forecasting, 2006.

[18] J. Jiang, C. Wilson, X. Wang, P. Huang, W. Sha, Y. Dai, and B. Y. Zhao. Understanding latent interactions in online social networks. In IMC, 2010.

[19] D. Kempe, J. Kleinberg, and É. Tardos. Maximizing the spread of influence through a social network. In Proceedings of the ninth ACM SIGKDD international conference on Knowledge discovery and data mining, 2003.

[20] W. O. Kermack and A. G. McKendrick. Contributions to the mathematical theory of epidemics. II. The problem of endemicity. Proc. of the Royal society of London. Series A, 1932.

[21] J. Leskovec, L. A. Adamic, and B. A. Huberman. The dynamics of viral marketing. ACM Trans. Web, 2007.

[22] J. Leskovec, D. Huttenlocher, and J. Kleinberg. Signed networks in social media. In CHI, 2010.

[23] J. Leskovec, J. Kleinberg, and C. Faloutsos. Graph evolution: Densification and shrinking diameters. ACM Trans. KDD, 2007.

[24] J. Leskovec, K. Lang, A. Dasgupta, and M. Mahoney. Community structure in large networks: Natural cluster sizes and the absence of large well-defined clusters. J. Int. Math., 2009.

[25] N. Litvak and R. van der Hofstad. Uncovering disassortativity in large scale-free networks. Phys. Review E, 2013.

[26] D. Maki and M. Thompson. Mathematical models and applications: with emphasis on the social, life, and management sciences. Prentice-Hall, 1973.

[27] Y. Matias, J. S. Vitter, and W.-C. Ni. Dynamic generation of discrete random variates. In SODA, 1993.

[28] M. E. J. Newman. Mixing patterns in networks. Phys. Rev. E, 2003.
[29] B. Pittel. On spreading a rumor. SIAM J. Appl. Math., 1987.
[30] A. Reka and Barabási. Statistical mechanics of complex networks. Rev. Mod. Phys., 2002.
[31] M. Richardson, R. Agrawal, and P. Domingos. Trust management for the semantic web. International Semantic Web Conference, 2003.
[32] L. Takac and M. Zabovsky. Data analysis in public social networks. In Int. Scientific Conf. Present Day Trends of Innovations, 2012.
[33] J. Ugander, B. Karrer, L. Backstrom, and C. Marlow. The anatomy of the facebook social graph. CoRR, 2011.
[34] B. Viswanath, A. Mislove, M. Cha, and K. P. Gummadi. On the evolution of user interaction in facebook. In WOSN, 2009.
[35] A. J. Walker. An efficient method for generating discrete random variables with general distributions. ACM Trans. Math. Softw., 1977.
[36] C. Wong and M. Easton. An efficient method for weighted sampling without replacement. SIAM J. on Computing, 1980.
[37] N. Wormald. Models of random regular graphs. In Surveys in Combinatorics. Cambridge U. Press, 1999.

Popularity Dynamics of Foursquare Micro-Reviews

Marisa Vasconcelos, Jussara Almeida, Marcos Gonçalves,
Daniel Souza, Guilherme Gomes
{marisav,jussara,mgoncalv,daniel.reis,gcm.gomes}@dcc.ufmg.br
Universidade Federal de Minas Gerais, Belo Horizonte, Brazil

ABSTRACT

Foursquare, the currently most popular location-based social network, allows users not only to share the places (venues) they visit but also post micro-reviews (tips) about their previous experiences at specific venues as well as "like" previously posted tips. The number of "likes" a tip receives ultimately reflects its popularity among users, providing valuable feedback to venue owners and other users.

In this paper, we provide an extensive analysis of the popularity dynamics of Foursquare tips using a large dataset containing over 10 million tips and 9 million likes posted by over 13,5 million users. Our results show that, unlike other types of online content such as news and photos, Foursquare tips experience very slow popularity evolution, attracting user likes through longer periods of time. Moreover, we find that the social network of the user who posted the tip plays an important role on the tip popularity throughout its lifetime, but particularly at earlier periods after posting time. We also find that most tips experience their daily popularity peaks within the first month in the system, although most of their likes are received after the peak. Moreover, compared to other types of online content (e.g., videos), we observe a weaker presence of the rich-get-richer effect in our data, demonstrating a lower correlation between the early and late popularities. Finally, we evaluate the stability of the tip popularity ranking over time, assessing to which extent the current popularity ranking of a set of tips can be used to predict their popularity ranking at a future time. To that end, we compare a prediction approach based solely on the current popularity ranking against a method that exploits a linear regression model using a multidimensional set of predictors as input. Our results show that use of the richer set of features can indeed improve the prediction accuracy, provided that enough data is available to train the regression model.

COSN'14, October 1–2, 2014, Dublin, Ireland.

http://dx.doi.org/10.1145/2660460.2660484.

Categories and Subject Descriptors

H.3.5 [**Online Information Services**]: Web-based services; J.4 [**Computer Applications**]: Social and behavioral sciences

Keywords

Popularity dynamics; online micro-reviews; location-based social networks

1. INTRODUCTION

Understanding the popularity dynamics of online content, particularly user generated content (UGC), is quite a challenge due to the various factors that might affect how the popularity of a particular piece of content (here referred to as an object) evolves over time. Moreover, the processes that govern UGC popularity evolution may vary greatly depending not only on the type of content but also on characteristics of the particular application where the content is shared. For example, mechanisms employed by the application, such as search and recommendation, social links among users, and even elements of the application that might favor the visibility of some objects over the others, may affect how content popularity evolves.

We here analyze the popularity dynamics of an increasingly popular type of UGC, namely Foursquare micro-reviews, also called *tips*, estimating the popularity of a tip at a certain time t by the number of likes it received from posting time until t.

A study of how the popularity of a tip evolves over time allows us to compare tips against other types of content whose popularity and dissemination dynamics have already been studied, such as videos [28, 31], photos [6, 34], and tweets and news articles [32]. Tips have inherent characteristics that distinguish them from these other types of content and that might impact their popularity evolution. For example, tips are associated with specific venues, and thus are visible to all users that visit the venue, including those that are drawn to it by other reasons (e.g., other tips). Also, tips usually contain opinions that might interest others for much longer periods of time than news and tweets. Thus, tips may remain live in the system, attracting attention (and likes), for longer periods.

The present effort also complements prior studies on the automatic assessment of the helpfulness (or quality) of online reviews, which focused mainly on traditional (longer) reviews, often exploiting textual features [17, 38]. Unlike such reviews, tips are more concise (constrained to 200 characters), often containing more subjective and informal content. Thus, attributes used by existing solutions, particularly those related to the textual content, may not be adequate for assessing the popularity of shorter reviews. Moreover, we are not aware of any prior study that analyzed the temporal popularity evolution of online reviews.

The study of tip popularity dynamics (as of any other type of content) can also provide valuable insights into improvements to the system. For example, it can guide the future design of tip popularity prediction methods [35], which in turn, can benefit various other services, including content filtering and recommendation, as well as more cost-effective marketing strategies. In the particular context of Foursquare tips, such predictions can benefit both users and venue owners as they can react quickly to opinions that may have a greater impact on decision making. For example, business owners are able to more quickly identify (and fix) aspects of their services or products that may affect revenues most.

In this context, we here provide an extensive analysis of the popularity dynamics of Foursquare tips. Using a large dataset containing over 10 million tips and 9 million likes posted by over 13,5 million users, we characterize how the popularity of different sets of tips evolves over time, and how it is affected by the social network of the user who posted the tip (its author). We observe that tips experience a very slow popularity evolution, compared to other types of UGC. While news articles acquire most of their comments within the first day of publication [32] and Flickr photos obtain half of their views within two days [34], tips take a couple of months to attract their likes. The social network of the tip's author has an important influence on the tip popularity throughout its lifetime, but especially in earlier periods after posting. For example, 62% of the likes received by the most popular tips during the first hour come from the social network of the user who posted them. This fraction is even larger for the less popular tips.

We also analyze tip popularity at and around the daily peak, and assess to which extent the rich-get-richer phenomenon impacts the popularity evolution of tips. We find that most tips experience their daily popularity peak within a month in the system. Yet, these peaks usually correspond to a small fraction of the total popularity, as most likes are received after the daily peak. Compared to YouTube videos [4], we observe a weaker presence of the rich-get-richer phenomenon in the popularity evolution of tips, suggesting that other factors, but the current popularity, may significantly impact the tip's future popularity.

Finally, we assess to which extent the future relative popularity of a set of Foursquare tips can be *predicted* based only on their popularity ranking at the prediction time, or, in other words, to which extent the tip popularity ranking remains stable over time. To that end, we compare two prediction strategies: one based solely on the current popularity ranking, and one that exploits a regression model and a much richer and multidimensional set of features, capturing aspects related to the user who posted the tip, the venue where it was posted, and its content. Our experimental results indicate that these features can improve the prediction accuracy, given that enough training data is available.

The rest of this paper is as follows. We review related work in Section 2 and describe our Foursquare dataset in Section 3. We analyze the dynamics of tip popularity in Section 4 and tackle the popularity ranking prediction problem in Section 5. Section 6 offers conclusions and directions for future work.

2. RELATED WORK

Our work is focused on analyzing the popularity evolution of Foursquare tips, estimated by the number of likes received. Previous related efforts can be grouped into: analyses of online content popularity, and methods to assess the helpfulness of online reviews.

Online Content Popularity. A number of studies on popularity dynamics were conducted analyzing the role of the social networks in the spread of news, videos [7, 20, 4], images [6] and tweets [20, 36]. Crane and Sornette [7] described four classes (memoryless, viral, quality and junk) of YouTube videos characterized by how their popularity evolves over time. The authors defined these classes according to the degree of influence of endogenous user interactions and external events. In contrast, Yang and Leskovec [36] proposed a clustering algorithm to classify the temporal evolution patterns of online content popularity, finding six "curves" that explain the popularity dynamics of tweets and news documents.

Lerman and Gosh [20] performed an empirical study to measure how popular news spread on Digg and Twitter. They observed that the number of votes and retweets accumulated by stories on both sites increases quickly within a short period of time and saturates after a day. In contrast, Cha et al. [6] showed that popular photos on Flickr, with popularity estimated by the number of favorite marks, spread neither widely nor rapidly through the network, contrary to the viral marketing intuition. Complementarily, Borghol et al. [4] assessed the impact of content-agnostic factors on the popularity of YouTube videos. They focused on groups of videos that have the same content (clones), finding a strong linear "rich-get-richer" behavior with the number of previous views as the most important factor.

Other studies have addressed the prediction of popularity of online content [1, 14, 28, 32]. Bandari et al. [1] and Hong et al. [14] exploited textual features extracted from messages (e.g., hashtags or URLs) or the topic of the message, and user related features to predict popularity of news and tweets. Tatar et.al [32] modeled the problem of predicting the popularity of a news article based on user comments as a ranking problem. Pinto et al. [28] proposed a multivariate regression model to predict the long-term popularity of YouTube videos based on measurements of user accesses during an early monitoring period. In [23], the authors proposed a unifying model for popularity evolution of blogs and tweets, showing that it can be used for tail-part forecasts.

Our current effort complements these prior studies by focusing on an inherently different type of content. Unlike news, videos and tweets, tips are associated with specific venues, and tend to be less ephemeral (particularly compared to news and tweets), as they remain associated with the venue (and thus visible to users) for a longer time. Thus, the analysis of tip popularity dynamics may lead to new insights. Also, towards analyzing the stability of popularity ranking over time, we tackle a different prediction task. While most prior efforts aim at predicting the future popularity of a given piece of content, we here explore strategies to predict the future popularity *ranking* of a set of tips.

Quality of Online Reviews. Most previous efforts to automatically assess the helpfulness or quality of online reviews

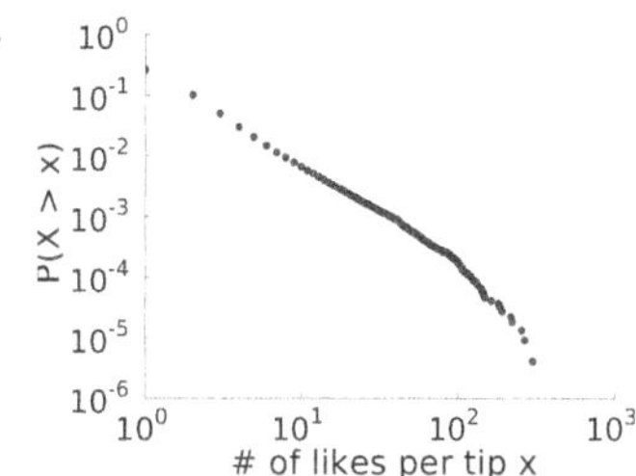

Figure 1: Distribution of Number of Likes per Tip

employ classification or regression-based models. For example, Kim et al. [17] used Support Vector regression (SVR) to rank reviews according to their helpfulness, exploiting features such as the length and the unigrams of a review and the reviewers' ratings. Mahony et al. [26] proposed a classification-based system to recommend the most helpful hotel reviews in Trip Advisor using features related to the user reviewing history and the scores previously assigned to the hotels. Zhang et al. [38], in turn, found that syntactic features (e.g., number of nouns, comparatives and modal verbs) extracted from the text reviews are the most effective predictors for SVR and linear regression to predict the utility of Amazon reviews. Ghose and Ipeirotis [13] applied a Random Forests classifier on a variety of textual features to predict if an Amazon product review is helpful or not. Hong et al. [15] built a binary helpfulness based system to classify Amazon reviews using textual features and features related to user preferences, and used this classification to rank product reviews. Finally, Momeni et al. [24] developed a "usefulness" classifier for predicting useful comments on YouTube and Flickr based on textual features as well as features that describe the author's posting and social behavior.

These prior studies focused on longer reviews, often exploiting textual features and, in some cases, aiming at a binary classification of reviews (helpful or not). Instead, we here tackle the ranking of tips based on the predicted number of likes. Tips have length constraints which lead users to write reviews using non-standard textual artifacts and informal language [3]. Thus, textual features often exploited are not adequate in our context. Moreover, previous work has not addressed how the helpfulness as perceived by users (or popularity) of the reviews evolve over time, as we do here.

The only prior study of tip popularity is a recent work of ours [35] which proposed regression and classification methods to predict, at posting time, the *popularity level* (high or low) of a given tip at a future time. We here greatly extend this work by: (1) providing an extensive analysis of tip popularity dynamics, and (2) tackling a different prediction task: the *ranking* of a set of tips based on their predicted popularity. Ranking and classification tasks support different applications. For example, tip ranking supports filtering and recommendation at a finer granularity (as opposed to 2 popularity levels) which is useful to users and venue owners.

3. FOURSQUARE DATASET

Our experiments are performed on a dataset consisting of more than 10 million tips posted by 13,5 million users at almost 16 million different venues. This dataset was crawled from Foursquare using the system's API from August to October 2011.

Figure 1 shows the complementary cumulative distribution of the number of likes received by each tip. The distribution is highly skewed, and only 34% of the tips received at least one like. As discussed in [35], this distribution, as the distributions of numbers of tips per user, likes per user, and tips per venue, are heavy tailed.

For the sake of analyzing tip popularity dynamics, we group tips with at least one like by breaking their popularity distribution into 10 slices, each one containing tips whose popularity fall into a certain range of the distribution[1]. For example, slice 0-10% contains the top-10% most popular tips, while slice 10%-20% contains the tips whose popularities fall between the 10th and 20th percentile of the popularity distribution. This partitioning is the same used in [34] for analyzing Flickr photos, since it is more balanced and less biased towards the more popular tips. Table 1 shows the number tips as well as total number of likes per slice.

Table 1: Distribution of Likes for Groups of Tips

Slice	# of Tips	Total # of Likes	% Social Likes	Group
0-10%	23,746	202,804	30.8%	G_1
10-20%	23,746	72,824	48.4%	G_2
20-30%	23,746	47,492	49.0%	G_3
30-40%	23,746	47,492	49.0%	G_3
40-50%	23,746	24,163	48.2%	G_4
50-60%	23,746	23,746	49.1%	G_4
60-70%	23,746	23,746	48.5%	G_4
70-80%	23,746	23,746	48.2%	G_4
80-90%	23,746	23,746	48.5%	G_4
90-100%	23,750	23,750	48.4%	G_4

We also examine the fraction of likes coming from the social network (friends and followers) of the user who posted the tip (i.e., the tip's author). Table 1 shows the percentages of likes coming from the social network, referred to as *social likes*, for tips in each slice. We note that for all slices but the first one, almost half of the likes received by tips come from the user's social network, highlighting the importance of friends and followers to the popularity of those tips. In contrast, for the most popular tips, the fraction of social likes is smaller (31%), suggesting that most likes probably come from venue visitors. We further analyze the importance of the social network to tip popularity in Section 4.2.

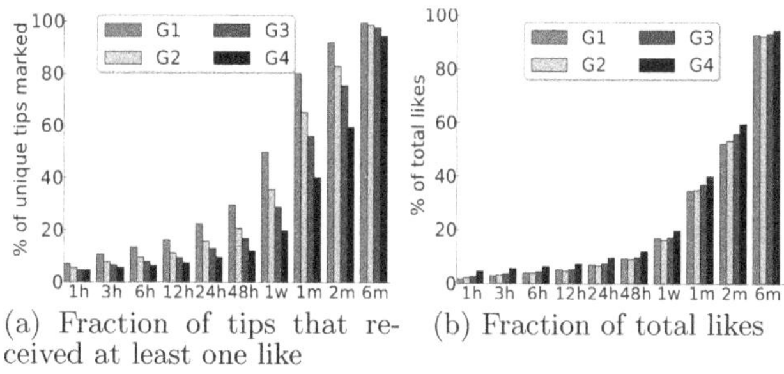

(a) Fraction of tips that received at least one like (b) Fraction of total likes

Figure 2: Distribution of Tip Popularity over Time

We aggregate the slices into 4 major groups, as shown in Table 1. Groups 3 and 4 contain tips that received, on average, 2 and 1 likes, respectively. We analyze tip popularity

[1]Note that we exclude tips with no likes from these slices.

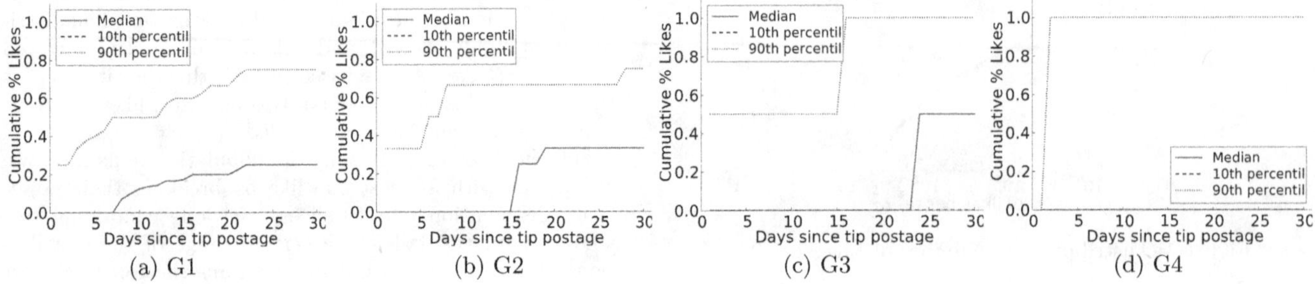

Figure 3: Distribution of Percentage of Likes Received During the First Month after Posting Time

separately for each slice. However, as the same conclusions hold for tips in different slices of the same group, we present results for each group only.

4. DYNAMICS OF TIP POPULARITY

In this section, we analyze the dynamics of tip popularity in Foursquare. We start by discussing how the number of likes of a tip evolves over time (Section 4.1), and how it is affected by the social network of the tip's author (Section 4.2). We then analyze tip popularity at and around the peak (Section 4.3), and assess to which extent the rich-get-richer phenomenon is present in the popularity evolution of tips (Section 4.4).

4.1 Popularity Evolution

We start by analyzing how the popularity of tips in each group of slices defined in Table 1 evolves over time. We focus on the first six months after the tip is posted. Figure 2a plots the fraction of unique tips in each group that received at least one like within the first x hours (h), week (w) or months (m) after posting time. We observe that within the first 48 hours, 29% of the tips in the most popular group (G1) received at least one like, while in one and two months this fraction grows up to 80% and 92%, respectively. That is, 20% of the top-10% most popular tips take more than one month to attract their first likes. This slow popularity evolution is even more clear for tips in the other (less popular) groups. Figure 2b shows the cumulative fraction of the total number of likes (as observed in our dataset) received by tips in each group over time. Note that, for all four groups, between 41% and 48% of the likes are received *after* 2 months since posting time.

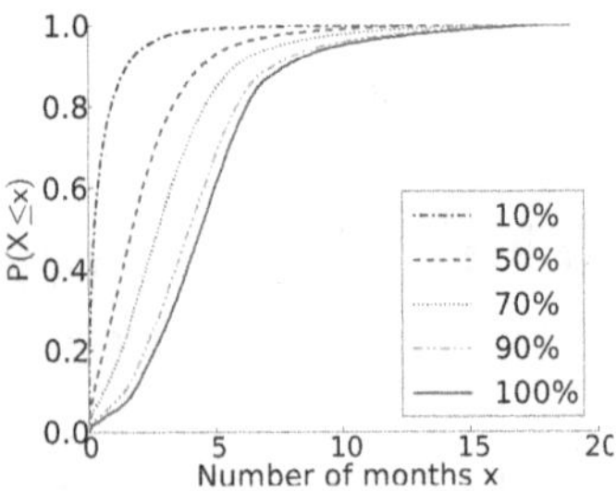

Figure 4: Distribution of time until x% of total likes are received for the most popular tips (G1)

Thus, in general, tips tend to live long in the system, presenting a gradual increase of interest. Indeed, tip popularity evolves much more slowly compared to other types of content, even for tips that end up becoming very popular. For example, news articles have a very short lifespan [32] acquiring all comments within the first day of publication, while a large fraction of views of Flickr photos are generated within the first two days after upload[34]. In contrast, we here find a significant fraction of tips that can take quite months to attract likes and become popular. This longer lifecycle was also observed in the acquisition of *fans* by Flickr photos [6].

We further analyze the popularity evolution of tips in each group by showing in Figure 3 the curves of the 10th and 90th percentiles as well as the median of number of likes over time during the first one month since the tip was posted. For all groups, the 10th percentile curve is equal to zero through the whole period, implying 10% of the tips in each group did not receive any like within the first month in the system. Around half of the most popular tips (G1) starts receiving likes after 7 days since posting time, achieving only 20% of the total likes after a month. For the second most popular group (G2), we note half of the tips start receiving likes after 15 days while tips in group G3 and G4 take more than 20 and 30 days, respectively, to start attracting likes.

We also analyze the amount of time it takes for a tip to receive at least X% of their total likes, for X equal to 10, 50, 70, 90 and 100%. Figure 4 shows those distributions for the most popular tips (G1). Note that 57% of the tips in this group take at least 2 (3) months to reach 50% (70%) of its total observed popularity. In sum, many tips do take a few months to attract likes, even those that end up being the most popular ones.

4.2 The Role of the Social Network

The popularity evolution of a tip is directly related to how users find the tip: either by visiting the venue page or through activity notifications from their friends and followees. Thus, the number of likes received by a tip depends on a combination of its visibility and interest by the social network of the tip's author and by others.

In this section, we discuss the role of the social network of the tip's author on its popularity evolution. To that end, we revisit Figure 2b by separating likes coming from the author's social network (social likes) and likes coming from other users (non-social likes). Figure 5 shows the cumulative fraction of likes, in both categories, for tips in each group. Note that the author's social network has an important influence on the popularity of a tip throughout its lifetime: at least half of all likes received in any period of time (up to 6 months since posting) come from the author's social net-

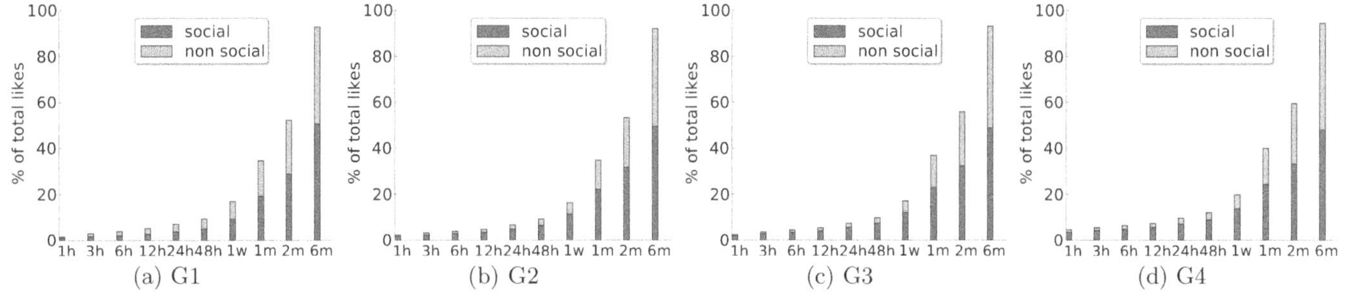

(a) G1 (b) G2 (c) G3 (d) G4

Figure 5: Social vs. Non Social Likes: Distribution of Percentage of Likes Received over Time

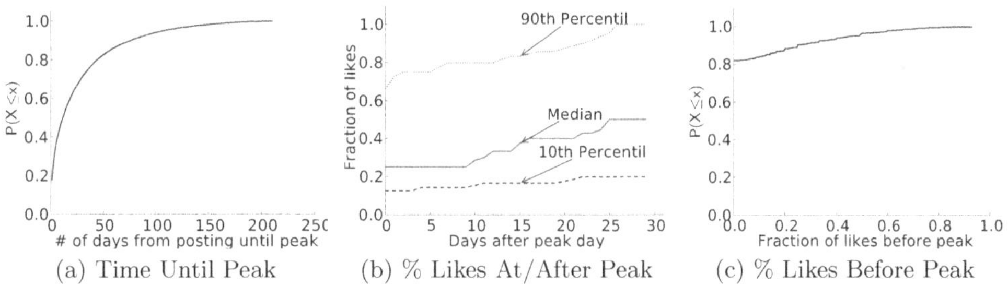

(a) Time Until Peak (b) % Likes At/After Peak (c) % Likes Before Peak

Figure 6: Cumulative Distributions of Popularity Peak for Most Popular Tips (G1)

work, for tips in *all* four groups. This fraction is higher in the earlier periods after posting time, and tends to decrease with time as the tip becomes visible to other users (e.g., venue visitors). For example, the social likes correspond to 62% of all likes received by the most popular tips (G1) in the 1st hour since posting time, decreasing to 54% after 6 hours. Interestingly, the social network seems to have an even more important role for the least popular tips. For example, for tips in G2, G3 and G4, the social likes correspond to more than 70% of all likes received by a tip in the first week in the system.

These results indicate that the social network of a tip's author may be responsible for boosting its popularity, particularly during early periods after posting. As consequence, they also suggest that it might be possible for a recently posted tip to become more popular than other tips that had already attracted many likes and thus gained visibility in the system.

4.3 Popularity Peak

We further analyze tip popularity evolution by focusing on the popularity peak. Considering the daily popularity time series of each tip, we define the peak k_{p_i} of tip p_i as the largest number of likes received by p_i on a single day. We then compute the time (in number of days) it takes for p_i to reach is popularity peak[2]. We also measure the fraction of the total likes p_i received at, *before* and *after* the peak. For this analysis we focus on the most popular tips (G1).

Figure 6a shows the cumulative distribution of the time until the popularity peak. Around 18% of the tips experience its popularity peak one day after posting time, and around 72% of the tips reach their popularity peak within a month since posting. This implies that most tips do not take too long (less than a month) to reach its daily popularity peak. Yet, we observe that, for many tips, this peak represents only a small fraction of the total observed popularity. This is illustrated in Figure 6b, which presents the cumulative distributions of the median, 10th and 90th percentiles of the fraction of likes received at and after the peak day. As a complement, Figure 6c shows the cumulative distribution of the fraction of likes received *before* the peak day. Like observed for other types of online content (e.g., videos and news [7, 28, 32]), some tips do experience heavy bursts of popularity on the peak day: for 10% of the tips, the daily peak corresponds to at least 67% of their total popularity (see 90th percentile curve in Figure 6b).

However, for half of the tips (median curve), the peak corresponds to only 25% of all likes. Moreover, Figure 6c shows that most tips (82%) receives their first like in the peak day, and only a very small fraction of the tips (3.3%) receive more than 50% of the likes before the peak day. Thus, a large fraction of tips receive most of their likes *after* the peak day, suggesting, once again, that tips experience a slow popularity evolution.

Contrasting our findings with the acquisition of fans by Flickr photos [6], we observe that both fans and likes are acquired after a longer period of time after posting/upload, compared to, for example, tweets. Also, as in [6], we do not observe an exponential growth on popularity as suggested by existing models of information diffusion [33]. However, comparing our results (particularly Figure 3), with similar ones presented in [6], we find that tip popularity seems to increase even more slowly than photo fan acquisition. For example, we do not observe a period of steady linear popularity growth during the first month, as observed for photos.

[2]In case of ties, we pick the first day with k_{p_i} likes.

4.4 The Rich-Get-Richer Phenomenon

Most online systems offer their users the option to see different pieces of content (or *objects*) sorted by their posting dates or by some estimate of their popularity. The adopted strategy may have a direct impact on the visibility of different objects. For example, by displaying objects sorted in decreasing order of popularity, a website may contribute to further increasing the popularity of an object that is already very popular, a phenomenon that is known as *rich-get-richer* [2]. Indeed, prior work has already suggested that popularity of some types of online content (e.g., video) evolves according to this phenomenon [4, 31].

Foursquare tips may be sorted by the number of likes (in increasing/decreasing order) or by posting time, but only the former is available in the mobile application. Thus, we here assess to which extent the rich-get-richer phenomenon can explain tip popularity evolution.

The rich-get-richer, or preferential attachment, models define that the probability of a tip p_i experiencing an increase in popularity is directly proportional to p_i's current popularity [2]. As in [4], we consider a model where the probability that a tip p_i with l_{p_i} likes receives a new like is a power law, i.e., $Prob(p_i) \propto l_{p_i}^{\alpha}$.

We analyze the rich-get-richer effect using a univariate linear regression to observe the impact of the number of likes of a tip after a monitoring time t_r (predictor variable) in the total number of likes of the tip at target time $t_r + \delta$ (response variable), using log-transformed data. The case of α=1 corresponds to a linear preferential selection [2], and $\alpha > 1$ implies in a case where the rich gets much richer with time. The sublinear case ($\alpha < 1$) results in a (stretched) exponential popularity distribution, which reflects a much weaker presence of the rich-get-richer effect [19]. We perform this analysis separately for tips in each group as well as for all tips.

Table 2 shows the coefficients α (along with 95% confidence intervals) and the coefficients of determination R^2 of the univariate regressions performed using various predictor and response variables, for tips in G1 as well as for all tips. For all considered cases, we find $\alpha < 1$, which indicates an exponential popularity evolution that could result in a much more even popularity distribution than suggested by the pure (linear) rich-get-richer dynamics. This has also been observed for a set of different YouTube videos [4], although the values of α found in that case (0.93 on average) are much larger than those we observed in all considered scenarios. This suggests that the rich-get-richer effect might be weaker in Foursquare tips than in YouTube videos, even considering all tips jointly. This also implies that other factors might strongly impact tip popularity. Indeed, as discussed in Section 4.2, the social network of the tip's author is responsible for a significant fraction of the likes received by the tip, and thus might contribute to reduce the impact of the rich-get-richer effect.

The univariate regression model has also been proposed as a means to predict the future popularity of YouTube videos and Digg stories [31]. This prediction strategy was motivated by a strong linear correlation observed between the (log-transformed) popularity of objects and earlier measures of user accesses (also log-transformed). For example, the authors observed Pearson linear correlations above 0.90 between the popularity of Digg stories measured at 1 hour and at 30 days after upload as well as between the popularity

Table 2: Rich-get-richer Analysis: coefficients α (and 95% confidence intervals) and R^2 of linear regressions from (log) popularity in t_r to (log) popularity $t_r + \delta$.

		Tips in G1		All tips	
$t_r+\delta$	t_r	α	R^2	α	R^2
1 mo	1 hr	0.799 ± 0.033	0.09	0.749 ± 0.011	0.07
1 mo	1 day	0.763 ± 0.016	0.26	0.822 ± 0.006	0.21
1 mo	1 wk	0.838 ± 0.009	0.57	0.887 ± 0.004	0.49
2 mo	1 day	0.594 ± 0.017	0.17	0.673 ± 0.007	0.13
2 mo	1 wk	0.681 ± 0.011	0.40	0.753 ± 0.004	0.31
2 mo	1 mo	0.834 ± 0.006	0.74	0.856 ± 0.003	0.65
6 mo	1 day	0.309 ± 0.015	0.07	0.397 ± 0.007	0.05
6 mo	1 wk	0.394 ± 0.010	0.20	0.489 ± 0.005	0.16
6 mo	1 mo	0.504 ± 0.008	0.40	0.562 ± 0.003	0.33

of YouTube videos measured at 7 and 30 days after upload. These correlations are stronger than those observed for tips. For example, the R^2 value of the regression from popularity in 1 week to popularity in 1 month is only 0.57 (for tips in G1) and 0.49 (for all tips), which correspond to linear correlations of 0.75 and 0.7, respectively[3]. For shorter monitoring periods t_r or longer values of δ, the R^2 values are much lower, indicating that popularity at time t_r can only explain a small fraction of the total popularity acquired by the tip at $t_r + \delta$.

This result motivates the development of more sophisticated prediction models, such as those proposed in [35], which exploit other factors (e.g., characteristics of the user who posted the tip, the venue where it was posted and its content) to estimate the future popularity of a given tip. Yet, a different prediction task consists of estimating the ranking *by popularity* of a given *set* of tips at a future time. This is a possibly easier task, as it requires predicting not the actual popularity (or popularity level, as in [35]) of a tip but rather its relative popularity according to others. The prediction of popularity ranking supports various applications such as tip filtering and recommendation. Next, we evaluate the stability of tip popularity ranking over time, and assess to which extent the current popularity of a set of tips can be used to predict their future popularity ranking, and to which extent such prediction can be improved by also exploiting other features.

5. PREDICTING THE FUTURE

In the previous section, we observed that tips have longer lifespans than other types of online content (e.g, tweets, photos), and that tip popularity dynamics may be more strongly influenced by factors other than simply their current popularity (e.g., social network). We now further analyze this issue by assessing to which extent the *relative* popularity of a set of Foursquare tips can be predicted using only their popularity at prediction time, and to which extent the use of other attributes may improve prediction accuracy. In [35], we tackled the problem of predicting the popularity level of a given tip at posting time, formulating it as a classification task, and showed the importance of taking into account attributes of both the user who posted the tip and the venue where the tip was posted for that task.

[3]The R^2 is the square of the linear correlation between predictor and response variables.

We here focus on a different task, modeling the prediction as a *ranking task*, which aims at ranking a group of tips based on their predicted popularity at a future time. The ranking of the most popular tips helps to summarize a large set of tips focusing on the most popular ones for a scenario of interest (e.g., a city, a venue), instead of looking at the tips individually. By focusing on this task, we complement not only our prior prediction effort [35] but also our current analyses of tip popularity dynamics. Our ultimate goal is to assess to which extent the popularity ranking of a group of tips remains stable over time, and thus can be used to predict the ranking at a future time.

We first define our prediction task (Section 5.1), present the ranking strategies (Section 5.2) and the set of features (Section 5.3) used. We then discuss our experimental setup (Section 5.4) and results (Section 5.5).

5.1 Popularity Prediction Task

The problem we tackle can be formally defined as follows. Given a set P_d of tips posted in the previous d time units ($d \in (0, \infty)$) that meet a certain criterion c, rank those tips according to their expected popularity, measured in terms of the total number of likes they will receive up to time $t_r + \delta$, where t_r is the time when the ranking is performed. Criterion c may be, for example, tips posted at venues of a given city and/or category (e.g., Food), or even at a given venue. An empty criterion implies in no further constraint on set P_d.

Note that different tips in P_d may have been posted at different times within the time window $[t_r - d, t_r]$. Thus, we associate a posting time t_{p_i} with each tip p_i in P_d. We also consider sets V and U of venues and users, respectively, where $u_i \in U$ is the user who posted p_i, and $v_i \in V$ is the venue where it was posted. For evaluation purposes, we consider that each tip $p_i \in P_d$ is *labeled* with a numeric value that represents the number of likes received by p_i in the time interval $[t_{p_i}, t_r + \delta]$ (i.e., the true popularity acquired by p_i up to $t_r + \delta$), as discussed in Section 5.4. Each entity in P_d, U and V has a set of features F associated with it. Collectively, the features associated with p_i, u_i and v_i are used as inputs to a ranking model (see below) representing the given tip instance. The values of these features for a tip p_i are computed considering all the information available up to the time when the ranking is performed (t_r).

The choice of criterion c allows for different scenarios where the tip ranking problem becomes relevant. One scenario is that of a user who is interested in quickly finding tips with greater potential of becoming popular, and thus of containing valuable information, posted in any venue in her home city. A different scenario is that of a user who is particularly interested in retrieving tips regarding restaurants in her home city (or neighborhood). A business owner can also benefit from a ranking restricted to tips posted at venues of a specific category to get feedback about her business and about her competitors. Also, changes in the current and future tip popularity rankings can help with indirect analysis such as the influence of certain users whose tips got promoted in the future and the potential market share gains or losses for certain venues or venue categories.

5.2 Ranking Strategies

Recall that our goal is to assess to which extent using only the tips' current popularity ranking is enough to accurately predict their ranking at a future time. Thus, we here consider two ranking strategies. The first approach simply uses the ranking of the tips at prediction time (t_r) as an estimate of their ranking at the future time $t_r + \delta$. If the popularity ranking is stable, this approach should lead to perfect predictions. Thus, by analyzing the effectiveness of this approach we are indirectly assessing the stability of tip popularity ranking. We refer to this approach as *baseline*.

In order to assess the potential benefit of exploiting other factors to this prediction task, we consider a second approach that combines multiple features. To that end, we rely on an ordinary least square (OLS) multivariate regression model to predict the popularity of each tip p_i in P_d at time $t_r + \delta$ and then rank the tips by their predictions. In this approach, the logarithm of the number of likes of a tip p_i, $\mathcal{R}_t$, is estimated as a linear function of k predictor variables or features (presented in the next section), i.e.: $\mathcal{R}_t = \beta_0 + \beta_1 x_1 + \beta_2 x_2 + \cdots \beta_k x_k$. Model parameters β_i (i=0..k) are determined by the minimization of the least squared errors [16] in the training data, as will be discussed in Section 5.4.

We note that various other algorithms could be used to exploit multiple features to predict the popularity ranking of a set of tips. Indeed, we did experiment with more sophisticated regression algorithms (notably Support Vector Regression (SVR) with radial basis function kernel [8], which handles non-linear relationships) as well as with a state-of-the-art learning-to-rank algorithm called Random Forests [5]. However, when applied with the same set of features, their results are similar (or even worse in some cases) than those obtained with the simpler OLS regression[4]. Thus, in order to avoid hurt readability, we present only OLS results.

5.3 Features

We consider a large set of features related to the three central entities which, intuitively, should be related to the popularity of a tip: textual content, user (i.e., tip's author), and venue. Specifically, we represent each tip p_i by $k = 53$ features related to the user u_i who posted p_i, the venue v_i where p_i was posted, and to the content of p_i. The values of these features are computed at the time when the ranking is performed (t_r). Table 3 shows the complete set of features. We have exploited most of these features for classifying a tip into low or high (predicted) popularity [35], although some features are novel and specific to the task of ranking multiple tips, as further discussed below. Some of these features, such as average number of likes received by all previous tips of user u_i and size of the tip p_i, have also been previously explored to analyze the helpfulness of online reviews [17, 38] and predict the ratings of (long) reviews [22, 29].

User features describe the tip's author past behavior and degree of activity in the system. Features related to the numbers of tips previously posted, number of likes received or given, and her social network are considered. Similarly, venue features capture the activity at the venue or its visibility to other users. For example, a tip may have a higher chance of becoming popular if it is posted at a venue that has more visibility. We also try to capture the strategy adopted by Foursquare to display the tips posted at the same venue,

[4]We note that we also found OLS to be as good as (if not better than) SVR when applied to the (different) task of predicting the popularity level of a given tip [35].

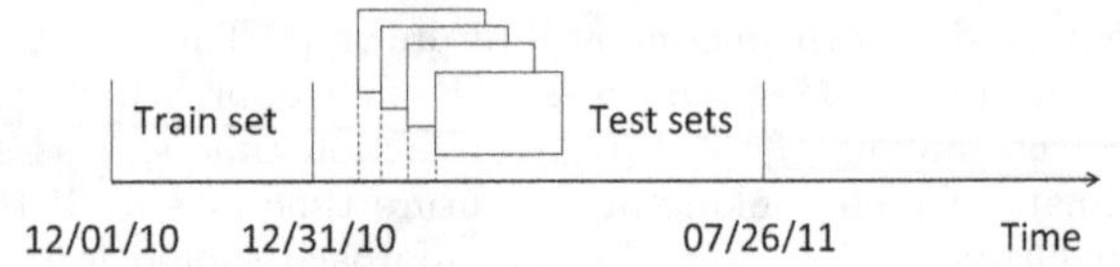

Figure 7: Temporal Data Split into Train and Test Sets

which may also impact the visibility of a tip by including the position of the tip in the rankings of tips of the venue.

We also consider features related to the tip's content. Numbers of characters and words, number of URLs or e-mails, as well as the fractions of words of each grammatical class are included. The latter are computed using the Stanford Part of Speech tagger[5], which employs probabilistic methods to build parse trees for sentences aiming at representing their grammatical structure, as in [21, 22]. We also include three features to represent sentiment scores obtained from SentiWordNet [9]. SentiWordNet is a lexical resource for supporting opinion mining by assigning three scores (positive, negative and neutral) to each synset (set of one or more synonyms) in the WordNet lexical database of English [11]. The scores are in the range of [0,1] and sum up to 1 for each word. We compute a positive, a negative and a neutral score for each tip by taking the average of the respective scores for each word in the tip that has an entry in SentiWordNet, as in [29]. To handle negation, we add the tag NOT to every word between a negation word (e.g., "no", "didn't") and the first punctuation mark following it [27], which implies that the positive scores of these words are converted to negative ones. Since some of our textual features are computed based on tools that were developed for English language only, we used a Linux dictionary (*myspell*) to filter tips with fewer than 60% of the words in English out from our datasets.

Since different tips in set P_d may have been posted at different times, we also add the age of the tip (in number of hours since posting time t_{p_i}) and the number of likes it has already received. These features are novel and have not been exploited in [35].

Tips can also be evaluated for their credibility as source of information. Fogg et al. [12] described credibility as a perceived quality composed by multiple dimensions, and showed that four website design elements – *Real-World Feel*, *Ease of Use*, *Expertise*, and *Trustworthiness* – impact credibility. Some of our features are based on these elements, as indicated in Table 3.

5.4 Experimental Setup

We build two scenarios to evaluate the prediction strategies: ranking all tips recently posted at venues located in New York, the city for which we have the largest number of tips, and ranking tips posted at venues of a specific category (Food) (also the largest category) located in New York [6]. In both scenarios, we consider only tips posted in the previous month (i.e., d = 30 days), and produce rankings based on their predicted popularity δ days later. We compare the effectiveness of both prediction strategies for various values of

[5]www-nlp.stanford.edu/software/corenlp.shtml

[6]Other scenarios, such as ranking tips posted at a venue, are also possible. However, the highly skewed distribution of tips per venue leads to severe data sparsity, which, in turn, poses a challenge to the training of the regression model.

Table 3: Features Used by the OLS Regression Model

Type	Description
User	Total # of tips posted by the user
	Number of of venues where the author posted tips
	Total # of likes received by previous tips of the author[1,c]
	Total # of likes given by the tip's author
	Number of friends or followers of the author
	Ratio of all likes received by the author coming from his friends and followers
	Total # of tips posted by the author's social network[1]
	# likes given by author's social network (in any tip)[1]
	Fraction of all likes received by the tip's author that are associated with tips posted at the same venue of the current tip but after it was posted[1]
	User category defined by Foursquare
	Total # of mayorships won by the author[a]
	If the author was mayor of the venue where tip was posted[a]
Venue	Total # of tips posted at the venue[b]
	Total # of likes received by tips posted at the venue[1,b]
	Total # of checkins at the venue[b]
	Total # of unique visitors[b]
	If the tipped venue was verified by Foursquare[c]
	Venue category defined by Foursquare
	Position of the tip in the tips of the venue sorted by # of likes in ascending order
	Position of the tip in the ranking of the venue sorted by # of likes in descending order
	Position of the tip in the ranking of the venue sorted by date in ascending order
Content	# of likes received until time t_r
	Hours since posting until time t_r
	Length of the text of the tip, in characters
	Length of the text of the tip, in number of words
	# of URLs or emails address contained on a tip
	Fraction of nouns in the tip
	Fraction of adjectives in the tip
	Fraction of adverbs in the tip
	Fraction of comparatives in the tip
	Fraction of verbs in the tip
	Fraction of non-English words in the tip
	Fraction of numbers in the tip
	Fraction of superlatives in the tip
	Fraction of symbols in the tip
	Fraction of punctuation in the tip
	Average positive score over all words in the tip
	Average neutral score over all words in the tip
	Average negative score over all words in the tip

[1] Median, average and standard deviation are also included.
[a] Based on Fogg's design element Expertise.
[b] Based on the Fogg's design element Trustworthiness.
[c] Based on the Fogg's design element Real-world feel.

δ. Table 4 summarizes these two datasets, presenting the total numbers of tips, venues and users in each of them (the two rightmost columns are discussed below).

Unlike the baseline, the regression model needs to be parameterized. Thus, our experimental setup consists, in general terms, of dividing the data into training and test sets, using the former to learn the model parameters and the latter to evaluate the learned model. We split the tips chronologically into training and test sets, rather than randomly, to avoid including in the training tips that were posted after the tips for which predictions will be performed (test set). Figure 7 illustrates this chronological splitting used. For comparison purposes, we also evaluate the baseline only in the test sets.

The training set is composed of all tips posted from December 1st to 30th, 2010. These tips are used to learn the (regression-based) ranking model. We assume the ranking of the training instances is done on December 30th, and thus use the total number of likes received by these tips at the target date (i.e., δ days later) as the ground truth to build the regression model.

Table 4: Overview of Datasets and Scenarios of Evaluation

Scenarios	# of tips	# of users	# of venues	# of tips in training sets	Avg # of tips in test sets
NY	169,393	55,149	31,737	516	4,697.87
NY Food	81,742	32,961	8,927	244	2,365.0

Recall that the distribution of number of likes per tip is highly skewed towards very few number of likes (Section 3), which might bias the regression model and ultimately hurt its accuracy[7]. Thus, we adopt the following approach to reduce this skew. We group tips in the *training set* according to a threshold τ for the number of likes received by the tip at the target date. Two classes are defined: all tips with at least τ likes are grouped into the high popularity class, and the others are grouped into the low popularity class. We then build balanced training sets according to these two classes by performing under-sampling: we randomly select n tips from the low popularity class, whereas n is the number of tips in the high popularity class[8]. We repeat this process r times, thus building multiple (balanced) training sets. We experiment with various values of τ finding best results with τ=5. This was also the threshold used in [35] to predict the *popularity level* of a tip at a future target date. However, whereas in that work the classification task was the core of the prediction strategy, here it is employed simply for evaluation purposes (i.e., for balancing the training set). We also use r=5 replications, which allows us to assess the variability of our results. We note that this under-sampling approach (and threshold τ) is applied *only to the training set*. The test sets (described next) remains unchanged (imbalanced). Table 4 (5th column) presents the total number of tips in the training sets for each scenario.

We then use tips posted from December 31st until February 27th 2011 to build 30 different test sets, as follows. Since tips can be continually liked, the predicted ranking may become stale. Thus, we evaluate the effectiveness of the ranking methods by using them to build a new ranking by the end of each day (starting on January 29th), always considering the tips posted in the previous d = 30 days. Thus, 30 test sets are built by considering a window of 30 days and sliding it 1 day at a time, 30 times. Table 4 (6th column) shows the average number of tips in each test set[9]. For each test set, we report average results produced by all 5 training sets, and corresponding 95% confidence intervals.

For both training and test sets, the features of each tip are computed using all data collected up to the time when ranking is performed (t_r), including (for the regression model) information associated with tips posted before the beginning of each training set. Moreover, feature values are computed by first applying a logarithm transformation on the raw numbers to reduce their large variability, and then scaling these results between 0 and 1. We note that, in order to have enough historical data about users who posted tips, for both training and test sets, we consider only tips posted by users with at least five tips. We determine the best parameters of the regression models by minimizing the least squared errors of predictions for the candidate tips in the training set.

We evaluate each ranking method by computing the Kendall τ rank distance of the top-k tips in the rankings produced by it (i.e., Kτ@k). Since we are comparing two top-k lists (τ_1 and τ_2), we use a modified Kendall τ metric [18], that uses a penalty parameter p, with $0 \leq p \leq 1$, to account for the distances between non-overlapping tips in τ_1 and τ_2[10]. The modified Kendall τ is defined as follows:

$$K\tau(\tau_1,\tau_2)@k = (k - |\tau_1 \cap \tau_2|)((2+p)k - p|\tau_1 \cap \tau_2| + 1 - p) + \sum_{i \in \tau_i \cap \tau_2} \kappa_{i,j}(\tau_1, \tau_1) - \sum_{i \in \tau_1 - \tau_2} \tau_1(i) - \sum_{i \in \tau_2 - \tau_1} \tau_2(i) \quad (1)$$

where $\tau_1(i)$ or $\tau_2(i)$ is the position in the rank of the ith item and $\kappa_{i,j}(\tau_1,\tau_2) = 0$ if $\tau_1(i) < \tau_1(j)$ and $\tau_2(i) < \tau_2(j)$, or $\kappa_{i,j}(\tau_1,\tau_2) = 1$, otherwise. K$\tau$@k ranges from 0 to 1, with values close to 1 indicating greater disagreement between the predicted ranking and an ideal ranking defined by the actual number of likes accumulated by each tip until t_r+δ (i.e., the tip's label).

5.5 Experimental Results

We discuss our results by first assessing how the popularity ranking of tips varies over time (Section 5.5.1), and then comparing the prediction based only on the current ranking (baseline) and the regression-based prediction that uses a richer set of features (Section 5.5.2).

5.5.1 Ranking Stability

Using the experimental setup described in Section 5.4, we investigate the differences between the *true* popularity rankings of tips at times t_r and $t_r + \delta$, for various values of δ. To that end, we quantify the correlation between these two rankings using Kendall's τ coefficient. Recall that the closer to 1 the value of Kτ is, the larger the disagreements between both rankings.

Figure 8 shows the Kτ@k for each day in the test fold of both NY and NY Food scenarios, for values of δ varying from 1 to 5 months. We focus on the top-10 most popular tips (k=10). Focusing first on the NY scenario, Figure 8a shows that the disagreements between both rankings increase as we increase δ. Indeed, for a fixed test day (fixed set of tips), the Kτ@10 varies from 0.26 to 0.72 as we increase δ from 1 to 5 months. Moreover, we can still observe some discrepancies even if we predict for only one month ahead in the future (δ=1 month). Indeed, as discussed in Section 4, over 40% of the likes of most tips arrive after two months since posting time. Since the tips in each test fold are at most 1 month old, most of them are still at very early stages of their popularity curves, and the popularity ranking, even considering only the top-10 tips, will change. Very similar results were also observed for the NY Food scenario, as shown in Figure

[7]Great imbalance in the training set, as observed in our datasets, is known to have a detrimental impact on the effectiveness of classification and regression algorithms.

[8]For illustration purposes, we note that the original training set for the NY scenario had 5,225 tips in the low popularity class and only 258 tips in the other (smaller) class.

[9]The results are qualitatively similar when ranking is performed at lower frequencies, once each k days ($k > 1$).

[10]We use $p = 0.5$ which was recommended by [10].

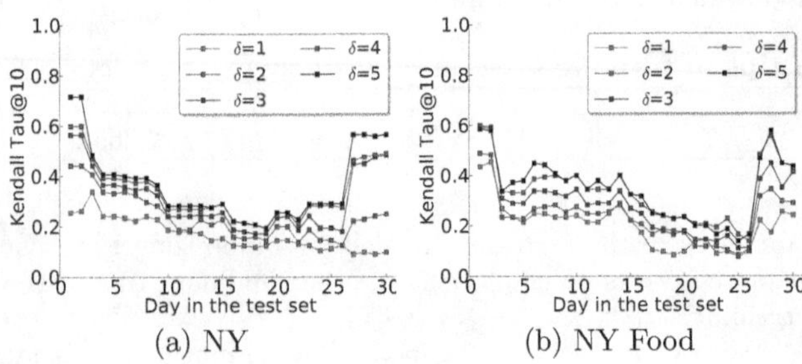

(a) NY (b) NY Food

Figure 8: Correlations between the top-10 most popular tips at time t_r and at time $t_r + \delta$ (δ in months).

8b, although the values of Kτ@10 (and thus the disagreements between current and future rankings) seem somewhat smaller on some days, particularly for larger values of δ.

Examining the top most popular tips in each test fold for the NY scenario, we found that some of them referred to special events occurring in the city. These tips exhibit a somewhat different pattern: all of their likes are received until the event occurs. Thus, once they reach the top of the ranking, they tend to remain there for a while, which contributes to lower the discrepancies between predicted and future rankings.

Overall, these results corroborate our discussion in Section 4, and suggest that there are some noticeable discrepancies between the current and the long-term popularity of tips (even within the top-10 most popular tips). Thus, models that use only early measurements may lead to inaccurate predictions not only of popularity measures (as discussed in Section 4.4) but also of popularity ranking. Next, we assess to which extent such ranking predictions can be improved by exploiting a multidimensional set of predictors.

5.5.2 Prediction Results

We now compare the prediction results using only the popularity ranking at t_r (baseline) against the prediction produced by using the OLS regression model jointly with the features defined in Section 5.3. Figure 9 shows the average daily Kτ@10 along with 95% confidence intervals for the two ranking methods and each value of δ, for the NY scenario. For δ equal to 1 month, both methods produce τ@k results below 0.4, showing a high correlation between the predicted ranking and the true popularity ranking at $t_r + \delta$. However, the OLS regression model produces results that are significantly better (lower Kτ@10) than those produced by the baseline in 67% of the days (reductions in up to 69%).

Moreover, as we predict further into the future, increasing δ to 2, 5 and 6 months, we observe increasing values of Kτ@10 for both methods. This implies that the discrepancies with the true ranking tend to increase as both methods start using outdated and possibly inaccurate data. Yet, the gap between the baseline and the OLS regression model tends to increase (reaching up to 65% for δ equal to 6 months). This result shows that taking factors other than simply the current popularity of the tips into account is important and can improve prediction accuracy of the long-term popularity ranking.

We note, however, that there are some cases where the baseline performs as good as the more sophisticated OLS model. These specific cases are explained by the following: some of the most popular tips (which referred to real events), acquired most of their likes very early on before time t_r (before the event). Thus, they quickly reached top positions of the ranking, remaining there until t_r+δ. For such cases, the use of other features produces only marginal improvements in prediction.

Figure 10 shows similar results for the NY Food scenario. In this case, we see smaller differences between both methods. In most cases, the baseline is just as good as the more sophisticated OLS method, although the use of the extra features does provide improvements (up to 30%) in some of the days for large values of δ. These results reflect the higher stability of the tip popularity ranking in the NY Food scenario (Section 5.5.1). Moreover, as shown in Table 4, the number of tips in the training set of this scenario is almost half of that used in the NY scenario, which also impacts the accuracy of the regression model. That is, the benefits from using more features are constrained by the limited amount of data to train an accurate model[11]

These results highlight that the accurate popularity prediction of tips is a challenging task. Although tip popularity ranking remains roughly stable over short periods of time (e.g., 1 month), there are still significant discrepancies that occur in the top of the ranking. Moreover, the use of other features related to the tip's author, venue and tip's content can improve prediction accuracy to some extent, provided that enough information about the features is available to train the model.

Finally, we sorted the features used by the OLS method using the Information Gain feature selection technique [37]. We found that the most important feature is, unsurprisingly, the current popularity of the tip. It is followed by features related to the user's popularity, such as the total number of likes in previous tips. Features related to the social network of the tip's author (number of followers and friends, and average number of tips posted by them) are also in the top-10 most important features, consistently with our results in Section 4.2.

The most important venue feature is the total number of check-ins, followed by the current position of the tip in the ranking of tips of the venue sorted by increasing number of likes. However, these features, like the other venue related features, are much less important than the user features, occupying only the 24th and 25th positions of the ranking. Similarly, the most important content feature is the number of characters in the tip, but it occupies only the 21st position of the ranking. Thus, like observed in [35] and unlike in other efforts to assess the helpfulness of online reviews [17, 38], textual features play a much less important role in the tip popularity ranking prediction task, possibly due to the inherent different nature of these pieces of content.

We did test whether multicollinearity exists among different predictors, which could affect robustness of the results of the OLS model. In our analysis, we use two methods: variance inflation factors (VIF) [30] and tolerance [25]. For each predictor variable j, $VIF_j = \frac{1}{1-R_j^2}$, where R_i^2 is the coefficient of determination from a regression using predictor j as response variable and all the other predictors as independent variables. A VIF value greater than 10 is a indication

[11]Recall that we did experiment with other prediction strategies based on SVR and Random Forests, but OLS provided the best results across all scenarios.

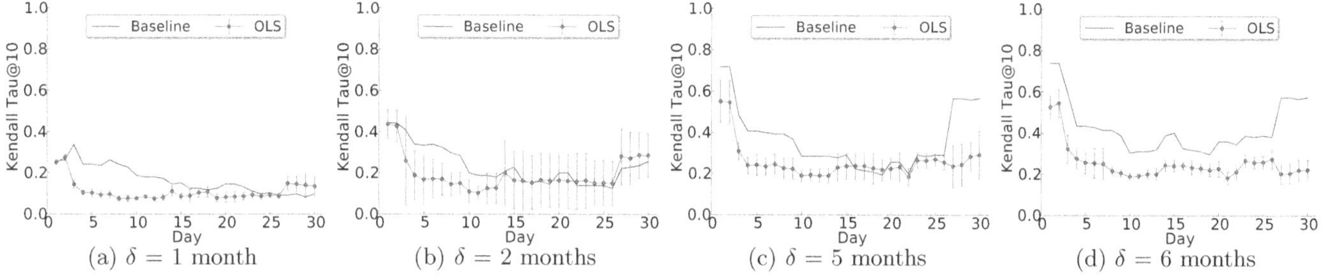

(a) $\delta = 1$ month (b) $\delta = 2$ months (c) $\delta = 5$ months (d) $\delta = 6$ months

Figure 9: Effectiveness of Ranking for Varying Target Time $t_r+\delta$: NY Scenario (average and 95% confidence intervals)

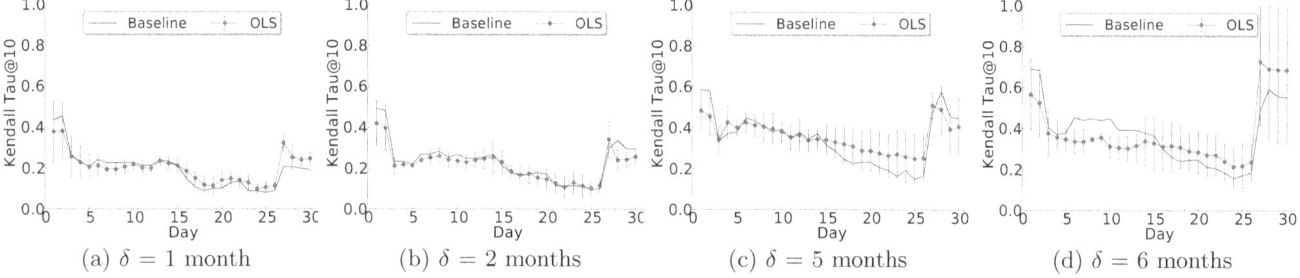

(a) $\delta = 1$ month (b) $\delta = 2$ months (c) $\delta = 5$ months (d) $\delta = 6$ months

Figure 10: Effectiveness of Ranking for Varying Target Time $t_r+\delta$: NY Food Scenario (average and 95% confidence intervals)

of potential multicollinearity problem [30]. The tolerance is the reciprocal of VIF, and is computed as $1 - VIF$. The smaller the tolerance value (< 0.10), the higher the degree of collinearity [25]. We compute the VIFs and tolerances for all features of our OLS model and we found that despite the strong correlations between some pairs of predictors, removing some of these variables from the model does not have impact on the accuracy (Kτ@10).

6. CONCLUSION AND FUTURE WORK

We presented an extensive study of tip popularity dynamics using a large dataset collected from Foursquare. Although prior work has tackled the popularity dynamics of various types of user generated content, we are not aware of prior temporal analysis of online reviews. We found that most tips have a slow popularity evolution, acquiring most of their likes after a few months, and that the social network of the tip's author plays an important role to draw attention to the tip, particularly soon after posting time. We also found that most tips reach their daily popularity peak within a month in the system, although most of their likes are received after the peak. Moreover, compared to other types of content, we observed a weaker presence of the rich-get-richer phenomenon, indicating a lower correlation between the early and long-term popularities of the tip. This suggests that the tip popularity prediction may require more sophisticated models, exploring other factors related to the tip, besides their current popularity.

We further analyzed this issue by looking into the stability of the popularity ranking over time, observing that there are some noticeable disagreements between the current and future popularity rankings, even when considering only the top-10 most popular tips and a time window of only 1 month. This suggests that predicting the future ranking based only on the current ranking may not be accurate. We thus investigated to which extent we can improve such predictions by using a regression model and exploiting a multidimensional set of features related to the tip's author, the venue where it was posted and its content. Our results show that the use of these features can improve the prediction accuracy, given that enough training data is available.

As future work, we intend to analyze the temporal dynamics of user tipping and "liking" activities, and their correlations with tip popularity, and investigate the benefits for prediction of adding new features, particularly geographic related features, such as the distance between different venues where a user posts tips.

7. ACKNOWLEDGEMENTS

This research is partially funded by the Brazilian National Institute of Science and Technology for Web Research (MCT/CNPq/ INCT grant number 573871/2008-6), CNPq, CAPES and Fapemig.

8. REFERENCES

[1] R. Bandari, S. Asur, and B. Huberman. The Pulse of News in Social Media: Forecasting Popularity. In *Proc. of ICWSM*, 2012.

[2] A.-L. Barabasi and R. Albert. Emergence of scaling in random networks. *Science*, 286(5439):509–512, 1999.

[3] A. Bermingham and A. Smeaton. Classifying Sentiment in Microblogs: is Brevity an Advantage? In *Proc. of CIKM*, 2010.

[4] Y. Borghol, S. Ardon, N. Carlsson, D. L. Eager, and A. Mahanti. The Untold Story of the Clones: Content-Agnostic Factors that Impact YouTube Video Popularity. In *Proc. of SIGKDD*, 2012.

[5] L. Breiman. Random Forests. *Machine Learning*, 45(1):5–32, Oct. 2001.

[6] M. Cha, A. Mislove, and K. P. Gummadi. A Measurement-driven Analysis of Information Propagation in the Flickr Social Network. In *Proc. of WWW*, 2009.

[7] R. Crane and D. Sornette. Robust Dynamic Classes Revealed by Measuring the Response Function of a Social System. In *Proc. of PNAS*, volume 105, pages 15649–15653, 2008.

[8] H. Drucker, C. Burges, L. Kaufman, A. Smola, and V. Vladimir. Support Vector Regression Machines. In *Proc. of NIPS*, 1997.

[9] A. Esuli and F. Sebastiani. SentiWordNet: A Publicly Available Lexical Resource for Opinion Mining. In *In Proc. of LREC*, 2006.

[10] R. Fagin, R. Kumar, and D. Sivakumar. Comparing Top K Lists. In *Proc. of SODA*, 2003.

[11] C. Fellbaum. *WordNet: An Electronical Lexical Database.* The MIT Press, Cambridge, MA, 1998.

[12] B. Fogg, J. Marshall, O. Laraki, A. Osipovich, et al. What Makes Web Sites Credible?: a Report on a Large Quantitative Study. In *Proc. of CHI*, 2001.

[13] A. Ghose and P. Ipeirotis. Estimating the helpfulness and economic impact of product reviews: Mining text and reviewer characteristics. *IEEE TKDE*, 23(10):1498–1512, 2011.

[14] L. Hong, O. Dan, and B. D. Davison. Predicting Popular Messages in Twitter. In *Proc. of WWW*, 2011.

[15] Y. Hong, J. Lu, J. Yao, Q. Zhu, and G. Zhou. What Reviews are Satisfactory: Novel Features for Automatic Helpfulness Voting. In *Proc. of SIGIR*, 2012.

[16] R. Jain. *The Art of Computer Systems Performance Analysis: Techniques for Experimental Design, Measurement, Simulation, and Modeling.* Wiley, 1991.

[17] S.-M. Kim, P. Pantel, T. Chklovski, and M. Pennacchiotti. Automatically Assessing Review Helpfulness. In *Proc. of EMNLP*, 2006.

[18] A. Konagurthu and J. Collier. An Information Measure for Comparing Top k Lists. *CoRR*, abs/1310.0110, 2013.

[19] P. L. Krapivsky, S. Redner, and F. Leyvraz. Connectivity of Growing Random Networks. *Physical Review Letters*, 85(21):4629–4632, Nov. 2000.

[20] K. Lerman and R. Ghosh. Information Contagion: An Empirical Study of the Spread of News on Digg and Twitter Social Networks. In *ICWSM*, 2010.

[21] Y. Liu, X. Huang, A. An, and X. Yu. Modeling and Predicting The Helpfulness of Online Reviews. In *Proc. of the ICDM*, 2008.

[22] Y. Lu, P. Tsaparas, A. Ntoulas, and L. Polanyi. Exploiting Social Context for Review Quality Prediction. In *Proc. of WWW*, 2010.

[23] Y. Matsubara, Y. Sakurai, A. Prakash, L. Li, and C. Faloutsos. Rise and Fall Patterns of Information Diffusion: Model and Implications. In *Proc. of the KDD*, 2012.

[24] E. Momeni, C. Cardie, and M. Ott. Properties, Prediction, and Prevalence of Useful User-Generated Comments for Descriptive Annotation of Social Media Objects. In *Proc. of ICWSM*, 2013.

[25] R. O'Brien. A Caution Regarding Rules of Thumb for Variance Inflation Factors. *Quality & Quantity: International Journal of Methodology*, 41(5):673–690, October 2007.

[26] M. O'Mahony and B. Smyth. Learning to Recommend Helpful Hotel Reviews. In *Proc. of RecSys*, 2009.

[27] B. Pang, L. Lee, and S. Vaithyanathan. Thumbs Up? Sentiment Classification Using Machine Learning Techniques. In *Proc. of EMNLP*, 2002.

[28] H. Pinto, J. Almeida, and M. Gonçalves. Using Early View Patterns to Predict the Popularity of YouTube Videos. In *Proc. of WSDM*, 2013.

[29] S. Siersdorfer, S. Chelaru, W. Nejdl, and J. San Pedro. How Useful are Your Comments?: Analyzing and Predicting YouTube Comments and Comment Ratings. In *Proc. of WWW*, 2010.

[30] J. Stevens. *Applied Multivariate Statistics for The Social Sciences.* L. Erlbaum Associates Inc., Hillsdale, NJ, USA, 2002.

[31] G. Szabo and B. A. Huberman. Predicting the Popularity of Online Content. *Communications of the ACM*, 53(8):80–88, Aug. 2010.

[32] A. Tatar, P. Antoniadis, M. Amorim, and S. Fdida. From Popularity Prediction to Ranking Online News. *Soc. Netw. Anal. and Min.*, page 4:174, Jan. 2014.

[33] T. Valente. *Network Models of the Diffusion of Inovations.* Hampton Press, Cresskill, NJ, 1995.

[34] R. van Zwol. Flickr: Who is Looking? In *Web Intelligence*, 2007.

[35] M. Vasconcelos, J. Almeida, and G. Marcos. What Makes your Opinion Popular? Predicting the Popularity of Micro-Reviews in Foursquare. In *Proc. of SAC*, 2014.

[36] J. Yang and J. Leskovec. Patterns of Temporal Variation in Online Media. In *Proc. of*, 2009.

[37] Y. Yang and J. Pedersen. A Comparative Study on Feature Selection in Text Categorization. In *Proc. of ICML*, 1997.

[38] Z. Zhang and B. Varadarajan. Utility Scoring of Product Reviews. In *Proc. of CIKM*, 2006.

Modeling Non-Progressive Phenomena for Influence Propagation

Vincent Yun Lou
Stanford University
yunlou@stanford.edu

Smriti Bhagat
Technicolor
smriti.bhagat@technicolor.com

Laks V.S. Lakshmanan Sharan Vaswani
University of British Columbia
{laks,sharanv}@cs.ubc.ca

ABSTRACT

Most previous work on modeling influence propagation has focused on progressive models, i.e., once a node is influenced (active) the node stays in that state and cannot become inactive. However, this assumption is unrealistic in many settings where nodes can transition between active and inactive states. For instance, a user of a social network may stop using an app and become inactive, but again activate when instigated by a friend, or when the app adds a new feature or releases a new version. In this work, we study such non-progressive phenomena and propose an efficient model of influence propagation. Specifically, we model influence propagation as a continuous-time Markov process with 2 states: active and inactive. Such a model is both highly scalable (we evaluated on graphs with over 2 million nodes), 17-20 times faster, and more accurate for estimating the spread of influence, as compared with state-of-the-art progressive models for several applications where nodes may switch states.

1. INTRODUCTION

Study of information and influence propagation over social networks has attracted significant research interest over the past decade, driven by applications such as viral marketing [?, ?], social feed ranking [?], contamination detection [?, ?, ?], and spread of innovation [?] to name a few. A prototypical problem that has received wide attention is *influence maximization*: given a social network along with pairwise influence probabilities between peers, and a number k, find k seed nodes such that activating them at start will eventually lead to the largest number of activated nodes in the network in the expected sense. Following the early work of Domingos and Richardson [?] and Kempe et al. [?], there has been a burst of activity in this area (e.g., see [?, ?, ?, ?, ?, ?, ?]). While the majority of previous studies employ propagation models with discrete time, in recent work, continuous time models have been shown to be more accurate at modeling influence propagation phenomena [?, ?, ?]. We refer the reader to the book [?] for a comprehensive survey and a detailed discussion of recent advances in influence maximization.

As discussed in [?], the propagation models can be classified into *progressive* and *non-progressive* (NP) models. In progressive models, an inactive node can become active, but once active, a node cannot become inactive. Non-progressive models relax this restriction and allow nodes to repeatedly transition between active and inactive states.

Indeed, an overwhelming majority of studies of information propagation have confined themselves to progressive models. For applications such as buying a product, the progressive assumption makes perfect sense: buying a product is not easily reversible in many cases. On the other hand, there are real applications which are not naturally captured by progressive models. For example, consider a user adopting a mobile app. Over time, its appeal may fade and her usage of the app may decline over time. Her interest in the app may be rejuvenated by a friend telling her about a new cool feature being added to the app at which point, she decides to try the app again and may continue using it once again. Alternatively, whenever a new version of the app is released, the user feels tempted to try it again and may, with some probability, decide to continue using it again. As a second example, it is well known that fashion follows cycles. Choices that are in fashion at the moment may fall out of fashion and may again become fashionable in the future, as it has been recognized that social choices follow cyclic trends [?]. As a third example, there are many applications where users may become active and stay in that state for a period of time before deactivating, such as, adopting a feature on a content sharing site where the feature may be the "like" or "favorite" button for a post, filters (sepia, sketch, outline) for photo editing, or "check-in" to a location or a show. Finally, in epidemiology, it is well known that an infected person may recover from a disease but not necessarily acquire lifelong immunity from the disease, thus being susceptible to the disease. In all the above examples, the phenomena in question are subject to spreading via influence. As we will show with experiments on real datasets in this paper, the use of progressive models for capturing such phenomena leads to considerable error. There is a clear need for a non-progressive model for studying these phenomena.

In their seminal paper, Kempe et al. [?] propose a non-progressive model and show that it can be reduced to a progressive model by replicating each node for every timestamp in the time horizon under consideration, and connecting each node to its neighbors in the previous timestamp. They show

COSN'14, October 1–2, 2014, Dublin, Ireland.

http://dx.doi.org/10.1145/2660460.2660483 .

that this reduction preserves equivalence, which implies all techniques developed for progressive models can in principle be applied to non-progressive models. However, replicating a large network for each timestamp over a large time horizon will clearly make this approach impractical for large social networks containing millions of nodes. Thus, this approach is largely of theoretical interest.

Another related area is *competitive* influence maximization, where competing parties choose seed nodes in order to maximize the adoption of their product or opinion [?]. Non-progressiveness arises naturally from the perspective of any one party involved in the competition. Our focus in this paper is not competition. As illustrated above, there are several example applications where propagation of information or influence happens in a non-progressive manner and it is our goal to model and study them in this paper.

Influence maximization is known to be a computationally hard problem, even over the relatively simpler progressive models. We don't expect influence maximization to be easier over non-progressive models. We face the challenge, *whether we can design approximation algorithms for influence maximization over non-progressive models that scale to large data sets.* To this end, we first propose a discrete time non-progressive model called DNP. It will turn out that DNP, while accurate at modeling non-progressive phenomena, does not lead to a scalable solution for estimating influence spread. To mitigate this, we propose a *continuous time non-progressive model* (CNP), which models the underlying influence propagation as a Markov process. This model can also capture progressive phenomena by appropriately setting the model parameters. We call this variant CNP-Progressive (CP for short). It is interesting to investigate how CP compares with the state-of-the-art progressive continuous time models such as [?, ?].

A second challenge centers on the question, what should the objective be when selecting seeds with respect to non-progressive models. As opposed to maximizing the *number* of active nodes at some time, as done in progressive models, we argue that it is more appropriate to maximize the *expected time during which nodes may have been active.*

Finally, while example applications demonstrating the value of and need for non-progressive models exist, to date, no empirical studies have compared non-progressive models with their progressive counterparts with an aim of calibrating their accuracy for explaining propagation phenomena over real data sets. This is partly exacerbated by the fact that real non-progressive data sets are relatively difficult to obtain. Can we establish the value of non-progressive models using any publicly available data sets?

In this paper, we address all the above challenges. Specifically, we make the following contributions.

- We propose a discrete time non-progressive model and implement it without graph replication (Section ??).
- We propose an efficient continuous time non-progressive model (Section ??).
- We define the objective of influence maximization as choosing seeds so as to maximize the total expected activation time of nodes. We show that the objective function of total expected activation time is both monotone and submodular. This implies the classic greedy seed selection algorithm, combined with our direct approach for computing expected total activation time, provides a $(1 - 1/e)$-approximation to the optimal solution (Section ??).
- Through experiments on synthetic and real datasets, we show that the accuracy of our non-progressive model for estimating expected total activation time is much higher than its progressive counterparts, including the recently proposed continuous time model [?]. Further, we show that our method is more than one order of magnitude faster than an efficient implementation of the DNP model, whose accuracy is comparable to that of CNP. We also show that on datasets that have no deactivations (i.e., progressive setting), our method using CP is 17-20 times faster than the continuous time progressive model of [?] (Section ??).

We start by presenting related work in Section ??, and conclude with a summary of the paper and a discussion on future work in Section ??. The major bottleneck in scaling influence maximization is in estimating the spread (in our case, expected active time). Our CNP model significantly outperforms the competition on this step and it's trivial to see this advantage will carry over to influence maximization.

2. RELATED WORK

Bharathi et al. [?] use exponential distribution to model the information propagation delay between nodes, and use this to avoid tie-breaking for simultaneous activation attempts by multiple neighbors. We share with them the use of exponential distribution to model activation delays in our CNP model. However, their main goal is designing response strategies to competing cascades rather than maximizing the spread. Considerable work on non-progressive models has been done by the economics community [?]. But they do not focus on computational issues, especially in relation to influence spread computation and maximization.

Kempe et al. [?] proposed several propagation models, including non-progressive ones, but all based on discrete time. Indeed, the DNP model we describe is fashioned after the non-progressive LT model they describe. As we show, our continuous time model CNP significantly outperforms DNP in terms of scalability. Our model and contributions are orthogonal to theirs. In particular, our efficient sampling strategy enables a scalable implementation of influence maximization. Recently, non-progressive models have received attention from the research community [?, ?, ?, ?]. As observed in [?], progressive models are not accurate and there is scalability issue with non-progressive models. Their model is a simplistic model based on strict majority. While theoretically appealing, it's easy to show it's not submodular and no scalable influence maximization algorithm is provided. Furthermore, they focus on finding a perfect target set, one that ends up activating every node, not a realistic goal. Maximizing the overall activation times of nodes is more realistic goal for a business, which is what we study. Other works such as [?, ?, ?, ?] study related problems where nodes have active and inactive states. However, these are significantly different from influence maximization. See [?] for a detailed survey.

Finally, a continuous-time Markov chain based progressive model was proposed by Rodriguez et al. [?], and more recently improved upon by Du et al. [?]. The model in [?], assumes exponential activation time delays on edges and thus the action time of a node is the shortest path distance from any seed node to that node. [?] avoids calculating the shortest paths and instead uses a randomized algorithm for estimating the neighborhood size of a single source node for estimating the influence spread within a given time horizon.In our experiments, we compare our CNP and its progressive variant CP with the method in [?]. On data sets corresponding to progressive phenomena, both [?] and CP have a comparable accuracy (which is very high). On data sets corresponding to non-progressive phenomena, both CP and [?] suffer from high error rates while CNP enjoys a very high level of accuracy. In all experiments, both CP and CNP run 17-20 times faster than [?].

3. DISCRETE TIME NP MODEL

There are two popular influence propagation models [?]: independent cascade (IC) and linear threshold (LT). In [?], Kempe et al. also described an intuitive non-progressive extension of the discrete time LT model. Fundamentally, the models we propose in the next sections are close to the IC model. To set the proper context, in this section, we describe a discrete time non-progressive model that is inspired by the framework given in [?], but closer to the framework we will follow for our CNP model.

Let $G = (V, E, P)$ be a weighted, directed graph representing a social network, with nodes (users) V and edges (social ties) E, with the function $P : E \to [0, 1]$ representing the probability of influence along edges: $P(u, v) := P_{u,v}$ on edge $(u, v) \in E$ is the probability that node v will be activated at time $t + 1$ given that u is active at time t. Additionally, the function $q : V \to [0, 1]$ associates each node $u \in V$ with a deactivation probability: $q(u) := q_u$ represents the probability that u will deactivate at time $t+1$ given that it's active at t. These are the key ingredients of our discrete time non-progressive model. Given the social network graph and a seed set of nodes S that are active at the start of the propagation process, time unfolds in discrete steps. At time $t = 0$, nodes in S are active. At any time $t > 0$, each of the currently active nodes u makes one attempt at activating each of its neighbors v and succeeds with probability $P_{u,v}$. At any time, an active node u can deactivate with probability q_u. We refer to this model as the *discrete-time non-progressive* (DNP) model.

In non-progressive models, nodes can get activated and deactivated infinitely often, so the influence propagation process can continue indefinitely. Thus, we need to consider a fixed *time horizon* as the time period within which we would like to study the propagation process. Kempe et al. [?] showed that their non-progressive (LT) model's behavior over a given time horizon T can be simulated using a progressive model. The key is to replicate the social network graph for each timestamp. However, a naïve implementation with replicated graphs is not practical. We describe a space efficient implementation that avoids graph replication in our tech report [?]. We show that the DNP model still suffers from a serious inefficiency that at each time step, each node needs to make the decision of whether or not it changes its state. Thus, at each time step, n nodes need to sample a Bernoulli distribution to determine their state at the next time step. Several nodes may stay in their current state for long periods of time. Hence, sampling at each time step at each node is extremely inefficient. We therefore move to the continuous-time regime for efficiently modeling the non-progressive phenomena.

4. CONTINUOUS-TIME NP MODEL

4.1 Model description

We model influence propagation as a continuous-time Markov process with nodes being in one of two states: *active* and *inactive*. As in classical propagation models, in our model, events trigger state changes and happen probabilistically. We start with a seed set of active nodes. At any time, there are two events that may happen at an active node: the node may activate its neighbor, or may deactivate itself. Similarly, for any inactive node, the node may get activated by one of its active neighbors, or stay inactive. We refer to an event that activates an inactive node as an *activation event* and one that deactivates an already active node as a *deactivation event*. It is these deactivation events that allow the model to be non-progressive.

More specifically, there are two parameters, one for activation and the other for deactivation, both being exponentially distributed random variables. Each edge $(u, v) \in E$ has an associated activation rate parameter $\gamma_{+,u,v}$, and each node u has a deactivation rate parameter $\gamma_{-,u}$. We start with a seed set of nodes that are, by definition, active at time 0. For each node u that is activated at time t, (a) a time τ sampled according to rate parameter $\gamma_{+,u,v}$ has the semantic that v will be activated no later than $t + \tau$, and (b) a time τ' sampled according to rate parameter $\gamma_{-,u}$, has the semantic that node u will deactivate at time $t + \tau'$. Notice that another neighbor of v may activate it sooner. In particular, an inactive node v that is reachable from one or more active nodes activates at a time equal to the shortest path from those active nodes, that is shortest in terms of the sum of sampled propagation times of the edges forming the path. However, each activation or deactivation with its associated rate parameter is one *local* event. That is, only the ego-centric network of a node is involved in any event. This observation is key to the scalability of our proposed method. In particular, unlike the recently proposed continuous time (but progressive) models [?, ?], we don't need to compute or even estimate the shortest path length directly.

4.2 Semantics of the propagation

During an influence propagation cascade, there are multiple activation and deactivation events that may happen. In order to model the cascade, we need to find the one that happens first and update the activation status of the corresponding node. For instance, if u is active, it deactivates with some rate parameter, however, it is also trying to activate its inactive neighbor v with some rate parameter. If u deactivates before activating v, then v may not have a chance to activate (assuming it has only one neighbor) unless u activates again. Further, if there are multiple neighbors trying to activate a node v, it will get activated by the local event that happens first, i.e., by the neighbor that first activates it. Therefore, it is important to understand and model the order of events. We crucially make use of two key properties of exponential distributions for modeling the time and order of events.

PROPERTY 1. *For n different events with rate parameters $\gamma_1, \gamma_2 \dots \gamma_n$, the probability that the ith event will happen first is $\frac{\gamma_i}{\sum_{i=1}^{n} \gamma_i}$.*

PROPERTY 2. *For different events with rate parameters $\gamma_1, \gamma_2 \ldots \gamma_n$, the time of the first event is exponentially distributed with rate parameter: $\sum_{i=1}^{n} \gamma_i$.*

We keep track of the current time t_{cur} during a propagation process. At each iteration, the categorical distribution in Property ?? is sampled to determine the event that happens first (or next). Then, the exponential distribution with rate parameter $\sum_{i=1}^{n} \gamma_i$ is sampled (Property ??) to obtain the time elapsed τ between last event and this event. The current time is then updated as $t_{cur} = t_{cur} + \tau$, and we proceed to the next iteration if $t_{cur} < T$, where T is the time horizon, and stop otherwise. In other words, even though the model is continuous time, it has a clear interpretation in terms of discrete steps, namely the occurrence of events.

Another way to understand the model semantics is in terms of possible worlds. A deterministic possible world for our model can be constructed as follows: For each edge $(u, v) \in E$ we sample an array of timestamps and sort it. A timestamp in the array indicates that if u is active at that time, it will activate node v. We call this array the *schedule of activations*. Similarly, for each node $u \in V$, we sample an array of deactivation times. If u is active at those timestamps, it will get deactivated. We refer to this array as the *schedule of deactivations*. The set of possible worlds for a given instance of our CNP model is the set of all such edge activation schedules and node deactivation schedules, for every edge and node in the given social graph. Such a construction of possible world aptly covers all possibilities in our random process. We will use these semantics to prove monotonicity and submodularity of the spread under the CNP model in Section ??.

4.3 Advantages of CNP over DNP

If we correctly map the rate parameters in CNP model to the probabilities in DNP model, the simulation results of two models will be similar. We note that the models are not equivalent, but have similar accuracy in terms of the expected spread, when the following mapping holds. In CNP, for any edge (u, v) where u is active but v is not, the probability that u activates v within the next time unit is equal to the CDF$(1, \gamma)$, where CDF is the cumulative distribution function of the exponential distribution, γ is the rate parameter associated with (u, v), and 1 is the time unit. The corresponding edge probabilities in the DNP model would be CDF$(1, \gamma)$. Similarly, we map the deactivation rates in CNP to deactivation probabilities in DNP. Then, the resulting DNP model will be a discrete-time approximation of the CNP model. Therefore, we expect the accuracy of CNP and DNP to be similar. We now compare the two models in terms of the computational cost incurred at each activation and deactivation. In the discrete time case, for each active node, we need to sample from a uniform distribution once at each timestamp to determine whether or not the node deactivates. In the continuous-time setting, however, we first need to randomly choose the event that occurs with probability governed by Property 1, then we need to sample the exponential distribution to get the time at which it occurs, using Property 2. Therefore, for nodes that do not deactivate in the time window, their cost of (attempted) deactivation is zero in the continuous-time setting, again, a significant saving from the discrete-time regime.

5. INFLUENCE MAXIMIZATION

Next, we discuss influence maximization, i.e., the process of seed selection to maximize the spread of influence under the CNP model. The influence maximization problem for non-progressive models is similar to that described in [?]. However, since nodes can deactivate, the *spread*, traditionally defined as the expected number of active nodes, changes with time. Thus, maximizing the expected number of active nodes at a given timestamp, or at the time horizon may not be ideal from the point of view of a company initiating a viral marketing campaign. We start by proposing an intuitive objective function for spread under a non-progressive model. Importantly, we show that our proposed spread function is monotone and submodular, hence the greedy approach yields a $(1 - 1/e)$-approximation to the optimal solution.

Objective Function. In a non-progressive world, an intuitive objective from the point of view of a marketer is to maximize the "active time" of its customers in a given social network. That is, maximize the total amount of time that nodes in the network are active, in expectation. Given a seed set A,

$$spread_A = \sum_{v \in V} \tau_v$$

where τ_v is the sum of time intervals within T for which node v is active. Then, the influence maximization problem [?] is defined as: select a seed set of nodes $A \subseteq V$ to be activated such that the expected $spread_A$ is maximized over a chosen time horizon T, given the non-progressive influence propagation model.

Monotonicity and Submodularity. As an important step towards solving the influence maximization problem, we show that the expected *spread* is monotone and submodular. Then, we can use the state-of-the-art greedy algorithm, such as CELF [?] and CELF++ [?], to guarantee a $(1 - 1/e)$-approximation. It is easy to see that,

$$\mathrm{E}[spread_A] = \sum_{v \in V} \mathrm{E}[\tau_v] = \int_{t=0}^{T} \mathrm{E}[\sigma(A, t)]dt$$

where $\sigma(A, t) = |S|$, S is the set of nodes activated from the seed set A at timestamp t, and $\sigma(A, t)$ is the number such nodes or the cardinality of set S. Therefore, we can prove monotonicity and submodularity of the expected spread, by showing that these properties hold for $\mathrm{E}[\sigma(A, t)]$. For this, we follow the proof guidelines in [?] to construct a deterministic possible world from the random process that we are modeling. Let X be the set of all possible worlds, and given $x \in X$, let $pdf(x)$ denote the probability density function of x. Then,

$$\mathrm{E}[\sigma(A, t)] = \int_{x \in X} pdf(x) \times \sigma_x(A, t)dx$$

Thus, we only need to prove that $\sigma_x(A, t)$ is monotone and submodular. Note, that we need to integrate over the possible worlds, as opposed to a summation performed in [?], because the number of deterministic possible worlds is uncountable in our setting.

LEMMA 1. *Additivity of spreads: Given two sets of seed nodes A, B, timestamp t, and a possible world x,*

$$S_x(A \cup B, t) = S_x(A, t) \cup S_x(B, t)$$

where $S_x(A,t)$ denotes the set of nodes activated by seed set A in possible world x at timestamp t.

THEOREM 1. *Given lemma ??, $\sigma_x(A,t) = |S_x(A,t)|$ is monotone and submodular.*

The proofs are presented in our tech report [?].

6. EXPERIMENTAL EVALUATION

In this section we compare the accuracy and running time of: traditional IC model, state-of-the-art continuous time progressive model ConTinEst[?], DNP and CNP, for estimating the spread as defined in Section ??. We evaluate our model on synthetically generated data and two real datasets: Flixster and Flickr, for which we have a social network, and an action log which contains the timestamps of users' actions. The synthetically generated dataset consists of a 500 node graph, and randomly generated cascades and deactivation events. The Flixster dataset [?] has 1 million nodes (users) and 26.7 million edges (social connections). An activation event is the act of *rating a movie from a specific genre.* We divide the action log into one year training and one year test set. Finally, the Flickr dataset [?] has 2.3 million nodes and 33.1 million edges. An action corresponds to using the "favorite photo" feature. The associated action log is over 138 days, of which we use the first 70 days as our training set for learning parameters, and the next 68 days as our test set. Given a training set in the form of an action log with <user,action,timestamp> tuples, we define the activation and deactivation events as: 1) when a user performs an action we call it an activation event and mark the user active 2) at each activation we start a timer, the event of the timer running out before another activation occurs, is called a deactivation, and the user is said to be deactivated. The timer is set for a length equal to the *deactivation time window.* We provide a detailed description of how our model parameters can be learned from data, and our experimental setup in our tech report [?]. For implementing the sampling without replacement procedure for a categorical distribution, see methods described in [?, ?].

6.1 Comparison Across Models

We start with presenting an overview of our results comparing different models: progressive vs. non-progressive models, and discrete vs. continuous time models, across two axes: accuracy of spread estimation and running time. Figure ?? illustrates this comparison for Flixster dataset. See detailed numbers for both datasets in Table ??. We make the following key observations, and substantiate these with details through the remainder of this section.

- Progressive models, here IC model and state-of-the-art ConTinEst, overestimate the spread and result in an error of 80-194% compared with the ground truth.
- Non-progressive models, DNP and CNP, are highly accurate in estimating the spread with very small errors of 0.1-3%. Notice that DNP is the non-progressive counterpart of the progressive IC model model and improves the accuracy of estimating spread by a 100%.
- Continuous models ConTinEst and CNP are slightly better at estimating accuracy than the discrete models IC and DNP.

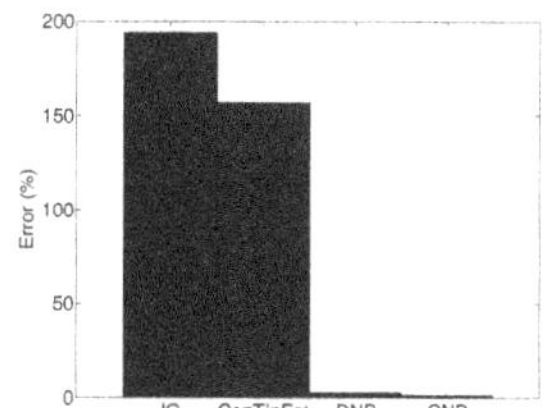

(a) Error in Spread estimation

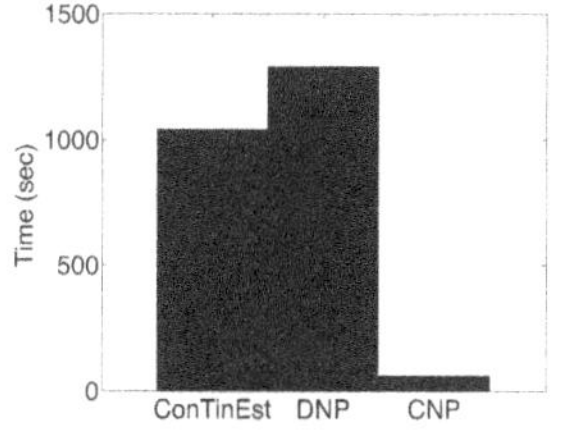

(b) Running time

Figure 1: Spread estimation error and time comparison for progressive (IC, ConTinEst) and non-progressive models (DNP, CNP) for Flixster dataset

Dataset	Ground Truth	CNP	DNP	ConTinEst [?]	IC
Flixster	964013	949750 (1.5%)	991141 (2.8%)	2477678 (157%)	2833860 (194%)
Flickr	2435663	2432053 (0.148%)	2409695 (1.07%)	4423372 (81%)	4922860 (102%)

Table 1: Spread estimated by progressive (IC, ConTinEst) and non-progressive models (DNP, CNP) and error percentage w.r.t. ground truth

- Our model CNP is not just more accurate but also an order of magnitude faster than the state-of-the-art continuous time model ConTinEst (Figure ??). These results are for running 100 Monte-Carlo simulations.

Evaluating Accuracy. We evaluate the accuracy of the estimation of spread of our model by simulating the propagation, starting at the state of the network at the last timestamp in our training set, and evaluating against the ground truth of spread achieved in the test set. In other words, the nodes active at the end of the training set are treated as the seed set, and the propagation is run for the time horizon equal to the length of the test set. The *ground truth* of spread is computed as the total active time of all nodes for the test set. Table ?? shows the spread as estimated by our model compared with the ground truth. For our model, error in spread estimation is just 1.5% and 0.1% over the Flixster and Flickr datasets resp. The difference between IC model and non-progressive models is two orders of magnitude. This validates that deactivation occurs in real datasets, and that modeling deactivation properly is critical for a reasonable estimation of influence spread in non-progressive settings.

Next, we perform an experiment on synthetic data to show the impact of number of deactivations on the spread estimates by a progressive model (ConTinEst [?]) and our CNP model. Figure ?? shows this the error (%) in estimating the spread. As the deactivations increase, the gap in the accuracy of the two methods increase, with CNP performing over 83% better than the competitor, establishing that in the presence of deactivations, non-progressive phenomena are modeled accurately by CNP.

Evaluating Computational Cost. We compare the running time of ConTinEst with CNP for our two real datasets Flickr and Flixster for running 100 Monte-Carlo simulations. As seen in Figure ??, our model is an order of magnitude faster than its progressive competitor.

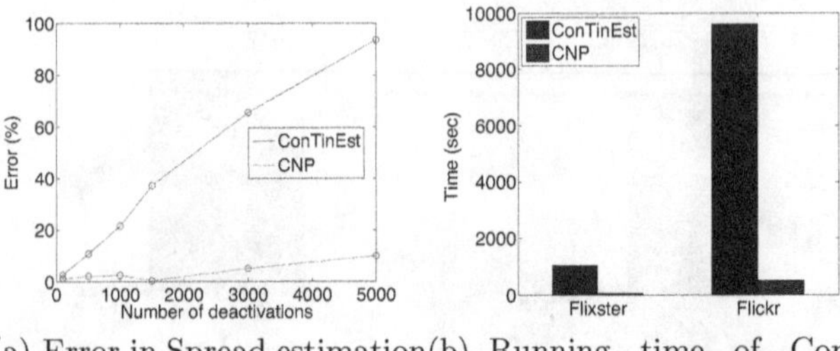

(a) Error in Spread estimation for synthetic data (b) Running time of ConTinEst vs. CNP on real data

Figure 2: Accuracy comparison for progressive (IC, ConTinEst) and non-progressive models (DNP, CNP)

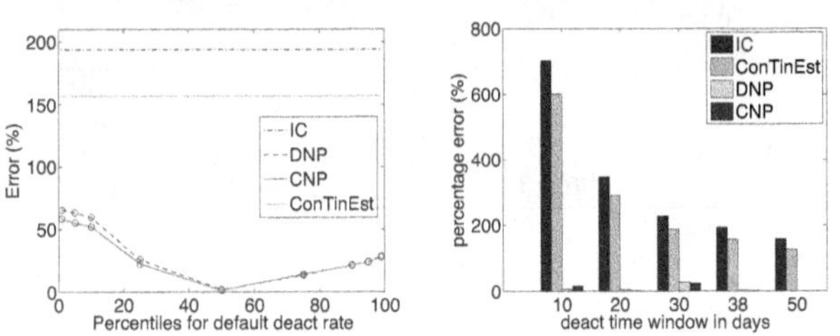

(a) Varying deactivation rate (b) Varying deactivation time window

Figure 3: Accuracy comparison for progressive (IC, ConTinEst) and non-progressive models (DNP, CNP) with varying deactivation parameters for Flixster dataset

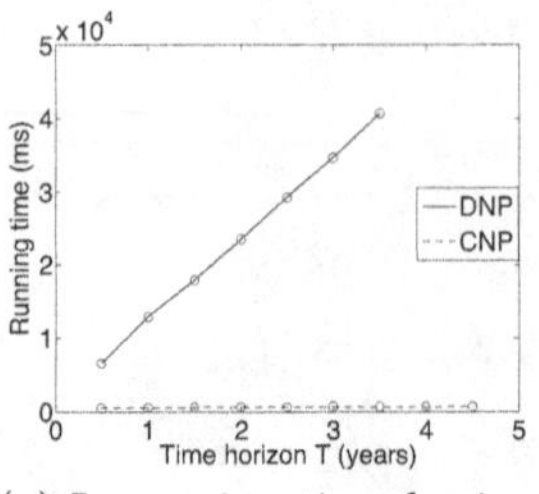

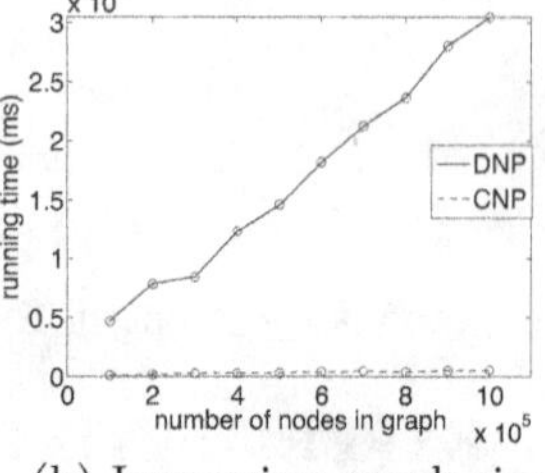

(a) Increasing time horizon (b) Increasing graph size

Figure 4: Running time comparisons on Flixster dataset for non-progressive models: DNP and CNP

6.2 Varying Parameter Values

Effect of deactivation parameters on accuracy. For Flickr, we observe that 98% of the nodes perform no action in our training set, and hence get a zero deactivation rate. This is an artifact of the short timespan of the training data. Filtering those nodes would result in a disconnected graph. To overcome this shortcoming of the data sample and to avoid overfitting, we assign a *default deactivation rate* to all such nodes. We use the set of non-zero deactivation rates (as learned from the data) as a guideline, and test different percentiles of this set as the default deactivation rate. Instead of fixing the value, we evaluate its impact on the accuracy by varying it. As seen in Figure ??, the default deactivation rate does impact the accuracy slightly, still the estimates by CNP are orders of magnitude more accurate than IC model and ConTinEst. Also notice that the estimated spread for DNP and CNP is very similar validating our argument in Section ?? that DNP is an approximation of CNP. The plots for Flickr are skipped for brevity, but the methodology adopted and results were similar. For the remainder of the experiments we set the default deactivation rate for Flixster and Flickr to the best obtained, i.e., 50th and 1 percentile resp. of the unique non-zero deactivation rates learned.

Next, we show using Figure ?? that changing the deactivation time window does not significantly impact the accuracy of CNP model. Although the progressive models are unaffected by the deactivation window, the ground truth computed is different across windows, and this change is reflected in the error percentage.

Effect of varying parameters on running time. The two factors that affect the computational cost of simulating the non-progressive models are: time horizon and graph size. We compare the computational cost for CNP and DNP for increasing time horizon on the full graphs of the two datasets. As seen in Figure ??, the running time for DNP increases linearly over increasing time horizon, while that for CNP changes only slightly. For instance, for Flickr, the running time for CNP is 73% less than DNP at 27 month time horizon. Finally, we set time horizon as 2 years for Flixster and show the running time with increasing graph size in Figure ??. Again, CNP scales up very well. The results for Flickr were similar and skipped for brevity.

Progressive Setting. We ask the question, "What if the world is progressive, i.e., there are no deactivations, how well would CNP perform?" To this end we perform an experiment of setting the deactivation time window to the end of the time horizon, essentially saying no nodes deactivate. We then compare this model we call CP for the continuous progressive version of our proposed model against ConTinEst and CNP. We observe that the running time on Flixster for CP, CNP and ConTinEst are 60, 64 and 1041s resp. The running time results for Flickr for the CP, CNP and ConTinEst were 498, 606 and 9605s resp. This illustrates that despite the data being progressive in nature, our model is 17-20 times faster than the state-of-the-art progressive continuous model.

7. CONCLUSIONS

There are applications where the propagation phenomena are more accurately captured using non-progressive models. We proposed a non-progressive model and showed that its behavior over a time horizon can be simulated without any need for graph replication [?]. The resulting discrete time non-progressive model is still not scalable owing to the prohibitive number of samplings necessary in order to monitor the state of nodes at every time. We proposed an alternative continuous time non-progressive model and showed that it permits a highly efficient implementation. In addition, we motivated the expected total amount of time the nodes in the network are active, as the right notion of spread, which a seed selection algorithm should optimize. We showed that this objective function is monotone and submodular in the set of seed nodes. By extensive experiments on two data sets, we show that our model significantly outperforms the state of the art progressive model ConTinEst [?] both on accuracy of spread estimating and on running time. It would be interesting to study non-progressive continuous time models in the competitive setting, where competitors may be adversarial.

8. REFERENCES

[1] J. G. U. A. Ostfeld and E. Salomons. Battle of water sensor networks: A design challenge for engineers and algorithms. In *WSDA*, 2006.

[2] S. Bharathi, D. Kempe, and M. Salek. Competitive influence maximization in social networks. In *WINE*, 2007.

[3] G.-I. Bischi and U. Merlone. Global dynamics in adaptive models of collective choice with social influence. In *Mathematical modeling of collective behavior in socio-economic and life sciences*, pages 223–244. Springer, 2010.

[4] L. Blume. The statistical mechanics of strategic interaction. *Games and Economic behavior*, 1993.

[5] C. Budak, D. Agrawal, and A. E. Abbadi. Limiting the spread of misinformation in social networks. In *WWW'11*.

[6] M. Cha, A. Mislove, and P. K. Gummadi. A measurement-driven analysis of information propagation in the flickr social network. In *WWW*, 2009.

[7] W. Chen, L. V. S. Lakshmanan, and C. Castillo. *Information and Influence Propagation in Social Networks*. Synthesis Lectures on Data Management. Morgan & Claypool Publishers, 2013.

[8] W. Chen, Y. Wang, and S. Yang. Effcient influence maximization in social networks. In *KDD*, 2009.

[9] W. Chen, Y. Wang, and L. Zhang. Scalable influence maximization in social networks under linear threshold model. In *ICDM*, 2010.

[10] P. Domingos and M. Richardson. Mining the network value of customers. In *KDD*, 2001.

[11] Nan Du, Yingyu Liang, M. F. Balcan and L. Song. Continuous-time influence maximization for multiple items. *CoRR*, abs/1312.2164, 2013.

[12] N. Du, L. Song, M. Gomez-Rodriguez, and H. Zha. Scalable influence estimation in continuous-time diffusion networks. In *NIPS*. 2013.

[13] E. Even-Dar and A. Shapira. A note on maximizing the spread of influence in social networks. In *Internet and Network Economics*, volume 4858. Springer Berlin Heidelberg, 2007.

[14] M. Fazli, M. Godsi, J. Habibi, P. J. Khalilabadi, V. Mirrokni, and S. S. Sadeghabad. On the non-progressive spread of influence through social networks. In *LATIN'12*.

[15] A. Ganesh, L. Massoulié, and D. Towsley. The effect of network topology on the spread of epidemics. In *INFOCOM 2005. 24th Annual Joint Conference of the IEEE Computer and Communications Societies. Proceedings IEEE*, volume 2, pages 1455–1466. IEEE, 2005.

[16] M. Gomez-Rodriguez and B. Scholkopf. Influence maximization in continuous time diffusion networks. In *ICML*, 2012.

[17] A. Goyal, F. Bonchi, and L. V. Lakshmanan. Learning influence probabilities in social networks. In *WSDM*, 2010.

[18] A. Goyal, F. Bonchi, and L. V. S. Lakshmanan. A data-based approach to social influence maximization. *Proc. VLDB Endow.*, 2011.

[19] A. Goyal, W. Lu, and L. V. Lakshmanan. Celf++:optimizing the greedy algorithm for influence maximization in social networks. In *WWW*, 2011.

[20] M. Jamali and M. Ester. A matrix factorization technique with trust propagation for recommendation in social networks. In *RecSys*, 2010.

[21] D. Kempe, J. Kleinbery, and E. Tardos. Maximizing the spread of influence through a social network. In *KDD*, 2003.

[22] C. Kuhlman, V. Kumar, M. Marathe, S. Swarup, G. Tuli, S. Ravi, and D. Rosenkrantz. Inhibiting the diffusion of contagions in bi-threshold systems: Analytical and experimental results. In *Proceedings of the AAAI Fall 2011 Symposium on Complex Adaptive Systems (CAS-AAAI 2011)*, pages 91–100, 2011.

[23] J. Leskovec, A. Kraus, C. Guestrin, C. Faloutsos, J. M. VanBriesen, and N. S. Glance. Cost-efficiective outbreak detection in networks. In *KDD*, 2007.

[24] Y. Li, W. Chen, Y. Wang, and Z.-L. Zhang. Influence diffusion dynamics and influence maximization in social networks with friend and foe relationships. In *WSDM*, 2013.

[25] V. Lou, S. Bhagat, L. V. S. Lakshmanan, and S. Vaswani. Modeling non-progressive phenomena for influence propagation. ArXiv, 2014. `http://arxiv.org/abs/1408.6466`.

[26] Y. Matias, J. S. Vitter, and W.-C. Ni. Dynamic generation of discrete random variates. In *SODA*, pages 361–370, 1993.

[27] A. Ostfeld and E. Salomons. Optimal layout of early warning detection stations for water distribution systems security. In *J. Water Resources Planning and Management*, 2004.

[28] N. Pathak, A. Banerjee, and J. Srivastava. A generalized linear threshold model for multiple cascades. In *ICDM*, 2010.

[29] B. A. Prakash, D. Chakrabarti, N. C. Valler, M. Faloutsos, and C. Faloutsos. Threshold conditions for arbitrary cascade models on arbitrary networks. *Knowledge and information systems*, 2012.

[30] A. D. Sarma, S. Gollapudi, R. Panigrahy, and L. Zhang. Understanding cyclic trends in social choices. In *WSDM*, pages 593–602, 2012.

[31] R. Schenkel, T. Crecelius, M. Kacimi, S. Michel, T. Neumann, J. X. Parreira, and G. Weikum. Efficient top-k querying over social-tagging networks. In *SIGIR'08*.

[32] T. Valente. Network models and methods for studying the diffusion of innovations. In *Models and methods in social network analysis*. Cambridge Univ. Press, 2005.

Measurement and Analysis of OSN Ad Auctions

Yabing Liu
Northeastern University
Boston, MA
ybliu@ccs.neu.edu

Chloe Kliman-Silver
Brown University
Providence, RI
chloe.klimansilver@gmail.com

Robert Bell
AT&T Labs–Research
Florham Park, NJ
rbell@research.att.com

Balachander Krishnamurthy
AT&T Labs–Research
Florham Park, NJ
bala@research.att.com

Alan Mislove
Northeastern University
Boston, MA
amislove@ccs.neu.edu

ABSTRACT

Advertising is ubiquitous on the Web; numerous ad networks serve billions of ads daily via keyword or search term auctions. Recently, online social networks (OSNs) such as Facebook have created site-specific ad services that differ from traditional ad networks by letting advertisers bid on *users* rather than *keywords*. With Facebook's annual ad revenue exceeding $4 billion, OSN-based ad services are emerging to be a significant fraction of the online ad market. In contrast to other online ad markets (e.g., Google's ad market), there has been little academic study of OSN ad services, and OSNs have released very little data about their advertising markets; as a result, researchers currently lack the tools to measure and understand these markets.

In this paper, our goal is to bring visibility to OSN ad markets, focusing on Facebook. We demonstrate that the (undocumented) feature that suggests bids to advertisers is most likely calculated via sampling recent winning bids. We then show how this feature can be used to explore the relative value of different user demographics and the overall stability of the advertising market. Through the exploration of suggested bid data for different demographics, we find dramatic differences in prices paid across different user interests and locations. Finally, we show that the ad market shows long-term variability, suggesting that OSN ad services have yet to mature.

Categories and Subject Descriptors

J.4 [**Social and Behavioral Sciences**]: Economics; H.3.5 [**Information Storage and Retrieval**]: Online Information Services—*Web-based services*; J.4 [**Social and Behavioral Sciences**]: Sociology

General Terms

Measurement, Experimentation, Economics

COSN'14, October 1–2, 2014, Dublin, Ireland.
Copyright 2014 ACM 978-1-4503-3198-2/14/10 ...$15.00.
http://dx.doi.org/10.1145/2660460.2660475.

Keywords

Online advertising; Online social networks; User demographics; Suggested bid

1. INTRODUCTION

Advertising is now the economic underpinning of much of the Web; large advertising networks (e.g., Google's Ad Network [22]) serve advertisements for millions of Web sites. Many of these advertising services are implemented as auctions, with individual advertisers bidding on specific keywords, pages, or search terms. These auctions are extremely popular with advertisers (Google alone earned over $50 billion in advertising revenue in 2013 [21]) and are well-studied in the research literature [15,33,37,39].

Recently, a new type of advertising network has emerged [24]: closed-site advertising services run by online social networks (OSNs) such as Facebook. Unlike prior systems, where the advertising network was forced to infer user information from cookies, browsing history, and search terms, OSN-based advertising services are provided demographic information directly by the users themselves. As a result, advertisers are able to target *users* directly (via profile attributes), rather than targeting keywords or search terms. Although OSN-based advertising services are nascent, they already carry a significant number of ads: Facebook alone had over $7.8 billion in advertising revenue in 2013 [10].

Unfortunately, there has been little academic study of these ad networks, and OSNs have released very little data about their advertising markets; the most in-depth numbers are from U.S. Securities and Exchange Commission (SEC) filings by the OSNs, which are typically at per-continent-per-fiscal-quarter granularity. Thus, researchers have little visibility into the dynamics of these markets, and it remains unclear which user demographics are the most valuable to advertisers (and therefore to the OSNs) and how stable these values are over time.

In this paper, our goal is to develop techniques that will allow researchers to measure and understand OSN ad markets. We focus on Facebook (currently the largest OSN ad market) and make three contributions: First, we explore how the *suggested bid*—a common feature of ad services that suggests prices to bid for a given target demographic—can provide insights on the revenue attainable from different users. On Facebook, the suggested bid is an undocumented feature, and the internal algorithm that Facebook uses is not public.

Basic Fields	Parameters/Examples
Location	Country, State, City, Postal code
Gender	Male, Female, All
Age	Range (from 13–65)
Precise Interest[1]	Travel, Science, Music, ...
Broad Category[2]	Cooking, Gardening, iPhone 5, ...
Interested In	Male, Female, All
Relationship Status	All, Single, In a relationship, Married, Engaged, Not specified
Language	English, Spanish, French, ...
Education	Anyone, In high school, In College, College Grad
Workplaces	Google, Facebook, AT&T, ...

Table 1: Facebook's targeting parameters made available to advertisers.

However, we demonstrate that this feature is likely based on a sample of the recent winning bids on users in the target demographic, and we provide strong supporting evidence for this hypothesis by conducting an experiment where we actively participate in the ad market.

Second, we demonstrate how researchers can use the suggested bid data. The raw data returned from the queries are noisy due to the sampling methodology, but we demonstrate that repeated sampling of the ad market can provide consistent results with distinctive trends. We verify that our derived relative revenue per user correlates well with ground-truth figures from Facebook's SEC filings [14]. While our methodology focuses on Facebook, it likely can be applied to other OSNs that provide suggested bids for placing advertisements. We make all of our code and data available to the research community.

Third, we use the suggested bid mechanism to explore two questions about how different users contribute to Facebook's revenue: How do the advertising prices compare across different demographics, and how stable are the prices for different target demographics over time? We explore different attributes, including location, age, and user interests, and provide a summary of the distribution of prices paid to advertise to different user demographics. We find significant differences in ad prices across different locations and user interests, and fewer differences by age. We also find prices to be variable over the long-term, but with distinct trends; this is consistent with OSN-based advertising markets being in a nascent phase.

The rest of this paper is organized as follows: Section 2 provides background information on Facebook's advertising model and an overview of related work that studies online advertising. Section 3 describes our data collection methodology, examines the properties of the suggested bid data, and explores how it can be interpreted and used. Section 4 presents an analysis of the current Facebook ad market, exploring the prices of different demographics and the stability over time. Finally, Section 5 provides a concluding discussion.

[1]Precise interests are interests explicitly stated by the user in their profile; broad interests are inferred by Facebook based on user activity.

[2]Broad Categories are pre-defined targeting categories provided by Facebook that group users according to their Likes, interests, applications, and other profile content they have provided. Recently, Facebook changed the interface by merging existing categories into a more general "Interests and Behaviors".

2. BACKGROUND

We now provide background on Internet advertising and detail related work on measuring online advertising auctions.

2.1 Online advertising

Most online advertising today is placed via *auctions*, where advertisers bid on keywords, search terms, or (in the case of OSNs) user demographics. The advertising network selects the winning bidders and presents their ads to the users. In different online advertising platforms, the underlying auction mechanism varies: many traditional ad networks, such as Google and Yahoo, use Generalized Second Price (GSP) auctions [9], whereas Facebook uses Vickrey–Clarke–Groves (VCG) auctions [36]. These two mechanisms primarily differ in how they calculate the price that a winning bidder should pay.

Advertisers typically bid using either CPM (Cost Per Mille, the cost of 1,000 ad impressions) or CPC (Cost Per Click). In order to support both bidding mechanisms at once, ad networks will typically record each advertiser's click-through rate (CTR, the fraction of impressions that result in a click), providing a way to compute an estimated CPM bid given a CPC bid (i.e., the estimated CPM bid is simply the CPC bid multiplied by the advertiser's CTR). In this paper, we focus only on CPM ad prices, as reasoning about CPC requires knowing an advertiser's CTR (which is not always available).

2.2 Facebook advertising

Advertisers can place ads on Facebook by creating *campaigns*; each campaign consists of a specific ad, a target demographic, a CPC or CPM bid, and a budget. After an advertiser creates a campaign, it must first be approved by Facebook (this process typically takes less than one day). Once the ad campaign is active, the advertiser participates in the ad auctions that occur whenever a user in the target demographic is shown an ad. An advertiser can view their campaign's status on Facebook's Web site to see details on the number of impressions, clicks, unique users, and overall cost, and can pause or cancel their campaign at any time.

Unlike traditional ad networks, OSNs such as Facebook have significant data about each user, including their personal information (demographics, interests, educational history, relationship status, etc), identities of friends, and their activity on the OSN. An overview of the currently available

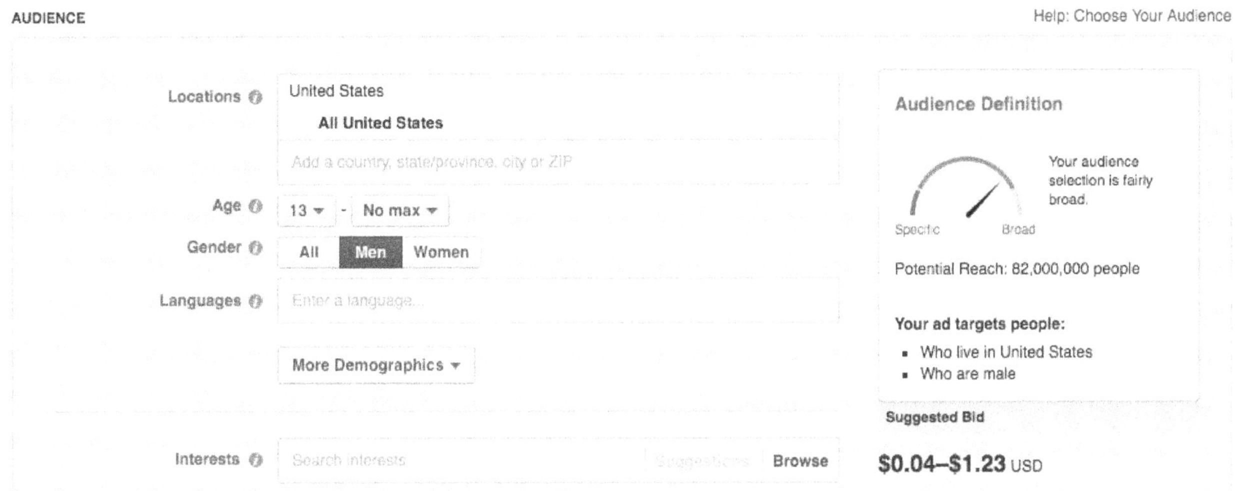

Figure 1: Screenshot of Facebook's ad creation webpage, showing the suggested bid (bottom right) for the selected targeting parameters. We programmatically collect the suggested bid information.

targeting parameters[3] are shown in Table 1. Advertisers can target any combination of these parameters, and are only required to specify at least one country.[4]

2.3 Related work

There is surprisingly little research work on OSN ad auctions. Researchers have studied existing Web-search-based advertising networks (e.g., Google's ad market) [15,32,39], prediction markets run by Google, Ford and others [5], and have used "estimated prices" [17] from Google's Traffic Estimator Tool [23] (similar to our suggested bids) as a mechanism for understanding the network. Noti et al. [29] demonstrated that bidders with some explicit knowledge during an initial learning phase can bid with better valuations than those without such knowledge; this implies that suggested bids can provide useful guidance for bidders. A related study [11] has developed a new analytical model of GSP auctions in order to predict the number of clicks and the total price the advertiser can expect, using the advertiser's bid and the distribution of the number of opponents and their relative weighted bids. Our work provides another methodology for the advertiser to estimate the price they need to pay when targeting users with different demographics in OSNs, in which the information of opponents are not available. Furthermore, we provide a way for advertisers to estimate and compare the prices for targeting different demographics of users in an automatic way; previously, advertisers needed to manually select a combination of interests, age, gender, and other options to obtain Facebook's suggestions.

Researchers have also examined and improved auction mechanisms, including better CTR estimates [6,16], usage of reserve prices in ad auction [30,34], and optimization in multiplicative bidding [3]. Using a sample from a week's worth of data across all keywords on Bing, other work [4] showed how to optimize linear combinations of the stakeholder utilities, showing that these can be tackled through a GSP auction with a per-click reserve price. There has also been much work proposing new models for conducting online auctions [19,20,28,39].

Prior work [18] has shown that the contribution of users to advertising revenue is skewed (20% of users accounting for 80% of revenue), which provides supports for our observations that the OSN ad market prices vary widely across different user interests and locations. Another study [2] has utilized AdReveal, a browser based tool to provide measurements of 139K online display ads and analysis of 103K Web pages. They demonstrated that up to 65% of ad categories received by users are behaviorally targeted using users' online interests. Our study has shown similar result: targeting users with specified interests is more expensive, implying more competition among advertisers.

Much of this work is orthogonal to ours, as we present a mechanism for measuring the OSN ad network itself. Others have explored ways of identifying influential users in OSNs [1,8]; our work is complementary to these. Additionally, there are nascent systems for leveraging unique features of OSNs for advertising (e.g., `adby.me` [25] allows users to create their own ads, shown to their friends). Finally, a few companies (e.g., AdParlor) have used Facebook's suggested bid data to provide clients with information on the ad market. Unfortunately, there are few published details of how their analysis is conducted.

3. SUGGESTED BIDS

We now describe our approach for measuring the Facebook Advertising Platform using suggested bids. We analyze the properties of the suggested bid data, with a goal of determining what the suggested bids represent and how they are calculated by Facebook. Finally, we describe how we interpret and use the data for our analysis in the following section.

[3] `https://developers.facebook.com/docs/reference/ads-api/targeting-specs/`

[4] Facebook provides different granularities of location information in different countries: the US includes ZIP code, most western European countries include city/town, and most developing countries only allow targeting at the country level.

Query:

https://graph.facebook.com/reachestimate?targeting_spec=
{"countries":["US"],"age_min":21,"age_max":30,genders=[1]}
¤cy=USD&accountId=XXX&access_token=XXXX

Response:

{"data": {"users":62984500,"bid_estimations":
[{"location":3,"cpc_min":54,"cpc_median":82,"cpc_max":144,
"cpm_min":3,"cpm_median":14,"cpm_max":83}]}}

Figure 2: Example query targeting U.S. males between 21 and 30. Also shown is the suggested bid response (in JSON format).

3.1 Collecting suggested bids

Facebook provides an API[5] that allows advertisers to create and manage ads efficiently by making different API queries. Unfortunately, the Ads API is restricted to high-volume advertisers and we were unable to obtain access. Instead, we obtain suggested bid data from Facebook's Ad Creation Web page,[6] a screenshot of which is shown in Figure 1.

We programmatically send HTTP GET requests to the Facebook URL that serves the suggested bid data presented on the page. This URL accepts arguments representing the desired targeting parameters and returns a suggested bid to the user. A user must be logged in to make the suggested bid request, so we create a pool of three accounts to place the queries. These accounts have no prior advertising history or uploaded content.[7]

The suggested bid response from Facebook actually contains 7 different values: the estimated *audience size*[8] (i.e., the number of Facebook users in the target demographic), the CPC min/med/max, and the CPM min/med/max. An example of query and response data is shown in Figure 2.[9] It is important to note that all suggested bid data is public for all advertisers, and contains no personally identifiable information for either the other advertisers or other Facebook users.

3.2 Suggested bid observations

Given the suggested bid data made available by Facebook, we now provide five observations about the bid data. To help illustrate these observations, we collect a data set consisting of 1,000 suggested bids in quick succession (i.e., issuing 1,000 queries back-to-back within 30 seconds), separately targeting each of the 204 countries that Facebook supports. Thus, for each country, we collect a set of 1,000 suggested bids obtained in quick succession, where each bid uses the default targeting parameters with the exception of specifying the respective country (e.g., the default gender parameter targets both male and female users).

Country	Coefficient of Variation CPM min	CPM med	CPM max
US	0.176	0.143	0.260
NZ	0.143	0.110	0.273
AG	0.0	0.308	0.358

Table 2: Comparison of the coefficient of variation of the CPM values for the three different countries. Significant variance is observed, especially for the CPM maximum values.

Skewed distribution Our first observation is that the suggested bid data is highly skewed, with the median of the suggested CPM almost always being significantly closer to the minimum than the maximum. For example, if we target users in the United States, the minimum of the suggested CPM is typically between \$0.03 and \$0.07, the median is typically between \$0.08 and \$0.18, and the maximum is typically between \$0.80 and \$2.00. This property holds regardless of the targeting parameters that we choose.

Significant variance Our next observation is that multiple suggested bids with the same targeting parameters show significant variance over short time periods. For example, consider the graphs presented in Figure 3, which shows the 1,000 suggested CPM bids for three different countries with very different populations (United States, 159M users; New Zealand, 2.2M users; and Antigua and Barbuda, 29K users). In all three cases, the minimum, median, and maximum values show significant variance,[10] even from query to query (queries were roughly spaced 35 milliseconds apart). To quantify the variance, we calculate the *coefficient of variation* (the standard deviation divided by the mean) of the distribution, and present the results in Table 2. In almost all cases, significant variance is observed, with the CPM maximum always showing the highest coefficient of variation.

Variance independent of audience size Our third observation is that the variance observed is independent of the audience size. We compare the audience size versus the coefficient of variation of the CPM minimum, median, and maximum values for each country in Figure 4. Across suggested bids from the 204 countries, we observe no correlation between the audience size and the coefficient of variation of any of the CPM values: the correlation coefficients are -0.02 (CPM minimum), -0.08 (CPM median), and -0.03 (CPM maximum). We observe similar results with audiences derived from over 100 different sets of targeting parameters including US states and zip codes, user interests, and relationship status.

Variance across accounts Our fourth observation is that the suggested bids queried at the same time from different accounts show no correlation. To explore this, we used our multiple Facebook accounts described above and queried for suggested bids for the same target demographic at the same time from multiple accounts. Despite using a range of tar-

[5]https://developers.facebook.com/docs/ads-api/

[6]https://www.facebook.com/advertising/

[7]The advertising history of accounts could be a factor in determining the suggested prices. To control for this, we tested with different accounts and observed no significant differences in characteristics of the returned suggested bid data.

[8]The audience size is returned with a granularity of 20 users, presumably to provide user privacy.

[9]The `location` parameter that is provided in the result is undocumented, but likely to the different locations on Facebook in which the ad will be shown.

[10]The minimum and median values for Antigua and Barbuda take on fewer values, but this is likely an artifact of the \$0.01-granularity of the data returned.

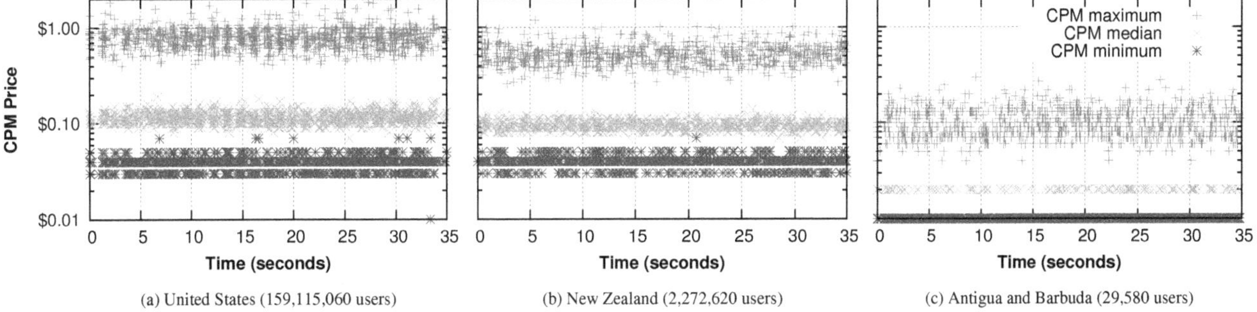

(a) United States (159,115,060 users) (b) New Zealand (2,272,620 users) (c) Antigua and Barbuda (29,580 users)

Figure 3: 1,000 suggested bids for three different sets of targeting parameters with massively different audience sizes (note the log-scale on the y-axis). Significant variance is observed, as well as a skewed distribution, across all three countries.

geting parameters (resulting in a variety of audience sizes), we did not find any correlation between the suggested bids received by the different accounts (despite the fact that the queries were issued at the same time).

An example is shown in Figure 5, containing the CPM maximum value received by two accounts targeting US users. Visually, we can observe little correlation between the values returned by the two accounts; for example, the spike around 85 seconds observed by account 2 is never reflected in account 1's results. Moreover, the Pearson's correlation coefficient between the values received by the two accounts is -0.01, further indicating the lack of a correlation.

Non-persistence of min or max Our final observation is that the CPM minimum and maximum values do not "persist" from query to query. For example, consider the graph in Figure 3 (c), which shows the CPM data for Antigua and Barbuda. While there are only 29,580 Facebook users in the country (as measured by the audience size), the CPM maximum value varies repeatedly between \$0.04 and \$0.30 in less than 100 milliseconds. This indicates that the minimum and maximum are very likely not calculated from the same pool (or a rolling pool) each time; instead, as we describe in Section 3.4, we believe they are calculated by *sampling* from the pool of recent winning bids.

3.3 Reverse-engineering suggested bids

The suggested bid feature is not documented by Facebook; the most relevant documentation describes the purpose of the feature as helping advertisers select a bid that is likely to cause their ads to be shown to users [13]. We requested additional information from Facebook's Advertising Support Team on how the suggested bids are calculated and received the following information (emphasis ours):

> The suggested bid range you see when creating your ads is based on the bids that are *currently winning the ad auction* for the users you've chosen to target.

Thus, it is clear that the suggested bids are derived from the *recent winning bids* on the target users, but it is not quite clear *exactly how* they are derived.

Ultimately, the suggested bid algorithm is a black box; we are unlikely to be able to definitively reverse-engineer how they are calculated. Instead, we look for the most reasonable explanation for how suggested bids are derived given our observations. We present three hypotheses below and rule out two as unlikely.

Hypothesis 1: Winning bids change rapidly The first hypothesis is that the suggested bids are derived from the most-recent-k winning bids for the target users (for some value of k). If this were the case, the observed variance would be due to the set of recently-won bids changing rapidly. However, this hypothesis does not explain the significant variance observed on very short timescales for countries with very small audience sizes (e.g., the Antigua and Barbuda CPM from Figure 3 (c)); with such small audiences, it is unlikely that ads are served to these users quickly

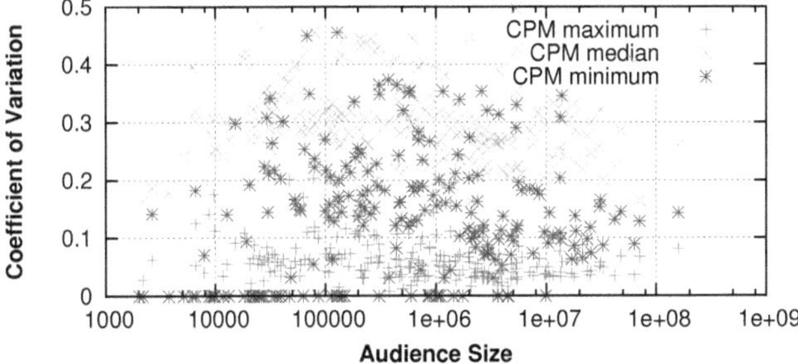

Figure 4: Audience size vs. coefficient of variation (standard deviation divided by mean) of suggested CPM bids for all 204 countries. No correlation is observed for CPM minimum, median, or maximum.

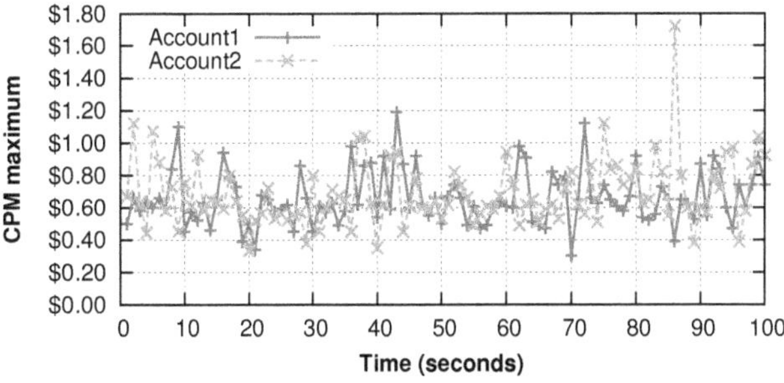

Figure 5: CPM maximum values for 100 successive suggested bids targeting US users, queried from 2 different accounts at the same time. The prices received by the two different accounts show no correlation.

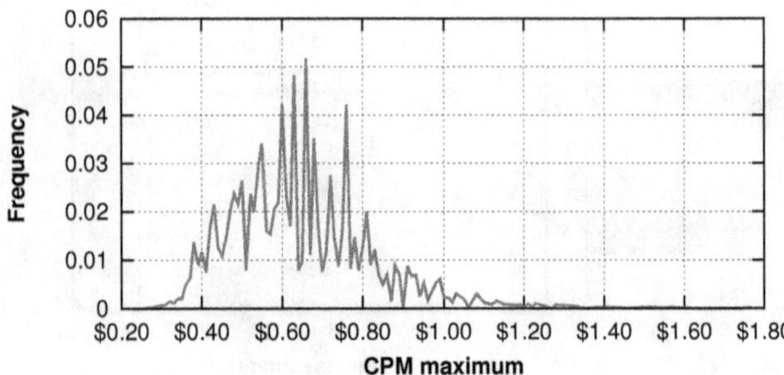

Figure 6: Example probability distribution function of CPM maximum values for 20,000 successive suggested bids (US 25-year-old females interested in computer programming; 179,760 users). This distribution fails statistical tests for multiple common distributions, suggesting the absence of random noise.

enough to account for the rapidly changing minimum and maximum values.

Hypothesis 2: Adding random noise The second hypothesis is that Facebook is adding random noise to the returned suggested bid data (possibly to obfuscate the true value). To explore this hypothesis, we collected 20,000 suggested bids in quick succession for a small target population (25-year-old U.S. females interested in computer programming; 179K users); we then ran a number of statistical tests to see if the data matched a number of common statistical distributions (as would be expected were Facebook adding random noise): Uniform random, Gaussian, Cauchy, Log-Normal, or Logistic distributions. We found a poor fit for all distributions, with a p-value of less than 10^{-16}. An example probability distribution function of one of these suggested bid sets is shown in Figure 6.

Hypothesis 3: Sampling winning bids The third hypothesis is that Facebook is *sampling* from the recent-k winning bids, and is reporting the minimum, median, and maximum of the sample; a diagram of this process is presented in Figure 8. This hypothesis is consistent with the format of the returned data (i.e., the fact that Facebook returns a minimum, median, and maximum) and is also consistent with our observations: we would expect to see significant variance from query to query, as different samples of the recent winning bids are used to generate each response. Moreover, this hypothesis is compatible with the variance being independent of audience size if the same k is used.

While verifying the correctness of Hypothesis 3 is likely only possible if one has access to Facebook's internal systems, we rely on the fact that it is both a logical mechanism for calculating suggested bids and is consistent with all of our observations on the properties of suggested bids.

3.4 Validating suggested bids

We now validate that suggested bids can be used to measure the overall Facebook ad market by showing that suggested bids reflect changes to the marketplace and that they correlate with Facebook's revenue.

Changes to the market To test our hypothesis that suggested bids are generated using recent winning bid data, we ran an experiment where we actively participate in the advertising market to see how quickly changes propagate into the suggested bids. To do so, we chose a small country (Seychelles, 26K Facebook users) with a low suggested CPM. We then created three accounts[11] to advertise with, and submitted one ad campaign from each targeting Seychelles users. To visibly affect the market, each of our three advertising accounts bid a significantly higher CPM ($1.00) than the suggested CPM maximum ($0.16). We ran the advertising campaigns concurrently for 8 hours, receiving an average of 19,903 impressions to 3,543 users.

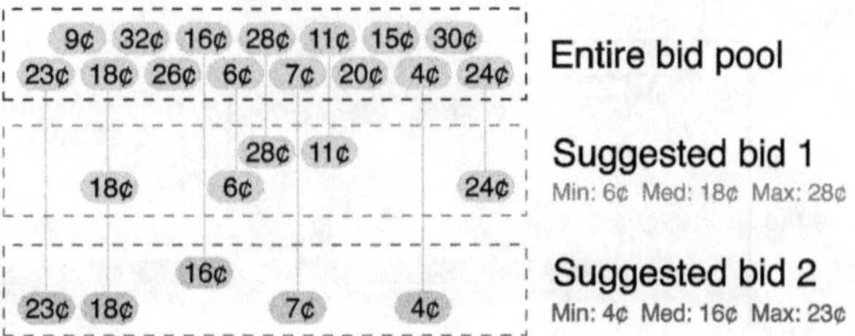

Figure 8: Diagram of Hypothesis 3: Sampling winning bids. To generate each suggested bid, Facebook selects a sample of bids from the set of all bids, and returns the median, minimum, and maximum from the sample.

To measure the effect the campaigns had on suggested bids for Seychelles users, we also collected data on the suggested bids for targeting Seychelles users every 5 minutes using a separate account. In order to observe the changes, we started collecting this data 8 hours *before* all three of the advertisement campaigns became active; we also collected suggested bid data for the 8 hours during the campaign and for 44 hours *after* the campaigns ended.

Figure 7 presents the results[12] of this experiment, showing the CPM medians and maximums before, during, and after our campaigns (the campaign was running during the shaded region). From Figure 7 (a), we observe that the CPM median value was stable at $0.01 before we started our campaigns, rose up to $0.07 within 18 hours after our campaigns, before returning back to $0.01. Examining Figure 7 (b), we find that the suggested bids maximum rose dramatically from $0.16 up to $7.64; after we paused our campaigns, it fell back to a low price $1.47. Overall, this experiment shows that changes to the ad market are reflected in the suggested bids, and provides evidence for our hypothesis that the suggested bids data comes from a sample of the recent winning bids.

Comparison with Facebook's revenue Finally, we compare the data we observe via suggested bids to the only ground-truth that we know of: Facebook's SEC filings. In Facebook's March 2013 10-Q filing, Facebook reports the Average Revenue Per User (ARPU) at the granularity of region (US+Canada, Europe, Asia, and the Rest of the World). To compare the suggested bid data to Facebook's ARPU, we aggregate our CPM median data into the same regions and take the average across all countries in the region

[11]We choose to create three accounts, rather than one, as Facebook places multiple advertisements from different advertisers on each page.

[12]The fractional values result from a change by Facebook on May 1, 2013 to provide more precise suggested bids.

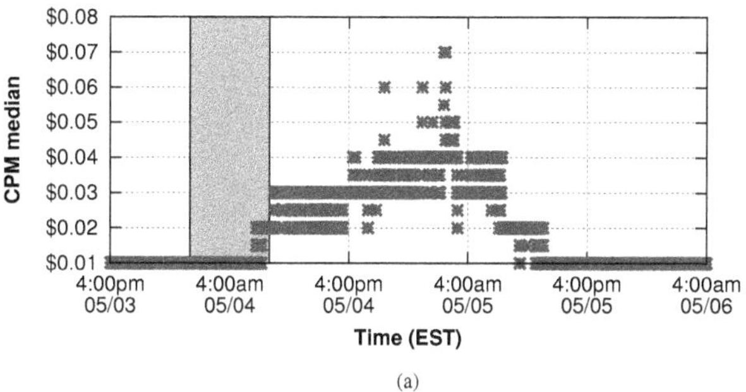

(a)

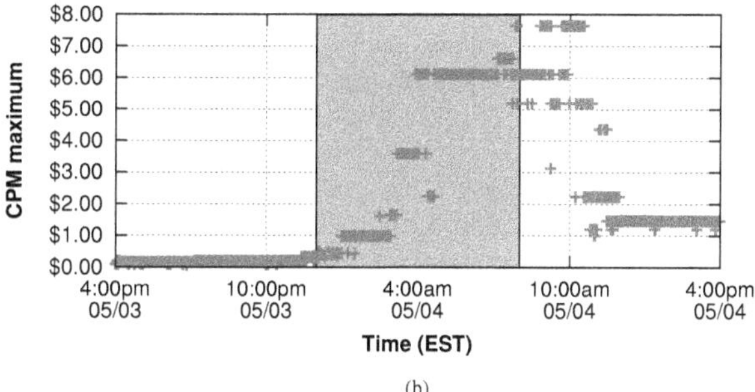

(b)

Figure 7: (a) CPM median values and (b) CPM maximum values before, during, and after our three advertising campaigns targeting Seychelles users (the shaded region represents the time of the ad campaigns. We observed that our advertising campaigns were quickly reflected in the suggested bids.

(weighted by audience size). We then scale both Facebook's ARPU and our aggregated suggested bid data relative to the US+Canada region. Of course, aggregating suggested bids in this way ignores many aspects of how revenue is generated (e.g., the activity level of different demographics), but can provide rough guidance on the relative revenue for different regions.

The results of this experiment are presented in Table 3. We observe similar trends between the two measures: Both Facebook's ARPU and the suggested bids rank the regions in the same order, with the Europe and Rest of the World regions at approximately the same ratios. While our results are far from being conclusive, this result indicates that the suggested bid data that we obtain from Facebook's advertising pages at least correlates with the distribution of Facebook's revenue.

3.5 Using suggested bids

From the previous section, we conclude that the suggested bid data is most likely calculated by sampling from the recent winning bids for the target users. Since the properties of the suggested bids are somewhat unique, we now explore how researchers can use suggested bids to measure the Facebook ad market.

Multiple samples Given that each suggested bid is most likely generated from a sample of the recent winning bids, it is clear that a single suggested bid may misrepresent the overall bid distribution. Instead, we collate multiple samples together, extracting the overall minimum, median, and maximum from the collated samples (i.e., for the remainder of the paper, all reported minima are the minimum across multiple suggested bid minima; the same holds for median and maximum).

Convergence The next step is to choose *how many* samples to collate together. To do so, we examine how quickly different numbers of collated suggested bids converge towards the overall "true" minimum, median, and maximum. To explore this question, we use the 204-countries data from the previous section. Since we do not know the true distribution of the recent winning bids, we instead use the overall minimum, median, and maximum of each country's 1,000 samples in its place.

Figure 9 presents the convergence of each of the 204 countries towards its overall minimum (bottom), median (mid-

Region	Facebook ARPU Raw	Facebook ARPU Scaled	Suggested Bid Scaled
US, Canada	$3.50	1.00	1.00
Europe	$1.60	0.45	0.42
Asia	$0.64	0.18	0.30
Rest of World	$0.50	0.14	0.15

Table 3: Comparison of Facebook's ARPU and CPM median suggested bids. We scale all values relative to the US+Canada region. We observe the same ranking of regions.

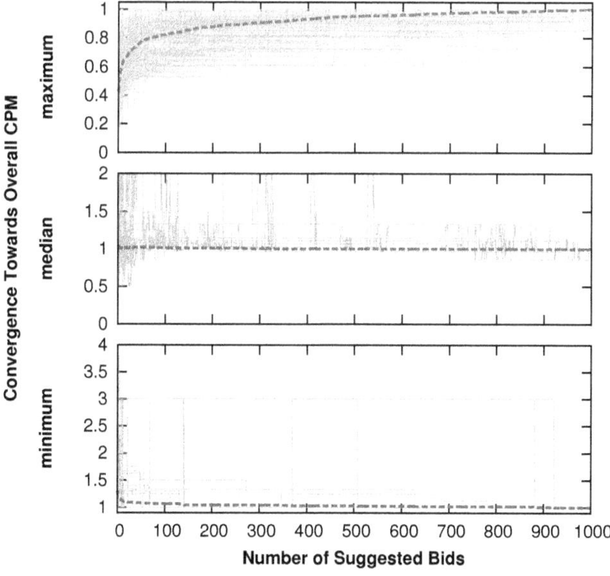

Figure 9: Convergence of different numbers of collated suggested bids towards overall CPM minimum, median, and maximum values for each of the 204 countries (each country is represented by a line in each graph). The average value across all countries is shown as the dark dashed line. Very quick convergence is observed for minimum and median, as expected.

dle), and maximum (top) values. Each country is represented by a thin line, and the average across all countries is shown as the dark, dashed line.

We observe that the minimum and median converge quite quickly: after only 25 suggested bids, both the minimum and median are within 15% of their eventual value (on average). Second, the maximum value converges more slowly (after 25 suggested bids, the maximum is within 30% of its eventual value, on average), which is expected due to the high variance and skewed distribution.

Choosing the number of suggested bids to collate together represents a tradeoff between accuracy and the load we place on Facebook. For the remainder of the paper, all of our reported data is the result of 25 collated suggested bids.

3.6 Limitations

Before examining the results for suggested bids for different user demographics, we first discuss a few of the limitations of our methodology.

User accounts As mentioned before, the advertising history of accounts could be a factor in determining the suggested prices (i.e., Facebook may show different suggested bids to different advertisers). Unfortunately, it is difficult (and expensive) to build an account with successful advertising history, as a result, to control any impact of this factor, all the user accounts used in our experiment are new created with no prior advertising history or uploaded content. Thus, the results in this paper are all comparable to each other, and we leave an exploration of the effect of advertising history on suggested bids for future work.

Facebook changes Our observations and methodology in this paper are based on the current advertising model used by Facebook; if Facebook makes internal changes in their advertising model, the suggested bid model, or the way they utilize the user data, our results may no longer be valid. However, we believe that our work provides researchers with a new approach for determining how suggested bids are calculated by Facebook, as well as ground-truth data to compare against.

Correlation versus causation In our analysis in the next section, we examine how the suggested bids are correlated with different user demographics. Of course, correlation does not imply causation, and it is possible that other, unknown factors are responsible for our observed correlations. Regardless, our analysis presents the first measurements of the relative value of different user demographics in OSNs.

4. ANALYSIS OF BID DATA

We now explore the properties of Facebook's ad auctions, using the suggested bid data.

4.1 Location

We examine how the *location* of the target demographic influences the ad auction winning bids, using the data set on 204 countries. We examine how the ad market CPM prices (represented by CPM median) correlate with the relative wealth of countries. To quantify the latter, we use GDP per capita [7], which is widely used in economics literature. The results are presented in Figure 10. As expected, we observe a correlation of 0.37 (statistically significant at the 0.001 level) between the GDP per capita and CPM prices. One

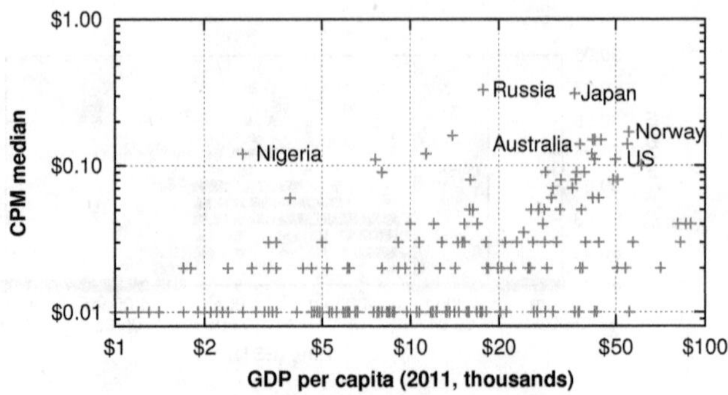

Figure 10: Scatterplot of CPM median versus GDP per capita for the 204 countries Facebook supports. Labeled are some of the countries with high CPM median values. All but a few countries have ad markets with very low CPMs.

notable outlier is Nigeria, which shows a CPM maximum on par with the U.S. while have a GDP per capita over an order of magnitude lower.

We now dig deeper into a single country and explore the differences in CPM prices between multiple cities in the same country. We choose to focus on the U.S., as it is the most mature Facebook ad market with the largest number of users. We query for the CPM prices of all U.S. cities with a population over 100,000 (285 cities). The results are presented in graphical form in Figure 11, plotting both CPM maximum (more red color representing higher values) and population (circle size) for each city. We observe that certain cities such as Las Vegas, NV and Hartford, CT show CPM maximums significantly higher than other cities like Cambridge, MA and Ann Arbor, MI, suggesting that certain cities have much more desirable users for advertisers to target.

Overall, we see dramatic differences in ad auction prices across different locations, with the most dramatic differences coming between users in different countries. As Facebook's ad markets continue to evolve, we can use our suggested bid methodology to measure their relatively maturity.

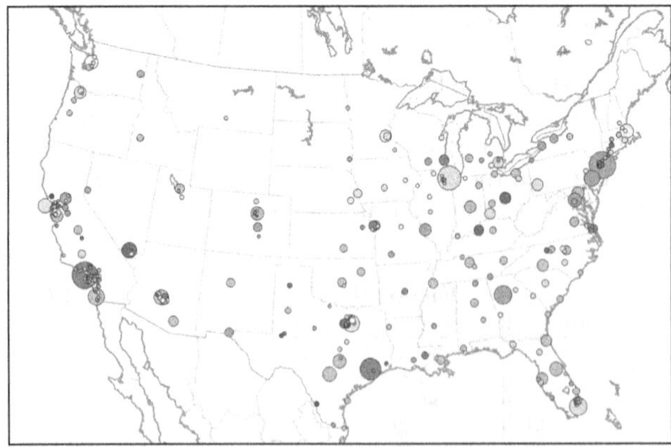

Figure 11: CPM maximum prices for all U.S. cities with population over 100,000. The color of each city corresponds to CPM maximum price (yellow to red represents increasing prices, and the size of the circle is in proportion to the number of Facebook users in each city.

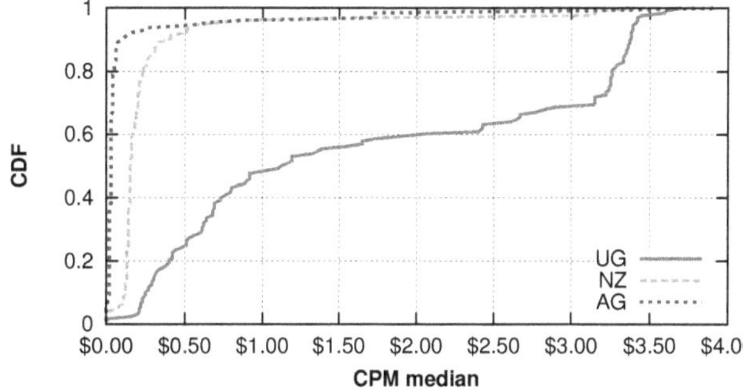

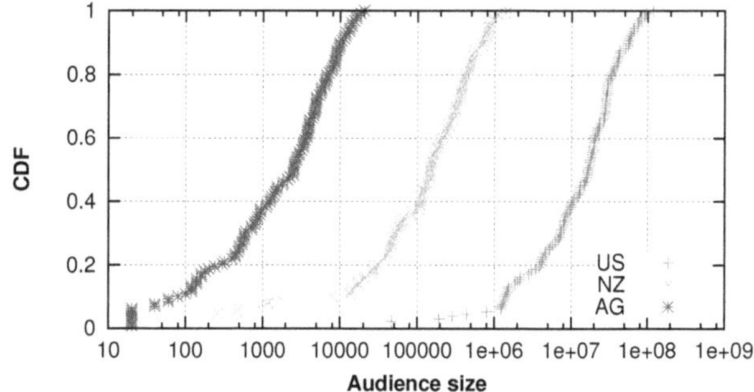

Figure 12: (a) Cumulative distribution of CPM median values for 129 interest categories for three countries. (b) Cumulative distribution of audience size for three countries (United States, New Zealand, and Antigua and Barbuda).

4.2 Age

We next explore how CPM median price is correlated with user *age*. We select the same three countries as before (the U.S., New Zealand, and Antigua and Barbuda), and retrieve suggested bids for users with different ages in each country. We note that Facebook's age policies come into effect here: the smallest age that an advertiser can target is 13, and targeting age 65 (the largest age one can target) encompasses all users 65 and over. The results of this experiment are presented in Figure 13 (top), showing the CPM median for different ages. We observe that in both the U.S. and New Zealand, as the age of target users increases, the CPM median price increases as well. The trend is less clear for Antigua and Barbuda, which we suspect is due to the smaller user population and less-well-developed ad market.

From Figure 13 (bottom), we observe that in all three countries, there is a rapid rise in the audience size (the number of Facebook users) between 13 to 18, followed by a slow decline over the remaining ages.[13] This observation corresponds strongly with previous studies about the age distribution of users in OSNs [35,38].

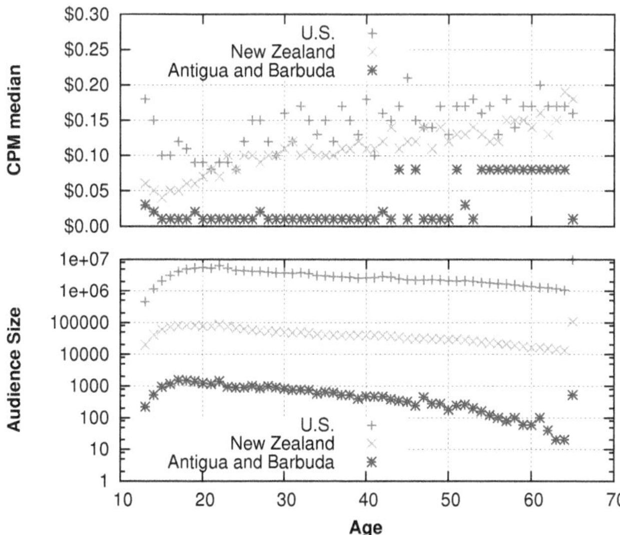

Figure 13: (a) CPM median versus Age (b) Audience Size versus Age for three countries. CPM prices increase significantly with age for the United States and New Zealand, and massively different user populations are observed (note the log scale on the y-axis of the lower graph).

4.3 Interests

For our final user attribute, we examine user *interests* in order to determine whether there are segments of the user population—based on particular interests—that are highly valued by advertisers. We are inspired by the wealth of studies on Web search auctions [26,27,31], which show there are certain keywords (e.g., "mesothelioma") that command prices thousands of times more than the average. For this experiment, we focus on *broad interests*, which are interests derived by Facebook based on user activity.

We retrieve suggested bids on all 129 Facebook-provided broad interest categories in each of the three countries that we have considered so far, and present the cumulative distribution across categories in Figure 12 (a). Surprisingly, the distribution of CPM median prices are rather broad: the most-expensive category is more than 20 times more expensive than the least-expensive category in all three countries. Interestingly, the most expensive categories in all three countries correspond to users who are traveling, recently engaged, or who like Apple products.

In Figure 12 (b), we observe that the distribution of audience size across different broad categories are widespread for all the three countries (note the log-scale on the x-axis). There are a significant number of broad categories are very popular within each country, for example, the largest categories in the United States are Mobile Users (All), Travelers, and Music (All).

4.4 Price stability

In addition to studying the CPM prices of different demographics, we also study the stability of different market prices over time. To do so, we select four different sets of targeting parameters, designed to cover a variety of targeting parameter types and audience sizes: G_1: U.S. users (167M users), G_2: 21-50 year-old Canadian users (11M users), G_3: 25-40 year-old college graduated Brazilian users (4.7M users), and G_4: 13-15 year-old British users (1.2M users). We track each of these sets of targeting parameters by retrieving 25 suggested bids each hour for a period of three weeks (April 3rd, 2013 through April 23rd, 2013).

[13] The "jump" in audience size at age 65 is because 65 represents "65 and older."

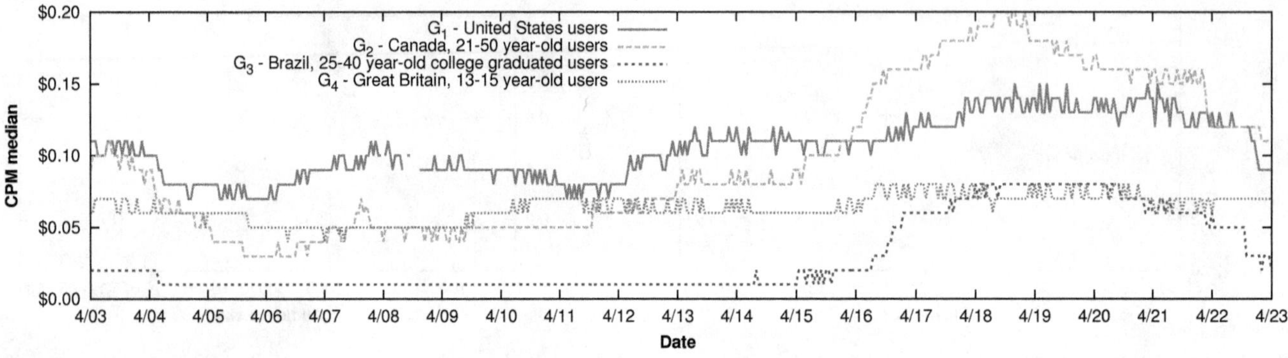

Figure 14: Long-term tracking of CPM median prices over three weeks for four different sets of targeting parameters that show different properties with distinct trends over time.

Figure 14 plots the CPM median values for these groups during our period of observation. We observe that while there is significant short-term variance in many of the groups, there are also a number of longer-term trends present. For example, group G_1 shows a periodic increases spaced out approximately one week apart, and groups G_2 and G_3 shows a multi-day increase starting approximately on 04/16. Moreover, certain groups—such as groups G_2 and G_3—show significant fluctuations in price (up to six-fold), while others—such as G_4—do not vary much over the study period. Overall, our results suggest that there are significant short-term and long-term dynamics present in Facebook's ad auctions, which may be explained by the relative immaturity of different sectors of the market.

5. CONCLUSION

Advertising is now ubiquitous on the Web; most of the popular OSNs are funded via advertising on their site. While OSNs themselves have all information of their advertising models as well as how they utilize all the user data, there is little information that is shared with external researchers, advertisers, even the users themselves. Thus, OSN advertising markets remain quite difficult for researchers to study, even as these markets are growing in prominence.

In this paper, we have explored Facebook ad auctions through the *suggested bid* feature, showing how this feature can be used by researchers to make inferences on properties of the ad market. While we have only presented a subset of our experiments here, we have explored suggested bids for many other targeting parameters that Facebook provides, including gender, precise interests, relationship status, education, and workplaces. In all cases, we observed fewer differences than for the targeting parameters presented.

While we are far from covering the entire space—the set of possible targeting parameters is prohibitively large—our results suggest that advertiser interest is focused on location, user interest, and age parameters (consistent with ads in other media). Though our results are not necessarily surprising, we present the first mechanism for quantifying the relative value of different user demographics on today's OSNs. For advertisers, our work offers some guidance especially when they start to advertise on Facebook users; for users themselves, we provide them a basic idea about how valuable they are towards advertisers and Facebook, based on their own demographic information and activities which fall under different interests.

As the Facebook ad market continues to mature, we plan to repeat our analysis to study the evolution of the market. Moreover, as more OSNs develop advertising markets, our approach can be used to measure these markets as well; it is typical for ad markets to provide suggested bids. In other words, we can apply the proposed methodology to analyze the underlying models, and compare user value. For example, Facebook recently launched a real-time bidding ad system Facebook Exchange [12]; we aim to extend our methodology to measure this network as well. Additionally, both LinkedIn and Twitter have recently developed and deployed advertising markets; we hope to be able to apply our methodology to those sites.

Finally, we make all of our suggested bid collection code and collected data available to the research community at

`http://osn-ads.ccs.neu.edu`

6. REFERENCES

[1] S. Aral and D. Walker. Identifying Social Influence in Networks Using Randomized Experiments. *IEEE IS*, 26(5):91–96, 2011.

[2] L. Bin, S. Anmol, W. Udi, C. Jaideep, and G. Ramesh. AdReveal: Improving Transparency into Online Targeted Advertising. *HotNets*, College Park, MD, Nov. 2013.

[3] M. Bateni, J. Feldman, V. Mirrokni, and S. C.-w. Wong. Multiplicative Bidding in Online Advertising. *EC*, Palo Alto, CA, June 2014.

[4] Y. Bachrach, S. Ceppi, I. A. Kash, P. Key, and D. Kurokawa. Optimising Trade-offs Among Stakeholders in Ad Auctions. *EC*, Palo Alto, CA, June 2014.

[5] B. Cowgill and E. Zitzewitz. Corporate Prediction Markets: Evidence from Google, Ford, and Firm X. *EC*, Palo Alto, CA, June 2014.

[6] H. Cheng and E. C. Paz. Personalized click prediction in sponsored search. *WSDM*, New York, NY, Feb. 2010.

[7] CIA the World Facebook. `https://www.cia.gov/library/publications/the-world-factbook/index.html`.

[8] B. Eytan, E. Dean, Y. Rong, and R. Itamar. Social influence in social advertising: evidence from field experiments. *EC*, Valencia, Spain, June 2012.

[9] B. Edelman, M. Ostrovsky, M. Schwarz, T. D. Fudenberg, L. Kaplow, R. Lee, P. Milgrom, M. Niederle, and A. Pakes. Internet Advertising and the Generalized Second Price Auction: Selling Billions of Dollars Worth of Keywords. *Am. Econ. Rev.*, 97(1):242–259, 2007.

[10] J. Edwards. Facebook Shares Surge on First Ever $1 Billion Mobile Ad Revenue Quarter. 2013. `http://www.businessinsider.com/facebook-q4-2013-earnings-2014-1`.

[11] P. Furcy and K. Peter. Stochastic Variability in Sponsored Search Auctions: Observations and Models. *EC*, San Jose, CA, June 2011.

[12] Facebook Exchange: A New Way for Advertisers to Target Specific Users with Real-Time Bid Ads. `http://techcrunch.com/2012/06/13/facebook-exchange/`.

[13] Facebook Help: What is the Suggested Bid Range and how does Facebook calculate it? `https://www.facebook.com/help/213140778716849`.

[14] Facebook SEC Filings. `http://investor.fb.com/sec.cfm/`.

[15] A. Ghose and S. Yang. An empirical analysis of sponsored search performance in search engine advertising. *WSDM*, Stanford, CA, Feb. 2008.

[16] A. Ghose and S. Yang. An Empirical Analysis of Search Engine Advertising: Sponsored Search in Electronic Markets. *Manage. Sci.*, 55(10):1605–1622, 2009.

[17] A. Goldfarb and C. Tucker. Search Engine Advertising: Channel Substitution When Pricing Ads to Context. *Manage. Sci.*, 57(3):458–470, 2011.

[18] P. Gill, V. Erramilli, A. Chaintreau, B. Krishnamurthy, K. Papagiannaki, and P. Rodriguez. Follow the Money: Understanding Economics of Online Aggregation and Advertising. *IMC*, Barcelona, Spain, Oct. 2013.

[19] D. G. Goldstein, R. P. McAfee, and S. Suri. The Effects of Exposure Time on Memory of Display Advertisements. *EC*, San Jose, CA, June 2011.

[20] D. G. Goldstein, R. P. McAfee, and S. Suri. Improving the Effectiveness of Time-based Display Advertising. *EC*, Valencia, Spain, June 2012.

[21] Google. 2013 Financial Tables. 2013. `http://investor.google.com/financial/2013/tables.html`.

[22] Google AdWords. `https://adwords.google.com/`.

[23] Traffic Estimator. *Google AdWords*. `https://adwords.google.com/o/TrafficEstimator`.

[24] R. D. Hof. Advertisers Flock to Social Networks. *MIT Technology Review*, 2011. `http://www.technologyreview.com/article/424409/advertisers-flock-to-social-networks/`.

[25] J. Kim. adby.me. 2011. `http://adby.me`.

[26] L. Kim. The Most Expensive Keywords in Google AdWords. 2011. `http://www.wordstream.com/blog/ws/2011/07/18/most-expensive-google-adwords-keywords/`.

[27] Kidgas. Twenty Keywords with CPC More Than $20. 2011. `http://kidgas.hubpages.com/hub/Twenty-Keywords-with-CPC-More-Than-20`.

[28] S. Muthukrishnan, M. Pál, and Z. Svitkina. Stochastic Models for Budget Optimization in Search-Based Advertising. *Algorithmica*, 58(4):1022–1044, 2010.

[29] G. Noti, N. Nisan, and I. Yaniv. An Experimental Evaluation of Bidders' Behavior in Ad Auctions. *WWW*, Seoul, Korea, Apr. 2014.

[30] M. Ostrovsky and M. Schwarz. Reserve Prices in Internet Advertising Auctions: A Field Experiment. *EC*, San Jose, CA, June 2011.

[31] SpyFu. Keywords with Highest Cost Per Click (CPC). 2014. `http://www.spyfu.com/TopList.aspx?listId=3`.

[32] C. Tucker. Social Advertising. *SSRN*, Feb. 2012.

[33] D. Turnbull and L. F. Bright. Advertising academia with sponsored search: an exploratory study examining the effectiveness of Google AdWords at the local and global level. *IJEB*, 6(2):149–171, 2008.

[34] D. R. M. Thompson and K. Leyton-Brown. Revenue Optimization in the Generalized Second-price Auction. *EC*, Philadelphia, PA, June 2013.

[35] US Social Network Users by Age Group - New Statistics from Pew. `http://bit.ly/1tGTpso`.

[36] W. Vickrey. Counterspeculation, auctions, and competitive sealed tenders. *J. Finance*, 16(1):8–37, 1961.

[37] H. R. Varian. Online Ad Auctions. *Am. Econ. Rev.*, 99(2):430–434, 2009.

[38] S. Wolfram. Data Science of the Facebook World. Apr. 2013. `http://blog.stephenwolfram.com/2013/04/data-science-of-the-facebook-world/`.

[39] S. Yao and C. F. Mela. A Dynamic Model of Sponsored Search Advertising. *Marketing Science*, 30(3):447–468, 2011.

Invite Your Friends and Get Rewards: Dynamics of Incentivized Friend Invitation in KakaoTalk Mobile Games

Jiwan Jeong
KAIST & Netmarble
Daejeon, Korea
jiwanjeong@gmail.com

Sue Moon
KAIST
Daejeon, Korea
sbmoon@kaist.edu

ABSTRACT

Incentivized friend invitation is an efficient and effective user growth mechanism, more so when combined with social platforms, such as online social networks (OSNs) or mobile instant messengers (MIMs). KakaoGame, a two-year-old mobile game platform based on a dominant MIM called KakaoTalk, brought 5.2 billion sign-ups over 520 games with quota-based reward schemes. How does the reward scheme help the spread of services?

In this paper, we analyze the friend invitation logs from 4 mobile games on KakaoGame, consisting of 330 million invitations from 8.4 million users to 36 million users. Our analysis aims at answering the following three key questions. (a) How do quota-based reward schemes stimulate invitation behavior? (b) How many invitations trigger the invitee to sign up for the game or become an annoyance to make the invitee turn a blind eye? (c) How fast are the invitations sent out and how does the diffusion slow down? Based on the analysis, we provide practical insights for viral marketing.

Categories and Subject Descriptors

J.4 [**Social and Behavioral Sciences**]: Economics

General Terms

Economoics

Keywords

Word-of-mouth; viral marketing; incentive; social network

Acknowledgements

This research was partially supported by Next-Generation Information Computing Development Program through the National Research Foundation of Korea (NRF) funded by the Ministry of Science, ICT & Future Planning (NRF-2012M3C4A7033342).

COSN'14, October 1–2, 2014, Dublin, Ireland.

ACM 978-1-4503-3198-2/14/10 ...$15.00.
http://dx.doi.org/10.1145/2660460.2660468.

1. INTRODUCTION

Word-of-mouth (WOM) is frequent and trustworthy. People talk about news, gossips, and products with friends all the time. Internet technologies, such as e-mail, online social networks (OSNs), and mobile instant messengers (MIMs) facilitate WOM, creating convenient forums for information sharing. According to Nielsen, 92% of consumers trust recommendations from their friends, while 67% do not trust online advertising [19]. WOM marketing is attracting attention from both the practitioners and the researchers, while traditional means of advertising is losing effectiveness [21].

Previous studies characterize WOM as an oral, person-to-person communication between customers, regarding a brand, a product, or a service [2, 5]. Businesses often exploit WOM by compensating social referrals with explicit incentives. Dropbox provides 250MB of bonus space for every successful referral. World of Warcraft gives one month of free game time when the user's recruit buys a month of game time. The auction site eBay provides a $5 voucher to recruiters. Moreover, such referral programs are becoming more powerful than ever before, being combined with social platforms based on OSNs and MIMs [9, 18, 22]. Accordingly, understanding user behavior under various reward schemes create opportunities for new designs in viral marketing.

KakaoGame, a mobile game platform based on a hugely popular MIM called KakaoTalk, is one of the most successful cases with 37 million users out of 50 million in Korea. KakaoGame users invite their KakaoTalk friends to a game by sending person-to-person private messages. The invitations are often compensated by quota-based rewards regardless of the success, *i.e.*, if a user invites 10, 20, and 30 friends cumulatively, then the user gets rewards, R_1, R_2, and R_3 respectively, no matter whether the invitee signs up for the game or not. In contrast to such a commercial success, the underlying incentive mechanism of WOM marketing has not received much attention.

In this paper, we analyze the friend invitation logs from four mobile games on KakaoGame. Our analysis aims at answering the following questions:

- *Inviter's behavior*: How do quota-based reward schemes stimulate spontaneous invitation behavior? How do users select whom to invite among their friends? How many friends do users invite comfortably?
- *Invitee's reaction*: Invitation even from a friend can be construed as spam and is controversial. How do invitees react to multiple invitations over time? When

should the system stop or advise a user to stop sending invitations to a friend?

- *Propagation speed*: How quickly are the invitations adopted and reproduced?

- *Causes for saturation*: How does the diffusion process slow down and terminate?

The questions listed above are intuitive and yet the answers should bring novel and fundamental insight into quota-based reward schemes for online e-commerce. The remainder of this paper is organized as follows. Section 2 describes the KakaoTalk service, its game platform, and our datasets. Section 3 examines the inviter's behavior in terms of the invitation rate and count, the invitee selection process, and mental mechanics. Section 4 looks at the invitee's reaction. In Section 5 we investigate the temporal aspects of the invitation behavior and in Section 6 the slowdown of diffusion. We discuss related work in Section 7, then conclude this paper in Section 8.

2. BACKGROUND

Before presenting our analysis, we give a brief introduction about the MIM, KakaoTalk, and its mobile game platform, KakaoGame. Then we describe our dataset and the history of our game user growth.

2.1 KakaoTalk and KakaoGame

Google. FedEx. Xerox. These companies got so successful that their brand names became synonymous with the services they provide. KakaoTalk reached that level of success and Koreans say "KaTalk me!" instead of "Send me a text message!"

MIMs, such as WhatsApp, WeChat, LINE, and KakaoTalk, have emerged as a key medium for communication, along with the popularization of smartphones. KakaoTalk is the most widely-used one in Korea, claiming 37 million registered users from the population of 50 million. Everyday 27 million people send 4.2 billion KakaoTalk messages, which is equivalent to 156 messages per person a day [9].

KakaoGame is a KakaoTalk-based mobile game platform launched in July 2012. It has brought 5.2 billion sign-ups over 520 mobile games, and generated USD 860 million in sales in 2013 [15], monopolizing the mobile application market as shown in Table 1. The games on KakaoGame have a few common characteristics. Most of them are single-player games, but users can interact with their friends by sharing activities via person-to-person private messages. Many are often score-based games providing each user with a personalized leaderboard involving only the user's friends. Also, most of them are *freemium*[1] games, and incentivize social referrals at a nominal cost by providing in-game items or coupons.

Quota-based reward schemes encourage users to invite friends and compensate for the act even when the invitations do not materialize to sign-ups. In order to prevent users from abusing the quota-based reward schemes, KakaoGame disallows inviting friends who have already joined a game or inviting more than twenty friends a day. Also a user cannot invite the same friend again to the same game within a month. The general convention in KakaoGame is to set the quotas at 10, 20, and 30 for reward schemes.

[1]Freemium is a pricing strategy by which a product or service (typically a digital offering, such as software, media, games or web services) is provided free of charge, but proprietary features, such as functionalities and virtual goods, are for fee.

Rank	Application	Publisher
1	Taming Monsters *for Kakao*	Netmarble
2	Cookie Run *for Kakao*	Devisisters
3	Candy Crush Saga *for Kakao*	King.com
4	Everybody's Marble *for Kakao*	Netmarble
5	Pokopang *for Kakao*	NHN
6	Anipang *for Kakao*	Sundaytoz
7	Everytown *for Kakao*	WeMade
8	KakaoTalk	Kakao
9	Anipang Mahjong *for Kakao*	Sundaytoz
10	Water Margin *for Kakao*	4:33
11	Five 2013 *for Kakao*	Netmarble
12	Zenonia Online *for Kakao*	Gamevil
13	Action Puzzle Family *for Kakao*	Com2us
14	Dragon Flight *for Kakao*	Next Floor
15	Atlan Story *for Kakao*	WeMade

Table 1: Top grossing applications on Korean Google Play Market captured on Jan 1, 2014. Except for KakaoTalk, all other applications are KakaoTalk mobile games.

2.2 Dataset Description

In this paper, we analyze the referral logs of four mobile games on KakaoGame. The datasets were provided by the game publisher, Netmarble. Per Netmarble's request we do not divulge the names of the games and instead refer to them as A, B, C, and D. All the games were launched on both Android and iOS in mid 2013, and we have logs for the first 20 weeks from the release dates. The datasets consist of user registration logs and friend invitation logs. The former includes the signed-up user's ID (encrypted) and the timestamp, and the latter has the inviter's ID (encrypted), the invitee's ID (encrypted differently), and the timestamp per invitation. Note that the IDs of the signed-up users including inviters follow different numbering schemes from the IDs of invitees. This idiosyncrasy of ID mismatch in the logs bars us from studying the cascading behavior of invitations. The game publisher has provided us with a mapping for a limited number of $10,000$ user IDs between the two encrypted IDs out of the 7 million invitees of C. We do not know the sampling mechanism for the $10,000$ users and cannot quantify the sampling error. But the sample size is large enough that we expect the error to be within a reasonable limit. We use these users in our analysis in Section 4 and part of Section 5 and 6.

All the games have similar, but slightly different quotas for rewards. All the games have quotas at 10, 20, and 30, but B and C have additional quotas at 3 and 5, and D has at 5, 15, and 25. There are reward resets that cleared all user's invitation counts to zero and users could get rewards again. A reset reward in the 15th week from its release, B in the 11th and 15th week, and C and D in the 6th week. Note that B changed the reward quotas to 5, 10, 20, 30, and 40 at the second reward reset. In Table 2 we summarize the dataset statistics and reward schemes.

	Dataset Statistics				Reward Schemes		
	n_{user}	n_{inviter}	n_{invitee}	$n_{\text{invitation}}$	Reward Quotas	Reward Resets	Notes
A	13,413K	7,762K	33,668K	268,123K	10/20/30	15th week	B changed the quotas to 5/10/20/30/40 at the 2nd reward reset
B	2,510K	1,270K	17,111K	42,419K	3/5/10/20/30	11th & 15th weeks	
C	872K	393K	7,567K	12,816K	3/5/10/20/30	6th week	
D	648K	253K	4,934K	7,680K	5/10/15/20/25/30	6th week	

Table 2: Dataset statistics and reward schemes.

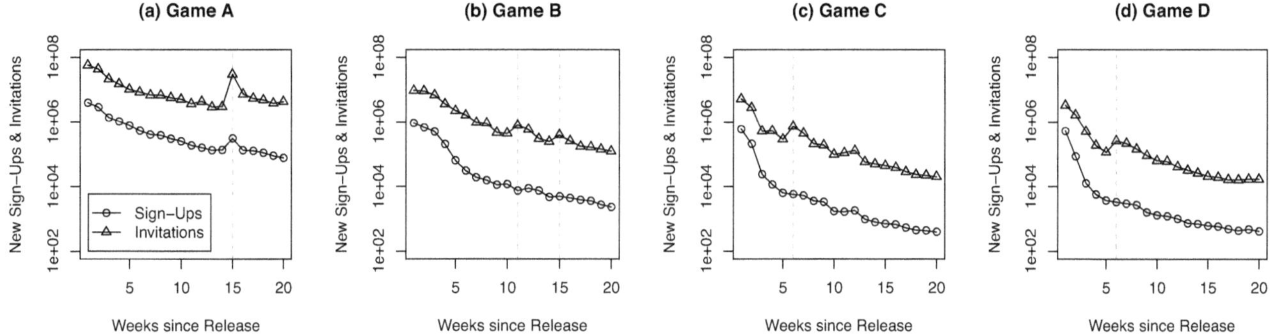

Figure 1: Weekly new sign-ups and invitations.

2.3 Friend Invitation and User Growth

KakaoGame has won its fame for its fast user growth mechanism. Figure 1 plots the weekly numbers of new sign-ups and invitations of the four games. The two numbers are highly correlated; the Pearson correlation coefficient is 0.94. Both numbers are the highest during the first week of the game release. In case of A, 4 million users joined the game and sent out 58 million invitations only in the first week. In contrast to the explosive growth in the early stage, both numbers drop exponentially (the y-axis of the graph is in log scale) over time. The dotted vertical lines represent reward resets. Even with the reward resets, the numbers of invitations and new sign-ups decrease by two orders of magnitude in 20 weeks after the initial release.

How does the quota-based reward scheme bring explosive user growth in the beginning? How does the user growth slow down exponentially over time? How do the inviters and invitees affect the diffusion dynamics? We answer these questions one by one in the following sections.

3. INVITER'S BEHAVIOR

3.1 Invitation Rate and Count

How do the quota-based reward schemes affect the invitation behavior? We begin by examining the *invitation rate*, the proportion of inviters among signed-up users, and the *invitation count*, the number of friends an inviter invites to a game. The reward scheme is not the only factor that affects the invitation behavior. For example, the player population of a game can limit invitation because users cannot invite friends who already signed up. Also, the reward resets that clear the quotas can stimulate invitations by encouraging users who have reached the maximum quota previously.

To observe the invitation behavior at an early stage with no reward reset, we use only the first 28 days of data after the sign-up for the first 100,000 users. Table 3 summarizes the statistics. The invitation rates vary from a low of 30% to a high of 90%, corresponding to popularity of the games. However, all the games show similar invitation count statistics, as they have similar reward schemes. For all four games, the median of invitation count is exactly 30, and the average and the 3rd quartile are also around 30, which is the maximum quota.

	Invitation Rate		Invitation Count			
	n_{user}	n_{inviter}	1Q	Avg.	Med.	3Q
A	100K	87K	30	28.9	30	31
B	100K	40K	20	30.2	30	31
C	100K	32K	20	27.2	30	30
D	100K	31K	20	28.8	30	30

Table 3: Invitation rate and count statistics from the first 28 days of data after the sign-up for the first 100,000 users.

In Figure 2, we plot the complementary cumulative distribution function (CCDF) of the invitation count for each game. The CCDFs show marked discontinuations at quotas of the games. A is the most popular game with the total of 13 million signed-up users, and 75% of its users sent out the maximum quota or more. In all four games, more than half of the inviters have sent out equal to or more invitations than the maximum quota of 30. Beyond the maximum quota, A offers no more reward, while the other games give away a coin[2] per invitation. Possibly due to the coins, games other than A have heavy inviters who sent out hundreds of invitations.

So far, we have seen the invitation behavior at the early stage. How does the invitation behavior change over time, with growing gamer population and reward resets? In Fig-

[2]Users play a game with a coin. (Usually,) a user gets a free coin every 10 minutes, but cannot accumulate more than 5 coins at any point. When a user runs out of coins, the user must wait until a refill or purchase coins to continue playing.

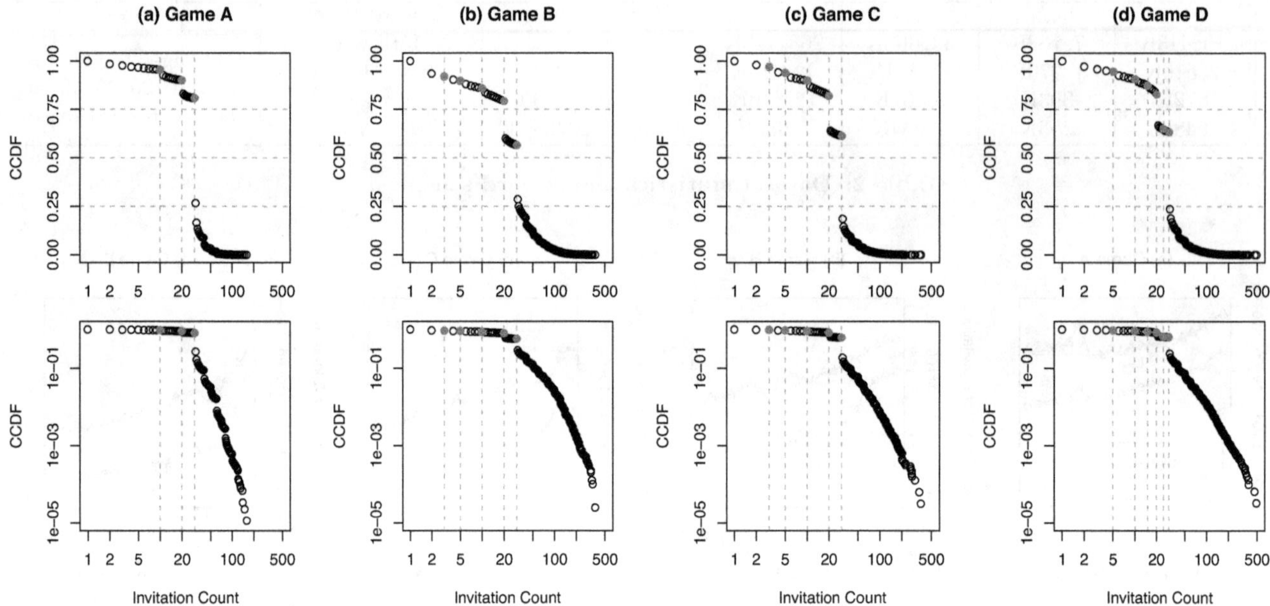

Figure 2: CCDF of invitation counts of the first 100,000 users in the first 28 days after each user's sign-up.

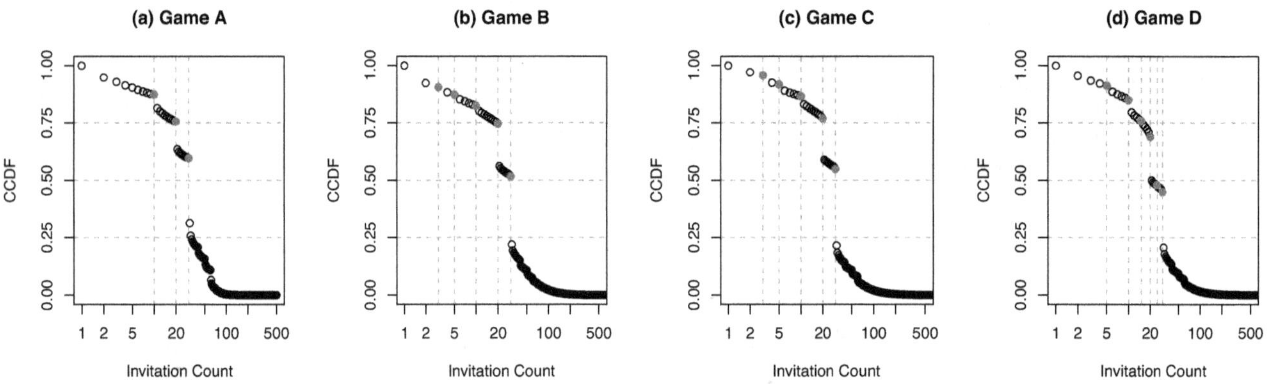

Figure 3: CCDF of invitation counts of all users in 20 weeks.

ure 3 we inspect the CCDFs of all users for the full 20 weeks of data. The percentage of users who have sent out equal to or more invitations than the maximum quota in game A decreases from 80% in Figure 2(a) to 60% in Figure 3(a). In the other games with less user growth, the drops are smaller but still manifest. The later a user joins a game, the more likely the user's friends have already signed up for the game and the more limited the user is in the choices of invitations. Thus less percentage of users have fulfilled the maximum quota of invitations compared to Figure 2. As the invitation count is reset to 0, users who have reached the maximum quota previously are encouraged to invite more. As a result in game A with reward intervals of 10, additional discontinuations appear between 30 and 60 in Figure 3.2(a).

Many types of human interaction, such as phone calls, e-mails, sexual relationships, and OSN friendships follow power-law distribution [1, 11, 17]. Recent studies of friend invitation counts report highly skewed distributions similar to power-law [18, 22]. Also, person-to-person product recommendations show power-law [16]. In our datasets there are a good number of users who continue to invite beyond the maximum quota of rewards. Unsurprisingly, the tails of the CCDFs in Figures 2 display power-law behavior.

The reward scheme alone does not motivate users to start inviting friends as the proportion of inviters varies from a game to another. Yet, we confirm that the quota-based reward scheme is quite effective in pushing users to invite up to the quotas, irrespective of game popularity. That is, *motivated* users who found the game interesting enough to entice friends and made up their minds to invite friends max out invitations to get rewards. Therefore we conclude that quota-based reward schemes are effective in exposing the game to a great user population, often 5x or more than the signed-up users as shown in Table 2.

3.2 Invitee Selection

Now, how do users select whom to invite? There is a trade-off between the cost of invitation and reward, where the cost includes emotional pressure for sending unsolicited messages to friends. How does a user minimize the cost? Here we present the following two possible strategies.

- **Strategy #1:** Users invite the same set of friends to different games repeatedly, thereby limiting the damage to a small circle of friends.
- **Strategy #2:** Users invite different sets of friends to different games, thus spreading the damage widely and imposing less on individual friends.

Which is a more dominant strategy? To answer the question, we examine the overlap between a user's invitees between games. For a user u who invites friends to games X and Y, let u_X and u_Y be the invitees for games X and Y, respectively. We define the user's invitee similarity for the game pair X and Y, $\mathcal{S}^u_{XY}$, as following:

$$\mathcal{S}^u_{XY} = \frac{|u_X \cap u_Y|}{\min(|u_X|, |u_Y|)}$$

Since users cannot invite friends who have already signed up for the game, the invitee selection can be severely restricted in popular games. A stands out among the four games with its popularity claiming 36% of all KakaoTalk users. To have a fair comparison of the user's emotional pressure, the two games under examination should have comparable rate of adoption. Therefore we exclude the game A in this analysis and consider only the remaining three.

For every pair of games, we select the users who have invited friends in both games. B and C have 179K common inviters, C and D have 55K, and D and B have 104K. Then we calculate $\mathcal{S}^u_{XY}$ for all three game pairs. Figure 4 shows the CCDF of the invitee similarities. For all three game pairs, about 80% of users invite more than 60% of same friends to two different games, and for about 50% of users more than 80% of invitees are the same. In summary, users are highly likely to invite the same set of friends to different games. Also, the distributions of users' invitee similarity for all three game pairs are analogous to each other.

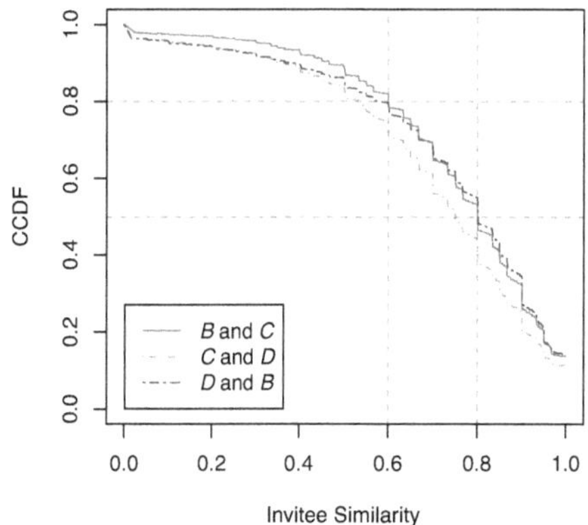

Figure 4: CCDF of invitee similarity.

Our observation above supports Strategy #1, but why do people use Strategy #1? One possible explanation is that gamers' preference to those games are similar. To examine the preference similarity among games, we compute the member and inviter overlaps between games as follows. Let $\mathcal{M}_{XY}$ be the member similarity and $\mathcal{I}_{XY}$ be the inviter similarity between games X and Y,

$$\mathcal{M}_{XY} = \frac{|\mathcal{M}_X \cap \mathcal{M}_Y|}{\min(|\mathcal{M}_X|, |\mathcal{M}_Y|)}, \; \mathcal{I}_{XY} = \frac{|\mathcal{I}_X \cap \mathcal{I}_Y|}{\min(|\mathcal{I}_X|, |\mathcal{I}_Y|)}$$

where $\mathcal{M}_G$ is the set of members in game G, and $\mathcal{I}_G$ is the set of inviters in game G. Not all members have invited friends, and thus $\mathcal{M}_G \supset \mathcal{I}_G$.

Table 4 summarizes the member similarities and inviter similarities among the three games, and compares them with average invitee similarities. The member and inviter similarities vary from a low of 0.2651 to a high of 0.5891. Yet, the average invitee similarity remains high, over 0.7. Therefore, we conclude that users invite the same set of friends, regardless of the preference for games.

X	Y	$\mathcal{M}_{XY}$	$\mathcal{I}_{XY}$	Avg. $\mathcal{S}^u_{XY}$
B	C	0.5214	0.4544	0.7529
C	D	0.3280	0.2177	0.7388
D	B	0.5891	0.2651	0.7022

Table 4: Similarities between games.

For the curiosity for the personal motivation behind Strategy #1, we conducted an informal survey among 50 gamers and 47 of them answered that they invite closest friends regardless of the game. We leave a rigorous user study for the motivation for future work.

3.3 Mental Mechanics of Inviters

If you are a compensation plan designer for a WOM marketing campaign with quota-based rewards, setting a proper quota is critical for the success. Too low a quota, for example, 5 friends to invite for the reward, may not bring enough exposure. On the other hand, too high a quota, for example 100, may actually discourage users and lead them to abandon the effort altogether. We investigate the time it takes for a user to invite friends to understand the mental mechanics of inviters.

In the previous section we have seen that most users invite the same set of close friends repeatedly. Then how big is the circle of close friends? Or to put it differently, how long does a person take to name the close friends? From the logs we mine the timestamps between invitations and plot them in Figure 5. The data points are grouped in 5 along the x-axis. The y-axis is the inter-invitation time between two consecutive invitations. The boxes represent the quartiles and the upper and lower marks represent the 5 and 95 percentiles of the inter-invitation time. Results from all four games are very similar, and here we only present the results from A.

Figure 5(a) pictures the inter-invitation time evolution of those who invited exactly 20 friends. The inter-invitation time dips if very minutely from the 5-th to the 10-th invitee in all three figures in Figure 5. We believe this slight decrease in invitation time is likely to be due to user's improved familiarity with the invitation mechanism. A conspicuous jump in the 95-percentile takes place from the 15-th to 20-th invitee in Figure 5(a). A bigger jump is from the 20th to 25-th in Figure 5(b). In Figure 5(b) the third quartile and median also increase, representing the extra mental cost users experience in listing 10 more friends beyond 20.

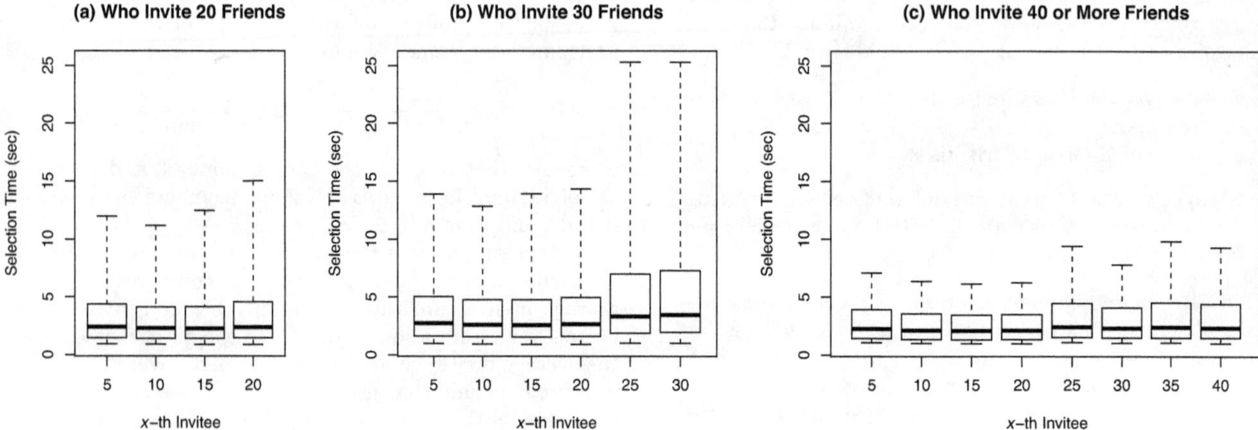

Figure 5: Time it takes an inviter to select x-th invitee in A. (a) For those who invited exactly 20 friends. (b) For those who invited exactly 30 friends. (c) For those who invited 40 or more friends. The x-axis is grouped in units of 5. The boxes represent the quartiles and the upper and lower marks represent the 5 and 95 percentiles.

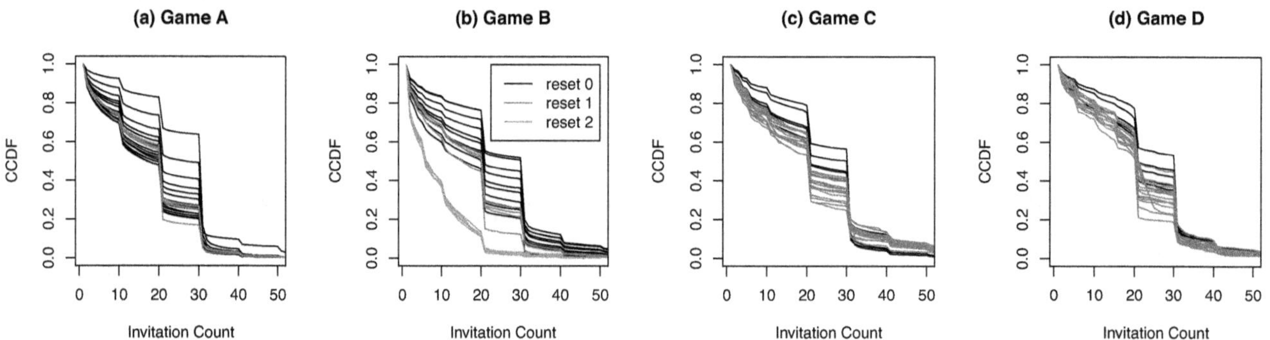

Figure 6: Weekly CCDF of the invitation counts. Black lines for the weeks before the first reward reset, red lines for after the first reward reset, and green lines for the weeks after the second reward reset for B (best viewed in color).

Apparently, those who invite beyond the maximum reward quota feel much less pressure about friend invitation. In Figure 5(c) for those who invite 40 or more friends, the selection time is much lower than the previous groups. Nevertheless, there is also a slight bump after 20. Thus we conclude that there is a mental hurdle somewhere between 21 to 30 in naming close friends.

Another angle to study the inviter's mental mechanics is to see the reaction to the quota over time. How has the user's invitation behavior changed? As more users sign up for the game over time, there remain fewer users to invite. Thus the number of friends a user invites should decrease over time. Is the change incremental? Figure 6 show the weekly CCDF of the invitation counts. As all games have had reward resets, we use black lines for weeks before the reset, and red for after.

During the course of our log collection, B had reset the quota in the 11th week and reset again with its maximum quota change from 30 to 40 in the 15th week. For B, we use a third color green for the weeks after the second reset.

For A, C, and D, graphs in black or weeks before the reset tend to be above the red lines. That is, the earlier users invite friends, the more they invite. In the case of B, we see a stark drop for the graphs in green. Since the second reset, almost no one has the heart to invite up to the quota and gave up around 20.

It is too premature to draw a conclusion on the mental capacity for human social networking from this data alone, and we only note the above as interesting observations that require further study.

4. INVITEE'S REACTION

Friend invitations arrive unsolicited, and that alone could trouble the invitee, whether it comes from a close friend or not. Worse yet, a user may get multiple invitations to the same game. It would be interesting to understand the user's reaction to multiple invitations. In this section, we analyze the invitee's reaction in 10,000 sampled invitees in C.

The response to social referrals has been studied in a few platforms, but the results are not consistent. In an online retailer's referral program, the probability of buying a book peaks at receiving two recommendations and then drops [16]. In an online social network experiment, the probability of adopting a health community activity increases up to four social signals [6]. In a social game diffusion case on Facebook, the probability of joining a game steadily increases as one gets more invitations [22].

All of the above studies only consider the number of incoming invitations per user. Yet, the temporal aspect in the invitation is another important factor. Receiving a number of invitations in a short period of time may be more attractive than receiving them staggered over time. Figure 7 shows the probability of signing up for C after receiving x invitations over time. When we do not consider the time interval between incoming invitations, the probability of joining decreases as one receives more invitations as in Figure 7(a), which is consistent to Leskovec *et al.*'s observation [16]. However, if we set the limit to a week, the probability of signing up for the game increases up to receiving 4 invitations, supporting Centola's observation [6].

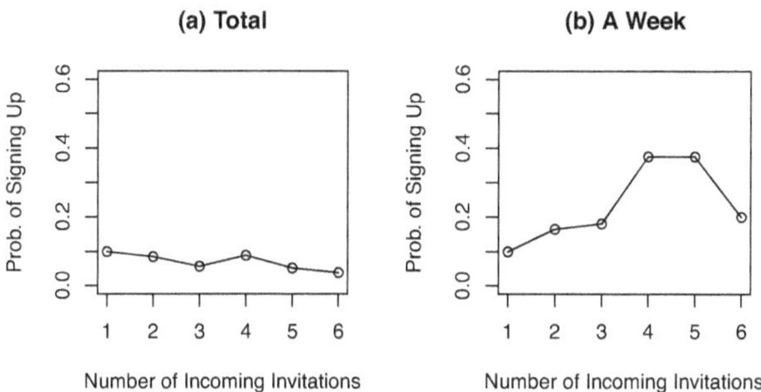

Figure 7: Probability of signing up given a number of incoming invitations for C. (a) In total. (b) In a week.

In Figure 7 we see that the time intervals between incoming invitations play a key role as well as the number of incoming invitations. In order to study the temporal aspect of invitations, we define $p(n, d)$ as the ratio of those who sign up over the total number of people who received exactly n invitations spanning d days. Then, $p(1, 1)$ means the ratio of sign-ups among invitees who received only one invitation. If $p(n, d) > p(1, 1)$, sending an invitation message to an invitee who received $n - 1$ invitations within d days is more effective than inviting a new person. If $p(n, d) < p(n-1, d)$, sending n-th invitation to an invitee is not that effective.

Table 5 shows $p(n, d)$ values, where the rows represent n and columns represent d. The first observation from the table is in a row the values increase when d decreases from right to left: invitations are more persuasive when they arrive in a shorter time span. Or for the same number of invitations, the longer it takes to receive them, the less likely the user signs up. At what point does it become not worthwhile to send an additional invitation? Using $p(1, 1)$ as the cut-off point, the dark shaded area represent the region of not effective invitation. If an additional invitation does not amount to the marginal utility of $p(1, 1)$, the invitation might as well be spent on a user never invited before.

More invitations for the same period of time do not always have a positive effect on the invitee. Except for $d = 1$, if the number of invitations goes over 4, the probability of sign-up starts to decrease. Why four invitations? Either

		d					
		1	2	3	4	5	≥6
n	1	10.0	-	-	-	-	-
	2	29.2	23.2	12.3	9.2	6.8	2.9
	3	83.3	20.7	16.7	12.2	6.7	2.0
	4	100.0	88.9	50.0	20.0	25.0	2.2
	5	100.0	85.7	20.0	-	-	-

Table 5: Table of $p(n, d)$, the percentage of those who sign up over the total number of people who received exactly n invitations spanning d days. The shaded area represents not effective invitations.

by coincidence or not, our number is consistent with that reported by Centola [6]. We envision the need for controlled experiments to verify the psychological threshold of four and leave it for future work.

Based on the observations in this section, game companies can improve the effectiveness of friend invitations. For example, they can put recently invited people on top of the friend list as long as they have fewer than four invitations from friends. As time passes and if a user has received four invitations or more, the user should be demoted off the top in the friend's list of the recommended.

5. PROPAGATION SPEED

Previous sections describe how inviters and invitees behave in the quota-based reward schemes. Now we begin to examine how quickly the invitations are sent out and propagated. Our datasets are well suited for the study of game propagation, because the invitation and the act of sign-up are both explicit and timestamped with millisecond accuracy. In this section, we investigate the diffusion speed of game C. We divide the invitation cascading process into three phases, and examine the distributions of the time intervals for the three stages.

- t_1: Time interval from receiving an invitation to joining the game. (If a user received multiple invitations, we consider only the last one.)
- t_2: Time interval from joining the game to sending the first invitation.
- t_3: Time interval between consecutive invitations sent by a user.

We plot the distribution of each time interval in Figure 8. In Figure 8(a) about 20% of the sign-ups occurred within an hour after the last invitation received, 50% occurred within a day, and 80% occurred within a week. It seems like the CDF is linearly proportional to logarithm of the time intervals, $F(t_1) \propto \log t_1$, implying $P(t_1) \propto 1/t_1$.

After joining a game, users start inviting in very quick succession. As shown in Figure 8(b), about 50% of inviters start inviting friends within 5 minutes after joining the game, while only about 20% of users invite friends half a day after sign-ups. Most of the users invite friends right after the tutorial or a few additional plays.

After sending the first invitation, the users send consecutive invitations in a bursty manner. In Figure 8(c), about 50% of the invitations occurred within 6 seconds from the previous one, and more than 90% occurred within 1 minute.

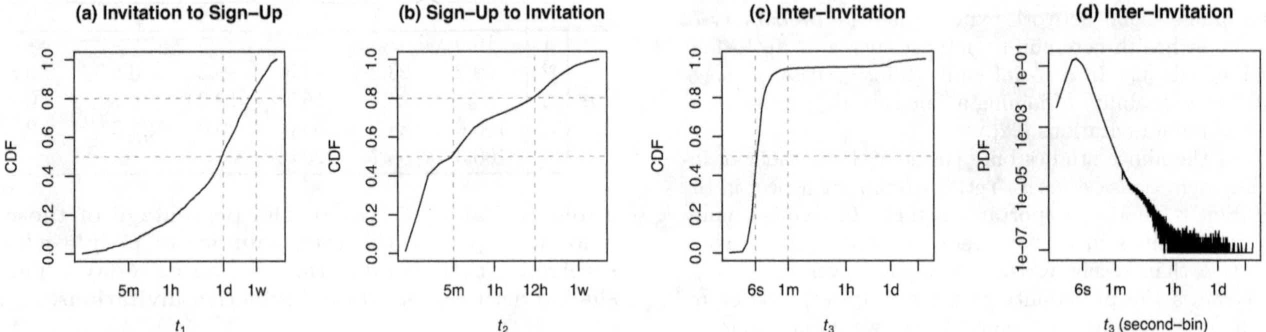

Figure 8: Timing of invitation cascading. (a) Time interval from receiving an an invitation to joining the game. (b) Time interval from joining the game to sending the first invitation. (c), (d) Time interval between consecutive invitations sent by a user.

As shown in Figure 8(d), the PDF of t_3 follows power-law, indicating that an individual's invitation pattern has a bursty nature. Barabasi models the bursty nature of human activities as a priority-based decision process [3]. In quota-based reward schemes, invitations up to reward quotas have high priority than the remainders. Users send several invitations during a single session in quick succession to meet the reward quotas, followed by a long period of no invitation activity. The immediate and bursty nature of the invitation behavior can be explained by the law of diminishing marginal utility. The utility of a reward is greater at the beginning of the game playing, because users have limited ability and experience to earn commodity such as game money or items.

Quota-based reward schemes not only motivate users to invite many friends, but also spur the pace of its propagation. This makes the explosive growth of the games at the very early stage, as we have witnessed new sign-ups and invitations occur in an explosive manner in the first week of the game launch as Figure 1.

6. CAUSES FOR SATURATION

In previous sections we have learned that friend invitations are a very effective mechanism for game advertisement and recruiting. However, the user growth soon reaches saturation regardless of the popularity (in Figure 1, new sign-ups decrease exponentially). Earlier studies characterize what drives ongoing WOM [4, 8, 10, 20], but none of them investigate what causes its termination. There are still millions of people not yet registered for the services, but why does the WOM spread no more? In this section, we study the causes for slowdown in the diffusion of the games, using data C.

The diffusion of the games arises from aggregation of each individual's decisions about the invitation. There are three decision points an individual faces. First, after signing up and playing a few matches, the user decides whether or not to invite friends. Then, the user decides whom and how many friends to invite. In next turn, each of the invitees decides whether or not to sign up for the game, and if so, the decision process repeats. To reveal where the slowdown occurs most at among the three decision points, we look at the temporal changes of the following measures.

- *Invitation rate*: what proportion of the signed-up users start inviting friends?
- *Average invitation count*: how many friends do the inviters invite on average?
- *Acceptance rate*: what proportion of the invitees actually sign up for the game?

Figure 9 shows the temporal changes of the invitation rate and the average invitation count for 10 weeks, and the acceptance rate for 3 weeks in C. Surprisingly, whenever users joined the game, constant proportion ($mean = 0.48, sd = 0.04$) of the users start inviting friends as in Figure 9(a). Also they invite a similar number ($mean = 24.21, sd = 1.32$) of friends on average as in Figure 9(b). However, the acceptance rate drops dramatically by the day. Invitees who did not sign up for the game are continuously exposed to additional invitations, while the signed-up invitees are not. This may cause the decreasing acceptance rate. Thus, we plot the acceptance rates for all invitees and new invitees who received the first invitation separately in Figure 9(c), and the acceptance rates for both groups drop rapidly.

With the sampled data, we could only check the acceptance rate for C. However, we show the time series of the invitation rate and the average invitation count of the other games in Figure 10. In A, the invitation rate decreases from 0.8 to 0.4, but still a significant proportion of users actually invite friends. The decreases in A arise from its popularity. Because most of the people have already signed up for the game, the users have limited friends to invite. Other games shows similar patterns to C, resulting in constant invitation rates and average invitation counts for ten weeks.

The result is striking because of the decrease in acceptance rate brings all the slowdown of diffusion. It is natural to expect that the termination of diffusion comes from a combination of three factors, but our analysis result points at only the acceptance rate.

One possible explanation for this result is homophilic nature of social network formation. In this incentivized WOM referral program, users invite closest friends as we have seen in Section 3.2. The diffusion of games may be initiated by a small number of the game fans at the beginning. Their close friends are likely to have similar preferences, and they are likely to accept the invitation. However the preferences

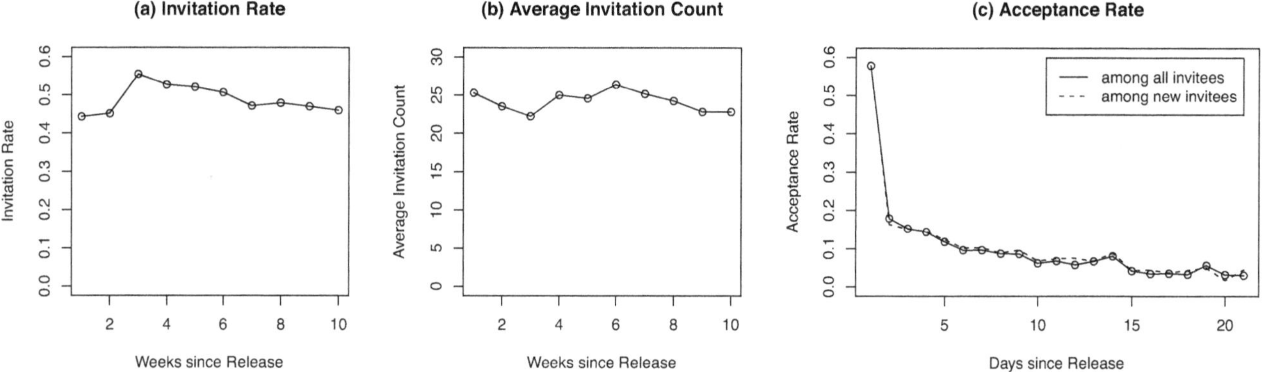

Figure 9: Time series showing the changes in the diffusion statistics of C. (a) The proportion of inviters among new sign-ups. (b) The average number of invitations a new inviter sent during a week. (c) The proportion of sign-ups among invitees. We plot the acceptance rate in daily binning to show its rapid decrease.

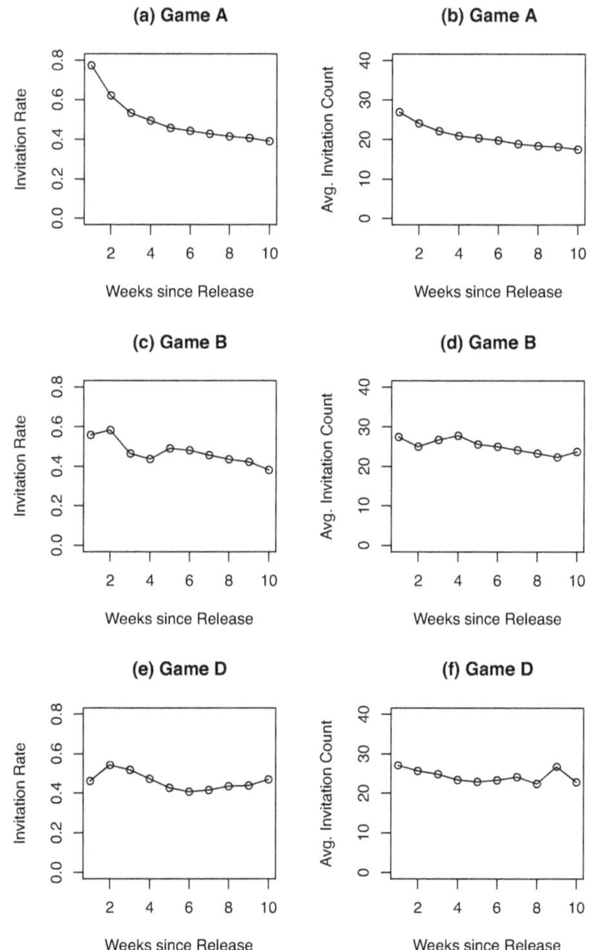

Figure 10: Time series showing the diffusion statistics of A, B, and D. (left) The proportion of inviters among new sign-ups. (right) The average number of invitations a new inviter sent during a week.

drop as the invitations spread through the network. Eventually, most of the incentivized friend invitation cascading terminates. Nevertheless, it is efficient and effective because it draws a large number of people explosively at the early stage of a game launch.

7. RELATED WORK

WOM marketing is attracting massive interest with emerging social platforms, but studies on the influence of WOM go as far back as decades. Earliest studies on WOM effect were survey-based, and reported that WOM affects not only purchase decisions, but also pre- and post-purchase perceptions [2, 12, 14]. Recently, the survey-based work begins to focus on the online and, in particular, the mobile environment [10, 20].

As OSNs have emerged providing venues for content sharing, a number of studies characterized content dissemination on OSNs. Guhl *et al.* studied information diffusion on blogspace based on keywords and links [13]. Cha *et al.* investigated the photo propagation on Flickr from favorite marking activities [7]. However, these works have limitation that they infer WOM rather than directly observe it.

Investigating direct WOM is rare because of the lack in public data. Leskovec *et al.*, reported an analysis of person-to-person recommendation via e-mail on an online retailer, as the first empirical study with large-scale data [16]. On the other hand, Centola designed an experiment about spread of behavior on artificially generated social networks [6]. With the recent advent of social platforms based on existing social networks such as Facebook, Wei *et al.*, studied diffusion of social games on Facebook platform via friend invitation [22].

8. CONCLUSIONS

In this paper, we analyze the user behavior and diffusion dynamics in friend invitation programs compensated with quota-based rewards.

The incentives motivate users to invite their friends up to reward quotas, only beyond which we start to see power-law tail behavior. Users tend to invite their closest friends to different genres of games, regardless of the game popularity or one's own preference. In general, users invite 20 friends *comfortably*.

The acceptance rate increases up to 4 incoming invitations, but more than 4 invitations are not effective. Also the time interval between multiple incoming invitations is critical to the success. Generally, 2 invitations within 3 days, 3 invitations within 4 days, and 4 invitations within 5 days are more effective than just a single invitation, and multiple invitations spanning longer than 5 days are regarded not as persuasive.

Once a user receives an invitation, the user signs up quickly, and starts inviting people in a few minutes. As they start inviting, the consecutive invitations are sent in a bursty manner, showing a power-law time interval distribution.

However, the diffusion of games soon terminates. We have found that only the acceptance rate decreases rapidly, but the invitation rate and the average invitation count remain constant. However, incentivized friend invitation still makes sense because it draws attention to potential sign-ups immediately after the game launch.

Mobile social platforms are growing rapidly. KakaoGame already has two-thirds of Korean population as registered users, and LINE and WeChat are following suit. Accordingly, understanding the user behavior in mobile social context has a far-reaching impact on marketing, psychology, sociology, and beyond. In this paper, we have analyzed a novel dataset from KakaoTalk mobile games. We have found practical insights for viral marketing which we hope will bring a new spin to the social network research community.

9. REFERENCES

[1] Y.-Y. Ahn, S. Han, H. Kwak, S. Moon, and H. Jeong. Analysis of topological characteristics of huge online social networking services. In *Proceedings of the 16th International Conference on World Wide Web*, pages 835–844. ACM, 2007.

[2] J. Arndt. Role of product-related conversations in the diffusion of a new product. *Journal of Marketing Research*, 4(3):291–295, 1967.

[3] A.-L. Barabasi. The origin of bursts and heavy tails in human dynamics. *Nature*, 435(7039):207–211, 2005.

[4] J. Berger and E. M. Schwartz. What drives immediate and ongoing word of mouth? *Journal of Marketing Research*, 48(5):869–880, 2011.

[5] F. A. Buttle. Word of mouth: understanding and managing referral marketing. *Journal of Strategic Marketing*, 6(3):241–254, 1998.

[6] D. Centola. The spread of behavior in an online social network experiment. *Science*, 329(5996):1194–1197, 2010.

[7] M. Cha, A. Mislove, and K. P. Gummadi. A measurement-driven analysis of information propagation in the Flickr social network. In *Proceedings of the 18th International Conference on World Wide Web*, pages 721–730. ACM, 2009.

[8] J. Cheng, L. Adamic, P. A. Dow, J. M. Kleinberg, and J. Leskovec. Can cascades be predicted? In *Proceedings of the 23rd International Conference on World Wide Web*, pages 925–936. International World Wide Web Conferences Steering Committee, 2014.

[9] E. Choi. Kakaotalk, a mobile social platform pioneer. *SERI Quarterly*, 6(1):63–69, 2013.

[10] S.-C. Chu and Y. Kim. Determinants of consumer engagement in electronic word-of-mouth (eWOM) in social networking sites. *International Journal of Advertising*, 30(1):47–75, 2011.

[11] A. Clauset, C. R. Shalizi, and M. E. Newman. Power-law distributions in empirical data. *SIAM Review*, 51(4):661–703, 2009.

[12] P. Fitzgerald Bone. Determinants of word-of-mouth communications during product consumption. *Advances in Consumer Research*, 19(1), 1992.

[13] D. Gruhl, R. Guha, D. Liben-Nowell, and A. Tomkins. Information diffusion through blogspace. In *Proceedings of the 13th International Conference on World Wide Web*, pages 491–501, New York, NY, USA, 2004. ACM.

[14] P. M. Herr, F. R. Kardes, and J. Kim. Effects of word-of-mouth and product-attribute information on persuasion: An accessibility-diagnosticity perspective. *Journal of Consumer Research*, 17(4):454, 1991.

[15] Kakao Corp. *Kakao Annual Report*, 2014.

[16] J. Leskovec, L. A. Adamic, and B. A. Huberman. The dynamics of viral marketing. *ACM Transactions on the Web*, 1(1):5, 2007.

[17] F. Liljeros, C. R. Edling, L. A. N. Amaral, H. E. Stanley, and Y. Åberg. The web of human sexual contacts. *Nature*, 411(6840):907–908, 2001.

[18] A. Nazir, A. Waagen, V. S. Vijayaraghavan, C.-N. Chuah, R. M. D'Souza, and B. Krishnamurthy. Beyond friendship: modeling user activity graphs on social network-based gifting applications. In *Proceedings of the 12th ACM Internet Measurement Conference*, pages 467–480. ACM, 2012.

[19] Nielsen Media Research. *Nielsen Global Trust in Advertising Survey*, Q3, 2013.

[20] W. Palka, K. Pousttchi, and D. G. Wiedemann. Mobile word-of-mouth: A grounded theory of mobile viral marketing. *Journal of Information Technology*, 24(2):172–185, 2009.

[21] M. Trusov, R. E. Bucklin, and K. Pauwels. Effects of word-of-mouth versus traditional marketing: Findings from an Internet social networking site. *Journal of Marketing*, 73(5):90–102, 2009.

[22] X. Wei, J. Yang, L. A. Adamic, R. M. de Araújo, and M. Rekhi. Diffusion dynamics of games on online social networks. In *Proceedings of the 3rd Workshop on Online Social Networks*. USENIX Association, 2010.

Beyond CPM and CPC: Determining the Value of Users on OSNs

Diego Saez-Trumper
Yahoo Labs
Barcelona, Spain
dsaez-trumper@acm.org

Yabing Liu
Northeastern University
Boston, USA
ybliu@ccs.neu.edu

Ricardo Baeza-Yates
Yahoo Labs
Barcelona, Spain
rbaeza@acm.org

Balachander Krishnamurthy
AT&T Labs–Research
Florham Park, USA
bala@research.att.com

Alan Mislove
Northeastern University
Boston, USA
amislove@ccs.neu.edu

ABSTRACT

Not all of the over one billion users of online social networks (OSNs) are equally valuable to the OSNs. The current business model of monetizing advertisements targeted to users does not appear to be based on any visible grouping of the users. The primary metrics remain CPM (cost per mille—i.e., thousand impressions) and CPC (cost per click) of ads that are shown to users. However, there is significant diversity in the actions of users—some users upload interesting content triggering additional views and comments leading to further cascades of action. Beyond direct impressions, a user's action can generate indirect impressions by actions induced on friends and other users. Identifying the valuable user segments requires examination of profile data, friendships, and most importantly, their activity. Here we explore an alternate approach for measuring the value of users in OSNs by proposing a framework from the viewpoint of a popular OSN. Using a real dataset on the social network and activities of users, we show that a small subset of actions are likely to be key indicators of a user's value. Additionally, by examining the current targeting demographics available in Facebook, we are able to explore the relative (monetary) value that different users represent to the OSN.

Categories and Subject Descriptors

I.6 [**Simulation and Modeling**]: Applications; J.4 [**Social and Behavioral Sciences**]: Sociology; H.3.5 [**Information Storage and Retrieval**]: Online Information Services—*Web-based services.*

General Terms

Theory, Measurement, Economics.

Keywords

Online advertising; Online social networks; User value

COSN'14, October 1–2, 2014, Dublin, Ireland.

http://dx.doi.org/10.1145/2660460.2660477.

1. INTRODUCTION

Online advertising underlies much of the economic basis of the Web today; many sites provide free services supported by advertising. Google—far and away the largest advertising network on the Web—reported over $50 billion in 2013 [15] in advertising revenue alone. Typically, advertisers place ads on Google by specifying keywords of interest; different keywords have different values with their market price determined via a dynamic auction. The cost to advertisers when using networks like Google is generally expressed in terms of CPM (Cost per Mille, or the cost of 1,000 ad impressions) or CPC (Cost per Click, or the cost to receive a single ad click independent of the number of impressions).

Recently, online social networks (OSNs) such as Facebook have also seen an advertising market develop. For example, Facebook's most recently quarterly report indicated advertising revenue of over $7.8 billion in 2013 [12]. Advertising on OSNs works in a manner similar to advertising on Google: advertisers specify targeting parameters (i.e., attributes that the advertisers desire users to have) and a CPM/CPC bid price, and the OSN ranks the ads to select the ones to be shown. The ranking is typically based on the bids and the click-through-rate (CTR) of the ad.

The strong similarity between advertising on the Web and OSNs is surprising given that OSNs are significantly different from a typical website or a search engine answer page. On Web-search-based ads such as Google, the ad network, by default, knows relatively little about the user. Instead, the network must track users using cookies and other techniques, extracting more information about users through data mining. For example, Google provides a significant number of services (e.g., email, calendar, etc.) to users, presumably to be able to gather additional information. However, in the case of OSN-based ads, users must have an account and be logged in, in order to even see ads. As part of participating in the OSN, users provide information about themselves in profiles (interests, identities of friends, demographics, educational history, etc.) and through interactions with the site (posting updates, "checking in", installing applications, etc.). Moreover, because the OSN is run by a single centralized entity, the OSN observes all user actions on the site.

We posit that users on OSNs have sharply different values—in terms of the revenue they generate through ad impressions—to both the OSN itself and advertisers. For example, influential users often have many friends, post significant amounts of content, and have their posts forwarded to many others; these users are likely to be more valuable than the average user. Such users are likely to bring more value to the OSN itself (as they afford more advertising opportunities) and to advertisers as well (as their activities offer more opportunities for the advertiser's message to be spread). However, little work has gone into studying how the value of users in OSNs varies, and determining the extent to which users' value contributions can be extracted, quantified, and presented to advertisers. Moreover, no one has come up with a framework for assigning different values to individual users; the focus is typically on aggregate user values.

We explore an alternate approach for measuring the value of users in OSNs such as Facebook via a framework for estimating their relative value. We do so from the perspective of the OSN operator, who both runs the advertising network and the OSN site. However, our analysis is constrained by the (very) limited visibility we have into the OSN's revenue (i.e., we are typically unable to know how many ad impressions each user receives, or how often they click on ads). Thus, we rely on the data available to us to parametrize our model, with the knowledge that the OSN operator likely has significantly better data available; this more accurate data could be used to further refine our model and the resulting predictions. It is worth noting that our goal is not to validate a specific model, but rather to propose a potential model and explore its feasibility given the limited data available to external observers.

We examine the wealth of information that the OSN operator receives about user activity on their site and present a methodology for reasoning about how different user actions correspond to revenue. We argue that a user's value can be divided into direct impressions (advertising opportunities that a user provides by browsing OSN site pages) and indirect impressions (advertising opportunities that a user provides by enticing others to browse OSN site pages). Indirect impressions can *cascade* via the network, where a user's actions ultimately cause other users to visit the OSN. For example, after one user uploads a photo, this action may cause her friends to log in to the OSN and view it (potentially causing more users to log in, etc.).

Having a proper understanding of the economic value of different users benefits both the OSN and advertisers. OSNs can enable targeting of such "more valuable" users, increasing revenues and making their advertising platform more attractive to advertisers. Additionally, uncovering the value of users will also benefit the users themselves, as they become aware of their relative value. In other types of networks, understanding which nodes are most central has proven quite valuable. For example, on the AS-level Internet topology, the peerings and traffic details of Internet Exchange Points (IXPs) were not widely known until recently [3]. It was revealed that each of largest European IXPs handles on a daily basis as much traffic as some of the global Tier-1 ISPs and supports a peering fabric that consists of more peering links than were previously believed to exist Internet-wide [32]. Locating high value users may likewise uncover a different microcosm in the OSN.

We explore our framework by leveraging a detailed data set from Facebook covering 90,269 users in the New Orleans metropolitan area [29]. We estimate the number of impressions attributable to users via activity, and show that users from our data set are likely to have sharply different values. We also show that our model can be extended to represent the user value in monetary terms beyond just the number of advertising impressions. We collect data from the Facebook Ads platform for each of the New Orleans users who have filled in basic demographic information, and use this as a basis for estimating revenue per user.

2. BACKGROUND

We now provide background on OSN advertising and cover work related to this study.

Facebook's Advertising Model. To study current advertising models in OSNs, we focus on Facebook, as it is the largest and most mature OSN. Facebook offers targeting parameters—such as location, gender, interests—and advertisers pay either per click or per impression for users who match the advertiser's specified targeting parameters. Although the parameters are quite detailed in terms of different demographics and interests, they currently do not relate directly to the target user's popularity or level of activity within the OSN (e.g., there is generally no mechanism for directly targeting "users who are influential").

The CPM and CPC ad prices are set through an auction, where each advertiser bids the maximum that she is willing to pay for impressions or clicks. Facebook selects the "best" ads to present to the user; while the ad selection algorithms are secret, the OSNs presumably use the highest bids in the case of CPM, or the highest expected revenues in the case of CPC (similar to the popular approach used in sponsored search advertisement auctions [17]). Thus, targeting parameters that are popular with advertisers are expected to have higher winning auction prices.

Information Diffusion. Much work has studied "influential" users in social networks; but deciding where to "seed" ads to reach the biggest possible audience remains a challenge. Social contagion has been studied from different angles: finding the set of users that maximize the probability of spreading [11], discovering topical authorities [31] or identifying trendsetters [26]. Other roles in the diffusion process include promoters [7], early adopters and imitators [5].

Beyond social contagion, cascading behavior is common in OSNs [9], and although the user's popularity does not necessarily create cascades [10], being popular is essential for direct influence [4] (popular users broadcast to a broader audience). Moreover, if we consider that cascades tend to be wider than deeper [25], the size of a user's audience (i.e., node in-degree) is key to estimating their value.

Auction mechanisms. Online advertising has been extensively studied due to its popularity and data availability [16, 30]. Researchers have studied the properties of advertisers [19, 23], and techniques for online advertisers to maximize their revenue [24]. Barford et al. [6] studied the features, mechanisms and dynamics of display advertising on the Web, demonstrating that a user's profile (i.e., browser and cookies) can have a significant impact on which ads are shown. Moreover, they demonstrated that the specific types of ads delivered generally correspond with the details of user profiles. Our work is complementary to these, as we focus on differentiating between more- and less-valuable users, rather than ad auctions or targeting. Beyond CPC and CPM [21, 22], there are other proposed pricing models [13, 14] that combine both (called impression-plus-click pricing). Other work has explored predicting the number of clicks—effectively, the CTR—for new ads [2, 18].

3. USER VALUE FRAMEWORK

Each page on the OSN that the user visits gives an opportunity to the OSN provider to show advertisements. As discussed above, the value of a user in an OSN is directly proportional to the number of advertising impressions and clicks that the user generates by their actions. The actions may be visible (such as uploading content or commenting on a friend's content) or invisible (such as visiting a friend's profile or browsing a friend's photos without commenting).

We call the advertisements shown directly to the user *direct impressions*. Thus, users who browse the OSN frequently are likely to generate many direct impressions. When a user perform actions that have effects visible to others in the OSN, the user has the potential to also generate *indirect impressions*. For example, a user commenting on a friend's photo may trigger other users to return to the OSN (thereby generating additional, indirect impressions). Thus, when more people browse the OSN as a result of one user's action, more impressions can be attributed to the action.

We argue that different user actions are likely to generate different numbers of impressions. The "place" where the action has been done (e.g., in the user's profile, friends' profiles, or on group/community pages) can result in generating different numbers of impressions.

Below, we propose a potential framework that considers all these factors and uses them to compute a user's value (in terms of the advertising revenue of the OSN that can be attributed to the user). First, we analyze why different actions produce different numbers of indirect impressions and how external observers or the OSN provider can measure this. Next, we show how users' characteristics and the places where they perform their actions affect their value. Finally, we propose a comprehensive methodology for computing users' values that can be applied to many OSNs.

3.1 The Value of Actions

Consider an OSN where the most common action is to browse photos of friends, but articles posted by friends are rarely read. In such an OSN, when a user uploads a photo, the user is generating more indirect impressions than by posting an article. The value of an action is thus related to the new actions triggered.

The primary challenge in measuring the value of actions is that many of the impressions cannot be directly observed; only the OSN knows when they occur and few OSNs provide visibility into how often other users browse content. An external observer, however, can estimate invisible actions, for example, by considering visible actions as a proxy for invisible actions [33]. Another option is to extrapolate this information from previous studies that have access to (private) invisible actions and show that most user activities on OSNs consist of visiting friend profiles and photos. We take this approach and use two studies [8, 28] that examined user's actions on popular OSNs. Each of these studies relied on clickstream data (e.g., records of requests to the OSN) in order to study how users spend their time in OSNs. Table 1 shows activity distribution of a large number of users in three different OSNs in these two studies. Although the actual distribution of user activities may vary with the OSN, we show in Section 4 that small variations in action value assignment are not likely to dramatically impact the final user value.

Facebook		Orkut		Hi5	
Category	Share	Category	Share	Category	Share
Home	35 %	Profile,Friends	41%	Photos	45%
Profile	16 %	Photos	31%	Profile	20%
Photos	16 %	Scrapbook	20%	Home	13%
Friends	4.7 %	Other	3%	Friends	13%
Groups	3 %	Communities	1%	Groups	1%

Table 1: Comparison of popular user activities across three OSN sites [8, 28].

3.2 Users Characteristics and Interactions

We next consider the information that external observers can collect to help estimate the value of users. Many OSN services make basic personal information provided by each user (gender, age, location, interests) public by default. It is also generally possible to obtain some information about the social graph, such as the number of friends and their identities. While the basic information is useful for targeting (e.g., an advertiser is targeting 30-year-old men in Barcelona), the latter is useful to estimate the indirect impressions. For example, when a user with thousands of friends posts an update, the user is broadcasting information to a wider audience than a user with only a few friends. As a user's friends tend to be similar in demographics and tastes to the user [1], it is conceivable that most of the indirect impressions would be shown to a similar target group.

3.3 Measuring User Value

We now present a framework for measuring the relative values of users, and begin by defining the value of user characteristics, activities, and friends' activities:

User characteristics (u_c): This term measures individual user characteristics and is composed of two elements: the targeting parameters t and the number of friends d (i.e., the user's degree). We can tailor t to a given target group; if the advertiser is seeking older demographics, t could be defined as being proportional to the age. If the target is related to a geographical location, t would be inversely proportional to (e.g., the logarithm of) the distance. All such targeting parameters can be combined depending on the advertiser requirements. Precision and granularity of targeting will depend on user's demographic information available on each OSN (for example gender, countries GDP, etc.). The second parameter d reflects the amplification of an action as a result of the direct audience reached by each user. To be conservative, we define d as the logarithm of the user's degree (as studies have shown that the fraction of a user's friends who the user interacts with is not a linear function of their degree [33]). Hence

$$u_c \propto t \cdot d \propto t \cdot \log(\#friends + 1) \tag{1}$$

Notice that this only captures the first hop on an activity cascade. The next hop will be captured by the activities of the users influenced by this user.

User activity in her own profile ($u_{a_{self}}$): This is a weighted sum of u actions (such as number of photos uploaded, number of articles posted, etc.) done by u in her own profile or home page.

$$u_{a_{self}} \propto \sum_i w_i \ \#action_i \quad (2)$$

where w_i is a weight proportional to the action value. Most likely, activities in a user's profile correspond to direct impressions.

Friends activity in a user's profile ($u_{a_{friends}}$): For all the users v that are friends with u, we measure their activity in u's profile. Given that each time v performs an action in u's profile this information is sent both to u and v friends by default (this can be changed through privacy settings but is rarely done), we weight all these actions by v's individual characteristics v_c:

$$u_{a_{friends}} \propto \sum_{v \in |u|} v_c \sum_i w_i \ \#action_i \quad (3)$$

As discussed earlier, most actions are reactive and thus most of them will correspond to indirect impressions.

User activity in their friends' profiles ($u_{a_{visitor}}$): When u carried out an action in her friends' profiles:

$$u_{a_{visitor}} \propto \sum_{v \in |u|} v_c \sum_i w_i \ \#action_i \quad (4)$$

As in the previous case, most of these activities will likely correspond to indirect impressions.

If we are targeting all users in the same way (that is, $t = 1$), then the final formula for the u_{value} is a function of her activity and her friends:

$$u_{value} \propto (u_{a_{self}} + u_{a_{friends}} + u_{a_{visitor}}) \ u_c \quad (5)$$

In Section 5, we analyze the case of the value of different users as per their different interests. Overall, the first weight captures mainly direct impressions while the other two capture mainly indirect impressions.

This simple definition could be extended to include different weights for friends based on tie strength (closer friends are more likely to see our actions and generate more impressions), privacy settings, and "circles" (groups of users see only partial information about our actions depending on our privacy configuration). Groups or community activity could also be included. However, an easy way to add group activity, is to consider the group as a friend, where all the group members would be friends of friends. Then, group activities can be included in the terms $u_{a_{friends}}$ and $u_{a_{visitor}}$.

4. APPLYING USER VALUE

Having defined a framework for reasoning about the value of users to the OSN, we now apply our model on a real OSN dataset. The goal is to explore how the relative value is distributed by our model across users, and how different strategies to measure invisible actions affect these results.

4.1 Dataset Description

We use a 2009 dataset collected from Facebook covering users in New Orleans [29]. We only consider the 50,564 users with public profiles out of the 90,269 users. As we are interested in classifying users by their interests and demographics, we use only those who share their age and gender, have at least one interest, and have at least one "post" on their wall. Most of the users divulge gender and age but only 23,950 users have at least one interest and an even smaller number (7,054) users have any posts.

4.2 Choosing Weights

Facebook's users can share different types of posts (status updates, posts, URLs, etc.), upload multimedia content (photos, videos), and perform actions within communities (join a group, event, fan page, etc.). To simplify our analysis, we group all these actions in three categories: posts, multimedia, and communities. We need a way to define the weights w_i described in Section 3 for each of these groups. This is difficult because the invisible actions (e.g. watching a video without leaving any comments) are unknown to external observers. Of course, the OSN operator is privy to much more detailed information and could likely derive many of the weights from the traces of user activity. Instead, we rely on externally-visible information in order to estimate the rough values of the weights.

Previous studies (see Table 1) have shown that visiting friend's profiles (corresponding to our "posts" category) is the most frequent activity, followed by browsing photos (multimedia), while group or community actions are infrequent. Although this ordering is consistent among different OSNs, the percentage of time spent in each category varies (e.g people spent 45% browsing photos in Hi5 vs only 16% on Facebook). Thus, we need to study the sensitivity of u_{value} to different w_i values. To understand how these weights affect the results, we can check to see if correlation among these three groups of actions is high, indicating that the weights are less important. If user's activities are equally distributed, weights are less important, because the numbers of actions ($\#action_i$) will be proportional.

We found a strong correlation between posts and multimedia actions but a lower correlation between multimedia and communities. Users uploading significant multimedia content are thus also creating many "wall posts" but do not necessarily engage in group activities. Thus, we normalize by the three categories of actions and group "home", "profile" and "friends" activities in the posts category; we then assign weights of 0.75 for posts, 0.21 for multimedia, and 0.04 for communities.

4.3 Value Distributions

Next, we want to study how value is distributed among users after applying our model and how they are related to user attributes (age, gender, and interests). Our hypothesis is that the number of impressions (i.e. value) generated by each user varies over a wide range. We expect a small fraction of users to create a lot of impressions and many users generating only a handful.

To test our hypothesis, we first compute the value for each user in our dataset. Next, we normalize these values, with 1 being the most valuable user. Not too surprisingly, we found users' value distribution is Zipfian, confirming our hypothesis that a small subset generates most of the impressions.

Next, we identify the high value users. In our experiment, we are considering all the users in our New Orleans dataset as the target group. Thus, t in equation 1 does not depend on age, gender or interests and so u_c only depends on the number of friends. We want to compute a generic value that allows us to compare the impressions generated by different demographic groups. For example, do women generate more

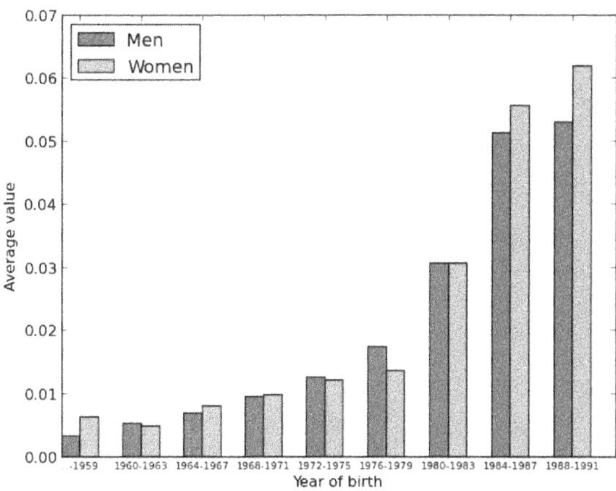

Figure 1: Users' relative value predicted by our model, broken down by age and gender. Younger users appear to be significantly more valuable, largely due to their higher level of activity.

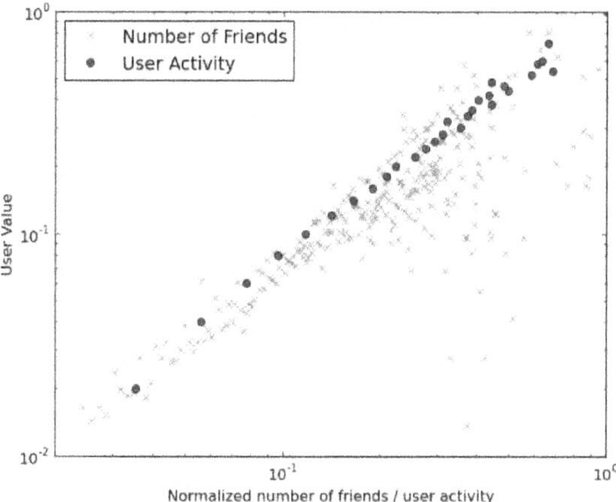

Figure 2: User's value vs. number of friends and activity.

impressions than men? We find that women are more valuable in our model than men, and young people generate more impressions than more mature users (see Figure 1). Given that the difference between the least valuable group (males born after 1959) and the most valuable group (women born between 1989-1991) is less than 10%—with large standard deviation in each group—we can assume that high and low value users are spread across different demographic groups.

A previous study [27] suggests that there is a strong correlation between the number of friends and user activity; users that post/upload more information have more friends. Our experiments show that popular users are more active and valuable (see Figure 2), which is partly a consequence of using friends and activity to compute the user's value. However the correlation is much higher for the activity than for the number of friends; activity produces impressions while the number of friends is only a potential amplifier of activity.

5. FROM VALUE TO REVENUE

The model that we have proposed and evaluated so far has considered ad impressions as the metric for valuing users, as OSNs are typically ad-supported. However, we would also like to be able to reason about the actual (monetary) value of each user so that the OSN provider and advertisers can determine which users are profitable. The mechanism we propose here is only one way of doing so; there may be others that are more attractive if additional data is available.

5.1 Using Ad Auction Data

To map user value to revenue we need to translate ad impressions to monetary revenue. An approach that assumes that all ad impressions provide equal revenue is unrealistic as certain user attributes are likely to be much more valuable (i.e., we know that there are certain demographics that are much more valuable to advertisers, and users in different countries are likely to provide significantly different revenue). Fortunately, Facebook provides advertisers with a "suggested bid" [20] for a given set of targeting parameters; this suggested bid is expressed as a range (min, median, and max) over the current bids for the target demographic. Thus, for a given user, we can determine the current revenue that Facebook receives for each ad impression shown to that user by querying for the suggested bid.

5.2 Collecting Data

To demonstrate this approach in practice, we use the same Facebook New Orleans data set from 2009 from Section 3. For each of the users, we extract as many profile attributes as possible, including basic attributes like gender and age, and free-form attributes like user interests. Recall that we only consider users who provided their age, gender, and at least one interest; leaving us with 7,054 users. We map each of the free-form interests to Facebook's "precise interests"; we found a match to a Facebook-supported interest category 60.4% of the time (4,265 users).

We query Facebook's Ads platform for the suggested bid of each of the 4,265 users, using *all* available targeting parameters [20]. For users with multiple interests that we could match, we queried multiple times (once for each interest).

Examining the bid data, we make two interesting observations. First, the distribution is remarkably even, with the CPC of 99% of users' interests ranging between \$0.62 and \$1.53 and the CPM for 99% of users' interests ranging between \$0.07 and \$0.31. This suggests that there are not specific interests that are significantly more highly valued by advertisers than others. Second, we observe that the prices are quite stable over time (see an example in Figure 3), indicating that our methodology is likely to hold over at least short periods of time.

5.3 Putting It All Together

We demonstrated in the previous section that a user's value (in terms of ad impressions) can be modeled based on the user's actions. Here we showed that these ad impressions can be translated into actual revenue received by the OSN. Now, we use the New Orleans data set to estimate the potential ad revenues brought in by the different users (i.e., we estimate the value of the users to Facebook). To do so, we first use the model of user value to assign credit for ad impressions to different users. Then, we use the advertising revenue for each user, and translate credit for ad impressions to credit for revenue (basically, using a different t per user).

We present the results in Figure 4. Recall that for users with multiple interests, we obtained multiple CPM/CPC

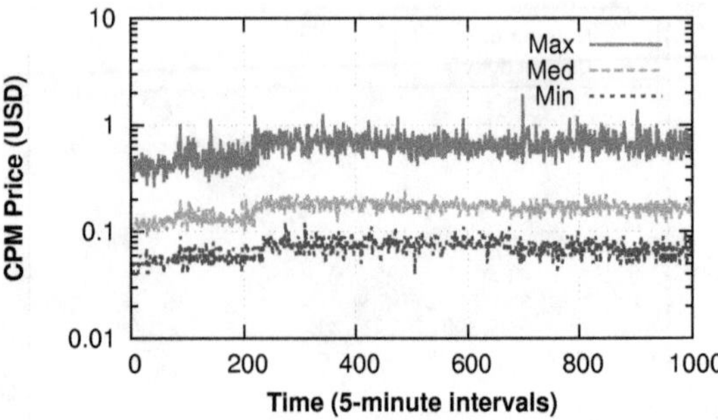

Figure 3: Facebook's suggested CPM bids from one particular set of parameters over three days, showing price stability over time (note y-axis in log-scale).

values (one for each interest). We present two separate means of aggregating these values together for such users: (a) we *average* of all of their interest prices together and (b) we *sum* all of their interest prices together (e.g. the overall potential value of a user). Since most users have only one matched interest, the two cases do not differ significantly.

We observe that there is a surprisingly wide variety in the user value to the OSN. For example, there are users who are over 10,000 times more valuable than other users. In fact, over 95% of the users have a value of less than one-tenth of the most valuable users. This result suggests that the value of different users to the OSN is quite different, and that it would be beneficial for both the OSN and advertisers to focus more on these highly valuable users.

6. CONCLUDING DISCUSSION

Popular OSNs provide "free" access to users in return for revenue generated by advertising impressions shown to them. We explored how different classes of actions result in different advertising impression counts and corresponding revenue. Implicitly, our goal was to demonstrate through our model that users on OSNs have an intrinsic value that varies with the extent of their participation on OSNs. Our two-stage approach first identifies the actions that are key to generating direct and indirect impressions. We then map these actions to actual revenue, showing the feasibility using real-world data sets. Our model is extensible, applicable to other OSNs and adaptable to alternate revenue mapping.

The results of our initial study are intriguing: a small subset of actions on OSNs are responsible for most of the advertising impressions, and a small fraction of users are key to the overall advertising revenue. Identifying these users can benefit OSNs (who may provide more services for such users), advertisers (who can target the more valuable users directly), and users (who will have understand how their actions are actually valued on OSNs). We can imagine an economic *modus vivendi* where there is an explicit trade between user's actions and profile information and the resulting service from the OSN.

Limitations. Our work has several limitations, starting with the heuristic nature of our proposed model and the assignment of parameters. Both of these are due to limited data availability on the actual views and clicks in the OSN. With better data, we could include additional activities and better parametrize the model. Additionally, validating the proposed model also requires data (such as more detailed breakdowns of the advertising revenue) that is currently in the possession of the OSNs. We leave addressing both of these to future work.

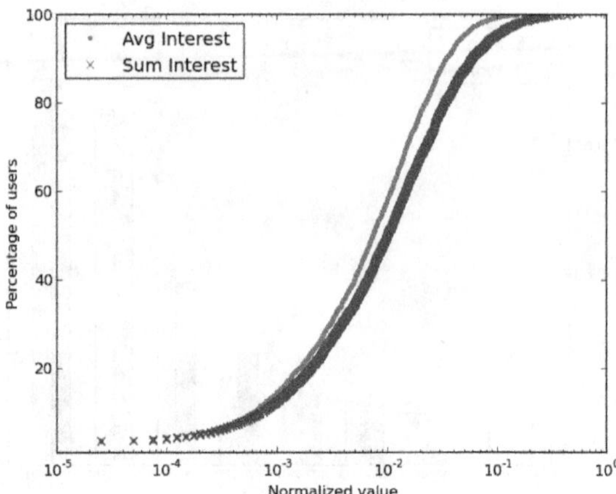

Figure 4: Average and potential (sum) value of users as per their interests and the advertising bids.

Leveraging user value. While advertisers are clearly interested in the value of users, we believe that it is actually the OSN provider who is best positioned to make direct use of this knowledge. This is due to three reasons: First, the OSN provider is clearly best able to make accurate estimates of user value; the provider observes all user activity, and typically only makes a portion (if any) available to advertisers or other third-parties. Second, the OSN provider is able to encourage "high value" behavior by its users by directly rewarding them or by more prominently featuring the more highly valued friends. By doing this, the OSN increases the value of all users and by proxy the OSN platform itself, and also encourages emulation by other users. Third, the OSN provider is able to charge higher prices for advertising to such users, providing benefits for both advertisers and the provider. Note that users can also benefit by becoming aware of their relative value.

7. REFERENCES

[1] P. Adams. *Grouped: How Small Groups of Friends Are the Key to Influence on the Social Web.* Voices That Matter. Pearson Education, 2011.

[2] V. Aksakallı. Optimizing direct response in internet display advertising. *Electron. Commer. Rec. Appl.*, 11(3):229–240, May 2012.

[3] B. Augustin, B. Krishnamurthy and W. Willinger. Ixps: Mapped? In *IMC*, 2009.

[4] E. Bakshy, J. M. Hofman, W. A. Mason and D. J. Watts. Everyone's an influencer: quantifying influence on twitter. In *WSDM*, 2011.

[5] E. Bakshy, B. Karrer and L. Adamic. Social influence and the diffusion of user-created content. In *EC*, 2009.

[6] P. Barford, I. Canadi, D. Krushevskaja, Q. Ma and S. Muthukrishnan. Adscape: Harvesting and analyzing online display ads. In *WWW*, 2014.

[7] F. Benevenuto, T. Rodrigues, V. Almeida, J. Almeida and M. Gonçalves. Detecting spammers and content

promoters in online video social networks. In *SIGIR*, July 2009.

[8] F. Benevenuto, T. Rodrigues, M. Cha and V. Almeida. Characterizing user behavior in online social networks. In *IMC*, 2009.

[9] M. Cha, F. Benevenuto, Y.-Y. Ahn and K. P. Gummadi. Delayed information cascades in Flickr: Measurement, analysis, and modeling. *Computer Networks*, 56(3):1066–1076, 2012.

[10] M. Cha, H. Haddadi, F. Benevenuto and K. P. Gummadi. Measuring User Influence in Twitter: The Million Follower Fallacy. In *ICWSM*, 2010.

[11] P. Domingos and M. Richardson. Mining the network value of customers. In *KDD*, 2001.

[12] J. Edwards. Facebook shares surge on first ever $1 billion mobile ad revenue quarter, 2013. http://www.businessinsider.com/facebook-q4-2013-earnings-2014-1.

[13] A. Goel and K. Munagala. Hybrid keyword search auctions. In *WWW*, 2009.

[14] S. Goel, S. Lahaie and S. Vassilvitskii. Contract auctions for sponsored search. In *WINE*, 2009.

[15] Google. 2013 financial tables, 2013. http://investor.google.com/financial/2013/tables.html.

[16] S. Guha, B. Cheng and P. Francis. Challenges in measuring online advertising systems. In *IMC*, 2010.

[17] B. J. Jansen, T. Flaherty, R. A. Baeza-Yates, L. Hunter, B. Kitts and J. Murphy. The components and impact of sponsored search. *IEEE Computer*, 42(5), 2009.

[18] A. C. König, M. Gamon and Q. Wu. Click-through prediction for news queries. In *SIGIR '09*, 2009.

[19] K. J. Lang, B. Moseley and S. Vassilvitskii. Handling forecast errors while bidding for display advertising. In *WWW*, 2012.

[20] Y. Liu, C. Kliman-Silver, B. Krishnamurthy, R. Bell and A. Mislove. Measurement and analysis of osn ad auctions. In *COSN*, 2014.

[21] Y. Moon and C. Kwon. Online advertisement service pricing and an option contract. *Electron. Commer. Rec. Appl.*, 10(1):38–48, Jan. 2011.

[22] H. Nazerzadeh, A. Saberi and R. Vohra. Dynamic cost-per-action mechanisms and applications to online advertising. In *WWW*, 2008.

[23] C. Perlich, B. Dalessandro, R. Hook, O. Stitelman, T. Raeder and F. Provost. Bid optimizing and inventory scoring in targeted online advertising. In *KDD*, 2012.

[24] A. Radovanovic and W. D. Heavlin. Risk-aware revenue maximization in display advertising. In *WWW*, 2012.

[25] T. Rodrigues, F. Benevenuto, M. Cha, K. Gummadi and V. Almeida. On word-of-mouth based discovery of the Web. In *IMC*, 2011.

[26] D. Saez-Trumper, G. Comarela, V. Almeida, R. Baeza-Yates and F. Benevenuto. Finding trendsetters in information networks. In *KDD*, 2012.

[27] D. Saez-Trumper, D. Nettleton and R. Baeza-Yates. High correlation between incoming and outgoing activity: a distinctive property of OSNs? In *ICWSM*, 2011.

[28] F. Schneider, A. Feldmann, B. Krishnamurthy and W. Willinger. Understanding online social network usage from a network perspective. In *IMC*, 2009.

[29] B. Viswanath, A. Mislove, M. Cha and K. P. Gummadi. On the Evolution of User Interaction in Facebook. In *WOSN*, 2009.

[30] Y. Wang, D. Burgener, A. Kuzmanovic and G. Maciá-Fernández. Understanding the network and user-targeting properties of web advertising networks. In *ICDCS*, 2011.

[31] J. Weng, E.-P. Lim, J. Jiang and Q. He. Twitterrank: finding topic-sensitive influential twitterers. In *WSDM*, 2010.

[32] W. Willinger, B. Ager, N. Chatzis, A. Feldmann, N. Sarrar and S. Uhlig. Anatomy of a large european ixp. In *SIGCOMM*, 2012.

[33] C. Wilson, A. Sala, K. P. Puttaswamy and B. Y. Zhao. Beyond social graphs: User interactions in online social networks and their implications. *ACM Transactions on the Web*, 6(4), 2012.

Price Trade-offs in Social Media Advertising

Milad Eftekhar†, Saravanan Thirumuruganathan‡, Gautam Das‡, and Nick Koudas†
†Department of Computer Science, University of Toronto
Toronto, ON, Canada
‡Computer Science and Engineering Department, University of Texas at Arlington
Arlington, Texas, USA
milad@cs.toronto.edu, saravanan.thirumuruganathan@mavs.uta.edu,
gdas@cse.uta.edu, koudas@cs.toronto.edu

ABSTRACT

The prevalence of social media has sparked novel advertising models, vastly different from the traditional keyword based bidding model adopted by search engines. One such model is topic based advertising, popular with micro-blogging sites. Instead of bidding on keywords, the approach is based on bidding on topics, with the winning bid allowed to disseminate messages to users interested in the specific topic.

Naturally topics have varying costs depending on multiple factors (e.g., how popular or prevalent they are). Similarly users in a micro-blogging site have diverse interests. Assuming one wishes to disseminate a message to a set V of users interested in a specific topic, a question arises whether it is possible to disseminate the same message by bidding on a set of topics that collectively reach the same users in V albeit at a cheaper cost.

In this paper, we show how an alternative set of topics R with a lower cost can be identified to target (most) users in V. Two approximation algorithms are presented to address the problem with strong bounds. Theoretical analysis and extensive quantitative and qualitative experiments over real-world data sets at realistic scale containing millions of users and topics demonstrate the effectiveness of our approach.

Categories and Subject Descriptors

I.1.2 [**Computing Methodologies**]: Symbolic and algebraic manipulation, Algorithms, Analysis of algorithms; J.4 [**Computer Applications**]: Social and behavioral sciences, Economics; G.1.2 [**Mathematics of Computing**]: Numerical analysis, Approximation

Keywords

Social advertising; Topic-based advertising; Alternate topics

1. INTRODUCTION

Online advertising is a multi-billion dollar business and has attracted a lot of attention among many advertisers all over the world. Online display ads are ubiquitous (e.g. popular on prevalent sites such as CNN, BBC, Reuters, blogs, search engines' result pages, etc.). Several methods are utilized to deliver ads, the most popular approach is keyword bidding. Popular web portals and search engines have created platforms (e.g., Google AdWords) to display online ads based on a keyword bidding methodology. Typically multiple people may bid on a keyword and an auction is held for each keyword. The advertiser with the maximum bid wins the auction and its ad is shown to users who search for that keyword.

COSN'14, October 1–2, 2014, Dublin, Ireland.

ACM 978-1-4503-3198-2/14/10 ...$15.00.
http://dx.doi.org/10.1145/2660460.2660462.

Social networks had expansive growth over the last decade. Facebook with over 1 billion users and Twitter with half a billion registered users are just two examples of successful social platforms hosting billions of messages posted every week. Users spend considerable time on social networks. Thus advertisers recently started to focus on advertising opportunities on such platforms.

Since time spent on social networks does not involve information search (keywords queries) but information production and consumption (generating posts, reading posts from social connections, and interacting with social connections), new models of advertising emerged. For example, recently Twitter introduced a new advertising platform [25] that provides advertisers several options for user targeting. One of them is to design advertising campaigns on specific topics (topic-based advertising). Utilizing this feature, an advertiser chooses a topic, places a bid value, and provides a tweet (called a "promoted tweet") to the system. If the bid is granted, the tweet provided is shown to a set of related users. In other words, the tweet is shown to a user (*appears in user's timeline*) if the chosen topic is relevant to that user. We say that these users are *targeted* by the chosen topic. Moreover, we refer to this set of users, as the *target set* of the topic. Similarly Facebook utilizes promoted stories with overall functionality related to that of promoted tweets.

Since social platforms have hundreds of millions of users, the type of topics in which these users produce or consume contents is expected to be highly diverse. In a micro-blogging platform for example, one would typically produce content on topics one knows well (maybe profess) and also consume content in topics one is interested in, by following other users who are producers of contents of such topics. Thus, if a user u is a producer (or consumer) of topics such as "soccer" and "computer science", we may target u by advertising on either "soccer" or "computer science". It is evident that there is not just a single way to target a user, but indeed, several ways exist utilizing different topics that are relevant to u.

Different topics have different costs however (exactly as different keywords have varying costs in the keyword based advertising model). Given that a user can be targeted possibly by multiple topics, an interesting question to ask is the following: Given a topic t with a target set S_t (the set of users targeted by t), is it possible to reach the same target set S_t by bidding on topics other than t in a more economical way? If that is possible and the new topics are less expensive compared to t, obviously this would be beneficial. We aim to identify a set of less expensive topics that target approximately (for a quantitatively measurable notion of approximation) the same set of users as the target set of t (i.e., they have approximately the same target sets). In doing so, we are interested to avoid targeting users outside S_t as that would not be beneficial. In particular we focus on a tight targeting model. Under this model, we aim to locate a set of topics with a target set as close as possible to t's target set. The key property is to prevent targeting users who are not in t's target set (e.g., users for whom t is not relevant). We penalize the method to avoid spamming these users. Therefore, a penalty cost (according to a *penalty cost function*) is associated with any instance of targeting a user outside t's target set. We aim to identify an alternative topic set R (obviously not including t) such that the number of users in t's target set that are targeted by at least one topic in R is maximized provided that the sum of the costs of topics in R and the sum of the penalty costs is not greater than a maximum budget.

The problem of identifying alternative topics is inspired by Twitter and Facebook advertising platforms. However, we would like to emphasize that as the details of these social advertising platforms are not known to public, the problem we discuss in this paper is a general problem and is *not* designed for or based on *any* specific social media platform including Twitter and Facebook.

Under this model, we show that if the penalty cost function is non-decreasing and convex, we identify solutions and propose algorithms with guaranteed approximation bounds.

Our techniques create a win-win situation for both advertisers and the advertising platforms. By providing more options (i.e., topics with approximately the same audience) for each advertiser to target, we prevent the situation where a single popular topic (that is very expensive) exists alongside several cheaper topics that no one bids on. Therefore by utilizing our techniques, more advertisers afford to target their desirable audience. Hence the revenue of the advertising platform may significantly increase (since more advertisers pay) while advertisers also obtain more savings per advertisement.

2. RELATED WORKS

Social based analytics: Many works have been done on micro-blogging platforms in recent years. Sankaranarayanan et al [24] use these platforms to identify breaking news as well as to consume news [17]. Micro-blogging platforms have also been used to monitor trends with novel applications such as predicting stock prices [23]. They have also been used to detect communities based on interests [14] or bursts [11] and to rank users based on their influence [27] within their community or based on their topical expertise [21]. Behavior of users on the social platforms and communities has also been studied [1, 19].

Advertising: Twitter has joined the likes of Google and Facebook to start an online advertising platform [25]. Recent research has shown that Twitter users respond favorably to advertising [6]. Broadly, existing work on social networks have studied three different types of advertising. The first is behavioral targeting [2, 29] where the aim is to show relevant advertisements based on user behavior over a given site or over a set of mutually co-ordinating sites. The second is influence based [4, 7, 18, 28] advertising. In this approach, the aim is to identify influential users whose tweets or posts serve as an endorsement influencing his/her followers to indulge in an activity. The final type of advertisement is topic based [8, 13, 16, 22, 27]. In this approach, advertisers bid on a topic and a promoted tweet is shown to users who are interested in the topic. In this paper, we focused on such an approach as it is closer to the Twitter advertising platform.

Set, Max and Budgeted Coverage Problems: From a theoretical perspective, our solutions are akin to the set cover and its variants - Max-Cover and Budgeted Set cover all of which have been proven to be NP-Complete [20]. Refer to [26] for a discussion on efficient approximation algorithms for set cover. Khuller et al., [15] proposed two approximation algorithms for the budgeted maximum coverage problem. We adopt these algorithms as a basis towards designing algorithms to address Problem 1. The online variant of set cover has been studied in [3] while [9] studied adoptions of the approximation algorithm for set cover to very large datasets. Bonchi et. al. [5] studied decompositions of a single query to a small set of queries whose result union approximates the original query result.

3. THE TARGETING PROBLEM

The online advertising platform offered by micro-blogging services enables advertisers to target users based on topics. The cost of advertising on different topics is, clearly, not the same. Some topics are costly since they are popular and attract the attention of advertisers, while some other topics are cheaper. On the other hand, a user may be targeted by many topics. If a user belongs to the target set of several topics, advertising on any of these topics will target this user.

Let U represent a set of users and T represent a set of topics. For a topic $t \in T$, let S_t represent the target set of t. The target set S_t is the set of users who are targeted by bidding on topic t. The target sets can be identified by different approaches such as user-defined lists [8, 10]. We note that the sets U, T, and the target sets S_t are inputs of the problem and can be computed by any means one prefers without changing any part of the problem and the algorithms proposed in this paper.

Let the cost of advertising on t be C_t. The cost of a topic depends on the payment method adopted. Two popular payment methods are *pay per impression* and *pay per click*. Utilizing *pay per impression* method, the advertiser pays an amount b_t (identified based on bid values) for each impression of its ad. In *pay per click* method, the advertiser pays an amount b_t when a user clicks on its ad. Assuming that the ad is shown to all users in the target set S_t, the cost of t is $C_t = |S_t| \times b_t$ in case of pay per impression technique and $C_t = |S_t| \times b_t \times f_t$ in case of pay per click technique. Here, f_t is the fraction of users in S_t who click on the ad.

Suppose one wishes to advertise on topic t with a budget of B at hand and $C_t > B$. Two cases exist. First, the cost C_t should be paid by the advertiser so that the advertisement carry on. Second, the ad of the winning bidder is shown to users in S_t till the budget is exhausted. In the former case, one cannot advertise on t as one does not have enough budget to do so. In the latter, one can target just a portion $\frac{B}{C_t}$ of the target set S_t, for both *pay per impression* and *pay per click* methods providing that users in S_t click on the ad uniformly at random.

Given that users can be targeted by multiple topics, a natural question arises. Is it possible to target more users in S_t by determining alternative topics without exceeding the budget? For example, one might conclude that when the goal is to advertise on topic "music", by choosing topic "wine" instead, we reach 70% of users in the target set of "music" while we pay half the cost of C_{music}.

By identifying these alternative topics, the advertising platform can provide the advertiser with multiple options to choose with different cost and coverage values. As explained in Section 1, providing these options is beneficial to both advertisers and the advertising platform. We note that the topics that are targeted by advertisers are unknown to the users. In other words, a targeted user u just sees the ad (e.g., the promoted tweet) and is unaware of the topic that is utilized by the advertiser to target u. Therefore, utilizing alternative topics leads to no change in users' experience. As a further step, an advertiser may choose to target the alternative topic while creating advertisements on events related to both the main topic and the alternative topic (e.g., events on "music & wine"). Our intuition is that adopting this strategy even increases the engagement of users on the ad, hence increasing the click through rate (compared to the case where the ad just talks about music), as the ad would excite users in $S_{music} \cap S_{wine}$ (users who are interested in both music and wine).[1]

We aim to identify topics to (1) target as many users in S_t as possible and (2) avoid targeting users outside S_t. More formally, we associate a penalty cost when targeting users outside S_t (*unwanted targeting*). This penalty, that aids to avoid spamming these users, depends on the number of users targeted outside S_t, and the number of times each of these users is targeted. Let $u \notin S_t$; assume u is targeted x_u times. We denote the penalty cost as $f(x_u)$. Such cost depends on the number of times u is targeted. The goal of this cost is to capture the intuition that if a user does not belong to the target set of t, it is not supposed to be targeted for content related to t. Therefore, each time u is targeted incorrectly, we associate a penalty. This penalty increases as x_u increases. In particular we associate a penalty with a positive marginal increase (i.e., an increase following a convex trend) when the number of times a user is targeted increases. We utilize a function $f(x_u)$ that is (1) non-decreasing (the penalty cost does not decrease as a function of x_u), and (2) convex (the marginal cost does not decrease as a function of x_u). The penalty cost function captures the intuition that the penalty incurred when targeting a single user u, say, three times when $u \notin S_t$ for a topic t is higher than that of targeting three users not in S_t for a topic t only once. A non-decreasing convex function is appropriate to capture this behavior. We aim to maximize the number of users targeted in S_t with the lowest cost possible.

Problem 1. Let T be a set of topics, t be a specific topic, S_t be the target set of topic t, and B be the budget. Let $f(x_u)$ be the penalty cost for each user where x_u determines the number of times that the user u not in S_t is targeted. Identify a set $R \subseteq T - \{t\}$ to maximize

$$|S_R \cap S_t|$$

subject to $C_R + C'_R \leq B$ where $S_R = \bigcup_{r \in R} S_r$ is the union of the target set of all topics in R, $C_R = \sum_{r \in R} C_r$ is the cost of targeting all topics in R, $C'_R = \sum_{u \in S_R - S_t} f(x_u)$ is the total penalty cost, and for any user u outside S_t ($u \in S_R - S_t$), $x_u = |\{r | r \in R, u \in S_r\}|$ is the number of times u is targeted incorrectly (the number of topics in R that u belongs to their target set).

A reduction from the Set Cover problem shows that Problem 1 is NP-hard even in a very simple case where there is no penalty cost and the cost of targeting each topic is 1. The reduction is as follows. Consider a universe U, m sets $A_1, \cdots, A_m$, and an integer k. The set cover decision problem aims to determine whether there exists k sets among $A_1, \cdots, A_m$ with a union equal to U. We create an instance of Problem 1. Let t be a topic with $S_t = U$. For each A_i ($1 \leq i \leq m$), let t_i be a topic in T with $S_{t_i} = A_i$, and $C_{t_i} = 1$. Moreover, let $B = k$ and $f(x) = 0$ for any x. The answer to the set cover decision problem is *yes* if and only if $|S_R| = |S_t|$.

[1]Validation of this intuition needs psychological experiments and is out of the scope of this paper.

We present two algorithms to address Problem 1 and identify set R. Section 3.1 explains TG, a faster algorithm that provides a $1 - 1/\sqrt{e}$ approximation factor. Section 3.2 presents TG3 that provides a tighter bound of $1 - 1/e$.

3.1 The Tight Greedy algorithm (TG)

Let t be the given topic, and *coverage* of any set $A \subseteq T$ be the number of users that are targeted in set S_t when advertising on topics in A. Thus, the coverage of set A is $|S_A \cap S_t|$ where S_A is the union of the target set of all topics in A. The main idea in TG is (1) to identify a set of topics R_1 by iteratively adding the topic t' achieving the maximum ratio of marginal coverage over marginal cost ($\frac{|S_{R_1 \cup \{t'\}} \cap S_t| - |S_{R_1} \cap S_t|}{C_{t'} + C'_{R_1 \cup \{t'\}} - C'_{R_1}}$) as long as $C_{R_1 \cup \{t'\}} + C'_{R_1 \cup \{t'\}} \leq B$, (2) to identify a topic $q^* \in T$ with the maximum coverage (i.e., $|S_{q^*} \cap S_t|$) such that $C_{q^*} + C'_{q^*} \leq B$, and (3) to report the set with the maximum coverage, among R_1 and $\{q^*\}$, as the set R. The pseudo code of TG is presented as Algorithm 1.

Algorithm 1: The Tight Greedy algorithm (TG) for alternative topic set identification

Input: t: the original topic,
T: the set of topics (not including t),
U: the set of users,
$S_{t'}$: the target set of any arbitrary topic t',
$C_{t'}$: the cost of targeting any arbitrary topic t',
$C'_{t'}$: the penalty cost of any topic t',
B: budget
Output: R^*: a subset of topics

$q^* = \arg\max_{q \in T} |S_t \cap S_q|$ s.t. $C_q + C'_q \leq B$
$R_1 = \{\}$
while *T is not empty* **do**
  $t^* = \arg\max_{t' \in T} \frac{|S_{R_1 \cup \{t'\}} \cap S_t| - |S_{R_1} \cap S_t|}{C_{t'} + C'_{R_1 \cup \{t'\}} - C'_{R_1}}$
  if $C_{R_1 \cup \{t'\}} + C'_{R_1 \cup \{t'\}} \leq B$ **then**
    $R_1 = R_1 \cup \{t^*\}$
  $T = T - \{t^*\}$
return $R^* = \arg\max_{R \in \{\{q^*\}, R_1\}} |S_R \cap S_t|$

As Algorithm 1 shows TG first identifies a set R_1 created by greedily adding the best available topic; second it identifies the topic q^* with maximum coverage; and finally it compares the coverage of these two options to identify the alternative topic set. A simpler algorithm that just identifies the set R_1 and reports it as the alternative topic set (we call it *simpleGreedy*) leads to arbitrarily bad approximation results as the following example clarifies.

Example 1. Assume the original topic is t with a target set of $S_t = \{u_1, u_2, \cdots, u_n\}$ and a very high cost. Suppose there exist two topics t_1 and t_2. Topic t_1 has a target set of $S_{t_1} = \{u_1\}$ and a cost of $C_{t_1} = 1$. Topic t_2 has a target set of $S_{t_2} = \{u_2, u_3, \cdots, u_n\}$ and a cost of $C_{t_2} = 2n$. Moreover, the budget is $B = 2n$. The *simpleGreedy* algorithm reports $\{t_1\}$ as the alternative set with a coverage of 1, while the optimal answer is $\{t_2\}$ with a coverage of $n - 1$. Thus, the approximation factor in this example is $\frac{1}{n-1}$. Clearly the approximation factor approaches 0 when n approaches infinity.

By comparing the set R_1 with the optimal topic q^*, we show that TG can lead to an approximation bound of $1 - 1/\sqrt{e}$.

THEOREM 1. *Utilizing any non-decreasing convex penalty function $f(x)$ in Problem 1 (i.e., $\frac{\partial f}{\partial x} \geq 0$ and $\frac{\partial^2 f}{\partial^2 x} \geq 0$), algorithm TG identifies an alternative topic set with an approximation factor of* $1 - 1/\sqrt{e}$.[2]

THEOREM 2. *The run time complexity of TG is $\mathcal{O}(|T|^2 \times |U|)$ where $|T|$ is the number of topics and $|U|$ is the number of users.*

PROOF. Line 1 takes $\mathcal{O}(|T| \times |U|)$ time since we measure the coverage of each topic; there are $|T|$ topics and calculating the coverage takes $\mathcal{O}(|U|)$ (note that the maximum size of a target set S can be $|U|$).

The while loop runs for $\mathcal{O}(|T|)$ iterations since in each iteration we remove exactly one topic from T and there are $|T|$ topics. In each iteration, we calculate the marginal increase in coverage and cost. This calculation takes $\mathcal{O}(|U|)$ for each topic. Hence, line 4 takes $\mathcal{O}(|T| \times |U|)$. The calculations in lines 5-7 takes $\mathcal{O}(|T|)$. Thus, The while loop in lines 3-7 takes $\mathcal{O}(|T|^2 \times |U|)$.

Overall, the run time complexity of TG is $\mathcal{O}(|T|^2 \times |U|)$. □

3.2 The Tight Greedy algorithm on a basis of 3 (TG3)

As Theorem 1 suggests the approximation bound of TG is $1 - 1/\sqrt{e}$. We can improve this bound utilizing algorithm TG3. The intuition in TG3 is to consider all sets of size 3, expand these sets greedily, and identify the set with the highest coverage. The algorithm TG3 (1) locates a subset R_1 of size not greater than 3 with maximum coverage such that $C_{R_1} + C'_{R_1} \leq B$, (2) locates sets R_2 that are created by iteratively adding topic t' achieving the maximum ratio of marginal coverage over marginal cost to any initial set of size 3 as long as the sum of the total cost and the total penalty cost does not exceed the budget B, and (3) reports the set with the highest coverage, among R_1 and all R_2 sets, as the set R. The pseudo code of TG3 is presented as Algorithm 2.

THEOREM 3. *Utilizing any non-decreasing convex penalty function $f(x)$ in Problem 1 (i.e., $\frac{\partial f}{\partial x} \geq 0$ and $\frac{\partial^2 f}{\partial^2 x} \geq 0$), algorithm TG3 results in an approximation factor of* $1 - 1/e$.

THEOREM 4. *The run time complexity of TG3 is $\mathcal{O}(|T|^5 \times |U|)$ where $|T|$ is the number of topics and $|U|$ is the number of users.*

PROOF. To identify R_1 we need to compute the coverage for any subset T with a size at most 3. There are $\mathcal{O}(|T|^3)$ subsets and for each subset it takes $\mathcal{O}(|U|)$ to compute the coverage. Hence identifying R_1 takes $\mathcal{O}(|T|^3 \times |U|)$.

To identify R_2, we need to expand all subsets of T of size 3 using the while loop. There are $\mathcal{O}(|T|^3)$ subsets. For each subset, the while loop runs for $\mathcal{O}(|T|)$ iterations. Each iteration evaluates all topics in T_{temp} that takes $\mathcal{O}(|T| \times |U|)$. Hence the second part of the algorithm (identifying R_2) takes $\mathcal{O}(|T|^3 \times |T| \times |T| \times |U|) = \mathcal{O}(|T|^5 \times |U|)$.

Therefore, the run time complexity of TG3 is $\mathcal{O}(|T|^5 \times |U|)$. □

4. EXPERIMENTS

We conduct a comprehensive set of performance and quality experiments using realistic, large scale datasets derived from Twitter. We first describe our dataset in Section 4.1, followed by quantitative results on the run time, coverage, and cost of all proposed algorithms in Section 4.2; qualitative results of their output are discussed in Section 4.3.

[2] Long proofs are omitted due to space limitations. Please see our technical report for these proofs [12].

Algorithm 2: The Tight Greedy algorithm on a basis of 3 (TG3) to identify an alternative topic set

Input: t: the original topic,
T: the set of topics (not including t),
U: the set of users,
$S_{t'}$: the target set of any arbitrary topic t',
$C_{t'}$: the cost of targeting any arbitrary topic t',
$C'_{t'}$: the penalty cost of any topic t',
B: budget
Output: R: a subset of topics

```
R_1 = arg max_{X ⊆ T & |X| ≤ 3 & C_X + C'_X ≤ B} |S_X ∩ S_t|
R_2 = ∅
foreach X ⊆ T s.t. |X| = 3 and C_X + C'_X ≤ B do
    J = X
    T_temp = T − X
    while |T_temp| > 0 do
        Select t' ∈ T_temp maximizing (|S_{J∪{t'}} ∩ S_t| − |S_J ∩ S_t|) / (C_{t'} + C'_{J∪{t'}} − C'_J)
        if C_{J∪{t'}} + C'_{J∪{t'}} ≤ B then
            J = J ∪ {t'}
        T_temp = T_temp − {t'}
    if |S_J ∩ S_t| > |S_{R_2} ∩ S_t| then
        R_2 = J
if |S_{R_1} ∩ S_t| > |S_{R_2} ∩ S_t| then
    return R_1
else
    return R_2
```

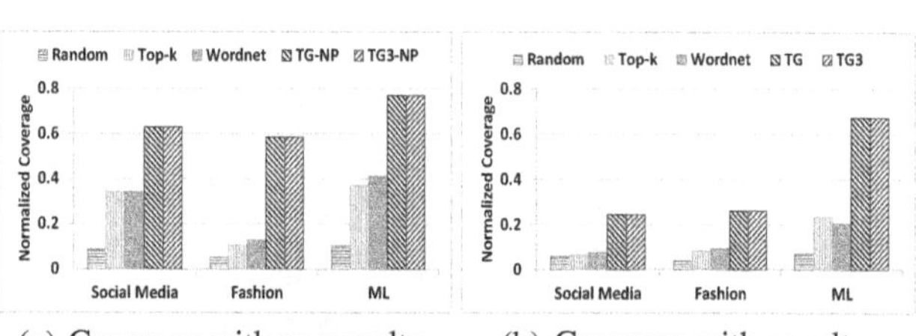

(a) Coverage with no penalty (b) Coverage with penalty

Figure 1: Comparison of our algorithms with baseline algorithms with and without penalty

4.1 Experimental Setup

Hardware and Platform: The algorithms were coded in Java and evaluated on a quad core 2.4 GHz computer (AMD Opteron™ Processor 850) with 100 GB on memory running CentOS 5.5 with kernel version 2.6.18-194.11.1.el5. All algorithms are single-threaded.

Topics and Users : Recall that the major input to our problem is a set of topics and the target sets. Other relevant parameters include the expected bidding costs for each of the topics and a penalty function that determines the penalty cost of unwanted targeting.

For the case of Twitter, utilizing the standard APIs, we collected all Twitter lists and the users belonging to these lists. List names are adopted to identify topics [8, 10]. We collected a set of approximately 4.5 million topics and their target sets. For the case of our experiments, target sets include users that belong to these lists. Overall, the total number of users in these target sets is 150 million of which about 13.5 million accounts are distinct. On average, each user is in the target set of 11 topics.

Cost Model for Topics: While collecting users and topics was relatively straightforward, identifying the costs was not. Most com-

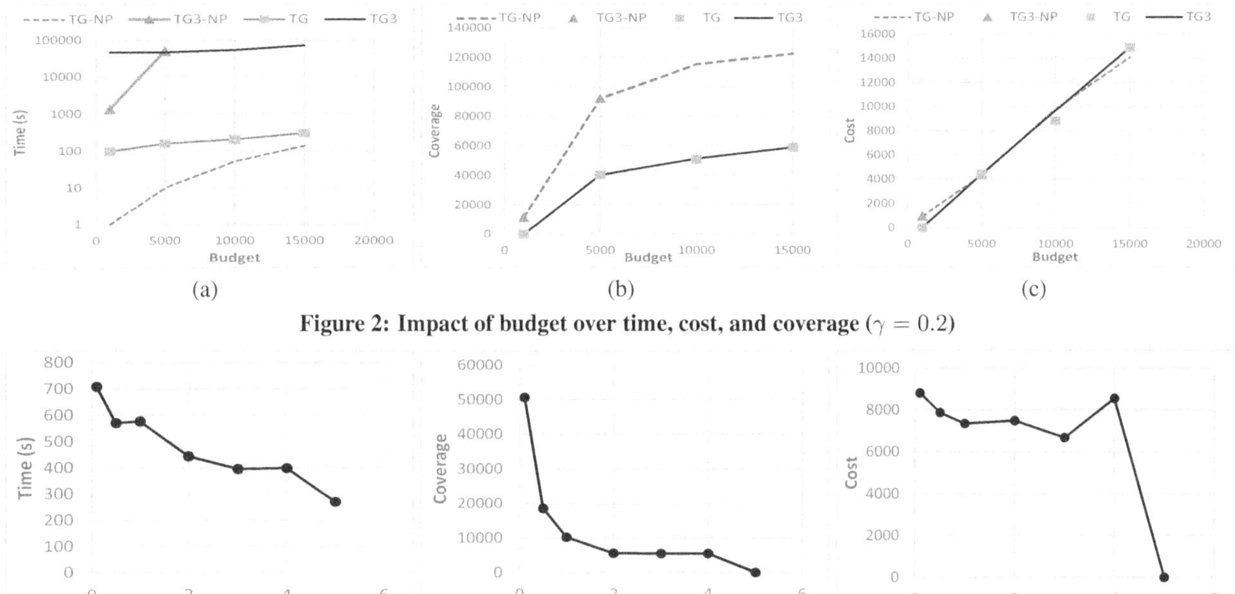

Figure 2: Impact of budget over time, cost, and coverage ($\gamma = 0.2$)

Figure 3: Impact of linear penalty cost over time, coverage, and bidding cost ($\gamma = 0.1$)

panies including Twitter do not reveal the bidding costs for their topics. Hence we adopt a diverse set of analytical but realistic cost models to estimate the cost of a topic. At a high level, our cost models can be partitioned into those that are independent of the target set size and those that are dependent on it.

For the former case, we generated costs for topics based on uniform and normal distributions. For the latter case, we generated costs based on a power law (size of target sets for different topics follows a power law) cost model. The rationale is that topics that are generic and have a large target set have a higher cost.

Penalty Function: We study two cases a) the penalty for any instance of unwanted targeting (covering a user outside S_t) is 0, and b) it is not. We studied three intuitive penalty functions. First a *linear* penalty function that assigns a penalty as ax where a is a constant (10 cents in our experiments except Figure 3) and x is the number of times the user was incorrectly targeted. Second is the *polynomial* cost function that assigns penalty as x^a where the parameters are as defined above. We also evaluated our algorithm on *exponential* cost functions according to a^x.

Performance Measures: There are multiple relevant metrics that could be used to evaluate our algorithms. The first is *runtime performance* which measures the time it takes to run our targeting algorithm. The second is the *coverage*, namely, how many users in the target set of t (the original query) are present in the target set of the alternative topic set R. Since our objective is to replace an expensive topic with multiple others relatively inexpensive ones, this is a crucial metric. Third is the *bidding cost* of the alternative topic set R (i.e. C_R). We would also like to reduce our *penalty cost* by minimizing the number of instances of unwanted targeting that are caused by our alternate topic set (C'_R). Experiments are performed on several original topics. The results are consistent with those presented below. In this section, due to space limitations, we report the results of the experiments done for the original topic of `social media` which has a target set of approximately 160,000 users.

Algorithms Evaluated: In this section, we evaluate two major algorithms that trade-off approximation bounds for speed: algorithms TG and TG3. In addition, both algorithms are affected by penalty function and we evaluated both scenarios with zero (TG-NP and TG3-NP where NP means no penalty) and non-zero penalty cost (TG and TG3). To speed up the algorithms, we also apply pruning techniques to remove irrelevant or costly topics. Given a topic t, the first pruning technique (we name it the *coverage-based* pruning technique) is to remove all topics with a coverage less than γ fraction of S_t. The alternative pruning technique (*ratio-based*) is to remove all topics with a coverage over cost ratio less than γ fraction of the maximum coverage over cost value among all topics. We have shown that these pruning techniques provide an approximation guarantee and a significant speedup in run time of the algorithms.[3] In all experiments, loading target sets in memory and conducting pruning require, respectively, 7 and 1 minute.

We compare these algorithms with baseline algorithms (Random, Top-k, WordNet) and demonstrate that the proposed algorithms outperform the baselines.

In all experiments except those reported in Figure 2, the budget is set to \$10000.

4.2 Performance Analysis

Comparison with baseline algorithms: We start by comparing our algorithms TG and TG3 with 3 baseline algorithms:

Random: Randomly pick topics until the budget is exhausted. Repeat this process for 10 times and pick the best.

Top-k: Order candidate topics based on their coverage. Pick topics in this order until the budget is exhausted.

WordNet: Given a query, do basic stemming, perform synonym expansion using Lucene-WordNet index and order results based on similarity. Pick topics in this order until the budget is exhausted.

Figure 1 reports the normalized coverage of the alternative topic sets identified by different algorithms when a coverage-based pruning technique is utilized with a pruning fraction of $\gamma = 0.5$. The normalized coverage of a topic set S with respect to a query topic t is the fraction of users in the target set of t that is targeted by S. The results for other pruning fraction values are consistent with those in Figure 1. Figure 1(a) displays the results when the penalty

[3]Please see [12] for an extensive set of experiments on the accuracy and performance of these pruning techniques.

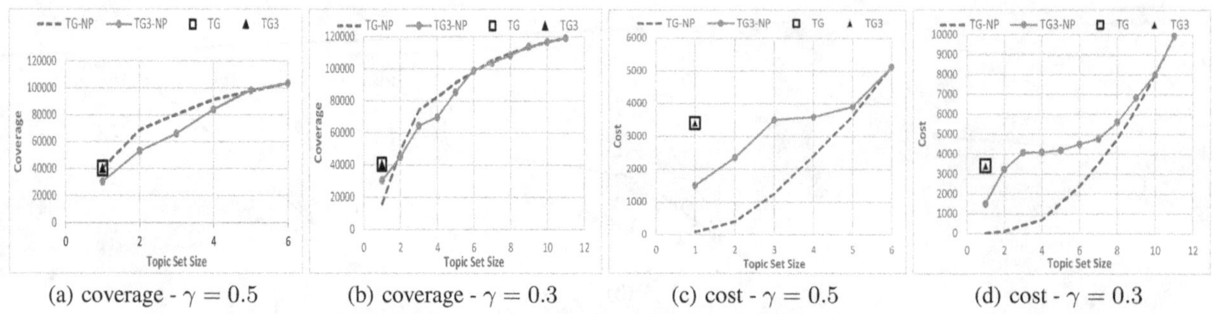

(a) coverage - $\gamma = 0.5$ (b) coverage - $\gamma = 0.3$ (c) cost - $\gamma = 0.5$ (d) cost - $\gamma = 0.3$

Figure 4: Impact of topic set size on coverage and cost for different pruning fractions

for any unwanted targeting is zero; Figure 1(b) depicts the results adopting a linear penalty function. We observe that in both cases our algorithms TG and TG3 significantly outperform all baseline algorithms. While the baseline algorithms have normalized coverage values of 7%, 20%, and 21% in average, our algorithms result in normalized coverage values of up to 80%.

Impact of budget over time, cost, and coverage: We test how budget impacts the run time, cost, and coverage of the alternative topic set R. We decided to run experiments not taking more than a few hours. Figure 2 shows the results. As expected, as the budget increases, it is possible to afford a larger alternative topic set which in turn increases the run time, cost, and coverage. As the budget increases, the running time of the algorithms increases as they have to run additional iterations to choose more alternative topics (Figure 2(a)). The total cost also increases linearly, according to Figure 2(c), with budget increases. These changes are linear as the algorithms could utilize all the budget to cover more users. Note that since our algorithms choose topics with higher coverage to cost ratio in the first iterations, as we proceed we cover less and less new users by paying more and more, that explains the concave shape of coverage in Figure 2(b).

Impact of penalty cost over time, cost and coverage: We evaluate how the different penalty cost models affect the outcome of algorithms. We start with a *linear* penalty cost function $f(x_u) = a \times x_u$ for a non-negative constant a where x_u is the number of times user u is targeted by different topics. The results are provided in Figures 3(a)-3(c). When the cost of incorrect targeting (parameter a) increases, the algorithms become "risk-averse" and try to choose only topics that are very similar to the query topic and the size of the alternative topic set R would be smaller. This results in a drop in run time, coverage, and bidding cost C_R and an increase in penalty cost C'_R. We also evaluated our algorithms for other cost functions such as polynomial and exponential cost functions $f(x) = x^a$ and $f(x) = a^x$. We found the behavior to be similar to the linear function except the fact that the drop rate in run time, coverage, and bidding cost is much sharper.

Impact of alternative topic set size on coverage and cost: We also aim to understand how total coverage and cost changes when the algorithms add more topics in subsequent iterations to the alternative topic set R. We evaluate this experiment utilizing different pruning fractions. Figure 4 details this behavior. As we add more topics, coverage follows a concave shape while the total cost of this set increases following a *convex* behavior. This is expected since in later iterations the algorithms add topics with lower coverage to cost ratio. Further, we can observe that as the pruning fraction decreases, the size of target set increases (from a size of 6 for a pruning fraction 0.5 to a size of 11 for a pruning fraction 0.3) thereby increasing both the cost and coverage. Intuitively, a less aggressive pruning strategy results in more topics that are not necessarily cost or coverage optimal.

Table 1: Case Study of Alternate Topics (the words are stemmed)

Machine Learning	Fashion	Social Media
strata	beauti fashion	market pr
machinelearn(ing)	fashion peopl	socialmedia
ai	style fashion	communiti
info engin(e)	fashion blog	seo
ai ppl	shoe	blog
researchnew	fashion world	onlin(e) market
nosql	apparel	
nlp ml	stylist	
inform(ation) retriev(al)	fashion brand	
analytics research data dev		
data analyt(ics)		
aier		
fourtytwo		
data scientist		

4.3 Qualitative Results

In this section, we show that the output of our algorithms are quite realistic using three sample topics. For this purpose, we choose three diverse topics - `social media`, `fashion` and `machine learning`. Table 1 shows the alternate topics identified by our algorithms. We can see that the topics are intuitively similar to the original topic and expected to have users of related expertise. For example, our algorithms identify that users who produces content in topics such as `strata` (a data analysis language), `ai`, `ml`, etc. are also producing content in the topic `machine learning`. Also, topics such as `apparel`, `shoe`, `fashion blog` are good proxies if you wish to target producers in `Fashion`. Moreover, topics such as `online market`, `seo`, `blog` target similar users as `social media`.

5. CONCLUSION AND FUTURE WORKS

In this paper, we initiate a study into a targeting problem in social media advertising. We introduced a taxonomy of relevant parameters (such as cost and penalty function) and studied the feasibility of our problem for various scenarios. We show that the problem is NP-hard, present two algorithms to solve it, and prove that they provide good approximation guarantees. Finally, we conduct a comprehensive set of experiments that demonstrate the efficacy of our algorithms and the quality of the results.

As a future work, we are interested to analyze the impact of our techniques when all advertisers adopt our proposed strategy and to study costs' changes in equilibrium state. We also aim to evaluate the practicality of our approaches when real cost values are available.

6. REFERENCES

[1] A. Acquisti and R. Gross. Imagined communities: Awareness, information sharing, and privacy on the Facebook. In *Privacy enhancing technologies*, pages 36–58. Springer, 2006.

[2] A. Ahmed, Y. Low, M. Aly, V. Josifovski, and A. J. Smola. Scalable distributed inference of dynamic user interests for behavioral targeting. In *KDD*, pages 114–122, 2011.

[3] N. Alon, B. Awerbuch, and Y. Azar. The online set cover problem. In *STOC*, pages 100–105. ACM, 2003.

[4] E. Bakshy, J. M. Hofman, W. A. Mason, and D. J. Watts. Everyone's an influencer: Quantifying influence on Twitter. WSDM, pages 65–74. ACM, 2011.

[5] F. Bonchi, C. Castillo, D. Donato, and A. Gionis. Topical query decomposition. In *SIGKDD*, pages 52–60. ACM, 2008.

[6] A. L. Brooks and C. Cheshire. Ad-itudes: Twitter users & advertising. In *Proceedings of the ACM 2012 conference on Computer Supported Cooperative Work Companion*, pages 63–66. ACM, 2012.

[7] M. Cha, H. Haddadi, F. Benevenuto, and P. K. Gummadi. Measuring user influence in Twitter: The million follower fallacy. *ICWSM*, 10:10–17, 2010.

[8] A. Cheng, N. Bansal, and N. Koudas. Peckalytics: Analyzing experts and interests on Twitter. SIGMOD Demo Track, pages 973–976. ACM, 2013.

[9] G. Cormode, H. Karloff, and A. Wirth. Set cover algorithms for very large datasets. In *CIKM*, pages 479–488. ACM, 2010.

[10] M. Eftekhar and N. Koudas. Some research opportunities on Twitter advertising. *IEEE Data Eng. Bull.*, 36(3):77–82, 2013.

[11] M. Eftekhar, N. Koudas, and Y. Ganjali. Bursty subgraphs in social networks. In *WSDM*, pages 213–222. ACM, 2013.

[12] M. Eftekhar, S. Thirumuruganathan, G. Das, and N. Koudas. Price trade-offs in social media advertising. Technical Report TR-DM-UT-14-05-00, University of Toronto, 2014. Available at: `http://www.cs.toronto.edu/~milad/paper/economical_bidding-TR.pdf`.

[13] D. Ferreira, M. Freitas, J. Rodrigues, and V. Ferreira. Twitviz-exploring Twitter network for your interests. *UMA*, pages 1–8, 2009.

[14] A. Java, X. Song, T. Finin, and B. Tseng. Why we Twitter: understanding microblogging usage and communities. In *WebKDD and SNA-KDD*, pages 56–65. ACM, 2007.

[15] S. Khuller, A. Moss, and J. Naor. The budgeted maximum coverage problem. *Information Processing Letters*, 70(1):39 – 45, 1999.

[16] D. Kim, Y. Jo, I.-C. Moon, and A. Oh. Analysis of Twitter lists as a potential source for discovering latent characteristics of users. In *ACM CHI Workshop on Microblogging*, 2010.

[17] H. Kwak, C. Lee, H. Park, and S. Moon. What is Twitter, a social network or a news media? In *WWW*, pages 591–600. ACM, 2010.

[18] C. Lee, H. Kwak, H. Park, and S. Moon. Finding influentials based on the temporal order of information adoption in Twitter. In *WWW*, pages 1137–1138. ACM, 2010.

[19] K. Lewis, J. Kaufman, M. Gonzalez, A. Wimmer, and N. Christakis. Tastes, ties, and time: A new social network dataset using facebook. com. *Social networks*, 30(4):330–342, 2008.

[20] R. G. Michael and D. S. Johnson. Computers and intractability: A guide to the theory of NP-completeness. *WH Freeman & Co., San Francisco*, 1979.

[21] A. Pal and S. Counts. Identifying topical authorities in microblogs. In *WSDM*, pages 45–54. ACM, 2011.

[22] M. Pennacchiotti, F. Silvestri, H. Vahabi, and R. Venturini. Making your interests follow you on Twitter. CIKM '12, pages 165–174, New York, NY, USA, 2012. ACM.

[23] E. J. Ruiz, V. Hristidis, C. Castillo, A. Gionis, and A. Jaimes. Correlating financial time series with micro-blogging activity. In *WSDM*, pages 513–522. ACM, 2012.

[24] J. Sankaranarayanan, H. Samet, B. E. Teitler, M. D. Lieberman, and J. Sperling. Twitterstand: news in tweets. In *GIS*, pages 42–51. ACM, 2009.

[25] Twitter. Start Advertising | Twitter for Business. `https://business.twitter.com/start-advertising`.

[26] V. V. Vazirani. *Approximation algorithms*. springer, 2001.

[27] J. Weng, E.-P. Lim, J. Jiang, and Q. He. Twitterrank: finding topic-sensitive influential Twitterers. In *WSDM*, pages 261–270. ACM, 2010.

[28] S. Wu, J. M. Hofman, W. A. Mason, and D. J. Watts. Who says what to whom on Twitter. In *WWW*, pages 705–714. ACM, 2011.

[29] J. Yan, N. Liu, G. Wang, W. Zhang, Y. Jiang, and Z. Chen. How much can behavioral targeting help online advertising? WWW, pages 261–270, New York, NY, USA, 2009. ACM.

Ranking Twitter Discussion Groups

James Cook
UC Berkeley
jcook@cs.berkeley.edu

Abhimanyu Das
Microsoft Research
abhidas@microsoft.com

Krishnaram Kenthapadi
Microsoft Research
krisken@microsoft.com

Nina Mishra
Microsoft Research
ninam@microsoft.com

ABSTRACT

A discussion group is a repeated, synchronized conversation organized around a specific topic. Groups are extremely valuable to the attendees, creating a sense of community among like-minded users. While groups may involve many users, there are many outside the group that would benefit from participation. However, finding the right group is not easy given their quantity and given topic overlap. We study the following problem: given a search query, find a good ranking of discussion groups. We describe a random walk model for how users select groups: starting with a group relevant to the query, a hypothetical user repeatedly selects an authoritative user in the group and then moves to a group according to what the authoritative user prefers. The stationary distribution of this walk yields a group ranking. We analyze this random walk model, demonstrating that it enjoys many natural properties of a desirable ranking algorithm. We study groups on Twitter where conversations can be organized via pre-designated hashtags. These groups are an emerging phenomenon and there are at least tens of thousands in existence today according to our calculations. Via an extensive collection of experiments on one year of tweets, we show that our model effectively ranks groups, outperforming several baseline solutions.

Categories and Subject Descriptors

H.3.3 [**Information Systems**]: Information Search and Retrieval; J.4 [**Computer Applications**]: Social and Behavioral Sciences

Keywords

discussion groups; group chats; Twitter groups; online communities; ranking groups; group search; group preference

COSN'14, October 1–2, 2014, Dublin, Ireland.
Copyright 2014 ACM 978-1-4503-3198-2/14/10 ...$15.00.
http://dx.doi.org/10.1145/2660460.2660473.

1. INTRODUCTION

Many venues exist for holding group conversations on the Internet. For example, forum sites, Internet Relay Chat, newsgroups and Yahoo groups have been widely studied. In this paper, we study *discussion groups*, which are groups that repeatedly meet at a mutually agreed upon time with the goal of discussing a particular topic.

We specifically study Twitter discussion groups where prior work shows that some discussions may be organized via pre-designated hashtags [13]. For example, wine aficionados append the hashtag `#winechat` during their conversations. Those interested follow the hashtag to listen during the pre-agreed upon time. The topics of these chats span multiple categories, from arts to education, entertainment and hobbies.

Our goal is to develop a method that will enable new users to search for discussion groups. A key question is given a search query, how can we rank discussion groups according to where the query is best discussed?

A natural approach is to treat the question as a classical web page ranking problem. In other words, treat the content of all messages exchanged in a discussion group as a web page and order the web pages using traditional information retrieval metrics such as TFIDF [42]. We study such approaches as a baseline upon which our methods should improve. But in the case of Twitter, and other social networks, we have more information at our disposal beyond the content of the message. For example, we know who contributed to which discussion group, as well as some indication of the authoritativeness of a user. We study how these additional signals can be used to generate an improved ranking.

We are not aware of any existing work on ranking discussion groups. There is related work in the area of ranking threads within a discussion, where the goal is to prevent new users from posting the same question twice [17] but, to our knowledge, nothing in the area of ordering groups.

In this paper, we begin by defining a discussion group, which is a generalization of a group chat [13]. We seek groups that have repeatedly met in a short window of time, where a group meets if a significant fraction of the traffic generated by the group takes place in a narrow window of time. This more general definition will give users of a group ranking engine the ability to search over a larger collection of groups.

We describe a new model for ranking groups called the group preference model: for a given search query, a hypothetical user starts with a group where the topic is discussed and repeatedly finds an authoritative user in the group and walks to a random group according to what the authoritative user prefers. With small probability the hypothetical user jumps to a random group. The model resembles PageRank [4] where a random surfer repeatedly follows outgoing links and jumps to a random node with small probability. A key difference is that in our model the hypothetical user bounces back and forth between groups and authoritative participants.

The technical exploration of this paper is devoted to understanding how our ranking algorithm responds to small perturbations in the input. Observe that the data that feeds our group preference model is constantly changing: *e.g.*, meeting attendance patterns may shift over time and a user's authoritativeness may rise and fall over time. We still want good groups to remain near the top of the ranking, particularly if the underlying data continues to support it. One notion of such good behavior is *rank stability* [37], but this turns out to be a very strong requirement: for example, the well-known PageRank and HITS algorithms are not rank-stable. Instead, we make a more specific list of desirable properties, and show that our algorithm satisfies them. For example, if one group is universally preferred to another according to a dataset and we add a new user to the dataset who holds the same preference, then our algorithm will also retain the preference. In a similar vein, if a user has an exclusive preference for some group, then increasing that user's authority cannot hurt that group's ranking.

We conduct an experiment on one year of tweets. We identify a collection of 27K discussion groups (hashtags) from this data. We create a set of group queries based on queries posed to Yahoo groups and a ground truth ranking of hashtags for these queries. We compare the performance of our algorithm with the performance of several natural baseline algorithms in terms of precision, recall, mean average precision, and NDCG and show that our algorithm outperforms the baselines on all of these metrics.

2. RELATED WORK

Our work sits in the context of other work in online forums, ranking, recommendation, group membership and group chats. We describe findings in these areas, as well as how our work relates.

Search in Online Forums While we are not aware of previous work on ranking discussion groups, there is work addressing related search problems. Online forums are similar to discussion groups, but generally involve parallel, asynchronous discussion threads instead of synchronized meetings. There is work on finding forum threads relevant to a query [17], as well as matching questions to answers [12]. The goal of this line of research is to prevent people from posting the same question twice. In contrast, the unit of retrieval in our work is a discussion group, rather than a thread. Also, we seek to a connect a user to a like-minded community of individuals where they can engage in repeated conversations, rather than find a closely matching question.

Ranking Models Given a search query, our group preference model describes a user (the *seeker*) who starts at a random group where the query is discussed, then repeatedly finds an authoritative participant in that group and then a group where that person discusses the query. The model is related to the Random Surfer Model [4] where a random walk repeatedly follows outgoing links on a directed graph. Our model differs in that we are bouncing back and forth between two kinds of nodes (groups and authoritative participants). Also, the transition probabilities depend on the query, and are determined by social interactions instead of links between documents. Both models include a *teleport* probability that the walk jumps to a completely random node, and in both models, the walk's stationary distribution is used to rank nodes. Our model is similar to personalized PageRank [25] in that the probability of teleporting to a group can depend on features such as how often the query is discussed in the group. Some of the mathematics developed for PageRank regarding how small changes to a graph affect the stationary distribution [10] are useful in our work (§5.1).

The group preference model is also related to HITS [32] which assigns hub and authority values to each node on a graph. The hub and authority scores complement each other in much the same way that the group preference seeker spends more time on participants with authority in highly ranked discussion groups, and groups preferred by highly-ranked participants. One important difference is that the HITS algorithm computes each new hub or authority score as a sum of neighboring values, whereas our model, since it follows a random walk, averages the values. Averaging has the advantage that a discussion group with very many participants but only marginally related to a query can be ranked lower than a collection of groups very related to a query that comes from a community of groups and participants who reinforce each other with evidence of preference and authority (§5.2). Another difference is that we allow the group preference seeker, when jumping from a person to a group, to use the previous group visited to inform the decision. For example, it is within the scope of our model for the seeker to only jump to groups that the person prefers to the previous group.

Implementing our model to serve a large number of queries would introduce scalability challenges similar to those faced by the HITS algorithm. For example, both models use a different graph for every query. There is past work on improving the efficiency of the HITS and related MAX and SALSA algorithms [36, 39, 47]. There has also been work on the similarly challenging problem of pre-computing personalized PageRank results for every starting node [14, 25].

The random shopper model [23] was developed in the context of online shopping and is also related. Each feature is represented as a directed graph over products with an edge from one product to another if it is better according to that feature. For example, if the feature is "lower price", then the user will walk to a cheaper product. The process of selecting a product starts at a random one, and then repeatedly selects a feature according to its importance and walks to a better product according to that feature. The principle goal is to learn the relative importance of each feature. One can view the features as authoritative participants and the walk within a feature as selecting a group according to the participants' preferences. The random choice of feature to select is independent of which product the random shopper has reached. In our work, the group that the seeker walks to intentionally depends on which authoritative participant was selected. In our work, the technical emphasis is in demonstrating that under reasonable changes to the underlying data, the ranking will remain unchanged, while in that work the emphasis was on showing how the ordering can and should flip [48] depending on which other products are shown.

Learning to Rank There is a large body of work in the learning to rank literature [6, 7, 11, 27] that on the surface seems relevant to the discussion group ranking problem. These techniques learn a function that given a search query and URL produce a score for how well the URL matches the query. However, these techniques require training data indicating how well a URL matches a given query. This training data can either be editorially judged or inferred from click activity [1, 28]. We note that obtaining training data for our search problem is quite challenging. For a human judge who is external to a search query and a group to evaluate the relevance of a group to a query is quite difficult and time-consuming, as we ourselves discovered as candidate judges. Furthermore, since no discussion group ranking system is in existence today, no click activity exists for inferring relevance. Instead, we use meeting attendance patterns, message content and user authority to drive a model of group preference.

Recommending Hashtags and Groups The general problem of recommending hashtags has been previously studied where given a tweet, the goal is to find a relevant hashtag. In one approach, the text of the tweet is used to identify similar tweets, and then a hashtag is recommended based on those found in similar tweets [34]. In other methods, the users who tweet about the subject may be used to find a relevant hashtag [20]. Note that arbitrary hashtags may never meet again. Indeed, prior work shows that 86% of hashtags have been used less than five times [52]. Such hashtags are not relevant to our problem of helping a new user find a future conversation. Further, since prior techniques are applied to arbitrary hashtags, the work does not take advantage of the fact that some of these hashtags are discussion groups — whose richer structure can be exploited to deduce higher quality rankings. We are motivated by applications where a new user seeks a future conversation. The hashtag prediction problem — given a user, predict which hashtags they will use in the future — has also been studied [51]. Many interesting characteristics of a hashtag are identified as useful for effective prediction, such as the prestige of a hashtag. These characteristics could also be used to create richer models of group preference.

There is also past work on recommending groups in online social networks [45], based on a user's existing social links and without any query. In our work, we hope to introduce a user with a topic of interest (query) to relevant discussion groups, even if the user is not yet a member of the system that hosts the groups.

Group Membership There is a substantial body of work in understanding why people join and remain in online communities. The size of a group is known to affect whether a user joins a group. Too many messages drive people away [8, 29], while having too few inhibits community responsiveness [38]. The level of moderation also plays a role [44]. The more friends a user has in a group, the more likely they are to join [33], and this likelihood increases if their friends are in turn connected [2]. If a user receives a response to their first message to a community, it increases the likelihood that they will subsequently interact with the community [3, 30]. A first response is also known to increase the speed at which a second message is posted [35]. Linguistic complexity reduces the chance of a response [50], and linguistic discrepancy can signal a user's departure from a group [15]. Our work differs in that we seek to connect a user to a group that was previously unknown to them. Our goal is to rank the best groups for discussing a particular topic. Richer contextual clues (friends in the group, linguistic coherence, etc.) that are known to drive group membership could lead to better and more personalized rankings.

Group Chats A group chat [13] is defined by three properties that we state for completeness. (1) REGULAR: In a group, people who share an interest meet on a regular basis over a prolonged period of time. (2) SYNCHRONIZED: In a group, meetings occur for a fixed duration at a specified time. (3) COHESIVE: Members in a group communicate with each other over the course of many meetings. In contrast, the definition of a discussion group explored in this paper is looser and focuses on the second property. We replace the notion of a regular meeting, *e.g.*, once a week, with one where the group meets multiple times. We also remove the requirement that the group be cohesive. The resulting set of groups is much larger – 1500 group chats versus 27K discussion groups, though still not as large as the number of Yahoo groups (~6M according to [3]). Where the previous work was concerned with measuring the number and variety of group chats, and therefore called for a more conservative definition, the goal of the current work is to provide a comprehensive discussion group ranking algorithm, and is best served by a broader definition, providing a large number of candidates as input. The goal of [13] was to design algorithms that could automatically find group chats on Twitter. The emphasis of our work is on ranking discussion groups so that we can connect a new user to a group.

3. PROBLEM FORMULATION

Consider any setting where many groups $g_1, \ldots, g_n$ meet often to discuss various topics. Our goal is to help a user with a topic of interest (the *query*) to find a relevant discussion group in which to participate. We hope that such an algorithm will help people to find others with similar interests, and give them a place to ask questions and share stories.

Discussion Groups We begin by describing the kind of group we seek. Since we wish to find a place for the user to have discussions, we restrict our attention to groups that have proved themselves by holding meetings in the past:

DEFINITION 3.1 (DISCUSSION GROUP). *A* meeting *is a span of time at most w hours long during which at least a γ fraction of all of the group's interactions in a specified time period happen. A collection of meetings constitutes a candidate* discussion group *if there have been at least m different meetings.*

In other words, a discussion group should have many discussions that last for some short period of time, typically one or two hours.

Problem Statement Given a query topic q that a user is interested in, we have two closely related goals. First, to understand which discussion group the user would choose to attend after spending some time on their own exploring groups related to topic q. Second, to develop an algorithm to predict these preferences, in order to save time or to suggest discussion groups to a user who would not otherwise embark on such an exploration.

PROBLEM 3.2. *Given a query topic q, we wish to find a set of discussion groups $g_1, \ldots, g_r$ relevant to q, together with a ranking on those groups: we say $g_i >_q g_j$ if our algorithm determines that group g_i is preferable to g_j in the context of topic q.*

We also seek to understand what characteristics influence a user's decision to prefer one discussion group over another. To this end, we will investigate a variety of characteristics.

Twitter Interpretation To interpret Definition 3.1 in the context of Twitter, we say that a *meeting* is a w-hour window of time that contains at least a γ fraction of all tweets sent during that week, and a set of tweets forms a *chat* if there are at least m weeks that contain a meeting. We make the simplifying assumption that every chat has a hashtag that is not used by any other chat — this is usually the case in our experience. In this work, we set out to solve Problem 3.2 via Twitter discussion groups.

4. MODEL

To solve Problem 3.2, we propose a model called the *group preference model* for the process a user (the *seeker*) interested in a topic q might follow to choose among the relevant discussion groups. The seeker begins by finding an arbitrary relevant group g_0. They then find a participant p_0 who holds some degree of *authority* in the group g_0. By looking at p_0's profile page, they look at the other discussion groups that p_0 participates in, and choose a group g_1 that p_0 shows a *preference* for. The seeker continues alternating between discussion groups and people $g_0, p_0, g_1, p_1, \ldots$ and eventually stops on one of the discussion groups.

An important feature of this model is that it makes use of social signals. This allows a community of discussion groups and people around a topic to be promoted through a feedback effect (§5.2). The model also satisfies several desirable properties described in §5.1. See §2 for a comparison to some similar ranking models.

We begin our precise description of the model by describing in more detail the steps of jumping from a discussion group to a participant and from a participant to a group.

4.1 Authority Score $A_{q,g}(p)$

After arriving at a discussion group g, the seeker chooses a participant to jump to according to their *authority score*. The authority of different participants p within a group g is quantified by authority scores $A_{q,g}(p)$ which form a probability distribution. The scores could be determined in many different ways. For example, we could assign equal weight to every person who has participated in g. Alternatively, we could assign weight proportional to the number of followers, or the number of @-mentions received by the person.

4.2 Preference Score $P_{q,p,g}(g')$

After arriving at a participant p from a group g, the seeker looks at various discussion groups p has participated in and jumps to one according to the *preference score*. For a query q, participant p, and last group g, the preference scores $P_{q,p,g}(g')$ of participant p for different groups g' form a probability distribution (that is, $\sum_{g'} P_{q,p,g}(g') = 1$). One simple way to determine $P_{q,p,g}(g')$ is to make it proportional to the number of meetings of group g' that p took the time to attend. We may also wish the preference score to depend on the last group g that the seeker visited. In particular, our implementation (described in §6.2) requires that the seeker never jump to a group g' if p is less active in g' than in g.

4.3 Teleport Distribution D_q

After each step, with some probability $\lambda \in (0, 1)$ the seeker decides to cut short their current exploration, and chooses a new random discussion group to start from. For example, in the context of Twitter, the seeker might use Twitter's search feature to find a new potential group. This is analogous to the teleportation step of PageRank, where the surfer sometimes jumps to a uniformly random web page. The probability distribution the seeker uses to jump to a new discussion group is a parameter of our model, called the *teleport distribution* D_q, and is over discussion groups relevant to the topic q. D_q plays the same role as the preference vector in personalized PageRank [25, 40]. As with PageRank, one simple choice is to set $D_q(g) = \frac{1}{n}$ for every relevant group g, where n is the number of such groups. Alternatively, we may wish to capture the notion that the seeker is more likely to start at discussion groups which are more strongly relevant to the topic q. In the context of Twitter, we could set the teleport probability $D_q(c)$ of a chat c to be proportional to the number of tweets in chat c where q is mentioned divided by the total number of tweets in chat c. However D_q is determined, it should be normalized so that the sum of probabilities is one. We require $D_q(g) > 0$ for every relevant group g in order to ensure that the model gives a well-defined solution, in a sense that will become clear when we describe our algorithm in §5.

4.4 The Group Preference Model

Given a query q, the seeker follows this process, which is parameterized by a teleportation parameter $\lambda \in (0, 1)$.

1. Choose an arbitrary starting group g.
2. Select a participant p at random using the probability distribution $A_{q,g}(p)$.
3. Select a group g' at random using the probability distribution $P_{q,p,g}(g')$.
4. With probability λ, sample a discussion group g from the teleport distribution D_q, and go to step 2.
5. Otherwise, go to step 2 using g' as the new g.

Eventually, the seeker stops and chooses the discussion group that they most recently jumped to. Figure 1 illustrates the first three steps of the process in the context of Twitter. We are not claiming that real users follow this process, only that it may model part of the behavior we observe.

5. ALGORITHM AND ANALYSIS

We now describe our algorithm for solving Problem 3.2 using the group preference model. The key observation is that even though the seeker visits both discussion groups

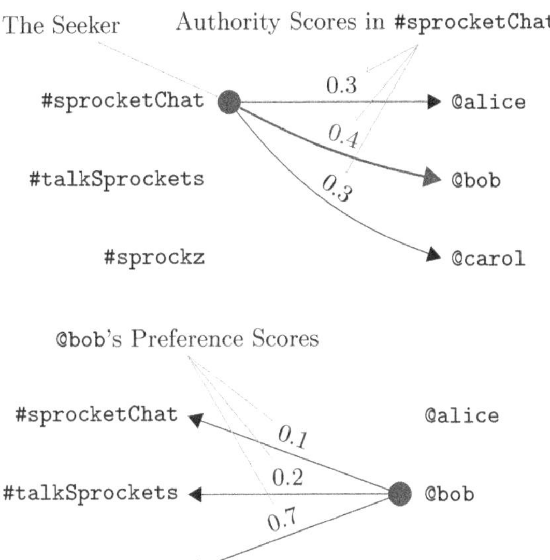

Figure 1: The first steps of the group preference model in the context of Twitter. Starting from a random discussion group (#sprocketChat), the seeker jumps to a user randomly using authority scores in that group, then to a new group according to that user's preferences over the current group.

and participants, the model can be represented by the following Markov process over just the groups with the matrix of transition probabilities $M(q)$ computed as follows:

$$M(q)_{g_1,g_2} = \lambda D_q(g_2) + (1-\lambda)\sum_{p\in U} A_{q,g_1}(p)P_{q,p,g_1}(g_2) \quad (1)$$

Where U is the set of people who participate in any relevant group. Each transition probability $M(q)_{g_1,g_2}$ in (1) is then equal to the probability that the seeker lands on g_2 given that the last group they landed on was g_1. To understand why this is true, note that the seeker can land on g_2 either by (a) landing on a participant with a positive preference for g_2, or (b) teleporting directly. Case (b) happens with probability $\lambda D_q(g_2)$, where $D_q(g_2)$ is the teleport distribution parameter of the model. To compute the probability of (a), note that the probability of arriving at g_2 through a participant p is $(1-\lambda)A_{q,g_1}(p) \cdot P_{q,p,g_1}(g_2)$, and sum over all participants p. Notice that every query q gives rise to a different Markov process, and that $M(q)$ is regular so long as $\lambda > 0$. (If we generalize to an arbitrary teleport distribution D_q, this is why we require (§4.3) that every probability is positive.)

Given a query q, Algorithm 1 (GroupPreference) computes the stationary distribution of $M(q)$ and ranks the discussion groups by their stationary probabilities.

5.1 Properties of Algorithm GroupPreference

To help understand the behavior of Algorithm 1 (GroupPreference), we study how changes in the input data can affect the ranking. The stationary distribution of a Markov process can change in unintuitive ways as a result of changes to the transition probabilities. For example, increasing a transition probability to one state can increase the stationary probabilities of many other states, and when λ is near 0, a small change can have a large effect. In this section, we show that our algorithm has many simple and desirable properties: for example, if a participant shows an increased preference for a discussion group g, then g's ranking will not be negatively affected (Theorem 5.5).

Algorithm 1 GroupPreference

Parameters: Authority score function $A_{q,g}(.)$; Preference score function $P_{q,p,g}(.)$; Teleport parameter $\lambda \in (0,1)$; Teleport distribution D_q.
Input: A set of candidate discussion groups (Def. 3.1); A dataset of group interactions; A query q.
Output: A ranking of discussion groups relevant to topic q.
1: Find all groups $g_1, \ldots, g_n$ where the topic q is mentioned in some group interaction.
2: Compute the authority and preference scores and teleport probabilities $A_{q,g}(p)$, $P_{q,p,g}(g')$, $D_q(g)$ for every g, g', p.
3: Compute the stationary distribution π of the Markov process $M(q)$ defined in (1).
4: **return** Groups ranked so $g_1 >_q g_2$ iff $\pi(g_1) > \pi(g_2)$.

Our first property describes what happens when every participant prefers one group g_1 over another group g_2. The property holds when the teleport distribution is uniform, or at least does not favor g_2 over g_1.

THEOREM 5.1. *If for topic q, every participant always assigns a higher preference score to group g_1 than g_2, and g_2 does not have a higher teleport probability, then $g_1 >_q g_2$.*

PROOF. The proof is guided by the intuition that whenever the seeker is at a participant, the next group they jump to is more likely to be g_1 than g_2. Looking at (1), we see that for every group g, $M(q)_{g,g_1} > M(q)_{g,g_2}$. It follows that after one step of the Markov process, the seeker is more likely to end up at group g_1 than g_2 — in particular, taking π to be the stationary distribution, we have $(\pi M(q))(g_1) > (\pi M(q))(g_2)$. Since $\pi = \pi M(q)$, we have $\pi(g_1) > \pi(g_2)$, so the algorithm will rank $g_1 >_q g_2$. □

Instead of comparing two groups, we can describe what happens if every user's preference for one group g_1 is high. This property holds if the teleport distribution is uniform.

THEOREM 5.2. *Suppose that for topic q, every participant has a preference of at least α for group g_1, regardless of the previous group g'. If the teleport distribution D_q is uniform, then no more than $1/\alpha - 1$ other groups will be ranked higher than g_1.*

PROOF. First, notice that the stationary probability of g_1 is at least $\gamma = \lambda\frac{1}{n} + (1-\lambda)\alpha$. This is true because, looking at (1), $M(q)_{g,g_1} \geq \gamma$ for every group g. Hence, $\pi(g_1) = \sum_g(\pi(g) \cdot M(q)_{g,g_1}) \geq (\sum_g \pi(g)) \cdot \gamma = \gamma$. Using a similar argument, for every group g, $\pi(g) \geq \lambda\frac{1}{n}$ since $M(q)_{g',g} \geq \lambda\frac{1}{n}$ for any g' and g. Based on these two lower bounds on the stationary probabilities, we next obtain an upper bound on the number of groups with large stationary probability. It is not possible for more than $1/\alpha$ groups to have a stationary probability as high as γ: otherwise, the sum of all stationary probabilities would be more than $n\lambda\frac{1}{n} + (1/\alpha)(1-\lambda)\alpha = 1$. □

The remaining properties restrict how the algorithm's ranking can change if the input data changes. In each case, we will consider two datasets T and T' of discussion group interactions. We will assume the preference or authority scores which result from these datasets (§4.1, §4.2) differ in some small way. Notationally, we will add T as a parameter to the authority and preference scores $A_{T,q,g}(p)$ and $P_{T,q,p,g}(g')$; the teleport distribution $D_{T,q}$; the transition matrix $M(T,q)_{g_1,g_2}$; and the resulting judgments $g_1 >_q^T g_2$.

Next, we show that if we add to the dataset a new participant who shares a preference with all existing participants, that preference will still be reflected in the new ranking. Also, if we add a participant with a preference of α for a group g_1 to a dataset where all existing participants have such a preference, then g_1 will still be ranked in the top $1/\alpha$.

COROLLARY 5.3. *Suppose that in T, every participant assigns a higher preference score to g_1 than g_2 and g_2 does not have a higher teleport probability. If the only change from T to T' is the addition of a new person p_* who also prefers g_1 to g_2 (that is, teleport probabilities, and preference scores as well as the proportions between authority scores not involving p_*, are unchanged), then $g_1 >_q^{T'} g_2$.*

Similarly, suppose that in T, every participant assigns a preference of at least α to g_1, and the teleport distribution is uniform. If the only change from T to T' is the addition of a new person who also has a preference of at least α for g_1, then g_1 will be ranked in the top $1/\alpha$ groups.

This corollary follows because the hypotheses of Theorem 5.1 and Theorem 5.2 are still respectively true in dataset T'.

Our next two theorems will make use of a result by Chien et al. [10] about Markov processes, that increasing the transition probability to a state at the expense of other states cannot negatively affect that state's ranking. We re-formulate their result to be more immediately applicable to our setting.

THEOREM 5.4 (CHIEN ET AL. [10, THEOREM 2.9]). *Consider a regular Markov chain M. Fix some state s_1 in M. Let M' be a regular Markov chain over the same set of states as M, obtained by modifying M as follows. Transition probabilities to states other than s_1 are either decreased or kept unchanged in M', compared to M. Correspondingly, transition probabilities to s_1 are either increased or kept unchanged (so that the transition probabilites out of any state sum to 1). In other words, for every $s_2 \neq s_1$ and every s_3, $M'_{s_3,s_2} \leq M_{s_3,s_2}$ (and since the transition probabilities out of s_3 sum to 1, $M'_{s_3,s_1} \geq M_{s_3,s_1}$).*

Let π and π' be the stationary distributions of M and M' respectively. Then, for any state s_4, if $\pi_{s_1} > \pi_{s_4}$, then $\pi'_{s_1} > \pi'_{s_4}$.

Theorem 5.4 allows us to understand the consequences of various changes by studying their effects on the transition matrix $M(q)$. Our next two properties say that the algorithm is monotonic in ways that one would expect: the rank of a discussion group g must not decrease when a participant's demonstrated preference for it increases (for example, because they attended more meetings) or when an avid fan of the group gains authority.

THEOREM 5.5. *Suppose that the only change from T to T' is that participant p_1 shows an increased preference for group g_1 and a decreased preference for other groups for a given query q. That is: $P_{T',q,p_1,g'}(g_1) \geq P_{T,q,p_1,g'}(g_1)$ for all g'; $P_{T',q,p_1,g'}(g) \leq P_{T,q,p_1,g'}(g)$ for all $g \neq g_1$ and all g'; and all other authority and preference scores and teleport probabilities are unchanged. Then for any group g_2, if $g_1 >_q^T g_2$, then $g_1 >_q^{T'} g_2$.*

PROOF. Since the authority scores and teleport probabilities are unchanged, and preference scores for participants other than p_1 are also unchanged, we can express the change in the Markov transition matrix (1) as: $\forall h_1, h_2$,

$$\begin{aligned}&M(T',q)_{h_1,h_2} - M(T,q)_{h_1,h_2}\\&=(1-\lambda)A_{T,q,h_1}(p_1)(P_{T',q,p_1,h_1}(h_2) - P_{T,q,p_1,h_1}(h_2)).\end{aligned}$$

This change is nonnegative when $h_2 = g_1$ and nonpositive otherwise. So by Theorem 5.4, for any group g_2, if $g_1 >_q^T g_2$, then $g_1 >_q^{T'} g_2$. □

Finally, increasing the authority of group's fan cannot negatively impact the group's ranking.

THEOREM 5.6. *Suppose that participant p_1 has an exclusive preference for group g_1: $P_{T,q,p_1,g'}(g_1) = 1$ for all g'. Assume that the only change from T to T' is that p_1 gains authority. That is: for every group g, $A_{T',q,g}(p_1) \geq A_{T,q,g}(p_1)$; for every group g and participant $p \neq p_1$, $A_{T',q,g}(p) \leq A_{T,q,g}(p)$; and all other authority and preference scores and teleport probabilities are unchanged. Then for any group g_2, if $g_1 >_q^T g_2$, then $g_1 >_q^{T'} g_2$.*

PROOF. Notice that for any groups g and g' where $g' \neq g_1$, and any participant p,

$$A_{T',q,g}(p)P_{T',q,p}(g') \leq A_{T,q,g}(p)P_{T,q,p}(g').$$

(For user p_1, this is true because p_1's preference for g' is zero.) It follows that $M(T',q)_{g,g'} \leq M(T,q)_{g,g'}$. So by Theorem 5.4, for any group g_2, if $g_1 >_q^T g_2$, then $g_1 >_q^{T'} g_2$. □

In §5.2, we describe a scenario showing an advantage of Algorithm 1 over simpler approaches. In §6, we evaluate the algorithm experimentally.

5.2 Comparing to the Naive Approach

Instead of using Algorithm 1, one could rank the discussion groups relevant to a topic q based simply on the number of people who attend meetings, the number of interactions in the groups, or some similar metric. One problem with such naïve rankings is that very popular groups which are not about topic q, but where topic q arises incidentally, can dominate smaller groups whose main focus is q. For example, if q is a disease and a celebrity is diagnosed with it, then a Twitter chat about celebrities might see a surge of messages about q that is much greater in volume then any discussion on the Twitter chats that are focused on topic q.

To understand the advantage of Algorithm 1, consider the following scenario, illustrated in Figure 2:

SCENARIO 5.7. *There is a set of discussion groups G_{pop}, which we think of as being* popular*, but barely related to the topic q. There is a very large set F of participants whom we think of as* fans *of groups in G_{pop} and uninterested in q. We assume the following two properties:*

- *Non-fans $p \notin F$ who mention topic q give small preference scores to G_{pop}: $\forall g'$, $\sum_{g \in G_{\text{pop}}} P_{q,p,g'}(g) < \epsilon$.*
- *Fans $p \in F$ do not have a strong interest in q, so they have small authority scores in the groups that are focused on the topic: $\forall g \notin G_{\text{pop}}$, $\sum_{p \in F} A_{q,g}(p) < \epsilon$.*

THEOREM 5.8. *In Scenario 5.7, let $D_{\text{pop}} = \sum_{g \in G_{\text{pop}}} D_q(g)$ be the total teleport probability of the non-relevant groups. Suppose that there is some relevant group $g_* \notin G_{\text{pop}}$ for which every non-fan $p \notin F$ has a preference of at least $\frac{8}{7}(\beta + \frac{\lambda}{1-\lambda} D_{\text{pop}})/(1-\beta)$, where $\beta = D_{\text{pop}} + \frac{2\epsilon}{\lambda}$. Then, if $\epsilon < \frac{1}{8}$ and $\lambda < 1$, then Algorithm 1 will rank group g_* above every group in G_{pop}. (This holds true even if there are many more fans than non-fans and the groups in G_{pop} have many more tweets than the other groups.)*

PROOF. Let π be the stationary distribution of $M(q)$. For a group g, let π_g denote its probability under distribution π, and for a set of groups G let $\pi_G = \sum_{g \in G} \pi(g)$. We will first show that $\pi_{G_{\text{pop}}}$ is small and then show that π_{g_*} is large.

For any $g_1 \notin G_{\text{pop}}$ and $g_2 \in G_{\text{pop}}$,

$$\begin{aligned} M(q)_{g_1,g_2} \leq & \lambda D_q(g_2) + (1-\lambda)(\sum_{p \in F} A_{q,g}(p) + \sum_{p \notin F} A_{q,g}(p)\epsilon) \\ \leq & \lambda D_q(g_2) + (1-\lambda)(2\epsilon), \end{aligned}$$

and similarly, for $g_1, g_2 \in G_{\text{pop}}$,

$$M(q)_{g_1,g_2} \leq \lambda D_q(g_2) + (1-\lambda).$$

For any distribution d and $g_2 \in G_{\text{pop}}$, it follows that

$$(dM(q))_{g_2} \leq \lambda D_q(g_2) + (1-\lambda)(d_{G_{\text{pop}}} + 2\epsilon(1 - d_{G_{\text{pop}}})),$$

and so $(dM(q))_{G_{\text{pop}}} \leq \lambda D_{\text{pop}} + (1-\lambda)(d_{G_{\text{pop}}} + 2\epsilon(1-d_{G_{\text{pop}}}))$.

In particular, the total stationary probability of G_{pop} satisfies

$$\pi_{G_{\text{pop}}} = (\pi M(q))_{G_{\text{pop}}} \leq \lambda D_{\text{pop}} + (1-\lambda)(\pi_{G_{\text{pop}}} + 2\epsilon(1-\pi_{G_{\text{pop}}}))$$

so $\pi_{G_{\text{pop}}}(1 - (1-\lambda)(1-2\epsilon)) \leq \lambda D_{\text{pop}} + (1-\lambda)2\epsilon$, and so

$$\pi_{G_{\text{pop}}} \leq D_{\text{pop}} + 2\epsilon \tfrac{1-\lambda}{\lambda} = \beta - 2\epsilon. \qquad (2)$$

Now, let's show that the stationary probability of g_* is high. For any discussion group $g \notin G_{\text{pop}}$, we have

$$\begin{aligned} M(q)_{g,g_*} \geq & (1-\lambda) \sum_{p \notin F} A_{q,g}(p) P_{q,p,g}(g_*) \\ \geq & \tfrac{8}{7}(1-\lambda) \tfrac{\beta + \lambda D_{\text{pop}}/(1-\lambda)}{1-\beta} \sum_{p \notin F} A_{q,g}(p) \end{aligned}$$

(Recall that $\sum_{p \notin F} A_{q,g}(p) \geq 1 - \epsilon > \frac{7}{8}$.)

$$> (1-\lambda) \tfrac{\beta + \lambda D_{\text{pop}}/(1-\lambda)}{1-\beta}$$

and so for any distribution d,

$$(dM(q))_{g_*} \geq (1-\lambda)(1 - d_{G_{\text{pop}}}) \tfrac{\beta + \lambda D_{\text{pop}}/(1-\lambda)}{1-\beta}.$$

We have:

$$\begin{aligned} \pi_{g_*} = (\pi M(q))_{g_*} \geq & (1-\lambda)(1 - \pi_{G_{\text{pop}}}) \tfrac{\beta + \lambda D_{\text{pop}}/(1-\lambda)}{1-\beta} \\ > & (1-\lambda)(1-\beta) \tfrac{\beta + \lambda D_{\text{pop}}/(1-\lambda)}{1-\beta} \\ = & \beta - 2\epsilon \geq \pi_{G_{\text{pop}}}. \quad \square \end{aligned}$$

People interested in q don't prefer popular but irrelevant groups, and fans of popular groups don't have authority in relevant groups.

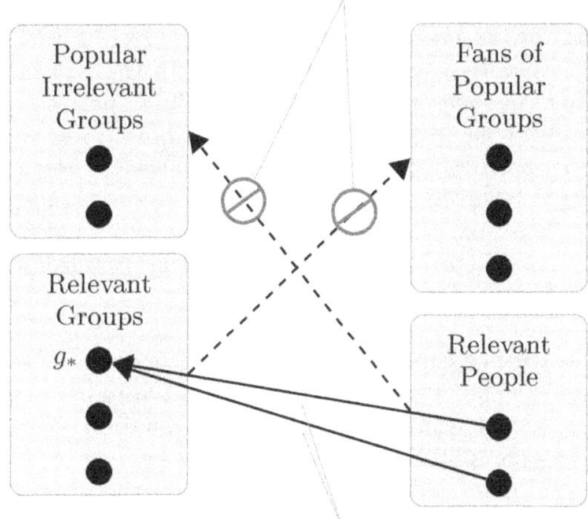

People interested in q support the best group g_*, and have high authority scores in relevant groups.

Figure 2: Illustration of Scenario 5.7. A set of popular but irrelevant groups has many fans. The most relevant group g_* has fewer supporters, but the whole community of relevant groups gives authority to them. Under the right conditions, g_* will be ranked at the top (Thm. 5.8).

6. EXPERIMENTS

We present the results of running our algorithm on one year of tweets. We begin with the experimental setup and data description, and then explain our evaluation methodology. We show empirically that our algorithm performs significantly better than the baseline with respect to different performance measures. We also present qualitative results.

6.1 Experimental Setup

We obtained the set of all English language tweets posted in a 12 month time period starting from 6/2012. Given the scale of this data (several petabytes), we implemented our algorithm in the SCOPE language [9] and ran it offline over a large distributed computing cluster. We extracted the set of all distinct hashtags used in this timeframe, and the tweets associated with each hashtag, along with their corresponding users and timestamps. We processed each tweet message to extract the hashtags and the noun phrases present in the tweet (using a Part-of-Speech Tagger). The noun phrases serve to capture the potential queries that the tweet contains. Underutilized hashtags were removed (present in less than 60 tweets or used by less than 10 people), as were underutilized queries (less than 100 tweets).

Identifying Twitter Discussion Groups The set of Twitter Discussion Groups was determined as per §3. We consider the activity for the hashtag during each week, and analyze the fraction of the activity occurring during every possible duration of a short window of time each. In our implementation, we used $w = 2$ hours as the window length, and considered discrete time windows starting at every hour and half hour (since participants are likely to agree to meet at a round time such as 3:30 or 4:00). We then check if there is significant activity in the window with the largest activity during the week. We denote the window with the largest activity during the week as a "meeting" if at least $\gamma = 20\%$ of the activity for the hashtag in that week occurred during this window. We only consider the window with the largest activity during the week under the reasonable assumption that a large group of people are unlikely to have time to participate in multiple meetings in the same week. For a hashtag to be considered a discussion group, there should have been at least $m = 10$ weeks containing valid meetings. We obtained a total of $27K$ discussion groups using the above process.

Selecting candidate queries for ranking Since our algorithm is query-specific, we need to identify a set of representative queries against which to perform our evaluation. The union of all the noun phrases in the tweets gave us a set of 27 million potential queries, but a large fraction of them were phrases that were unrealistic as real queries (for example, phrases such as "someone", "next week" or "great day"). We sought a list of queries that capture how seekers query for groups, and queries posed to Yahoo Groups provided such a collection. We collected queries posed to Yahoo Groups based on five months of browsing behavior. After intersecting these queries with the set that we gathered from tweets, we were left with 2K queries.

A limitation of using Yahoo Group queries is that there may be Yahoo Groups not present on Twitter, and Twitter Discussion groups not present in Yahoo. Note that since no Twitter Discussion Group search engine exists, we are unable to use an existing query log for the purpose of our experiment. Rather, we are using Yahoo Group queries as a proxy for how people seek online communities.

Ground Truth Creation To evaluate the performance of our algorithm, we next need to obtain a ground truth ranked hashtag list for each query. However, given the number of candidate hashtags, this is clearly impossible to create manually — even for a few of the 2K candidate queries. Instead, we rely on an approach to obtain a (noisy) list of ground truth hashtags for each of a small set of queries, and then manually clean the list. For each candidate query, we identify a list of Twitter self-declared enthusiasts by selecting people who mention the query phrase in their Twitter profile. This is a simple approach and quite prone to error, *e.g.*, Jimmy Fallon (comedian) claims to be an astrophysicist in his Twitter profile [19]. We note that better techniques exist for identifying true experts, *e.g.*, [16, 19, 21, 26, 31, 41, 43] and these could perform better. We leave this as a potential direction for future work. Nevertheless, given the limited space allowed for a Twitter profile, people who explicitly mention the query (for example, "camera") in their Twitter profile, are more likely to be enthused (enjoy photography) than a random person who has merely used the query in a few tweets. For each query, we then rank hashtags based on their popularity among the tweets of the enthusiasts corresponding to the query. More specifically, we obtain a ranked list of hashtags for each query, where the ranking is based on the number of enthusiasts that have written tweets containing the query and the hashtag.

From among the $2K$ candidate queries, we were able to obtain this enthusiast ranking for only around 600 queries (for the remaining queries, we could not find enough enthusiasts who mentioned the query in their profile). Note that this coverage issue is another critical shortcoming of this method, and is the main reason why this cannot be a candidate algorithm for the discussion group ranking problem, even though it is used in creating the ground truth and (as seen later) has very good performance on the queries for which it returns an answer.

A manual evaluation of the enthusiast based ranking revealed that while the ranking had good precision for most queries, it had two shortcomings: first, it did not have sufficient recall and failed to report hashtags that we manually found to be very relevant to the query (*e.g.*, `#photography-chat` for the query, "camera" and `#tl_chat` for the query "travel", both of which are highly relevant Twitter discussion groups) and second, there were some queries on which its precision was quite poor.

To resolve these issues, we resorted to the pooling method in information retrieval [49] and manually created the final ground truth as follows: for each query, we pooled together the top 10 hashtags output by the above enthusiast ranking, the baselines, and our algorithm. We then asked a human assessor to consider each of these candidate hashtags in the pool, and manually annotate the hashtag (by scanning through the set of tweets corresponding to the hashtag, and performing a web search for information related to the hashtag) on a four-point graded relevance scale (with 3-being most relevant to the query, and 0 being irrelevant). Note that the human assessor did not have access to any information about which algorithm(s) generated the candidate hashtag in the pool. Since this process is extremely labor-intensive, we considered only the top 10 results from each algorithm for a given query, and restricted the set of queries for which we generated ground-truth rankings by sampling 50 queries from among the 600 candidate queries.

6.2 Implementation choices

Next we list the various implementation choices related to our model.

Authority Score We consider four different methods for assigning participants an authority score to capture how authoritative they are with respect to the discussion group and the query. (1) Noun-Frequency based Authority (NounFreqWeights): For each query and hashtag, we compute the authority score of a participant according to how many of their tweets contain both the query and the hashtag. A participant that tweets a lot about the query in the context of that hashtag is considered more authoritative than a participant with only a few tweets containing the (query, hashtag) pair. (2) @-mention Authority (@-mentionWeights): For each query and hashtag, we compute a participant's authority score according to the number of times the participant is @-mentioned in the context of the query and the hashtag. A participant that is @-messaged frequently in tweets containing the (query, hashtag) pair is considered more authoritative. (3) Follower Authority (FollowerWeights): We compute a participant's authority score according to how many followers they have on Twitter. A snapshot of the complete Twitter follower group was used to obtain follower counts. (4) Equal Authority (EqualWeights): For each query and hashtag, we give equal weights to all participants.

We report the performance of our algorithm with respect to each of these authority scores.

Teleport Distribution As described in §4, the teleport distribution for the random jumps in our group preference model can be either unweighted, or weighted according to the hashtag to which we are teleporting. We experiment with both options. For the unweighted case, the probability is divided among all hashtags equally. For the weighted case, we divide this probability among hashtags based on the fraction of tweets of this hashtag that contain the specific query. That is, the teleportation process is biased towards hashtags in which the query occurs more frequently. The intuition behind weighing the teleportation process is that if the input graph for the PageRank computation contains a few disjoint connected components, then ranking the hashtags across these two clusters would normally (in the unweighted case) depend only on the relative sizes of the components. By weighing the teleport distribution, we can factor in the query-specific popularity of hashtags when comparing hashtags from different connected components. As we will observe in the experimental results, weighting the teleport process significantly improves the quality of our rankings.

Preference Score As described in §4, a key component of our GROUPPREFERENCE algorithm is the computation of *preference scores*. For any fixed query, participant, and last group g, these scores form a probability distribution representing the participant's preference for different groups g'. Hence, for a fixed query and a fixed participant, these scores can be viewed as a probability transition matrix over groups. For computing a participant's preference between hashtags (groups) g and g', we wish to only use Twitter data corresponding to the time when the participant was "aware" of *both* the hashtags. We define the participant's awareness-time for a hashtag as the first time when they tweeted with that hashtag. Using this definition, we then restrict the tweets of the participant to the time-period starting from the *later* of the awareness time for g and g'. For this time-period, we compute the number of meetings of g and g' attended by the participant for the given query (*i.e.*, the number of two-hour windows within which the participant posted at least one tweet containing the hashtag and the query). We define the transition from g to g' (resp. g' to g) to be valid, if the participant has attended "significantly more" (we use a relative difference threshold of 0.1 for estimating significance) meetings of g' compared to g (resp. g compared to g'). The combined transition probability of 1 from g is then equally divided among all valid transitions from g. If the participant does not have a significant preference for any group g' over g (and hence there is no valid transition from g), we assign a transition probability of 1 from g to itself. Formally, for query q and participant p, let $G^{pref}_{q,p,g}$ denote the set of groups for which p has significant preference over group g. If $G^{pref}_{q,p,g}$ is non-empty, then we set $P_{q,p,g}(g') = 1/|G^{pref}_{q,p,g}|$ for $g' \in G^{pref}_{q,p,g}$, and $P_{q,p,g}(g') = 0$ for $g' \notin G^{pref}_{q,p,g}$. If $G^{pref}_{q,p,g}$ is empty, then we set $P_{q,p,g}(g) = 1$ and $P_{q,p,g}(g') = 0$ for any g' different from g.

6.3 Baseline Algorithms

We compared our GROUPPREFERENCE algorithm against the following baselines, all of which correspond to various intuitive notions of the popularity of a discussion group on Twitter with respect to a given query.

User Frequency-based Ranking Algorithm (UFA): For each query, we assign a score to each hashtag based on the number of distinct participants that have posted tweets containing the given hashtag and query.

TFIDF Algorithm (TFIDF): We treat all tweets corresponding to a hashtag as a document. For each query, we rank hashtags by their TFIDF scores [42].

Tweet Ratio-based Ranking Algorithm (TRA): For each query, we assign a score to each hashtag based on the ratio of the number of tweets containing that hashtag divided by the number of tweets containing both the hashtag and the query.

In addition to the above three baselines, we also compare our algorithm against the enthusiast ranking (ENTHUSIASTPREFERENCE) algorithm mentioned previously, that was used for creating the ground truth. As mentioned previously, while this is not a practical algorithm due to its extremely low coverage of queries, we still use it as an upper bound for a practical ranking algorithm and compare our algorithms against the performance of ENTHUSIASTPREFERENCE.

6.4 Evaluation Metrics

For our evaluation, we compute metrics for each algorithm by comparing it with the ground truth ranking. For a given query, let A and G be the ranked list of discussion groups identified by an algorithm and by the ground truth respectively, with $A[i]$ (resp. $G[i]$) being the ith discussion group. For every discussion group p, let $R(p) \in [0, 3]$ be the ground truth relevance rating provided by the human assessor. We define the following metrics [46]:

Weighted Precision: The WeightedPrecision @K of the algorithm at the top K rank is $\frac{\sum_{i=1}^{K} R(A[i])}{3K}$.

Weighted Recall: The WeightedRecall @K of the algorithm at the top K rank is $\frac{\sum_{i=1}^{K} R(A[i])}{\sum_{p \in G} R(p)}$

Weighted Mean Average Precision: The WeightedMAP of the algorithm is $\frac{1}{|G|} \cdot \sum_{p \in (G \cap A)} \text{WeightedPrecision } @\text{r}_{\text{p,A}}$, where $r_{p,A}$ is the rank of group p in A.

NDCG: The NDCG@K of the algorithm at the top K rank is $\frac{\text{DCG(A)}}{\text{DCG(G)}}$, where $\text{DCG(A)} = R(A[1]) + \sum_{i=2}^{K} \frac{R(A[i])}{\log_2 i}$.

In addition, we also compute the unweighted versions of the above metrics corresponding to precision (Precision @K), recall (Recall @K) and Mean Average Precision (MAP).

For the unweighted metrics, the relevance rating of a group is rounded to 1 if $R(p) \geq 2$ and 0 otherwise. We set $K = 5$.

6.5 Results of Implementation Choices

Teleport Distribution We first study the effect of varying the teleport probability from 0 to 1, with NOUNFREQWEIGHTS as the authority score. From Table 1, we first observe the significant benefit of having a non-zero teleport probability. This observation can be explained by the presence of several disjoint connected components of varying sizes in the graph formed over hashtags. For example, the graph over hashtags for the query "photography" consists of two large connected components: the first component consists of highly relevant groups such as **`#photographytips`**, **`#phototips`**, **`#photog`** and **`#photochat`**, while the second component consists of several less relevant hashtags such as **`#northeasthour`**, **`#yorkshirehour`**, **`#bathhour`** and **`#devonhour`**. In the absence of the option to teleport, the surfer may get stuck in the less relevant component. Even with a small teleport probability, the surfer is able to explore components containing relevant hashtags, and consequently, our algorithm is able to rank such hashtags higher.

As the teleport probability is increased, the performance improves initially, maximizing at 0.25, and then drops because the surfer teleports too often instead of moving towards better hashtags. Hence, we chose 0.25 as the teleport probability for further analysis. We next validate the benefit of having a biased teleport distribution (Table 2), confirming that it is desirable to factor in the query-specific popularity of hashtags instead of teleporting uniformly.

Authority Score We present a comparison of different authority scores in Table 3. We were at first surprised to observe similar performance across different authority scores, since these scores correspond to orthogonal signals. In fact, giving equal weight to all participants performed slightly better than the other three authority scores. A possible explanation is that for a given query, the signal to discriminate highly relevant hashtags from highly irrelevant hashtags are spread across many participants, and the aggregate preference captures this signal irrespective of the weights given to the participants. The participants may differ in their finer preferences over relevant hashtags (*e.g.*, between `#rosechat` and `#gardenchat` for the query "garden"), and hence, while the authority scores can influence the final relative ordering of two highly relevant hashtags, our metrics are unaffected if the positions of two such groups are swapped. Even though the authority scores did not significantly influence the performance measures at the aggregate level, we did observe relatively large variance in performance at the level of individual queries.

6.6 Performance Results

We next compare the performance of our algorithm (with NOUNFREQWEIGHTS as the authority score) with the three baselines, and the enthusiast-based ranking in Table 4. We observe that our algorithm significantly outperforms the best baseline, TFIDF along all seven metrics. Our algorithm improves TFIDF by 30% with respect to mean average precision (0.437 vs 0.336), about 25% with respect to weighted mean average precision (0.309 vs 0.246), and about 20% with respect to NDCG (0.488 vs 0.404). With respect to these three metrics, our algorithm achieves about 70% of the performance of ENTHUSIASTPREFERENCE, which, as noted earlier, is not a practical algorithm but can serve as an upper bound.

Qualitative Evaluation of Rankings

To provide qualitative insights into the ranking algorithms, we next highlight the top-3 Twitter hashtags retrieved by the different algorithms for 4 representative queries, in Table 5. (We omitted the UFA baseline due to its poor performance.) A quick scan on Twitter of the tweets related to the retrieved hashtags will reveal that for most of these queries, the GROUPPREFERENCE algorithm clearly retrieves more relevant groups compared to the baselines, and performs almost as well as ENTHUSIASTPREFERENCE. For example, for the query "garden", both GROUPPREFERENCE and ENTHUSIASTPREFERENCE retrieve a weekly Twitter group about gardening enthusiasts (`#gardenchat`) as the top hashtag (though ENTHUSIASTPREFERENCE also retrieves another related Twitter group related to roses (`#rosechat`). On the other hand, the baselines results are not very relevant. Indeed, TFIDF returns a hashtag related to Justin Bieber's "Believe Tour" at Madison Square Garden, simply due to the sheer number of tweets containing both "`#believetour`" and "garden". Similarly, for the query "resume", GROUPPREFERENCE returns three relevant weekly Twitter groups about jobs and hiring (`#omcchat`, `#animalchat` and `#hfchat`), and outperforms all the other algorithms that return at least one group that is not a discussion group (for example, `#jobfair` or `#forbesgreatesthits`). For the query "hotels", both GROUPPREFERENCE and ENTHUSIASTPREFERENCE return a travel-related weekly Twitter group as the top-ranked hashtag (`#tni` and `#ttot` respectively), whereas the baselines' top hashtag is not as relevant (`#dimiami` is a Miami-specific travel hashtag).

7. DISCUSSION AND FUTURE WORK

Group selection is admittedly more complicated than combining preference with authoritativeness. For example, among two groups that equally discuss a topic, the group that is more open to outsiders may be more preferable. The age and size of a group may also play a role in that mature, sizeable groups may be less welcome to newbies than younger, smaller groups. There are other potential factors [24]: for example, the quality of the relationships in the group (both online and offline), whether participant privacy is respected, and how conflict is handled (netiquette). Our work implicitly uses these signals by following the trail of participation left by authoritative users, but explicit use of such signals may lead to better solutions.

Personalized group ranking is another potential direction. For example, the demographic makeup of a group (race, gender, age) may be used to match a user's demographic. The language/vocabulary of a group is known to impact further participation [5, 18] and consequently may be used to improve ranking. The nature of groups that a user already participates in may also be an indication of the kinds of groups the user wishes to join. Richer graph structure signals such as the number of friends that a person has in the group and how connected their friends are could also be useful [2].

Furthermore, varying query types may call for varying groups. If the query suggests a user seeking knowledge or new expertise about a subject, then groups that frequently invite outside experts to answer questions may be more desirable. Other queries may suggest users seeking groups for humor or entertainment, and this could be another factor that improves ranking.

Moreover, the dynamic nature of Twitter implies that the best venue to discuss a topic may shift over time. In addition, participant authoritativeness may rise and fall over time. It would be valuable to understand and characterize when and how often these changes occur. If the ground truth changes repeatedly, then methods may be needed to quickly detect these shifts and rerank groups accordingly.

Our goal in ranking groups is to connect a new user to a group of like-minded users. The true test of whether our algorithm works is if users positively respond to our ranking. To that end, a practical direction is to build a system that runs our ranking algorithm periodically, and allows users to obtain the most recently computed ranked lists of discussion groups corresponding to their issued queries. One concern that needs to be addressed prior to deployment is determining which groups want to be found. Even though these conversations take place in "public", some participants may hide in obscurity [22], *e.g.*, believe that their conversations are invisible to current search engines, or communicate with fake accounts. Another concern is the potential consequences of overwhelming these groups with new members, *e.g.*, message overload [8, 29]. Historically, groups have found ways to cope with large membership, *e.g.*, by splitting into smaller groups, by geography or subtopic.

8. REFERENCES

[1] R. Agrawal, A. Halverson, K. Kenthapadi, N. Mishra, and P. Tsaparas. Generating labels from clicks. In *WSDM*, 2009.

[2] L. Backstrom, D. Huttenlocher, J. Kleinberg, and X. Lan. Group formation in large social networks: Membership, growth, and evolution. In *KDD*, 2006.

[3] L. Backstrom, R. Kumar, C. Marlow, J. Novak, and A. Tomkins. Preferential behavior in online groups. In *WSDM*, 2008.

[4] S. Brin and L. Page. The anatomy of a large-scale hypertextual Web search engine. *Computer Networks and ISDN Systems*, 30, 1998.

[5] C. Budak and R. Agrawal. Participation in group chats on Twitter. In *WWW*, 2013.

[6] C. Burges, R. Ragno, and Q. V. Le. Learning to rank with nonsmooth cost functions. In *NIPS*, 2006.

[7] C. Burges, T. Shaked, E. Renshaw, A. Lazier, M. Deeds, N. Hamilton, and G. Hullender. Learning to rank using gradient descent. In *ICML*, 2005.

[8] B. S. Butler. Membership size, communication activity, and sustainability: A resource-based model of online social structures. *Info. Sys. Research*, 12(4), Dec. 2001.

[9] R. Chaiken, B. Jenkins, P. Larson, B. Ramsey, D. Shakib, S. Weaver, and J. Zhou. SCOPE: Easy and efficient parallel processing of massive data sets. *PVLDB*, 1(2), 2008.

[10] S. Chien, C. Dwork, R. Kumar, D. R. Simon, and D. Sivakumar. Link evolution: Analysis and algorithms. *Internet Mathematics*, 1(3), 2003.

[11] W. Cohen, R. Schapire, and Y. Singer. Learning to order things. *JAIR*, 10, 1999.

[12] G. Cong, L. Wang, C.-Y. Lin, Y.-I. Song, and Y. Sun. Finding question-answer pairs from online forums. In *SIGIR*, 2008.

[13] J. Cook, K. Kenthapadi, and N. Mishra. Group chats on Twitter. In *WWW*, 2013.

[14] K. Csalogány, D. Fogaras, B. Rácz, and T. Sarlós. Towards scaling fully personalized pagerank: Algorithms, lower bounds, and experiments, 2005.

[15] C. Danescu-Niculescu-Mizil, R. West, D. Jurafsky, J. Leskovec, and C. Potts. No country for old members: User lifecycle and linguistic change in online communities. In *WWW*, 2013.

[16] K. Ehrlich, C.-Y. Lin, and V. Griffiths-Fisher. Searching for experts in the enterprise: Combining text and social network analysis. In *GROUP*, 2007.

[17] J. L. Elsas and J. G. Carbonell. It pays to be picky: An evaluation of thread retrieval in online forums. In *SIGIR*, 2009.

[18] D. Forsyth. *Group dynamics*. Wadsworth, 2009.

[19] S. Ghosh, N. K. Sharma, F. Benevenuto, N. Ganguly, and P. K. Gummadi. Cognos: Crowdsourcing search for topic experts in microblogs. In *SIGIR*, 2012.

[20] F. Godin, V. Slavkovikj, W. D. Neve, B. Schrauwen, and R. V. de Walle. Using topic models for Twitter hashtag recommendation. In *WWW (Companion Volume)*, 2013.

[21] P. Gupta, A. Goel, J. Lin, A. Sharma, D. Wang, and R. Zadeh. WTF: The who to follow service at Twitter. In *WWW*, 2013.

[22] W. Hartzog and F. Stutzman. The case for online obscurity. *California Law Review*, 101(1), 2013.

[23] S. Ieong, N. Mishra, and O. Sheffet. Predicting preference flips in commerce search. In *ICML*, 2012.

[24] A. Iriberri and G. Leroy. A life-cycle perspective on online community success. *CSUR*, 41(2), 2009.

[25] G. Jeh and J. Widom. Scaling personalized web search. In *WWW*, 2003.

[26] J. Jiao, J. Yan, H. Zhao, and W. Fan. Expertrank: An expert user ranking algorithm in online communities. In *NISS*, 2009.

[27] T. Joachims. Optimizing search engines using clickthrough data. In *KDD*, 2002.

[28] T. Joachims, L. Granka, B. Pan, H. Hembrooke, F. Radlinski, and G. Gay. Evaluating the accuracy of implicit feedback from clicks and query reformulations in web search. *ACM Trans. Inf. Syst*, 25(2), 2007.

[29] Q. Jones, G. Ravid, and S. Rafaeli. Information overload and the message dynamics of online interaction spaces: A theoretical model and empirical exploration. *Info. Sys. Research*, 15(2), 2004.

[30] E. Joyce and R. Kraut. Predicting continued participation in newsgroups. *J. Comput. Mediat. Comm*, 11(3), 2006.

[31] H. Kautz, B. Selman, and M. Shah. Referral web: Combining social networks and collaborative filtering. *Commun. ACM*, 40(3), 1997.

[32] J. Kleinberg. Authoritative sources in a hyperlinked environment. In *SODA*, 1998.

[33] G. Kossinets and D. J. Watts. Empirical analysis of an evolving social network. *Science*, 311(5757), 2006.

[34] S. M. Kywe, T. A. Hoang, E. P. Lim, and F. Zhu. On recommending hashtags in Twitter networks. In *SocInfo*, 2012.

[35] C. Lampe and E. Johnston. Follow the (slash) dot: Effects of feedback on new members in an online community. In *GROUP*, 2005.

[36] R. Lempel and S. Moran. Salsa: The stochastic approach for link-structure analysis. *ACM TOIS*, 19(2), 2001.

[37] R. Lempel and S. Moran. Rank-stability and rank-similarity of link-based web ranking algorithms in authority-connected graphs. *Information Retrieval*, 8(2), 2005.

[38] M. L. Markus. Toward a "critical mass" theory of interactive media universal access, interdependence and diffusion. *Communication research*, 14(5), 1987.

[39] M. Najork, S. Gollapudi, and R. Panigrahy. Less is more: Sampling the neighborhood graph makes SALSA better and faster. In *WSDM*, 2009.

[40] L. Page, S. Brin, R. Motwani, and T. Winograd. The PageRank citation ranking: Bringing order to the web. Technical report, Stanford InfoLab, 1999.

[41] A. Pal and S. Counts. Identifying topical authorities in microblogs. In *WSDM*, 2011.

[42] A. Rajaraman and J. D. Ullman. *Mining of massive datasets.* Cambridge University Press, 2011.

[43] T. Reichling, K. Schubert, and V. Wulf. Matching human actors based on their texts: Design and evaluation of an instance of the expertfinding framework. In *GROUP*, 2005.

[44] Y. Ren and R. E. Kraut. A simulation for designing online community: Member motivation, contribution, and discussion moderation. *Info. Sys. Research*, 2011.

[45] B. Saha and L. Getoor. Group proximity measure for recommending groups in online social networks. In *SNA-KDD Workshop*, 2008.

[46] T. Sakai. On the reliability of information retrieval metrics based on graded relevance. *Inform. Process. Manag*, 2007.

[47] P. Tsaparas. Using non-linear dynamical systems for web searching and ranking. In *PODS*, 2004.

[48] A. Tversky. Elimination by aspects: A theory of choice. *Psychological review*, 79(4), 1972.

[49] E. M. Voorhees and D. K. Harman. *TREC: Experiment and evaluation in information retrieval.* MIT Press, 2005.

[50] S. Whittaker, L. Terveen, W. Hill, and L. Cherny. The dynamics of mass interaction. In *From Usenet to CoWebs.* Springer London, 2003.

[51] L. Yang, T. Sun, M. Zhang, and Q. Mei. We know what @you #tag: Does the dual role affect hashtag adoption? In *WWW*, 2012.

[52] E. Zangerle and W. Gassler. Recommending #-tags in Twitter. In *CEUR Workshop*, 2011.

Teleport Probability	Precision	Recall	MAP	Weighted Precision	Weighted Recall	Weighted MAP
0.00	0.091	0.110	0.083	0.092	0.117	0.068
0.15	0.395	0.486	0.425	0.347	0.437	0.303
0.25	0.395	0.491	0.437	0.350	0.447	0.309
0.50	0.382	0.463	0.423	0.332	0.412	0.297
0.75	0.364	0.451	0.414	0.323	0.408	0.288
1.00	0.350	0.440	0.391	0.306	0.395	0.271

Table 1: Effect of Varying Teleport Probability

Teleport Bias	Precision	Recall	MAP	Weighted Precision	Weighted Recall	Weighted MAP
Uniform	0.177	0.224	0.169	0.171	0.211	0.131
Biased	0.395	0.491	0.437	0.350	0.447	0.309

Table 2: Benefit of Non-uniform Teleport Distribution

Authority Score	Precision	Recall	MAP	Weighted Precision	Weighted Recall	Weighted MAP
NounFreqWeights	0.395	0.491	0.437	0.350	0.447	0.309
FollowerWeights	0.377	0.467	0.461	0.345	0.433	0.330
@-mentionWeights	0.382	0.467	0.467	0.341	0.423	0.332
EqualWeights	0.400	0.485	0.479	0.359	0.446	0.340

Table 3: Empirical Analysis of Different Authority Scores

Algorithm	Precision	Recall	MAP	Weighted Precision	Weighted Recall	Weighted MAP	NDCG
UFA	0.236	0.280	0.232	0.212	0.277	0.168	0.301
TRA	0.273	0.377	0.313	0.245	0.348	0.217	0.362
TFIDF	0.309	0.362	0.336	0.288	0.366	0.246	0.404
GroupPreference	0.395	0.491	0.437	0.350	0.447	0.309	0.488
EnthusiastPreference	0.532	0.706	0.611	0.480	0.636	0.446	0.691

Table 4: Performance of Different Algorithms

Query	TFIDF	TRA	GroupPreference	EnthusiastPreference
garden	#believetour #beastmode #knicks	#fuego #joedirt #count	#gardenchat #fuego #joedirt	#gardenchat #growyourown #rosechat
hotels	#dimiami #united #ttot	#dimiami #tunehotelquiz #dolcehotels	#tl_chat #traveltuesday #tni	#ttot #traveltuesday #barcelona
photographers	#photog #togchat #phototips	#photographychat #togchat #thegridlive	#photographychat #phototips #togchat	#photog #scotland #sbs
resume	#forbesgreatesthits #hfchat #sctop10	#momken #resuchat #hfchat	#omcchat #animalchat #hfchat	#hfchat #jobhuntchat #jobfair

Table 5: Sample Discussion Group Rankings using Different Algorithms

Inferring Coarse Views of Connectivity in Very Large Graphs

Reza Motamedi
University of Oregon
motamedi@cs.uoregon.edu

Reza Rejaie
University of Oregon
reza@cs.uoregon.edu

Walter Willinger
Niksun, Inc.
wwillinger@niksun.com

Daniel Lowd
University of Oregon
lowd@cs.uoregon.edu

Roberto Gonzalez
NEC Europe Ltd.
roberto.gonzalez@neclab.eu

ABSTRACT

This paper presents a simple framework, called *WalkAbout*, to infer a coarse view of connectivity in very large graphs; that is, identify well-connected "regions" with different edge densities and determine the corresponding inter- and intra-region connectivity. We leverage the transient behavior of many short random walks (RW) on a large graph that is assumed to have regions of varying edge density but whose structure is otherwise unknown. The key idea is that as RWs approach the mixing time of a region, the ratio of the number of visits by all RWs to the degree for nodes in that region converges to a value proportional to the average node degree in that region. Leveraging this indirect sign of connectivity enables our proposed framework to effectively scale with graph size.

After describing the design of *WalkAbout*, we demonstrate the capabilities of *WalkAbout* by applying it to three major OSNs (*i.e.*, Flickr, Twitter, and Google+) and obtaining a coarse view of their connectivity structure. In addition, we illustrate how the communities that are obtained by running a popular community detection method on these OSNs stack up against the *WalkAbout*-discovered regions. Finally, we examine the "meaning" of the regions obtained by *WalkAbout*, and demonstrate that users in the identified regions exhibit common social attributes.

Categories and Subject Descriptors

E.1 [**Data Structures**]: Graphs and networks

General Terms

Algorithms, Design

Keywords

Graph Coarsening; Community Detection; Clustering; Graph Partitioning; Scalability

COSN'14, October 1–2, 2014, Dublin, Ireland.

http://dx.doi.org/10.1145/2660460.2660480.

1. INTRODUCTION

Large-scale, networked systems such as the World Wide Web or Online Social Networks (OSNs) can be represented as graphs where nodes represent individual entities, such as web pages or users, and directed or undirected edges represent relations between these entities, such as interaction or friendship between users [14, 18, 24]. Characterizing the connectivity structure of such a graph, in particular at scale, often provides deeper insight into the corresponding networked system and has motivated many researchers to analyze graph representations of large networked systems (*e.g.*, [1]).

It is often very useful to obtain a coarse view of the connectivity structure of a huge graph that shows a few major tightly connected components or *regions* of the graph along with the inter- and intra-region connectivity. Such a regional view also enables a natural top-down approach to the analysis of large graphs, where one first examines the regional connectivity of a huge graph and then zooms in to individual regions to explore their structure in further detail. However, capturing a regional view of a huge graph is a non-trivial task that existing tools and techniques are not able to achieve. While many techniques exist for graph clustering [26, 6], graph partitioning [12], and community detection [4, 22, 9], these approaches do not work well for discovering coarse regional views in very large graphs. These methods usually scale poorly, force regions to have similar size, or find communities that are too small. For example, existing techniques (*e.g.*, Louvain [4]) are likely to identify tens of thousands of communities in the structure of a large OSN that is still too complex for high-level analysis to determine the full picture of inter-community connectivity.

This paper presents a simple top-down framework, called *WalkAbout*, to identify tightly connected regions in a large unknown graph and subsequently characterize the regional view of its connectivity structure. The main idea is to leverage the behavior of an army of short random walks (RW) on a graph to identify nodes that are located in the same region. When the random walks are longer than the mixing time of an individual region and shorter than the mixing time of the overall graph, the ratio of node degree to expected number of visits is proportional to the edge density of that region. We refer to this quantity as the degree/visit ratio (*dvr*). If individual regions in a graph have different edge densities and shorter mixing times than the entire graph, we can leverage the *dvr* "signal" to identify the regions, their corresponding nodes and their intra- and inter-region connectivity. The main novelty of *WalkAbout* is to leverage this indirect sign of connectivity to identify tightly connected nodes in a region. This leads to a very scalable method: in a graph with $|V|$ nodes, $|E|$ edges, and a regional mixing time of wl, *WalkAbout* requires only $O(wl \times |E|)$ time and $O(|V|)$ space. A few parameters in *WalkAbout* enable one to explore different aspects of the regional connectivity in order to produce the outcome with the desired resolution.

In our empirical evaluation, we apply *WalkAbout* to three major OSNs: Flickr, Twitter and Google+. Compared to Louvain [4], the gold standard for scalable community detection, *WalkAbout* runs faster and finds larger, coarser regions. Most communities discovered by Louvain can be mapped to a single one of *WalkAbout*'s regions, suggesting that *WalkAbout* is providing a higher-level view of the network than Louvain. Finally, we analyze the regions in Flickr and show that different regions discovered by *WalkAbout* correspond to different interest groups, providing a meaningful coarse view of this OSN.

The remainder of our paper is organized as follows. Section 2 provides the background for the paper and an overview of related work. Section 3 explores the behavior of short random walks and *dvr* on graphs with a single region. Section 4 extends this analysis to multiple region graphs and motivates using *dvr* for region identification. In Section 5, we present the full details of *WalkAbout*, our step-by-step framework for identifying regions in large graphs. To demonstrate and evaluate *WalkAbout*, we apply it to three major OSNs in Section 6. In Section 7, we compare the characteristics of Louvain communities with *WalkAbout* regions. We show that the regions discovered by *WalkAbout* are indeed meaningful in Section 8. We conclude the paper in Section 9 and summarize our future plans.

2. BACKGROUND & RELATED WORK

We begin with a brief overview of related work in community detection and graph partitioning. Most methods work by optimizing an objective function. Since this is typically NP-hard, greedy or heuristic methods are usually necessary. One of the most popular metrics for community detection is modularity, which relates the number of edges within a cluster to the expected number for a random graph. For optimizing modularity, one of the most scalable and effective algorithms is the Louvain method [4]. The Louvain method greedily assigns nodes to communities based on their local connectivity, then coarsens the graph by replacing each community with a single node. This procedure repeats until it reaches a local optimum of modularity. However, in most real-world graphs, modularity tends to favor smaller communities of around 100 nodes [16]. Other measures such as conductance also tend to favor small clusters in real-world graphs, limiting their effectiveness at describing high-level structure.

Community detection methods based on RWs and "flows" have been proposed as well [25, 22, 23]. These methods use RWs or the associated transition matrix to compute some kind of distance or similarity relationship between each pair of nodes. However, even computing and storing sparse pairwise information is usually too expensive on large graphs with millions of nodes.

Graph partitioning or global clustering techniques [12, 13] adopt a top-down approach, dividing a graph into strongly connected partitions and optionally recursing within each partition to obtain the desired granularity [8, 12, 13]. While this does discover larger regions than the bottom-up approaches, these regions may or may not faithfully represent the overall graph structure. For example, methods that optimize the popular normalized cut criterion tend to produce regions of approximately equal size, even when this leads to poorly separated regions. Furthermore, some approaches require specifying seed instances for each partition [2] or the total number of partitions, both of which can be difficult to determine a priori. Finally, many of these techniques, including spectral clustering [11], do not scale with graph size and often require a complete snapshot of the target graph or its adjacency matrix.

WalkAbout is different from the prior approaches as it is not optimizing a single metric or objective function. Rather, it is a heuristic approach that relies on an interesting transient phenomenon to explore the coarse view of structure in very large graphs. More specifically, *WalkAbout* does not only produce a single coarse view of connectivity, but also its parameters allow a user to explore the connectivity structure to identify proper view at the desired resolution.

3. THE BEHAVIOR OF MANY SHORT RWS

Random Walks (RW) are a well-known technique for sampling graphs. A RW on a graph starts from an arbitrary node and at each step moves to a randomly chosen neighbor of the current node. Consider a graph $G = [V, E]$ where V and E denote the set of graph vertices and edges, respectively. In an undirected, connected, and non-bipartite graph, the probability that a sufficiently long RW would be at a particular node x converges to $\frac{deg(x)}{2\times|E|}$ [17]. The *mixing time* $T_G(\epsilon)$ of a graph G is the walk length at which the probability of being at each node is within ϵ of the stationary distribution. In this paper, we will use this term somewhat informally, without specifying a particular value of ϵ.

Suppose we run $|V|$ RWs in parallel, one starting at each node. Let $V(x, wl)$ denote the expected number of RWs that are at a particular node x after wl number of steps (e.g., *walk length* of wl). Since one RW is started at each node, $V(x, 0) = 1$. For other values of wl, we can define $V(x, k)$ inductively:

$$V(x,0) = 1$$

$$V(x,wl) = \sum_{n\in\text{Neighbors}(x)} \frac{V(n,wl-1)}{\deg(n)} \qquad \text{for } wl > 0 \quad (1)$$

This function can be computed iteratively with complexity $O(|E|wl)$. As wl reaches the *mixing time*, $V(x, wl)$ converges to $|V|\frac{deg(x)}{2\times|E|}$. Hence, when wl is sufficiently long, the following holds for all nodes:

$$\frac{deg(x)}{V(x,wl)} \approx \frac{2\times|E|}{|V|} \quad (2)$$

We refer to the fraction $\frac{deg(x)}{V(x,wl)}$ as the *degree/visit ratio* or *dvr*. Equation (2) indicates that the *dvr* converges to the average degree of the graph.

In practice, estimating the mixing time for an arbitrary graph is a known hard problem. In this section, we will explore the dependency of *dvr* on wl through simulations

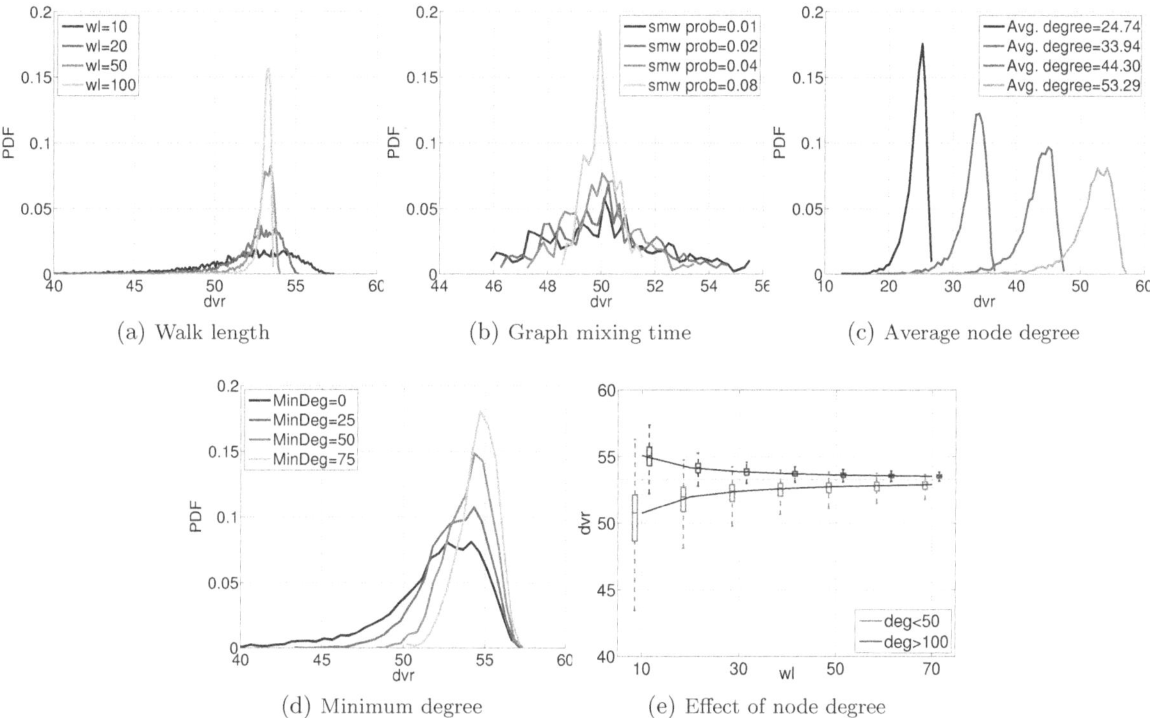

Figure 1: The effect of main parameters on the shape of the dvr histogram

on different synthetically-generated graphs. The graphs are generated by selecting the range of node degrees, the distribution of node degrees across this range, and then randomly connecting the nodes until all half-edges are connected. For each simulation, we show a normalized histogram of dvr values across all nodes, which represents the empirical distribution of dvr values for that simulation.

Effect of Walk Length: Figure 1(a) shows the evolution of the dvr histogram as we increase walk length over a generic random graph. As the walk length increases, the variation in dvr across different nodes decreases, leading to the formation of a narrower peak in the histogram. As wl reaches the mixing time, the probability of visiting each node becomes approximately proportional to its degree.

Effect of Mixing Time: To explore the effect of mixing time on the dvr histogram, we show in Figure 1(b) the evolution of the dvr histogram for a small-world graph as we increase the level of clustering (and thus the mixing time) for a particular walk length ($wl = 20$). As the mixing time becomes longer, the variation in dvr values increases because the RWs are farther from convergence.

Effect of Average Node Degree (E): Figure 1(c) presents the effect of average node degree ($i.e.$, changing $|E|$ when $|V|$ is fixed) on the shape of the dvr histogram at a given walk length ($wl = 20$). Increasing the average node degree shifts the corresponding peak to higher dvr values. It is worth noting that the placement of each peak is in perfect agreement with the average degree of each graph.

Effect of Minimum Node Degree: Figure 1(d) shows the contribution of low degree nodes to the shape of the dvr histogram by plotting the histogram only for nodes whose degree is larger than a threshold D_{min}. We find that higher degree nodes show less variation in dvr than low degree nodes, $i.e.$, filtering low degree nodes leads to a sharper peak in the histogram. Figure 1(e) depicts the evolution of summary distribution of dvr across two groups of nodes with different degrees which shows that the range of dvr is inversely proportional with node degree and rapidly decreases with the walk length. This property is due to the fact that higher degree nodes are averaging over more neighbors in each update of $V(x, wl)$, thus reducing the variation.

4. DETECTING REGIONS IN A GRAPH

To infer a coarse view of graph connectivity, we assume that each graph consists of a number of weakly inter-connected regions, where individual regions have varying edge density. We use the term "region" instead of "community" to emphasize the fact that regions are often much larger in size than typical communities, and are identified based on a heuristic rather than optimizing an objective function or a metric.

We have no a priori knowledge of either the number of regions or their relative size and make no assumptions about the precise nature of the inter-region connectivity or intra-region connections.

4.1 The Key Idea

Our approach is to leverage the behavior of RWs that are shorter than the mixing time of the graph to identify nodes in each region of the graph. To this end, consider RWs that start from randomly selected nodes of a graph $G = [V, E]$ that has multiple regions. Based on our discussion in Section 3, the fraction of RWs that start in region i ($G_i = [V_i, E_i]$) of the graph is equal to the fraction of nodes in that region ($i.e.$, $\frac{|V_i|}{|V|}$). If the length of those RWs is approximately equal to the mixing time of regions G_i, a majority of RWs will remain within that starting region, and for all practical purposes, we can view the different regions of the graph as disconnected partitions. Thus, we can use

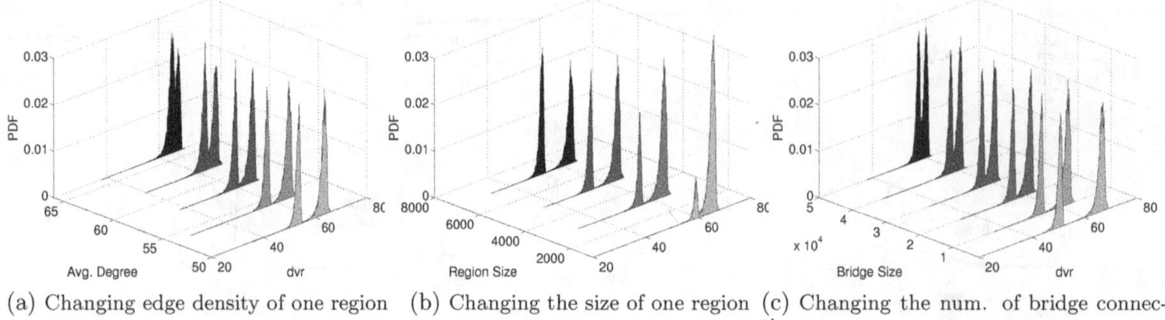

(a) Changing edge density of one region (b) Changing the size of one region (c) Changing the num. of bridge connections

Figure 2: The effect of connectivity features of a two-region graph on the *dvr* histogram ($wl = 20$)

Equation (2) to determine the value of the *dvr* ratio to which node x in region i converges to as follows:

$$dvr_i(x) = \frac{deg(x)}{E[V(x, wl)]} = \frac{(2 \times |E_i|)}{|V_i|}, \quad (3)$$

Equation (3) shows that the degree-to-visit ratio for nodes x in region i equals $\frac{2 \times |E_i|}{|V_i|}$ which is the average node degree for region i. Therefore, if regions of the graph have different average node degrees, the $dvr_i(x)$ values for nodes in each region converge to a different *dvr* value, *i.e.*, form a peak at a different location in the *dvr* histogram across all nodes. We can represent each region with its associated non-overlapping range of *dvr* values and then map visited nodes to a region based on their *dvr* values. Furthermore, as discussed earlier, other key connectivity features of a region i (*e.g.*, mixing time and size) affect the shape of the corresponding peak.

As the length of the RWs increases beyond the mixing time of individual regions, the RWs are likely to leave their starting regions and contribute to the number of visits for nodes in other regions of the graph. This in turn decreases the gap in the $dvr_i(x)$ values for different regions and the *dvrs* values for all nodes converge to a single value (determined by Equation (2) as soon as the walk length of the RWs agrees approximately with the mixing time of the entire graph. Therefore, the separation between peaks in the *dvr* histogram that are associated with different regions of a graph is a *transient* phenomenon that occurs for RWs whose walk lengths are between region-specific mixing times and the mixing time for the entire graph. The more pronounced the regions, the larger the gaps between the mixing times of individual regions and the entire graph, which in turn translates to a longer transient phase and simplifies the detection of different regions. *In a nutshell, the similarity in dvr value serves as a promising indirect signal that reveals a tight connectivity among a group of nodes in a graph. The indirect nature of the dvr signal coupled with the ability to efficiently obtain dvr values using short random walks enables our approach to scale with graph size.*

4.2 Validation with Synthetic Graphs

Next we use synthetic graphs to demonstrate how our basic idea can reveal (or decode) the regional connectivity features within a graph. To this end, we consider a graph G with two regions, R_0 and R_1, both with 4K nodes and random connectivity and an average degree of 70 and 60, respectively. We connect these two regions with b bridge connections, where each bridge connection is between a pair of random nodes from these regions, and its default value is b=10k. In essence, the value of b controls the inter-region connectivity and thus the mixing time of the entire graph. To illustrate the effect of regional connectivity features on the shape of the *dvr* histogram, we keep region R_0 fixed and systematically change features of R_1 and the value of b.

Figure 2(a) shows the evolution of the *dvr* histogram as we vary the average node degree in R_1 between 50 and 66. We observe that as the average degree of $R1$ increases, the corresponding peak gradually moves to higher *dvr* values and blends into the peak for R_0 until individual peaks are no longer distinguishable. Figure 2(b) shows how varying the size of R_1 from 1K to 8K nodes affects the shape of the *dvr* histogram when all other parameters remain constant. Increasing the size of a region proportionally increases the number of RWs that start from that region which in turn leads to a proportionally larger peak. Since we normalize *dvr* and plot the PDF, the peak corresponding to R_0 decreases in size. Finally, Figure 2(c) illustrates the effect of increasing the number of bridge edges (or bridge width) between the two regions from 5K to 50k. We note that as the bridge width increases, the two peaks gradually merge and become less and less distinguishable. This is due to the fact that increasing bridge width decreases the mixing time of the entire graph and thus shrinks the transition phase where the peaks for two regions can be clearly identified.

In summary, these examples illustrate that the behavior of many short RWs on a single graph can be extended to multi-region graphs as long as the mixing time of the entire graph is sufficiently larger than the the mixing time of individual regions.

5. WALKABOUT

In this section, we present *WalkAbout*, our proposed method for inferring and exploring a regional (*i.e.*, coarse) view of connectivity for large graphs. We first discuss some of the basic challenges in designing such a methodology and then describe our approach and how it addresses these challenges.

5.1 Basic Challenges

The behavior of many short RWs on a large graph motivates the idea of using the similarity of *dvr* values to identify individual regions of a graph where regions are represented as a collection of nodes with non-overlapping ranges of *dvr* values. To implement this idea in practice, a number of challenges arise. First, we recall that the variation of *dvr* values across nodes with degree d in a given region decreases monotonically while the median value converges towards the average node degree of the region. More importantly, the degree of variation and its rate of convergence is inversely proportional to the node degree d, *i.e.*, *dvr* values of higher degree nodes exhibit smaller variations and convergence faster than lower degree nodes. The typically large fraction of low degree nodes in big graphs coupled with the wider variation and slower convergence rate of their *dvr* values make it difficult to accurately associate a set of nodes with their corresponding region. This problem is further exacerbated by the fact that different regions may have a different mixing time and overlapping ranges of *dvr* values.

5.2 Main Steps of WalkAbout

Given a large graph $G[V, E]$, the goal of *WalkAbout* is to identify the number of regions, map all nodes to their corresponding region, and determine the inter- and intra-region connectivity (*i.e.*, fraction of edges that are connecting nodes in different regions or the same region). We call such a representation of a large graph a *regional (or coarse) view* of the graph. To overcome the above-mentioned challenges, *WalkAbout* identifies individual regions in two steps. First, it identifies a "core" component for each region. Such a component consists of a collection of high degree nodes in that region based on the similarity of their *dvr* values. Second, it considers each of these core components, views their elements as "anchors" and maps the remaining low degree nodes to the various regions based on the nodes' relative reachability to each core. This approach can effectively cope with the variations of the *dvr* values for low degree nodes and is less sensitive to the walk length. The *WalkAbout* technique comes with a set of parameters/options that enable the exploration of the regional connectivity of a graph and support experimentation with different coarse views of a graph. In the following, we describe the five main steps of the *WalkAbout* technique.

1) Determining *dvr* Values for Individual Nodes: We emulate the behavior of $|V|$ short RWs starting from individual nodes in the graph and derive the probability of visits and use that probability to determine the degree-to-visit ratio for individual nodes at walk length wl, similar to Equation (1).

2) Creating the *dvr* Histogram: Given the *dvr* values of different nodes, our goal is to group nodes with similar *dvr* values and use them as the core elements for the corresponding region. To this end, we bin the nodes based on their *dvr* values and generate a histogram to identify the most common values (*i.e.*, "peaks") which in turn suggest the existence of different regions. To reduce the noise that the wide variation of *dvr* values for low degree nodes introduces, we first filter out all nodes whose degree is smaller than a threshold D_{min}. In fact D_{min} is a parameter that can be used to control the visibility of nodes that are under possible consideration for being selected as core elements. It provides a knob for examining the trade-offs that result from increasing the level of noise caused by a larger number of low degree nodes (*i.e.*, small D_{min} values) – allowing for more noise typically results in the identification of a larger number of less reliable core elements and hence regions. Next, while the *dvr* values for higher degree nodes are significantly more reliable, these nodes may not have a profound impact on the shape of the histogram due to the often small fraction of high degree nodes. We deal with this issue by introducing a bias towards the *dvr* values of high degree nodes. In particular, for each high degree node, we multiply its *dvr* value by its node degree. In effect, we simply increase the frequency of the *dvr* values of the high degree nodes proportional to their node degree. The resulting conditioned histogram is in general more amenable to reveal the presence of reliable regions since it has more pronounced peaks that are less sensitive to the value of D_{min} parameter.

3) Identifying Core of a Region From the Histogram: Identifying regions from a *dvr* histogram requires *(i)* determining a proper walk length that generates the best histogram, and *(ii)* detecting the regions from the resulting histogram. To deal with item *(i)*, we progressively increase the walk length and repeat steps (1) and (2) to generate the resulting histogram. We carefully examine the evolution of the histogram as a function of walk length and select the histogram where the peaks are most pronounced and most separated. By definition, such a histogram should be formed when the walk length is close to the mixing time of individual regions. In such a histogram, each peak (*i.e.*, a local maximum that is surrounded by two local minimum values) represents a region's core whose range of *dvr* values is specified by the *dvr* values corresponding to the two minimum values. This heuristic can be viewed as a naive one-dimensional clustering technique. We examine the connectivity among nodes that are part of each core to ensure that they form a connected component[1] This check also reveals whether the cores of two separate regions with overlapping *dvr* ranges appear as a single peak which makes it difficult to distinguish them from the histogram in the first place. At the end of this step, we have the number of regions and the list of high degree nodes that form the core of each region.

4) Mapping Low-Degree Nodes to Cores: We use the relative reachability of low degree nodes to identified cores in order to map them. To this end, we start N RWs from each node where each RW walk continues until it hits a node in one of the cores. Each walk provides a sample of reachability for this node. The node is mapped to the core with the highest reachability. The fraction of RWs that hit the most reachable core indicates our confidence in mapping a node to that region.

5) Producing the Regional View: Once nodes in each region of the graph are identified, we determine the edges that are within each region or connecting two different regions. Then we produce a diagram that incorporates all the information about regional connectivity of a graph including *(i)* a circle represents a region with the area logarithmically proportional to the size of the region, *(ii)* arrows between two regions indicate the inter-region connectivity and their width as well as color is proportional with the relative fraction of directed half-edges between two regions. Intra region half-edges are represented with the modularity of a region and thus are not shown in the regional view to keep this less crowded.

[1]It is not a required condition that core nodes form a connected component. However, forming a connected component does indicate that the core is coherent.

Table 1: Characteristics of LCC snapshots of target OSNs

	FL	TW	G+
Nodes	$1.6M$	$41.6M$	$51.7M$
Edges	$31.1M$	$1,468M$	$869.4M$
Louvain Communities	$264.4K$	$9,9M$	$43.6K$

5.3 Inferring vs. Exploring Regions

The design of *WalkAbout* provides several parameters or knobs that can be tuned to explore different coarse views of a given graph. These parameters include the walk length, the D_{min} threshold, and the precise nature of determining how low degree nodes get mapped to regions (core anchors). In essence, examining the effect of these parameters on the resulting regional views facilitates studying the quality of a given regional view in terms of its robustness to the choices *WalkAbout* offers to its users. In this sense, *WalkAbout* can be viewed as a framework for exploring regional connectivity in an interactive manner rather than a technique for producing a single regional view.

It is also important to emphasize that since *WalkAbout* is not trying to optimize an explicit objective function (*e.g.*, modularity [21], the regional view that results from running *WalkAbout* for a given graph is not unique. Instead, by harvesting a transient phenomenon, we face a new challenge in the form of deciding on a proper walk length. Our approach to deal with this challenge is to gain an understanding of the sensitivity of a resulting regional view to the choice of the walk length to minimize potential mistakes at each step.

By varying the D_{min} parameter, we are able to explore the trade-off between level of coarsening and the accuracy of the regional view. Large values of this parameter typically result in few but reliable regions (*i.e.*, coarse and stable view), while smaller values of D_{min} produce in general many more but less reliable regions (*i.e.*, fine but unstable views). Alternatively, D_{min} can be set based on domain knowledge to only include nodes that are considered central for a given context. For example, in an OSN graph, nodes with degree larger than 500 or even 1000 may be viewed as core nodes. In this paper, we primarily focus on the application of *WalkAbout* to OSN and set D_{min} to 500.[2]

We have developed *WalkAbout* as an interactive tool with GUI that allows users to arbitrarily slice the histogram and generate the resulting regional view in an interactive manner. This publicly available tool can be downloaded from the project web site [20].

6. WALKABOUT IN ACTION

In this section, we use our proposed technique to characterize coarse views of large popular OSNs such as Flickr, Twitter, and Google+. In the process, we not only demonstrate the key features and capabilities of our technique, but also show what sort of coarse views *WalkAbout* produces for the well-known OSNs.

6.1 Datasets and Methodology

In the following, we rely on anonymized snapshots of the largest connected component (LCC) of the connectivity structure for Flickr (FL) that was captured by Mislove et al. [18], a snapshot of the Twitter (TW) social graph that was collected by Kwak et al. [15], and a snapshot of Google+ (G+) from a recent study by Gonzalez et al. [10]. Table 1 summarizes the main characteristics of these snapshots.

When applying the *WalkAbout* technique to each OSN, we consider these snapshots as as undirected graphs, *i.e.*, converting any directed edge between two nodes (for TW and G+) into an undirected edge. For each OSN, we apply *WalkAbout* and show the following results: *(i)* the evolution of the conditioned *dvr* histogram (see Section 5) as a function of walk length to illustrate the selection of target walk length. *(ii)* the shape of the modified histogram at the target walk length that shows the peaks used for identifying individual regions, *(iii)* a table that summarizes the main features of the identified cores (number of nodes and the average degree in each core) and the corresponding regions (the percentage of total nodes and edges, average degree and modularity), and *(iv)* a sketch the regional view of the OSN.

We refer to the collection of specified values for the *WalkAbout* parameters, namely D_{min} and wl, as the *target setting*. In particular, we used $D_{min} = 500$ throughout this analysis. To examine the robustness of our results to different choices of D_{min} values, we repeated our analysis with D_{min} values that are 10% larger or smaller and observed no significant differences. For a more detailed account of this robustness analysis, refer to our related technical report [19].

Table 2: FL – Basic features of identified regions

	cores		region			
#Region	Size	Avg.Deg	%Nodes	%Edges	Avg.Deg.	Mod.
$R0$	4.04E+03	1.10E+03	92.8	58.2	11.9	0.4
$R1$	5.69E+02	1.01E+03	1.2	3.2	50.1	0.5
$R2$	3.01E+03	1.12E+03	4.0	17.6	83.7	0.7
$R3$	2.12E+03	1.35E+03	1.8	16.6	174.2	0.6
$R4$	1.14E+03	1.10E+03	0.2	4.4	431.0	0.3

6.2 OSNs and Their Regional Views

Regional View of Flicker (FL): Figure 3(a) shows the evolution of *dvr* histogram for a FL snapshot as a function of walk length around the selected target setting ($wl = 30$, $D_{min} = 500$). We observe that $wl = 30$ reveals the largest number of pronounced peaks; *i.e.*, a total of five peaks. Figure 3(b) shows the shape of *dvr* histogram at our selected target setting for FL ($wl = 30$, $D_{min} = 500$) where the five major peaks are marked and their associated ranges of *dvr*-values are colored. Note that regions R_3 and R_4 could have been considered as a single region. However, because of the observed dip around $dvr = 35$, we split that peak into two regions. We later discuss the effect of this decision. Due to their small sizes and to keep the number of regions within limits, we did not consider several very small peaks in the middle of the histogram whose *dvr* was $21.96 < dvr < 33.4$ and contained between 1 to 100 nodes (with the median of 8 nodes). This is indeed one way to explore the tradeoff between the accuracy or resolution (by keeping many core components) and complexity of the resulting view. Note that *WalkAbout* reveals these peaks and allows us to explore them if a higher resolution is desired.

Table 2 summarizes the key features of the five identified cores and their corresponding regions. We observe that the cores include between 500-4000 nodes and collectively contain less than 1% of nodes of the graph. Except for R_1,

[2]We have examined the effect of D_{min} on the *dvr* histogram and our findings are reported in the related technical report [19].

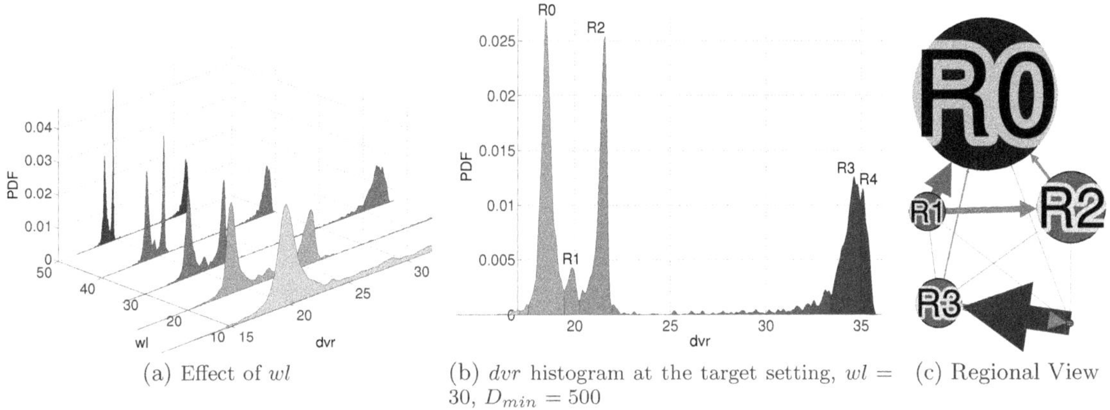

(a) Effect of wl (b) dvr histogram at the target setting, wl = 30, D_{min} = 500 (c) Regional View

Figure 3: Applying *WalkAbout* to Flickr snapshot

Table 3: TW – Basic features of identified regions

	cores		region			
#Region	Size	Avg.Deg	%Nodes	%Edges	Avg.Deg.	Mod.
$R0$	8.05E+04	1.02E+03	2.6	4.5	124.2	0.4
$R1$	2.75E+05	1.47E+03	54.1	31.0	40.4	0.3
$R2$	2.72E+05	2.16E+03	40.8	42.6	73.5	0.2
$R3$	1.20E+05	4.70E+03	2.5	20.7	596.2	0.4
$R4$	4.57E+03	5.21E+03	0.01	0.8	3,167.7	0.4
$R5$	1.90E+03	5.83E+03	0.002	0.4	4,066.3	0.4

Table 4: G+ – Basic features of identified regions

	cores		region			
#Region	Size	Avg.Deg	%Nodes	%Edges	Avg.Deg.	Mod.
$R0$	2.18E+05	1.73E+03	82.0	62.8	25.8	0.3
$R1$	4.00E+04	7.13E+03	16.3	33.5	69.2	0.6
$R2$	6.51E+03	1.70E+03	0.6	1.0	54.2	0.7
$R3$	9.94E+03	2.28E+03	0.9	1.9	73.8	0.8
$R4$	7.40E+01	3.71E+04	0.2	0.5	74.5	0.7
$R5$	1.45E+02	1.78E+04	0.1	0.3	175.4	0.6

they are all of similar size. The resulting regions are very imbalanced, with R_0 containing more than 92% of all nodes and 58% of all edges and having average degree of 11.9 and modularity of 0.4. The other regions are very small and contain only some 0.2%-4% of all nodes. However, regions R_2 and R_3 have a high average degree and thus include a much larger fraction of edges. At the same time, regions R_2 and R_3 have a much higher modularity than R_0. All the identified cores and regions form connected components. Figure 3(c) sketches the regional view of the FL structure. This figure shows that for all practical purposes, regions R_3 and R_4 are weakly connected to the other three regions. We recall that these two regions are created as a result of splitting the right most peak of the dvr histogram into two parts. Given their strong inter-connectivity, an option would be to merge these two regions together and consider them as a single region, thus producing a yet coarser view of the FL connectivity structure.

Regional View of Twitter (TW): Figure 5(a) depicts the evolution of the dvr histogram for the TW structure as a function of wl where D_{min} = 500. We observe that the transition phase for the formation of peaks for different regions is rather short, between wl values of 14 and 22. We select wl = 18 for our target setting as it reveals the most clear set of peaks in the histogram. Figure 4(b) depicts six peaks in the dvr histogram at our target setting.

Table 3 summarizes the main characteristics of the identified cores and their corresponding regions. We observe that the cores have between 1.9K and 275K nodes. There are two large (R_1 and R_2), two small (R_0 and R_3), and two tiny (R_4 and R_5) regions. The regions generally exhibit low modularity ($\leq$0.4). The low level of modularity for regions in TW indicates that regions do not exhibit tight internal connectivity. An interesting fact about the two tiny regions is that they have an order of magnitude larger average degree than the other regions but still exhibit the same modularity. Figure 4(c) depicts the resulting regional view for the TW structure and reveals that regions R_1 and R_2 have strong mutual connectivity and play a central role in the graph. R_0 is connected to R_1 and R_2 from one side while R_5, R_4 and R_3 form a triangle structure that connect to the rest of the regions primarily through R_2.

Regional View of Google+ (G+): Figure 5(a) depicts the evolution of the dvr histogram for the G+ graph as we change wl. The histogram which most clearly reveals different regions is formed around wl = 20. Therefore, we select this wl as our target setting. The corresponding histogram is shown in Figure 5(b) and reveals the existence of six distinguishable peaks. While the regions R_4 and R_5 result from rather small peaks, we still use them as cores because they are clearly separated from other peaks and also have a large average degree.

Table 4 summarizes the main features of the identified cores and regions. We observe that the core sizes vary between 74 and 218k which is much more skewed compared to the other OSNs. These cores lead to a dominant region R_0, a moderate-sized region R_1, and four tiny regions. All regions except for R_0 exhibit a rather high modularity (0.6-0.8). Figure 5(c) plots the regional view of the connectivity structure for G+. We observe that R_4 and R_5 are tightly inter-connected but have a weak connectivity to the other regions. The other four regions have a moderate chain-like inter-connectivity structure of the form R_2-R_3-R_1-R_0.

6.3 Lessons Learned

The obtained regional views of the connectivity structures of some of the most popular OSNs provide a novel and useful

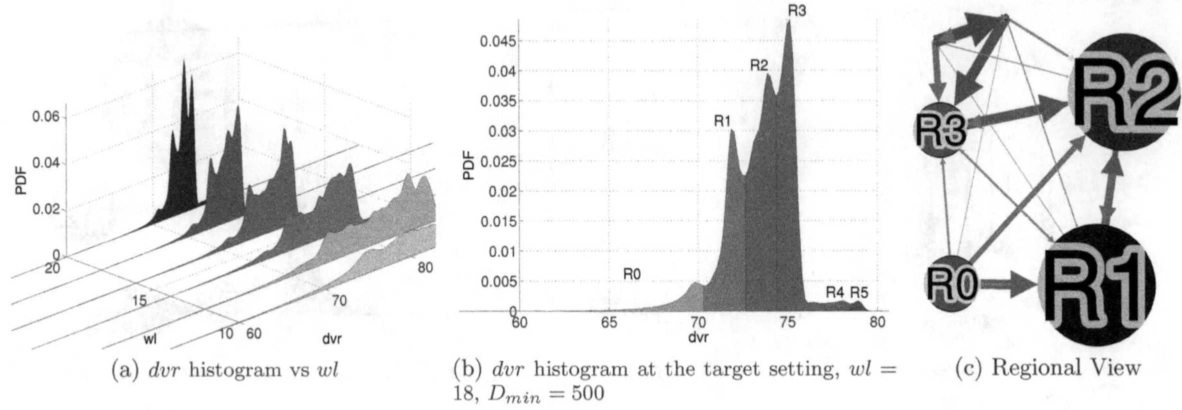

(a) *dvr* histogram vs *wl*

(b) *dvr* histogram at the target setting, $wl = 18$, $D_{min} = 500$

(c) Regional View

Figure 4: Applying *WalkAbout* to Twitter snapshot

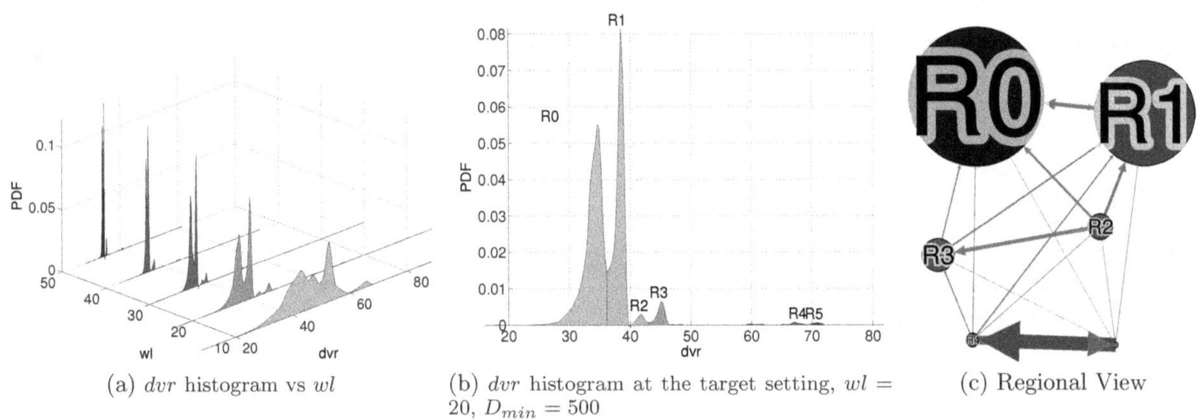

(a) *dvr* histogram vs *wl*

(b) *dvr* histogram at the target setting, $wl = 20$, $D_{min} = 500$

(c) Regional View

Figure 5: Applying *WalkAbout* to Google+ snapshot

abstraction of the large-scale real-world systems. They offer a manageable high-order view of how nodes are mapped into various regions of different sizes, along with a quantitative assessment of the corresponding inter- and intra-region connectivity.

A common observation from applying *WalkAbout* to the three OSNs is that separate regions (peaks) with close-by *dvr* values tend to have stronger inter-region connectivity than regions that result from clearly separated peaks in the *dvr* histogram. Such behavior is to be expected for real-world graphs. For one, our approach for mapping high degree nodes to cores based on slicing peaks in the histogram is ambiguous for high degree nodes whose *dvr* values are close to the border value of a region. Moreover, the size of a region and its mixing time can vary widely across different regions of a large graph. This in turn makes the selection of a proper walk length challenging. For example, a particular walk length that is close to a region's mixing time and thus clearly reveals the associated peak in the *dvr* histogram could be too long for other regions. This behavior can cause some of the RWs of other regions to leave their starting points and move to other close-by regions. The fraction of such "misbehaving" RWS depends on the walk length and the relative connectivity between starting and neighboring regions. Both of the above factors tend to decrease the gap between the *dvr* ranges of close-by regions proportional to their pairwise connectivity. However, given the coarse resolution of the considered regional views of a graph, the resulting ambiguities do not significantly impact the value that can be derived from examining such coarse views of large-scale graphs.

Also note that the number of peaks that appear in a *dvr* histogram changes with the walk length which, in turn, can change the perspective of what peak size should be considered to be significant. Our focus here has been on considering only a handful of regions so that the resulting regional views are manageable. *WalkAbout* is clearly an interactive framework and can be used to identify a different number of regions and examine how such selections affect the characteristics of the resulting regional views.

As our results show, the identified regions by *WalkAbout* could be very imbalanced in size. In particular, a large region may consist of two or more smaller regions that are not properly recognizable during the first round. One way to explore the structure of these larger regions is to apply *WalkAbout* to each identified regions. This hierarchical application might be able to identify the internal structure (sub-regions) of a large region if they have sufficiently distinct average de-

Table 5: FL

region	comm.
$R0$	26,987
$R1$	173
$R2$	639
$R3$	251
$R4$	7

Table 6: TW

region	comm.
$R0$	142
$R1$	13,171
$R2$	10,003
$R3$	724
$R4$	9
$R5$	5

Table 7: G+

region	comm.
$R0$	29,577
$R1$	9,545
$R2$	93
$R3$	32
$R4$	18
$R5$	2

grees and shorter mixing time than the entire region. This issue remains as a future work for us to explore in more detail.

6.4 *WalkAbout* as an Interactive Tool

We have implemented *WalkAbout* as an interactive tool for browsing coarse-view of connectivity for large graphs. Our tool accepts the edge view of a large graph and produces *dvr* histogram. A user can browse through the evolution of the histogram as a function of the walk length and D_{min} to select its desired parameters, and then focus on the desired histogram to interactively determine the number and location of individual peaks (regions). Our tool then generates the input for viewing the resulting regional view on an existing visualization program (such as Gephi [3]). The key feature of our tool is the ability for a user to interact with the process to determine the proper parameters based on those interactions. Our tool is publicly available at the project web site [20].

7. REGIONS & COMMUNITIES

Community detection in graphs is a commonly used technique that can also be viewed as providing a coarse view of a graph (*i.e.*, community-level instead of regional-level view). Community detection techniques typically group nodes into tightly connected groups, called a community, based on an objective function (*e.g.*, modularity) and present characteristics of the detected communities without emphasis on the inter-community connectivity. In this section, we compare and contrast the regional view that *WalkAbout* produces with the community view of a large graph. Given the similarity between the notion of a "community" and a "region", and the popularity of applying community detection techniques for graph analysis, this comparison helps us relate the regional view of the graph with a related concept (*i.e.*, community) that is widely used. To this end, we have to run a community detection technique on our large target graphs. Unfortunately, most of the commonly-used community detection techniques do not scale to graphs with more than tens of millions of nodes [7], or require the number of communities as an input (*e.g.*, Metis [12, 13]), or recursively partition the graph into balanced communities that may not lead to the most tightly connected communities [12]. Due to these limitations, we use the *Louvain community detection technique* [4] that implements a greedy method to optimize the "modularity" of identified partitions. The Louvain technique is often considered to be the gold standard for scalable community detection and has a publicly available and robust implementation.

We applied Louvain to our targeted OSN structures and identified 28K, 39K, and 24K communities of various sizes in FL, G+, and TW, respectively. Importantly, these results show that *the number of communities in these graphs are several orders of magnitude larger than the number of regions. This large number of communities implies that the graph connectivity at the community level is still too complex for high-level analysis* (e.g., *determining the full picture of inter-community connectivity.)*

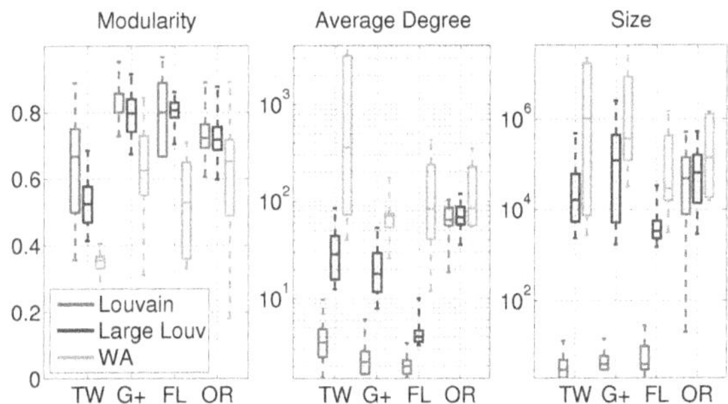

Figure 6: Comparison of Louvain communities and *WalkAbout* regions.

Figure 6 presents the summary distribution of the main features (modularity, size and average degree) across all regions and all communities associated with each each OSN. To examine the effect of community size, we have also included the results where we only consider the large communities that consist of 1000 or more nodes. We observe that communities are typically more than four orders of magnitude smaller than regions. However, size-wise, the largest communities clearly have an overlap with the obtained regions. While the modularity of communities is typically higher than the modularity of regions, this gap is more pronounced in less clustered graphs (*e.g.*, TW) than in more clustered graphs like FL and G+. Also, the large communities exhibit higher modularity than the *WaltAbout*-derived regions, and the average degree of the communities is smaller than its counterpart for regions (irrespective of community size).

To gain more insight into connectivity-related features, we examine the placement of the 1000 nodes with the highest degree in each region across the different communities. Interestingly, we find that in all three OSNs, the top 1000 nodes are located in 5 or 6 communities, with some of those communities attracting significantly more nodes than others. Moreover, both the size (15K-359K for FL, 72K-22M for TW, and 336K-16M for G+) and the modularity of these few communities (0.48-0.75 for FL, 0.28-0.78 for TW, and 0.35-0.89 for G+) are comparable with typical values for the *WaltAbout*-derived regions. *These results suggest that the large communities that are needed for accommodating high-degree nodes exhibit characteristics very similar to the* WaltAbout*-identified regions.*

7.1 Mapping Communities to Regions

To further explore the relationship between the community- and regional-level views of these graphs, we map individual Louvain communities to the identified regions for the same graph. In particular, for each community c, we determine the region where each node of this community is located and identify the region R that contains a majority of nodes in that community. Then community c is mapped to that region R that hosts a majority of its nodes, and the confi-

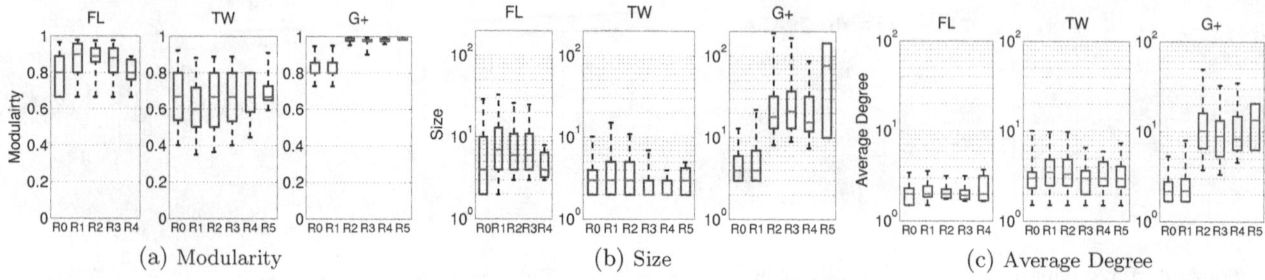

(a) Modularity (b) Size (c) Average Degree

Figure 7: Characteristics of Louvain communities mapped to different *WalkAbout* regions

dence for this mapping is equal to the fraction of c's nodes that are located in R. Tables 5 through 6 summarize the number of communities that are mapped to the individual regions of each OSN. In the extreme case, if the nodes in each community are randomly located in different regions, then all communities are mapped to the largest region(s) with a confidence equal to the region's relative size. We observe that the mapping confidence for 75% of the communities in every single region is 100%, and for 90% of communities, all but one small region in FL (R_4) has a mapping confidence higher than 80%. Even for the large communities with more than 1K nodes, the mapping confidence for 90% of them is larger than 80% for all regions of all OSNs except for TW, where it is 60% . *These results clearly demonstrate that the vast majority of nodes in most communities are mapped into a single region. This in turn suggests that a region can be viewed as a collection of connected communities and thus offer a coarser view of the graph.*

7.2 Per-region Analysis of Communities:

We now examine the group of communities that are mapped to each region to determine whether they exhibit any distinguishing features. Figure 7 uses box-plots to summarize the distribution of modularity, size and average node degree across all communities that are mapped to each region of individual OSNs. These figures illustrate that there does not appear to be a strong correlation between the modularity of communities in a region and the modularity of the entire region. This observation is explained by the fact that the modularity of a region depends, among other factors, on the inter-community connectivity. We also observe that in general, there is no significant difference in the modularity, size and average degree of the communities that are mapped to each region, *i.e.*, regions are not generally distinguishable based on the characteristics of their communities despite the difference in their average degree and size. The only exceptions to this observation are regions R_3, R_4 and R_5 in G+ that contain communities with a significantly higher and more homogeneous modularity, larger size and higher average degree. This is intriguing since larger size or higher node degree could lead to lower modularity in a single community. *These findings suggest that identifying individual regions by merging communities in a bottom-up fashion (using modularity) is in general challenging. Alternatively, a top-down approach to region detection such as* WalkAbout *shows more promise.*

7.3 Comparing Run-time:

Finally, we compare the run times of *WalkAbout* and the Louvain community detection technique on an Intel X5650 2.66GHz computer with 72GB RAM which is sufficient to hold the entire graph in memory. Figure 7.2 shows the comparison of the run time per individual technique over each OSN using log scale for the x-axis. We further split the run time of *WalkAbout* into two components: *(i)* the calculation of the *dvr* values for high degree nodes to detect cores and *(ii)* mapping of low-degree nodes to those cores. These results show that the run times of both techniques are similar over small graphs (*e.g.*, 10 second difference for FL). However, as the graph size increases, Louvain requires a significantly longer run time and the gap between *WalkAbout* and Louvain seems to be widening. We also recall that for graphs of the size of these OSNs, many popular community detection or clustering techniques (including spectral clustering [5]) quickly run into scalability issues and cannot be used at all [9].

8. A NEW KIND OF VALIDATION

So far we have primarily focused on the connectivity features of regions and how they are aligned with smaller entities in a large graph such as communities. Since regions are not derived based on an objective function, there is no obvious way to validate/examine their accuracy. To tackle the challenging problem of "validation" of *WalkAbout* -derived regions, we conduct a case study to investigate *whether users in each identified region exhibit similar social attributes that act as the underlying factors for the formation of the region.*

8.1 Are Regions Meaningful?

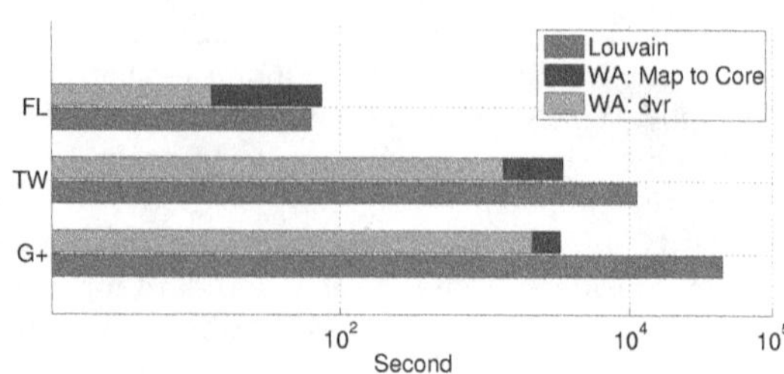

Figure 8: The comparison of the execution time for different techniques.

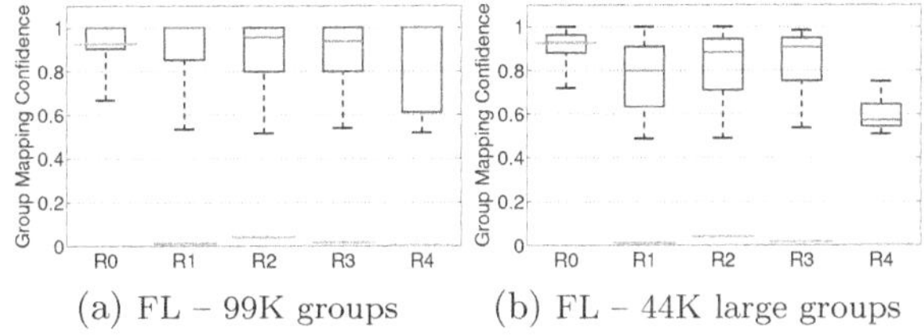

(a) FL – 99K groups (b) FL – 44K large groups

Figure 9: Distribution of confidence in mapping groups to identified regions. Large groups have more than 10 members.

Our ability to answer the posed question depends on the availability of semantically-rich metadata that contains social context. However, given adequate metadata, answering the above question will shed light on whether an identified region represents a meaningful portion of an OSN. In our case study, we focus on FL because of the availability of rich metadata with social context for this OSN.

More precisely, for our FL snapshot, we have a list of 99K social groups (with their names) where each group consists of a collection of users with common interest. A user can be a member of multiple groups. The name of most groups provides a great deal of information about the groups' interests or context (*e.g.*, big_and_hot, bigblkmuscles, bigbulls, boys, everydaymen, fatboys). Similarly to the mapping of communities to regions (Section 7), we map each group to a region where most of their users are located. Figure 9(a) and 9(b) shows the summary distribution of mapping confidence for all groups and for the 44K groups with more than 10 users to the five regions in FL, respectively. We observe that groups that are mapped to regions R_1-R_4 exhibit a very high confidence despite the small size of these regions. The mapping confidence drops for larger groups but it is still a couple of orders of magnitude larger than the relative size of the group. More specifically, regions R_1, R_2, R_3 and R_4 make up 1.2%, 4% 1.8%, and 0.2% of nodes in the graph but the typical confidence for their mapped groups is 0.8, 0.9, 0.92, and 0.58, respectively. These results suggest that the social context of each group is likely a driving force for its mapping to these four regions. In contrast, the typical confidence for mapped groups to region R_0 is comparable to its relative size. This indicates that social forces discernible from our data may not be primarily responsible for the mapping of groups to region R_0. To learn the context of individual regions, we manually examined the names of groups that are mapped to that region. Our examination reveals a very pronounced pattern among group names associated with the following regions[3]: Group names in R_1 are mostly related to male nudity and adult content, group names in R_2 are hinting at female nudity and adult content, and group names in both R_3 and R_4 have a common ethnic attribute, *i.e.*, either have Arabic name or post in Arabic. As expected, group names in R_0 do not show a coherent theme.

[3]The spreadsheet of FL group names that are mapped to each FL regions (or community) are available online at `http://onrg.cs.uoregon.edu/WalkAbout/group_per_region/`

8.2 Are Communities Meaningful?

We use the same methodology to examine the "validity" of communities; *i.e.*, checking whether the names of mapped groups to individual communities indicate any common social theme. In the case of regions without any pronounced social theme (*e.g.*, R_0), one of their large communities may indeed have a social context whereas for regions with an existing social context (*e.g.*, R_1), a community may offer an even more specific context. The large number and diverse size of communities in each graph make it difficult to examine all communities. Since small communities do not provide sufficient information to identify their social theme, we only focus on the three largest communities that are mapped to each region of FL. Careful examination of group names for groups that are mapped to each one of these large communities reveals that large communities in R_0 do not seem to have any social theme and large communities in all other regions often exhibit a theme that is very similar to the identified theme for the whole region. The only exception is a community in R_2 that contains groups with clearly more specific group names. In summary, our preliminary investigations suggest that some large communities that are embedded within a region are not "meaningful" in the sense that they exhibit rather diverse social themes that makes them the opposite of a "community."

9. CONCLUSION & OUTLOOK

In this paper, we present a new scalable framework called *WalkAbout* for examining and inferring regional views of connectivity for very large graph and demonstrate its application to three well-known OSNs. Moreover, we conduct a comparison between regional- and community-level views of large OSN and present a case study where we "validate" the individual regions and communities; *i.e.*, examining in detail the available meta-data for social themes that are associated with the obtained groupings of nodes in an OSN and are prime candidates for the root cause(s) behind the formation of these groupings.

The presented design of *WalkAbout* and the experience we gained from applying it to real-world OSNs suggest a number of extensions and improvements. For one, we plan to explore the recursive application of *WalkAbout* to identify potential sub-regions within each identified region. In the same vein, we intend to examine how the regional- and community-level views of a large graph can inform each other to yield a hybrid approach for a "multi-scale" exploration of the graph's connectivity (*e.g.*, examining the connectivity between large communities within a given region to obtain a higher-resolution view of graph connectivity). Extending *WalkAbout* to allow for overlapping regions and collecting semantically rich meta-data that enables the illustrated validations of groupings such as regions, clusters, or communities are other items on our research agenda in this area.

10. ACKNOWLEDGEMENTS

The authors would like to thank Mojtaba Torkjazi and Mauro Maggioni for their efforts in the early stages of this project. Roberto Gonzalez contributed to this project during his internship at the University of Oregon. Miles Nerenberg has packaged our research prototype into a publicly available interactive tool for exploring coarse views of large graphs. This project is funded by the National Science Foundation (NSF) grant no. IIS-0917381 and IIS-1342477. Any opinions, findings, and conclusions or recommendations expressed in this material are those of the author(s) and do not necessarily reflect the views of the National Science Foundation.

11. REFERENCES

[1] Y. Y. Ahn, S. Han, H. Kwak, S. Moon, and H. Jeong. Analysis of Topological Characteristics of Huge Online Social Networking Services. In *Proc. of ACM WWW*, pages 835–844, 2007.

[2] R. Andersen, F. Chung, and K. Lang. Local Graph Partitioning using Pagerank Vectors. In *Proc. of IEEE FoCS*, pages 475–486, 2006.

[3] M. Bastian, S. Heymann, M. Jacomy, et al. Gephi : An Open Source Software for Exploring and Manipulating Networks. *ICWSM*, 8:361–362, 2009.

[4] V. D. Blondel, J.-L. Guillaume, R. Lambiotte, and E. Lefebvre. Fast unfolding of communities in large networks. *Journal of Statistical Mechanics: Theory and Experiment*, 2008(10):P10008, 2008.

[5] F. Chung. *Spectral Graph Theory*. CBMS Regional Conference Series. Conference Board of the Mathematical Sciences, 1997.

[6] I. S. Dhillon, Y. Guan, and B. Kulis. Kernel k-means: Spectral Clustering and Normalized Cuts. In *Proc. of ACM SIGKDD*, pages 551–556, 2004.

[7] I. S. Dhillon, Y. Guan, and B. Kulis. Weighted Graph Cuts without Eigenvectors: A Multilevel Approach. *IEEE Transactions on Pattern Analysis and Machine Intelligence*, 29(11):1944–1957, 2007.

[8] H. N. Djidjev. A Scalable Multilevel Algorithm for Graph Clustering and Community Structure Detection. In *Algorithms and Models for the Web-Graph*, pages 117–128. Springer, 2008.

[9] S. Fortunato. Community detection in graphs. *Physics Reports*, 486(3):75–174, 2010.

[10] R. Gonzalez, R. Cuevas, R. Motamedi, R. Rejaie, and A. Cuevas. Google+ or Google-?: Dissecting the Evolution of the New OSN in its First Year. In *Proc. of ACM WWW*, 2013.

[11] R. Kannan, S. Vempala, and A. Vetta. On Clusterings: Good, Bad and Spectral. *Journal of the ACM*, 51(3):497–515, 2004.

[12] G. Karypis and V. Kumar. METIS - Unstructured Graph Partitioning and Sparse Matrix Ordering System, Version 2.0, 1995.

[13] G. Karypis and V. Kumar. A FAST AND HIGH QUALITY MULTILEVEL SCHEME FOR PARTITIONING IRREGULAR GRAPHS. *SIAM Journal on scientific Computing*, 20(1):359–392, 1998.

[14] J. M. Kleinberg, R. Kumar, P. Raghavan, S. Rajagopalan, and A. S. Tomkins. The Web as a graph: measurements, models, and methods. In *Computing and combinatorics*, pages 1–17. Springer, 1999.

[15] H. Kwak, C. Lee, H. Park, and S. Moon. What is Twitter, a Social Network or a News Media? In *Proc. of ACM WWW*, pages 591–600, 2010.

[16] J. Leskovec, K. J. Lang, A. Dasgupta, and M. W. Mahoney. Community Structure in Large Networks: Natural Cluster Sizes and The Absence of Large Well-Defined Clusters. *Internet Mathematics*, 6(1):29–123, 2009.

[17] L. Lovász. Random Walks on Graphs: A Survey. *Combinatorics, Paul erdos is eighty*, 2(1):1–46, 1993.

[18] A. Mislove, M. Marcon, K. P. Gummadi, P. Druschel, and B. Bhattacharjee. Measurement and Analysis of Online Social Networks. In *Proc. of ACM IMC*, pages 29–42, 2007.

[19] R. Motamedi, R. Rejaie, D. Lowd, and W. Willinger. WalkAbout: Exploring the Regional Connectivity of Large Graphs and Its Application to OSNs. Technical report available at: `http://onrg.cs.uoregon.edu/pub/tr13-06.pdf`, University of Oregon, 2014.

[20] M. Nerenberg, R. Motamedi, and R. Rejaie. Interactive Graph Coarsening by WalkAbout. Code available at: `http://onrg.cs.uoregon.edu/WalkAbout`, University of Oregon, 2014.

[21] M. E. Newman. Modularity and community structure in networks. *Proc. of the National Academy of Sciences*, 103(23):8577–8582, 2006.

[22] P. Pons and M. Latapy. Computing communities in large networks using random walks. *Journal of Graph Algorithms and Applications*, 10(2), 2006.

[23] V. Satuluri and S. Parthasarathy. Scalable Graph Clustering Using Stochastic Flows: Applications to Community Discovery. In *Proc. of ACM SIGKDD*, pages 737–746, 2009.

[24] D. Stutzbach, R. Rejaie, and S. Sen. Characterizing Unstructured Overlay Topologies in Modern P2P File-Sharing Systems. *IEEE/ACM Transactions on Networking*, 16(2):267–280, 2008.

[25] S. Van Dongen. A cluster algorithm for graphs. *Report-Information systems*, (10):1–40, 2000.

[26] S. White and P. Smyth. A Spectral Clustering Approach To Finding Communities in Graph. In *Proc. of SIAM SDM*, volume 5, pages 76–84, 2005.

Simultaneous Detection of Communities and Roles from Large Networks

Yiye Ruan
ruan@cse.ohio-state.edu

Srinivasan Parthasarathy
srini@cse.ohio-state.edu

Department of Computer Science and Engineering
The Ohio State University

ABSTRACT

Community detection and structural role detection are two distinct but closely-related perspectives in network analytics. In this paper, we propose RC-Joint, a novel algorithm to simultaneously identify community and structural role assignments in a network. Rather than being agnostic to one assignment while inferring the other, RC-Joint employs a principled approach to guide the detection process in a nonparametric fashion and ensures that the two sets of assignments are sufficiently different from each other. Roles and communities generated by RC-Joint are both soft assignments, reflecting the fact that many real-world networks have overlapping community structures and role memberships. By comparing with state-of-the-art methods in community detection and structural role detection, we demonstrate that RC-Joint harvests the best of two worlds and outperforms existing approaches, while still being competitive in efficiency. We also investigate the effect of different initialization schemes, and find that using the results of RC-Joint on a sparse network as the seed often leads to faster convergence and higher quality.

Categories and Subject Descriptors

H.2.8 [**Database Management**]: Database Applications—*Data mining*

Keywords

community detection; structural role; role detection; social networks

1. INTRODUCTION

Community detection and structural role detection are two essential tasks in the realm of network analytics, and they have received extensive research interests. Community detection, with its roots in graph partitioning is concerned with the inter-connectivity among nodes, as it aims at identifying groups of nodes that are densely connected compared with their neighbors. Exemplar applications include finding clusters of users from social networks and functional protein complexes from bioinformatics networks. On the other hand, structural role detection focuses on finding sets of nodes (i.e. roles) that share similar structural properties (such as degree, clustering coefficient, and betweenness) and characterizing different roles. Structural roles can often be associated with various functions in a network. For example, hub nodes with high degree in an epidemic network are more likely to spread diseases, whereas bridge nodes with low degree and high betweenness are gatekeepers and important candidates for immunization. Recent work has leveraged role detection techniques for identity resolution [11, 9], exploratory network analysis [9], and anomaly detection [20].

To date, however, studies on these two topics have been performed independently, and there has been little synergy between them. When an algorithm is performing community (role) detection, it often ignores any role (community) information that is available. In this work we argue that community and structural role discovery should be interdependent and complementary to each other. Real-world communities often contain nodes with various roles for it to function, such as ones that interface with other communities and ones that are peripheral to community cores. On the other hand, the role assignment of a node also depends on the communities it, its neighbors and beyond belong to. Therefore there exists a strong and crucial need to detect communities and roles jointly, and we provide such a method in this paper. As shown in the following sections, the joint discovery of communities and roles can generate communities and roles of higher quality, as compared with identifying them separately.

Problem statement: Given an undirected, unweighted network $G(V, E)$ as the input, our goal is to design an algorithm that outputs both community and structural role assignments for nodes simultaneously. To overcome limitations in prior work, we state the following desiderata:

- **Nonparametric Guidance**: Utilize role information when inferring community assignment, and vice versa, so that assignment information is able to provide guidance to the detection process in a nonparametric fashion.
- **Iterative update**: Improve community and role assignments iteratively, so that the guidance is no longer static and always using the latest assignment information.

COSN'14, October 1–2, 2014, Dublin, Ireland.

http://dx.doi.org/10.1145/2660460.2660482.

- **Overlapping communities and roles**: Generate soft assignments for both community and role, since in many real-world networks nodes naturally belong to multiple communities and share multiple roles, though not uniformly. For example, one researcher can have several research interests, and a star node also acts as a bridge when connecting multiple tight knit communities.

- **Diversity**: Produce heterogeneous role assignment in each community, and vice versa, so that community and role assignments are as diverse from each other as possible.

The last desideratum regarding diversity is because community and role assignments are expected to characterize graph nodes from two different aspects, and thus nodes in the same community are expected to possess diverse roles. To illustrate the validity of this assumption in practice, we studied the composition of roles in several networks that have ground truth community assignments. Specifically, we download three networks (Google Plus, Facebook, and Twitter) from the SNAP network repository[1], and run RolX [11], a role detection algorithm, on them. The number of roles is set to 4, as is automatically determined by RolX. In Google Plus, among all large communities that altogether cover more than 95% of all labeled nodes, 94% of them contain nodes that altogether have at least 2 majority roles, and 48% of them have nodes that altogether have all 4 majority roles. Similar results are found on Facebook and Twitter, where 92% and 62%, respectively, of large communities contain nodes that belong to at least 2 majority roles. This shows that many real world communities indeed have diverse role assignment inherently.

Building on those observations and desiderata, we present `RC-Joint`, our algorithmic solution to the above problem. It treats community detection as a likelihood maximization problem with diversity constraints by role assignment, and it updates role assignment by performing soft clustering of nodes with features derived from community memberships. One iteration of each process is performed alternately, until both community and role assignments converge. This bootstrapping paradigm satisfies all four desiderata, and is therefore able to mine community and role assignments with the up-to-date knowledge of each other. We will describe `RC-Joint` in details in Section 3. An added benefit is that `RC-Joint` is naturally parallel since inference is done on each node, therefore parallel computing paradigms (such as OpenMP) can be easily leveraged. This fact makes it possible to scale `RC-Joint` to large networks.

In Section 4, we will discuss several optimizations in the implementation of `RC-Joint`, including parallelism, that yield significant speedup. We also investigate efficient initialization schemes for `RC-Joint`, which lead to faster execution and often higher accuracy. We demonstrate the efficacy of `RC-Joint` by experimenting on a wide array of real and synthetic networks (Section 5). We compare `RC-Joint` with state-of-the-art algorithms in both community detection and role detection, including BigClam [26], Markov Clustering [22], Graclus [7], RolX [11] and GLRD [9]. Quality of the output are measured by F-score using ground truth information. Results show that `RC-Joint` is able to detect communities and roles of higher quality, compared with existing methods. The improvement is up to 15% on real networks and 75% on synthetic networks.

[1] `http://snap.stanford.edu/data/index.html`

2. RELATED WORK

2.1 Community Detection

Community detection, with its root in graph clustering and graph partitioning, has been pivotal to network science. A plethora of algorithms have been proposed to address this task over the years, be it heuristic-motivated [14], cut-based [7], modularity-based [6], information theoretic [21], or stochastic flow-driven [22]. To cover all community detection algorithms is beyond the scope of this paper, and interested readers can refer to survey articles such as [8].

Among many challenges faced in the community detection literature, a prominent one is the need to find overlapping communities. That is, community assignment is rather "soft". This desideratum is motivated by the observation on many real-world networks that, by nature, community memberships are not mutually exclusive. Various algorithms have been proposed to address this need [25]. For example, clique percolation method by Palla et al. [18] operates on the assumption that overlapping communities consist of adjacent small cliques. Airoldi et al. [2] extend the standard stochastic block model [24] by letting a node's community indicator vector be drawn from a multinomial distribution, creating the mixed membership stochastic block model.

Another family of methods approach the problem by converting edges in a network to nodes in a new graph (called *line graph*) and then applying regular non-overlapping community detection algorithms to create clusters of new nodes [1]. Since a node in the input network is incident to multiple edges which may in turn be assigned to various clusters in the line graph, it may belong to multiple communities. The line graph, however, contains significantly more nodes than the original network, making the algorithm too costly for large networks.

Recently, Yang and Leskovec propose an affiliation-based model to handle overlapping communities [26]. Each node has an affiliation score with each community, and the affiliation strength is decided by its value. The probability that an edge exists between two nodes is decided by the nodes' community affiliations. Compared with block models, this approach grants individual nodes more flexibility since the linkage probability is no longer subject to the community-specific values. None of those methods, however, consider the structural roles of individual nodes.

2.2 Role Detection

While having a shorter history than community detection, role detection is a field of growing research interest. Here, we focus on *structural* roles in a network, although role has also been used to encompass latent topics in document corpus [17]. Henderson et al. have proposed RolX, a non-negative matrix factorization-based (NMF) approach to decompose a node-feature matrix into node-role and role-feature matrices [11]. They show that RolX is able to find roles with distinct characteristics, and the role representation learned on one network can be transferred to another.

Rossi et al. extend role analyses to the dynamic environment, where a series of network snapshots are available [20]. By performing role detection on each snapshot first and then calculating the transition of roles over snapshots, temporal patterns of nodes are extracted. Here role detection serves to provide high-level features for temporal behavior extraction, and its end applications include anomaly detection and nodal behavior prediction.

Recently, Gilpin et al. study the possibility of supplying extra guidance to role detection in order to incorporate external knowledge or requirements [9]. Their framework, *GLRD*, models role detection as a constrained NMF problem, where the guidance is provided as convex constraints and specified per role. Instead of optimizing matrices as a whole, they opt for an alternating least square formulation to improve the efficiency. Three types of guidance are described: sparsity (role assignment and/or representation being sparse for each role), diversity (role assignment and/or representation being different among roles), and alternative role discovery (role assignment and/or representation being different from a given assignment/representation). There are still two limitations in GLRD: (1) It treats community assignment as static input; (2) The recursive feature extraction scheme [11] it relies on incurs a complexity that is cubic to the number of nodes.

Lastly, one common drawback in existing literature of role detection is the absence of direct quality evaluation on proposed algorithms, possibly due to the lack of network data with ground truth on roles. Therefore previous work is confined to exploratory analyses or transfer learning tasks where roles themselves are utilized as high-level features.

3. ALGORITHM

Key intuitions: We view edges in the network as a result of nodes being affiliated to communities. The stronger two nodes are associated with a same community, the more likely it is to observe an edge between them. Furthermore, nodes in one community have diverse structural roles, thus the assignment vectors of any community and any role ought to be dissimilar. As for a node's role assignment, we consider it to be dependent on how clique-like the node is as well as how many of the node's neighbors belong to the same community as it does. We will elaborate on the materialization of those intuitions in the following sections.

As mentioned in Section 1, `RC-Joint` is an iterative algorithm that improves community and role assignments alternately. It takes as input a connected, undirected, unweighted graph $G = (V, E)$, the number of communities (N_c) and the number of roles (N_r). The convergence threshold (δ_{comm} and δ_{role}) and maximal number of iterations can also be specified. The output is a community score c_{vi} for each node $v \in V$ and each community $i = 1 \cdots N_c$, and a role score r_{vj} for each $v \in V$ and each role $j = 1 \cdots N_r$. Both community and role scores are non-negative. Table 1 lists notations used in the rest of the paper.

Algorithm 1 shows the pseudo code of the workflow, and each component will be introduced below. `RC-Joint` starts by initializing community and role assignments, and they can be either specified by some user-provided configurations (e.g. results from a previous run) or inferred automatically (Sections 3.1 and 3.2). After that, community and role assignments are updated one after each other iteratively. The algorithm stops when both communities and roles converge, or if the maximal number of iterations has been reached[2]. For the convergence check of community assignment, we impose that the relative improvement on network likelihood is less than δ_{comm}, since its value range is network-dependent. When checking the convergence of roles, we require the maximal change of any role score itself is less than δ_{role}, since role scores are always in the range [0, 1].

$G(V, E)$	Network with the vertex set V and edge set E
N_c	Number of communities to detect
N_r	Number of roles to detect
δ_{comm}	Community assignment convergence threshold
δ_{role}	Role assignment convergence threshold
$\mathbf{C}$	$\lvert V\rvert$-by-N_c non-negative matrix of community scores
$\mathbf{c}_{\bullet i}$	Column vector of community scores for community i
$\mathbf{c}_{v\bullet}$	Row vector of community scores for node v
$\mathbf{R}$	$\lvert V\rvert$-by-N_r non-negative matrix of role scores
$\mathbf{r}_{\bullet j}$	Column vector of role scores for role j
$\mathbf{r}_{v\bullet}$	Row vector of role scores for node v
Γ_v	Set of nodes adjacent to node v
π	Permutation on the set V (Equation 1)
$\mathbf{f}_v$	Feature vector of v for role assignment (Equation 3)
β	Softness parameter for role assignment (Equation 3)
ϵ	Angular cosine threshold for the diversity constraint (Equation 8)

Table 1: Table of notations

Algorithm 1 Workflow of `RC-Joint`

Require: G, N_c, N_r, δ_{comm}, δ_{role}
$\mathbf{C^0} \leftarrow$ `InitComm`(G, N_c)
$\mathbf{R^0} \leftarrow$ `InitRole`(G, N_r)

$i \leftarrow 1$

while not $(conv_{comm}$ **and** $conv_{role})$ **and** $i \leq$ `MaxIter` **do**
  $\mathbf{C^i} =$ `UpdateComm`$(G, \mathbf{C^{i-1}}, \mathbf{R^{i-1}}, N_c)$
  if $\frac{\texttt{Likelihood}(G,\mathbf{C^i}) - \texttt{Likelihood}(G,\mathbf{C^{i-1}})}{\texttt{Likelihood}(G,\mathbf{C^{i-1}})} < \delta_{comm}$ **then**
    $conv_{comm} \leftarrow$ **true** ▷ Communities converge
  end if

  $\mathbf{R^i} =$ `UpdateComm`$(G, \mathbf{R^{i-1}}, \mathbf{C^i}, N_r)$
  if $\lvert\lvert R^i - R^{i-1} \rvert\rvert_{max} < \delta_{role}$ **then**
    $conv_{role} \leftarrow$ **true** ▷ Roles converge
  end if

  `iter` $\leftarrow$ `iter` $+ 1$
end while

return $\mathbf{C^{i-1}}, \mathbf{R^{i-1}}$

3.1 Initializing Community Assignment

One naive way to initialize community scores of nodes is to randomly assign community labels ($1 \cdots N_c$) to nodes. Though fast, this method does not leverage the network's

[2]Empirically the algorithm often converges within far fewer iterations.

connectivity information, and it is highly probable that nodes sharing the same initial label are far apart. Another simple approach is to choose several vantage points, and to send their labels via breadth-first traversal. While this guarantees connectivity in each initial community, it does not always capture community structures since high-degree hub nodes will pass a label to a large number of nodes with little inter-connectivity. On the other hand, the initialization scheme should be lightweight, otherwise it defeats the purpose of creating an efficient algorithm. For example, we find empirically that identifying neighborhoods with minimal local conductance [10] runs three orders of magnitude slower than our proposed initialization method below, on the Google Plus network (with 108K nodes and 12M edges).

Our solution (`InitComm`) hinges on the intuition that two nodes are likely to belong to the same community if they share a large number of common neighbors. Therefore, we want to group nodes according to relative amount of neighbors they are sharing with each other, and to treat those groups as initial communities.

One established method to efficiently calculate the proportion of shared neighbors is via min-wise hashing [3]. The adjacency list of a node can be viewed as a set, whose elements are from the universe of V, and we can generate one min-wise hash of the adjacency list by applying π, a permutation of V, on the set and taking the minimal value after the permutation. Let Γ_v be the neighborhood of node v, then its min-wise hash value under π, $h_\pi(\Gamma_v)$ (or $h_\pi(v)$ for short), is:

$$h_\pi(v) \equiv h_\pi(\Gamma_v) = \min_{u \in \Gamma_v} (\pi(u)) \ , \tag{1}$$

where $\pi(u)$ is the value of u after permutation π. A min-wise hash signature of length k for v is generated by randomly drawing k permutations $\pi_1 \cdots \pi_k$ and concatenating the corresponding hash values $h_{\pi_1}(v) \cdots h_{\pi_k}(v)$. The same set of permutations are applied to all adjacency lists to generate the corresponding length-k signature for each node.

Given all min-wise hash signatures, we create a top-down hierarchy of nodes according to signature values. This process will be referred to as *grouping* below. We start with the first hash value ($h_{\pi_1}(v)$, $\forall v \in V$), and split nodes into groups such that all nodes in one group have the same hash value. If a group is small enough (we use a size threshold of $\frac{|V|}{N_c}$), all nodes in it are given one initial community label. Otherwise, the group is further split based on the second hash value, and so on. This continues until either all k hash values are used, or no more split is required. After grouping, each node has one and only one initial community label.

If there are more than N_c initial community labels, we merge nodes in the smaller groups to larger groups. To achieve this, we perform a *label propagation* algorithm in the following manner. We rank all groups in the descending order of their sizes, and visit them in sequence. When visiting a group, we assign its group label to the immediate neighborhood of each member node. It is further required that if a node has received any label from its neighbors, it can no longer propagate labels to its neighbors. This makes sure that labels "stay" within the local neighborhood.Label propagation terminates when N_c labels have been successfully propagated, after which a node can possibly have multiple community labels. For a node v and each label i it has, we let the initial community score $c^0_{vi} = 1$, otherwise it is 0.

Lemma 1 below shows that after `InitComm`, any node in the network will find some other nodes belonging to the same initial community in close proximity.

LEMMA 1. *Given a connected, undirected, unweighted network $G(V, E)$, and `InitComm` is run to produce the initial community score matrix $\mathbf{C}^0$. For any node v and community i such that $c^0_{vi} = 1$, if there exist a non-empty set of other nodes ϕ_{vi} such that such that $c^0_{ui} = 1$, $\forall u \in \phi_{vi}$, then there is at least one node $u \in \phi_{vi}$ whose shortest path distance to v on G is at most 2.*

PROOF. There are three different scenarios:

I. v obtains label i after the grouping process, and it has propagated i to its neighbors. Then any node $u \in \Gamma_u$ also has label i, and their shortest path distance is 1.

II. v obtains label i after the grouping process, and it does not propagate i. Since ϕ_{vi} is non-empty, there exists at least one node u that also obtains label i after the grouping process because v does not propagate i. Since v and u are in the same group in the grouping process, $h_{\pi_1}(v) = h_{\pi_1}(u)$. Because any π (including π_1) is a one-to-one self-mapping on V, there is at least one element that exists in the adjacency lists of both v and u, i.e. $\Gamma_v \cap \Gamma_u \neq \emptyset$. Therefore, v and u have at least one common neighbor, and the shortest path distance between them is at most 2.

III. v receives label i from the propagation of one of its neighbors, u. Therefore $v \in \Gamma_u$, and their shortest path distance is 1.

To conclude, for any node v and label i such that $c^0_{vi} = 1$, if $\phi_{vi} \neq \emptyset$, there always exists a node u such that v and u have the same label and the shortest path distance between them is at most 2. □

3.2 Initializing Role Assignment

Role detection in `RC-Joint` is achieved by soft k-means clustering on nodes using various structural features described below. During the initialization stage, we assume no knowledge of communities, and therefore we do not use any feature that is derived from the community assignment. While recursive feature aggregation [12] has been shown to capture richer structural information than local features (e.g. degree) alone, we choose not to use it because its complexity is cubic to the number of nodes. To trade off between feature richness and efficiency, we reuse the min-wise hash signatures created in Section 3.1 to effectively approximate the similarity of a node's adjacency list and its neighbors' adjacency lists.

The purpose of using adjacency list similarity as node features is to gauge the distribution of a node's structural similarity with its neighbors. Intuitively, the more similar two nodes' adjacency lists are, the more triangles there are that consist of both nodes. If a node has high similarity with most of its neighbors, then it is more likely to be part of a clique-like substructure. In contrast, a node having low similarity with most of its neighbors resembles a star, and it connects multiple communities.

Assuming the hash signatures for nodes v and u have length k, then according to [3], the following statistic is an unbiased estimator of the Jaccard similarity between Γ_v and Γ_u:

$$\hat{sim}(v,u) \equiv \frac{1}{k}\sum_{n=1}^{k} I[h_{\pi_n}(v) = h_{\pi_n}(u)] \quad (2)$$
$$E[\hat{sim}(v,u)] = \frac{|\Gamma_v \cap \Gamma_u|}{|\Gamma_v \cup \Gamma_u|}$$

where $I[\bullet]$ is the identity function. For each node, we use the minimum, maximum and three quantiles of the estimated Jaccard similarity with all neighbors as its features.[3] We also include the logarithm of a node's degree as a feature in order to alleviate the large variance of node degree itself. We note that there exist other definitions of structural similarity that one can possibly employ, such as SimRank [13] and its variants. However, they do not fit our purpose because the costly computation is performed for all pairs of nodes, and we will not be able to reuse hash signatures either.

To assign initial role information to nodes, we randomly choose N_r nodes as centroids of k-means, and calculate a node v's role affiliation r_{vj} with each centroid j using an exponential kernel. Affiliation scores are L1-normalized over all centroid for each node, that is:

$$r_{vj} = \frac{\exp(-\beta||\mathbf{f}_v - \mathbf{f}_{s_j}||_2)}{\sum_{n=1}^{N_r}\exp(-\beta||\mathbf{f}_v - \mathbf{f}_{s_n}||_2)} \quad (3)$$

where $\mathbf{f}_v$ ($\mathbf{f}_{s_j}$) denotes the feature vector of node v (centroid s_j). The parameter β is used to control the "softness" of the assignment, and a larger β value suppresses minor affiliation scores. In our implementation the default value for β is 1.

3.3 Updating Community Assignment

Our goal in updating community assignment is to increase the likelihood of network's edge set E, given the community affiliation of nodes. At the same time, we want the community assignment to be diverse with regard to the role assignment by imposing the requirement of diversity in any pair of community and role.

Formally, the goal can be expressed as a constrained optimization problem:

$$\max_{\mathbf{C}}(\texttt{Likelihood}(G,\mathbf{C})) \quad (4)$$
$$\text{subject to } \mathbf{c}_{\bullet i}\cdot \mathbf{r}_{\bullet j} < \epsilon_{ij}, \forall i \in 1\cdots N_c, j \in 1\cdots N_r$$

Note that the desideratum of diversity is implemented as constraints to the optimization problem, and this is where role information is introduced to facilitate community detection. For each community i and role j, it is required that their inner product is less than a specified threshold value ϵ_{ij}.

We use the following setting to model the relationship between $\mathbf{C}$ and the network G. Given the community affiliation score matrix $\mathbf{C}$, we define the probability of an edge existing between v and u as a result of their affiliations with the community i:

$$P[(v,u)\in E \mid c_{vi}, c_{ui}] \equiv 1 - \exp(-c_{vi}\cdot c_{ui}) \ . \quad (5)$$

By treating the edge probability as independent when conditioned on each community, it is easy to show that the probability of observing the edge (v,u) with regard to the whole community assignment matrix $\mathbf{C}$ is:

$$P[(v,u)\in E \mid \mathbf{C}] = 1 - \exp(-\mathbf{c}_{v\bullet}\cdot \mathbf{c}_{u\bullet})$$

[3]We find that $k = 30$ is sufficient for the hash signature length.

Intuitively, the larger affiliation scores to the same community two nodes v and u have, the more likely it is to observe the edge (v,u).

This setting can also be explained by viewing the multiplicity of edge (v,u) under community i as a Poisson random variable with parameter $c_{vi}\cdot c_{ui}$. Due to the additivity of Poisson distribution, the total multiplicity of edge (v,u) in G is also a Poisson random variable with parameter $\mathbf{c}_{v\bullet}\cdot\mathbf{c}_{u\bullet}$. Therefore, higher community affiliation scores lead to higher edge multiplicity, and in terms of unweighted edge, higher possibility of observing the edge.

Given $\mathbf{C}$, the log-likelihood of the whole network is:

$$\texttt{Likelihood}(G,\mathbf{C}) = \sum_{(v,u)\in E}\log(1 - e^{-\mathbf{c}_{v\bullet}\cdot\mathbf{c}_{u\bullet}}) - \sum_{(v,u)\notin E}\mathbf{c}_{v\bullet}\cdot\mathbf{c}_{u\bullet} \quad (6)$$

For a specific node v, when the community affiliation scores of all other nodes $\mathbf{c}_{-v\bullet}$ are fixed, the unconstrained version of Equation 4 becomes convex on $\mathbf{c}_{v\bullet}$, and gradient ascent (lines 1 to 6 in Algorithm 2) can be utilized to solve it since the likelihood's gradient has a closed form:

$$\nabla c_{vi} = \sum_{u\in\Gamma_v} c_{ui}\cdot\frac{\exp(-\mathbf{c}_{v\bullet}\cdot\mathbf{c}_{u\bullet})}{1-\exp(-\mathbf{c}_{v\bullet}\cdot\mathbf{c}_{u\bullet})} - \sum_{u\notin\Gamma_v} c_{ui} \quad (7)$$

Because the gradient ascent algorithm optimizes the community assignment for one node each time, it is difficult to directly factor in the diversity constraints in Equation 4, each of which is community-specific. Therefore, we purpose to relax the problem by first solving the unconstrained version as described above, and then projecting the updated community assignment to the closest possible point in the feasible region that satisfies all diversity constraints. For each community, the projection can be viewed as a quadratic programming problem with inequality constraints (lines 7 to 9 in Algorithm 2), and it can be handled by various high-level solvers.

ϵ_{ij} in the constraints are threshold parameters of the inner product between each pair of community and role vectors. Since $\epsilon_{ij} = \cos(\angle(\mathbf{c}_{\bullet i}, \mathbf{r}_{\bullet j}))\cdot||\mathbf{c}_{\bullet i}||_2\cdot||\mathbf{r}_{\bullet j}||_2$, all ϵ_{ij} parameter values can be controlled by one single parameter ϵ:

$$\epsilon_{ij} \equiv \epsilon\cdot||\mathbf{c}_{\bullet i}||_2\cdot||\mathbf{r}_{\bullet j}||_2 \quad (8)$$

where ϵ represents the angular cosine between two vectors, and its domain is $[0,1]$ since community and role affiliation scores are all non-negative. $\epsilon = 0$ means the community and role vectors are strictly orthogonal whereas $\epsilon = 1$ indicates no constraint. In our experiments we use $\epsilon = 0.5$ (i.e. the angle is no less than $\frac{\pi}{3}$) as the default.

Algorithm 2 outlines the two steps to update communities in each iteration.

3.4 Updating Role Assignment

In RC-Joint, influences of community and role assignments go both ways. In order to let up-to-date community information have impact on the role detection process, we need to incorporate it into node features. To this end, we append to $\mathbf{f}_v$, the feature vector of node v, one extra feature: the proportion of v's neighbors that have the same dominant community label as v has.

$$\frac{|\{u\in\Gamma_v \mid \arg\max_{i'}(c_{ui'}) = \arg\max_{i'}(c_{vi'})\}|}{|\Gamma_v|} \quad (9)$$

Intuitively, a gateway node is more likely to belong to a different community than most of its neighbors, while a cen-

Algorithm 2 $\texttt{UpdateComm}(G, \mathbf{C}, \mathbf{R}, N_c)$

Require: Learning rate l (fixed or learned from line search)
for $v \in V$ **do** ▷ Gradient ascent
  Calculate $\nabla \mathbf{c}_{v\bullet}$ according to Equation 7
  for $i \in 1 \cdots N_c$ **do**
    $c_{vi} \leftarrow \max(c_{vi} + l\nabla c_{vi}, 0)$
  end for
end for

for $i \in 1 \cdots N_c$ **do** ▷ Diversity constraints by roles
  $\mathbf{c}'_{\bullet i} \leftarrow \arg\min_{\hat{\mathbf{c}}} ||\hat{\mathbf{c}} - \mathbf{c}_{\bullet i}||_2$,
    s.t. $\hat{\mathbf{c}} \cdot \mathbf{r}_{\bullet j} < \epsilon_{ij}, \forall j \in 1 \cdots N_r$ and $\hat{\mathbf{c}} \geq \mathbf{0}$
end for

return $\mathbf{C}'$

tral node in one community will mostly connect to other core nodes in the same community.

Given updated feature values for each node, the next step is to update all N_r centroids. Features of centroids are recalculated as the sum of feature values from all nodes, weighted by their role affiliation scores. The step of adjusting role affiliation scores for nodes has the same form as Equation 3, except that the underlying feature vector is slightly different since the feature from Equation 9 was not used during role initialization. Algorithm 3 lists the steps to update roles.

Algorithm 3 $\texttt{UpdateRole}(G, \mathbf{C}, \mathbf{R}, N_r)$

for $v \in V$ **do** ▷ Update node features
  $\mathbf{f}_v$[intra-community neighbor ratio] $\leftarrow$ Equation 9
end for

for $j \in 1 \cdots N_r$ **do** ▷ Update centroids
  $\mathbf{f}_{s_j} = \frac{\sum_{v \in V} r_{vj} \mathbf{f}_v}{\sum_{v \in V} r_{vj}}$
end for

for $v \in V$ **do** ▷ Update role assignment
  for $j \in 1 \cdots N_r$ **do**
    $r'_{vj} \leftarrow$ Equation 3
  end for
end for

return $\mathbf{R}'$

4. DESIGN CHOICES AND TECHNIQUES FOR SPEEDUP

We dedicate this section to how RC-Joint can be implemented efficiently and the selection of parameters. First we show how results of RC-Joint on a sparse network can be used to initialize the algorithm on the original network. Then we discuss leveraging the inherent parallelism in RC-Joint via parallel computing paradigms. Reusing computed results and reducing subroutine's problem size also help decrease the computation cost. Finally we shed light on the process of selecting N_c and N_r values.

4.1 Initialization with Results from Sparse Networks

In Sections 3.1 and 3.2 we present our default methods of initializing communities and roles. Here we present a refinement that is analogous to the use of sampling in initializing various clustering algorithms such as K-means, Expectation-Maximization and even Graph Clustering [23]. Specifically, here we first sample (sparsify) the edges of the original graph. Next we run RC-Joint on the sampled (sparse) graph and obtain the community membership and role associations. We refer to this as the *first run*. We use the results of the *first run* to initialize a second run of RC-Joint on the full network. We refer to the latter as the *second run*.

Given the network $G = (V, E)$, the sampled or sparse version of it is denoted $G_{sparse} = (V, E_{sparse})$ has the same set of nodes but a smaller set of edges ($E_{sparse} \subset E$). The process of deciding which edges to keep in E_{sparse} can be viewed as a sparsification exercise. We examine two strategies described below:

- **Random Sparsification:** Sample edges uniformly at random. Retain sampled edges in E_{sparse}.
- **Local Rank Sparsification:** Rank all edges according to an edge similarity metric (e.g. estimate of the Jaccard similarity in Equation 3). Edges that have a higher triangle density (participate in a greater number of triangles within the network) will be ranked higher. For each node, rank its incident edges according to the above metric, and retain a number of top-ranked edges. This approach has been shown to preserve salient community structure especially in graphs with communities of varying densities, and to deliver high-quality results at a fraction of the cost [23]. Our hope is this strategy can also help in our context.

To reiterate, given a sparse network G_{sparse}, we first supply it to RC-Joint and obtain community and role score matrices $\mathbf{C}_{sparse}$ and $\mathbf{R}_{sparse}$. Then RC-Joint is run on the original network G, using $\mathbf{C}^0 = \mathbf{C}_{sparse}$ and $\mathbf{R}^0 = \mathbf{R}_{sparse}$. The **key intuition** here is that using those initial values will allow the second run to finish much faster than using the default because (1) $\mathbf{C}_{sparse}$ and $\mathbf{R}_{sparse}$ yield better objective function values, so that fewer iterations are needed to converge, and (2) $\mathbf{C}_{sparse}$ and $\mathbf{R}_{sparse}$ are more sparse (i.e. more zeros in affiliation scores), thus fewer operations are performed when updating communities and roles iteratively.

In Section 5.3, we will report results from this sparse graph initialization approach. The default strategy we adopt is local rank sparsification, and for a node of degree d, $\lceil \sqrt{d} \rceil$ incident edges of the highest Jaccard similarity are preserved. As expected, using $\mathbf{C}_{sparse}$ and $\mathbf{R}_{sparse}$ indeed reduces the total running time of RC-Joint (two runs combined), and on several datasets it also improves the quality of detected communities and roles.

4.2 Parallelizing RC-Joint

Main stages of UpdateComm (Algorithm 2) and UpdateRole (Algorithm 3) are inherently parallelizable. When computing the community assignment, gradient calculation can be performed on each node independently. Quadratic programming with diversity constraints can also be done on each community separately. During the process of updating role affiliation scores, each node can be updated individually. Lastly, updating centroids in role detection are parallelizable as well, although in practice the improvement may not be as significant since N_r is usually quite small.

In our implementation, we use OpenMP to exploit such parallelism, and the speedup is significant. Distributed computing architecture such as MPI can also be used, and we leave this as one direction of future work.

4.3 Reusing Computed Results

We have already mentioned one instance of result reusing, where min-wise hash signatures are used for both community initialization and role feature calculation. Another case is introduced in [26], where the authors point out that when calculating the gradient of a node's community affiliation scores (Equation 7), the last item can be rewritten as

$$\sum_{u \notin \Gamma_v} c_{ui} = \sum_{v \in V} c_{vi} - \sum_{u \in \Gamma_v} c_{ui}$$

and that $\sum_{v \in V} c_{vi}$ remains the same in each iteration. This reduces the complexity of gradient calculation from $O(|V|^2)$ to $O(|E|)$.

4.4 Reducing Quadratic Programming Problem Size

In the second part of Algorithm 2, community affiliation scores for each community are adjusted by being projected to the closest point in the feasible region that satisfies all N_r diversity constraints (one for each role). In its original form, each quadratic programming problem need to solve for $|V|$ variables, and this becomes a performance bottleneck when the network is large. However, the following lemma shows that the problem size can be reduced to the number of nonzeros in each community.

LEMMA 2. *For a community i, let*

$$\mathbf{c'}_{\bullet i} = \arg\min_{\hat{\mathbf{c}}} ||\hat{\mathbf{c}} - \mathbf{c}_{\bullet i}||_2$$

such that $\hat{\mathbf{c}} \cdot \mathbf{r}_{\bullet j} < \epsilon_{ij}, \forall j \in 1 \cdots N_r$ and $\hat{\mathbf{c}} \geq \mathbf{0}$. For any $v \in V$, if $c_{vi} = 0$, then $c'_{vi} = 0$.

PROOF. Assume there exists a node $v \in V$ such that $c_{vi} = 0$ and $c'_{vi} > 0$. Let another assignment vector $\mathbf{c''}_{\bullet i}$ be that $\mathbf{c''}_{-vi} = \mathbf{c'}_{-vi}$ and $c''_{vi} = 0$. Apparently $\mathbf{c''}_{\bullet i}$ satisfies the non-negativity constraint.

For any role $j \in 1 \cdots N_r$, $\mathbf{c''}_{\bullet i} \cdot \mathbf{r}_{\bullet j} = \mathbf{c'}_{\bullet i} \cdot \mathbf{r}_{\bullet j} - c'_{vi} r_{vj} \leq \mathbf{c'}_{\bullet i} \cdot \mathbf{r}_{\bullet j} < \epsilon_{ij}$. Therefore $\mathbf{c''}_{\bullet i}$ also satisfies all diversity constraints.

Finally,

$$\begin{aligned}
&||\mathbf{c''}_{\bullet i} - \mathbf{c}_{\bullet i}||_2 \\
=&\sqrt{\sum_{v' \neq v} (c''_{v'i} - c_{v'i})^2 + (c''_{vi} - c_{vi})^2} \\
=&\sqrt{\sum_{v' \neq v} (c'_{v'i} - c_{v'i})^2 + (c''_{vi} - c_{vi})^2} \\
<&\sqrt{\sum_{v' \neq v} (c'_{v'i} - c_{v'i})^2 + (c'_{vi} - c_{vi})^2} \\
=&||\mathbf{c'}_{\bullet i} - \mathbf{c}_{\bullet i}||_2
\end{aligned}$$

which contradicts with the claim that $\mathbf{c'}_{\bullet i}$ is closest to $\mathbf{c}_{\bullet i}$.

Therefore, if $c_{vi} = 0$, c'_{vi} must be 0, too. □

From Lemma 2, it is easy to see that one can obtain $\mathbf{c'}_{\bullet i}$ by:

1. Creating a compact vector $\tilde{\mathbf{c}}_i$ from $\mathbf{c}_{\bullet i}$ by keeping only all non-zero elements.
2. Finding $\tilde{\mathbf{c}}'_i$, the closest projection of $\tilde{\mathbf{c}}_i$ in the feasible region.
3. Expanding $\tilde{\mathbf{c}}'_i$ back to length $|V|$ by filling corresponding elements with 0.

Here, the number of variables in the optimization problem is only the number of non-zeros in $\mathbf{c}_{\bullet i}$, which is much smaller than $|V|$.

4.5 Choosing N_c and N_r

The number of communities and roles to find are two parameters provided by end users to `RC-Joint`, and there are several strategies to select them. One can perform grid search of N_c and N_r on a held-out development set, and choose values that result in the highest likelihood. Alternatively, measures like Bayesian Information Criterion (BIC) or Minimum Description Length (MDL) can be calculated, and N_c, N_r that minimize the combination of modeling and error costs can be selected.

For our network dataset, we compare total numbers of bits under different N_r values as in RolX [11], and find that $N_r = 4$ often yields the minimum description length. Therefore we use this value for all networks in experiments. For networks without ground truth of communities, we pick N_c by following the empirical evidence that community structure is most pronounced when the community size is approximately 100 [16].

5. EXPERIMENTS AND EVALUATION

In this section, we apply `RC-Joint` to both real and synthetic networks, aiming to understand its performance on both community detection and role detection under various scenarios. We first evaluate `RC-Joint` and state-of-the-art algorithms on the community detection task (Section 5.1), then compare it with existent role detection algorithms (Section 5.2). We also investigate the effects of different initialization schemes on the algorithm's execution and performance (Section 5.3).

5.1 Performance on Community Detection

5.1.1 Networks for Community Detection

We download a collection of real-world networks that have ground truth on the community membership[4], and discard edge directions if the original network is directed. The type of networks varies from social network to product network, and they have different levels of density as well as community size. Table 2 summarizes the basic information of those networks. All networks considered have ground truth on overlapping communities.

5.1.2 Evaluation Metric and Comparisons

Because ground truth information is available, we can gauge the performance of each community that an algorithm has discovered and whether a ground truth community has been successfully identified.

Since affiliation scores are real values instead of binary, we filter off nodes with low affiliation scores from each community to get a compact representation of communities. The

[4]They are all available from the SNAP network repository.

Network	$\|V\|$	$\|E\|$	Number of Communities	Avg. Community Size	Community Ground Truth Definition
Facebook	4039	88234	193	23	Facebook friend list
Twitter	81306	1342303	4065	14	Twitter list
Google Plus	107614	12238285	468	136	Google Plus list
Amazon	334863	925872	120999	20	Product category
YouTube	1134890	2987624	14870	8	User group
LiveJournal	3997962	34681189	576120	12	User-defined group

Table 2: Information of networks for community detection. Communities may be overlapping.

filtering threshold can be set to $\sqrt{\frac{2|E|}{|V|^2}}$, square root of the empirical edge probability [26].

For each ground truth community $c_{\tilde{i}}$, we create a length-$|V|$ vector $\tilde{\mathbf{c}}_{\bullet\tilde{i}}$ where $\tilde{c}_{v\tilde{i}} = 1$ if v belongs to $c_{\tilde{i}}$, or 0 otherwise. The standard F-score formula is then extended to handle affiliation scores (assuming $\mathbf{C}$ and $\tilde{\mathbf{C}}$ have been L1-normalized over nodes):

$$\text{precision}(i,\tilde{i}) = \frac{\mathbf{c}_{\bullet i}\cdot\tilde{\mathbf{c}}_{\bullet\tilde{i}}}{||\mathbf{c}_{\bullet i}||_1}, \text{recall}(i,\tilde{i}) = \frac{\mathbf{c}_{\bullet i}\cdot\tilde{\mathbf{c}}_{\bullet\tilde{i}}}{||\tilde{\mathbf{c}}_{\bullet\tilde{i}}||_1},$$

$$\text{f-score}(i,\tilde{i}) = \frac{2\cdot\text{precision}(i,\tilde{i})\cdot\text{recall}(i,\tilde{i})}{\text{precision}(i,\tilde{i})+\text{recall}(i,\tilde{i})}$$

Let $\tilde{N}_c$ be the total number of ground truth communities, we then calculate the overall F-score using the following formula:

$$F(\mathbf{C},\tilde{\mathbf{C}}) = \frac{1}{2}\Big(\frac{\sum_{i=1}^{N_c}\max_{\tilde{i}=1}^{\tilde{N}_c}(\text{f-score}(i,\tilde{i}))}{N_c} + \frac{\sum_{\tilde{i}=1}^{\tilde{N}_c}\max_{i=1}^{N_c}(\text{f-score}(i,\tilde{i}))}{\tilde{N}_c}\Big) \tag{10}$$

We compare `RC-Joint` with three representative community detection algorithms, BigClam [26], MLR-MCL [22], and Graclus [7]. BigClam employs the same setting of community affiliation scores in Section 3.3 to discover overlapping communities. It has been shown that BigClam outperforms many existing overlapping community detection algorithms, including line graph clustering [1], clique percolation model [18], and mixed membership stochastic block model [2]. However, it does not detect roles, nor does it exploit the influence of roles on communities. MLR-MCL takes a multi-level approach and identifies communities by propagating stochastic flows over a network and identifying each flow attractor as well as its contributors as one cluster. Similarly, Graclus performs multi-level clustering where at each level kernel k-means is run to optimize a partitioning's normalized cut. MLR-MCL and Graclus do not have the ability to detect overlapping communities.

5.1.3 Results

Table 3 summarizes the evaluation results, with F-scores of all algorithms on each network. We provide the actual number of communities in each network as the input parameter to each algorithm.

The largest network, LiveJournal, only successfully finishes on `RC-Joint` with local rank sparsification, and MLR-MCL. This demonstrates the benefits of using proper initialization, which will be further discussed in Section 5.3. Moreover, Graclus crashes when running on Amazon and YouTube, too. Comparing with BigClam, we find that `RC-Joint` has better performance on most networks. This demonstrates the efficacy of `RC-Joint`'s inherent design to provide auxiliary information via the role assignment, in order to facilitate the process of community detection. When initializing `RC-Joint` with communities and roles identified from a sparse network, the results are still highly competitive, and for Google Plus the performance is significantly improved. On the other hand, non-overlapping community detection methods do not fare well in general, except for MLR-MCL on Amazon.

The advantage of `RC-Joint` is also reflected in the log likelihood of the network edge set (Equation 6), as we find that `RC-Joint` achieves better log likelihood values than BigClam on all networks except Google Plus (Table 4). This shows the same trend as in Table 3.

	`RC-Joint`	`RC-Joint` w/ sparse init.	BigClam
Facebook	-171085	**-167758**	-182284
Twitter	**-3305980**	-3341592	-3381248
Google+	-57249698	**-49624553**	-52169083
Amazon	-5452800	**-5434790**	-5476358
YouTube	-19101405	**-18713629**	-19138838

Table 4: Log likelihood of the network, given the extracted community assignment values. The closer the log likelihood value is to 0, the higher the quality.

5.2 Performance on Role Detection

In this section, we investigate the performance of `RC-Joint` on its second task: role detection.

5.2.1 Networks for Role Detection

Real-world networks: One challenge that the role detection literature has been facing is the availability of ground truth on roles for real-world networks, and most work [11, 20] has to use some relevant tasks to indirectly measure the quality and meaningfulness of roles extracted. To alleviate the problem, we propose to use a node's behavior in diffusing and blocking information flows as the surrogate of its role.

Specifically, we calculate two sets of measures for each node and use them to define ground truth on roles. The first set is influence and passivity values of each node, as described in [19], where nodes (i.e. users) of information networks start and/or selectively relay cascades (e.g. URLs, photos, memes). The influence of a user is based on how many users it mobilizes and how difficult to mobilize those users are. The passivity of a user, on the other hand, is determined by how unlikely it is for him to forward information and how influential his friends are. For a network, we rank influence and passivity values over all users and divide both into two bins, respectively. Bin combinations (four types) are then considered to be the ground truth label for

	Facebook	Twitter	Google+	Amazon	YouTube	LJ
`RC-Joint`	**0.3928** (7%)	0.2431 (2%)	0.2160 (-11%)	0.4765 (2%)	**0.0503** (2%)	N/A
`RC-Joint` w/ sparse init.	0.3843 (5%)	**0.2506** (5%)	**0.2499** (3%)	0.4688 (1%)	0.0491 (0%)	0.1632
BigClam	0.3660	0.2381	0.2416	0.4664	0.0491	N/A
MLR-MCL	0.2701 (-26%)	0.1146 (-52%)	0.0100 (-96%)	**0.5001** (7%)	0.0068 (-86%)	0.1497
Graclus	0.3026 (-17%)	0.2147 (-10%)	0.1789 (-26%)	N/A	N/A	N/A

Table 3: F-scores on community detection, and the value in brackets is the percentage of improvement from BigClam. LiveJournal ("LJ") is only finished on `RC-Joint` with sparse network initialization and MLR-MCL. Graclus also crashes on Amazon and YouTube.

the network's role assignment. The second set of measures is influence and blockade, as defined in [5]. Influence is defined as the proportion of re-shares a user receives among all information he has shared. Blockade is calculated as the ratio of the number of cascades a user does not re-share to the total number of cascades he has received. Similarly, influence and blockade values are binned to create role labels. Both sets of measures attempt to capture the duality of propagating and impeding information flows, though the former set is updated iteratively until convergence and the latter is not.

We use two information networks for our experiments: Digg [15] and Flickr [4]. The Digg network has 19609 nodes and 161650 edges, where all votes on a particular story is viewed as a cascade. The Flickr network has 33887 nodes and 2441316 edges, where all favorites of a particular photo is considered to be a cascade.

Synthetic networks: Apart from information networks, we also create a collection of synthetic networks where role assignments are known in advance. We consider four different nodal types here:

- Member of a 10-clique. We create five such cliques, corresponding to 50 nodes in total.
- Member of a 5-clique. We create ten such cliques, corresponding to 50 nodes in total.
- Bridge of degree 2. We create 25 of them.
- Star of degree 10. We create 25 of them.

Bridges and starts are randomly connected to cliques, in order to make the whole network connected. The last step is to add noise edges between any pair of nodes with a fixed probability ρ. The value of ρ is ranged to generate networks with varying difficulty. Each node type described above is treated as one role, and this forms the ground truth for all synthetic networks.

5.2.2 Evaluation Metric and Comparisons

We use the same formula (Equation 10) to calculate the F-score on role detection. Apart from `RC-Joint`, we also compare with RolX and three variants of GLRD (sparsity, diversity[5], alternative role discovery constraints on role vectors). Because details on the selection of constraint thresholds in GLRD are not specified, we choose them in the following manner. For the sparsity constraint (on the target role vector's L1-norm), we let the threshold be $\frac{|V|}{N_r}$. For the diversity constraint (on the inner product of the target role vector and every other role vector) and alternative role discovery (on the inner product of the target role vector and any externally-specified vector), we set the threshold of angular cosine (similar to ϵ in Equation 8) to 0.5. We use communities identified by BigClam as the guideline for GLRD's alternative role discovery.

[5]This is different from the *diversity* constraints in `RC-Joint` (Equation 4).

5.2.3 Results

F-scores of various algorithms on Digg and Flickr are reported in Table 5. Results for synthetic networks are listed in Table 6. We separate the results on real networks and synthetic networks because the sources of ground truth are different.

	Influence/Passivity [19]		Influence/Blockade [5]	
	Digg	Flickr	Digg	Flickr
`RC-Joint`	0.2032 (8%)	**0.1372** (5%)	**0.1407** (15%)	**0.0565** (14%)
`RC-Joint` w/ sparse init.	**0.2033** (8%)	0.1371 (5%)	0.1406 (15%)	0.0563 (14%)
RolX	0.1886	0.1301	0.1225	0.0496
GLRD Alternative	0.1885 (0%)	0.1291 (-1%)	0.1228 (2%)	0.0536 (8%)
GLRD Sparsity	0.1792 (-5%)	0.1295 (0%)	0.1217 (-1%)	0.0509 (3%)
GLRD Diversity	0.1866 (-1%)	0.1304 (0%)	0.1231 (0%)	0.0522 (5%)

Table 5: F-scores on role detection on real-world networks with two sets of influence-induced ground truth labels, and the value in brackets is the percentage of improvement from RolX.

	$\rho = 0.01$	$\rho = 0.05$	$\rho = 0.10$
`RC-Joint`	0.7189 (35%)	**0.5531** (75%)	**0.3735** (34%)
`RC-Joint` w/ sparse init.	**0.7275** (37%)	0.5132 (62%)	0.3689 (33%)
RolX	0.5314	0.3168	0.2782
GLRD Alternative	0.4877 (-8%)	0.3182 (0%)	0.2822 (1%)
GLRD Sparsity	0.5044 (-5%)	0.3186 (1%)	0.2808 (1%)
GLRD Diversity	0.5061 (-5%)	0.3270 (3%)	0.2787 (0%)

Table 6: F-scores on role detection on synthetic networks with different amount of noise edges, and the value in brackets is the percentage of improvement from RolX.

It can be seen that RC-Joint obtains results of higher quality than both RolX and GLRD, uniformly. Initialization using sparse network also performs well. F-scores of GLRD fall between those of RC-Joint and RolX, demonstrating the power of providing community information to guide role detection, and the downside of treating community information as static input.

5.3 Effects of Initializing with Sparse Networks

5.3.1 *Local Ranking*

Previously in Section 4.1, we discuss the possibility of seeding RC-Joint with results from a preliminary run on a sparse version of the network. Moreover, we have already seen the quality improvement this technique can provide in Sections 5.1 and 5.2. Those sparse networks are produced by local rank sparsification, where each node of degree d keeps $\lceil \sqrt{d} \rceil$ incident edges with the highest Jaccard similarity of adjacency lists.

In this section, we report the impact on RC-Joint's time consumption by this technique. Figure 1 shows the amount of time it takes to run RC-Joint (with and without sparse network initialization) as well as BigClam. Implementations of both RC-Joint and BigClam are in C/C++, using OpenMP with 8 threads. Experiments are run on a desktop with an Intel i7 quad-core processor and 16GB of RAM.

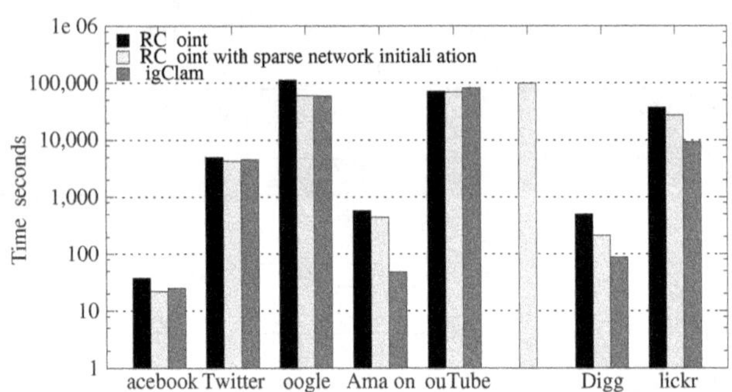

Figure 1: Comparison of time consumption (OpenMP with 8 threads). For RC-Joint with sparse network initialization, the running time include both runs.

As the plot suggests, using initialization from results of the sparse network always leads to lower total running time (both runs combined), as anticipated in Section 4.1. In the cases of Facebook, Twitter, Google Plus and YouTube, it is also faster than BigClam. This could be because proper initialization lets RC-Joint start at a state closer to convergence.

It is worth pointing out again that using sparse network initialization enables us to operate on even larger networks when RC-Joint itself or other methods becomes too slow. For example, experiments on the LiveJournal network do not finish in two days with either RC-Joint or BigClam. However, by first processing on the sparse version of it and then initializing another run with those results, RC-Joint manages to finish the computation in 25 hours.

5.3.2 *Benefits of Sparsification*

One may ask if the benefits of edge sparsification to RC-Joint can be precisely quantified with respect to efficiency and quality. To evaluate, we consider Twitter, Google Plus, two networks in our study. Similar results are observed for other networks in our study. Edge retention probability values are set up so that both strategies retain roughly the same number of edges in each network. Table 7 summarizes the amount of time each edge sparsification strategy takes for two runs, as well as the quality of results. F-score of the first run is from the results of RC-Joint on the sparse network itself, and F-score of the second run is from the results of RC-Joint on the original network. We also calculate the percentage of time saved and F-score increased compared with the default RC-Joint, and report those values in corresponding brackets.

Not all edge sparsification strategies are equal in terms of efficiency and quality. Edge ranking leveraging similarity information and local sparsification is more efficient than random sparsification, and the results have higher F-scores. Intuitively, local ranking is effective in capturing the skeleton of the network and enables faster convergence. In terms of quality of communities and roles, results from the local edge ranking sparsification procedure is also significantly better than random sparsification.

We note that numbers of RC-Joint iterations in the second run of local ranking for Twitter and Google Plus are 55 and 66, respectively (not shown in the table). In contrast, RC-Joint with default initialization takes 64 on Twitter and 100 on Google Plus. The reduction in number of iterations is consistent with the speedup in running time. Therefore, the first run on the sparse network helps to find a better initialization, decrease the number of iterations required, and therefore reduce the total running time.

6. DISCUSSION

Across the board, RC-Joint achieves higher quality than baseline methods which identify only communities or roles. Existing single-tasked community (role) detection algorithms suffer from not exploiting the latest knowledge on roles (communities), accounting for lower performance. For all experiments, we have reported absolute F-score values as well as relative improvements over baseline methods. We note that, in general, the problem we tackle is quite challenging (the absolute F-score values are not very high, also observed in other contemporary studies [26]). This reflects the inherent difficulty of community and role detection as well as room for future improvement.

Different initialization schemes also impact the efficiency and performance of RC-Joint, and we investigate the potential of edge sparsification techniques in the context of creating good seeds of communities and roles. We find that edge sparsification based on structural similarity is more effective than selecting edges by random, and local edge sparsification yields the most speedup and performance gain.

The RC-Joint approach we describe offers a marked departure from most existing algorithms. In terms of community discovery, BigClam [26] is somewhat related in that the relationship between community affiliation scores and the edge set has a similar formulation. However, BigClam only optimizes likelihood of the network without any constraint, and RC-Joint differs from it by being able to adjust the community assignment to accommodate the latest role assignment after each iteration. This difference we believe accounts for RC-Joint's qualitative improvements over BigClam. With respect to role discovery, RC-Joint also bears

	Local					Random				
	First run		Second run			First run		Second run		
	Time	F-score	Time	F-score	Total time	Time	F-score	Time	F-score	Total time
Twitter	90	0.2172	4175	0.2506 (5%)	4265 (13%)	1268	0.1746	8612	0.2390 (0%)	9880 (-116%)
Google Plus	1042	0.1938	58844	0.2499 (3%)	59886 (46%)	8858	0.1311	89069	0.2360 (-2%)	97927 (12%)

Table 7: Running time (in seconds) and F-score of two runs of RC-Joint. The first run is on the sparse network, and the second run is on the original network using results from the first run. Improvement of running time and F-score over RC-Joint with no sparse network initialization are included in brackets.

important difference from existing NMF-based role detection algorithms, such as RolX [11] and GLRD [9], as it uses soft k-means to identify roles, and it considers guidance from the community structure. The guidance is nonparametric and does not require extrinsic input from the domain. Essentially, in RC-Joint, roles are treated as the external knowledge to guide community detection, and such external knowledge is dynamically updated after each iteration.

7. CONCLUSION

We propose RC-Joint, a principled algorithm to mine communities and structural roles from networks simultaneously. RC-Joint operates on the observation that community and role assignments are complement to each other, and utilizing information from one component can benefit the discovery process of another. During each iteration, RC-Joint updates communities and roles alternately by improving the network likelihood and soft k-means objective function, respectively. The end result is an algorithm that is capable of identifying overlapping community and role assignments simultaneously. Empirical evaluations of RC-Joint and other state-of-the-art single-tasked mining algorithms on real-world as well as synthetic networks show that RC-Joint indeed produces communities and roles that have higher quality with regard to the gold standard. Furthermore, we find that algorithm speedup as well as quality improvement can be achieved by running RC-Joint on a sparse version of the network and using its results to initialize another run on the original network.

For future work, it will be beneficial to extend RC-Joint to directed and weighted networks because some real-world networks also have those properties. Another direction is to explore other community-induced node features to be used in updating role affiliation scores. Finally, implementations of RC-Joint using other more sophisticated parallel computing paradigms need to be investigated to realize even more speedup.

8. ACKNOWLEDGEMENTS

We heartily thank Lu Wang and the reviewers for their feedbacks, and Jaewon Yang for providing the implementation of BigClam. This work is sponsored by NSF Award IIS-1111118 "SoCS: Collaborative Research: Social Media Enhanced Organizational Sensemaking in Emergency Response" and NSF Award DMS-1418265 "Sampling and Inference in Network Analysis".

9. REFERENCES

[1] Y.-Y. Ahn, J. P. Bagrow, and S. Lehmann. Link communities reveal multiscale complexity in networks. *Nature*, 466(7307):761–764, 2010.

[2] E. M. Airoldi, D. M. Blei, S. E. Fienberg, and E. P. Xing. Mixed membership stochastic blockmodels. *Journal of Machine Learning Research*, 9(1981-2014):3, 2008.

[3] A. Z. Broder, M. Charikar, A. M. Frieze, and M. Mitzenmacher. Min-wise independent permutations. In *Proceedings of the thirtieth annual ACM symposium on Theory of computing*, pages 327–336. ACM, 1998.

[4] M. Cha, A. Mislove, and K. P. Gummadi. A measurement-driven analysis of information propagation in the flickr social network. In *Proceedings of the 18th international conference on World wide web*, pages 721–730. ACM, 2009.

[5] S. Choobdar, P. Rebeiro, S. Parthasarathy, and F. Silva. Dynamic inference of social roles in information cascades. *Under review*.

[6] A. Clauset, M. E. Newman, and C. Moore. Finding community structure in very large networks. *Physical review E*, 70(6):066111, 2004.

[7] I. S. Dhillon, Y. Guan, and B. Kulis. Weighted graph cuts without eigenvectors a multilevel approach. *IEEE Trans. Pattern Anal. Mach. Intell.*, 29(11):1944–1957, 2007.

[8] S. Fortunato. Community detection in graphs. *Physics Reports*, 486(3):75–174, 2010.

[9] S. Gilpin, T. Eliassi-Rad, and I. Davidson. Guided learning for role discovery (glrd): framework, algorithms, and applications. In *Proceedings of the 19th ACM SIGKDD international conference on Knowledge discovery and data mining*, pages 113–121. ACM, 2013.

[10] D. F. Gleich and C. Seshadhri. Vertex neighborhoods, low conductance cuts, and good seeds for local community methods. In *Proceedings of the 18th ACM SIGKDD international conference on Knowledge discovery and data mining*, pages 597–605. ACM, 2012.

[11] K. Henderson, B. Gallagher, T. Eliassi-Rad, H. Tong, S. Basu, L. Akoglu, D. Koutra, C. Faloutsos, and L. Li. Rolx: structural role extraction & mining in large graphs. In *Proceedings of the 18th ACM SIGKDD international conference on Knowledge discovery and data mining*, pages 1231–1239. ACM, 2012.

[12] K. Henderson, B. Gallagher, L. Li, L. Akoglu, T. Eliassi-Rad, H. Tong, and C. Faloutsos. It's who you know: graph mining using recursive structural features. In *Proceedings of the 17th ACM SIGKDD international conference on Knowledge discovery and data mining*, pages 663–671. ACM, 2011.

[13] G. Jeh and J. Widom. Simrank: a measure of structural-context similarity. In *Proceedings of the eighth ACM SIGKDD international conference on Knowledge discovery and data mining*, pages 538–543. ACM, 2002.

[14] G. Karypis and V. Kumar. A fast and high quality multilevel scheme for partitioning irregular graphs. *SIAM Journal on scientific Computing*, 20(1):359–392, 1998.

[15] K. Lerman and R. Ghosh. Information contagion: An empirical study of the spread of news on digg and twitter social networks. *ICWSM*, 10:90–97, 2010.

[16] J. Leskovec, K. J. Lang, and M. Mahoney. Empirical comparison of algorithms for network community detection. In *Proceedings of the 19th international conference on World wide web*, pages 631–640. ACM, 2010.

[17] A. McCallum, X. Wang, and A. Corrada-Emmanuel. Topic and role discovery in social networks with experiments on enron and academic email. *J. Artif. Intell. Res.(JAIR)*, 30:249–272, 2007.

[18] G. Palla, I. Derényi, I. Farkas, and T. Vicsek. Uncovering the overlapping community structure of complex networks in nature and society. *Nature*, 435(7043):814–818, 2005.

[19] D. M. Romero, W. Galuba, S. Asur, and B. A. Huberman. Influence and passivity in social media. *Machine learning and knowledge discovery in databases*, pages 18–33, 2011.

[20] R. A. Rossi, B. Gallagher, J. Neville, and K. Henderson. Modeling dynamic behavior in large evolving graphs. In *Proceedings of the sixth ACM international conference on Web search and data mining*, pages 667–676. ACM, 2013.

[21] M. Rosvall and C. T. Bergstrom. Multilevel compression of random walks on networks reveals hierarchical organization in large integrated systems. *PloS one*, 6(4):e18209, 2011.

[22] V. Satuluri and S. Parthasarathy. Scalable graph clustering using stochastic flows: applications to community discovery. In *Proceedings of the 15th ACM SIGKDD international conference on Knowledge discovery and data mining*, pages 737–746. ACM, 2009.

[23] V. Satuluri, S. Parthasarathy, and Y. Ruan. Local graph sparsification for scalable clustering. In *Proceedings of the 2011 international conference on Management of data*, pages 721–732. ACM, 2011.

[24] T. A. Snijders and K. Nowicki. Estimation and prediction for stochastic blockmodels for graphs with latent block structure. *Journal of Classification*, 14(1):75–100, 1997.

[25] J. Xie, S. Kelley, and B. K. Szymanski. Overlapping community detection in networks: The state-of-the-art and comparative study. *ACM Computing Surveys (CSUR)*, 45(4):43, 2013.

[26] J. Yang and J. Leskovec. Overlapping community detection at scale: a nonnegative matrix factorization approach. In *Proceedings of the sixth ACM international conference on Web search and data mining*, pages 587–596. ACM, 2013.

It's the Way you Check-in: Identifying Users in Location-Based Social Networks

Luca Rossi
School of Computer Science
University of Birmingham, UK
l.rossi@cs.bham.ac.uk

Mirco Musolesi
School of Computer Science
University of Birmingham, UK
m.musolesi@cs.bham.ac.uk

ABSTRACT

In recent years, the rapid spread of smartphones has led to the increasing popularity of Location-Based Social Networks (LBSNs). Although a number of research studies and articles in the press have shown the dangers of exposing personal location data, the inherent nature of LBSNs encourages users to publish information about their current location (i.e., their *check-ins*). The same is true for the majority of the most popular social networking websites, which offer the possibility of associating the current location of users to their posts and photos. Moreover, some LBSNs, such as Foursquare, let users tag their friends in their check-ins, thus potentially releasing location information of individuals that have no control over the published data. This raises additional privacy concerns for the management of location information in LBSNs.

In this paper we propose and evaluate a series of techniques for the identification of users from their check-in data. More specifically, we first present two strategies according to which users are characterized by the spatio-temporal trajectory emerging from their check-ins over time and the frequency of visit to specific locations, respectively. In addition to these approaches, we also propose a hybrid strategy that is able to exploit both types of information. It is worth noting that these techniques can be applied to a more general class of problems where locations and social links of individuals are available in a given dataset. We evaluate our techniques by means of three real-world LBSNs datasets, demonstrating that a very limited amount of data points is sufficient to identify a user with a high degree of accuracy. For instance, we show that in some datasets we are able to classify more than 80% of the users correctly.

Categories and Subject Descriptors

K.4 [**Computers and Society**]: Public Policy Issues—*Privacy*; H.3 [**Information Storage and Retrieval**]: Online Information Services—*Data sharing, Web-based services*

Keywords

Location-based social networks; User identification; Privacy

COSN'14, October 1–2, 2014, Dublin, Ireland.

ACM 978-1-4503-3198-2/14/10 ...$15.00.
http://dx.doi.org/10.1145/2660460.2660485.

1. INTRODUCTION

With the proliferation of GPS and Internet enabled smartphones over the last years, Location-Based Social Networks (LBSNs) have been increasingly popular and have attracted millions of users. Examples of LBSNs include BrightKite[1], Gowalla[2], Facebook Places [3] and Foursquare[4]. While BrightKite and Gowalla have been discontinued, Foursquare is now one of the most popular and widely used LBSNs with nearly 30 million users and over 3 billion check-ins.

These systems are based on the concept of *check-in*: a user can register in a certain location and share this information with his/her friends with the possibility of leaving recommendations and comments about shops, restaurants and so on. However, a great deal of research has highlighted the dangers of exposing personal location information [2, 5, 20]. In particular, the problem of protecting privacy in LBSNs has also been the subject of several studies, such as [4, 17, 19, 33, 7, 22, 28, 29]. The social nature of LBSNs inevitably introduces new concerns, as users are encouraged to disseminate location information on the network [31]. Moreover, as noted by Ruiz et al., the practice of tagging users can lead to the release of location information about other individuals that have no control over the published data [31]. For instance, in August 2012 Foursquare announced the possibility of tagging friends belonging to other social networks, i.e., Facebook, even when these are not Foursquare users[5]. In general, there is an increasing concern about the possibility of identifying users from the information that can be extracted from geo-social media.

In this paper, we address the problem of identifying a user through location information from a LBSN. Our aim is to elaborate a number of strategies for the identification of users given their check-in data. More specifically, we firstly propose a trajectory-based approach where a user is identified simply considering the trajectory of spatio-temporal points given by his/her check-in activity. In addition to this, we propose a series of alternative probabilistic Bayesian approaches where a user is characterized by his/her check-in frequency at each location. We also propose to exploit the social ties of the LBSNs by augmenting the frequency information of a user with that of his/her neighbors in the social graph. Finally, we combine the trajectory-based and the frequency-based techniques and propose a hybrid identification strategy. In order to evaluate these techniques, we measure experimentally the loss of victims' privacy as a function of the available anonymized infor-

[1]http://techcrunch.com/2011/12/20/brightkite-winds-down-says-it-will-come-back-with-something-better-again/
[2]http://blog.gowalla.com/
[3]https://www.facebook.com/about/location
[4]https://foursquare.com
[5]http://aboutfoursquare.com/foursquare-extends-friend-tagging-to-facebook/

	l_1	l_2	l_3	l_4
Alice	4	4	4	4
Bob	1	1	1	4
Charlie	5	1	2	0

id	Trace	Other
u_1	l_4, l_1, l_4	s_1
u_2	l_1, l_1, l_1	s_2
u_3	l_1, l_2, l_3	s_3

Table 1: Linking location information across different databases allows the attacker to break users' privacy.

mation. We also propose to quantify the complexity of the identification task by means of the generalized Jensen-Shannon divergence [21] between the frequency histograms of the users.

To the best of our knowledge, this is the first work concerning the problem of identification of users through LBNS location data. We find that the check-in data of the neighbors of a user, depending on the dataset being used, have a limited impact on the ability of identifying that user, which fits with what previous studies have observed on the interaction between mobility and social ties in LBSNs [6, 13, 14]. We also show that the more unique a GPS position is (i.e., the less shared it is among users), the more efficient the trajectory-based strategy is when the number of check-ins that we intend to classify is small. Overall, however, we find that the hybrid approach yields the best classification performance, with an accuracy of more than 90% in some of the selected datasets.

We should stress that the identification strategies proposed in this paper can be generally applied to any setting in which location information and social ties are available. One example is the case of a dataset composed of "significant places" [1] and social connections for a set of users. Significant places of a specific user are usually extracted by means of clustering techniques (see, for example, the seminal work by Ashbrook et al. [1]) and they can be interpreted as his/her check-in locations.

One can argue that by choosing to participate in a LBSN, the user implicitly accepts the respective privacy disclosure agreement. In fact, LBSNs users willingly share their location data on the network, where their identity is publicly visible to all the other users. However, it is possible to note that a potential attacker who intends to break the privacy of an additional source of anonymized location information may use the LBSNs data to transfer the identity information to the anonymized dataset [11]. As a consequence, we believe that it is of pivotal importance to investigate the threats posed by identification attacks of users from their check-in data.

The remainder of this paper is organized as follows. Section 2 defines the identification problem and the motivations for the present work. Section 3 gives an overview of the three datasets selected for this study. In Section 4 we introduce the techniques proposed in this paper for identifying a user given a set of check-ins and we propose a way to measure the complexity of the identification task over a given dataset. In Section 5 we provide an extensive experimental evaluation of the classification accuracy using data from three different LBSNs and we review our main findings and the related work in Section 6. Finally, we conclude the paper in Section 7 and we outline our future research agenda.

2. PROBLEM DEFINITION

We assume that an attacker has access to both unanonymized LBSN data and a source of anonymized location information[6]. This database is anonymized in that the true identities of its participants are replaced by unique random identifiers. Note that such a database may also contain other potentially sensitive data, e.g., health or financial information. Given this setting, the attacker tries to reveal the identities of the participants by linking the location information in the LBSN, where the users' identities are revealed, to the anonymized database.

Let us introduce the problem by means of a toy example illustrated in Table 1. The left part shows, for each user, the number of times that he or she has checked-in at location l_i, whereas the right part shows an additional database of location data in which the identities of the participants have been masked using random identifiers. More specifically, each row of this database consists of an identifier u_i, a sequence of visited locations l_j and an additional sensitive attribute denoted as s_i. The task of the attacker is that of linking the information across the two databases using the location data. In this example, we note that u_1's presence has been recorded 2 out of 3 times at l_4, which suggests that u_1 is either *Alice* or *Bob*, as *Charlie* has never checked-in at l_4. The uncertainty can be further reduced by observing that while the check-in history of *Alice* suggests that she has an equal probability of checking-in at any location, the frequency histogram of *Bob* is sharply peaked at l_4, which fits better the sequence of locations visited by u_1.

Note that the issues that arise from linking information across different databases have been widely investigated in recent years by the community working on differential privacy [33, 26, 11, 7, 22]. The problem we consider in this paper, however, differs from the previous work by being focused on the identity privacy leakage of LBSNs data. With respect to other source of mobility data, in fact, *LBSNs add a further social dimension that can be exploited when trying to break the privacy of an individual.*

3. OVERVIEW OF THE DATASETS

We choose to validate the proposed techniques on three different LBSNs, namely Brightkite, Gowalla and Foursquare. More specifically, we use the Brightkite and Gowalla data collected by Cho et al. [6] and the Foursquare data collected by Gao et al. [13, 14].

The Brightkite data contains 4,491,143 check-ins from 58,228 users over 772,764 location, from April 2008 to October 2010. The Gowalla dataset is composed of 6,442,890 check-ins from 196,591 users over 1,280,969 locations, collected from February 2009 to October 2010. Finally, the Foursquare dataset is a collection of 2,073,740 check-ins from 18,107 users over 43,063 locations, from August 2010 to November 2011. Due to the lack of an API to collect personal check-ins from Foursquare, the authors of [13, 14] collected the data using Twitter's REST API, while the social ties were collected directly from Foursquare. BrightKite and Gowalla instead used to provide an API to directly access the publicly available data.

For each check-in, we have the (anonymized) user identifier, the location identifier, the timestamp and the GPS coordinates where the check-in was made. Note, however, that while in the Foursquare dataset these are precisely the spatial coordinates where the user shared his/her position, in the other datasets these actually refer to the GPS coordinates of the venue itself. As a consequence, the location information in the Foursquare dataset is in a sense much more *unique* [9] than in the other two datasets. By uniqueness, we mean the extent to which a location in a dataset is shared among different individuals, i.e., the less shared a location is, the more unique it is. In this sense, the precise GPS location of a user where he/she performed his/her check-in is more unique than the GPS coordinates of the venue itself, as the latter will be shared in the records of all the users that checked-in at that venue. As a result, the less unique a piece of information is, i.e., the more shared it is among several users, the less discriminative it will be when exploited to identify users.

[6]This could be in the form of check-in data or sequences of GPS points. These can be reduced to a finite set of venues by extracting the set of significant places as in [1].

	SF_B	NY_B	LA_B	SF_G	NY_G	LA_G	SF_F	NY_F	LA_F
number of users	525	494	371	2,203	1,280	690	697	2,592	473
number of check-ins	66,593	61,607	63,923	340,366	136,548	79,616	65,092	258,469	42,011
number of locations	12,929	13,592	11,329	15,673	4,074	2,695	1,173	4,484	1,177

Table 2: Number of users and locations in the the selected cities. The subscript denotes the initial of the name of the LBSN dataset (Brighkite, Gowalla and Foursquare).

Note that, given the nature of our task, identifying users from check-ins scattered all over the world may be considered as an almost trivial task, due to the sparsity of the location information and the lack of a substantial overlap between different users in their check-ins habits. For this reason, we decide to restrict our analysis to the users that are active in San Francisco, New York and Los Angeles, considering only the check-ins in the urban boundaries of these cities. More specifically, given the latitude and longitude of the city center of a city[7], we keep all the users and locations within a 20km radius from it. We select these cities since they have the highest number of active users, so as to render the identification task as hard as possible. Table 2 shows the number of users and locations in each selected city. Note that for each city we consider only the users that performed at least 10 check-ins, as explained in Section 5.

4. IDENTIFICATION METHODS

In this section, we propose a set of techniques to identify a user given a series of check-ins data. Let $C = \{c_1 \dots c_n\}$ denote a set of check-ins. In our dataset, each check-in c_i is labeled with a user identifier u_id_i, a location identifier l_id_i, a timestamp t_i and a GPS point p_i indicating where the user performed the check-in. Let $C(u)$ denote the set of check-ins c_i with $u\_id_i = u$ and $u \in U$, where U is the set of users. For each user u, we divide $C(u)$ into a training test $C_{train}(u)$ and a test set $C_{test}(u)$, where in the latter we remove the user identifier attribute. Given $C_{test}(u)$, our task is that of recovering the identity of the original user. We propose to solve this task by using location data at different levels of granularity. More specifically, we use both the trajectory of high-resolution GPS coordinates visited by the users and the frequency of visits to the different locations. We conclude the section introducing a simple yet effective way to measure the complexity of the identification task over a given dataset.

4.1 Trajectory-based Identification

Since every check-in action is labeled with the precise GPS position where the user was located at that moment, we firstly explore an identification technique based on the analysis of the spatio-temporal information alone. More precisely, let the set of time labeled points p_i in $C_{train}(u)$ and $C_{test}(u)$ be denoted as $T_{train}(u)$ and $T_{test}(u)$ respectively. In other words, $T_{train}(u)$ and $T_{test}(u)$ are spatio-temporal trajectories induced by the check-ins of u. Then, given the spatio-temporal trajectory $T_{test}(u)$, we assign it to the user $v \in U$ who minimizes the distance $dist(T_{train}(v), T_{test}(u))$ defined as follows. Recall that the Hausdorff distance between two finite set of points $A = \{a_1, \cdots, a_m\}$ and $B = \{b_1, \cdots, b_n\}$ is defined as

$$H(A, B) = \max(h(A, B), h(B, A)) \tag{1}$$

where $h(A, B)$ is the directed Hausdorff distance from set A to B

$$h(A, B) = \max_{a \in A} \min_{b \in B} ||a - b|| \tag{2}$$

[7]http://www.census.gov/geo/maps-data/data/gazetteer.html

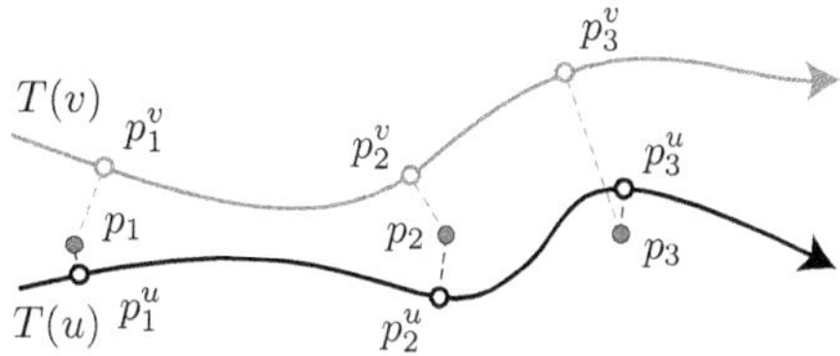

Figure 1: Two users v and u and their traces $T(v)$ (grey) and $T(u)$ (black) along with a set of three points (red) sampled from $T(u)$. These points are classified as belonging to $T(u)$ because the average distance to the corresponding nearest points in $T(u)$ is lower than the average distance to the nearest points in $T(v)$.

and $||\cdot||$ denotes the norm on the underlying space. The modified Hausdorff distance is introduced by Dubuisson et al. [10] as

$$h_m(A, B) = \frac{1}{|A|} \sum_{a \in A} \min_{b \in B} ||a - b|| \tag{3}$$

where $|A|$ denotes the number of points in A. We then define the spatio-temporal distance $d_{st}(p_1, p_2)$ between two points p_1 and p_2 as

$$d_{st}(p_1, p_2) = d_s(p_1, p_2) e^{\frac{d_t(p_1, p_2)}{\tau}} \tag{4}$$

where d_s denotes the distance computed using the Haversine formula [30], while d_t denotes the absolute time difference between two points. Here the exponential is used to smooth the distance between two points according to the absolute difference of their timestamps. Note that by setting $\tau \to \infty$ we ignore the temporal dimension, i.e., the distance between two spatio-temporal points is equivalent to their Haversine distance. As it turns out, due to the spatial and temporal sparsity of the check-in data, the best identification accuracy is achieved for $\tau \to \infty$, and thus we define the distance between a user's trajectory $T_{train}(v)$ and a set of check-in coordinates $T_{test}(u)$ as

$$dist(T_{train}(v), T_{test}(u)) = \frac{1}{|T_{test}(u)|} \sum_{p_1 \in T_{test}(u)} \min_{p_2 \in T_{train}(v)} d_s(p_1, p_2). \tag{5}$$

We stress that the modified Hausdorff distance is not properly a metric, as it is not symmetric. We choose the modified Hausdorff distance over other commonly used distances such as the Hausdorff [32], Fréchet [12], or Dynamic Time Warping distance [3], for its simplicity and robustness to outliers. Note in fact that the Hausdorff distance between $T_{train}(v)$ and $T_{test}(u)$ is low only if every point of either set is close to some point of the other set. This is clearly not true in our case, as we expect $T_{test}(u)$ to contain much fewer points than $T_{train}(v)$, and thus a large portion of $T_{train}(v)$ consists of outliers with respect to $T_{test}(u)$. More specifically, we need to compute the distance between a subset of points and an entire trajectory. The Fréchet and DTW distances, on the other hand, are designed to evaluate the distance between two trajectories of

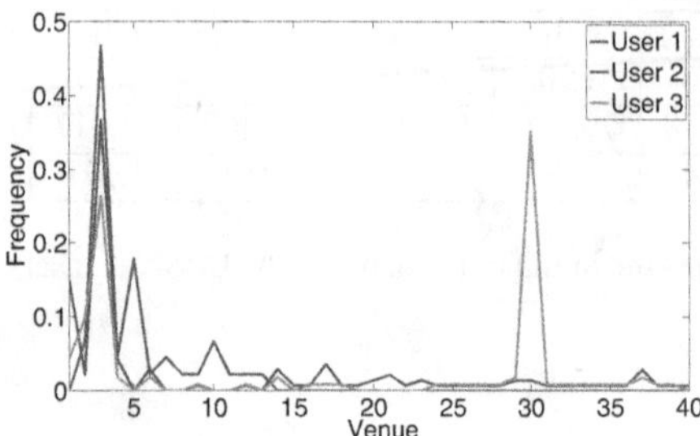

Figure 2: The multinomial models (without Laplace smoothing) for three users in the city of San Francisco.

points, while here the set of points $T_{test}(u)$ can contain as little as a single point. Figure 1 shows the intuition behind the use of the modified Hausdorff distance.

4.2 Frequency-based Identification

Although the GPS points p_i describing a user in the trajectory based model are generally considered to be distinct, they are actually clustered around a limited number of locations. Hence, we can characterize a user with the frequency of visit to this set of locations, rather than the trajectory of spatio-temporal points. In particular, given a set of check-ins $C_{test}(u) = \{c_1 \dots c_m\}$ where the user attribute has been removed, we propose to solve the identification task by selecting the user v which maximizes the posterior probability

$$v^* = \arg\max_{v \in U} P(v|c_1 \dots c_m) \tag{6}$$

where $P(v|c_1 \dots c_m)$ denotes the probability of $v \in U$ being the user who generated the check-in series $C_{test}(u)$.

4.2.1 Multinomial Model

We also develop an identification method based on a multinomial naïve Bayes model, widely used for several classification tasks, such as text classification [25]. By applying Bayes theorem and making the naïve assumption that each check-in c_i is conditionally independent of the others given the user v, we can rewrite Eq. 6 as

$$v^* = \arg\max_{v \in U} P(v) \prod_{i=1}^{m} P(c_i|v) \tag{7}$$

where $P(v)$ is the user prior and $P(c_i|v)$ is the probability of c_i being a check-in generated by v. Here we assume a uniform distribution for the user prior, while we apply a standard maximum likelihood approach to estimate the multinomial distribution associated to each user, i.e.,

$$P(c_i|v) = \frac{N_i^v}{\sum_{j=1}^{n} N_j^v} \tag{8}$$

where N_i^v denotes the number check-ins of v at the location l_id_i in $C_{train}(v)$.

We eliminate zero probabilities by applying Laplace smoothing [24], i.e.,

$$P(c_i|v) = \frac{N_i^v + \alpha}{\sum_{j=1}^{n} N_j^v + \alpha|L|} \tag{9}$$

where $\alpha > 0$ is the smoothing parameter and $|L|$ is the number of locations in our dataset. In other words, we assume a uniform prior over the set of locations. Figure 2 shows the probability distributions over the set of locations of three different users in the city of San Francisco. For the sake of clarity, only the locations visited by at least one of the users are shown.

4.2.2 Time-dependent Multinomial Model

The multinomial model can be enhanced by exploiting the temporal information of the check-ins. In fact, we know that people tend to check-in at the same locations at similar times, yet different people may exhibit different temporal habits. Here, we propose to use 4 time units of 6 hours each to characterise the daily activity of users. Let $\xi \in \Xi = \{1, 2, 3, 4\}$ be a discrete variable denoting the parts of the day. We model each user with 4 different multinomial distributions describing the time dependent check-in frequency over the locations, i.e.,

$$P_\xi(c_i|v) = \frac{N_i^v(\xi) + \alpha}{\sum_{j=1}^{n} N_j^v(\xi) + \alpha|L|} \tag{10}$$

where $P_\xi(c_i|v)$ denotes the time dependent probability of performing a check-in at l_id_i during the time interval ξ and $N_i^v(\xi)$ is the number of check-ins of user v at location l_id_i during the time interval ξ.

4.2.3 Social Smoothing

Given the social nature of LBSNs, it is reasonable to expect that the activity of a user may be influenced by that of his/her friends in the network [14, 13]. Hence, we explore the possibility of exploiting the check-in distributions of the social neighbors of u to augment the previous models. More formally, let $h_u \in \mathcal{R}^n$ be a vector such that $h_u(i)$ denotes the number of check-ins performed by user u at the location i. We first define the similarity between two users u and v as the cosine similarity between h_u and h_v, i.e.,

$$s(u, v) = \frac{h_u^\top h_v}{||h_u|| \, ||h_v||} \tag{11}$$

where $a^\top b$ denotes the dot product between a and b and $||a||$ is the Euclidean norm of a. The underlying intuition is that the more similar two users are the more likely they are to influence each other.

We then apply a "social smoothing" to the check-in data of v as follows:

$$P(c_i|v) = \frac{N_i^v + \mu \sum_{w \in \mathcal{S}(v)} s(v, w) N_i^w + \alpha}{\sum_{j=1}^{n} N_j^v + \mu \sum_{w \in \mathcal{S}(v)} \sum_{j=1}^{n} s(v, w) N_j^w + \alpha|L|} \tag{12}$$

where $\mathcal{S}(v)$ denotes the social neighborhood of v and μ is a parameter that controls the impact of the social smoothing. The rationale behind the social smoothing is that if a location has not been visited by v, it has a higher chance to be visited in the future if it has been visited by some of his/her friends. However, care should be given to the choice of the value of μ, as large values would introduce too much smoothing, effectively rendering a user indistinguishable from his/her social neighborhood. Note also that we still need to apply Laplace smoothing to avoid zero probabilities.

4.2.4 Hybrid Model

Finally, we propose to merge the spatial and frequency information in a single hybrid model. Given a set of check-ins $C_{test}(u)$ and a user v, we assign the pair a value which is a convex combination of the probability of $C_{test}(u)$ being generated by v with the inverse of the distance to v defined in Eq. 5, i.e.,

$$\gamma(v, C_{test}(u)) = w_{prob} P(C_{test}(u)|v) + \frac{w_{dist}}{1 + dist(T_{train}(v), T_{test}(u))} \tag{13}$$

where w_{prob} and w_{dist} are non negative weights such that $w_{prob} + w_{dist} = 1$. The second term of Equation 13 encodes the spatial similarity between the two trajectories, and it is bounded between 0 and 1. Since we also have that $0 \leq P(C_{test}(u)|v) \leq 1$, it follows that $\gamma(v, C_{test}(u))$ itself will be a real number between 0 and 1.

4.3 Measuring the Complexity of the Identification Task

We conclude this part by introducing a simple yet effective way to quantify the complexity of the identification task over a given dataset, under the assumption that a Bayesian approach is used to break the privacy of the dataset as described in the previous subsection. This in turn requires computing the Jensen-Shannon divergence [21] between the multinomial distributions associated with the users, i.e., their check-in frequency histograms. Unlike other pairwise divergence measures, such as the relative entropy [8], the Jensen-Shannon divergence is designed to deal with $n \geq 2$ probability distributions. Since in our case the number of users n is indeed larger than 2, the choice of the Jensen-Shannon divergence seemed the most appropriate.

Let $P_1, P_2, \cdots, P_n$, with $P_i = \{p_{ij}, j = 1, \cdots, k\}$, be n probability distributions over some finite set X, where $\pi = \{\pi_1, \pi_2, \cdots, \pi_n | \pi_i > 0, \sum \pi_i = 1\}$ is a set of weights, i.e., a set of priors. The generalized Jensen-Shannon divergence of the set $P_1, P_2, \cdots, P_n$ is defined as

$$JS_\pi(P_1, \cdots, P_n) = H(\sum_{i=1}^{n} \pi_i P_i) - \sum_{i=1}^{n} \pi_i H(P_i) \quad (14)$$

where $H(\cdot)$ denotes the Shannon entropy. Eq. 14 is essentially measuring the irregularity of the set $P_1, \cdots, P_n$ as the difference between the entropy of the convex combination of the P_i and the convex combination of the respective entropies. Interestingly, when all the P_i are equal we have that $JS_\pi = 0$. For the case $n = 2$, Lin [21] has shown that the Jensen-Shannon divergence is bounded between 0 and 1, symmetric and non-negative. However, in the general case where $n > 2$, the upper bound of the Jensen-Shannon divergence becomes $\log(\min(n, k))$ [15].

As a first attempt to rigorously measure the complexity measure of the complexity task, we decided to use the Jensen-Shannon divergence to compute lower and upper bounds of the multiclass Bayes error as shown by Lin [21]. In fact, the Bayes error can be seen as a measure of the hardness of a classification problem. More specifically, the Bayes error estimates the probability of misclassifying an observation in a Bayesian framework, i.e., in our case, the probability of misidentifying an individual. Given a multiclass problem with n classes $c_1, \cdots, c_n$, class conditional distributions $P_1, \cdots, P_n$ and priors $\pi = (\pi_1, \cdots, \pi_n)$, the following relationship between the Jensen-Shannon divergence and the Bayes probability of error $P(e)$ holds:

$$\frac{J_n^2}{4(n-1)} \leq P(e) \leq \frac{J_n}{2}, \quad (15)$$

where $J_n = H(\pi) - JS_\pi(P_1, \cdots, P_n)$. However, our experimental evaluation found that the bounds to be not tight enough to be informative. In particular, we found the upper bound to be larger than 1, over all the cities and datasets. This may be a consequence of the fact that, in order to reflect the lack of knowledge on the prior probability of the different users, we set $\pi = (\frac{1}{n}, \frac{1}{n}, \cdots, \frac{1}{n})$. Note in fact that $H(\pi) \leq \log(n)$, and in our specific case equality holds. On the other hand, the upper bound of $JS_\pi(P_1, \cdots, P_n)$ is $\log(\min(n, k))$, and, as a consequence, we have that $J_n \leq \log \frac{n}{\min(n,k)}$. In particular, J_n is certainly greater than 1 whenever $k < n$ and $H(\pi) = \log(n)$. Unfortunately, although in our case $n < k$ for all the cities and datasets, we still observe a value of $\frac{J_n}{2} > 1$, thus rendering the bound of limited interest. We also tried to estimate π_i as the frequency of the check-ins of users i with respect to the total number of check-ins, thus lowering $H(\pi)$, but the results were equally uninformative. For example, we found that for the city of New York (Foursquare) $0.011 < P(e) < 2.819$.

Given the limitations of Eq. 15, we propose a different way to measure the complexity of the classification task. Let D be a dataset holding the records of n users, each of which is characterized by a probability distribution P_i over a finite set X of size k. Then the complexity of discriminating the users of D is defined as

$$\mathcal{C}(D) = 1 - \frac{JS_\pi(P_1, \cdots, P_n)}{\log(\min(n, k))}. \quad (16)$$

Although not directly connected to the Bayes error, $\mathcal{C}(D)$ is bounded between 0 and 1 and it gives us a readily interpretable measure of the complexity of identifying the users of D. More specifically, $\mathcal{C}(D) = 1$ if and only if the values of P_i are equal for all i, i.e., it is impossible to discriminate between the users based on their check-in frequency. Moreover, when the distributions are maximally different, i.e., the frequency vectors P_i form an orthonormal set, then $\mathcal{C}(D) = 0$, i.e., it is trivial to discriminate between the users.

5. EXPERIMENTAL EVALUATION

In this section we will describe the evaluation of the methods presented above. We firstly describe the experimental settings and we then evaluate the performance of the proposed identification strategies.

5.1 Preliminaries

Given a city in our dataset (see Table 2), for each active user we randomly remove 10 check-ins from his/her history $C(u)$ and we use the remaining data to train our algorithms. That is, for each user u we separate $C(u)$ into a training test $C_{train}(u)$ and a test set $C_{test}(u)$. Hence, we are left with $|U|$ sets $C_{test}(u)$ of 10 check-ins, where $|U|$ is the number of users in the city. Given $C_{test}(u)$, the task consists in the identification of the user that originated the set of check-ins. We measure the performance of the different identification strategies in terms of classification accuracy, i.e., the ratio of successfully identified users. Moreover, we are interested in determining the score of each strategy, i.e., the number of guesses required to correctly identify a user. Here the baseline is a random guess, which has average score $|U|/2$. The results of the experiments are then averaged over 100 runs. Note that the scale of the standard error is generally too small to appear in our plots and it has been omitted from the tables as it is always smaller than 10^{-3}. Finally, note that, in the following experiments, we keep the size of $C_{test}(u)$ fixed to 10, but we vary the number of check-ins that we sample from it to identify the users, in order to measure how the performance of the proposed methods depends on the number of observed check-ins. We refer to the set of check-ins sampled from $C_{test}(u)$ as $C_{sample}(u)$.

Recall that the proposed strategies are dependent on the choice of a number of parameters, which include the smoothing parameter α, the social smoothing parameter μ and the interpolation weights w_{prob} and w_{dist}. The parameters are optimized by means of an exhaustive search over a manually defined subset of the parameters space. For each city and dataset, we run our experiments on the training set alone for different combinations of these parameters, and we select the optimal combination in terms of classification accuracy. To this end, we extract 5 check-ins from each user and we

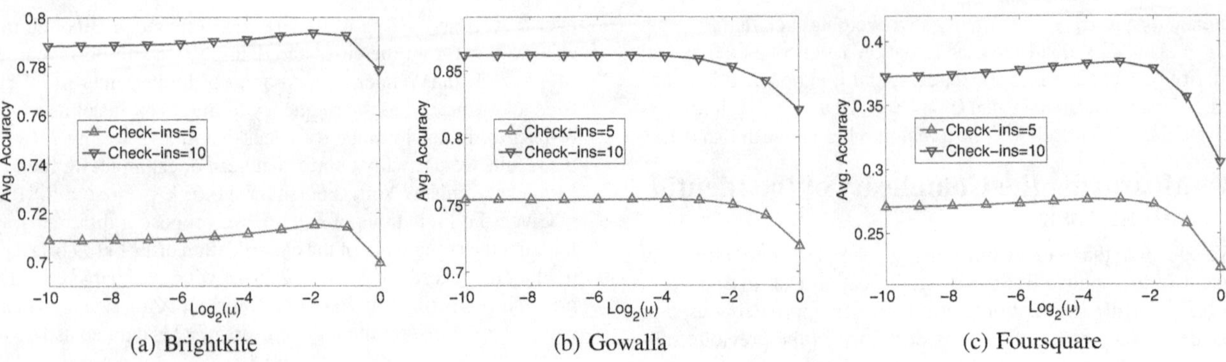

(a) Brightkite (b) Gowalla (c) Foursquare

Figure 3: The effect of the social smoothing on the average classification accuracy for the users in San Francisco.

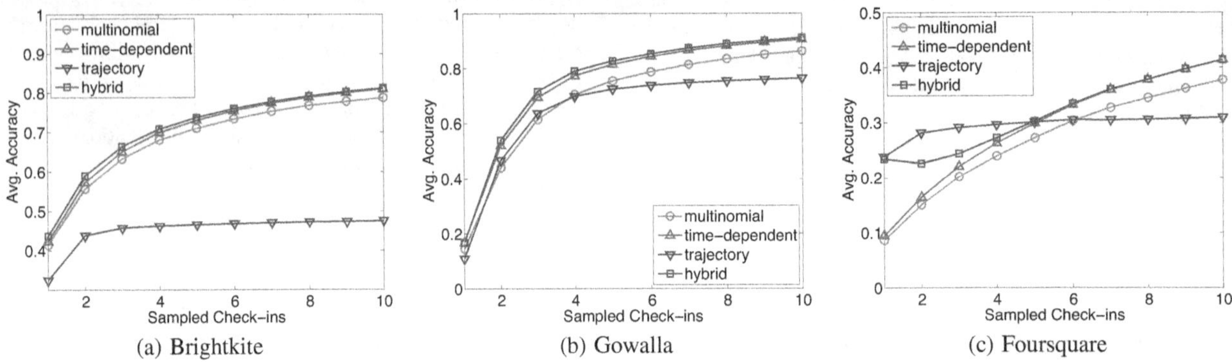

(a) Brightkite (b) Gowalla (c) Foursquare

Figure 4: The average classification accuracy in the city of San Francisco on the three datasets for increasing size of $C_{sample}(u)$. In the Foursquare dataset, the trajectory-based strategy is the best performing one when the number of sampled check-ins is small. Overall, the hybrid model is the best performing one: it consistently outperforms all the other methods in the Brightkite and Gowalla datasets.

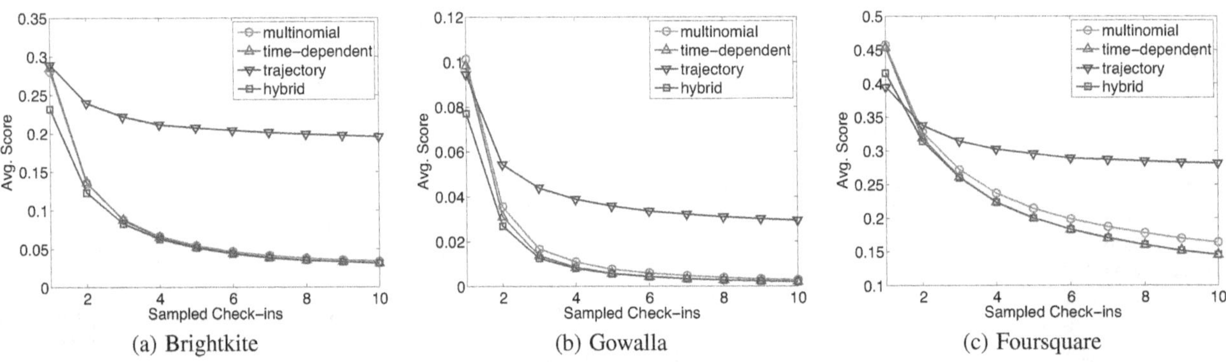

(a) Brightkite (b) Gowalla (c) Foursquare

Figure 5: The average score in the city of San Francisco on the three datasets for increasing size of $C_{sample}(u)$. In terms of average score, the hybrid model consistently outperforms all the other strategies. Also, in the Foursquare dataset the performance gap between the frequency-based strategies and the trajectory-based one is clearly reduced.

apply our identification strategies as described above. Note that, after the test check-ins are removed, the less active users can have as little as 1 check-in in the training set. Thus, we perform the exhaustive search using only those users with more than 5 check-ins in their training set, which in our experimental setting amount for more than 97% of the users. We find that the best classification accuracy is achieved for small values of α. In fact, α represents the prior probability of a user to visit any location in the dataset, independently from his/her check-in history and, therefore, choosing a high value of α would smooth the distribution too much, thus rendering the user harder to classify.

5.2 Experimental Results

Figure 3 shows the effect of applying the social smoothing to the frequency-based strategies. Here we show the average classification accuracy in the city of San Francisco as the value of μ varies. The impact of the social smoothing seems to be rather limited in Foursquare and Brightkite, while in Gowalla the best accuracy is achieved for $\mu = 0$, i.e., when no social smoothing is applied. As

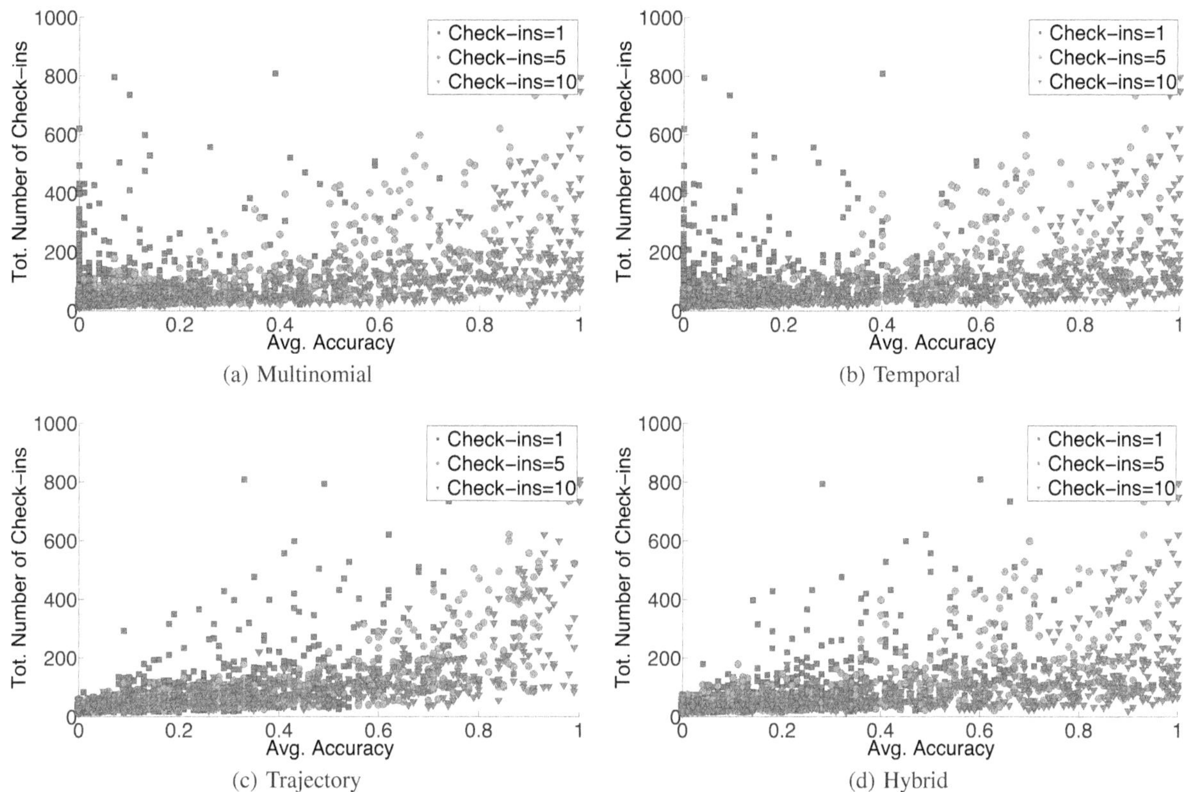

Figure 6: Activity versus average accuracy on the city of San Francisco (Foursquare). Less active users are more difficult to classify correctly, due to the limited number of check-ins available for the training, while very active users are easier to classify.

expected, on the other hand, for large values of μ the performance suddenly drops, as the smoothing starts to render the users indistinguishable from their social neighborhoods. The fact that the social smoothing does not result in a clear increase of the accuracy is not surprising and it fits with what previous studies have observed on the interaction between mobility and social ties in LBSNs [6, 13, 14]. In particular, Cho et al. [6] have found that friendship has a very limited influence on short distance movements (i.e., shorter than 25km, whereas the radius of the cities considered in this paper is 20km), and it is an order of magnitude lower than the influence on long distances (i.e., longer than 1,000km). In particular, they show that only 9.6% of all the check-ins in Gowalla and 4.1% of all the check-ins in Brightkite were first visited by a friend before being visited by a user. In Gao et al. [13, 14], on the other hand, the authors observe an improvement of the location prediction accuracy when the social information is taken into account. However, their study also shows that the impact of the social information is rather limited, and that historical check-in information is more crucial in terms of prediction accuracy.

Figures 4 and 5 show how the average classification accuracy and score on the city of San Francisco vary as we increase the size of $C_{sample}(u)$. The score is reported as a percentage of the baseline score $|U|/2$, i.e., a score of 1 indicates that the method has the same performance of a random guess. We observe that in the Foursquare dataset, when the number of sampled check-ins is smaller than 5, the best performing strategy in terms of accuracy is the trajectory-based one. This is likely due to the high precision and uniqueness of GPS data (the extent to which the data is shared among different users). Recall, in fact, that in this dataset a GPS position refers to the precise spatial coordinates where the user shared his/her position, rather than the coordinates of the venue itself. As a consequence, the spatial information may be sufficient to discriminate among different users who checked-in at the same venue but in positions corresponding to different geographic coordinates, i.e., different places in an urban or non-urban area. However, the same does not hold for Brightkite and Gowalla, where the GPS location of a check-in refers to a unique set of coordinates associated to each venue. In this case, the trajectory-based strategy is always the worst performing one, which confirms our intuition about the uniqueness of the spatial information. As for the frequency-based strategies, we see that the addition of the temporal dimension always yields an increase of the accuracy with respect to the standard multinomial model. Overall, the best performing method is the hybrid one. In the Foursquare dataset, the hybrid model seems to be able to combine the advantages of both the trajectory-based and the frequency-based strategies, by achieving a good performance when the number of sampled check-ins is small, and the best performance when $|C_{sample}(u)| \geq 6$. Conversely, in Brightkite and Gowalla, the hybrid method is consistently outperforming all the others.

In terms of score, Figure 5 also shows that the hybrid method consistently outperforms all the others, in all the three datasets. Note also that, in terms of score, in the Foursquare dataset the advantage of the trajectory-based strategy over the frequency-based one seems to be greatly reduced. In other words, when a user is misclassified, the number of guesses needed to correctly identify him/her is generally higher in the trajectory-based approach than in the frequency-based ones. Interestingly, we also observe that the

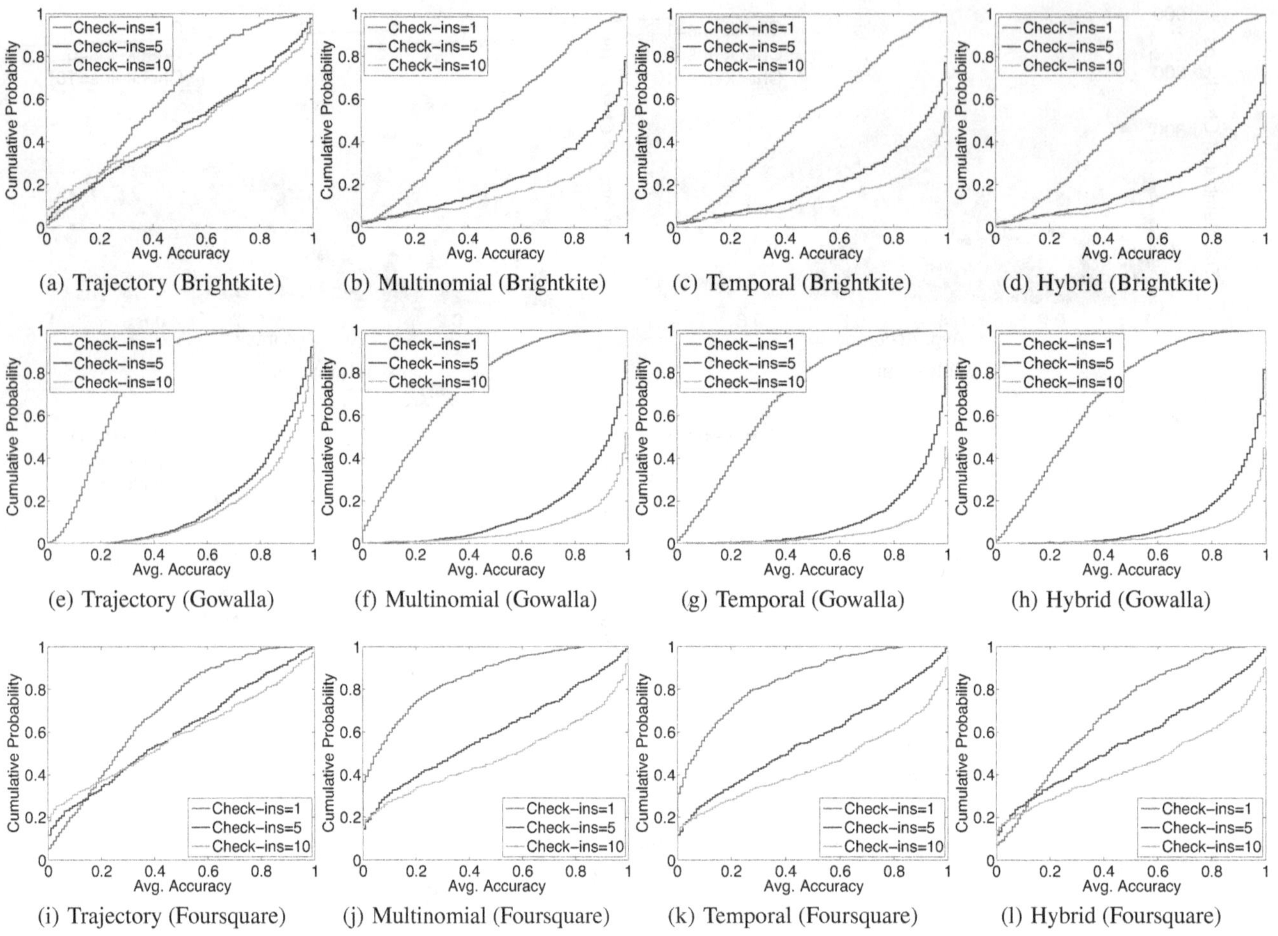

Figure 7: The empirical Cumulative Distribution Function of the user classification accuracies of all the methods on Los Angeles, for the three datasets. In the Gowalla dataset, the hybrid method can identify more than 90% of the users with an accuracy of at least 80%, with $|C_{sample}(u)| = 10$. Note that the results for the other cities show similar trends, and they are omitted due to space constraints.

average scores of the multinomial and its time-dependent version in the other datasets are very close.

The scatter plot of Figure 6 shows the user classification accuracies related to San Francisco (Foursquare), as a function of the users activity. Note that we present the results only for the city of San Francisco due to space limitations. However, the observations we make here hold also in the case of the other cities and datasets. We observe that for the most active users we get a better classification accuracy, as we have a large number of check-ins available to train our models. On the other hand, the performance in terms of classification of less active users can vary considerably. In fact, it would be trivial to identify a user who performed a single check-in at a location where nobody else checked-in. However, a user who performs a small number of check-ins all at very popular venues can be easily misclassified. Figure 6 also shows the advantage of the hybrid method over the other strategies. When the number of sampled check-ins is small, the multinomial and time-dependent models fail to identify most of the users. Instead, the hybrid model shows a distribution similar to that of the trajectory-based strategy, which is the best performing one for small values of $C_{sample}(u)$. When we increase the number of sampled check-ins, on the other hand, the hybrid model performs similarly to the frequency-based strategies, while the trajectory-based approach performs rather poorly, especially for less active users.

Figure 7 shows the empirical distribution function of the user classification accuracies for all the methods and datasets for the city of Los Angeles. These plots show that the classification task seems to be easier on the Brightkite and Gowalla datasets. In the latter, the hybrid method can identify more than 90% of the users with an accuracy of at least 80%, with $|C_{sample}(u)| = 10$. This may be partly due to the fact that, especially in Brightkite, we observe a very large number of locations, which might be the result of fake check-ins. In fact, in both datasets we find several instances of users performing a series of check-ins at locations having different identifiers but same GPS coordinates, and in a relatively short time interval. This in turn results in a very sparse dataset, where there is little overlap between the check-ins of different users, and thus an easier classification task for our strategies. We consider the presence of fake check-ins as a sort of natural feature of datasets extracted from LBSNs. Therefore, we do not perform any preprocessing on our datasets. The classification methodologies have to be robust enough and able to deal with the presence of spurious check-ins associated to a given user.

For the sake of completeness, we report the average classification accuracy and the score of all the strategies over all the cities for the

Trajectory	SF_B	NY_B	LA_B	SF_G	NY_G	LA_G	SF_F	NY_F	LA_F
$\lvert C_{sample}(u)\rvert = 1$	0.325	0.402	0.388	0.110	0.189	0.232	**0.238**	0.182	0.299
$\lvert C_{sample}(u)\rvert = 5$	0.465	0.493	0.530	0.724	0.730	0.815	0.301	**0.275**	0.402
$\lvert C_{sample}(u)\rvert = 10$	0.475	0.505	0.534	0.764	0.760	0.846	0.309	0.294	0.418
Multinomial	SF_B	NY_B	LA_B	SF_G	NY_G	LA_G	SF_F	NY_F	LA_F
$\lvert C_{sample}(u)\rvert = 1$	0.413	0.460	0.471	0.145	0.189	0.260	0.086	0.075	0.144
$\lvert C_{sample}(u)\rvert = 5$	0.710	0.766	0.769	0.754	0.771	0.850	0.272	0.227	0.404
$\lvert C_{sample}(u)\rvert = 10$	0.787	0.837	0.841	0.862	0.867	0.867	0.378	0.301	0.513
Temporal	SF_B	NY_B	LA_B	SF_G	NY_G	LA_G	SF_F	NY_F	LA_F
$\lvert C_{sample}(u)\rvert = 1$	0.423	0.467	0.478	0.167	0.224	0.300	0.095	0.079	0.155
$\lvert C_{sample}(u)\rvert = 5$	0.731	0.777	0.787	0.814	0.828	0.887	0.299	0.250	0.435
$\lvert C_{sample}(u)\rvert = 10$	0.810	0.850	0.860	0.906	0.909	0.948	0.414	0.335	0.552
Hybrid	SF_B	NY_B	LA_B	SF_G	NY_G	LA_G	SF_F	NY_F	LA_F
$\lvert C_{sample}(u)\rvert = 1$	**0.437**	**0.487**	**0.496**	**0.168**	**0.225**	**0.301**	0.234	**0.199**	**0.308**
$\lvert C_{sample}(u)\rvert = 5$	**0.738**	**0.781**	**0.792**	**0.828**	**0.835**	**0.894**	**0.303**	0.256	**0.439**
$\lvert C_{sample}(u)\rvert = 10$	**0.812**	**0.851**	**0.863**	**0.912**	**0.913**	**0.951**	**0.414**	**0.335**	**0.552**

Table 3: Average classification accuracy over all the cities of the three datasets. The best performing method for each city, dataset and size of $C_{sample}(u)$ is highlighted in bold. The standard error is not shown as it was always less than 10^{-3}.

	San Francisco	New York	Los Angeles
Brightkite	0.144	0.079	0.120
Gowalla	0.335	0.279	0.233
Foursquare	0.606	0.571	0.527

Table 4: The identification complexity $\mathcal{C}(D)$ over all the cities and datasets, using the multinomial model.

	San Francisco	New York	Los Angeles
Brightkite	0.083	0.018	0.061
Gowalla	0.190	0.126	0.094
Foursquare	0.469	0.448	0.397

Table 5: The identification complexity $\mathcal{C}(D)$ over all the cities and datasets, using the time-dependent multinomial model.

three datasets in Tables 3 and 6. Again, we see that in most of the cases the best performing method is the hybrid one. Note that we achieve a remarkably high accuracy on some cities: for example, in the city of Los Angeles (Gowalla), we obtain a 95% identification accuracy, when 10 anonymized points are observed. On the other hand, when as little as 1 anonymized point is observed, the maximum accuracy is achieved on the city of Los Angeles (Brightkite), where we can correctly identify nearly 50% of the users.

Finally, we compare these results with those obtained by measuring the identification complexity $\mathcal{C}(D)$ according to Eq. 16. Tables 4 and 5 show the average value of $\mathcal{C}(D)$ for each city and dataset, under the multinomial and time-dependent multinomial models, respectively. More specifically, each time we train the (time-dependent) multinomial model on a training set C_{train} we also compute $\mathcal{C}(C_{train})$. In other words, when computing $\mathcal{C}(C_{train})$ each individual is characterized by a (time-dependent) multinomial distribution p_i, and thus the results should be compared with the classification accuracy of the (time-dependent) multinomial model of Table 3. We should stress, however, that the proposed complexity measure is not restricted to these models and can be applied to any set of probability distributions p_i characterizing an ensemble of users. Finally, note that while in the frequency-based identification methods we applied Laplace smoothing to remove the occurrence of zero probabilities, when computing the Shannon entropy this step is not necessary. In fact, we followed the convention that $0 \log 0 = 0$, which is justified by continuity since $x \log x \to 0$ as $x \to 0$.

Tables 4 and 5 show that the cities in the Foursquare dataset are the most complex ones, which is in accordance with the low classification accuracy achieved by the multinomial model in this dataset. We also observe that the identification task over the cities in the Brighkite dataset seems to be less hard, which is only in partial agreement with the results of Table 3. In fact, when a single point is observed in $C_{sample}(u)$, the Brightkite dataset proves to be the less complex one, in terms of classification accuracy. However, when a larger sample of points is observed, the difference in classification accuracy between Brightkite and Gowalla completely disappears. This may be due to the Laplace smoothing that was applied when training the models. Finally, we observe that the addition of the temporal dimension invariably leads to a reduction of the identification complexity, as already observed in Table 3.

6. DISCUSSION AND RELATED WORK

The results of the experimental evaluation show that it is possible to classify a user from his/her check-in data with high accuracy given a small number of points. In general, the best identification accuracy is achieved by combining frequency and spatial information together. However, if the GPS data refers to the spatial coordinates where the user shared his/her position, the trajectory-based strategy outperforms all the others, when the number of check-ins to classify is small. On the other hand, we observe a negative impact if the GPS information refers to the coordinates of the venue itself, since it has less discriminatory power.

Moreover, in some cases the check-in activity of the friends of a user can be used to increase the identification accuracy, although the effect seems rather limited. The experimental results show that in Brightkite and Gowalla the proposed identification strategies can achieve an accuracy of more than 80% using only 10 check-ins. In Foursquare, we still obtain a classification performance between 30% and 50%, with the same number of check-ins. Given the rising popularity of LBSNs, we believe that our findings raise serious concerns on the privacy of their users. Moreover, we should stress again that the identification strategies proposed in this paper can be

Trajectory	SF_B	NY_B	LA_B	SF_G	NY_G	LA_G	SF_F	NY_F	LA_F
$\|C_{sample}(u)\| = 1$	0.289	0.275	0.222	0.094	0.090	0.063	**0.395**	**0.384**	**0.318**
$\|C_{sample}(u)\| = 5$	0.208	0.180	0.136	0.036	0.031	0.021	0.295	0.271	0.207
$\|C_{sample}(u)\| = 10$	0.195	0.158	0.113	0.029	0.024	0.016	0.281	0.250	0.181

Multinomial	SF_B	NY_B	LA_B	SF_G	NY_G	LA_G	SF_F	NY_F	LA_F
$\|C_{sample}(u)\| = 1$	0.280	0.303	0.250	0.101	0.114	0.085	0.457	0.442	0.376
$\|C_{sample}(u)\| = 5$	0.054	0.044	0.042	0.008	0.009	0.005	0.215	0.230	0.150
$\|C_{sample}(u)\| = 10$	0.034	0.023	0.023	0.003	0.004	0.003	0.164	0.194	0.111

Temporal	SF_B	NY_B	LA_B	SF_G	NY_G	LA_G	SF_F	NY_F	LA_F
$\|C_{sample}(u)\| = 1$	0.285	0.309	0.255	0.098	0.114	0.088	0.453	0.445	0.376
$\|C_{sample}(u)\| = 5$	0.052	0.042	0.040	0.006	0.007	0.004	0.200	0.216	0.141
$\|C_{sample}(u)\| = 10$	0.031	0.022	0.021	0.002	0.003	0.002	0.145	0.179	0.100

Hybrid	SF_B	NY_B	LA_B	SF_G	NY_G	LA_G	SF_F	NY_F	LA_F
$\|C_{sample}(u)\| = 1$	**0.231**	**0.245**	**0.209**	**0.007**	**0.081**	**0.063**	0.415	0.413	0.338
$\|C_{sample}(u)\| = 5$	**0.051**	**0.043**	**0.040**	**0.006**	**0.006**	**0.004**	**0.199**	**0.216**	**0.128**
$\|C_{sample}(u)\| = 10$	**0.031**	**0.022**	**0.021**	**0.002**	**0.002**	**0.002**	**0.145**	**0.178**	**0.099**

Table 6: Average score over all the cities of the three datasets. The best performing method for each city, dataset and size of $C_{sample}(u)$ is highlighted in bold. The standard error is not shown as it was always less than 10^{-3}.

generally applied to any identification problem in which location information and social ties are available. If the location information is in the form of GPS trajectories, it would be sufficient to extract the significant places using clustering techniques [1] and interpret them as the check-in locations.

The advent of mobile technologies has led to several studies concerning human mobility in a geographic space. Recent papers include the prediction of the future location of a person [1], their mode of transport [35] and the identification of individuals from a sample of their location data [9]. In [16] it was shown that there is a high degree of temporal and spatial regularity in human trajectories: users are more likely to visit an area if they have been frequently visited it in the past.

More recently, LBNSs have attracted an increasing interest, due to the massive volume of data generated by their users and their explicit social structure. Examples of applications go from the prediction of the next visited location [27] to the clustering of different types of behaviors of users [18]. Malmi et al. [23] present a transfer learning approach to integrate different types of movement data, including LBSNs check-ins, in order to address the next place prediction problem. Gao et al. [14], on the other hand, propose a geo-social correlation model to capture check-ins correlations between users at different geographical and social distances. Interestingly, they find that there is a higher correlation between users who are not friends but live in the same area rather than direct friends. Similarly, Cho et al. [6] study how the friendships in LBSNs can influence human mobility, and find that in general the influence is higher on long-range movements rather than short-range ones. In another paper, Gao et al. [13] propose a series of models that integrate social information in a location prediction task. Joseph et al. propose to use Latent Dirichlet Allocation to model the check-in activity of Foursquare users and cluster them into different groups with different interests [18]. Vasconcelos et al. [34] investigate the use of "tips", "dones" and "todos" in Foursquare to cluster users profiles. The problem of privacy in LBSNs is discussed and analyzed in Ruiz et al. [31]. In particular, the authors study a number of privacy issues related to the location and identity of LBSN users, and describe possible means of protecting privacy.

Finally, Pontes et al. [29, 28] focus on the inference of the user home location using publicly available information from Foursquare and two different online social networks, namely Google+ and Twitter. More specifically, in [29] the authors show that it is possible to infer with high accuracy where a user lives based on his or her set of Foursquare activities (such as "todos"). In [28], the analysis is extended to Google+ and Twitter, where a number of attributes including the location of the users' friends are used to infer the home city as well as their residence location of the individuals.

With respect to this body of work, to the best of our knowledge, our paper is the first attempt of studying the problem of user identification from LBSNs data. We believe that this issue will be increasingly important, given the ever growing popularity of smartphones running a plethora of location-aware (and usually socially-aware) applications.

7. CONCLUSIONS AND FUTURE WORK

In this paper we have introduced and evaluated a series of techniques for the identification of users in LBSNs. We have tested the proposed strategies using three datasets from different LBSNs, namely Brightkite, Gowalla and Foursquare. We have showed that both the GPS information contained in a user's check-ins and the frequency of visits to certain locations can be used to successfully identify him/her. In particular, we have demonstrated that it is possible to achieve a high level of accuracy with only 10 check-ins, thus raising serious concerns with respect to the privacy of LBSNs users. Finally, we have proposed a simple yet effective way to quantify the complexity of the identification task over a given dataset.

We plan to apply the proposed methods on different datasets, since we are aware of the possible peculiarities and limitations of those used in this study. Indeed, even if we believe that the proposed methodology can be applied to a vast number of identification problems for which geographic and social information are available, we aim to investigate the generalizability of the identification strategies presented in this work to larger and more challenging datasets, which may thus demand more scalable and efficient machine learning techniques. Our future research agenda also includes the definition, implementation and evaluation of obfuscation techniques based on the findings presented in this paper. We also intend to investigate the use of our identification complexity measure on different datasets and to extend it to more general scenarios, considering also additional information from users' profiles, if available.

Acknowledgement

This work was supported through the EPSRC Grant "The Uncertainty of Identity: Linking Spatiotemporal Information Between Virtual and Real Worlds" (EP/J005266/1)

8. REFERENCES

[1] D. Ashbrook and T. Starner. Using GPS to Learn Significant Locations and Predict Movement Across Multiple Users. *Personal and Ubiquitous Computing*, 7(5):275–286, 2003.

[2] A. R. Beresford and F. Stajano. Location privacy in pervasive computing. *IEEE Pervasive Computing*, 2(1):46–55, 2003.

[3] D. J. Berndt and J. Clifford. Using dynamic time warping to find patterns in time series. In *Proceedings of the AAAI-94 Workshop on Knowledge Discovery in Databases*, volume 10, pages 359–370. Seattle, WA, 1994.

[4] C. Bettini, X. S. Wang, and S. Jajodia. Protecting privacy against location-based personal identification. In *Secure Data Management*, pages 185–199. Springer, 2005.

[5] J. Bohn, V. Coroamă, M. Langheinrich, F. Mattern, and M. Rohs. Social, economic, and ethical implications of ambient intelligence and ubiquitous computing. In *Ambient Intelligence*, pages 5–29. Springer, 2005.

[6] E. Cho, S. A. Myers, and J. Leskovec. Friendship and mobility: User movement in location-based social networks. In *Proceedings of SIGKDD'11*, pages 1082–1090. ACM, 2011.

[7] C.-Y. Chow and M. F. Mokbel. Trajectory privacy in location-based services and data publication. *ACM SIGKDD Explorations Newsletter*, 13(1):19–29, 2011.

[8] T. M. Cover and J. A. Thomas. *Elements of information theory*. John Wiley & Sons, 2012.

[9] Y.-A. de Montjoye, C. A. Hidalgo, M. Verleysen, and V. D. Blondel. Unique in the crowd: The privacy bounds of human mobility. *Scientific Reports*, 3, 2013.

[10] M.-P. Dubuisson and A. K. Jain. A Modified Hausdorff Distance for Object Matching. In *Proceedings of ICPR'94*, pages 566–568, 1994.

[11] C. Dwork. Differential privacy: A survey of results. In *Theory and Applications of Models of Computation*, pages 1–19. Springer, 2008.

[12] T. Eiter and H. Mannila. Computing Discrete Fréchet Distance. Technical report, Technische Universitat Wien, 1994.

[13] H. Gao, J. Tang, and H. Liu. Exploring social-historical ties on location-based social networks. In *Proceedings of ICWSM'12*, 2012.

[14] H. Gao, J. Tang, and H. Liu. gSCorr: modeling geo-social correlations for new check-ins on location-based social networks. In *Proceedings of CIKM'12*, pages 1582–1586. ACM, 2012.

[15] J. F. Gómez-Lopera, J. Martínez-Aroza, A. M. Robles-Pérez, and R. Román-Roldán. An analysis of edge detection by using the jensen-shannon divergence. *Journal of Mathematical Imaging and Vision*, 13(1):35–56, 2000.

[16] M. C. Gonzalez, C. A. Hidalgo, and A.-L. Barabasi. Understanding individual human mobility patterns. *Nature*, 453(7196):779–782, 2008.

[17] M. Gruteser and D. Grunwald. Anonymous usage of location-based services through spatial and temporal cloaking. In *Proceedings of MobiSys'03*, pages 31–42. ACM, 2003.

[18] K. Joseph, C. H. Tan, and K. M. Carley. Beyond Local, Categories and Friends: Clustering Foursquare Users with Latent Topics. In *Proceedings of UbiComp'12*, pages 919–926. ACM, 2012.

[19] P. Kalnis, G. Ghinita, K. Mouratidis, and D. Papadias. Preventing location-based identity inference in anonymous spatial queries. *IEEE Transactions on Knowledge and Data Engineering*, 19(12):1719–1733, 2007.

[20] J. Krumm. A survey of computational location privacy. *Personal and Ubiquitous Computing*, 13(6):391–399, 2009.

[21] J. Lin. Divergence Measures based on the Shannon Entropy. *IEEE Transactions on Information Theory*, 37(1):145–151, 1991.

[22] C. Y. T. Ma, D. K. Y. Yau, N. K. Yip, and N. S. Rao. Privacy vulnerability of published anonymous mobility traces. *IEEE/ACM Transactions on Networking*, 21(3):720–733, 2013.

[23] E. Malmi, T. M. T. Do, and D. Gatica-Perez. From Foursquare to My Square: Learning Check-in Behavior from Multiple Sources. In *Proceedings of ICWSM'13*, 2013.

[24] C. D. Manning, P. Raghavan, and H. Schütze. *Introduction to Information Retrieval*. Cambridge University Press, 2008.

[25] A. McCallum and K. Nigam. A comparison of event models for naive bayes text classification. In *Proceeding of the AAAI-98 Workshop on Learning for Text Categorization*, volume 752, pages 41–48, 1998.

[26] A. Narayanan and V. Shmatikov. Robust de-anonymization of large sparse datasets. In *Proceedings of SP'08*, pages 111–125. IEEE, 2008.

[27] A. Noulas, S. Scellato, R. Lambiotte, M. Pontil, and C. Mascolo. A tale of many cities: Universal patterns in human urban mobility. *PLOS ONE*, 7(5):e37027, 2012.

[28] T. Pontes, G. Magno, M. Vasconcelos, A. Gupta, J. Almeida, P. Kumaraguru, and V. Almeida. Beware of what you share: Inferring home location in social networks. In *Proceedings of ICDM'12 Workshops*, pages 571–578. IEEE, 2012.

[29] T. Pontes, M. Vasconcelos, J. Almeida, P. Kumaraguru, and V. Almeida. We Know Where you Live: Privacy Characterization of Foursquare Behavior. In *Proceedings of UbiComp'12*, pages 898–905. ACM, 2012.

[30] C. C. Robusto. The Cosine-Haversine formula. *The American Mathematical Monthly*, 64(1):38–40, 1957.

[31] C. Ruiz Vicente, D. Freni, C. Bettini, and C. S. Jensen. Location-related privacy in geo-social networks. *IEEE Internet Computing*, 15(3):20–27, 2011.

[32] J.-R. Sack and J. Urrutia. *Handbook of Computational Geometry*. North Holland, 1999.

[33] L. Sweeney. k-anonymity: A model for protecting privacy. *International Journal of Uncertainty, Fuzziness and Knowledge-Based Systems*, 10(05):557–570, 2002.

[34] M. A. Vasconcelos, S. Ricci, J. Almeida, F. Benevenuto, and V. Almeida. Tips, Dones and Todos: Uncovering User Profiles in Foursquare. In *Proceedings of WSDM'12*, pages 653–662. ACM, 2012.

[35] Y. Zheng, Q. Li, Y. Chen, X. Xie, and W.-Y. Ma. Understanding Mobility based on GPS Data. In *Proceedings of UbiComp'08*, pages 312–321. ACM, 2008.

Estimating Heights from Photo Collections: A Data-Driven Approach

Ratan Dey
New York University
ratan@nyu.edu

Madhurya Nangia
New York University
madhurya27@gmail.com

Keith W. Ross
New York University
New York University Shanghai
keithwross@nyu.edu

Yong Liu
New York University
yongliu@nyu.edu

ABSTRACT

A photo can potentially reveal a tremendous amount of information about an individual, including the individual's height, weight, gender, ethnicity, hair color, skin condition, interests, and wealth. A *photo collection* – a set of inter-related photos including photos of many people appearing in two or more photos – could potentially reveal a more vivid picture of the individuals in the collection.

In this paper we consider the problem of estimating the heights of all the users in a photo collection, such as a collection of photos from a social network. The main ideas in our methodology are (i) for each individual photo, estimate the height differences among the people standing in the photo, (ii) from the photo collection, create a people graph, and combine this graph with the height difference estimates from the individual photos to generate height difference estimates among all the people in the collection, (iii) then use these height difference estimates, as well as an *a priori* distribution, to estimate the heights of all the people in the photo collection. Because many people will appear in multiple photos across the collection, height-difference estimates can be chained together, potentially reducing the errors in the estimates. To this end, we formulate a Maximum Likelihood Estimation (MLE) problem, which we show can be easily solved as a quadratic programming problem. Intuitively, this data-driven approach will improve as the number of photos and people in the collection increases. We apply the technique to estimating the heights of over 400 movie stars in the IMDb database and of about 30 graduate students.

Categories and Subject Descriptors

E.1 [**Data**]: Data Structures—*Graph and Networks*; I.4.7 [**Computing Methodologies**]: Image Processing and Computer Vision—*Feature Measurement*; H.4.m [**Information Systems Applications**]: Miscellaneous; K.4.1 [**Computers and Society**]: Public Policy Issues—*Privacy*

COSN'14, October 1–2, 2014, Dublin, Ireland.

http://dx.doi.org/10.1145/2660460.2660466 .

General Terms

Statistical Inference

Keywords

Height Estimate; Photo Collection; Privacy; Maximum Likelihood Estimation; People Graph; Image Processing; Concept extraction

1. INTRODUCTION

Many online social networks (OSNs) – such as Facebook, Instagram, WeChat, and Flickr – have access to vast collections of photos. For example, as of September 2013, more than 250 billion photos have been uploaded to Facebook, with 350 million photos being uploaded every day [8]. As of March 2004, more than 20 billion photos have been uploaded to Instagram with 60 million photos being uploaded every day [5]. A large fraction of these photos contain pictures of the users of these OSNs. A single photo can be mined to potentially reveal a tremendous amount of information about an individual, including the individual's height, weight, gender, ethnicity, hair color, skin condition, interests, and wealth. A *photo collection* – a set of inter-related photos including photos of many people appearing in two or more photos – could potentially reveal a more vivid picture of the individuals in the collection.

In this paper we will consider the problem of estimating one such attribute from a photo collection, namely, the heights of *all* the people appearing in the photo collection. There are many applications of inferring heights from photos in social networks:

- **Targeted Advertising:** Users of social networks often do not explicitly provide their heights in their profiles. Yet many advertisers would like to have access to height information. For example, many clothing retailers have specific product lines and marketing strategies for tall/large people and for small people, and some clothing retailers (such as Destinaion XL [3]) are entirely devoted to these markets. Similarly, furniture retailers often create product lines specifically for tall/large/small people (such as King Size Direct [4] and Brigger Furniture [1]). Along with many other possible sectors, airlines would like to identify tall people so that they can attempt to sell them economy plus and business class seats.
- **Match Making:** Many individuals seek dating partners in specific height ranges. Height information extracted from photos can be used to help with matchmaking.
- **Forensics for Law Enforcement:** Law enforcement officials have traditionally used the height attribute in profile

databases to help narrow down suspects in crimes. But for many individuals in these databases, height information is unavailable. By working directly with the OSN, or by scraping the photos themselves from the OSNs, law enforcement organizations can create world-wide profiles including valuable height information.

- **Height Validation:** Models, actors and athletes often make their heights known when marketing their services. But automatically estimating their height from photos, we can validate their advertised heights.

On the other hand, many people would consider the automatic extraction of users' height (and potentially other sensitive information) from photo collections as as a privacy violation. This paper also serves the role of putting the issue of extracting sensitive information from photo collections on the radar screen of privacy advocates.

Several research groups have previously attempted to estimate the height of a single person from a *single photo* with limited success. Some approaches require that the image include reference length in the background scene to indicate scale [20, 15, 14]. This approach has two main difficulties in practice: (i) a reference length may not always be available, and (ii) the results are strongly affected by camera perspective. Other approaches make use of human anthropometry, that is, estimating from the photo anthropometric ratios (such has neck height and head-to-chin distance, which are measured from the image) and anthropometric statistics [12]. This approach requires that the subject to be standing upright, be facing directly the camera, and that his/her upper body be present in the photo.

In this paper we minimally rely on image processing and computer vision techniques, and instead take a data-driven approach to the problem of height estimation. The approach not only has the potential of improving the estimates and relaxing the requirements of the traditional approaches, but also can provide estimates of thousands (potentially millions) of individuals. Specifically, in this paper we develop a novel approach for estimating the heights of all the users in a photo collection, such as a collection of photos from a social network. The main ideas in our methodology are (i) for each individual photo, estimate the height differences among the people standing in the photo, (ii) from the photo collection, create a people graph, and combine this graph with the height difference estimates from the individual photos to generate height difference estimates among all the people in the collection, (iii) then use these height difference estimates, as well as an *a priori* distribution, to estimate the heights of all the people in the photo collection. Due to camera angle and the possibility of some people slouching, for a single photo, some estimates may be overestimates and others may be underestimates. By chaining people across a large collection of photos, and exploiting the fact many people will appear in multiple photos, we will show that height estimation errors can be significantly reduced.

We formulate the estimation problem as a maximum likelihood estimation problem. Specifically, we find the height values of *all the subjects* in the photo collection that maximize the probability of the height-differences observations. The resulting problem becomes a quadratic programming problem, with constraints generated from an *a priori* mean and variance. We apply the technique to two data sets, for both of which we have ground-truth height information. The first data set consists of over 400 movie stars from 1,300 photos. The second data set consists of 30 graduate students from 25 photos. For both data sets, our technique was able to significantly reduce the baseline errors, in both cases to average error of less than 1.5 inches.

In addition to providing a novel methodology to estimating heights from photos, this paper also shows the potential of mining data from social networks in which the same people appear in multiple, but different, photos. In addition to features like height and weight, it may be possible to use photo collections to mine a story around the community people in the photos, such as examining how off-line friends revolve over time.

This paper is organized as follows. In Section 2, we describe the methodology used in this paper, including the methodology to obtain height-difference estimates from individual photos and the maximum likelihood estimation procedure to obtain the height estimates from the photo collection. In Section 3 we describe the datasets, including the celebrity dataset and the student dataset. In Section 4 we present and discuss the results for the two datasets. In Section 5, we analyze the errors in greater detail. In Section 6 we describe related work and in Section 7 we conclude.

2. METHODOLOGY

2.1 Overview of the "Data-Driven Approach"

In this paper we examine estimating heights of people from collections of group photos. A group photo is a photo in which more than one person appears. Group photos can be collected from many different sources on the Internet, including social networks such as Facebook and Instagram, photo sharing sites such as Flickr, and stills from video sharing sites such as YouTube. The basic idea is to automatically estimate people's heights using computer-estimated height differences of the people in the photo collection, combined with a priori population height distributions.

As an example, consider the four photos in Figure 1, which were collected from the Internet Movie Database (IMDb). This collection of photos contains six distinct people. In the case of IMDb, the people in each of the photos are labeled. (We will discuss how people in photo collections can be labeled in Section 2.3.) We now consider the problem of estimating the heights of all six people in this collection of photos.

To this end, we first consider estimating the heights in each of the photos *separately*, for example, the heights of Person 0 (P0) and Person 1 (P1) in photo 1(b). We consider the following two-step procedure:

1. We first assign each person in the photo the same height, namely, the global population mean across the whole population. For example, if the global mean of height of movie stars is 171 cm, then we assign the height of 171 cm to both P0 and P1.

2. We then adjust these heights by estimating the height difference between P0 and P1 from the photo. We will discuss a methodology for doing this in Section 2.2. For example, suppose we estimate that P1 is 4 centimeters taller than P0. Then we can adjust our original estimates for P0 and P1 to be 171 - 4/2 = 169 cm and 171 + 4/2 = 173 cm.

Intuitively, the adjustment Step 2 can significantly improve the baseline mean estimate in Step 1. But the resulting estimates can be still far from the correct heights for two classes of reasons:

1. Because the photo population is very small (two in this example), there is a high probability that the photo-population mean differs greatly from the global population mean. If the two means differ significantly, the estimates will have large errors.

(a) (b) (c) (d)

Figure 1: An example of a small collection of 4 photos with rectangles around faces

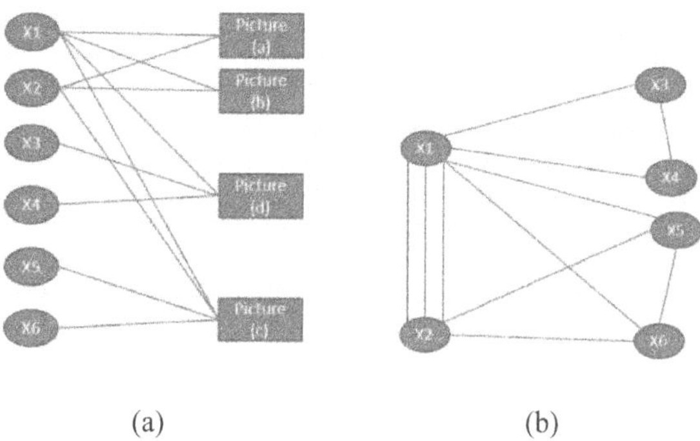

(a) (b)

Figure 2: Two network depictions of photo collection in Figure 1. The first network representation shows for each of the six persons, which photos he or she appears in. The second network representation has a node for each of the six persons, and a link between two nodes if the two corresponding persons appear in the same photo.

2. The estimates for the height differences may also be inaccurate. These inaccuracies can be due to people slouching, the ground level where the various people stand, the camera angle, and the heel sizes.

In order to respond to these two classes of error sources, we explore in this paper taking a "data-driven approach", namely, estimating people's heights from a large collection of inter-related photos. To this end, Figure 2 shows two network representations of the photo collection from Figure 1. There are a total of six people in the collection. The first network representation shows for the six persons, which photos they appear in. The second network representation has a node for each of the six persons, and a link between two nodes if the two corresponding persons appear in the same photo. Note that, for this example, this second network is fully connected, meaning that *it is possible to directly or indirectly compare the heights of all six persons throughout the collection.* Although in this example we are considering a small collection consisting of four photos, in practice we may have thousands of photos in a collection.

For the collection of photos, we now have a revised two-step procedure:

1. We first assign to each person in the collection the same height, namely, the global population mean calculated across the whole population. Because the number of people in the collection is much larger than the number of people in an individual photo, it is likely the collection mean will be relatively close to the global mean. In fact, as the number of individuals in the collection increases, the collection mean should approach the population mean due to the law of large numbers.

2. We then again adjust the estimates in Step 1 by examining the height differences in the various photos. But now, for any pair of persons, there can be multiple height difference estimates. For example, both P0 and P1 appear in Photo 1(a) and in Photo 1(b). So, for these two photos, we can obtain two height difference estimates for P0 and P1. As explained later in this section, we can obtain additional estimates by looking at chains of people across photos. By aggregating the various height-difference estimates, errors due to slouching and camera angles will potentially be reduced due to averaging.

In the following subsections, we will formulate and solve the height estimation problem as a data-driven problem.

2.2 Height Difference Estimation from Individual Photos

A central part of the methodology is *intra-photo height-difference estimation*, that is, finding height difference estimates among pairs of people in the same photo. For each photo with multiple persons, we use the OpenCV tool to detect the faces of all persons in the photo. For each detected face, this tool provides the x and y coordinates of the top left corner of each rectangle as well as the height and width of every detected face. We assign indexes to each detected face based on their positions in the photo. Figures 1 and 3 show the boxes along with their assigned indexes on the detected faces. We then use the boxes to calculate the height differences among all persons in the photo. Specifically:

- For each pair of persons, we calculate the vertical distance between the mid-points of the two corresponding face boxes. This results in a height difference value in units of pixels. Pixel values are very much dependent on the resolution of the photo and are not very useful in comparing heights across different photos.

- We then convert the height differences (in pixels) to average box size, which is the average height (in pixels) of all the detected head boxes in that photo. This results in height differences measured in units of "heads". For example, if person A is 35 pixels taller than person B and the average height of the boxes in the photo is 50 pixels, then person A is said to be $35/50 = 0.7$ heads taller than person B.

- In the end, we need to convert our height differences in "heads" to height differences in centimeters. One simple way of doing this is to assume a value in centimeters for the head height, and multiply this value by the number of heads taller. For example, suppose we assume that the average box head height corresponds to 20 cm. Then if person A is 0.7 heads

Figure 3: Example of a group picture of students with boxes around their faces

taller than person B, we can estimate that person A is $0.7 \cdot 20$ = 14 cm taller than person B. (We will describe a more systematic way of determining head size in centimeters. But for now let us assume that we are working with a given reasonable value.)

We mention briefly that in many real scenarios, the images collected from a social network are taken with an indirect camera angle, for example, from the left and below of the faces. Such indirect angles can introduce errors into the height difference estimates in the the individual photos. It should be possible to reduce these errors by preprocessing the photos, for example, by using calibration [2]. In this paper, however, we do not preprocess, as we are interested in exploring how well a pure data-driven technique can perform: If each person appears in many photos, then errors from different camera angles could cancel out (as in the law of large numbers). We leave preprocessing of the photos, and its potential to reducing errors, to future research.

2.3 Height Inference from a Photo Collection

Given a collection of photos, our goal is to infer the heights of the people in the collection based on all the height difference estimates within the individual photos. We refer to this as *inter-photo height estimation*. The first step is to extract group photos from the collection, that is, extract photos in which there are multiple people roughly standing next to each other. In this paper, we manually extracted such group photos from our collection; but it should be possible to find such photos automatically [17].

The second step is to label the people in the photos, so that we can link the same person in different photos to build graphs as in Figure 2. In many photo collections, the people appearing in the photos are explicitly labeled; for example, in the IMDb collection, each person in each photo is labeled. In other photo collections, not all the people in the photos are labeled, by a significant fraction may be. For example, in Facebook many photos are explicitly labeled via tagging. (Facebook encourages this by using face recognition to suggest tags.) Other photos, such as profile photos, are implicitly labeled. Even if the collection has no labels or tags, it should be possible to link many of the people across photos using face recognition technology. Stone et al. showed how social network contexts can enhance the performance of face recognition and hence can be used for automatically tagging millions of photos [22]. Linking people across photos using face recognition is an orthogonal problem and is not considered in this paper.

After making the associations between the same people in different photos, we can convert the height differences between positions into the height differences between actual people, thereby creating a graph as in Figure 2(b) with each link labeled with a height difference estimate in centimeters. Specifically, we create one node for each person who appears at least once in the photo collection. For each pair of persons (i, j) in picture p (without loss of generality suppose person i has lower ID than person j), we create a directed link from node i to node j, with the link weight d^p_{ij} being the estimated height difference of person i over person j in photo p. Note that if the pair (i, j) appear together in multiple group photos, they will be connected by multiple links with different weights.

We can now describe our procedure for estimating the heights of people in the collection of photos. Let $\mathcal{P}$ be the set of photos, $\mathcal{I}_p$ be the subset of individual persons who appear in photo $p \in \mathcal{P}$, and $\mathcal{I} = \cup_{p\in\mathcal{P}}\mathcal{I}_p$ be the set of persons who appear in at least one of the photos. In each photo p, we obtain $d^p_{ij}, i, j \in \mathcal{I}_p$, the estimated height difference of person i over person j, as described in Section 2.2. (For now, we will assume that these values were calculated with a given and fixed box head size in centimeters.) Let $x_i, i \in \mathcal{I}$, be our estimated height of person i. Our task is to obtain good estimates of $\{x_i, i \in \mathcal{I}\}$ based on $\{d^p_{ij}, i, j \in \mathcal{I}_p, p \in \mathcal{P}\}$.

2.4 Maximum Likelihood Estimate

The most natural error model is to assume the estimated height difference between a pair of persons in the same photo is a noisy measurement of their real height difference, with the error following a zero-mean Normal distribution. Let D^p_{ij} be the random variable of the measured height difference of i over j in photo p. Then

$$D^p_{ij} = x_i - x_j + E^p_{ij}, \tag{1}$$

where E^p_{ij} is the random error, and $E^p_{ij} \sim \mathcal{N}(0, \sigma^2_{ijp})$. Immediately, the density function of the height difference of i over j measured from photo p can be calculated as:

$$f(D^p_{ij} = d^p_{ij}|x_i, x_j) = C_{ij} \exp\left\{-\frac{(d^p_{ij} - x_i + x_j)^2}{2\sigma^2_{ijp}}\right\},$$

where $C_{ij} = 1/(2\pi\sigma^2_{ijp})^{1/2}$. For any pair of persons (i, j) in photo p, we can obtain their height difference d^p_{ij} using the procedure described in Section 2.2. Obviously the height differences are *dependent*, e.g., $D^p_{ij} = -D^p_{ji}$ and $D^p_{ij} + D^p_{jk} = D^p_{ik}$. We can select independent height differences by choosing a common reference point. Specifically, let p_0 be the person at the leftmost position in photo p. Any other pairwise height difference d^p_{ij} can be calculated as $d^p_{ip_0} - d^p_{jp_0}$. If we further assume that the error terms between different pairs are i.i.d, i.e., $E^p_{ip_0}$ is independent of $E^p_{jp_0}$, $\forall i \neq j$, and $\sigma^2_{ip_0p} = \sigma^2_p, \forall i \in \mathcal{I}_p$, then the joint density function of the measured height differences from photo p is:

$$\begin{aligned} & f\left(\{D^p_{ij} = d^p_{ij}, \forall i, j \in \mathcal{I}_p, i \neq j\} \mid \{x_i, i \in \mathcal{I}_p\}\right) && (2)\\ = \; & f\left(\{D^p_{ip_0} = d^p_{ip_0}, \forall i \in \mathcal{I}_p, i \neq p_0\} \mid \{x_i, i \in \mathcal{I}_p\}\right) && (3)\\ = \; & \textstyle\prod_{\forall i \in I_p, i\neq p_0} \frac{1}{(2\pi\sigma^2_p)^{1/2}} \exp\left\{-\frac{(d^p_{ip_0} - x_i + x_{p_0})^2}{2\sigma^2_p}\right\}. && (4)\end{aligned}$$

Finally, for the height differences observed from all photos $\mathcal{D} \triangleq \{\{D^p_{ij} = d^p_{ij}, i, j \in \mathcal{I}_p, i \neq j\}, p \in \mathcal{P}\}$, the joint distribution can be calculated as:

$$\begin{aligned} & f(\mathcal{D}|\{x_i, i \in \mathcal{I}\}) \\ = & \prod_{p\in\mathcal{P}} f(\{D^p_{ip_0} = d^p_{ip_0}, i \in I_p, i \neq p_0\}|\{x_i, i \in \mathcal{I}_p\}) \\ = & \prod_{p\in\mathcal{P}} \prod_{i\in I_p, i\neq p_0} \frac{1}{(2\pi\sigma_p^2)^{1/2}} \exp\left\{-\frac{(d^p_{ip_0} - x_i + x_{p_0})^2}{2\sigma_p^2}\right\} \end{aligned}$$

Then the Maximum Likelihood Estimate $\mathbf{x}_{ML}$ of $\mathbf{x} = \{x_i, i \in \mathcal{I}\}$ can be obtained as

$$\begin{aligned} & \mathop{\mathbf{argmax}}_{\mathbf{x}} \; f(\mathcal{D}|\mathbf{x}) \\ = & \mathop{\mathbf{argmax}}_{\mathbf{x}} \prod_{p\in\mathcal{P}} \prod_{i\in I_p, i\neq p_0} \exp\left\{-\frac{(d^p_{ip_0} - x_i + x_{p_0})^2}{2\sigma_p^2}\right\} \\ = & \mathop{\mathbf{argmin}}_{\mathbf{x}} \sum_{p\in\mathcal{P}} \sum_{i\in I_p, i\neq p_0} \frac{(d^p_{ip_0} - x_i + x_{p_0})^2}{2\sigma_p^2} \end{aligned}$$

If we further assume that $\sigma_p^2 = \sigma^2, \forall p$. Then we have

$$\mathbf{x}_{ML} = \mathop{\mathbf{argmin}}_{\mathbf{x}} \sum_{p\in\mathcal{P}} \sum_{i\in I_p, i\neq p_0} (d^p_{ip_0} - x_i + x_{p_0})^2 \qquad (5)$$

To obtain the MLE, we need to numerically solve the optimization problem (5). Since variables $\{x_i\}$ always appear in the objective in the difference form of $x_i - x_j$, $\vec{x}$ and $\vec{x} + c$ have the same objective value. We need an additional constraint to obtain the appropriate estimates. We use the sample mean to introduce additional constraints for the MLE optimization. For the sample mean, we simply require the average of the height estimates be equal to the average height of the global population.

$$\textit{Global Mean Constraint:} \quad \sum_{i\in\mathcal{I}} x_i = |\mathcal{I}|\bar{m}, \qquad (6)$$

where $\bar{m}$ is the average height of the global population. In this case, the MLE is obtained by solving a quadratic programming problem, namely, minimize (5) subject to the global mean constraint (6). It can be easily and rapidly solved for tens of thousands of variables.

If the genders of the people in the photos can be automatically identified, then an alternative is to introduce gender-based mean constraints. Let $\mathcal{I}^m$ be the set of males, and $\mathcal{I}^f$ be the set of females. In this case, we would have two gender-based constraints in the quadratic programming problem:

$$\sum_{i\in\mathcal{I}^m} x_i = |\mathcal{I}^m|\bar{m}_m, \quad \sum_{i\in\mathcal{I}^f} x_i = |\mathcal{I}^f|\bar{m}_f, \qquad (7)$$

where $\bar{m}_m$ and $\bar{m}_f$ are the average heights for male and female population, respectively.

2.5 Head Size

Recall from Section 2.2 we measure height differences from the photos in units of heads. We then convert this height difference into units of centimeters by multiplying the height difference in heads by an estimate of the head size in centimeters. Up until this point, to make this conversion, we have simply been using an assumed and fixed value for the box head size. In this section we present an adaptive approach for determining the head size. Let S be a variable denoting the head size in cm. Let b^p_{ij} in units of heads be the height difference between person i and j appearing in photo p. We now calculate the height difference (in centimeters) by multiplying the height difference b^p_{ij} by the head size variable S. Because we have added a new variable S, we also add a new constraint to automatically determine what the appropriate head size S should be. To this end, we now additionally require that the sample variance of the height estimates be equal to the a priori global population height variance. This technique, of course, requires that we have a good estimate of the global population variance. Using (5), the new optimization problem becomes minimizing:

$$\sum_{p\in\mathcal{P}} \sum_{\forall i\in I_p, i\neq p_0} (S \cdot b^p_{ip_0} - x_i + x_{p_0})^2 \qquad (8)$$

subject to

$$\textit{Global Mean Constraint:} \quad \sum_{i\in\mathcal{I}} x_i = |\mathcal{I}|\bar{m},$$

and

$$\textit{Global Variance Constraint:} \quad \sum_{i\in\mathcal{I}} (x_i - \bar{x})^2 = (|\mathcal{I}| - 1)\sigma^2,$$

where σ^2 is the height variance of the whole population. Similar to the gender-based mean constraints, we can also introduce gender-based variance constraints.

2.6 Evaluation and Baseline Methods

We used the *fmincon* optimization tool from Matlab to solve the constrained optimization problems and get MLE height estimates $\{x_i, i \in \mathcal{I}\}$ for all persons. To evaluate the performance of our technique, we compare the estimates with the ground-truth actual heights $\{h_i, i \in \mathcal{I}\}$. We calculate the Root Mean Squared Error (RMSE) as:

$$RMSE = \sqrt{\frac{\sum_{i\in\mathcal{I}} (x_i - h_i)^2}{|\mathcal{I}|}}$$

We will compare the RMSE error with the error of two baseline approaches. In **Baseline 0**, we assign everyone the same mean height, equal to the height of the global population. In **Baseline 0 with gender**, we also consider gender where we assign all males the average male population height and females the average female population height.

For Baseline 1, we estimate heights considering each of the photos separately using the height-difference techniques described in Section 2.2. *In Baseline 1, we take intra-photo height differences into account, but we do not the exploit inter-photo information from the collection.* Specifically, for the **Baseline 1 approach without gender**, for any given photo we first assign every person in the photo the same average height for global population. We then adjust these height estimates using the height-difference estimates *only within that single photo*. This estimate will typically have an error, as it will not be exactly equal to the ground-truth height. The overall average error is given by the RMSE values of these individual errors. For the **Baseline 1 approach with gender**, for a given photo we first identify the males and females and assign them each their respective global average heights. We then adjust the heights of the males (respectively, females) using the intra-photo height differences of the males (respectively, of the females). We then again average the errors as just described.

3. DATA SET

We tested the performance of our height estimation procedures using two datasets – the **celebrity dataset** and the **student dataset**, for both of which we have ground-truth height information. We also applied the baseline approaches to these two datasets.

Table 1: Basic Properties of Celebrity Dataset

Name	Number	Mean Heights (cm)	Standard Deviation (cm)
Sample Population	426	174.5	7.0
Sample Population: Male	230	180.9	7.5
Sample Population: Female	196	167.0	6.5
Global Population	1029	174.1	7.3
Global Population: Male	525	180.6	8.1
Global Population: Female	504	167.3	6.5

3.1 The Celebrity Dataset

The Internet Movie Database (IMDb) is an online database which stores movie, TV, and celebrity content. It has information on more than 2.5 million titles and 5.2 million people, which can be accessed from the IMDB website. For this project, we used IMDb to obtain publicly available information on celebrities. Each celebrity has a profile page with his or her biography, awards and nominations, credits, occupation, pictures, personal details, height, and so on. IMDb also has photo galleries for movies, TV shows, events, and people, all of which is publicly accessible on the website. For each photo, the names of the people in the photo are displayed along with links to their profiles.

We wrote a web crawler in Python to collect information on celebrities and collect their group pictures from IMDb.com. IMDb ranks the celebrities. We downloaded profile pages, including heights, as well as the "event photos" they appear in, for 450 popular celebrities, giving rise to 1,300 photos which contain multiple (two or more) people standing next to each other. We then constructed a graph, with one node for each of the 450 celebrities, as in Figure 2(b). The resulting graph contained one large component with 426 nodes and several smaller components with a small number of nodes. Figure 4 shows the graph for the largest component. Because we are interested in estimating the heights in large interconnected social groups, we estimate the height of these 426 celebrities in the large component only. We refer these 426 (230 are male and 196 are female) celebrities as the **sample population**. Although not easily seen in Figure 4, many of the node pairs have multiple links between them. For example, Angelina Jolie and Brad Pitt together appear in 15 photos.

To obtain global population statistics, we also collected heights and gender of other celebrities. All combined we collected gender and height information for 1,029 celebrities, which includes the 426 celebrities in our sample population. We refer to these 1,029 celebrities as our **global population**. The statistics of the celebrity dataset are summarized in Table 1.

3.2 Student Dataset

Table 2: Basic properties of Student Dataset

Name	Number	Mean Heights (cm)	Standard Deviation (cm)
Sample Population	30	172.3	5.6
Sample Population: Male	25	174.6	5.1
Sample Population: Female	5	160.8	8.1
Global Population	94	171.1	6.3
Global Population: Male	73	173.9	6.1
Global Population: Female	21	162.5	6.9

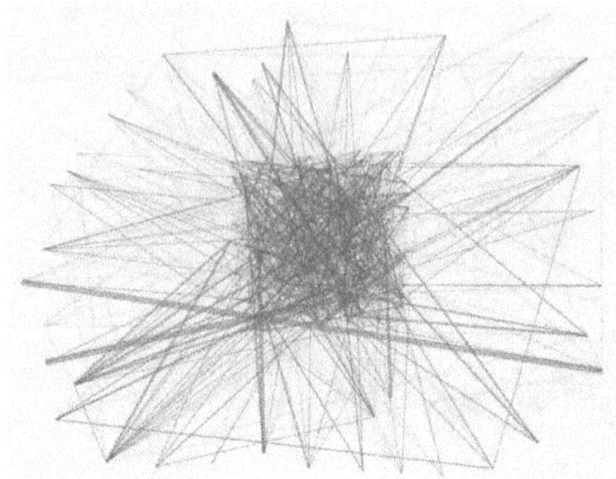

Figure 4: The largest connected component in the celebrity graph

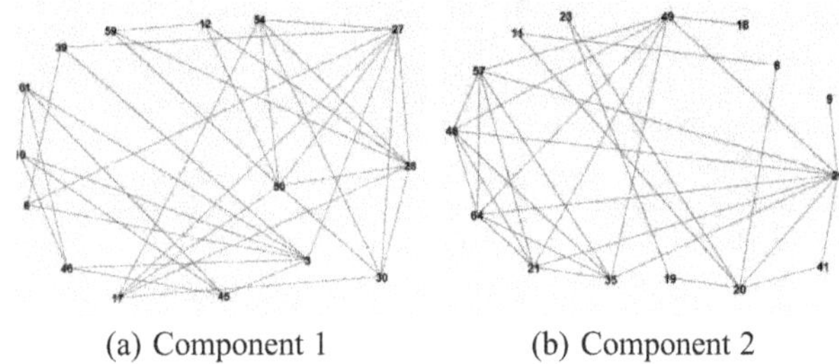

(a) Component 1 (b) Component 2

Figure 5: Components of Student Networks

In addition to studying a relatively large dataset, as in our celebrity dataset, is of interest to study the performance of our methodology for smaller dataset. From our university graduate students, we asked for volunteers to appear in group photos. We asked each student who volunteered to tell us his/her height. Thirty students volunteered to appear in 25 photos. We refer to these students as the **sample population.** The graph for these 30 students is shown in Figure 5. Note that the graph has two components. To obtain population statistics, we additionally asked for the heights and genders of other students. Totally, we obtained height and gender data for 94 students, including the 30 students in the sample population. We refer to these 94 students as our **global population**. The basic properties of our student dataset are shown in Table 2.

4. RESULTS

We now describe the results for our data-driven approach, which uses the constrained optimization problem (8) resulting from the MLE procedure. In the baseline and data-driven approaches, we initially consider the case where we cannot identify gender in the photos. For this case, we use aggregate statistics in the global mean and variance constraints. We then also consider the case when gender is available, which we call the baseline approach with gender and the data-driven approach with gender. In this latter approach, we use two gender-based mean constraints but one aggregate variance constraint.

With the celebrity dataset, many of the actors (female and male) wear high heels, with the heel sizes varying from actor to actor, and also possibly varying for the same actor across different photos. To deal with this issue, we make the rough assumption that women's heels are six centimeters higher on average than men's heels. This is accounted for by adding six centimeters to each women's ground truth height, then calculating global population means and variance accordingly. With the student dataset, the female students generally wear smaller heel lifts. We make the rough estimation that female students' heel sizes are two centimeters higher than men's heel sizes.

4.1 Results for the Celebrity Dataset

Table 3: Results found for celebrity dataset: Without Gender

Approach Name	RMSE Overall	RMSE Male	RMSE Female
Baseline 0	9.9	10.1	9.6
Baseline 1	7.0	7.0	7.1
Data-Driven	3.8	4.0	3.6

Table 4: Results found for celebrity dataset: With Gender

Approach Name	RMSE Overall	RMSE Male	RMSE Female
Baseline 0	7.0	7.6	6.4
Baseline 1	5.7	5.9	5.4
Data-Driven	3.9	4.1	3.6

Table 3 and 4 show the root mean square error (RMSE) for the celebrity dataset. We calculate RMSE for all of the celebrities, only for male celebrities, and only for female celebrities. Note that our Baseline 1 approach significantly reduces the error of the naive Baseline 0 approach, for when gender is identified and gender is not identified in the photos. Recall that our Baseline 1 approach takes advantage of intra-photo height differences but does not exploit inter-photo information.

Our data-driven approach exploits inter-photo information as well is intra-photo height differences. We see from Table 3 that when gender is not available, our data-driven approach gives a dramatic reduction in the error. The Baseline 1 error is further reduced from 7.0 cm to 3.8. In the case when gender can be identified (Table 4, our data-driven approach reduces the RMSE from 5.7 cm to 3.8 cm or 5.7 cm (baseline 1) to 3.9 cm. In both cases, our data-driven approach gives a substantial improvement over the baseline approaches. (Because there may be ground-truth errors for some of the celebrities as reported on IMDb, the actual estimation errors are likely lower than reported in this section; see Section 5.)

Note that when gender is available, the separate gender constraints do not improve the performance of our data-driven approach. We also note that all the estimation procedures (baseline and data-driven) are more accurate for females than for males. This is likely due to two reasons. First, the standard deviation for female heights is less than it is for male heights in the global population (see Table 1), making male heights more difficult to estimate. Second we believe there is more variation in male celebrity's heel sizes than in female celebrity's heel sizes. Note that for the data-driven approach with and without gender, we get the same optimal head size, namely, $S = 21.5$cm.

Table 5: Results found for male celebrities who appeared in small number of photos

Number of Photos (n)	1	2	3	4	5
Baseline 1: Average error over people with n photos	7.6	6.3	5.1	4.9	4.6
Data-Driven: Average error over people with n photos	3.9	4.2	3.7	2.6	2.4

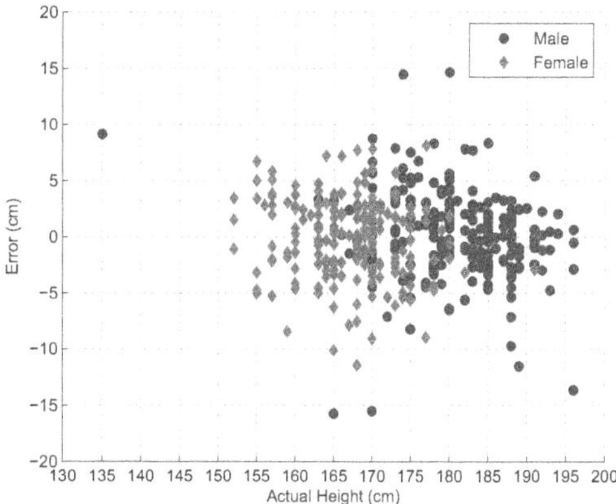

Figure 6: Actual height versus error using data-driven approach in celebrity dataset

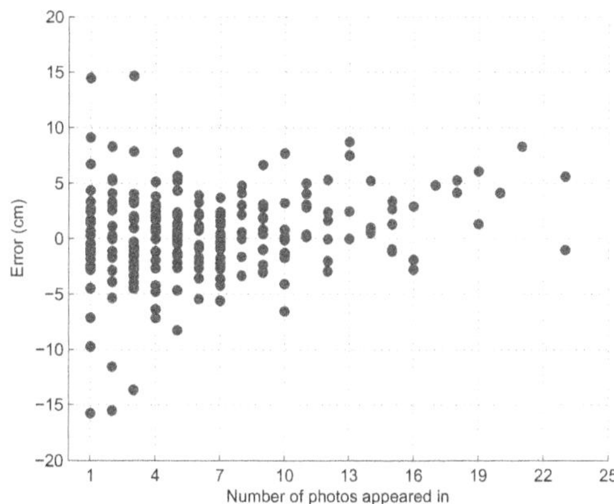

Figure 7: Celebrity Male: Number of photos appeared in vs error for data-driven approach

Figure 6 shows a scatter diagram for the data-driven approach, with actual heights on the x-axis and errors on the y-axis. If the difference between estimated height and actual height is positive, then we are overestimating the actual height; and if it is negative, we are underestimating the actual heights.

Note that for the data-driven approach, the errors are roughly uniformly distributed over the entire height range, whereas for the baseline 0 approaches, intuitively the taller and shorter people have the largest errors. For the data-driven approach, more than 85% of the celebrities are within an error of margin of 5 cm (2 inches), whereas for the baseline 0 approach, only 55% of the celebrities are within an error margin of 5 cm.

For the data-driven approach, most of the large errors (more than 10 cm) are for males. We believe that males may have larger errors because males may have a larger variation in heel size.

The scatter diagrams 7 and 8 investigate the error, for the data-driven approach, as a function of the number of photos a person appears in. In these diagrams, we show overestimation and underestimation of height for each celebrity vs. number of photos he/she appears in. We can clearly see a general trend of accuracy improving as the number of photos increases. Thus this confirms that as the data gets "bigger," the data-driven approach provides better results.

Many of the larger errors are simply due to individuals only appearing in 1-2 photos which have sloping camera angles or people not standing upright. For example Johnny Galecki and Simon Helberg have large errors, 15.8 cm and 15.6 cm, respectively. Galecki

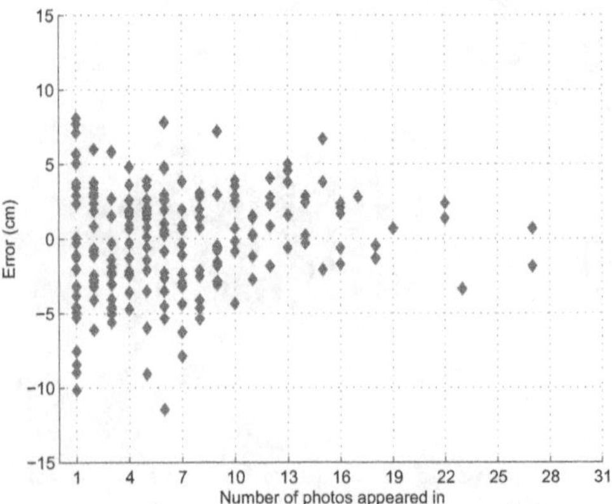

Figure 8: Celebrity Female: Number of photos appeared in vs error for data-driven approach

(a) (b)

Figure 9: Error analysis for Johnny Galecki and Simon Helberg

appears in one photo only, appearing with Helberg; Helberg appears in only one other photo, appearing with Kaley Cuoco. These two photos are shown in Figure 9. These two celebrities (Galecki and Helberg) form a hanging branch in the graph. The photo 9(a) with Cuoco and Helberg is problematic: due to the camera angle Helberg appears to be much shorter than Cuoco, which isn't the case. In photo 9(b), due to Galecki leaning into Helberg, Galecki also appears to much shorter than Helberg, which also isn't the case. The error for Galecki is therefore particularly large due to the cascading errors. If these two actors appeared in more photos, and if they also form a cycle rather than just a hanging branch, the errors would likely be significantly reduced.

But even for people who appear in a small number of photos, our data-driven approach does better than our Baseline 1 approach, as height comparisons are implicitly made over more people people. Table 5 compares the error averaged over male celebrities who appear in the same number of photos (1 to 5) for Baseline 1 and for the data-driven approaches. We can clearly see that performance of data-driven approach is significantly better. We find similar results in the case of female celebrities.

4.2 Results for Student Dataset

In Table 6 and 7, we have shown the results in terms of root mean square error (RMSE) for student dataset. As with the celebrities, our baseline 1 approach performs significantly better than the naive baseline 0 approach, and our data-driven approach performs better than our baseline 1 approach.From Table 7, we can see that when gender is considered, the error is reduced from 5.8 to 3.1, which is significant. Note that a significant portion of this error is due to the

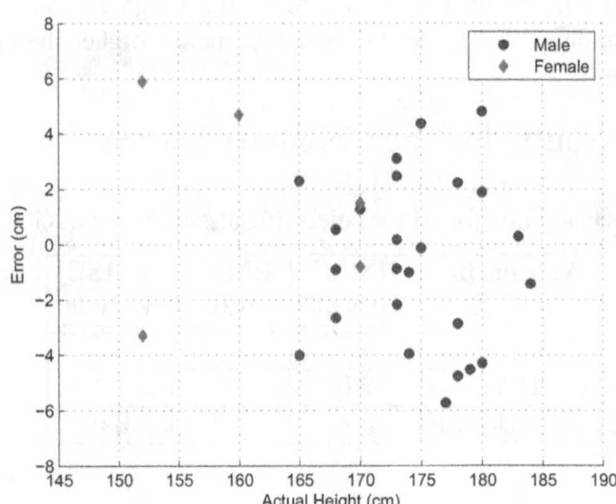

Figure 10: Actual height versus error for the student dataset using the data-driven approach

sample mean differing from the global mean by 1.2 cm. By using a larger photo collection, this error source would be eliminated, reducing the RMSE error to less than an inch. Also note that the error with the student dataset is less than it is with the celebrity dataest, even though the photo collection for the celebrities is much larger. This is likely because most students did not wear high heels, and the photos were taken in a more controlled environment. We found the same head size, $S = 14.25cm$ for the data-driven approaches (both with gender and without gender). Figure 10 shows the errors as a function of height.

Table 6: Results found for the student dataset: Without Gender

Approach Name	RMSE Overall	RMSE Male	RMSE Female
Baseline 0	7.7	5.7	13.8
Baseline 1	4.7	4.8	4.3
Data-Driven	3.1	3.0	3.8

Table 7: Results found for the student dataset: With Gender

Approach Name	RMSE Overall	RMSE Male	RMSE Female
Baseline 0	5.8	5.2	8.2
Baseline 1	4.0	3.6	5.9
Data-Driven	3.3	3.1	3.9

Figure 11 investigates the error, for the data-driven approach, as a function of the number of photos a student appears in. In this diagram, we show overestimation and underestimation of height for each student vs. number of photos he/she appears in. We can clearly see a general trend of accuracy improving as the number of photos increases.

4.3 Head size analysis

Recall that in our data-driven approach (8) we are choosing a head size S that matches the *a priori* global variance. We also examined the *optimal head size*, namely, the head size that gives the least RMSE. We did this for both the celebrity and student datasets. To this end, we solved the optimization problem using only the global mean constraint. In particular, we did not use the global variance constraint, but instead solved the problem repeatedly for different values of S ranging from 5 to 30. We then chose the value of the head size S that gives the lowest RMSE. For the celebrity

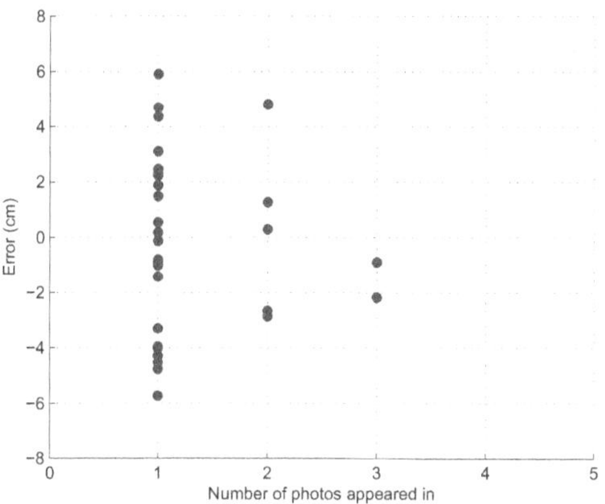

Figure 11: Student: Number of photos appeared in vs error for data-driven approach

dataset, the lowest RMSE was 3.6 (reduced from 3.8) with an optimal head size value 18 cm (instead of 21.5). For the student dataset, the lowest RMSE was 3.0 at head size value 13 cm. These RMSE values are only slightly smaller than what we obtain in Tables 3 and 6, for which we do not use a specific head size (which is difficult to obtain *a priori*).

4.4 Estimating males and females separately

Table 8: Statistics and results for male-only estimation

Name	Value
# of Images	289
# of Male Celebrities in Big component	160
RMSE for Data-Driven method	5.2
RMSE found for Data-Driven method in Table 4	4.1

To gain further insight into the problem, we considered estimating the heights of the males and females separately in the celebrity dataset. Specifically, we extract from the photo dataset only those photos that have only males in them, and then apply the data-driven approach to that subset of photos. We also do the same for the females. In this way, we can minimize the effects of heel size differences across genders.

For males, we have 289 photos in which only male celebrities appear, with 160 male celebrities in those photos. The statistics and results are summarized in Table 8. For females, we have 213 images where only female celebrities have appeared and in these images 119 female celebrities appear. The statistics and results are summarized in Table 9. We see that these RMSE values are significantly higher than for when the entire photo collection is used (that is, including photos in which males and females appear together). To gain further insight, in Figure 12 we show the scatter plots for actual heights versus errors for the case of estimating males and females separately. We see that, as compared with the case when using the entire photo collection, significantly more people have estimated height errors that are more than 5 cm. These results further argue for the data-driven approach: by using a larger dataset, which includes photos mixing males and females together, we can significantly reduce the error.

5. GROUND-TRUTH ANALYSIS

Simon Helberg is one of the celebrities for which our estimate has a large error. IMDb says he is 170 cm tall whereas we esti-

Table 9: Statistics and results for female-only estimation

Name	Value
# of Images	213
# of Female Celebrities in Big component	119
RMSE for Data-Driven method	4.9
RMSE found for Data-Driven method in Table 4	3.6

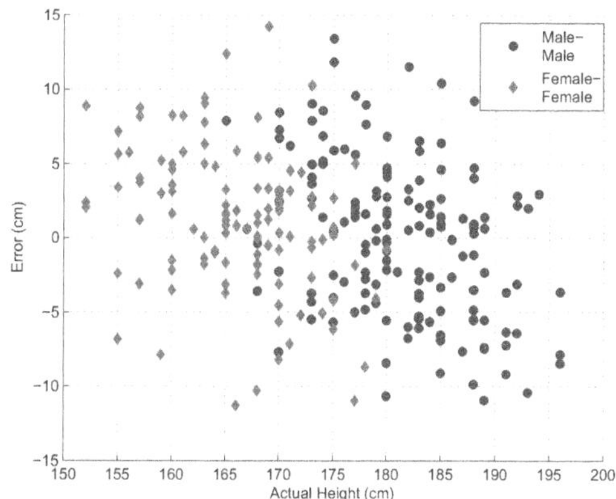

Figure 12: Actual height versus error: Estimating males and females separately

mate him to be 154.5 cm. With more than 15 cm estimation error and examining photos of him in our collection and outside of our collection, we became suspicious about his ground truth height as reported by IMDb. We then found that several other sites say he is 163 cm tall. Assuming his real height is indeed 163 cm, the estimation error for Helberg is reduced from 15.5 cm to 8.5 cm.

We then compared the IMDb values with height values from another site `http://www.celebheights.com`, from which we downloaded the heights of all 426 celebrities. We find mismatches for 244 celebrities, most of which are small but some rather big (such as for Simon Helberg). If we change the ground truth heights for these 244 celebrities, as given in celebheights.com, the RMSE error for males goes down from 4.0 cm to 3.8 cm, but stayed the same for females at 3.6 cm. More importantly, with the new ground-truth values, many of the larger errors significantly decrease. Figures 13 and 14 show the errors, calculated using the two sources of ground truth heights, for these 244 celebrities (i.e., with mismatches) as a function of the number of photos a person appears in. From these figures, we see that with the new ground-truth data, all men (in the mismatch set) have estimation errors less than 11 cm and all women have estimation errors less than 8 cm. By simply eyeballing many of the photos, we believe that the site `http://www.celebheights.com` is somewhat more accurate than IMDb. Thus the estimation methodology given in this paper can be used to crosscheck the ground-truth information given in various height datasets. The methodology can also be used to dispel myths about peoples' heights, whether they are famous or not.

6. RELATED WORK

6.1 Estimating Height

Several research groups have previously attempted to estimate the height of a single person from a *single photo* with limited success. One approach is to make use of human anthropometry,

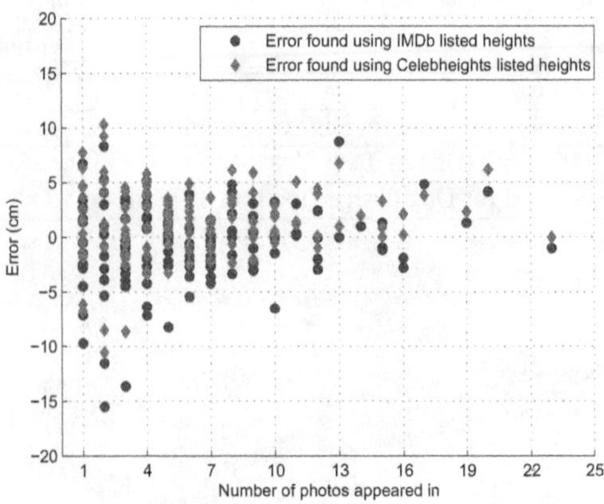

Figure 13: Celebrity Male for whom mismatch found in ground-truth heights: Number of photos appeared in vs error

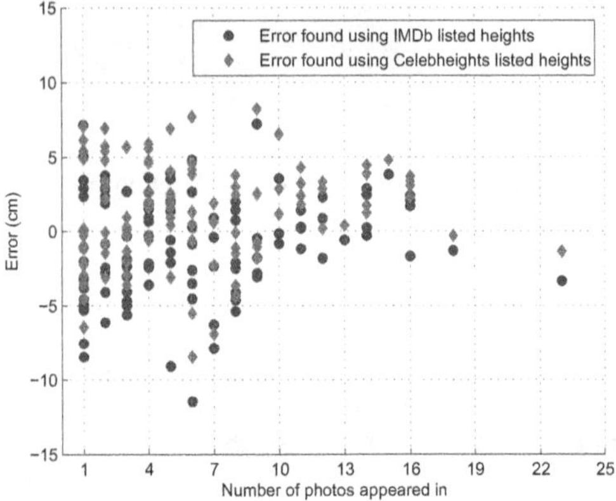

Figure 14: Celebrity Female for whom mismatch found in ground-truth heights: Number of photos appeared in vs error

that is, estimating from the photo anthropometric ratios (such as neck height and head-to-chin distance) and combining these estimates with anthropometric statistics to estimate height [12] [19]. This approach requires that the subject be standing upright, be facing directly the camera, and his/her upper body be present in the photo. BenAbdelkader and Yacoob [12] estimated height from full body images and from images which contain only the upper part. They evaluated their methodology on synthetic data (generated randomly) and real images. Their real image dataset consisted of 108 high-resolution full body photos of 27 adults. They compared there estimates with the same baseline estimates we use in this paper, namely, estimating each male's height simply as the male population mean and each female's height simply as the female population mean. In contrast, our methodology does not require the photos to be calibrated. For example, our celebrity dataset contains photos directly downloaded from IMDb, with photos taken from a variety of camera angles and subjects who are occasionally slumping or not facing the camera directly. They also manually located different body landmarks (top of head, chin, left corner etc) to measure anthropometric parameters, whereas we automated the measurements using off-the-shelf face detection tools.

Our data-driven approach gives significantly better results. As shown in Table 10 their methodology estimated heights for less than 60% of the cases within a 5 cm error, whereas our methodology estimated heights for 85% of the celebrities and 93% of the students within 5 cm. Similarly, their methodology estimated heights for less than 83% of the cases within a 10 cm error, whereas our methodology estimated heights for 98% of the celebrities and 100% of the students within 10 cm.

Table 10: Comparison of the results for the anthropometry approach with our data-driven approach for the celebrity and student datasets.

Error	**Anthropometry (at most)**	**Celebrity (at most)**	**Student (at most)**
Within 3 cm	40%	63%	60%
Within 5 cm	60%	85%	93%
Within 8 cm	80%	96%	100%
Within 10 cm	83%	98%	100%

Another approach is to exploit a known reference length in the background image to indicate scale [20, 15, 14]. This approach has two main difficulties in practice: (i) a reference length may not always be available, and (ii) the results are strongly affected by camera perspective. Criminsi et al. [15, 14] presented an algorithm which estimated height from a single known physical measurement in an image. They measured the vanishing line and vanishing plane directly from the image. Their methodology requires the reference height of a length in the vertical direction in the scene. They evaluated their methodology on a small number of subjects and achieved very small estimation errors. But this methodology is not applicable in our case as it requires reference heights of the images. Their evaluation dataset is also very small compared to our student and celebrity datasets.

A third approach for for estimating height requires a sequence of images from a single camera or multiple cameras (for example, from videos) [11]. Height estimates are obtained by segmenting the person from the background and fitting the height to a time-dependent model of stride. They evaluated their methodology on a dataset of frontal parallel sequences taken in a outdoor environment with 45 people. For each person, they used 4 samples of walking a 5 meter long path. Their height estimates had an average error of 3.5 cm, on the same order as the methodology presented in this paper. But this stride-matching approach requires not only a sequence of photos but also that the person is walking upright with a constant velocity for at least 3-4 seconds and that the camera is calibrated with respect to the ground plane. When obtaining a collection of photos from a social network, it is clearly not possible to meet all these conditions.

6.2 Estimating demographics and social information from group photos

Although to our knowledge there is no previous work on using photo collections to predict height, there is some previous work on using group photos and photo collections to infer demographic and social information from the photos. For example, Gallagher et al. [16] examined how positions of people in a group photo can be used to infer the genders and ages of the individuals in the photo. Shu et al. [18] proposed a methodology for classifying the type of group photo based on spatial arrangement and the predicted age and gender from the faces in the image. They demonstrated that face arrangement, when combined with age and gender prediction, is a useful clue in estimating the type of photo (family photo, sports team photo, friends hanging out, and so on).

6.3 Photos in Social Networks

Although we believe this is the first paper to use inter-photo techniques to mine information from online social networks, there has been significant work in using photos in social networks. Yardi el al. [24] have used Facebook graph and tagged photos to build web based authentication system. White [23] has discussed how travel photos posted by Facebook friends may influence the travel decisions of those who view these photos. Acquisti el al.[9] has mapped match.com users' profile to their corresponding Facebook profile using only photos posted in both websites and face recognition technology. Sedar et al. [21] have shown that intensity of smiling in Facebook photos may predict future life satisfaction. Other researchers also discuss privacy concerns associated with sharing and tagging photos in social networks. Facebook photos are already used by employers [7] to investigate job seekers and by law enforcement agencies [6] to resolve criminal cases. Besmer et al. [13] described various privacy concerns of Facebook users related to tagged photos and Ahern et al. [10] discussed Flickr users' privacy concerns and managing policies about uploaded photos.

7. CONCLUSION

In this paper we consider the problem of estimating the heights of all the users in a *photo collection*, such as a collection of photos from a social network. The main ideas in our methodology are (i) for each individual photo, estimate the height differences among the people standing in the photo (intra-photo estimation), (ii) from the photo collection, create a people graph, and combine this graph with the height difference estimates from the individual photos to generate height difference estimates among all the people in the collection (inter-photo estimation), (iii) then use these height difference estimates, as well as an *a priori* distribution, to estimate the heights of all the people in the photo collection. Because many people will appear in multiple photos across the collection, we showed that the height of each person can be compared with a much larger set of people (sometimes with most of the people in the collection), to significantly improve the estimates.

We formulated the problem as a MLE estimation problem, which when combined with a priori global mean and variance information, gives rise to a quadratic programming problem that can be easily solved with thousands of variables (people) at once. We applied the technique to estimating the heights of over 400 movie stars in the IMDb database and the heights of about 30 graduate students. Our results indicate that this data-driven approach can give good estimates, with significantly lower errors than the baseline approaches. We further found that as the photo collection increases, with people appearing in multiple photos, accuracy generally improves.

In addition to providing a novel methodology to estimating heights from photos, this paper also shows the great potential of mining data from photo collections in which the same people appear in multiple, but different, photos. In addition to features like height and weight, it may be possible to use photo collections to mine a story around the community people in the photos, such as determining kinship relationships and also current and past romantic relationships.

8. ACKNOWLEDGMENT

This work was supported in part by the NSF (under grant 0966187 and grant CNS-1318659). The views and conclusions contained in this document are those of the authors and should not be interpreted as necessarily representing the official policies, either expressed or implied, of any of the sponsors.

9. REFERENCES

[1] Brigger Furniture - Comfort Seats Made to Fit Your Body. `http://www.briggerfurniture.com/`.

[2] Camera Calibration With Opencv. `http://docs.opencv.org/doc/tutorials/calib3d/camera_calibration/camera_calibration.html#cameracalibrationopencv`.

[3] Destination XL - Men's Big and Tall Superstore. `http://www.destinationxl.com/mens-big-and-tall-store/`.

[4] King Size - The Big and Tall Experts. `http://www.kingsizedirect.com/`.

[5] Instagram reports 200m users, 20b photos shared, Gigacom, March 25, 2014. `http://gigaom.com/2014/03/25/instagram-reports-200m-users-20b-photos-shared/`.

[6] Walking a New Beat: Surfing Myspace.com helps cops crack the case, Newsweek, April 17, 2006. `http://www.informationliberation.com/?id=9643`.

[7] Face it: âĂŸbookâĂŹ no secret to employers, The Wastington Times, July 17, 2006. `http://www.washingtontimes.com/news/2006/jul/17/20060717-124952-1800r/?page=all`.

[8] A Focus on Efficiency, White Paper, September 23, 2013. `http://www.informationliberation.com/?id=9643`.

[9] A. Acquisti, R. Gross, and F. Stutzman. Faces of facebook: Privacy in the age of augmented reality. *BlackHat USA*, 2011.

[10] S. Ahern, D. Eckles, N. Good, S. King, M. Naaman, and R. Nair. Over-exposed?: privacy patterns and considerations in online and mobile photo sharing. In *CHI*, volume 7, pages 357–366, 2007.

[11] C. BenAbdelkader, R. Cutler, and L. Davis. Person Identification using Automatic Height and Stride Estimation. In *16th International Conference on Pattern Recognition*, volume 4, pages 377–380, 2002.

[12] C. BenAbdelkader and Y. Yacoob. Statistical Body Height Estimation from a Single Image. In *IEEE International Conference on Automatic Face and Gesture Recognition*, pages 1–7, 2008.

[13] A. Besmer and H. Richter Lipford. Moving beyond untagging: photo privacy in a tagged world. In *Proceedings of the SIGCHI Conference on Human Factors in Computing Systems*, pages 1563–1572. ACM, 2010.

[14] A. Criminisi, I. Reid, and A. Zisserman. Single view metrology. *Internation Journal on Computer Vision*, 40(2):123–148, Nov. 2000.

[15] A. Criminisia, A. Zisserman, L. Van Gool, S. Bramble, and D. Compton. New Approach to Obtain Height Measurements from Video. In *Proceedings of SPIE- The International Society for Optical Engineering*, volume 3576, 1999.

[16] A. Gallagher and T. Chen. Understanding Images of Groups of People. *IEEE Conference on Computer Vision and Pattern Recognition*, 0:256–263, 2009.

[17] A. C. Gallagher and T. Chen. Finding Rows of People in Group Images. In *IEEE international conference on Multimedia and Expo*, pages 602–605, 2009.

[18] H. C. Henry Shu, Andrew Gallagher and T. Chen. Face-graph Matching for Classifying Groups of People. In *International Conference on Image Processing*, 2013.

[19] K. Kato and A. Higashiyama. Estimation of Height for Persons in Pictures. *Perception and Psychophysics*, 60(8):1318–1328, 1998.

[20] N. Saitoh, K. Kurosawa, and K. Kuroki. Study on Height Measurement from a Single View. In *IEEE International Conference on Image Processing*, pages 523–526, 1999.

[21] J. P. Seder and S. Oishi. Intensity of smiling in facebook photos predicts future life satisfaction. *Social Psychological and Personality Science*, 3(4):407–413, 2012.

[22] Z. Stone, T. Zickler, and T. Darrell. Autotagging facebook: Social network context improves photo annotation. In *Computer Vision and Pattern Recognition Workshops, 2008. CVPRW'08. IEEE Computer Society Conference on*, pages 1–8. IEEE, 2008.

[23] L. White. Facebook, friends and photos: A snapshot into social networking for generating travel ideas. *Tourism informatics: Visual travel recommender systems, social communities and user interface design. Hershey, PA: IGI Global*, pages 115–129, 2010.

[24] S. Yardi, N. Feamster, and A. Bruckman. Photo-based authentication using social networks. In *Proceedings of the first workshop on Online social networks*, pages 55–60. ACM, 2008.

"I Knew They Clicked When I Saw Them With Their Friends"

Identifying your silent web visitors on social media

Arthi Ramachandran
Columbia University
New York, NY
arthir@cs.columbia.edu

Yunsung Kim
Columbia University
New York, NY
yk2553@columbia.edu

Augustin Chaintreau
Columbia University
New York, NY
augustin@cs.columbia.edu

ABSTRACT

An increasing fraction of users access content on the web from social media. Endorsements by microbloggers and public figures you connect with gradually replaces the curation originally in the hand of traditional media sources. One expects a social media provider to possess a unique ability to analyze audience and trends since they collect not only information about what you *actively* share, but also about what you *silently* watch. Your behavior in the latter seems safe from observations outside your online service provider, for privacy but also commercial reasons.

In this paper, we show that supposing that your passive web visits are anonymous to your host is a fragile assumption, or alternatively that third parties – content publishers or providers serving ads onto them – can efficiently reconciliate visitors with their social media identities. What is remarkable in this technique is that it need *no support* from the social media provider, it seamlessly applies to visitors who *never* post or endorse content, and a visitor's public identity become known after a *few* clicks. This method combines properties of the public follower graph with posting behaviors and recent time-based inference, making it difficult to evade without drastic or time-wasting measures. It potentially offers researchers working on traffic datasets a new view into who access content or through which channels.

1. INTRODUCTION

Most of the work on social media centers on a user's *explicit* activity with regard to one or several social network providers, and occasionally on how this leaks information between or beyond them. In contrast, *implicit* activities such as clicks and reads are under-explored. They are typically much harder to study: only providers of social networks have access to individual data about them, and they rarely reveal it for privacy and commercial reasons. Studying *implicit* activites requires bridging two worlds: Content producers maintain a detailed user profile for personalization and ads using cookies, but *a priori* have no information about the user outside their domain. Social media usually have a wider view of someone's interest, but may lack detailed information about a user in a domain.

Bridging this gap opens opportunity and concerns, of commercial and ethical nature. When this happens today it is set up *manually* with social media provider's *approval*, using APIs, unified logins, and less transparently, through endorsement buttons like "share" and "like". There are reasons to believe that social media providers may restrict what a third party can learn about a user, or even what the identity of that user is. As an example, when clicking a URL received on Twitter, your username is not communicated to the receiving domain. Intuitively, social media provider are rich in individual data and for legitimate privacy reason, as well as commercial interests, they have no incentive to share that data beyond what users expect of them: the network of their public connections and posting.

We focus on a simple yet central problem: "Can an independent first or third party (respectively hosting content or serving ads) recognizes a visitor as the owner of a profile in social media?" We consider the most general case: The third party has no individual information beyond this visitor's clicks on its site, and the visitor's social media profile may show no activity. We assume the third party monitors public information about its domain: public postings of URLs it hosts, and connections among users. Our goal is to identify web-visitors just by their clicks.

We make the following contributions.

- We first unearth a critical fact: Although links shared on social media exhibit extremely skewed popularity distribution with a few receiving most mentions, the set of links a user receive is highly distinguishable. Even if one takes only links to a single domain of moderate size, 96% of the social media traffic comes from users who are exposed to a unique set of links. We provide additional ways to strengthen this result. (§ 2)
- We design an original identification method that we test using hypotheses on the traffic that get exposed to a given domain. The method is proved to always work fast with a median of at most 10 clicks. However, as we show even such performance limits its applicability to small domains in the sparsest regime (very low link click rates). (§ 3)
- To address the most challenging cases, we introduce an extension of the baseline method, that we call Remember-

COSN'14, October 1–2, 2014, Dublin, Ireland.

http://dx.doi.org/10.1145/2660460.2660461.

Attribute-Intersect (RAI), using recent work on influence inference. We first show that when inference is accurate the method promises identification in less than 4 or 5 clicks, which makes it practical for a much larger set of smaller domains and even when click through rates (CTRs) are low. We finally show how errors in the attribution process can be handled. (§ 4)

Our work follows a long line of research exploiting sparsity in data in general [17, 18, 7] to identify or infer information about users of online services, and social media in particular [24, 15, 16]. What sets it apart is that our work exploits basic ingredients, common to any web-domain. Hence, our results apply more generally: Whenever a user follows information from a *public* social media such as Twitter she is instantly recognizable by the website she visits unless she (1) has not visited this domain more than 4 times, (2) takes action not to be appearing as the same visitor, or (3) creates multiple identities, makes her list of connections private, or delays her visits by a non-negligible time. While each of these actions or situations are deemed possible, they significantly limit a user's web experience.

In a different line of research, our results can be used to complement previous studies of cascades and information diffusion in social media [6, 13, 1, 21, 5, 25, 11]. Indeed, measuring and predicting the success of a cascade is still a matter of controversy [6, 3]. Validating those studies with individual data about *which* users clicked *which* links sent by *whom* requires data unavailable outside researchers at social media provider [26, 4]. This paper opens an alternative way, by inferring visitors from web traffic, to study the real success of social media in generating clicks.

2. OUR DISTINGUISHED FRIENDS

As a preliminary result to our method, we would like to prove a pervasive property that highlights the potential of social networks for re-identification using a *minimum* set of information. Previous results reported that four spatio-temporal points are enough to uniquely identify 96% of the individuals in large anonymous mobility datasets[7]. Similarly, records from the Netflix prize revealed that most of the time the set of items rated by a user overlaps with less than half of those from the *closest* users in these data [17].

Similarly, we ask here: "How unique is the set of people you follow and the content you receive from them?"

Datasets.

We gathered a week of all Twitter posts that contained a URL from the `nytimes.com` domain (*NYT*). We crawled in parallel the follower-followee relationship to construct for each user the URLs that they receive. The final datasets totals 346k unique users receiving a total 22m tweets with URL (if we include multiplicity) that contained 70k unique links posted by 328k of the users (more details in [14]).

For validation, we used an additional dataset consisting of the *entire* Twitter graph from August 2009 (*KAIST*) [6]. The entire network used consists of 8m users and 700m links receiving a total of 183m tweets from July 2009. Of these, we focused on the 37m tweets that contained URLs.

Finally, within KAIST we focused on the domain `digg.com` (*DIGG*). This dataset consists of 216k unique URLs tweeted by 44k unique users. These users represent the population that displays some interest in the domain. Hence, the associated network is derived from the 52m links connecting these individuals.

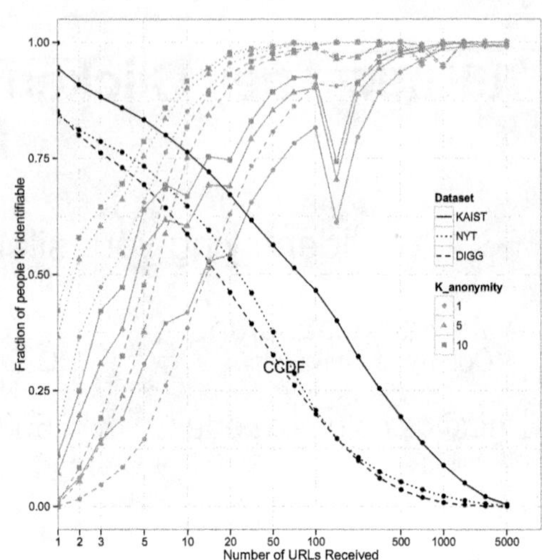

Figure 1: Fraction of social media users receiving more than n URLs, and those receiving a unique sets of URLs among them.

How unique are the links you receive?.

The first and most striking result is that users overwhelmingly receive a *distinguished* set of URLs. This is in spite that the majority of users receive few of them (*e.g.*, in *NYT* half of them receives less than 15 distinct URLs) and that URLs are concentrated on a few blockbuster links that are essentially received by everyone (*e.g.*, the top-15 URLs account together for 7% of all the tweets).

Figure 1 shows, for each number n on the x-axis in logscale, the fraction of users who received more than n URLs and, for those receiving exactly a subset of n, how much of them have a unique subset (i.e. one that no other user received). Note that, alternatively, when no more than $k \geq 1$ users receive this subset, we say the user is *k-anonymous*, and plot the fraction of such users for $k = 5$ and $k = 10$. We compare our datasets: the entire Twitter graph (*KAIST*), our crawled dataset based on the `nytimes.com` domain (*NYT*) and the twitter graph based on the `digg.com` domain (*DIGG*).

One observes that 15 URLs appears to be a turning point: A user receiving significantly less than that, especially below 5 URLs, is rarely distinguished by its set of urls (we observe, however, that it is typically only among a set of 20 people who received that combination). Users receiving above 50 URLs are unique at least 80% of the time. In general, we obtain overall consistent results across data-sets, with unicity or k-anonymity for small k more prevalent when one considers URLs from a specific domain (*NYT* or *DIGG*) than otherwise (*KAIST*). This indicates that the method we present extend to various domains, we will now focus on *NYT* data.

While for *KAIST* and *DIGG*, we looked at unicity by comparing the full sets of URLs received among individuals, in the *NYT*, we also considered unicity w.r.t. subset relationship. In this case and in the rest of the paper, we considered a user uniquely identified only if it is the only one that receives these URLs *or a superset of them*[1]. This property is stronger and makes this result more surprising given that some users received an enormous amount of information from the `nytimes.com` domain (we had more than 10 users receiving above 5,000 URLs each). Overall, 53% of all *NYT* users are unique with the above definition. As the users which are unique also tend to receive more content, they account together for 90% of the traffic that this social media can generate to this domain.

The unicity property of your set of URLs is derived from the long-tail property of the distribution [10]. According to this property, a very large fraction of the content you receive is common, while some items will be highly specific. The occurrence of one of these items (which is likely unless your set of received URLs is very small) is sufficient to offer information that makes you distinct.

Your distinguished set of "friends".

Given that the links that form your social media news feed are a direct consequence of the person you follow and their posts, it does not come as a surprise that this set of "friends" (as Twitter terminology refers to them) is unique. Indeed, were they not unique, several other people would enjoy what they post, hence the same content as yours, contradicting our results above. What is perhaps less obvious is that this set of friends distinguishes you even more than your content. The effect is significant and intuitively comes from the fact that multiple people may have received the same URLs from different "friends".

To measure that effect, we run a similar experiment on the New York Time dataset reported on Figure 2. The x-axis denotes the number n of friends posting URLs, and we plot the same distributions and unicity measures. The turning point for the unicity property moves significantly: With the exception of users whose set of active friends are extremely small (below 3), knowing who contributed to your feed distinguish you with overwhelming probability, even against supersets as discussed before. This translate into almost 70% of the users being unique in that regard; those users amount to 96% of the potential traffic to `nytimes.com`. In effect, knowing a small subset of your posting friends almost always makes you a unique person, except if you belong to a minority who is only rarely exposed to information from that source, and accounts for less than 5% of the traffic.

We run a similar experiment on a surrogate social media, reshuffling at random the edges of bipartite graph, while maintaining the overall friend and popularity distributions. The result shown in Figure 2 confirms most of the effect is not an artifact of specific structures of Twitter. An interesting point is to determine which "friends" are the most useful, we delay a discussion of this point until Section 4.

In summary, our results highlight a new promising domain of application of sparsity methods to identify social media users, which is based on the content that they receive and the individuals participating in it. We have shown that this has a high potential, as a very large fraction of the users, and overwhelming percentage of the traffic, is created by visitors with unique patterns. It remains to be seen how these facts can come together to constitute a proper and practical re-identification method for the web.

[1]Later this point is critical for identification as it is not in general easy to deduce that a user did *not* receive a URL.

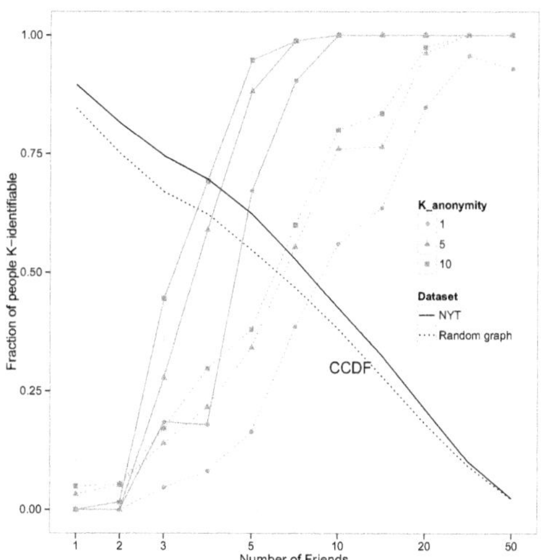

Figure 2: Fraction of user with at least n active friends, and those for which this set is unique.

3. WEB VISITOR RE-IDENTIFICATION

We have shown that content received on social media is highly distinctive. We now study several methods leveraging this fact, to allow a web domain receiving visits from social media to identify their visitors explicitly. They are multiple motivations for a domain owner to do that: learning additional information about its audience (demographics, interests, trending topics), monitoring the content its users receive from competitors, or even personalize your results (with or without user's knowledge) based on a visitor's infered social media profile.

Currently, there are three ways to identify your visitors: asking for *users* to sign in using the social network service, asking *social media providers* to reveal a user's identity whenever she clicks on this domain, or asking a *web-aggregator* to perform synchronization. Each is cumbersome as it poses usability concerns (*e.g.*, your visitors may leave or even lie if asked to provide a form of identification) and assumes cooperation (*e.g.*, a social network provider or web-aggregator may not want to reveal their users' identity to a domain, a domain may not want to reveal its audience to them). In contrast with previous work, we assume *no cooperation* of any sort. We aim at an identification scheme that bypasses all mechanisms mentioned above.

The state of web-tracking.

Web content publishers or third parties generally keep track of web visitors to inform personalization, targeted advertisement and general audience analytics. There is a clear tendency to aggregate identities for a user across domains, making it ever more difficult to evade tracking [23]. The result is the rise of *web aggregators*, a large class of services who typically observe a user's web itinerary on a large fraction of the web [9]. The HTTP protocol allows us to aggregate identities: A single webpage (*e.g.*, an article on `nytimes.com`) generates requests to multiples domains (*e.g.*, `admob.com`, `facebook.com`, `twitter.com`), each one keeping a *local* user identity. Since browser only blocks `set-cookies` in HTTP response – if they block third party at all – it means the user is recognized unless it was never called before in a first party transactions, a relatively rare case. Ad-networks allow cookies synchronization [19], further extending the reach of third party tracking. Evasion techniques exist, such as stronger third-party cookies blocking or reset, but each is met with an alternative forms of tracking: 1x1 pixel image forcing third party request, malicious use of web caching to provide pseudo identifiers in the `Etag` field, Flash cookies [2], or use of Browser Fingerprinting and Javascript [8].

Our assumptions, discussed immediately below, leverages common facts on tracking with *no third party cooperation*.

Problem Formulation & Assumptions.

We assume simply *first party tracking*: the provider can maintain a persistent identity for web visitor *only within its domain*. This applies to content publishers (*e.g.,* `nytimes.com`). This also captures aggregators who do not have such limitations (*e.g.,* `admob.com, bluekai.com`) by extending the domain considered to all those they can track.

In both cases, we assume that the domain knows only one thing: that the click was generated through a social media site (*e.g.,* from `twitter.com`). We note that this is commonly done today (*e.g.,* `nytimes.com` limits non-subscribers to 10 articles a month, but allow unlimited access from social media) in multiple ways: most commonly the HTTP referrer field[2], or by providing specific URLs to use in various social media. We do *not* assume, however, that the URL itself is indicative of which posts, tweets, or mention generated that click. It is sometimes possible to leverage that fact and make our method even more efficient, but we ignore it here. Note, however, that we assume that all clicks a user generates on the social media (*e.g.,* from `twitter.com`) comes from her feed and not search or special content promotion. We believe this would affect our results in the same way as attribution errors (see § 4 for more on that topic).

We assume that, in parallel, the domain also monitors *who* post links to its content in the social media. It seems legitimate as "active" users posting links expect it to be publicly known. Again, it's commonly done especially to promote a domain by retweeting users and celebrities mentioning its content or to follow what is said about the domain. Our last assumption is that the domain owner is able to access the graph of followers of each "active" users mentioning URLs from their domain. To simplify we first assume that this information is prior knowledge, but later on we discuss how to limit how much of that information is needed.

These assumptions are inspired from information made publicly available by Twitter. Our methods would extend to other social media with similar policies.

A simple method for re-identification.

Given what we have learned about content received on social media, the following scheme is promising: In the first phase, for every URL in the domain collect the set of people who received it in the social media (*i.e.,* the union of followers of "active" users who post it). In the second phase, for each visitor, collect URLs of all her HTTP requests generated from this social media, and intersect the URLs' received sets. This method can safely conclude the identity of this visitor when this intersection contains a single node.

[2]For aggregators, we assume that the content publisher relay that information.

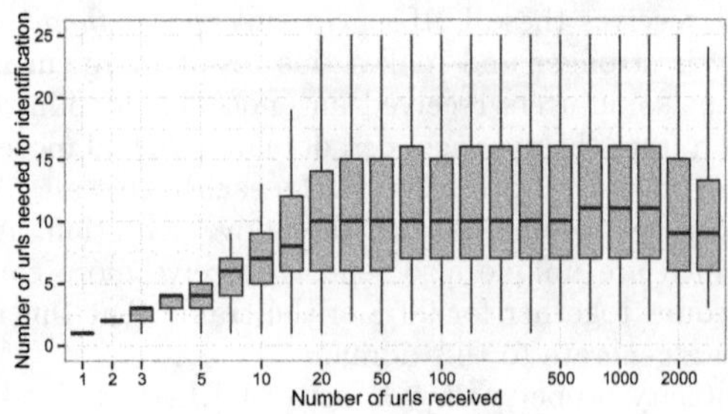

Figure 3: Distribution of the number of visits needed to successfully re-identify a node as a function of the size of its receiving URLs set.

Our preliminary analysis suggests this method terminates, as each user often is the unique node intersecting all the URLs she receives. But this raised two questions: How many URLs from each user are needed to reach this conclusion? As a consequence, how likely is this method to complete when only a subset of the content a user receive does generate a click to that domain? Figure 3 presents the results of a simulation where for each user in our dataset we look at URLs included one by one in random order and stop whenever the intersecting set is a singleton. Across the whole population the median user is identified after 8 URLs, and even for large sets 10 URLs suffice on average. It is unlikely that more than 15 or 20 intersections are needed.

In real life, however, an intersection step occurs when a user decides to clicks, and only a fraction of URLs received generate a HTTP request (except for users with browser/app prefetching that proactively load content). Besides, among URLs received, some may receive more clicks as they are simply more interesting. So we build the following click generation model: Many links were published using the URL shortener `bit.ly`, and we use this API to obtain the number of clicks that each of those URLs generated. Dividing by the number of times this URLs is received in our dataset yields for each URL a coefficient. We scaled these coefficients by a constant so that the effective Click-Through-Rate (CTR) experienced by URLs posted on Twitter is 1%, 2%, 5% and 10% overall, chosen to represent a range of plausible hypotheses on CTR [20, 27]. Note that our method is approximate (*i.e.,* the measured clicks may be generated through other sources than Twitter), but it still captures heterogeneous popularity of URLs, most notably that rare URLs are less likely to generate click, under normalized conditions.

Figure 4 assumes the above click generation model and it plots using dashed lines the fraction of users identified with the intersection method described above. The qualitative trend is not surprising, the identifiability of a node depends on the number of URLs it clicks and is also inversely proportional to the click rate. If one out of twenty URLs get clicked, we can successfully identify 40% of the traffic, and for a CTR of 1%, more than 99% are users are left unidentified, since the success probably is low for anyone unless they receive at least 1,500 URLs.

4. THE POWER OF ATTRIBUTION

Social media potentially produces a highly distinctive traffic, but it may not be enough to scale our methods for small

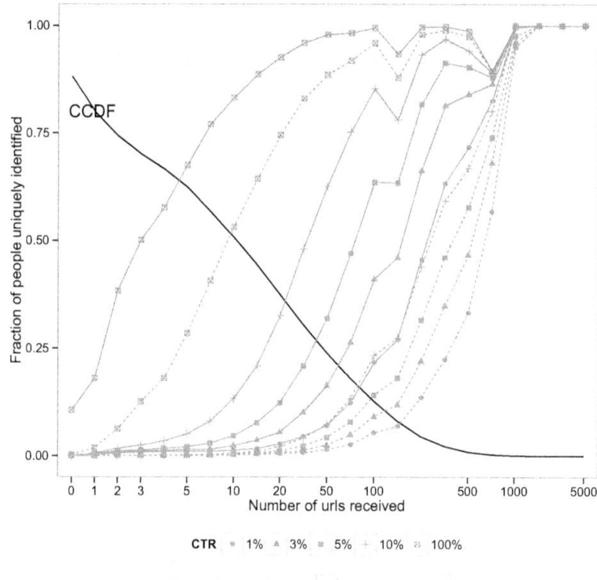

Figure 4: Fraction of users with at least n URLs received, and the proportion that are identified for various click generation rates and two methods.

ALGORITHM 1: Intersect Algorithm of RAI

Data: Social Network $G(V, E)$: Node $v \in V$; URLs visited $u \in URLs(v)$
Result: $I(v)$ = identity of v; $f \subseteq$ Friends(v) used for re-identification
Identities(v) $\leftarrow V$;
while *Identities(v)* > 1 *and* $\exists$ *url visit* u **do**
  I(v) $\leftarrow (\cup_{f \text{ post } u \,\&\, v \text{ visits } u \text{ via } f}\text{Followers}(f)) \cap \text{I}(v)$;
  $u \leftarrow$ next visited url;
end
if *Length(Identities(v))* $\neq 1$ **then** `// no unique identity found`
  while *Length(I(v))* > 1 *and* $\exists$ *url visit* u **do**
    I(v) $\leftarrow (\cup_{f \text{ post } u}\text{Followers}(f)) \cap \text{I}(v)$;
    $u \leftarrow$ next visited url;
  end
end

domains receiving typically less than 10 clicks on a regular basis. It is however possible to extract even more information from social media diffusion.

Refining the attribute step with time information.

Our next method is inspired by recent advances to use time in the inference of links and diffusion on social media [12, 22]. Leveraging the fact that most clicks occur within a very short time of the URLs being posted, one can reconstruct minimal graphs to account for the visit times using convex optimization techniques. These rely on the time differences between visits of users to estimate probabilities of follower relationships existing among them. The intuition is that visits that are closer together in time are more likely to be related to each other in the social graph.

We now utilize a method, Remember-Attribute-Intersect (RAI), a three phase algorithm which uses methods of influence detection to attribute URLs to their social media source. While simulating the entire inference relies on information about click times, which is difficult to obtain and beyond our paper, we conduct simulation assuming that the attribution steps succeeds with some probability in finding the source, or otherwise introduces an attribution error.

Results with perfect attribution.

We applied RAI to *NYT* and recovered a significant fraction of the individuals. Figure 4 compares the performance of the two methods – the baseline method using just URLs and the modified RAI method. Again, for more realistic performance, we examined the results with CTRs of 1%, 2%, 5% and 10%. We see that there is a significant advantage in using attribution over the baseline. Even at low clicks rates of 1% and 5%, we capture individuals receiving only 100 URLs, which is a more typical user. Note that attribution errors were ignored here.

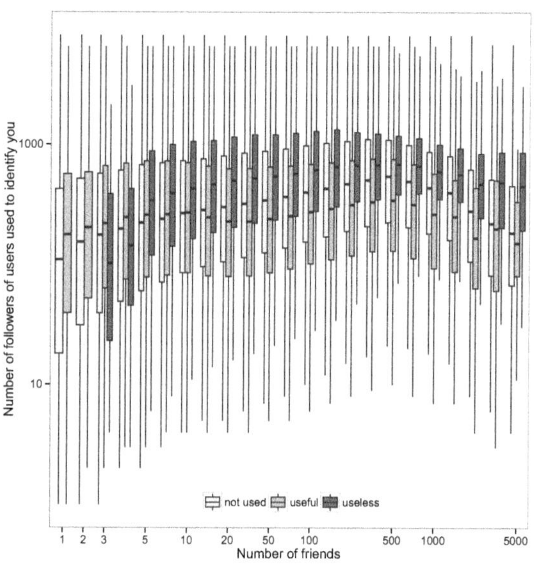

Figure 5: Distribution of followers for active friends used in re-identification.

We examined characteristics of the individuals used for re-identification. We would expect that the less popular and therefore more unusual individuals are more useful for identification. Figure 5 shows the distribution of the popularity for three classes of friends: those useful in re-identification, those who did not provide additional information for the re-identification and those who were not even examined before successful re-identification. We see that the less useful individuals tended to be more popular. Surprisingly, the set of individuals useful in identification were not significantly less popular than the others, indicating that our method does not rely on the inactive and less detectable individuals.

Effect of attribution error.

All of our previous analysis assume that the attribution of URLs works perfectly. However, this stage is susceptible to error from various sources. For instance, times of visits might not be sufficiently spread to effectively which of several sources is correct or multiple sources might have posted

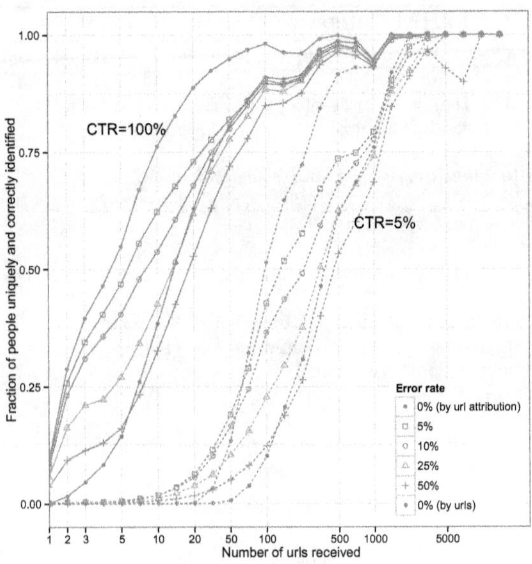

Figure 6: Fraction of nodes identified with attribution errors for two CTRs.

the same content at the same time. Here, we verify the performance of RAI under several error regimes.

We simulate errors as follows: for a certain error rate, we attribute a URL incorrectly to another user who also posted that URL. Note that the set of URLs received by a web visitor is always correct under the persistence assumption. We then run a modified version of RAI. With incorrect attribution, it is possible that the intersection of followers of the attributed sources are not consistent and lead to no possible identifications. In that case, we back off, and run our initial URL re-identification method which is not susceptible to errors. Thus we leverage the additional information from the attribution while still being error tolerant.

Figure 6 presents the results of RAI under error rates ranging from 5% to 45%. In addition, we account for imperfect detection by assuming a 5% uniform click through rate. The performance of RAI with errors falls somewhere between the two methods with perfect information. Indeed, for individuals receiving more than 1000 URLs, the performance is virtually unaffected by errors. In most cases, there are still gains in individuals identified with attribution which were previously not possibly by the URLs alone.

Table 1 shows the overall percentages of visits and people re-identified with both methods with varying CTRs and error rates. In a perfect information scenario, we can account for 97% of the visits. Even in more restrictive scenarios, with 5% CTR and significant error, we can account for about half of the visits and almost 20% of the whole population.

Limitations & Extensions.

Our method relies on identities being persistent over the time period being examined. In Section 3, we covered some of the means to do so and without this assumption, it is impossible to associate an individual with their identity.

Our analysis also relies on the content provider or aggregator observing posting behavior over a sufficient period of time. We found that a week was sufficient for a domain such as `nytimes.com` or `digg.com`. More generally our experiments indicate that one would need to collect enough data so that most users receive at least 8 posts. We required to crawl or obtain the associated social graph for that time period. For content providers invested in an analysis of their audience, this does not prove to be a major impediment but can be resource and time intensive. Since the intersection method use simple operations, it could be run on a selective set of URLs (*e.g.,* , ignoring the most popular ones posted many times) or to reidentify only some particular set of visitors. Both of these cases may reduce the cost of this step.

Error Rate		CTR 100%	30%	5%	1%
(a) 0%	% visits	97.0%	91.9%	70.3%	31.7%
	% visitors	69.1%	49.3%	19.5%	3.7%
(a) 5%	% visits	91.5%	83.1%	59.4%	
	% visitors	60.8%	43.4%	18.1%	
	(fals. pos.)	(8.5%)	(8.8%)	(5.7%)	
(a) 20%	% visits	89.5%	77.9%	47.6%	
	% visitors	52.6%	34.2%	11.9%	
	(fals. pos.)	(15.9%)	(18.1%)	(15.1%)	
(b) N/A	% visits	91.0%	79.2%	43.8%	11.8%
	% visitors	53.7%	30.5%	7.9%	0.8%

Table 1: Fraction of visits and visitors identified by (a) attributed URLs with varying error rates, and (b) unattributed URLs, for different CTRs.

We also assumed that clicks are generated from users of `twitter.com` via their feed and not through other means (*e.g.,* search or promoted content). If the latter occurs occasionally, one might detect that as an attribution error, ignoring that URLs and applying the method on the rest.

5. CONCLUSION

The large majority of links received on social media distinguish users, even when limited to a single domain like `nytimes.com` for a short time span of a week. This new observation redefines the possibility of being anonymous and socially connected. Half of the time, only 8 clicks are needed for unique identification. We have verified these results on another dataset based on the `digg.com` domain.

The case of low CTRs and occasional visitors appears to be particularly challenging, but even in these cases, one can hope for some percentage of the individuals to be identified. In the presence of attribution errors, fewer individuals can be identified but overall, a significant fraction of the users are not anonymous.

Here, we focused on a specific domain, mimicking a content provider. However, exploiting more information across domains and using click datasets are important next steps to assess the scale of this potential privacy threat.

Acknowledgment

We would like to thank Meeyoung Cha for providing access and help on the Twitter Data used for comparison. This material is based upon work supported by the National Science Foundation under grant no. CNS-1254035 and through a Graduate Research Fellowship to Arthi Ramachandran. This research was also funded by Microsoft Research under a Graduate Fellowship.

6. REFERENCES

[1] J. An, M. Cha, K. Gummadi, and J. Crowcroft. Media landscape in Twitter: A world of new conventions and political diversity. *Proceedings of the International Conference Weblogs and Social Media (ICWSM)*, 2011.

[2] M. Ayenson, D. J. Wambach, A. Soltani, N. Good, and C. J. Hoofnagle. Flash cookies and privacy II: Now with HTML5 and ETag respawning. *World Wide Web Internet And Web Information Systems*, 2011.

[3] E. Bakshy, J. M. Hofman, W. A. Mason, and D. J. Watts. Everyone's an influencer: quantifying influence on twitter. In *WSDM '11: Proceedings of the fourth ACM international conference on Web search and data mining*, 2011.

[4] E. Bakshy, I. Rosenn, C. Marlow, and L. A. Adamic. The Role of Social Networks in Information Diffusion. In *WWW '12: Proceedings of the 21st international conference on World Wide Web*, 2012.

[5] M. Cha, F. Benevenuto, H. Haddadi, and K. Gummadi. The World of Connections and Information Flow in Twitter. *Systems, Man and Cybernetics, Part A: Systems and Humans, IEEE Transactions on*, 2012.

[6] M. Cha, H. Haddadi, F. Benevenuto, and K. Gummadi. Measuring User Influence in Twitter: The Million Follower Fallacy. *Proceedings of the International Conference Weblogs and Social Media (ICWSM)*, 2010.

[7] Y.-A. de Montjoye, C. A. Hidalgo, M. Verleysen, and V. D. Blondel. Unique in the Crowd: The privacy bounds of human mobility. *Scientific Reports*, 2013.

[8] P. Eckersley. How unique is your web browser? *Privacy Enhancing Technologies*, 2010.

[9] P. Gill, V. Erramilli, A. Chaintreau, B. Krishnamurthy, K. Papagiannaki, and P. Rodriguez. Follow the money: understanding economics of online aggregation and advertising. *IMC '13: Proceedings of the 2013 conference on Internet measurement conference*, 2013.

[10] S. Goel, A. Broder, E. Gabrilovich, and B. Pang. Anatomy of the long tail: ordinary people with extraordinary tastes. *WSDM '10: Proceedings of the third ACM international conference on Web search and data mining*, 2010.

[11] S. Goel, D. J. Watts, and D. G. Goldstein. The structure of online diffusion networks. In *EC '12: Proceedings of the 13th ACM Conference on Electronic Commerce*, 2012.

[12] M. Gomez-Rodriguez, J. Leskovec, and A. Krause. Inferring Networks of Diffusion and Influence. *ACM Transactions on Knowledge Discovery from Data (TKDD)*, 2012.

[13] H. Kwak, C. Lee, H. Park, and S. Moon. What is Twitter, a social network or a news media? In *WWW '10: Proceedings of the 19th international conference on World wide web*, 2010.

[14] A. May, A. Chaintreau, N. Korula, and S. Lattanzi. Filter & Follow: How Social Media Foster Content Curation. In *SIGMETRICS '14: Proceedings of the ACM International conference on Measurement and modeling of computer systems*, 2014.

[15] B. Meeder, B. Karrer, A. Sayedi, R. Ravi, C. Borgs, and J. Chayes. We know who you followed last summer: inferring social link creation times in twitter. In *WWW '11: Proceedings of the 20th international conference on World wide web*, 2011.

[16] A. Mislove, B. Viswanath, K. Gummadi, and P. Druschel. You are who you know: inferring user profiles in online social networks. *WSDM '10: Proceedings of the third ACM international conference on Web search and data mining*, 2010.

[17] A. Narayanan and V. Shmatikov. Robust De-anonymization of Large Sparse Datasets. *Security and Privacy, 2008. SP 2008. IEEE Symposium on*, 2008.

[18] A. Narayanan and V. Shmatikov. De-anonymizing Social Networks. *Security and Privacy, 2009 30th IEEE Symposium on*, 2009.

[19] L. Olejnik. Selling Off Privacy at Auction. *In Proceedings of the Network and Distributed System Security Symposium (NDSS)*, 2014.

[20] M. Richardson, E. Dominowska, and R. Ragno. Predicting clicks: estimating the click-through rate for new ads. In *WWW '07: Proceedings of the 16th international conference on World Wide Web*, 2007.

[21] T. Rodrigues, F. Benevenuto, M. Cha, K. Gummadi, and V. Almeida. On word-of-mouth based discovery of the web. In *IMC '11: Proceedings of the 2011 ACM SIGCOMM conference on Internet measurement conference*, 2011.

[22] M. G. Rodriguez, J. Leskovec, and B. Schölkopf. Structure and dynamics of information pathways in online media. In *WSDM '13: Proceedings of the sixth ACM international conference on Web search and data mining*, 2013.

[23] F. Roesner, T. Kohno, and D. Wetherall. Detecting and defending against third-party tracking on the web. In *NSDI'12: Proceedings of the 9th USENIX conference on Networked Systems Design and Implementation*, 2012.

[24] N. K. Sharma, S. Ghosh, F. Benevenuto, N. Ganguly, and K. Gummadi. Inferring who-is-who in the Twitter social network. In *WOSN '12: Proceedings of the 2012 ACM workshop on Workshop on online social networks*, 2012.

[25] S. Wu, J. M. Hofman, W. A. Mason, and D. J. Watts. Who says what to whom on twitter. *WWW '11: Proceedings of the 20th international conference on World wide web*, 2011.

[26] R. B. Zadeh, A. Goel, K. Munagala, and A. Sharma. On the precision of social and information networks. In *COSN '13: Proceedings of the first ACM conference on Online social networks*, 2013.

[27] Y. Zhang, W. Chen, D. Wang, and Q. Yang. User-click modeling for understanding and predicting search-behavior. In *Proceedings of the 17th ACM SIGKDD International Conference on Knowledge Discovery and Data Mining*, KDD '11, pages 1388–1396, New York, NY, USA, 2011. ACM.

Cognitive Disconnect: Understanding Facebook Connect Login Permissions

Nicky Robinson
Princeton University
ncrobins@princeton.edu

Joseph Bonneau
Princeton University
jbonneau@princeton.edu

ABSTRACT

We study Facebook Connect's permissions system using crawling, experimentation, and user surveys. We find several areas in which it it works differently than many users and developers expect. More permissions can be granted than developers intend. In particular, permissions that allow a site to post to the user's profile are granted on an all-or-nothing basis. While users generally understand what data sites can read from their profile, they generally do not understand the full extent of what sites can post. In the case of write permissions, we show that user expectations are influenced by the identity of the requesting site although this has no impact on what is actually enforced. We also find that users generally do not understand the way Facebook Connect permissions interact with Facebook's privacy settings. Our results suggest that users understand detailed, granular messages better than those that are broad and vague.

Categories and Subject Descriptors

D.4.6 [**Security and Protection**]: Access Controls

General Terms

Security; Human Factors

Keywords

Online social networks; permissions; privacy; Facebook

1. INTRODUCTION

Single Sign-On (SSO) systems allow users to log in to websites (called *relying sites* or *relying parties*) using their username and password from a third-party *identity provider*. This creates fewer passwords for users to remember, theoretically meaning that they can have more complicated and therefore more secure passwords [21]. Facebook Connect[1] is perhaps the most popular SSO system on the web today. A key reason is that Facebook Connect, like many SSO systems based off of the OAuth protocol, does more than just allow a user to sign in: sites can request access to read parts of the user's Facebook profile or write data back their profile. This has been sufficient in practice to overcome the lack of adoption incentives for relying parties which has plagued many other SSO systems on the web [24].

An important selling point is that Facebook Connect requires relying sites to request a specific set of permissions from the user up front in order to read or write data from the user's profile. These are presented to the user in a series of dialogues (shown in Figure 1) which the user must approve prior to logging into a relying site for the first time. In the words of Facebook, *"The user will have total control of the permissions granted"* [18].

Effective user control relies both on Facebook granting only the permissions intended by developers and on users correctly understanding the permissions they approve. We explore both assumptions and show that:

- Facebook Connect sometimes asks the user to authorize more permissions than the developer intended to request.
- Write permissions are granted to sites on an all-or-nothing basis. For example, if a site wants the ability to update the user's status, it must also gain the ability to upload photos.
- Users generally understand which read permissions are being requested when they log in, although many do not realize they are granting access to data they have marked as private using their privacy settings.
- Users generally do not understand the variety of write permissions sites will receive upon authorization. This indicates that, despite Facebook's claim that all-or-nothing write permissions are "simpler" for users to understand, users understand the more granular read permissions better.
- Users are influenced by the identity of the relying site; for example, they are much more likely to understand a photo sharing website can upload photos to their account. This suggests users are assuming a *contextual integrity* model of privacy [19], although this is not implemented technically.

[1] Facebook Connect is now technically called Facebook Login but is still frequently referred to as Facebook Connect.

COSN'14, October 1–2, 2014, Dublin, Ireland.

http://dx.doi.org/10.1145/2660460.2660471.

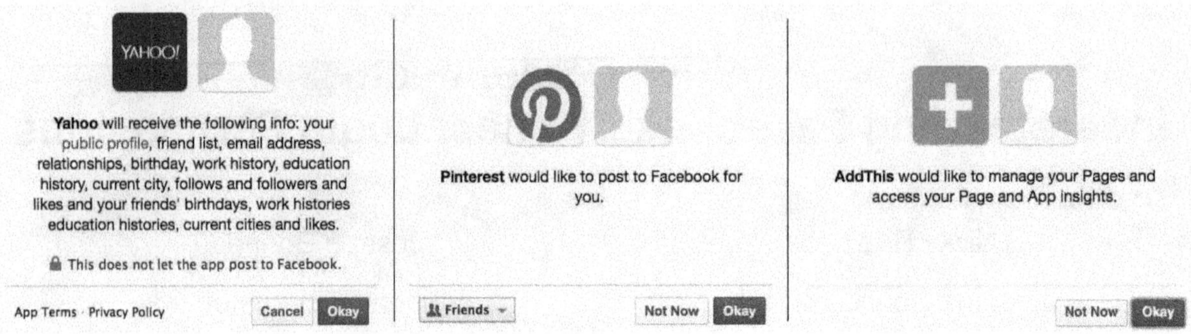

Figure 1: Examples of messages presented to the user. From left: Read permissions message from Yahoo.com, write permissions message from Pinterest.com, and extended permissions message from AddThis.com.

2. IMPLEMENTATION OF FACEBOOK CONNECT PERMISSIONS

The first step in determining whether the permissions system provides users with effective control is understanding which permissions are actually granted when a given authorization message is displayed. Facebook Connect's process of a site requesting permissions from a user can be broken down into three steps:

1. During login flow, relying parties request a set of permissions from the Facebook Connect API. We'll call this set the *requested permissions.*

2. Facebook receives the requested permissions and translates them into a set of permissions for approval which we'll call the *granted permissions.*

3. Facebook translates the the granted permissions into a dialogue presented to the user for approval. We'll call this text the *displayed permissions.*

Ideally, these three sets of permissions would be semantically identical and the text shown to the user would clearly represent them. In this section we'll explore the difference between the requested and granted permissions; we'll compare displayed and granted permissions in Section 3.

2.1 Methodology

Unfortunately, Facebook's documentation [3] is incomplete and sometimes outdated. As such, there is very little explanation of how requested permissions are eventually translated into permissions displayed to the user. To gain a better understanding, we combined information from the documentation with observations from integrating Facebook Connect login with a test site and crawled data from several hundred relying sites.

2.1.1 Obtaining a list of relying sites

To obtain a list of relying sites implementing Facebook Connect, we started with the most recent (October 2013) AppInspect [17] database of 25,000 Facebook apps. We filtered this list down to about 400 apps with an external site listed on the Facebook App Center. Finally, we manually idenitified 91 which had a Facebook Connect login.

Unfortunately, the AppInspect database does not include apps that are used solely for Facebook Connect, only those

https://www.facebook.com/dialogue/oauth?app_id=138615416238413
&domain=www.timecrunch.me&response_type=token%2Csigned_re
quest&scope=email%2Ccreate_event%2Coffline_access%2Cuser_gr
oups%2Cfriends_groups%2Cpublish_stream...

Figure 2: Example requested permissions (colored in red) in the scope parameter of the approval page URL.

that have native Facebook apps. To make up for these deficiencies, we took the Alexa Top 500[2] websites from February 27th, 2014 and manually identified those with Facebook Connect logins (112 sites). Combining these two lists gave us a total of 203 sites to study.

For crawling we used OpenWPM,[3] a Selenium-based[4] web crawler being developed by the Princeton Center for Information Technology Policy (CITP). We performed automated logins to all 203 sites and recorded the requested, granted, and displayed permissions. 26 of the 203 sites used an older version of Facebook Connect; we will focus only on the 177 using the current version.

2.2 Requested permissions

Developers request permissions in a parameter called "scope" or "data-scope" when the login process is initiated using Facebook's JavaScript SDK, Facebook's login button, or a manually built login system [7]. The developer can request any of the permissions listed in the documentation [6], although some are deprecated and will have no impact on the granted permissions.

The scope parameter is visible in the URL of the page where the user is asked to approve permissions (see Figure 2). We confirmed using our test site that this value is indeed exactly what the developer requested.

2.3 Granted permissions

Facebook receives the requested permissions and translates them into a set of granted permissions. The granted permissions may exclude requested permissions that are deprecated, or, in some cases, may add additional permissions. Two permissions, which Facebook calls "Basic Info/Default permissions"[7], are always added regardless of what is requested: *public_profile* and *user_friends*. The documenta-

[2]`http://www.alexa.com/topsites`
[3]`https://github.com/citp/OpenWPM/wiki`
[4]`https://github.com/cmwslw/selenium-crawler`

```
<input type="hidden" autocomplete="off" name=
"read" value="email,user_groups,friends_groups,
public_profile,user_friends,private" />

<input type="hidden" autocomplete="off" name=
"write" value="publish_stream,publish_actions,
create_note,photo_upload,publish_checkins,share_item,
status_update,video_upload" />

<input type="hidden" autocomplete="off" name=
"extended" value="create_event,rsvp_event" />
```

Figure 3: Example granted permissions (colored in red) shown by the *read*, *write*, and *extended* input elements on the permissions approval page for `timecrunch.me`.

Read Permissions
user_activities, user_about_me
friends_activities, friends_about_me
email, contact_email
read_stream, export_stream
Write Permissions
create_note, upload_photos, upload_videos, publish_actions, publish_checkins, publish_stream, share_item, status_update
Extended Permissions
rsvp_event, create_event

Table 1: Groups of permissions which area always granted together if any are requested.

tion does not mention any other permissions that may be granted outside of what the developer requested.

The approval page presented to the user has three hidden input HTML elements named *read*, *write*, and *extended* whose values are the granted permissions (see Figure 3). We confirmed with our test site that these permissions are actually granted and may be used by the relying site, regardless of the requested permissions.

We used these hidden elements to determine which permissions were granted in contrast to which were requested for all 177 sites we crawled. Our results are shown in Figure 4. First, we confirmed that with every site crawled the aforementioned default permissions (*public_profile* and *user_friends*) always appear in granted read permissions although they were never requested.

In addition, we identified several requested permissions which always cause extra permissions to be granted along with them (these will be discussed in more detail in the Section 2.3). For example, Facebook's documentation states that publishing a story (such as liking an article) requires the *publish_actions* permission. However, if the *create_note* permission is requested, *publish_actions* will also appear as a granted permission and this will allow stories to be published. Through experimentation with our test site, we determined exactly which permissions are always grouped together, listed in Table 1. If any one permission in a group is requested, all permissions in the group are granted. Grouped permissions are always displayed to the user with a single message, which we will discuss further in Section 2.4.

All of the grouped read and extended permissions are in pairs, so if the developer requests one they receive the other. However, all eight write permissions are in a single group, effectively making write permissions all-or-nothing.

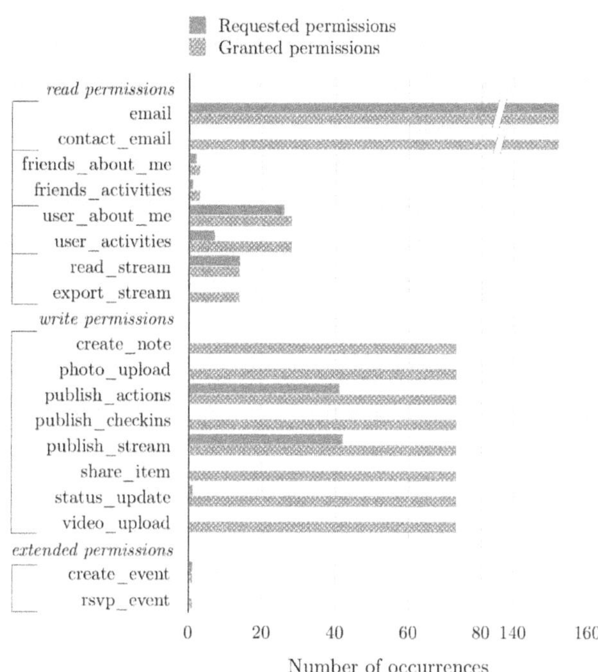

Figure 4: Permissions requested vs. permissions granted for permissions granted in groups, as listed in Table 1.

2.4 How permissions are presented to the user

As mentioned previously, when the user logs in to a site with Facebook Connect for the first time they are presented with up to three messages from Facebook asking them to approve the read, write, and/or extended permissions. We reverse-engineered the algorithm for generating the phrase or word in the displayed permissions message that corresponds to each granted permission using our test site and verified that it matched the data observed in our crawl. Most messages appear reasonably clear. However, the grouped permissions (see Table 1) are displayed with just one corresponding word or phrase indicating that *all* the permissions in that group are being requested. Table 2 presents these potentially unclear messages and their meaning according to the Facebook Connect documentation [6].

2.5 Facebook's response

We sent a security bug report to Facebook stating that we could use the *publish_actions* permission after requesting any other write permission. Facebook Security stated[5] that "this behavior is by design" and confirmed that when one permission is requested in the scope, they "translate them to a broader set of [permissions] which are easier for users to understand" [1]. When asked why this was done for write permissions but not read permissions, they responded that they "made this change to simplify the experience for developers and for users" and that "write permissions are more similar...whereas read permissions are more distinct." This motivated us to evaluate whether all-or-nothing write permissions are in fact easier for the user to understand.

[5]Our full correspondence with Facebook is in Appendix A.

Message	Permission	Meaning
Read Permissions: *Site_Name will receive the following info...*		
Message	**Permission**	**Meaning** [6]
email address	email	email
	contact_email	not listed
News Feed	read_stream	access my News Feed and Wall
	export_stream	export my posts and make them public. All posts will be exported, including status updates.
personal description	user_about_me	about me
	user_activities	activities
...and your friends'...		
personal descriptions	friends_about_me	'about me' details
	friends_activities	activities
Write Permissions: *Site_Name would like to...*		
Message	**Permission**	**Meaning**
post to Facebook for you. - *or** - post publicly to Facebook for you. - *or** - post privately to Facebook for you.	create_note	create and modify events
	photo_upload	add or modify photos
	publish_actions	publish my app activity to Facebook
	publish_checkins	publish checkins on my behalf
	publish_stream	publish content to my Wall
	share_item	share items on my behalf
	status_update	update my status
	video_upload	add or modify videos
Extended Permissions: *Site_Name would like to...*		
Message	**Permission**	**Meaning**
manage your events	create_event	create and modify events
	rsvp_event	RSVP to events

Table 2: Message decoder for permissions that are granted in groups. Italic text represents how the permissions are introduced when presented to the user. See Figure 1 for an example.
*Which of the three messages is presented depends on to whom the posts will be visible. This is controlled by the menu in the bottom left of the middle image in Figure 1.

3. USER UNDERSTANDING

The second critical component in effective user control on Facebook Connect is users' comprehension of the messages describing the permissions they're asked to approve. This is especially important given our findings in Section 2 that all write permissions are grouped together and displayed with a single somewhat-vague message. Previous research by Egelman [14] found that 88% of users have a general understanding of Facebook's read permissions dialogues; however, he studied only the read permissions dialogues. To our knowledge this is the first study evaluating comprehension of write permissions. Together with read permissions these make a fascinating natural experiment: are users better able to understand granular (but complicated) read permissions, or simpler (but vaguer) write permissions? To test this and other aspects of user comprehension, we ultimately conducted three studies:

1. One study tested general comprehension of read and write permissions and compared them to each other (see Section 3.2).[6]

2. One study tested how site identity affects interpretation of the write permissions message (see Section 3.3).

3. Our final study tested to see if users understand that they are giving access to data regardless of their profile privacy settings (see Section 3.4).

[6]We decided not to test extended permissions since they are presented similarly to read permissions and are relatively rare (only seven out of the 177 sites requested them).

3.1 Methodology

We conducted our surveys using Amazon Mechanical Turk, a service where workers can be paid to complete simple online tasks. This allowed a large and reasonably diverse response pool for little cost (we paid 10-15 cents per response). (See Section 3.5 for a discussion of Mechanical Turk's limitations.) All of our surveys took the basic format of presenting users with real dialogues that they might see when logging in to a site using Facebook Connect and asking questions about what actions that site may take if they authorize the login.

3.1.1 Pilot studies

We piloted three different methods of testing user comprehension. After verifying that the respondent had previously seen a Facebook Connect login, all pilots began by presenting the respondent with either a read or write permissions message that they might see when using Facebook Connect. No respondents were presented with both to ensure that no one got the two questions mixed up. Respondents were then presented with one of the following three question types:

1. A yes/no question asking if the site would be able to do something if they clicked okay, such as view their photos or update their status.

2. A list of things the site might be able to do if they clicked okay. The user was asked to select all those they thought the site would be able to do.

3. A free response question asking the user to describe what information they thought the site would be able to do if they clicked okay.

The free response question has the advantage of not prompting the user with any ideas that may not have occurred to them otherwise. However, pilots showed that answers to free response questions were frequently too vague to be useful and that respondents may not have put enough thought into their answers. While this may reflect how users pay little attention to permissions messages in real life when they log in to sites, it is not useful for this survey. There was no noticeable difference in responses between the yes/no questions and the multiple-selection questions, so we chose the latter to get results about more permissions.

We also experimented with showing the respondent messages from different sites. There was some indication that the site influenced the responses. For example, people appeared more likely to think photo-oriented sites like Flickr would be able to do photo-oriented things, such as uploading photos. To keep our independent variables separate, we conducted two different surveys. The first survey (Section 3.2) used the site name "Hooli.com" (Hooli is a fake tech company in HBO's *Silicon Valley*). The description of the site given to users was a description of a real site, *Splashscore.com*. This was one of the sites piloted and we determined it had an appropriately general-sounding description and could conceivably need a wide variety of permissions. Our second survey (Section 3.3) was designed to test write permission comprehension across different sites.

3.2 Read vs. write permissions

Our first study tests general comprehension of read and write permissions in such a way that they can be directly compared. For all questions, we used the site name "Hooli.com" to eliminate the site name as a variable. Our tests were designed to evaluate the the following null hypotheses:

Null Hypothesis 1. *Respondents' ability to identify which read permissions they are authorizing is no different than if they were randomly guessing.*

Null Hypothesis 2. *Respondents' ability to identify which write permissions they are authorizing is no different than if they were randomly guessing.*

Null Hypothesis 3. *Respondents' ability to identify which read permissions they are authorizing is no different than their ability to identify which write permissions they are authorizing.*

This survey was taken by 600 Mechanical Turk workers. All were first asked if they had seen a site use Facebook login before—nearly all had. Half of those who had[7] were presented with Facebook's standard write permissions message followed by 13 options of things they might be giving the site permission to do by clicking okay. Eight of the 13 were taken almost directly from the Facebook Connect documentation's permission descriptions [6], so they were all things the site would be able to do (since Facebook gives all write permissions together). The other five were things the site could not do. They were present not to be tested but to eliminate biases due to an aversion to selecting all available options. The 13 options were presented in 4 different orders.

[7]Respondents who had not seen a Facebook Connect login were not given the rest of the survey and were excluded from analysis, but were still paid for their participation.

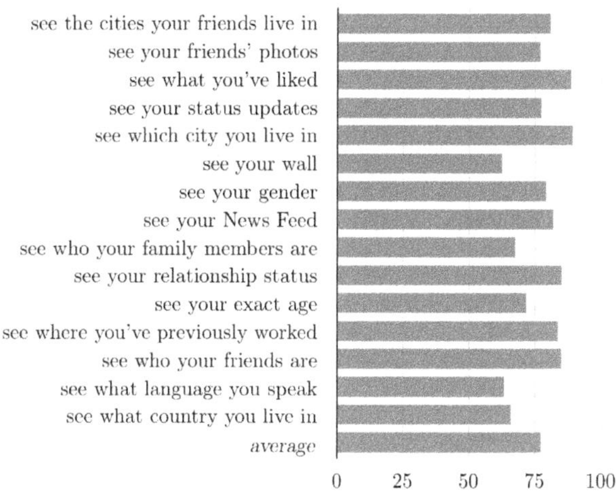

Figure 5: Percentage of people who correctly identified that each read permission would be granted to the site upon authorization.

The other half were presented with read permissions questions. Since read permissions messages vary, we used messages taken from four different real sites with varying numbers of permissions (*Jabong.com*, *Flickr.com*, *Splashscore.com*, and *TripAdvisor.com*). All were renamed "Hooli.com." Each message was followed with eight or nine options for things the site might be able to do. Four or five options were information on a Facebook profile that the site would be able to see. The other four were either things the site could not see or were write or extended permissions.[8] Again, the incorrect answers were only so the respondent did not have to select all options to be correct. There are too many different read permissions to effectively test them all without exhausting the respondents with too many questions, so the ones tested are some of the more common ones.

3.2.1 Read permissions results

Figure 5 illustrates the percentage of people who correctly identified that each permission would be given to the requesting site after they clicked okay.[9] Table 3 lists the numerical percentages as well as the 2-tailed p-value from a binomial test comparing the number of people who correctly identified a permission as being requested to the expected value with random guessing: half of the total number of people who were presented with that permission.

[8]It is difficult to determine what the site cannot see since the user's public profile could contain a lot of information if they have relaxed privacy settings, so only very clear-cut things like seeing private messages could be used.

[9]Only the real permissions being requested are presented. The incorrect answers we made up are not.

Permission	N	Percent Correct	2-tailed p-value
see the cities your friends live in	78	80.77	0.000
see your friends' photos	78	76.92	0.000
see what you've liked	78	88.46	0.000
see your status updates	150	77.33	0.000
see which city you live in	230	89.13	0.000
see your wall	72	62.50	0.044
see your gender	72	79.17	0.000
see your News Feed	72	81.94	0.000
see who your family members are	80	67.50	0.002
see your relationship status	80	85.00	0.000
see your exact age	159	71.70	0.000
see where you've previously worked	80	83.75	0.000
see who your friends are	79	84.81	0.000
see what language you speak	79	63.29	0.024
see what country you live in	79	65.82	0.007

Table 3: p-values for 2-tailed binomial test comparing the number of people who correctly selected each permission to Null Hypothesis 1 of random guessing.

For all tested read permissions, over half of people correctly identified that said permission would be granted based on the message presented. On average, individual permissions were correctly identified 79.72% of the time. This is comparable to Egelman's [14] conclusion that 88% of users understand generally which permissions are being requested.

Null Hypothesis 1, that respondents' ability to identify which read permissions they are authorizing is no different than if they were randomly guessing, can be rejected for all but two permissions with $p < .01$, suggesting that users have a significantly better understanding of which read permissions they are granting than if they were randomly guessing. We can also reject the possibility that users simply marked every survey option as visible to the website: an average of 81.96% of users correctly identified each of the options that would not be visible to the site. Null Hypothesis 1 for each of these options can be rejected with $p < .01$.

Null Hypothesis 1 for "see what language you speak" can be rejected with $p < .03$ and for "see your wall" with $p < .05$. A G-test[10] shows that respondents were worse at identifying "see your wall" than "see your status updates" (which had an accuracy rate roughly equal to the average) with $p < .04$ and a G-test statistic of 4.528. Recall that seeing one's Wall and seeing one's News Feed are both granted by the *read_stream* permission but the message presented to the user says only "News Feed" (see Section 4.1). This may have been the cause of some confusion. Respondents were also worse at identifying "see what language you speak" with $p < .04$ and a G-test statistic of 4.338, but the reason for this is unclear.

[10]The G-test is a likelihood-ratio statistical test of independence applicable in the same cases as a χ^2-test, but with lower approximation error in nearly all cases than the more traditional Pearson's χ^2-test.

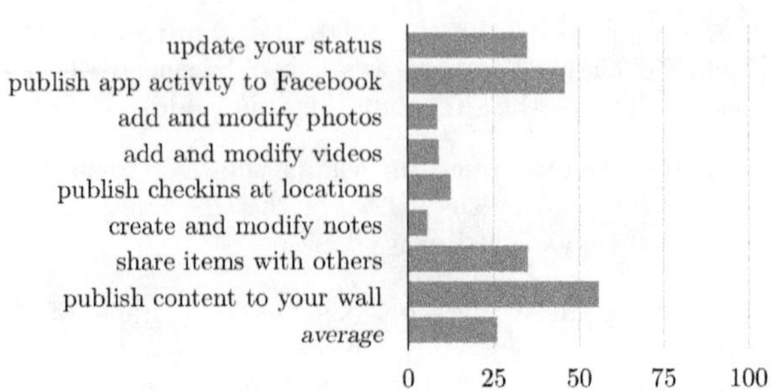

Figure 6: Percentage of people who correctly identified that each permission would be given to the site upon authorization.

Permission	Percent Correct	2-tailed p-value
update your status	34.88	0.000
publish app activity to Facebook	45.85	0.166
add and modify photos	8.64	0.000
add and modify videos	8.97	0.000
publish checkins at locations	12.62	0.000
create and modify notes	5.65	0.000
share items with others	34.88	0.000
publish content to your wall	55.81	0.050

Table 4: p-values for 2-tailed binomial test comparing the number of people who correctly selected each permission to Null Hypothesis 2 of random guessing. $N = 301$ for all permissions.

3.2.2 Write permissions results

Figure 6 illustrates the percentage of people who correctly identified that each permission would be given to the requesting site after they clicked okay. Table 4 lists the numerical percentages as well as the 2-tailed p-value from a binomial test comparing the number of people who correctly identified a permission as being requested to Null Hypothesis 2, that user's understanding would be equivalent to random guessing.

For all permissions except for "publish content to your wall," fewer than half of respondents answered correctly. For all of those except "publish app activity to Facebook," Null Hypothesis 2, that respondents' ability to identify which write permissions they are authorizing is no different than if they were randomly guessing, can be rejected with $p < .01$. That is, for these six permissions, people would have been significantly more likely to correctly identify whether they were granting the permission by randomly guessing.

The p-value for "publish app activity to Facebook" is too high to reject Null Hypothesis 2 with a reasonable level of confidence.

Over half of people correctly identified that the site would be able to "publish content to [their] wall," and Null Hypothesis 2 can be rejected with $p < .05$. People may have a better idea that this permission is being granted than if they were randomly guessing.

Worth noting is that the two permissions people did best with ("publish content to your wall" and "publish app activity to Facebook") are also the vaguest. (These are the *publish_stream* and *publish_actions* permissions that are intended to give nearly all publishing permissions.) Because they are so vague, the fact the more people selected them correctly probably does not mean that they fully understand the specific things the site can post on their profile—they include the functions of the other permissions, which most users were not successful at identifying.

3.2.3 Comparison of read and write permissions

It appears evident at this point that users understand read permissions messages significantly better than they understand write permissions messages: Respondents correctly identified whether a read permission would be granted 79.72% of the time, whereas write permissions were only correctly identified 25.91% of the time.

To evaluate Null Hypothesis 3, that respondents' ability to identify which read permissions they are authorizing is no different than their ability to identify which write permissions they are authorizing, we assigned a ranking to each respondent based on the percentage of permissions they correctly identified[11] and separated them into two groups, one for those asked about read permissions and one for those asked about write permissions. A Mann-Whitney U test of these two groups allows us to reject Null Hypothesis 3 with $p < 0.001$ and a test statistic of $U = 9163$.

3.3 Influence of relying site

As previously mentioned, our pilot surveys indicated that the site identity may influence how people interpret the write permissions message. We performed a separate survey with 300 Mechanical Turk workers to test this. The format of the survey was identical to the write permissions questions in the first survey and we provided the same options for the user to select. However, instead of using "Hooli.com" as the website in question, one third of respondents were presented with *Flickr.com* (a photo and video sharing site), one third with *TripAdvisor.com* (a travel site), and one third with *iFlikeU.com* (an anonymous messaging site). (Since there is only one write permissions message, the message presented to the user in all cases was identical aside from the site name and description.)

The results of this survey can be statistically analyzed with a G-test to see if the number of respondents who thought each permission would be granted varied across the four sites (the three mentioned here plus the data from "Hooli.com" from the first survey). Our null hypothesis is:

Null Hypothesis 4. *The relying site's identity does not affect how respondents interpret a requested permission.*

3.3.1 Results

Figure 7 illustrates the percentage of people who correctly identified that each permission would be given to each site after they clicked okay. Table 5 lists the numerical percentages as well as the p-values from a G-test comparing the variation in number of correct selections for each permission across all four sites.

For "publish app activity to Facebook," "add and modify photos," "add and modify videos," and "publish checkins at

[11]This counts only the real permissions and not the incorrect options since those were artificially created.

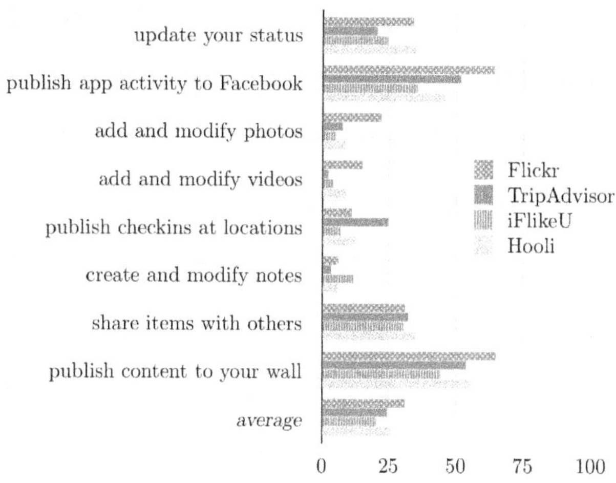

Figure 7: Percentage of people who correctly identified that each permission would be given to the site upon authorization for four sites.

locations," Null Hypothesis 4, that the relying site's identity does not affect how respondents interpret a requested permission, can be rejected with $p < .01$. More respondents thought Flickr would be able to add and modify photos and videos compared to other sites, which is reasonable since it is a photo and video sharing site. Likewise, many more people thought that TripAdvisor would be able to publish checkins at locations—a logical thing for a travel site to do.

Null Hypothesis 4 can be rejected for "update your status" with $p < .04$ and "publish content to your wall" with $p < .05$. It cannot be rejected for "share items with others" nor "create and modify notes" with a reasonable level of confidence.

3.4 Influence of privacy settings

In one pilot survey of the free response format, a respondent stated that the site would gain access to only a limited number of permissions because their Facebook settings prevented them from accessing the rest. This suggests a lack of understanding of how the read permissions work: A site can access nearly everything that is public with only the *public_profile* permission [9]. By granting the site additional permissions, a user is giving the site permission to access that information regardless of the user's privacy settings. Using the test site, we confirmed that we could see all user photo albums regardless of their privacy settings with the *user_photos* permission.

We surveyed 100 additional Mechanical Turk respondents to see if this confusion was widespread. The survey presented the user with the permission message for *Imgur.com*, which requests the *user_photos* permission. Users were asked to identify which photo albums Imgur would be able to see if they clicked okay. The options were those marked as visible to the public, those marked as visible to friends, and those marked as visible to only them (the correct answer is all three).

Our null hypothesis in this experiment is:

Null Hypothesis 5. *Respondents are equally likely to indicate that data can be read regardless of its privacy setting.*

Permission	Percent Correct				G-test statistic	p-value
	Flickr ($N = 100$)	TripAdvisor ($N = 93$)	iFlikeU ($N = 102$)	Hooli ($N = 301$)		
update your status	34	20.43	24.51	34.88	8.662	0.034
publish app activity to Facebook	64	51.61	35.29	45.85	16.733	0.001
add and modify photos	22	7.53	4.90	8.64	15.185	0.002
add and modify videos	15	2.15	3.92	8.97	11.783	0.008
publish checkins at locations	11	24.73	6.86	12.62	10.937	0.006
create and modify notes	6	3.23	11.76	5.65	4.783	0.188
share items with others	31	32.26	30.39	34.88	0.706	0.872
publish content to your wall	65	53.76	44.12	55.81	8.208	0.042

Table 5: p-values for G-test comparing the number of people who correctly selected each permission across four sites to Null Hypothesis 4 of no difference between sites.

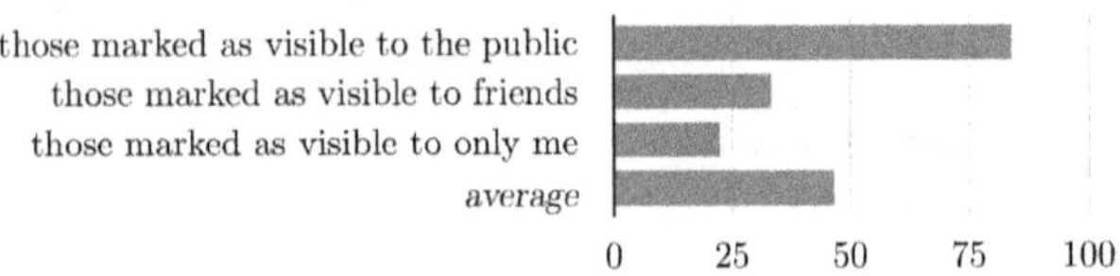

Figure 8: Percentage of people who correctly identified that Imgur.com would be able to see their photo albums of each privacy level upon authorization.

3.4.1 Results

Figure 8 illustrates the percentage of people who correctly identified that Imgur.com would be able to see their photo albums with various privacy settings if they clicked okay. It appears people are generally aware that they are giving access to their photo albums that are marked as public. However, they are generally unaware that they are also giving access to their photo albums that are marked as visible to their friends or only to themselves.

Using a G-test with three degrees of freedom to compare all three test conditions, Null Hypothesis 5, that respondents are equally likely to indicate that data can be read regardless of its privacy setting, can be rejected with $p < .001$ based on a G-test statistic of 86.31. Comparing each pair of conditions in turn using a G-test with two degrees of freedom, we can conclude with $p < .001$ that participants were significantly more likely to believe photos marked "visible to the public" could be read than either photos marked "visible to friends" or "visible to only me". However, we cannot conclude with high confidence ($p \approx .12$) that participants were significantly more likely to believe photos marked "visible to friends" could be read than photos marked "visible to only me". Thus we can reject Null Hypothesis 5 in general and conclude that users do believe privacy settings impact visibility of data to third-party sites, we cannot conclude if the specific privacy settings (visible to friends or only to the user) had a significant impact on user understanding.

Although our first set of surveys and Egelman's study [14] indicated that read permissions are understood decently well, this study suggests that these results may not actually be entirely representative of user understanding: although people know which types of information they are granting access to, most do not realize they are giving access to that information even if they have marked it with a privacy level other than public.

3.5 Limitations

There are several possible limitations to our surveys:

- As discussed previously, by giving respondents several options to select we suggested possible things the site could do that may not have occurred to them otherwise. In addition, in order to respond to our questions they may have paid more attention to the permissions dialogues than they normally would have. As a result, our survey may indicate that users are more aware of what permissions are being requested than they are in practice.
- If read and write permissions are fundamentally different in some non-obvious way, it may be invalid to compare understanding of read permissions to understanding of write permissions. It is possible that users would understand write permissions even more poorly if they were presented granularly rather than all-or-nothing.
- There may be some demographic bias in using Mechanical Turk to collect responses. We did not collect demographic information from respondents although we did restrict respondents to the United States (this was the only restriction we placed on respondents). Our use of Mechanical Turk is justified by previous research finding that "[Mechanical Turk] participants produced reliable results that are consistent with previous decision-making research" [16]. The most relevant concern they raise is of respondents not paying enough attention and becoming fatigued in longer surveys; the short length of our surveys hopefully ameliorated that to some degree. In addition, users are known to pay little attention to permissions messages in practice [14].
- When asking users which permissions were being granted, we had to make up some fake options so users did not have to select every option to be correct. If we did a poor job, this could have influenced results by distracting or unsettling users. We did not count these made up permissions in our statistical analysis for this reason.

4. DISCUSSION

Our study indicates that users have a decent understanding of read permissions messages but a significantly worse understanding of write permissions messages. As discussed in Section 2.5, Facebook claims that all-or-nothing write permissions are easier for the user to understand. However, comparison with the very granular read permissions suggests that users understand specific, distinct permissions better.

We also observe that grouped permissions cause confusion for developers who may receive more permissions than intended due to grouping of permissions. This appears contrary to Facebook's stated advice to developers that they should "only ask for the permissions that are essential to an app [or site]" [7]. Facebook's own research has demonstrated that "the more permissions an app requests, the less likely it is that people will use Facebook to log into [that] app"[7]. But because Facebook Connect often grants more permissions than the developer requested (even just by always granting *public_profile* and *user_friends*), the developer may have no choice but to receive unnecessary permissions.

We consider several possible explanations for why the system may be architected this way.

4.1 Evolution over time

Some of our findings around the permissions API appear likely to be artifacts of the API's evolution, many of which appear harmless. For example, two permissions for reading an email address exist (*email* and *contact_email*) and grouping them seems sensible.

It appears that the reason that all write permissions are presented together is that Facebook is gradually eliminating the distinction between different types of publishing under the hood. The description in the documentation for *publish_actions* is "publish my app activity to Facebook" and the description for *publish_stream* is "publish content to my Wall" [6]. These are quite vague, and seem as though they could encompass nearly anything. A blog post from a Facebook employee [12] helps explain these permissions: They are essentially the same thing (and are being merged into one) and allow a site to do any type of publishing to Facebook. The post mentions that they can be used to upload a photo, which one may have suspected required the *photo_upload* permission. Another post from a Facebook employee mentions that developers should only request *publish_actions* because it encompasses all other write permissions in an effort to "simplify the model" [26]. Furthermore, Facebook's Graph API lists *publish_actions* as the permission needed for all API calls that involve publishing [5].

This transition towards only one type of publishing is visible to anyone who has used Facebook for several years: updating one's status and uploading a photo used to be distinct actions, but now they are both performed by creating a post on one's Timeline. Perhaps at one point the six granular write permissions (*create_note*, *upload_photos*, *upload_videos*, *publish_checkins*, *share_item*, *status_update*) were the only write permissions. The read and extended permissions that are presented in groups may stem from similar changes in Facebook's structure and it may no longer be possible to separate them.

It is understandable that changes in the structure of Facebook necessitate changes in the Facebook Connect API to keep it simple and consistent. However, our results suggest user control may significantly harmed for the sake of simplicity. This threat does not appear purely academic, as there are many malicious Facebook apps that abuse the permissions they are given [13, 20].

4.2 Privacy salience

It is also possible that Facebook has evolved towards having a vague write permissions message as a strategy to decrease *privacy salience* [10]. If users thought too many permissions were being granted, they may not use the app or the Facebook Connect platform in general. A vague message allows developers to receive more permissions without losing users.

Evidence that this may be Facebook's intention can be seen by comparing the current write permissions messages to those from the previous implementation of Facebook Connect. As mentioned previously, 26 of the 203 websites we crawled used an older implementation. Table 6 presents a sampling of the messages we saw. These messages may be misleading since they provide examples of what the site can post based on the specific site even though all sites in the table request only *publish_actions*. However, these messages do distinctly identify several things the sites can post, unlike the vague messages in the current implementation. Facebook's choice to eliminate these descriptions may indicate an attempt to be less clear about what permissions are actually being granted.

By itself, limiting privacy salience cannot be a complete explanation because read permissions remain relatively detailed. It may be that read permissions are less concerning to users as write permissions can affect the user's profile on Facebook itself, so Facebook is less motivated to obscure them. Alternatively, it may be the case that read permissions are in fact more sensitive, since data cannot be un-read whereas unwanted posts from a third-party can be deleted. In this case, it may be that Facebook has decided that its more important to clearly indicate read permissions up front, whereas it isn't worth concerning users with detailed write permissions since posts can be deleted later.

Site	Write Permissions Message
Starpires.com	This app may post on your behalf, including status updates, photos and more.
PioneerLegends.com	This app may post on your behalf, including collections you completed, miles you collected and more.
Stratego.com	This app may post on your behalf, including achievements you earned and more.
OpenShuffle.com	This app may post on your behalf, including your high scores and more.
Fupa.com	This app may post on your behalf, including games you played and more.

Table 6: Write permissions messages from sites using an older version of Facebook Connect. All sites are gaming sites. The only write permission requested is *publish_actions*.

4.3 Ineffectiveness of user choice

It is possible that write messages are vague because users are unable to completely understand them (or simply do not pay attention to them [14]), so Facebook has decided it is better off protecting user privacy by policing developers.

Facebook has publicly attempted to address how general write permissions are by placing responsibility on the developer. The aforementioned Facebook blog post explaining the *publish_stream* and *publish_actions* permissions [12] states that since anything can be shared, "it will continue to be the developer's responsibility to make it clear to the user what content will be shared back to Facebook." Facebook's policy was updated to read: "If a user grants [the developer] a publishing permission, actions [the developer takes] on the user's behalf must be expected by the user and consistent with the user's actions within [the] app." This is especially important since our survey showed that users' interpretation of the write permissions message is influenced by the identity of the site even though there is no difference in the permissions being granted. As of the time of this writing, however, this is no longer mentioned in the Facebook policy [8].

5. FUTURE AREAS FOR RESEARCH

This research could be extended in a number of directions.

- The results of our survey testing whether users understand that sites are getting access to their information even if it is marked as private (see Figure 8) indicate that there is room for more research in the area. This should be tested with a variety of different permissions. One could also experiment with ways to make it clear to the user that all of their information is being shared, regardless of the privacy settings.

- We previously mentioned that our survey included options of things the sites could not actually do so the respondent would not have to select all options to be correct. However, many people selected these fake options. One could research what permissions users think are being requested beyond what is actually being requested. This is an important area of research because people may be unwilling to use the SSO service if they think too many permissions are being given.

- It is clear that users do not understand the full range of write permissions being requested. However, Egelman [14] determined that users make their decision to use Facebook Connect or not before they see the permissions requested. Egelman only tested read permissions, though. A similar study could see how the presence of write permissions affects users' decisions to use Facebook Connect.

- We observed that users understand the granular read permissions better than the single write permission. One could test whether granular write permissions are in fact more clear to users than the current system.

6. RELATED WORK

Many researchers have studied the security and permissions systems of various apps[12] and SSO systems. Sun and Beznosov [23] uncovered vulnerabilities in many major OAuth SSO implementations. Chaabane et al. [11] and Huber et al. [17] identified information leaks in Facebook and RenRen apps. There have also been several studies of what permissions sites request, such as Frank et al.'s study in which Facebook apps were grouped into categories based on the permissions they request [15].

Some studies have tested user comprehension of SSO systems as well. A 2011 audit of Facebook Ireland looked at, among other things, how clearly the Facebook app system is presented to users. It also states that it "is not possible for an application to access personal data over and above that to which an individual gives their consent or enabled by the relevant settings"—that is, Facebook's permissions do appropriately limit what data an app can access [2].

Sun et al. studied user understanding of the authentication process in general—for example, whether users understood that the site they are logging in to cannot see the password for the identity provider (Facebook, Google, etc.) [25]. The study most directly related to ours is Egelman [14], which studied whether users were willing to use Facebook Connect and how well they understand (and how much they pay attention to) the permissions messages. Egelman concluded that 88% of users have a general understanding that their profile information will be shared with the site they are logging in to, but that they typically do not pay attention to the specifics of the dialogues and do not make their decision whether to use Facebook Connect based on which permissions are being requested.

Our study differs from previous studies by determining what specific permissions correspond to the messages presented to the user and by evaluating user comprehension of these permissions. This lets us answer most precisely whether users understand exactly what information they are sharing by using Facebook Connect. In addition, Egelman only looked at read permissions. We found that write permissions are much more confusing to users.

7. CONCLUDING REMARKS

To maximize security and to ensure users feel comfortable using Facebook Connect, developers should minimize the number of permissions they request and the permissions should be presented to the user as clearly as possible. On both fronts, Facebook Connect could be improved.

When a developer designs their site to request certain permissions through Facebook Connect, the Facebook Connect system may translate certain permissions into broader groups of permissions that will all be granted if the user authorizes the site to access their profile. This may force users to give unnecessary permissions to a site in order to log in.

The messages presented to the user for read permissions are reasonably clear—our survey showed that a majority of users understand what data they are providing access to. However, many users are unaware that they are providing access even if this information is marked as private.

Write permissions, however, are much less clear. Facebook has simplified the write permissions process so that every site either gets all write permissions or none. Our survey shows that users do not understand the many things a site will be able to do to their profile if they authorize the vague message stating that the site "would like to post to Facebook for you." In addition, users' interpretations of this message vary depending on the identity of the site they are logging in to although this actually has no impact on the permissions granted. Given the relative success with which

[12]The Facebook Connect SSO system uses the same system as native Facebook apps—creating a Facebook login on a website requires creating a Facebook app [4].

users were able to identify the more distinct and well-defined read permissions, it appears users might actually understand write permissions better if they were split up.

On April 30, 2014 Facebook announced an update to their Facebook Login system to be rolled out over the following months that allows users to reject individual permissions or log in anonymously [22]. While this is a big step forward, it appears there is still only one publishing permission and it is presented with the same vague message that our survey respondents had trouble understanding. However, it does provide even more specific details about read permissions.

8. ACKNOWLEDGMENTS

Thanks to Arvind Narayanan for starting us on this research path. Thanks to Steven Englehardt, Dillon Reisman, Pete Zimmerman, and Christian Eubank for setting us up with the CITP's web crawling infrastructure. Steven originally discovering permissions in the hidden HTML input elements. Thanks to Markus Huber for providing us with the AppInspect dataset [17].

9. REFERENCES

[1] Personal correspondence with Facebook Security representative (Neal), April 2014.

[2] Report of Data Protection Audit of Facebook Ireland, December 2011.

[3] Facebook Developer Reference—Facebook Login. `https://developers.facebook.com/docs/facebook-login/`, 2014.

[4] Facebook Developer Reference—Getting Started with Custom Stories. `https://developers.facebook.com/docs/opengraph/getting-started/`, 2014.

[5] Facebook Developer Reference—Graph API Reference. `https://developers.facebook.com/docs/graph-api/reference/`, 2014.

[6] Facebook Developer Reference—Permissions. `https://developers.facebook.com/docs/reference/fql/permissions/`, 2014.

[7] Facebook Developer Reference—Permissions with Facebook Login. `https://developers.facebook.com/docs/facebook-login/permissions`, 2014.

[8] Facebook Developer Reference—Platform Policy. `https://developers.facebook.com/policy/`, 2014.

[9] Facebook Developer Reference—Privacy for Apps & Websites. `https://www.facebook.com/help/403786193017893`, 2014.

[10] J. Bonneau and S. Preibusch. The Privacy Jungle: On the Market for Privacy in Social Networks. In *WEIS '09: Proceedings of the 8th Workshop on the Economics of Information Security*, June 2009.

[11] A. Chaabane, Y. Ding, R. Dey, M. A. Kaafar, and K. W. Ross. A Closer Look at Third-Party OSN Applications: Are They Leaking Your Personal Information? In *Passive and Active Measurement Conference (2014)*, Los Angeles, March 2014. Springer.

[12] L. Chen. Streamlining publish_stream and publish_actions permissions. Facebook Blog, April 2012.

[13] P. H. Chia, Y. Yamamoto, and N. Asokan. Is This App Safe?: A Large Scale Study on Application Permissions and Risk Signals. In *WWW '12 Proceedings of the 21st International Conference on the World Wide Web*. ACM, April 2012.

[14] S. Egelman. My profile is my password, verify me!: The privacy/convenience tradeoff of Facebook Connect. In *CHI '13 Proceedings of the SIGCHI Conference on Human Factors in Computing Systems*. ACM, 2013.

[15] M. Frank, B. Dong, A. P. Felt, and D. Song. Mining Permission Request Patterns from Android and Facebook Applications. In *The 12th IEEE International Conference on Data Mining*. IEEE, 2012.

[16] J. K. Goodman, C. E. Cryder, and A. Cheema. Data Collection in a Flat World: The Strengths and Weaknesses of Mechanical Turk Samples. *Behavioral Decision Making*, 26(3):213–224, 2013.

[17] M. Huber, M. Mulazzani, S. Schrittwieser, and E. Weippl. AppInspect: Large-scale Evaluation of Social Networking Apps. In *COSN '13 Proceedings of the First ACM Conference on Online Social Networks*. ACM, 2013.

[18] D. Morin. Announcing Facebook Connect. Facebook Blog, May 2008.

[19] H. Nissenbaum. Privacy as contextual integrity. *Washington Law Review*, 79, 2004.

[20] M. S. Rahman, T.-K. Huang, H. V. Madhy, and M. Faloutsos. FRAppE: Detecting Malicious Facebook Applications. In *CoNEXT '12 Proceedings of the 8th International Conference on Emerging Networking Experiments and Technologies*. ACM, 2012.

[21] P. Sovis, F. Kohlar, and J. Schwenk. Security Analysis of OpenID. In *Securing Electronic Business Processes - Highlights of the Information Security Solutions Europe 2010 Conference*, 2010.

[22] J. Spehar. The New Facebook Login and Graph API 2.0. Facebook Blog, April 2014.

[23] S.-T. Sun and K. Beznosov. The Devil is in the (Implementation) Details: An Empirical Analysis of OAuth SSO Systems. In *Proceedings of ACM Conference on Computer and Communications Security '12*. LERSSE, October 2012.

[24] S.-T. Sun, Y. Boshmaf, K. Hawkey, and K. Beznosov. A Billion Keys, but Few Locks: The Crisis of Web Single Sign-On. In *NSPW '10: Proceedings of the 2010 New Security Paradigms Workshop*. ACM, 2010.

[25] S.-T. Sun, E. Pospisil, I. Muslukhov, N. Dindar, K. Hawkey, and K. Beznosov. Investigating User's Perspective of Web Single Sign-On: Conceptual Gaps, Alternative Design and Acceptance Model. *ACM Transactions on Internet Technology*, 2013.

[26] A. Wyler. Providing people greater clarity and control. Facebook Blog, December 2012.

APPENDIX

A. CORRESPONDENCE WITH FACEBOOK SECURITY

As mentioned in Section 2.5, we sent a security bug report to Facebook reporting that we could use the *publish_actions* permission after requesting any other write permission (see Section 2.3). Below is the full correspondence with Facebook Security [1].

Initial bug report
Description and Impact:
I can design a site with Facebook Connect that publishes a story with the 'publish_actions' permission. However, if I request any other write/publishing permission, such as 'create_note', I can still use the 'publish_actions' permission and publish the story. I believe this is a vulnerability because applications may be receiving more capability than they believe they are requesting.
Reproduction Instructions / Proof of Concept:

1. I followed the Facebook documentation instructions to create a story with the publish_actions permission: https://developers.facebook.com/docs/opengraph/getting-started/
2. If I replace publish_actions in data-scope with any other write permission, including create_note, I can still publish the story. (If I replace it with a read permission such as email I cannot.)

Facebook Security's response
Thanks for writing in. Can you send in some screenshots of the dialogue you see when requesting the different permissions? I'm curious to see if the wording changes between the two.

Our response
Below are screenshots of the two messages presented whether I request create_note or publish_actions. *[screenshots not shown here, roughly equivalent to Figure 1, center image]*

The HTML for these messages has three hidden input elements named read, write, and extended. The permissions requested appear in their value fields. However, if I request any of the 8 write permissions (publish_actions, publish_stream, status_update, video_upload, photo_upload, share_item, create_note, or publish_checkins), all 8 appear in the value of the input element named write. I've been researching this for a class project at Princeton University and I've confirmed that this is true on 73 of 73 different websites that request write permissions. The only two write permissions messages between the 73 sites are "App_Name would like to post to Facebook for you" and "App_Name would like to post publicly to Facebook for you." The presence of "publicly" is just determined by the selection on the menu on the bottom left of the message page (second screenshot), not by the permissions being requested.

Facebook Security's response
I'll confirm with the Platform team, but I believe this is intentional behavior: as you noted, while in the URL you're requesting one scope we actually translate them to a broader set of scopes which are easier for users to understand.

Facebook Security's followup
I just confirmed with our Platform team that this behavior is by design.

Our response
Ok, thanks for looking into that. Is there a reason you do that for the write permissions but not for read or extended permissions?

Facebook Security's response
The Platform team made this change to simplify the experience for developers and for users. My guess would be that generally, write permissions are more similar (ie: creating a note versus creating a video versus posting all are ways to create content on the site that are not very different) whereas read permissions are more distinct (ie: an app which can view your friends does not necessarily need to view your relationships unless major functionality changes).
[End of correspondence]

The Socio-monetary Incentives of Online Social Network Malware Campaigns

Ting-Kai Huang
Google
Mountain View, CA
tingkaih@google.com

Bruno Ribeiro
Carnegie Mellon University
Pittsburgh, PA
ribeiro@cs.cmu.edu

Harsha V. Madhyastha
University of California Riverside
Riverside, CA
harsha@cs.ucr.edu

Michalis Faloutsos
University of New Mexico
Albuquerque, NM
michalis@cs.unm.edu

ABSTRACT

Online social networks (OSNs) offer a rich medium of malware propagation. Unlike other forms of malware, OSN malware campaigns direct users to malicious websites that hijack their accounts, posting malicious messages on their behalf with the intent of luring their friends to the malicious website, thus triggering word-of-mouth infections that cascade through the network compromising thousands of accounts. *But how are OSN users lured to click on the malicious links?* In this work, we monitor 3.5 million Facebook accounts and explore the role of pure monetary, social, and combined socio-monetary psychological incentives in OSN malware campaigns. Among other findings we see that the majority of the malware campaigns rely on pure social incentives. However, we also observe that malware campaigns using socio-monetary incentives infect more accounts and last longer than campaigns with pure monetary or social incentives. The latter suggests the efficiency of an epidemic tactic surprisingly similar to the mechanism used by biological pathogens to cope with diverse gene pools.

Categories and Subject Descriptors

H.1.2 [**Information Systems**]: User/Machine Systems—*Human factors*

General Terms

Human Factors, Measurement

Keywords

OSN Malware; Social Incentives; Monetary Incentives; Labor Markets

COSN'14, October 1–2, 2014, Dublin, Ireland.

http://dx.doi.org/10.1145/2660460.2660478.

1. INTRODUCTION

In 1949 von Neumann first suggested the possibility of creating self-reproducing computer programs [42]. Thirty-five years later Cohen wrote one of the first computer malwares, which he named a *computer virus* [7]. Since then, the connection between computer malware and biological viruses has captivated the imagination of both researchers and the general public [10, 11, 12, 36], and the manner in which malware interacts with people and computers has evolved. The inception of e-mail in the 60's created a new medium for malware developers [5, 15, 30].

Today, online social networks (OSNs) offer another new medium for malware propagation that, as shown in this and some of other of our recent studies [19, 33], is profoundly changing the face of malware. In OSN malware, OSN users are lured into visiting malicious websites containing *click-jacking* attacks[1] or into installing malicious in-OSN apps (e.g., Facebook apps). Once infected, the victim is impersonated in the social network, unknowingly exposing his or her friends to the same campaign through bogus direct messages or broadcast posts, creating a word of mouth infection that cascades through the network [19, 33]. One of the key features of OSN malware (a.k.a. socware [19, 33]) is leveraging on the perceived "endorsement" of hijacked users from the in the eyes of that user's friends. OSN malware is more than just a nuisance, it enables identity theft and cybercrime with several reported cases resulting in financial losses for the victims [20, 35].

But how are OSN users lured to click on these malicious links in the first place? We leverage on our prior work on detecting malware posts through a combination of keywords, anomalous user behavior, and topological anomalies [19, 33] to study how OSN malware exploits psychological incentives. Following Heyman and Ariely [17] classification of behavioral incentives in labor markets, we divide incentives into *monetary*, *social*, and *socio-monetary* (the latter is a combination of monetary and social incentives). These social and monetary incentives are, for instance, a pure monetary posts that promises a "free iPad"; pure social posts related to improving or checking your social status such as "Can you beat me in this game ⟨*link*⟩?" and "OMG check

[1]Clickjacking and other attack mechanisms are described in Huang et al. [19]

if a friend has deleted you! Click ⟨*here*⟩, it works!", or of shared curiosity "This is shocking ⟨*link*⟩!"; and finally (socio-monetary) a combination of social and monetary incentives (e.g., a friend's challenge with the promise of a free iPad if you win).

Contributions

One of the main contributions of this work is to study the impact of distinct socio-monetary incentives in the size and duration of malware campaigns[2], covering the posts of nearly 3.5 million Facebook users collected over ten months between July 2011 and April 2012. With the help of MyPageKeeper malware post detection heuristics [19, 33] and 226 Mechanical Turk [3] volunteers we classify thousands of unique Facebook posts. We note, however, that our monitoring is restricted to both users that installed MyPageKeeper and the posts of their friends that are visible to these users. But while we are limited to users of one online social network (Facebook) that volunteer to have their accounts protected by MyPageKeeper, the data collected from this viewpoint (of 3.5 million users) is of great interest. Aside from truly random monitoring without user consent, data collection from volunteers is prone to unknown biases.

We observe that 67% of the malware campaigns in our dataset use pure social incentives. Interestingly, and despite Heyman and Ariely's observations that subjects exposed to socio-monetary incentives act like subjects exposed to monetary incentives [17], we observe that combined socio-monetary incentives are more effective – in fact, stochastically dominant with respect to number of infected users and campaign durations – than campaigns using pure social or pure monetary incentives. For instance, malware campaigns with socio-monetary incentives last on average 136% longer than pure monetary and pure social campaigns.

Relation to Biological Pathogens

A simple explanation for the effectiveness of combined socio-monetary incentives is a type of percolation effect observed in plant pathogen epidemics over mixed crops [28, 46]. Through simulations we show that even if the susceptibility to combined incentives is less than that of any one specialized incentive, combining incentives provide a tremendous advantage to percolate over the network. On Facebook the mix is the likely propensity of distinct users to be more attracted to either monetary or social incentives. While there are other plausible explanations to why campaigns with socio-monetary incentives infect more users and last longer than campaigns with pure incentives (e.g., posts with socio-monetary incentives could be more difficult to classify as spam), the percolation effect described does not need extra (unverifiable) assumptions.

Outline

This work is organized as follows. Section 2 presents the necessary background to understand Facebook malware and their incentives. Section 3 presents the related work. Section 4 introduces our dataset, the malware incentives together, and the definitions used throughout this work. Section 5 shows how we classified malware posts. Section 6 reports statistics of the observed incentives at the campaign level. Section 7 shows that simulations of epidemics on real OSN topologies using mixed incentives can indeed outperform pure incentives, even if mixed incentives are not as effective than pure incentives in infecting to the subpopulation of individuals susceptible to the pure incentive. Finally, Section 8 discusses our results and future work.

[2]Malware campaigns are precisely defined in Section 4 but can be roughly thought as the spread of a malware associated with a specific website.

2. PRELIMINARIES

Facebook is the largest online social network ever created in the Internet's short history. With over 1.11 billion active users as of March 2013 [9], Facebook is a prime source of online social network data. Through the analysis of posts of over 3.5 million Facebook users collected over ten months, we observe a new generation of computer malware that relies heavily on two factors to spread through word of mouth: (a) incentive mechanisms provided by the post and (b) people's cognitive capacity to distinguish between a legitimate request from a friend and a bogus request from an infected friend. Other security factors are also known to play a role in security threats [4, 18, 25, 45], such as users' belief that they are less at risk than others, the fact that privacy and security are abstract concepts, and that it is hard for non-experts to judge risk. We leave the analysis of the analysis of these other security factors as future work, so we can instead focus our analysis on the role of socio-monetary incentives.

A representative example of the kind of incentive used on Facebook malware campaigns[3] is the campaign whose posts include the text "*OMG check if a friend has deleted you! Click ⟨here⟩, it works!*". This campaign simultaneously exploits the reader's incentive to know his or her social status in the group and the credibility (and *social capital* [37]) of the impersonated victim. The latter is remarkably different from messages seen in e-mail spam, an effect broadly felt on the use of keywords. For instance, "viagra" and "pills" are popular keywords in e-mail spam, but out of the hundreds of thousands of malicious posts we collected on Facebook, not a single one contains these keywords [33].

Once the post appears legitimate to the victim, a combination of the incentives in the post and the victim's susceptibility to the incentive drive the victim's decision as to whether or not to click on the malicious link. The data shows that social incentives often target the victim's social capital – increasing one's social capital is known as one of the reasons why people join online social networks [37] – or the victim's social insecurities about his or her social status in their social group.

3. RELATED WORK

While we are unaware of other works analyzing the impact of social and monetary incentives on online social network cascades, there is a rich literature on both percolation phenomena and computer viruses. Recent work on percolation phenomena over interdependent networks shows that a virus or a failure spreading over distinct but interconnected networks has a lower critical threshold than the same phenomenon spreading over a single network [14, 23, 43].

The connection between traditional computer viruses and biological pathogens has been extensively studied in the lit-

[3]Facebook actively combats malware alongside with third party application such as MyPageKeeper, the application we used to collect the data used in this study [19].

erature [7, 12, 36]. But these works do not consider the true networked nature of the infection. In the last decade there has been great interest in the connection between computer viruses and networks (e.g. [13, 32, 38]) but these works tend to look at worms and computer viruses that do not depend on human intervention to spread.

The role of diverse gene pools in the containment of biological pathogens has been studied since the early 70s [2, 6, 39]. Recent works in the literature make the connection between diversity of types and computer viruses. For instance, recently Wang et al. [44] conjectured that the spreading of viruses on mobile phones was hindered by the existence of two distinct popular (but incompatible) smartphone platforms. Even more recently, Newell et al. [29] proposed the use of a diverse set of network routers with distinct software (and possibly distinct vulnerabilities) as a way to deter malicious attacks that could compromise the network. The above works also disregard incentives and the effect of human intervention on the infection process. In business environments Yves et al. [8] study how to mitigate social engineering or insider attacks by using different administrative personnel.

In contrast to the above works, we study online social network malware that relies on user intervention to spread. Unlike worms and similar computer viruses, OSN malware must provide incentives to convince a user to perform actions that allow the malware to hijack that user's account. We analyze the incentives used by malware developers classifying these as social and monetary. Interestingly, we observe that malware campaigns with both monetary and social incentive are able to last longer and infect more users.

Adamic et. al. [22] study the evolution of memes of Facebook. They found that memes were copied or mutated by people during transmission. In contrast, our work focus on how malware developers conduct their malware campaigns with different incentives and how these incentives affect the duration and the number of infected users. Note that unlike Adamic et. al., victims of OSN malware often do not spread it willingly. The textual changes observed in the posts of a single malware campaign are overwhelmingly for text obfuscation purposes (likely to fool Facebook's malware detection tools). In this work we classify campaigns by the URL used in the attack rather than the text of the post as to avoid problems with obfuscation (in the following section we provide more details about our methodology).

4. DATASET AND DEFINITIONS

In this section, we describe some of the definitions used throughout this work. After presenting the definitions, we introduce our dataset.

Definitions. A *post* is a broadcast message that a Facebook user writes on her *timeline* (a.k.a. *wall*) that can be seen by all of her friends (modulo Facebook's post recommendation algorithm and privacy filters that users may have in place). We consider a *post text* to be the collection of all texts of posts that show small Levenshtein distance [24]. For instance, "Click here and win an iPad2" and "Click here and win an iPhone5" are considered posts with identical post text. A *campaign* is defined as the set of Facebook posts with the same unique URL, i.e., we are aggregating posts according to the website they advertise. Using URLs to fingerprint a campaign avoids the caveats of text-based classification or mutating post text. Some URLs are shortened using URL shortening services such as goo.gl and bit.ly. However, Huang et al. [19] shows that assigning posts to ' campaigns based on their URLs is similar to aggregating campaigns by the address of the final landing webpage.

Observation period	Jul'11–Apr'12
Number of observed posts with links	111 million
Number of malicious posts	164,304
Number of posts with text content	120,455
Number of campaigns with text	3,110

Table 1: Dataset summary.

A single post may contain one or more distinct incentives. For instance, 22.52% of the posts contain both social and monetary incentives. These posts are *combined socio-monetary incentive* posts. Otherwise the post has a *single incentive*. Our classification method is designed to find combined social and monetary incentives. A campaign may have both social and monetary incentives in two forms. Either the campaign sends messages with combined social and monetary incentives, or it uses two or more posts containing different incentives.

MyPageKeeper Summary: MyPageKeeper evaluates every URL that it sees on any user's Wall or News Feed to determine if the URL points to OSN malware. MyPageKeeper classifies a URL as malware if it points to a web page that 1) is known to spread malware, 2) attempts to "phish" for personal information, 3) requests the user to carry out tasks (e.g., fill out surveys) that profit the owner of the website, 4) promises false rewards, or 5) attempts to entice the user to artificially inflate the reputation of the page (e.g., forcing the user to "Like" the page to access a false reward). MyPageKeeper evaluates each URL using a classifier which leverages on hand-annotated and examples and post features that take into account the social reaction (context) of posts associated with the URL. For any particular URL, the features used by the classifier are obtained by combining information from all posts (seen across users) containing that URL. Example features used by MyPageKeeper's classifier include the similarity of text messages across posts and the number of comments and Likes on those posts. MyPageKeeper has false positive and false negative rates of 0.005% and 3%, respectively. For more details about MyPageKeeper's implementation and accuracy, please see Rahman et al. [33].

Datasets. Our data was collected through our MyPageKeeper Facebook app [1] from July 2011 to April 2012. We monitored the activity of 3.5 million Facebook users through the news feeds of 16,240 of MyPageKeeper's users[4]. In total, we identified 164,304 malicious posts, which contain at least one link out of 4,389 unique URLs. Within these posts we found 3,110 distinct posts that contain both text and a unique URL, the remaining 1,279 posts contain only URLs. Table 1 summarizes the dataset.

Detailed Description of MyPageKeeper

In what follows we present details of the MyPageKeeper app. The reader uninterested in the inner workings of MyPageKeeper can safely skip to the next section. The key

[4]On any user's news feed, Facebook selectively shows only 12% of updates posted by the user's friends. Hence, we will not see all the updates of any user's friends.

novelty of MyPageKeeper lies in the classification module (summarized in Figure 1(b) of Rahman et al. [33]). The input to the classification module is a URL and the related social context features extracted from the posts that contain the URL. Our classification algorithm operates in two phases, with the expectation that URLs and related posts that make it through either phase with- out a match are likely benign and are treated as such. We use whitelists and blacklists. To improve the efficiency and accuracy of our classifier, we use lists of URLs and domains in the following two steps. First, MyPageKeeper matches every URL against a whitelist of popular reputable domains. We currently use a whitelist comprising the top 70 domains listed by Quantcast, excluding domains that host user-contributed content (e.g., OSNs and blogging sites). Any URL that matches this whitelist is deemed safe, and it is not processed further.

All the URLs that remain are then matched with several URL blacklists that list domains and URLs that have been identified as responsible for spam, phishing, or malware. Using machine learning algorithms (trained with social context features) we evaluate all URLs that do not match the whitelist or any of the blacklists are evaluated using a Support Vector Machines (SVM) based classifier. We train our system with a batch of manually labeled data, that we gathered over several months prior to the launch of MyPageKeeper. For every input URL and post, the classifier outputs a binary decision to indicate whether it is malicious or not.

Our SVM classifier uses the following features: (a) Spam keyword score: keywords such as "FREE", "Hurry", "Deal", and "Shocked". To compile a list of such keywords we collect words that 1) occur frequently in blacklisted URL posts, and 2) appear with a greater frequency in OSN malware as compared to their frequency in benign posts. (b) Timeline post count: the more successful a spam campaign, the greater the number of users will be infected. Therefore, for each URL, MyPageKeeper computes counts of the number of Facebook timelines that contain the URL. (c) Like and comment count. Facebook users can "Like" any post to indicate their interest or approval. Users can also post comments to follow up on the post, again indicating their interest. (d) Level of URL obfuscation: hackers often try to spread malicious links in an obfuscated form, e.g., by shortening it with a URL shortening service such as bit.ly or goo.gl. We store a binary feature with every URL that indicates whether the URL has been shortened or not; we maintain a list of URL shorteners. Further details on the inner workings of MyPageKeeper can be found in Rahman et al. [33].

5. CLASSIFYING INCENTIVES

We classify the different types of incentives into one of the fourteen different incentives shown as a hierarchical taxonomy tree in Figure 1. These categories help our volunteers define whether the post contains a social, a monetary, or a socio-monetary incentive. At the highest level, we divide incentives into two categories: *monetary incentives* and *social incentives*. Under these two main categories, we further divided them into subcategories based on the mechanisms that are used to attract new victims. Table 2 presents three of the most informative frequent words of some of our incentive categories.

We use Amazon's Mechanical Turk platform [3] to recruit volunteers to classify thousands of unique Facebook posts. We refers to these volunteers as *turkers* in the remaining of the study. Mechanical Turk's main advantage over automatic text classifiers is its ability to actually reflect the reactions of real users to the post text. Simultaneously, Mechanical Turk allows us to perform the classification in much larger scale than with in-campus volunteers; by recruiting 226 turkers on Mechanical Turk, we avoid potential biases resulting from the use of a few volunteers doing a tedious task.

5.1 Mechanical Turk Classification

A total of 26.88% of all malicious posts in our dataset are URLs that do not contain any text. Facebook automatically displays a snapshot of the webpage URL, and as a result, when users read the post, they are subject to an incentivized post even though there is no text content in the post. Unfortunately, we do not consider these posts in this study as these webpages are short-lived [19], making it challenging to collect the necessary information. We defer the analysis of the incentives of these kind of posts for future study.

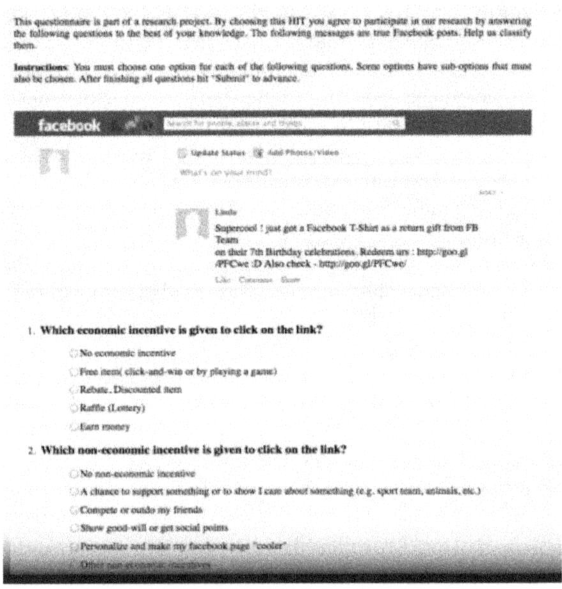

Figure 2: Screenshot of our Mechanical Turk survey.

From 120,455 malicious posts with text content, we identify 2,119 groups of posts, where posts in the same group contain text similar to each other with Levenshtein distance [24] less than 20. We select one post from each group to represent the group and ask workers two questions about the post:

1. Which monetary incentive is given to click on the link?

2. Which social incentive is given to click on the link?

On Amazon Mechanical Turk, tasks assigned to workers are called HITs (Human Intelligence Tasks). When we conduct our survey on Amazon Mechanical Turk, each HIT contains 19 different malicious posts and is assigned to 5 distinct *turkers*. To ensure the quality of the conducted survey, in each HIT, we add one control post with an obvious known incentive and one control question to each post. The results of a HIT completed by a *turker* are only valid if the

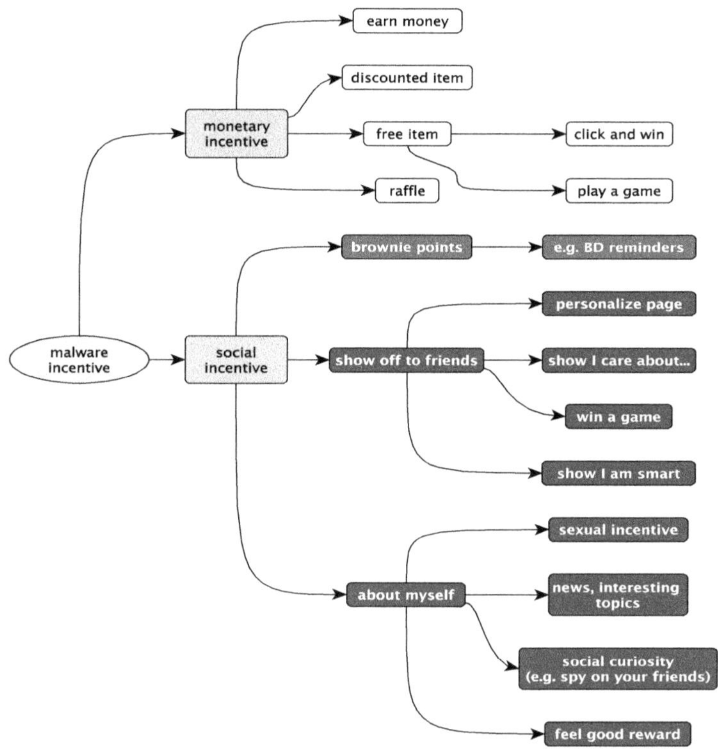

Figure 1: Taxonomy of malware post incentives.

Trait	Largest group	% of total
Age	25-34	39.42%
Gender	Male	55.29%
Education level	Some college	42.31%
Income	\$25K - \$37.5K	19.71%
Has FB account?	Yes	85.58%

Table 3: Demographical information of turkers

turker answers the control post and control questions correctly. Otherwise, we ignore it and assign the HIT to a new *turker*.

The content of a post is labeled social or non-social, monetary or non-monetary (socio-monetary are posts with both monetary and social labels) only if the majority of the *turkers* agree with the classification. In total, we successfully labeled 99.25% of all campaigns with a total disagreement rate of only 3%. Since these are malicious posts, we need to be careful with external links in the posts. To protect *turkers* we direct all links to our website explaining the nature of our study. To protect Facebook user's privacy, we do not include users' names on posts, replacing these names with some of the most common names and surnames in the U.S. population [40]. Figure. 2 shows a screenshot of our Mechanical Turk survey.

Each HIT consists of 19 malicious posts and one control post. Each post is rated by at least 5 *turkers*. We assign an incentive to a post by majority vote but to optimize labor costs we start assigning only 3 turkers to each HIT. We then create new HITs only for the posts where not all three

Control post	Get a free iPhone 4 Click here
Control question	$2+3=?$

Table 4: Sample of a control post and a control question.

turkers agreed on the incentive. We stop creating new assignments when all posts have at least 5 turker ratings.

Qualification of turkers.

To ensure that turkers are reliable we filter turkers that can accept on our HITs by: (1) Only allowing turkers who have "Assignments Approval rate" higher than 95%. (2) Only allowing turkers who register their location as the United States. to ensure consistency, and a common linguistic background. (3) No turker can work on two HITs that share the same posts. In total, we get 226 turkers. Table 3 shows the self-reported information about the turkers that helped us classify campaign incentives.

Human subject verification.

In order to ensure high quality in our classification results, we add one controlled message within each HIT and one controlled question in each post. Table 4 lists the control posts and sample of controlled questions. We design the incentive of the control post to be straightforward. If turkers cannot classify the controlled posts correctly the entire HIT is discarded.

We evaluate the quality of our survey by checking the design of the questions first. We want to make sure that turkers can understand our questions clearly. In the survey each question has 6-10 options. In total, $(85-90\%)$ of text

Category	Frequent Words
Click and win	Free, wow, offer
Play a game	contest, win, click
Discounted item	free, recharge, get
Best my friends in a game	context, win, click
Brownie points	just, got, miscrits
Raffle	cruise, win, holidays
Earn Money	make, moms, year
Sexual incentive	omg, shows, model
A chance to support something or to show I can about something (e.g. sport team, animals, etc.)	team, vote, favorite
Social curiosity (e.g., track profile visitors, monitor friend activities)	check, friend, deleted
News, interesting topics, etc. (e.g., Bin-Laden death video)	live, news, streaming
Feel-good reward (e.g., video of puppies)	freee, shirt, recharge
Personalize and make my Facebook page cooler	facebook, graphic, change

Table 2: Frequent words in each category

messages have at least 3 turkers voting the exact same answer according to our taxonomy in Figure 1 (e.g., the post contains a "Click-and-Win Rebate"). Second, we want to evaluate if our control questions are actually weeding out misbehaving turkers. Over the turkers that answered the control questions correctly, we select dissenting turkers who have at least one answer that disagrees with the majority of the other turkers of the same HIT. We found that $77-93\%$ of the remaining answers of the dissenting turkers agree with the majority, showing no consistent wrongdoing in the part of the dissenting turkers. Figure 3 lists the probability that the remaining answers of the dissenting turkers are the same as the majority. Based on the evaluation we just describe above, we believe that the results of our survey are trustworthy.

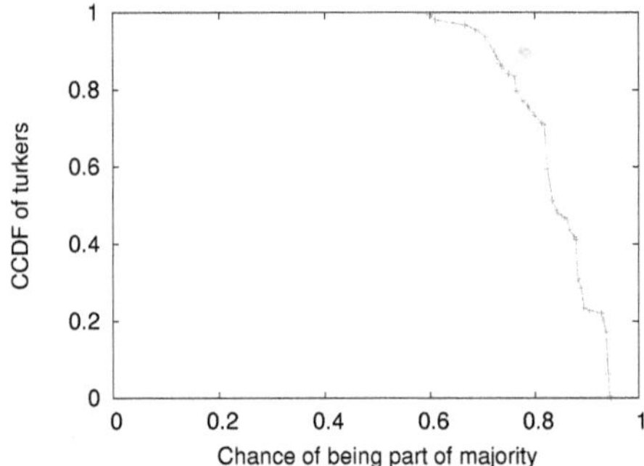

(a) Q: Which economic incentive is given to click on the link?

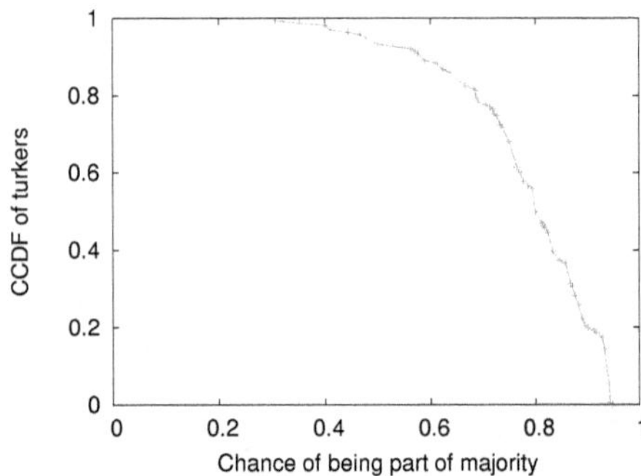

(b) Q: Which social (non-economic) incentive is given to click on the link?

Figure 3: Turker's classification performance.

6. USE OF INCENTIVES ON FACEBOOK MALWARE

In this section, we report the observed incentives at the campaign level. We also study these campaigns using metrics such as the number of infected accounts and duration of these campaigns. The duration of a campaign is defined as the period of time from the first day until the last day we observe newly infected users. Note that we consider a campaign to be alive only while it keeps infecting new users; we do not consider a campaign to be alive if it stops compromising new users. Figure 4 shows the evolution of the campaigns breaking them down into monetary, social, and socio-monetary incentivized campaigns relative to the total number of campaigns. The inset in Figure 4 shows the same plot with the absolute number of campaigns. Note that the overwhelming majority of the campaigns are social incentivized. Monetary and socio-monetary incentivized campaigns compete neck-in-neck.

Among campaigns with social incentives, we observe a sizable fraction of them lure users with social curiosity. For example, we observe 591 distinct campaigns—13% of all observed campaigns—with text content of the nature *"check if a friend has deleted you"*. Other representative text content of social curiosity campaigns—with observed 302 distinct campaigns—is *"Wow! l cant believe that you can check who is viewing your profile. l just checked my top proflle lookers (sic) and l am shocked at who is seeing my profile! You can also see who viewed your profile ⟨here⟩"*.

We use two measures of campaign success: campaign duration and the number of infected users of a campaign. Figure 5(a) shows a semi-log plot of the complementary cumulative distribution (CCDF) of campaign durations separated by incentive. Note that socio-monetary campaigns are stochastically dominant over the duration of monetary and social campaigns. The average duration of a socio-monetary campaign is 17.8 days while the durations of pure social

Campaign type	(Total campaigns)	
Social campaigns	2075	68%
Monetary campaigns	540	17%
Socio-monetary campaigns	414	13%
Unclassified	81	3%

Table 5: Breakdown of malware campaigns for each incentive type (unclassified campaigns are campaigns where there was no agreement on the type of incentive provided).

Campaign type	duration	reach
All campaigns	7.1 days	28.1 users
Social campaigns	4.8 days	26.2 users
Monetary campaigns	7.5 days	22.3 users
Socio-monetary campaigns	17.8 days	43.2 users

Table 6: Average duration and reach (number of infected users) of malware campaigns.

and monetary campaigns are 4.8 and 7.5, respectively. The duration average by campaign incentive is summarized in Table 6.

The total number of infected accounts with socio-monetary campaigns is also stochastically dominant over the number infected with only monetary or social campaigns (see the semi-log CCDF of number of infected users in Figure 5(b)). Interestingly, we observe that the conditional distribution of the number of infected users given campaign durations (Figure 6) shows that campaign durations and the number of infected users in a campaign are mostly independent of each other. In other words, campaigns that last long do not necessarily infect more users. On average socio-monetary campaigns infect almost twice as many users as pure monetary campaigns (43.2 v.s. 22.3) and 165% more users than pure social campaigns. The average number of infected users (reach) by campaign incentive is summarized in Table 6.

To exemplify the dominance of socio-monetary campaigns, we select two similar "play/win a game" subcategories that belong to monetary and social incentives, denoted "play a game" and "win a game" in Figure 1, respectively. Table 7 shows the statistics of these game campaigns along with a sample post content. Observe that socio-monetary campaigns infect 4.4 times more users than campaigns with

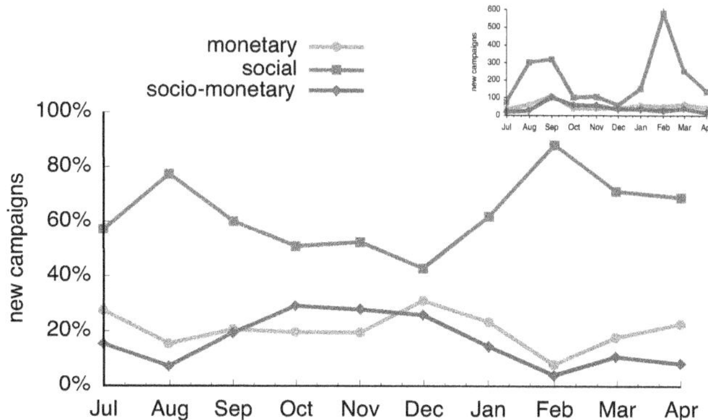

Figure 4: Evolution of the fraction (absolute numbers in the inset) of new campaigns per month per incentive.

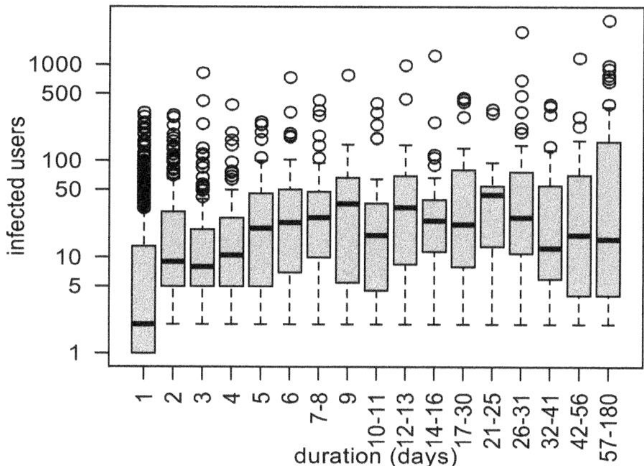

Figure 6: The number of infected users is loosely correlated with campaign durations. The graph shows the boxplot of the number of infected users of campaigns with a given duration. Duration values are sometimes binned to ensure that each bin has at least 31 samples.

pure incentives. Also note that, consistent with our general observations, there are more social game campaigns than monetary game campaigns, and that social campaigns are less effective than monetary campaigns.

These observations have remarkable real-world implications. For instance, stochastic dominance [16] implies that any rational agent betting on the outcome of a campaign whose utility function—for instance, the malware developer's revenue—increases according to the campaign duration or the number of infected (or any linear combination of the two) will choose socio-monetary campaigns. Another interesting observation is that while social incentivized campaigns are the majority of the observed campaigns, socio-monetary campaigns are superior and monetary campaigns are equally good if not better than social campaigns.

The observation that socio-monetary campaigns are more effective than pure monetary or pure social campaigns is rather surprising. Heyman and Ariely [17] show that subjects exposed to a combined socio-monetary incentive treat the incentive mostly as monetary and, thus, are less susceptible to the social incentive component. However, it is possible that the virulence of the monetary and social incentives that go into the socio-monetary campaign is more pronounced alone for certain users than when in combination. For instance, consider the following hypothetical scenario. Alice sees that her good friend Bob is challenging her to a game that also offers an iPad prize but is suspicious of the monetary prize (likely a scam) but would love to play the game with Bob. Carol is friends with Bob but does not know him very well and is not interested in the personal challenge but would love to play to win an iPad. In a scenario where socio-monetary incentives are not as virulent as pure incentives for a given set of users, could using socio-monetary incentives be still advantageous?

Without the possibility to infect users with malware we are unable to perform an experiment to answer the above question. However, we find a likely explanation can be found in a percolation phenomena well known in biological pathogens. Consider an extreme toy problem scenario. Fig-

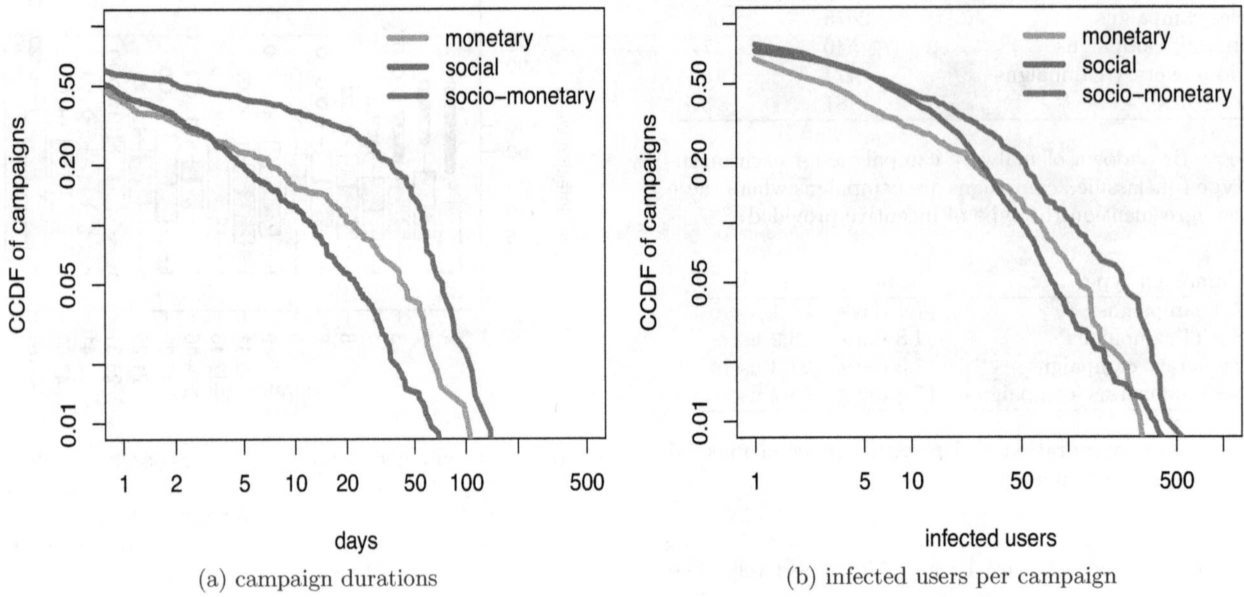

Figure 5: Impact of monetary, social, and socio-monetary incentives on the duration and size of malware campaigns.

incentive	infections per campaign	campaigns	sample post content
social (game)	2.46	24	Some People will dominate all the games and some are doomed to remain losers their whole life (*sic*): ⟨link⟩
monetary (game)	16.18	11	NEW GAME NOTICE! Come check out the awesome new Wild Wild Taxi contest that is available, you could win a Kindle Fire. Start playing⟨here⟩
socio-monetary (game)	71.33	51	CONTEST UPDATE: Currently in 10246th place in The Daily Addi's Gem Swap II contest to win a 16GB iPad2. Think you can do better? You should give it a try ⟨here⟩

Table 7: Statistics of social, monetary, and socio-monetary game campaigns.

ure 7(a) shows the original toy network where users have a pure incentive preference: social (blue) or monetary (green). While in real life people are susceptible to both social and monetary incentives with different intensities, in our toy example, we consider the extreme case where they have a strict preference for either social or monetary incentives. That is, a node with a social (monetary) incentive preference may not be infected by campaigns using pure monetary (social) incentive. Figs. 7(b-c) show the percolation paths that can be taken by pure incentive campaigns. In contrast, socio-monetary incentivized campaigns see the percolation paths as in Figure 7(d). However, despite the denser percolation paths, the virulence of a socio-monetary campaign may not be as high as the virulence of a pure incentive campaign. This is because users with social (monetary) incentive preference may be put off by the mix with a monetary (social) incentive.

While there is recent work on percolation phenomena over interdependent networks, showing that a virus spreading over distinct but interconnected networks is more virulent than the same virus spreading over a single network [14, 23, 43], the phenomenon of interest in this work is a different type of percolation. The percolation consists of a flexible "pathogen" (socio-monetary campaign) that can infect users with distinct incentive preferences, contrasting the latter with a more specialized "pathogen" (pure social or monetary campaigns) that is more virulent in infecting users of a specific incentive preference but less virulent to other users. We find a similar scenario looking at plant pathogens.

One of the most famous cases of the epidemiological impact of a single gene variant in crops is the blight disease that hit potatoes in Western Europe, particularly Ireland, in the middle of the 19th century (1845–1852). The widely used single variety of potato used in Europe allowed the disease to spread quickly through the continent [2]. Since then, some commercial farmers adopted mixed-strain crops.

The *E. graminis* is a fungus that causes powdery mildew on barley. *E. graminis* has genotypes that if specialized to attack one barley strand are known to be highly virulent on that strand but significantly less effective on other strands [6]. In the presence of mixed strands flexible *E. graminis* genotypes evolve to attack different barley strands, but this flexibility comes at the cost of limiting the pathogen's ability to adapt with increased virulence to individual strands. Despite the decreased virulence that comes with flexibility, *E. graminis* is known to suffer strong genetic pressure to

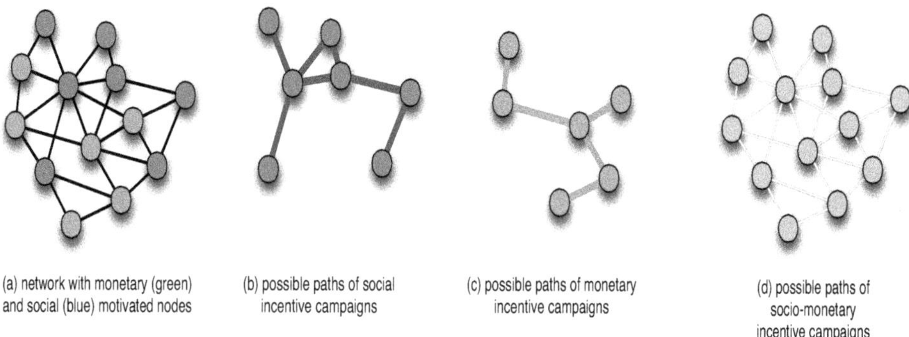

(a) network with monetary (green) and social (blue) motivated nodes
(b) possible paths of social incentive campaigns
(c) possible paths of monetary incentive campaigns
(d) possible paths of socio-monetary incentive campaigns

Figure 7: Malware spreading over a population with sharp incentive preferences such that users with one incentive preference may not be infected by the other incentive. Fig. (a) illustrates a network where users (nodes) prefer social (blue) or monetary (green) incentives. Figs. (b) and (c) show the possible edges that pure incentivized social and monetary campaigns can traverse, respectively. Fig. (d) shows the links that socio-monetary campaigns can traverse, however, with possibly lower virulence than pure incentive campaigns.

select flexible genotypes in mixed crops [6], an effect also extensively reported in simulations [28]. The percolation effect of specialized v.s. flexible pathogens on mixed crops is illustrated in Figure 8, showing why a more stable connectivity can tip the advantage towards flexibility. The reader is encouraged to see Mundt [28] for an interesting review on the effect of mixed crops on pathogen epidemics. This phenomenon is not limited to *E. graminis* [41] and provides an interesting mechanism to explain our observations: In populations with mixed susceptibilities to social and monetary incentives, flexible socio-monetary incentives are more effective due to percolation effects even if they are less virulent than pure incentives for some classes of users.

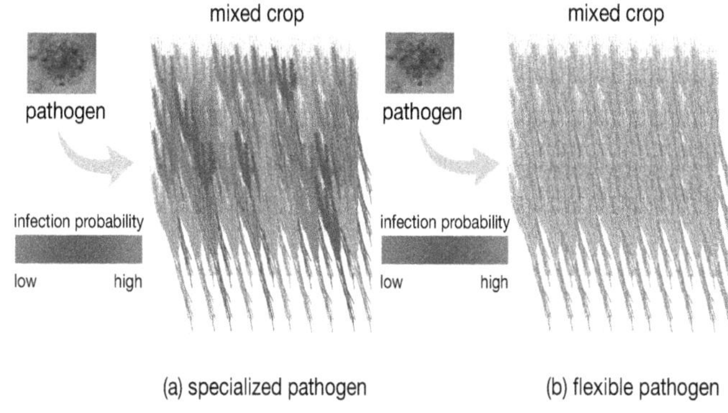

Figure 8: Percolation effect of specialized and flexible pathogens on mixed crops. In mixed crops, pathogen genotype flexibility reduces the infection probability variance, and possibly also its average. However, in most cases, the lower variability increases the percolation probability, facilitating the spread of the disease.

However, crops live in a two dimensional world—akin to a lattice—and small world effects of social networks can greatly impact epidemic cascades [27]. In what follows, we perform epidemic simulations over real social networks to show that, even in the presence of small world effects, the scale can also be tipped in favor of flexibility (i.e., socio-monetary incentives in our setting).

7. FLEXIBILITY V.S. VIRULENCE SIMULATIONS

We now use epidemic simulations over real social networks to show that, in the contest between flexibility (incentive combination) and virulence (pure incentive), the scale is tipped towards flexibility, thus providing a plausible explanation as to why socio-monetary campaigns outperform social and monetary campaigns. In other words, even if the combination of incentives reduces the virulence of each isolated incentive, incentive combination (flexibility) still produces larger cascades in most cases.

We simulate a variant of the Susceptible-Infected-Recovered (SIR) epidemic [31] that also takes into account user incentive preferences, a simple model to simulate the effects of different incentives over two distinct network datasets. The first network is the Enron e-mail network [21], which consists of 36,692 users. The Enron e-mail network is represented as an undirected graph between email senders and receivers. Malware campaign cascades are likely affected by trust relationships. To account for real (asymmetric) trust relationships, the second network dataset is the Epinions trust network [34], which consist of 75,879 users. The Epinion trust network shows a directed network of "who-trust-whom" among members of epinion.com. In our epidemic model, each user has a binary preference for social or monetary incentives, i.e., a purely socially incentivized campaign cannot infect monetary incentivized users and vice-versa. We randomly assign 60% of the users to prefer monetary incentives and the remaining 40% users to prefer social incentives.

At each time step, any infected user recovers with probability r. The recovery probability simulates the effect of the malware being discovered. Users that prefer social (monetary) incentives get infected with constant probability p by social (monetary) campaigns, but these same users cannot get infected by monetary (social) campaigns. The infection probability of socio-monetary campaigns is $p/2$ regardless of the incentive the user prefers. The latter captures the trade-off between flexibility and virulence.

Figure 9 shows box plots with the results of the average (over 300 campaigns) of number of infected nodes with different infection probabilities $p \in \{0.03, 0.05, 0.07, 0.09\}$. In

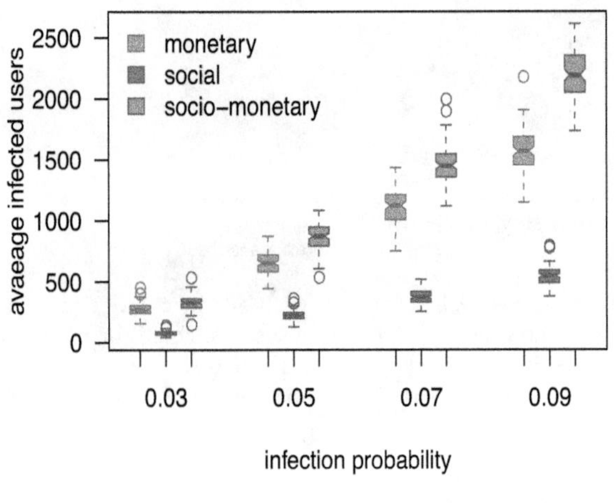

(a) The Enron network

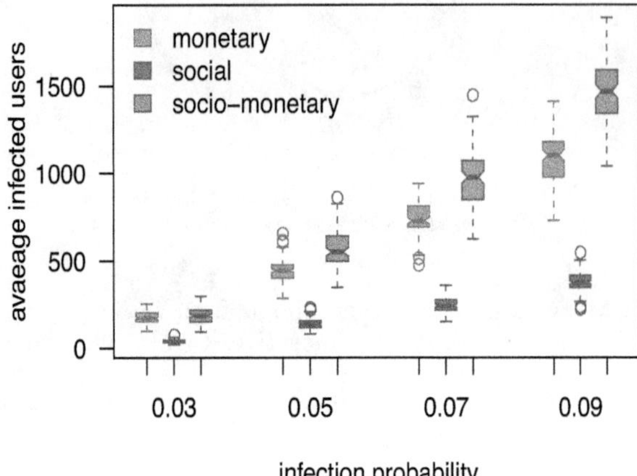

(b) The Epinions trust network

Figure 9: Simulation results showing the number of infected users of distinct incentive types.

these simulations, we set the recovery probability r to be 0.5. The box plots have a "notch" around the median that offer a rough guide to the significance of difference of medians; if the notches of two boxes do not overlap, this offers evidence of a statistically significant difference between the medians [26]. As observed in Facebook, the number of infected users in socio-monetary campaigns is larger than that of pure monetary or social campaigns in both Enron (Figure 9(a)) and Epinions (Figure 9(b)). Note, however, that the advantage between socio-monetary incentives and pure monetary incentives is more prominent as we increase the infection probability p. Observe that typically socio-monetary campaigns infect more users than campaigns with pure incentives with or without taking into account asymmetric trust relationships.

8. DISCUSSION

In this work, we observe that post incentives play a major role on the spread of malware campaigns over online social networks. We observe that while social incentives are prevalent in OSN malware, socio-monetary incentives are more effective—with respect to the number of infected users and campaign durations—than social or monetary incentives when used in isolation.

The effectiveness of combined socio-monetary incentives can be explained by percolation effects resulting from mixed incentive preferences in the population of users. Through simulations we show that even if the susceptibility to combined incentives is less than that of any one specialized incentive, combining incentives provide a tremendous advantage to percolate over the network. This phenomenon is also observed on plant pathogens [28, 46], to which we make a variety of connections in our conclusions. In mixed crops, natural selection dislikes highly virulent but specialized pathogen to promote less virulent but unspecialized pathogens [28, 46], a mechanisms used by biological pathogens to cope with diverse gene pools [2, 28, 46]. Thus, the diversity of incentive preferences of OSN users may be a key factor in impeding the further spread of OSN malware, which should put selective pressure on OSN malware to evolve towards socio-monetary incentives but, interestingly, we found no evidence of such evolution over our 10 months of data.

Acknowledgements

This work was partially supported by NSF grant CNS-1065133 and ARL Cooperative Agreement W911NF-09-2-0053. The views and conclusions contained in this document are those of the author and should not be interpreted as representing the official policies, either expressed or implied of the NSF, ARL, or the U.S. Government. The U.S. Government is authorized to reproduce and distribute reprints for Government purposes notwithstanding any copyright notation hereon.

9. REFERENCES

[1] MyPageKeeper. `https://apps.facebook.com/mypagekeeper/`.

[2] MW Adams, AH Ellingboe, and EC Rossman. Biological uniformity and disease epidemics. *BioScience*, pages 1067–1070, 1971.

[3] AWS. Amazon Mechanical Turk. `https://www.mturk.com/mturk/`, 2013.

[4] Kregg Aytes and Terry Connolly. Computer Security and Risky Computing Practices: A Rational Choice Perspective. *Journal of Organizational and End User Computing*, 16(3):22–40, 2004.

[5] J Balthrop. Technological Networks and the Spread of Computer Viruses. *science*, 304(5670):527–529, April 2004.

[6] K M Chin and M S Wolfe. Selection on Erysiphe graminis in pure and mixed stands of barley. *Plant Pathology*, 33(4):535–546, December 1984.

[7] Fred Cohen. Computer viruses: theory and experiments. *Computers & security*, 6(1):22–35, 1987.

[8] Yves Deswarte, Karama Kanoun, and Jean-Claude Laprie. Diversity against accidental and deliberate faults. In *Computer Security, Dependability, and Assurance*, pages 171–171. IEEE Computer Society, 1998.

[9] Inc. Facebook. Facebook reports first quarter 2013 results. March 2013.

[10] R Ford and E H Spafford. Computer science: Happy birthday, dear viruses. *Science*, 317(5835):210–211, July 2007.

[11] Stephanie Forrest and Catherine Beauchemin. Computer immunology. *Immunological Reviews*, 216(1):176–197, 2007.

[12] Stephanie Forrest, Steven A Hofmeyr, and Anil Somayaji. Computer immunology. *Communications of the ACM*, 40(10):88–96, 1997.

[13] a. Ganesh, L. Massoulié, and D. Towsley. The effect of network topology on the spread of epidemics. *IEEE INFOCOM*, 2(C):1455–1466, 2005.

[14] Jianxi Gao, Sergey V Buldyrev, H Eugene Stanley, and Shlomo Havlin. Networks formed from interdependent networks. *Nature Physics*, 8(1):40–48, December 2011.

[15] Jacob Goldenberg, Yuval Shavitt, Eran Shir, and Sorin Solomon. Distributive immunization of networks against viruses using the 'honey-pot' architecture. *Nature Physics*, 1(3):184–188, December 2005.

[16] Josef Hadar and William R Russell. Rules for Ordering Uncertain Prospects. *The American Economic Review*, 59(1):25–34, January 1969.

[17] James Heyman and Dan Ariely. Effort for payment a tale of two markets. *Psychological Science*, 15(11):787–793, 2004.

[18] A E Howe, I Ray, M Roberts, M Urbanska, and Z Byrne. The Psychology of Security for the Home Computer User. In *Security and Privacy (SP), 2012 IEEE Symposium on IS -*, pages 209–223. IEEE, 2012.

[19] Ting-Kai Huang, Md Sazzadur Rahman, Harsha Madhyastha, Michalis Faloutsos, and Bruno Ribeiro. An analysis of socware cascades in online social networks. In *WWW*, 2013.

[20] Hyphenet. Facebook phishing scam costs victims thousands of dollars, `http://goo.gl/4uVME4`.

[21] Bryan Klimt and Yiming Yang. Introducing the enron corpus. In *First conference on email and anti-spam (CEAS)*, 2004.

[22] Eytan Adar Lada Adamic, Thomas Lento and Pauline Ng. The evolution of memes on facebook, `http://goo.gl/JysRpD`.

[23] E A Leicht and Raissa M D'Souza. Percolation on interacting networks. *arXiv preprint arXiv:0907.0894*, 2009.

[24] V Levenshtein. Binary codes capable of correcting spurious insertions and deletions of ones. *Problems of Information Transmission*, 1(1):8–17, 1965.

[25] Hsi-Peng Lu, Chin-Lung Hsu, and Hsiu-Ying Hsu. An empirical study of the effect of perceived risk upon intention to use online applications. *Information Management & Computer Security*, 13(2):106–120, 2005.

[26] Robert McGill, John W Tukey, and Wayne A Larsen. Variations of box plots. *The American Statistician*, 32(1):12–16, 1978.

[27] Cristopher Moore and Mark EJ Newman. Epidemics and percolation in small-world networks. *Physical Review E*, 61(5):5678, 2000.

[28] C C Mundt. Use of multiline cultivars and cultivar mixtures for disease management. *Annual Review of Phytopathology*, 40(1):381–410, September 2002.

[29] Andrew Newell, Daniel Obenshain, Thomas Tantillo, Cristina Nita-Rotaru, and Yair Amir. Increasing network resiliency by optimally assigning diverse variants to routing nodes. In *IEEE/IFIP International Conference on Dependable Systems and Networks*, pages 1–12. IEEE, June 2013.

[30] M Newman, Stephanie Forrest, and Justin Balthrop. Email networks and the spread of computer viruses. *Physical Review E*, 66(3):035101, September 2002.

[31] Mark Newman. *Networks: An Introduction*. Oxford University Press, Inc., May 2010.

[32] B Aditya Prakash, Hanghang Tong, Nicholas Valler, Michalis Faloutsos, and Christos Faloutsos. Virus Propagation on Time-Varying Networks: Theory and Immunization Algorithms. In *Machine Learning and Knowledge Discovery in Databases*, volume 6323, pages 99–114. Springer Berlin Heidelberg, Berlin, Heidelberg, 2010.

[33] Md Sazzadur Rahman, Ting-Kai Huang, Harsha V Madhyastha, and Michalis Faloutsos. Efficient and scalable socware detection in online social networks. In *USENIX Security*, 2012.

[34] Matthew Richardson, Rakesh Agrawal, and Pedro Domingos. Trust management for the semantic web. In *The Semantic Web-ISWC 2003*, pages 351–368. Springer, 2003.

[35] Matt Russell. Facebook scam involves money transfers to the philippines, `http://goo.gl/SMLDyh`.

[36] Eugene H Spafford. Computer viruses as artificial life. *Artificial Life*, 1(3):249–265, 1994.

[37] Charles Steinfield, Nicole B Ellison, and Cliff Lampe. Social capital, self-esteem, and use of online social network sites: A longitudinal analysis. *Journal of Applied Developmental Psychology*, 29(6):434–445, November 2008.

[38] Hanghang Tong, B. Aditya Prakash, Charalampos Tsourakakis, Tina Eliassi-Rad, Christos Faloutsos, and Duen Horng Chau. On the Vulnerability of Large Graphs. In *ICDM*, pages 1091–1096. IEEE, December 2010.

[39] AJ Ullstrup. The impacts of the southern corn leaf blight epidemics of 1970-1971. *Annual Review of Phytopathology*, 10(1):37–50, 1972.

[40] U.S. Census Bureau. Genealogy Data: Frequently Occurring Surnames from Census 2000. `http://www.census.gov/genealogy/www/data/2000surnames/Top1000.xls`, 2000.

[41] Lorys M M A Villaréal and Christian Lannou. Selection for Increased Spore Efficacy by Host Genetic Background in a Wheat Powdery Mildew Population. *Phytopathology*, 90(12):1300–1306, December 2000.

[42] John Von Neumann and Arthur Walter Burks. *Theory of self-reproducing automata*. University of Illinois press Urbana, 1966.

[43] Huijuan Wang, Qian Li, Gregorio D'Agostino, Shlomo Havlin, H Eugene Stanley, and Piet Van Mieghem. Effect of the interconnected network structure on the epidemic threshold. *Physical Review E*, 88(2):022801, August 2013.

[44] P Wang, M C Gonzalez, C A Hidalgo, and A L Barabasi. Understanding the Spreading Patterns of Mobile Phone Viruses. *Science*, 324(5930):1071–1076, May 2009.

[45] Ryan West. The psychology of security. *Communications of the ACM*, 51(4):34–40, April 2008.

[46] X M Xu and M S Ridout. Stochastic simulation of the spread of race-specific and race-nonspecific aerial fungal pathogens in cultivar mixtures. *Plant Pathology*, 49(2):207–218, April 2000.

Application Impersonation: Problems of OAuth and API Design in Online Social Networks

Pili Hu[1], Ronghai Yang[1], Yue Li[2] and Wing Cheong Lau[1]
[1]Department of Information Engineering, The Chinese University of Hong Kong
[2]Department of Computer Science, College of William and Mary
{hupili,yr013}@ie.cuhk.edu.hk yli@cs.wm.edu wclau@ie.cuhk.edu.hk

ABSTRACT

OAuth 2.0 protocol has enjoyed wide adoption by Online Social Network (OSN) providers since its inception. Although the security guideline of OAuth 2.0 is well discussed in RFC6749 and RFC6819, many real-world attacks due to the implementation specifics of OAuth 2.0 in various OSNs have been discovered. To our knowledge, previously discovered loopholes are all based on the misuse of OAuth and many of them rely on provider side or application side vulnerabilities/ faults beyond the scope of the OAuth protocol. It was generally believed that correct use of OAuth 2.0 is secure. In this paper, we show that OAuth 2.0 is intrinsically vulnerable to App impersonation attack due to its provision of multiple authorization flows and token types. We start by reviewing and analyzing the OAuth 2.0 protocol and some common API design problems found in many 1st-tiered OSNs. We then propose the App impersonation attack and investigate its impact on 12 major OSN providers. We demonstrate that, App impersonation via OAuth 2.0, when combined with additional API design features/ deficiencies, make large-scale exploit and privacy-leak possible. For example, it becomes possible for an attacker to completely crawl a 200-million-user OSN within just one week and harvest data objects like the status list and friend list which are expected, by its users, to be private among only friends. We also propose fixes that can be readily deployed to tackle the OAuth2.0-based App impersonation problem.

Categories and Subject Descriptors

K.4.1 [**Computers and Society**]: Public Policy Issues—*Privacy*; K.6.5 [**Management of Computing and Information Systems**]: Security and Protection —*Unauthorized access, Authentication*

General Terms

Security, Measurement

* Pili Hu and Ronghai Yang have contributed equally to this work.
+ On May 22, 2014, we have notified all providers, to our knowledge, that are affected by the OAuth App Impersonation Attack.At the same time, we also sent the intial verison of this paper to all of these providers.

COSN'14, October 1–2, 2014, Dublin, Ireland.

http://dx.doi.org/10.1145/2660460.2660463.

Keywords

OAuth 2.0; App Impersonation Attack; API Design in OSN; Social Network Privacy; Single Sign On

1. INTRODUCTION

Many Online Social Networks (OSN) are using OAuth 2.0 to grant access to API endpoints nowadays. Despite of many thorough threat model analyses and security guidelines (e.g. RFC6819), most OSNs are still vulnerable to a variety of attacks. To our knowledge, previously discovered loopholes are all based on the misuse of OAuth 2.0 and some depend on provider-side or application-side faults beyond the scope of OAuth protocol, such as XSS and open redirector. It was generally believed that correct use of OAuth 2.0 (by OSN provider and application developer) is secure enough. However, we clarify this common misunderstanding by demonstrating various leakage of user data which roots from the blind-spot of the OAuth's fundamental design rationale: OAuth focuses on protecting the user, not the application.

We show that, even if OSN providers and application developers follow the current best practice in using OAuth 2.0, application impersonation is still inevitable on many OSN platforms: According to the OAuth 2.0 standard, they support implicit-grant flow and bearer-token usage. Although it has become common knowledge for application developers to use authorization-code-grant flow and use access token in a MAC-token style wherever possible, there is no mechanism for them to opt out from the support of implicit-grant flow and bearer-token usage in an OSN platform. Note that different applications may have different privileges like accessing permissions and rate limits. Towards this end, application impersonation in general enables privilege escalation and the extent of the actual damage would depend on platform-specific details. To summarize, this paper has made the following technical contributions:

- We found and formalized the forged-implicit-flow attack and forged-bearer-token attack, which lead to App impersonation attack, in OAuth 2.0 framework[1].
- We examined 12 major OSN providers and conducted proof-of-concept experiments to show the possible consequences of App impersonation attack. To our knowledge, these are the first demonstrations of massive attacks based on the design problem of OAuth, instead of the mis-use of OAuth.
- We propose immediate and deployable fixes to the App impersonation problem.

[1]For the rest of the paper, we use OAuth to denote OAuth 2.0 if not specified otherwise.

This paper is organized as follows. In Section 2, we survey related work in OAuth security and privacy issues on OSN. In Section 3, we discuss the authorization flows supported by OAuth 2.0, and propose the forged-implicit-flow attack. In Section 4, we discuss and analyze the two commonly used token types, and propose the forged-bearer-token attack. In Section 5, we discuss major issues related to API design. In Section 6, we summarize our findings on 12 major OSN providers and illustrate the feasibility of several large-scale exploits/ privacy-leaks. In Section 7, we conclude the paper and summarize the immediate fixes that OSN providers should adopt and deploy.

2. RELATED WORK

OAuth 1.0 is defined in RFC5849 [1] and obsoleted by OAuth 2.0 in RFC6749 [2]. RFC6749 devotes the whole chapter 10 to security considerations of the OAuth 2.0. The informational RFC6819 [3] further discusses OAuth security using a comprehensive threat model analysis. The access token obtained from the OAuth protocol can be used in two ways: bearer token defined in RFC6750 [4] and MAC token proposed in the draft [5].

Although OAuth itself has a sound security model, and the authorization code grant flow was cryptographically proved secure [6] under the assumption that TLS is used, many real-world attacks were found. This is mainly caused by the fact that many OSN providers implemented OAuth before the eventual standardization, and App developers are also likely to misuse the SDKs [7] due to undocumented assumptions in the SDKs. Motivated by formal protocol checking researches, [8] used automatic tools to discover a previously known security flaw from the specification of OAuth. [9] provided a finer-granulared modeling method of system components and was able to discover more concrete loopholes. Since the devil of OAuth (or more generally authentication/authorization protocols), is in the implementation details, researchers have recently used network-trace based approach [10] [11] [12] to discover security flaws, like fail of complete parameter checking, session swapping and Cross Site Request Forgery (CSRF), just to name a few. Many of the problems are ad-hoc in nature and some even depend on the existence of non-OAuth related fault components e.g. an open redirector on the Application site. Regardless of the details, previous demonstrable attacks are based on the misuse of OAuth and theoretically covered by RFC6819. On the contrary, we show that OAuth is intrinsically vulnerable to App impersonation attack. This was overlooked for a long time because the initial intention of OAuth is to protect users rather than applications.

In the field of user privacy study, there are qualitative or small-scale quantitative studies regarding privacy policy and settings on OSNs. It is shown that most users leave privacy settings as default [13] and those who ever tried to change the settings usually fail to achieve their goal [14] [15]. The consequence is that their social behaviour data is exposed to more audienaces than expected [16] [17]. In recent years, more concerns are raised regarding the potential leakage caused by 3rd-party Apps. [18] examined 150 popular Facebook Apps and found that 90% of them request user private data which were not actually needed. The App impersonation attack makes the problem worse, because un-used permissions might be exploited by attackers.

One of the most valuable assets generated by an OSN is the social-relationship graph. Based on the topology, one can conduct various privacy-breaking graph mining campaign like de-anonymizing a graph [19] and infer user ages [20]. Towards this end, protecting the social graph from massive and systematical leakage is of great importance for providers. We observed that all major providers gradually reinforced the crawling barriers over the years. For example, the million-level large-scale crawling methods used in [21] (1.7M Facebook) [20] (3M Facebook) [22] (40M Renren) [23] (70M Renren) were invalidated after some service upgrades. It is now usually costly (in terms of time and resources) to crawl a substantially large graph. Depending on the specific OSN, it may require a large amount of Sybil accounts, baiting applications, IP pools, etc. With the App impersonation flaw discovered in this paper, it is possible to conduct large-scale crawling in a rapid and cheap manner again.

3. OAUTH 2.0 AUTHORIZATION FLOWS

There are three parties in the OAuth eco-system: *Provider*, *User* and *App*. Users socialize on the OSN platform and create various data objects like statuses, photos and friendship graph. In order to read or write a User's object, the third-party App should get the corresponding authorization from User.

To solve this problem, RFC6749 [2] defines four types of authorization flows. Regardless of the authorization flow, the ultimate goal of OAuth is for App to get an *access token*, which is a proof that App can access to the associated resources (on behalf of User). In this section, we first introduce the two most common types of authorization flow, i.e. authorization code grant and implicit grant, and then we propose the forged-implicit-flow attack.

3.1 Authorization Code Grant Flow

The authorization code flow ("server flow" in some literature) plus the invocation of resource API is illustrated in Fig. 3.1. The steps are as follows:

1. User visits App;
2. App redirects User to Provider for authentication;
3. User reviews the permissions requested by App and present User credential to Provider for confirmation;
4. Once authenticated, Provider returns to User an authorization code;
5. User is redirected to App with the authorization code;
6. App exchanges authorization code for the access token by sending AppSecret to Provider.
7. After checking the validity of the authorization code and the App's identity (via the shared AppSecret), Provider responds to App with the access token.

After obtaining access token, the App can query the HTTP endpoints of resource APIs with this access token. There are two important properties of the authorization code grant flow.

- Access token is only shared between Provider and the App;
- Code alone is of no use to User because Provider requires proof of AppSecret before issuing the actual access token.

Note that the "+" sign in the figures just illustrate that AppSecret and/or access token is used in a request. The concrete process may involve signature using those elements.

3.2 Implicit Grant Flow

The high-level picture of the implicit grant flow ("client flow" in some literature) is shown in Fig. 3.2. The authorization steps are as follows:

1. User Visits App;

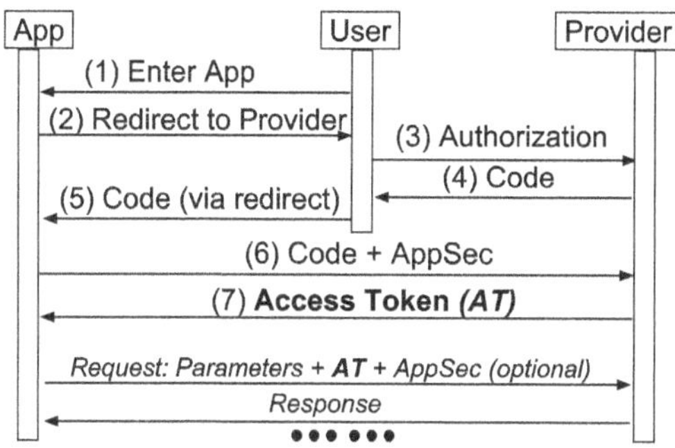

Figure 1: Authorization Code Grant Flow

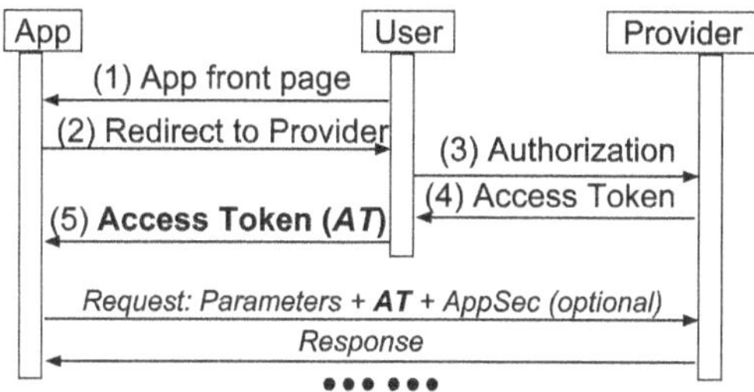

Figure 2: Implicit Grant Flow

2. App redirects User to Provider for authentication and declares to use implicit grant flow;
3. User reviews the permissions requested by App and show the credential to IdP for confirmation.
4. Once authenticated, Provider returns an access token;
5. Access token is redirected to App dirctly.

Unlike the authorization code flow, the access token issued by Provider is relayed through User to App directly. This authorization flow is intended to lower the barrier of App development. It is useful in cases where App can not protect the AppSecret or crypto primitives are too heavy for the execution environment of App. But it makes the authrization process less secure at the same time since IdP simply treats the access token holder as the App without further identity authentication (via AppSecret). Therefore, RFC6749 [2] suggested that implicit grant flow should be avoided whenever authorization code flow is available.

3.3 Forged-implicit-flow Attack

Comparing Fig. 3.1 and Fig. 3.2, it is easy to see that User can bypass App and use this access token to query Provider's resource APIs. This is the first key that enables App impersonation. Note that the problem here is the *availability of platform support* for implicit grant flow, regardless of whether an App would use it or not. Even if App follows the best practice of OAuth and employ the authorization code flow, User can enforce to use implicit flow instead as no mechanisms provided by Provider to opt out this flow. In order to accomplish Steps(1)-(4) of the implicit grant flow, A user only needs to know two public parameters from the App: `client_id` (AppID) and `redirect_uri` (callback URL). Even if App uses authorization code grant flow, User can still harvest these two parameters and forge an implicit grant flow.

For backward compatibility with a large number of existing 3rd-party Apps, OSN providers cannot totally remove the support of implicit grant flow. A practical and immediate fix for forged-implicit-flow attack is to let an App opt-out implicit grant flow if it is capable of performing authorization code flow.

4. OAUTH 2.0 TOKEN TYPES

Upon completion of OAuth protocol, an App obtains a valid access token. Regardless of the actual implementations, most providers use access token in (slight variation of) bearer token style or MAC token styles.

4.1 Bearer Token

Any party in possession of a bearer token [4] can use it to get access associated resource without identity assertion (AppSecret). An App simply puts the access token in the HTTP request as a header field or as part of the query-string. As long as the access token and other additional parameters are valid, Provider returns the requested resource.

4.2 MAC Token

Unlike bearer token, MAC token [5] requires the proof of the identity when making request. There are generally three steps to construct a request:

1. List all request parameters and the access token;
2. Concatenate those data as a single string in a canonical form;
3. Compute an HMAC [5] of the concatenated string using AppSecret as the key.

The Resource API endpoint verifies the authenticity and integrity of this request based on the shared secret AppSecret before returning results.

4.3 Forged-bearer-token Attack

One can see that MAC token is preferable from a security perspective. Since AppSecret is only shared between Provider and App, the HMAC output protects the authenticity and integrity of this request. On the contrary, bearer token is vulnerable to theft because anyone in possession of the access token can do whatever the original App can, as is defined by RFC6750 [4].

Similar to the forged-implicit-flow attack we point out in the previous sections, forged-bearer-token attack is feasible regardless of whether the App uses it or not. When these two attacks are combined, an attacker (a malicious User) can easily impersonate any App.

5. API DESIGN OF OSN

Using the aforementioned two attacks, one can launch App impersonation attack on any platform that supports, without opt-out, implicit-grant flow and bearer token usage. The consequence of App impersonation depends on the platform specifics, in particular how the API is designed. In this section, we discuss three general issues when designing the API.

5.1 Scope Design

The rights to access different resources is controlled by the "scope" parameter of OAuth. Although OAuth is originated and populated by large-scale OSNs, its use is not limited to the OSN scenario. Towards this end, how to design "scope" is not specified as part of the standard and every system should specify according to its own service nature. We have studied 12 major OSN providers (Table 1) and find the best practice is to make a three dimensional scope design, as illustrated in Fig. 3 and Fig. 4:

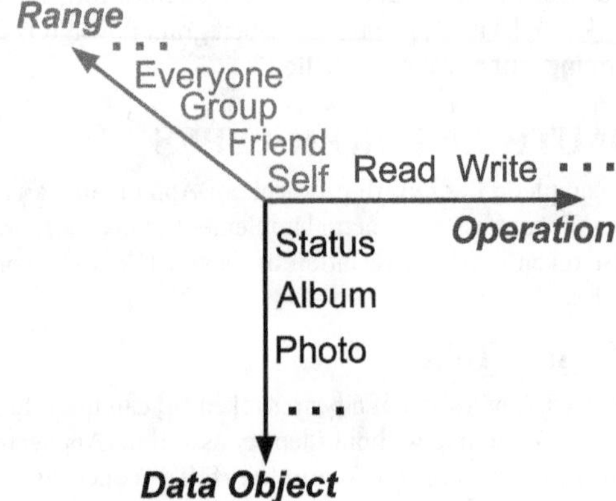

Figure 3: User Permissions

Figure 4: App Permissions

- Data Object – Examples are like status and photo.
- Operation – It can be coarsely classified as "read" or "write". Or, "write" can be further classified into "create", "modify" and "delete".
- Range – In the case of a User originated operation, e.g. "read status", the range can be "Self", "Friend", "Group" and "Everyone". In the case of an App originated operation, e.g. "send notification", the range can be "Installers" and "Everyone".

Note that not all combinations of the three dimensions are valid. For example, "write status of everyone" is a peculiar permission in the context of OSN. We have two remarks regarding scope:

- Permission systems for App originated and User originated operations should be separated. Or, malicious User can operate on behalf of the App as we will show in a proof-of-concept (POC) experiment later.
- Regardless of the dimensions of scope, there should be a way for Provider or App to constrain scope. This can make sure no unwanted permissions are granted and thus protect App from the abuse of access token when App credential is leaked.

5.2 Rate Limit

To avoid Denial of Service (DoS) attack, OSN providers should limit the API access rate. According to our study, the best practice should be to limit rate from four aspects:

Table 1: Statistics of Examined Providers

ID	Name	Registered Users	Alexa Rank*
P1	Provider 1	>300,000,000	≤ 10
P2	Provider 2	>200,000,000	≤ 1000
P3	Provider 3	>300,000,000	≤ 20
P4	Provider 4	>100,000,000	≤ 50
P5	Provider 5	>200,000,000	≤ 10
P6	Provider 6	>300,000,000	≤ 10
P8	Provider 8	Not Found	≤ 20
P7	Provider 7	>5,000,000	≤ 200
P9	Provider 9	>200,000,000	≤ 10
P10	Provider 10	>200,000,000	≤ 10
P11	Provider 11	>200,000,000	≤ 20
P12	Provider 12	>300,000,000	≤ 10

- *: Rank is for the root domain.
- Provider names are masked to avoid the concrete attacks being directly mapped back.

1. rate per IP (/IP);
2. rate per User per App (/User/App);
3. rate per App (/App);
4. rate per User (/User).

Since an access token is bound to a User and an App, those rate limit mechanisms are easy to implement. As we pointed out in the related work section, API rate limit model is of great interest to large-scale crawling campaigns. If not fully controlled from the four aspects, there is room for attackers to amplify crawling rate one way or the other.

5.3 App Differentiation

We find that some of the providers differentiate Apps and give them different access rate limit or access rights. For example, a test stage App may only get a rate limit of 10 queries/hour. After approved by the provider, the App may get 100 queries/hour. For another example, Provider can classify Apps into several categories and each category enjoys different permissions. App differentiation is the final trigger for most concrete attacks we found so far. If Apps are differentiated, App impersonation immediately means privilege escalation.

6. STUDY OF MAJOR PROVIDERS

We have systematically studied 12 major providers, whose statistics are shown in Table 1. In this section, we first summarize our findings of the features/problems of their OAuth/API implementations in Table 2 and then we perform case studies of concrete exploits.

6.1 Summary of Major OSN Providers

The features of 12 providers are summarized in Table 2. In order to review whether a provider is subject to the App impersonation attack, we focus what authorization flow it supports, what token type it supports, and whether it provides opt-outs for implicit flow and bearer token usage. The results are shown in the first 6 rows of Table 2. A simple way to check whether App impersonation attack is available is to examine row {1, 2, 4, 5} and see if the result is {Y,N,Y,N}. We find that 8 out of the 12 providers satisfy this condition.

Table 2: Summary Providers Properties

ID	P1	P2	P3	P4	P5	P6	P7	P8	P9	P10	P11	P12
Implicit Grant Flow	Y	Y	Y	Y	N	Y	N	Y	Y	Y	Y	N.A.
Implicit Grant Flow Opt-Out	Y[1]	N	N	N	N.A.	N	N.A.	N	N	N	N	N.A.
Authorization Code Grant Flow	Y	Y	Y	Y	Y	Y	Y	Y	Y	Y	Y	N.A.
Bearer Token	Y	Y	Y	Y	Y	Y	Y	Y	Y	Y	Y	N.A.
Bearer Token Opt-Out	Y[1]	N	N	N	N	N	N	N	N	N	N	N.A.
MAC Token	Y	Y	N	N	N	N	N	N	N	N	N	Y
Scope Dimensions	3D	2D	3D	2D	3D	3D	2D	3D	0D	3D	2D	2D
Scope Constraint	Y	N	Y	Y	N	N	N	N	N	Y	Y	Y
Rate Control (/IP)	Y[2]	N	Y	N	N	N	N	-	N	N	N	N
Rate Control (/User /App)	Y[2]	Y	Y	Y	N	N	N	-	N	N	Y	Y
Rate Control (/App)	Y[2]	N	N	Y	Y	Y	Y	-	Y	Y	N	N
Rate Control (/User)	N[2]	N	Y	N	Y	Y	N	-	N	N	N	Y
App Differentiation	-	Y	Y	-	-	-	-	-	Y	Y	Y	-

- [1]: Provider 1 did not support the two opt-outs proposed in this paper when we started the investigation. The two features were observed by our team in April 2014.
- [2]: No official rate control documentation is found for Provider 1. The control types are from other developers' tests on the forum.

In order to find more concrete and serious exploits, we investigate the API design issues from three aspects, namely, scope design, rate limit and App differentiation. For scope design, we emphasize two features: the dimensions and the constraints beyond protocol. For the former, we may find a problem once there is a missing dimension. For the latter, we mean whether Providers offer another way to limit the "scope" regardless of the "scope=xxx" parameter an (impersonated) App uses in the protocol sequence. This can be achieved by a request/approval process between App and Provider, or with a control panel for developers to self-limit the permissions. It helps to protect a legitimate App's access token from being abused.

The result of our study is summarized in Table 2. Following are the major observations:

- Out of the 12 major providers, only 3 of them support MAC token. Since there is only one token type in other platforms, Apps can not opt-out bearer token.
- Ideal dimensions of the scope is not a global constant. Instead, it depends on the service nature of one provider. For example, if one OSN is fully public, it does not hurt to remove the Range dimension we stated in Section 5.2.
- We find that no providers has actually implemented all the four types of rate control. Since all the four aspects increase the barrier for large-scale exploits, they should be enforced wherever possible.
- Although we focused systematic and documented difference of Apps in the survey, we did find Apps with undocumented difference. The surprisingly large power possessed by those Apps leads to serious exploits and some cases are shown in the next section.

6.2 Case Studies of Concrete Exploits

App impersonation has a great potential for various attacks especially when combined with additional design and/or implementation flaws of each specific platform. The consequence can be very serious, depending on the api design of a provider. In this section, we discuss some actual exemptified exploits enabled by App impersonation and show the corresponding implication.

6.2.1 App Reputation Attack

Many OSN providers will show the source when User performs a certain action, e.g. "message posted via XXX App" and "follower added via XXX App". This feature is useful for App to build up its brand if properly used. However, the attacker can perform some malicious actions to ruin the reputation of the impersonated App. For example, one can mention ("@") a user on some micro-blogging services. The attacker can post spams while mentioning other users. Form the victim user's point of view, the source (impersonated App) may look spammy. We have verified that this type of exploit is realizable on Provider 1, Provider 2, Provider 3, Provider 6, Provider 9, Provider 10 and Provider 11.

6.2.2 Privilege Escalation and Rate Amplification

Provider 3 supports scope constraint, which is a permission request/ approval process with this provider. Under this setup, the attacker can easily obtain advanced privileges without passing the request/ approval process, which is usually time consuming and may not always succeed. Furthermore, the permission to read the friend list of all users is only granted to a strictly selected set of "privileged" Apps, e.g. official client apps authored by the OSN provider itself or by some of its special business partners. An ordinary App can only get the authorizing User's friend list. It is not very useful because the authorizing User is a Sybil node in our App impersonation attack. Via a proof-of-concept App, we have demonstrated that it is possible to get the "friend list" of an arbitrary user by impersonating a "high-end" App. Worse still, the privileged App (which can get the friend list of any arbitrary user) possesses 40 times more API-based query rate quota than a standard App created by an ordinary user. When combined with App impersonation, the different treatment in access privilege and API query quota among different types of Apps becomes a flaw (or a feature) of severe consequence as it makes massive leakage of user data possible. In fact, we have found that at least Provider 2, Provider 3 and Provider 9 are vulnerable to such rate-amplification attacks as they can be tricked to give 10 to 1000 times more API-based query quota for a privileged impersonated App. Meanwhile, Provider 6, Provider 4,Provider 10 and Provider 11 are also vulnerable to access privilege escalation attack.

6.2.3 *Unauthorized Notification Delivery to Millions of App Users*

As we discussed in Section 5.1, the permission systems for User-originated operation and App-originated operation should be separated. The access token returned by the authorization grant code flow or implicit grant flow is bound to the User and the App. This access token should only be used when an App requests User-originated operation on behalf of the User. However, Provider 2 also uses this access token for a should-be App-originated operation, namely to send app notification to all the users who have installed the App. As a result, an attacker can impersonate an App and send notifications to *all* of its users with only a single Sybil user account. Since the notification message can contain a URL, this loophole can be used for massive spamming or delivery of malicious URLs or contents. To maximize the power of this attack, an attacker can first identify the popular Apps within the platform. The only remaining question is how to harvest the list of users who have installed one of these popular Apps. With some investigation of several popular Apps, we find that many App users also follow the public page of that App. To verify the feasibility of such a massive exploit, we have successfully conducted a proof-of-concept experiment as follows:

1. Send unauthorized notifications carrying arbitrary URLs to a list of our own accounts
2. Collect the IDs of 4 million users who have installed a popular App by examining the public fan list of the App.

6.2.4 *Massive Leakage of 200 Million+ User Data in a Matter of Weeks*

Provider 2 is supposed to be a closed OSN, i.e. user data objects like statuses and photos are shared among friend unless their access mode is set to public. We confirmed this perception by interviewing 20 active users. However, as noted in Table 2, the scope of access control in Provider 2 is only two-dimensional, i.e. it misses the Range dimension. In other words, as long as one valid access token with "read status" permission is granted, one can use it to perform actions like "read my status", "read my friends' statuses" and even "read one stranger's status". The same situation applies to other user data objects, e.g. albums and shared objects, on the same provider. We had reported this flawed API design to Provider 2 back in June 2013 but it claimed that the wide-open access control (collapsed dimensions in our terminology) is a feature rather than a bug. Instead, this provider seems to solely rely on rate throttling to prevent massive leakage, because it would take multiple years for a normal App to retrieve all the private data objects. However, we have verified that Provider 2 differentiates Apps and give them different API access rates. During the investigation of one privileged App, we discovered that the App possessed shockingly large API access quota of at least 1 million queries/hour. It is estimated to be close to 40% of the overall API server capacity of Provider 2[2] Given the size of the user base of Provider 2 (200 million), an attacker exhausting the full capacity can enumerate the whole network within one week. Considering CPU, memory (for ID deduplication in BFS), bandwidth and storage, the overall resource consumption can be well supported by a `m3.2xlarge` Amazon EC2 instance, which only costs US$150 per week.

6.2.5 *Massive Connection Establishment for Sybils*

Advertisers/Spammers on OSNs usually register many Sybil accounts on OSN. The more followers one account has, the more valuable it is. It has been shown in previous studies that reciprocal following is a common phenomenon on directed OSNs. That is, if A follows B, B will follow back as an acknowledgement. This is more likely to happen if B is a low-degree node. It is common knowledge for advertisers/spammers to automatically follow/unfollow other users in order to increase its number of followers. OSN providers already take action to limit the following rate. Prior to our discovery, the per-User per-App access rate limit is effective enough. One way to boost the "following" rate is to register more Apps, but it is more costly to register Sybil developer accounts than Sybil user accounts on many providers. Another way to increase aggregated rate is to register more Sybil user accounts and each account gets a small rate everyday. Neither is this alternative way preferable because of the preferential attachment effect on OSNs, namely, it is better to have one account with 10K followers than ten accounts with 1K followers. With App impersonation, it becomes very affordable (resource-wise) for an attacker to aggregate higher rate on a single user. As long as the provider does not have per-User rate limit, the attacker can easily launch a massive connection establishment campaign by using access token from different Apps and sending friend request to normal users. We have demonstated the feasibility of such an exploit via a POC experiment with our own unprivileged Apps on Provider 9 and Provider 11.

[2]The estimation is derived by observing the random drop rate of probing queries when the API-server is heavily loaded.

7. CONCLUSION

In this paper, we have identified and demonstrated the so-called App impersonation attack by leveraging OAuth 2.0's provisions of multiple authorization flows and token usage flavours. When implemented without opt-outs, attacker can easily launch forged-implicit-flow attacks and forged-bearer-token attacks. We have systematically examined 12 major OSN providers and found that 8 of them exhibited this vulnerability. The consequence is rather serious on some of the providers under study due to various platform-specific deficiencies in API design. Our findings show that it is high time for industrial practitioners to:

1. support the two opt-out policies we proposed for OAuth;
2. review the scope design in their access control architecture;
3. provide scope constraint mechanism beyond protocol;
4. review their rate control strategy;
5. review excessive power/ privileges they have been granting to some special/ partner Apps.

In the long run, this work calls for the re-examination of the need of providing application protection in the design of the next version of OAuth.

Responsible Disclosure

On May 22,2014, we have notified all providers, to our knowledge,that are affected by the OAuth App Impersonation Attack. At the same time, we also sent the intial version of this paper to all of these providers.

Acknowledgments

This work is supported in part by a CUHK-Hong Kong RGC Direct Grant - project number 4055031.

8. REFERENCES

[1] E. Hammer-Lahav, "The oauth 1.0 protocol," April 2010. RFC5849.

[2] D. Hardt, "The oauth 2.0 authorization framework," October 2012. RFC6749.

[3] T. Lodderstedt, M. McGloin, and P. Hunt, "Oauth 2.0 threat model and security considerations," January 2013. RFC6819.

[4] M. Jones and D. Hardt, "The oauth 2.0 authorization framework: Bearer token usage," October 2012. RFC6750.

[5] E. Hammer-Lahav, "HTTP authentication: MAC access authentication," Feb 2012.

[6] S. Chari, C. S. Jutla, and A. Roy, "Universally composable security analysis of oauth v2.0," *IACR Cryptology ePrint Archive*, vol. 2011, p. 526, 2011.

[7] R. Wang, Y. Zhou, S. Chen, S. Qadeer, D. Evans, and Y. Gurevich, "Explicating sdks: Uncovering assumptions underlying secure authentication and authorization," tech. rep., Microsoft Research Technical Report MSR-TR-2013, 2013.

[8] S. Pai, Y. Sharma, S. Kumar, R. M. Pai, and S. Singh, "Formal verification of oauth 2.0 using alloy framework," in *Communication Systems and Network Technologies (CSNT), 2011 International Conference on*, pp. 655–659, IEEE, 2011.

[9] C. Bansal, K. Bhargavan, and S. Maffeis, "Discovering concrete attacks on website authorization by formal analysis," in *Computer Security Foundations Symposium (CSF), 2012 IEEE 25th*, pp. 247–262, IEEE, 2012.

[10] R. Wang, S. Chen, and X. Wang, "Signing me onto your accounts through facebook and google: a traffic-guided security study of commercially deployed single-sign-on web services," in *Security and Privacy (SP), 2012 IEEE Symposium on*, pp. 365–379, IEEE, 2012.

[11] S.-T. Sun and K. Beznosov, "The devil is in the (implementation) details: an empirical analysis of oauth sso systems," in *Proceedings of the 2012 ACM conference on Computer and communications security*, pp. 378–390, ACM, 2012.

[12] G. Bai, J. Lei, G. Meng, S. S. Venkatraman, P. Saxena, J. Sun, Y. Liu, and J. S. Dong, "Authscan: Automatic extraction of web authentication protocols from implementations," in *Network and Distributed System Security Symposium*, 2013.

[13] R. Gross and A. Acquisti, "Information revelation and privacy in online social networks," in *Proceedings of the 2005 ACM workshop on Privacy in the electronic society*, 2005.

[14] M. Madejski, M. Johnson, and S. M. Bellovin, "A study of privacy settings errors in an online social network," in *PERCOM Workshops*, 2012.

[15] M. Madejski, M. L. Johnson, and S. M. Bellovin, "The failure of online social network privacy settings," Tech. Rep. CUCS-010-11, Department of Computer Science, Columbia University, 2011.

[16] Y. Liu, K. P. Gummadi, B. Krishnamurthy, and A. Mislove, "Analyzing Facebook privacy settings: user expectations vs. reality," in *IMC*, 2011.

[17] Y. Wang, G. Norcie, S. Komanduri, A. Acquisti, P. G. Leon, and L. F. Cranor, "I regretted the minute i pressed share: A qualitative study of regrets on facebook," in *Proceedings of the Seventh Symposium on Usable Privacy and Security*, p. 10, ACM, 2011.

[18] A. Felt and D. Evans, "Privacy protection for social networking apis," *W2SP*, 2008.

[19] A. Narayanan and V. Shmatikov, "De-anonymizing social networks," in *Security and Privacy, 2009 30th IEEE Symposium on*, pp. 173–187, IEEE, 2009.

[20] R. Dey, C. Tang, K. Ross, and N. Saxena, "Estimating age privacy leakage in online social networks," in *IEEE INFOCOM*, p. 3118, 2012.

[21] C. Wilson, B. Boe, A. Sala, K. P. Puttaswamy, and B. Y. Zhao, "User interactions in social networks and their implications," in *EuroSys*, 2009.

[22] J. Jiang, C. Wilson, X. Wang, P. Huang, W. Sha, Y. Dai, and B. Zhao, "Understanding latent interactions in online social networks," in *IMC*, 2010.

[23] Anonymous, "Crawling Renren by ID space enumeration." unpublished (Private Communication), 2010.

Author Index

www.ingramcontent.com/pod-product-compliance
Lightning Source LLC
Chambersburg PA
CBHW061348210326
41598CB00035B/5913
* 9 7 8 1 4 5 0 3 3 3 6 9 6 *